Cybersecurity and Data Laws of the Commonwealth

"As Walters points out, the digital economy is rapidly changing the way we work and live, and this brings considerable policy and legal challenges. His proposition is that the Commonwealth of Nations should have greater involvement in the areas of data, cybersecurity, and arbitration. And while there have been efforts to achieve legal convergence and cooperation among Commonwealth members, there is evidence, here in the author's research, a substantial level of divergence due to the varying stages of development among Commonwealth member countries. The book usefully compares the Commonwealth Model Privacy Bill, Model Bill on the Protection of Personal Information, and Model Bill on Computer-related Crime with all member countries' data and cyber laws, identifying the relevant divergences and (often) deficiencies. Walters argues that data and cyber law are crucial to international trade and the digital economy, and that the Commonwealth should consider undertaking further research to enhance and strengthen the respective Model Laws. He recommends, critically, that the Commonwealth broaden its role to include the active development of international law for data and cyber activities, and he calls for a deeper level of legal convergence and harmonization. Additionally, the work addresses international arbitration as it applies to data flows, data protection, and cybersecurity law, demonstrating the interconnectedness of international trade and investment with data and cybersecurity, and how arbitration can be an effective tool for resolving disputes."

—Prof. Dr. Michael Stuckey, *Former Dean Law, Victoria University*

Robert Walters

Cybersecurity and Data Laws of the Commonwealth

International Trade, Investment and Arbitration

Springer

Robert Walters
Victoria University
Melbourne, VIC, Australia

ISBN 978-981-99-3937-4 ISBN 978-981-99-3935-0 (eBook)
https://doi.org/10.1007/978-981-99-3935-0

This Springer imprint is published by the registered company Springer Nature Singapore Pte Ltd.
The registered company address is: 152 Beach Road, #21-01/04 Gateway East, Singapore 189721, Singapore

Foreword

The digital economy is rapidly changing the way we work and live. It is also changing the ways in which we protect both public and private data from misuse. These issues are central to public, social, and personal security across the global digital economy. This book highlights the diffuse and inconsistent legal protection that is accorded to data among nation states, drawing on data protection, data flows, and cybersecurity as a collective. They all support trade and investment not only across the digital economy, but also the traditional economy. The book highlights the increasing intersection between cybersecurity, data, and international arbitration. A final addition to this book is the inclusion of ethics into the regulatory discourse.

In demonstrating that inconsistency, it illustrates disparities in data protection across international and domestic legal systems, divergence in the principles underlying such protection, and the need for greater convergence among those laws. It stresses that guiding the search for solutions to these legal disparities is the need for greater understanding of the value of institutional reform in the regulation of data; enhanced trust and confidence in the institutional mechanisms that are used to accomplish such reform; and the use of ethical principles to guide such reform.

The book focuses on the need for greater compatibility in the legal principles by which to balance data transmission against data protection. It explores that balance through the freedom to communicate in the transmission of data, contrasted with freedom from data misuse in the collection, processing, and transmission of that data.

On the one side, it identifies the quandary over how to regulate the use of data, such as in preserving national security and inhibiting the unchecked disclosure of personal and commercial data to third parties. On the other side, it recognizes the need to avoid unduly trammeling the free flow of data.

The book illustrates the scope of data, cybersecurity, and arbitration laws globally and nationally. At the international level, it stresses the need for global organizations to further develop international principles that enhance trade and investment in the digital economy.

The book identifies the United Nations Commission on International Trade Law [UNCITRAL] as a primary institution capable of achieving these ends. At the national level, it demonstrates the mutual incompatibility in laws regulating the flow of data. Illustrating such divergence across national jurisdictions are the model privacy laws such the Protection of Personal Information and the Model Bill on Computer-related Crime (cybersecurity). It calls for countries that are not signatories to uniform data regulations to participate in developing uniform data and cyber laws in the future.

This book is an excellent resource for regulators, legal practitioners/scholars, students, and business community across the Commonwealth of Nations, seeking effective solutions to the immense uncertainty surrounding the use of personal, commercial data, cybersecurity, international arbitration, and ethics. It is a valuable resource for both data users and prospective targets of that use. It is a resource that encompasses, while transcending, national jurisdictions in recognizing that data transmission transcends geographic boundaries, however much it impacts upon governments, businesses, and individuals within those boundaries.

Sydney, Australia

Emeritus Professor Leon Trakman
Former Dean Law
University of New South Wales
International Arbitrator-Barrister

Acknowledgements

My personal friends, Emeritus Professor, Dr. Leon Trakman, former Dean of Law, University of New South Wales; Professor, Dr. Bruno Zeller, University of Western Australia; and Prof. Dr. Michael Stuckey, Dean of Law Victoria University.

This book acknowledges the work undertaken by Prof. Dr. Simon Chesterman, Dean of Law, Singapore National University, and Prof. Dr. Graham Greenleaf, University New South Wales. This book draws extensively on the work undertaken by both Prof. Greenleaf and Prof. Colin Bennett, University Victoria, Canada. It also acknowledges Prof. Dr. Sinta Dewi, Faculty of Law, University of Padjadjaran, Bandung, Indonesia.

Book Review

"This book seeks to enhance the engagement and strengthen the relationships among Commonwealth members through international and national cybersecurity, data, and arbitration law. The author has engaged three complex areas of the law and neatly articulated how they are interconnected. The commercial reality of data and cybersecurity has evolved rapidly over the past decade. The digital economy will provide Commonwealth members with many opportunities to work together and advance our respective nations. It will continue to grow in the forthcoming decade. As technology continues to evolve and change, the legal framework enabling international trade will need a high level of vigilance. I wish that the Commonwealth may pursue the proposals outlined in this book. With India being the largest member of the Commonwealth, this book comes at a time that will assist India in advancing our digital economy."

Prof. (Dr.) S. Shanthakumar
Director
Gujarat National Law University
Gandhinagar, Gujarat, India

This book is a comparative analysis of the current-day legislation in relation to data and cyber security. In some cases, the legislation has been directly transposed, and this has highlighted the differences between the laws. Generally, throughout the book, there has been a conscious effort to identify themes within the legislation; however, additional analysis is necessary to confirm this. The particularly affable thing about the book is that it is written in a simple language, and anyone can understand how the evolution of the Commonwealth took place and how the data and cybersecurity law came into existence. It also provides us with three case studies which help acknowledge the topic more effectively. This book extensively collates between the Model Privacy Bill and the Model Bill on the Protection of Personal Information, and the execution of the said laws in the member countries. Differences between national laws have also been identified, including in relation to arbitration. The book also conveys us the scenario regarding data and cybersecurity in investor-state arbitration. It calls our attention to the key postulation of arbitration that will need to be considered, as arguments and controversies across the web economy advance. The issue of a large number of the Commonwealth countries still being developed and not having a mature legal framework or economy, as the developed nations, is also handled quite well. The book also exhibits the intersection of international trade, investment, criminal and private law with a slight intricacy. The author also put forwards certain recommendations which will help intensify and build up the respective Model Laws. One of the recommendations it gives is to expand the role of Commonwealth, including the development of international law for data and cyber; as the cooperation lacks at the international level, but enjoys a good cooperation at the regional level. Though it also gives us a fair idea about how the member countries have a regional influence on them such as the African Union, European Union, etc. The influence at regional level directs the local needs, whereas at the international level, it takes in mind the universal viewpoint of the matter related to data and cybersecurity. Another recommendation given by the author is for the Commonwealth to work with relevant United Nation bodies, to further mature these areas of law, to augment trade and investment across the web economy.

The chapters provided/written are quite descriptive and accentuate the actual and specific provisions of the laws, with a high-level analysis at the end, which demarcate the differences in approach. A whole chapter is dedicated to the significance of data and cybersecurity law to the international digital economy. At law they are autonomous, be that as it may, in practice they are crucially tethered. The book highlights how compounded it has become to describe personal data and the varying methods taken to do so. The laws made by the member countries have been compared thoroughly with the Commonwealth MBP and MBPPI. The author explains the particular need to have a Regulator, who oversees the authority and governance of data law in the country. The topics of controller, consent, and processing were dealt astutely with clear distinctions of them being separated by law, but being the salient features of the current data laws. The author also asks well-grounded questions like "how can data subjects be confident in where and how their personal. Data is collected, stored, used and what other country it may be transferred to without their knowledge?" which further makes the reader question the extremities of protection one's content should have. The issue of data portability has also been discussed briefly due to its vulnerability to cyberattacks. The author also asserts how the Right To Be Forgotten must be made available to every person regardless of their country location. The author gives us a fair look at the respective laws of the member countries and the Commonwealth MBP and MBPPI, and lists some acceptable reasoning and schemes which may significantly benefit the member countries of the Commonwealth. Overall, the efforts taken by the author must be appreciated for his attempt to cover almost everything relating the current-day legislation in relation to data and cybersecurity with special reference to the Commonwealth countries. The book is a must read for those interested to explore this ever-evolving fields of data and cybersecurity.

Dr. Deesha Khaire
Associate Professor of Law
Maharashtra National Law University
Nagpur, Maharashtra, India

A comprehensive review of the law regulating digital connectivity across the Commonwealth, focussed on data and cyber law in commercial contexts and dispute resolution. It makes very useful recommendations for the reform of Commonwealth model laws on privacy, protection of personal information and cybersecurity. It recognises the two contemporary tipping points as IT is impacted by the accelerated development of artificial intelligence and changing geopolitics. Its relevance to Australian readers in these contexts is clear from the accounts of the Commonwealth nations in the Pacific and also South and South East Asia. It provides a blueprint on how to use the soft power of shared political and legal institutions and the membership of the Commonwealth. This should ensure that the peoples of these regional Commonwealth countries benefit from both the access to the technology and the security and prosperity it brings.

Emeritus Professor Neil Andrews
Victoria Law School
Victoria University,
Melbourne, VIC, Australia

Contents

Part I
Problem Definition

The digital economy is rapidly changing the way we work and live. It will come with significant policy and legal challenges. This book comes at a time when the world is being challenged by competing geopolitical and economic interests. It calls for greater collaboration by Commonwealth members in the future development of data, cybersecurity and arbitration (commercial and investor-state) law. This book is specifically highlights the divergence and fragmentation of these areas of law that, will be critical in and across the digital economy. The Commonwealth of nations emerged some decades ago, and since then there has been some highly important work undertaken to gain a level of legal convergence and cooperation in terms of data and cyber laws. However, today there continues to be a significant level of divergence amongst Commonwealth members. This is expected and unavoidable, since Commonwealth countries are at different stages of development and the Commonwealth itself, and that the Commonwealth itself is a voluntary organisation. That is, there are a large number of member countries that are still developing and do not have a mature legal framework or economy, unlike the developed nations.

Specifically, this book will compare the Commonwealth Model Privacy Bill,[1] Model Bill on the Protection of Personal Information[2] along with the Model Bill on Computer-related Crime (cybersecurity),[3] with all member countries data and cyber laws. It will demonstrate the shortcomings and complexity in the law between the respective jurisdictions. In reconciling the differences between the respective laws, it is argued that data and cyber law are very closely connected and are important to international trade and the digital economy. Significantly, it is argued that the

---

[1] The Commonwealth Model Privacy Bill, Office of Civil and Criminal Justice Reform, https://www.asianlaws.org/gcld/cyberlawdb/COM/P15370_9_ROL_Model_Privacy_Bill_0.pdf.

[2] The Commonwealth Model Bill on the Protection of Personal Information, Office of Civil and Criminal Justice Reform, https://www.asianlaws.org/gcld/cyberlawdb/COM/P15370_6_ROL_Model_Bill_Protection_Personal_Information_2.pdf.

[3] Model Law on Computer and Computer Related Crime, Office of Civil and Criminal Justice Reform, 2017, p 1 https://production-new-commonwealth-files.s3.eu-west2.amazonaws.com/migrated/key_reform_pdfs/P15370_11_ROL_Model_Law_Computer_Related_Crime.pdf

Ibid, sects. 5–9.

economic developments in and across the digital economy will need to be supported by robust data and cyber laws. Thus, this book is intended to demonstrate the intersection of international trade, investment, criminal, and private law, and how they will be important to the functioning of the digital economy. There are a number of areas where it is recommended that the Commonwealth consider undertaking further research that will enhance and strengthen the respective Model Laws.

A comparison of the data and cyber laws of Commonwealth nations reveals several common themes, particularly in relation to terms and terminology. In some cases, any differences are minor. On the other hand, there are instances where the approaches are significantly divergent. The divergences identified should be reconciled with a formal program of law reform across the Commonwealth. Doing so will lessen the complexity of understanding and locating the legal provisions. Moreover, some states do not have specific cyber laws. These states should reform their respective criminal laws and develop specific legislation for cyber and computer crime, in the same way as the majority of Commonwealth nations have done. The economic benefits of doing so will be important to the business community, even though the true financial impact from locating and interpreting and applying the laws is highly complex and has not been addressed in this book. This is an area requiring further research.

Another accentuating problem is the regional influences of entities such as the African Union, European Union (EU), Association of South East Nations and other less formal bodies, who have emerged and begun to shape and influence the development of data and cyber law and policy. Also, two Commonwealth members, Malta and Cyprus, are part of the EU and therefore are required to follow the EU laws and policies. The EU laws have arguably been the most influential in shaping the international legal landscape, particularly in relation to data protection and data flows. It is the data flows that underpin the digital economy, creating a new economic activity. While there is often good cooperation at a regional level, this is lacking at the international level. Therefore, it is recommended that the Commonwealth broaden its role to include the development of international law for data and cyber activities. The inclusion of this function will enable further and much needed international law to support the digital economy. Thus, the Commonwealth have a role and should call for the development of an international organisation for data and an international organisation for cybersecurity. In achieving this proposition, a starting point is the Commonwealth could work with relevant United Nation bodies to further develop these areas of law in order to strengthen trade and investment in the digital economy. The book calls for Commonwealth to engage non-member countries that are based on similar or the same values. It is not arguing for any one Commonwealth member to take control. Rather, the book is making the case for expanded engagement, collaboration, integration and convergence, through data, cybersecurity and arbitration. Doing so will enhance the digital economy as a collective and enrich the economic outcomes. The book calls for a deeper level of legal convergence and harmonisation. However, although this will not be easy to achieve, it is not insurmountable.

Finally, this book addresses the growing area of international arbitration as it applies to data flows, data protection and cybersecurity law. When coupled with the broader digital economy, and regulatory frameworks of nation states, the book confirms this proposition. Doing so demonstrates the deepening of the interconnectedness of international trade and investment with data and cybersecurity, and how arbitration can be an effective tool for resolving these disputes. The book also briefly identifies how ethics is increasingly being considered by scholars, government and the business community to build into legal frameworks and operational plans.

Chapter 1
Introduction

The Commonwealth of Nations (CON) has a long history. In 2013, The Commonwealth Charter (TCC) was presented to the United Kingdom 'Parliament by the Secretary of State for Foreign and Commonwealth Affairs by Command of Her Majesty'.[1] In my view, the TCC is one of the most important documents that espouses the values of the Commonwealth such as democracy, human rights, international peace and security, tolerance, respect and understanding, freedom of expression, separation of powers, rule of law, good governance, sustainable development, protecting the environment, access to health, education, food and shelter, gender equality, importance of young people, recognition of small states, recognition of vulnerable states and civil society.[2] These values cannot be underestimated. They have been instrumental in raising the standard of living for many countries. However, and across the Commonwealth there are significant differences in how these values are, and have been implemented. The Charter 'was agreed by all Commonwealth Heads of Government on 14 December 2012'.[3] It is 'an important outcome of the modernisation process and a milestone for the Commonwealth. For the first time in its 64-year history, the Commonwealth has a single document setting out the core values of the organisation and the aspiration of its members'.[4]

The core values above apply to all aspects of society, ranging from the economy to social justice and protection of the environment. Most significant is the reference to the rule of law. A salutary point in the contemporary world is how the rule of law is being challenged, and as the digital economy develops and evolves, the CON can play an important role in maintaining its application across nation states. This book calls for the CON to strengthen the economic, social and environmental relationship in order to address societal issues under a common set of rules and laws. The book calls

[1] The Commonwealth Charter, 2013, https://www.globalwps.org/data/GBR/files/Commonwealth%20Charter.pdf.

[2] Ibid.

[3] The Commonwealth Charter, https://www.gov.uk/government/publications/the-commonwealth-charter.

[4] Ibid.

R. Walters, *Cybersecurity and Data Laws of the Commonwealth*,
https://doi.org/10.1007/978-981-99-3935-0_1

for greater legal convergence and/or harmonisation, while not calling for members to accede any sovereignty to the Commonwealth, in the same way as member states of the European Union. The book is the first of its kind to compare all the data and cybersecurity laws of the nation states of the Commonwealth. Due to the divergence in approaches taken by the nation states being compared, the laws examined are at February 2023.

Notwithstanding the above, the evolution of the CON can traced to the '1918 Imperial War Conference was held in London and attempted to resolve the functions of governments across the Commonwealth, including Australia. There was a clear recognition from London that it was time for the Dominions, such as Australia, to have 'complete control over the composition'[5] of their community. This War Conference followed the outbreak of World War One (WWI), where, subjects from many of the Commonwealth nations fought in different theatres of war across the world.[6] Lord Lexton in a speech to the British Parliament stated:

> Within 10 days, New Zealand dispatched an expeditionary force of 8,000 men. Within two months, 31,000 Canadians had been recruited, drilled and sent to Europe. They were the vanguards of the mighty dominion contingents, whose enormous sacrifices on the Western Front won them lasting respect and gratitude. By the summer of 1918, Canada and Australia had each established its own army corps under outstanding national commanders. Their rigorously trained men—better, said many, than the English—were at the forefront in the Battle of Amiens and other great breakthroughs in the last months of the war. They were lauded as some of the best shock troops in the allied armies.[7]

This was a significant time in British history, and for the world. It paved the way for greater integration of countries that had common interests and values and encourage them to defend the British Empire. As summarised by Goodlad:

> My Lords, I congratulate my noble friend Lord Lexden on introducing this debate and share his hope that the Government will arrange to commemorate the contribution of Empire and Commonwealth troops during the First World War. It is estimated that about one-third of the troops raised by Britain were from what was then the Empire: Australia, New Zealand, Canada, South Africa, India, the Caribbean, Africa, Fiji, Hong Kong and so on. In the short time available I shall say a very few words about the Australian contribution, which was enormous and, in the final weeks on the Western Front, some would say decisive.[8]

Arguably, the contribution from Commonwealth states was not only well recognised, or understood to have assisted the British, for example, at Gallipoli by what would later become known as the Australian and New Zealand Army Core (ANZAC). Today, the ANZAC community is celebrated annually in both Gallipoli, Australia and New Zealand, with continued recognition from the UK. This strong military relationship between some of the Commonwealth countries enabled closer economic

[5] Arthur Berriedale Keith, Speeches and Documents on the British Dominions, 1879–1944.

[6] The Commonwealth and the First World War, https://www.nam.ac.uk/explore/commonwealth-and-first-world-war Also see, United Kingdom Parliament, Hansard, https://hansard.parliament.uk/lords/2018-06-04/debates/EA57B6BE-CEA6-4A13-9F3F-99B3DB24D332/FirstWorldWarEmpireAndCommonwealthTroops.

[7] Ibid., United Kingdom Parliament, Hansard.

[8] Ibid.

and social ties between all Commonwealth countries as the CON has developed over the past 100 years. Two years later in 1920, the League of Nations (LON) was formed, and consisted of the 'first intergovernmental organization established "to promote international cooperation and to achieve international peace and security". Moore goes further stating, it is often referred to as the "predecessor" of the United Nations'.[9] The LON, followed the 'Treaty of Versailles (which) was signed in the Palace of Versailles Hall of Mirrors on 28 June 1919. The Covenant of the League of Nations was integrated into the Treaty and all other peace settlements signed in Paris after World War I, and defined its main function to promote international co-operation and to achieve international peace and security'.[10] Yet, the LON was disbanded in 1945 and replaced by the United Nations. However, a question that did arise at the time was the status of Dominions within the League Council. Willian Moore makes the point that the:

> eligibility of Dominions to the Council of the League in view of the fact that the "British Empire" was a permanent member presented a question in some respects analogous one hand, there was a memorandum signed by M. Cleme President Wilson and Mr. Lloyd George definitely recognising the right; on the other, the notion, at first generally accepted that the "British Empire" in the Council was not limited to Great Britain and its dependencies, but was the whole group including the Dominions.[11]

Moore further highlights how Great Britain and its dependencies included considering the issues raised when the Irish Free State became a candidate, and the election first of Canada (1927) and then of the Irish Free State (1930) settled the matter.[12] Australia, New Zealand and South Africa regularly took their places at the Council.[13] It is argued that although the British retained a level of influence over the Dominions in this early period, the Dominions were afforded a level of autonomy, which they were able to engage in, and with, international institutions.

The formal and functional arrangements of the CON can also be traced to the Imperial Conference of 1926, which culminated in the Balfour Declaration.[14] The Conference sought to better understand the divide between the British Empire and its Dominions, with India being of special significance. To recall 'Resolution IX of the Imperial War Conference, 1917, due recognition was given to the important position held by India in the British Commonwealth. Where, in this Report, we have had occasion to consider the position of India, we have made particular reference

[9] The United Nations Office of Geneva, https://www.ungeneva.org/en/library-archives/league-of-nations.

[10] Ibid.

[11] William Harrison Moore, *The Dominions of the British Commonwealth in the League of Nations*, International Affairs (Royal Institute of International Affairs, Oxford University Press, Vol. 10, No. 3 (1931), p. 374.

[12] Ibid.

[13] Ibid.

[14] The Imperial Conference 1926, https://www.foundingdocs.gov.au/resources/transcripts/cth11_doc_1926.pdf.

to it'.[15] To clarify the connection between the Empire and its Dominions legislative programs, the Conference noted at the time the:

- present practice under which Acts of the Dominion Parliaments are sent each year to London, and it is intimated, through the Secretary of State for Dominion Affairs, that "His Majesty will not be advised to exercise his powers of disallowance" with regard to them.
- reservation of Dominion legislation, in certain circumstances, for the signification of His Majesty's pleasure which is signified on advice tendered by His Majesty's Government in Great Britain.
- difference between the legislative competence of the Parliament at Westminster and of the Dominion Parliaments in that Acts passed by the latter operate, as a general rule, only within the territorial area of the Dominion concerned.
- operation of legislation passed by the Parliament at Westminster in relation to the Dominions. In this connection special attention was called to such Statutes as the Colonial Laws Validity Act. It was suggested that in future uniformity of legislation as between Great Britain and the Dominions could best be secured by the enactment of reciprocal Statutes based upon consultation and agreement.[16]

The British Empire ad significant influences over the Dominions, with the adoption of the common law in nation states such as Australia, Singapore, India, New Zealand, Canada, and Malaysia to name a few. For instance, Australia was a young nation in 1926, having been constitutionalised in 1901. The common law of England had been transposed over the territory of the current day nation state of Australia. Under the international law of *terra nullius*, the British claimed the Australia territory was not inhabited. However, more than 90 years later after Australia becoming a federated state, the principle of *terra nullius* was overturned by the Australian High Court.[17] There are similar stories across the nations that make up the Commonwealth, where the British Empire had displaced the local indigenous inhabitants. This is far from being a criticism of the law and practices of the British Empire. They were, in my view like many other empires and dynasties before them, wanting to extend their economic and political reach. A year earlier, the Commonwealth Countries League (CCL), was founded in 1925 as the British Commonwealth League, which was a voluntary pan-Commonwealth civil society organisation,[18] promoting equality. This book is not calling for a return to the former British Empire, or the current day United Kingdom to assume a colonial level of control over member countries. Rather, the book is calling for greater integration, convergence and collaboration to address common societal challenges such as cybersecurity and data protection-data flows. The book is also calling for further convergence and harmonisation of

[15] Ibid., p. 4.

[16] Ibid., p. 5.

[17] *Mabo and others v Queensland* (No. 2) [1992] HCA 23; (1992) 175 CLR 1 F.C. 92/014 (3 June 1992).

[18] The Commonwealth, Commonwealth Countries League, https://thecommonwealth.org/organisations/commonwealth-countries-league-ccl.

the respective states arbitration laws, as it could increasingly be used to resolve commercial disputes across the digital economy that includes data and cybersecurity.

Most noteworthy was how the Balfour Declaration made a point of ensuring that 'Britain and its Dominions were constitutionally equal to each other'.[19] Yet in practice this could not be further from the truth. It further defined the 'group of self-governing communities composed of Great Britain and the Dominions as "autonomous Communities within the British Empire, equal in status, in no way subordinate one to another in any aspect of their domestic or external affairs, though united by a common allegiance to the Crown, and freely associated as members of the British Commonwealth of Nations". Moreover, the laws were made by the British Parliament in 1931 Statute of Westminster, which was the founding document of the modern Commonwealth.[20] The statute clarified the 'status and relations of Britain and the Dominions of Australia, South Africa, New Zealand, Newfoundland and Eire'.[21]

Not long after the implementation of the 1931 Statute of Westminster, World War Two (WWII) broke out in 1939. This marked the second world conflict in less than fifty years and, again, the theatres of war were across Europe. It has been described as the most significant and devastating conflict in history,[22] and Britain along with the Commonwealth nations committed more than ten million troops to active combat.[23] It began in 1939 and concluded in 1945. In the same year, the United Nations became the second international organisation established in the twentieth century that was worldwide in scope and membership.[24] For more than 50 years, the Commonwealth has been working alongside the United Nations (UN) to promote economic and social development, along with protecting the environment. More recently, in September 2022, the Commonwealth Secretary renewed its pledge to work with the UN on matters of mutual recognition and understanding, such as promoting and tackling 'present and future challenges in areas including disaster response, tackling climate change, conflict prevention and equality'.[25]

Significantly, WWII left deep scares on many nation states and the world economy was reshaped under the Bretton Woods framework. It was created by the 1944 Articles of Agreement at a global conference organised by the United States Treasury at the Mount Washington Hotel in Bretton Woods, New Hampshire, at the height of

[19] Jon Tattrie, Balfour Report [1926] United Kingdom, https://www.britannica.com/biography/W-L-Mackenzie-King.

[20] Ibid.

[21] Museum of Australian Democracy, https://www.foundingdocs.gov.au/item-sdid-96.html.

[22] Stuart Foster, The British Empire and Commonwealth in World War II: Selection and Omission in English History Textbooks Institute of Education. University of London, https://citeseerx.ist.psu.edu/document?repid=rep1&type=pdf&doi=096af9031d875455cba377657091d46b01ae836d.

[23] Ibid., p. 2.

[24] Karen Mingst, *United Nations International Organisation*, https://www.britannica.com/topic/United-Nations.

[25] The Commonwealth, The Commonwealth and United Nations Pledge to work together, September 2022, https://thecommonwealth.org/news/commonwealth-and-united-nations-pledge-work-partners.

WWII.[26] Following WWII, the 1951 Declaration by Commonwealth Prime Ministers United Kingdom, pledged to promote the peace and stability of all members.[27] Bordo is of the view that it was 'established to design a new international monetary order for the post war, and to avoid the perceived problems of the interwar period: protectionism, beggar-thy-neighbour devaluations, hot money flows, and unstable exchange rates. It also sought to provide a framework of monetary and financial stability to foster global economic growth and international trade'.[28] While the framework was only operational for a short period, it had all but fallen apart by 1971, it set up the beginnings of the current-day world order and rule of law pertaining to much of transnational trade and investment. During this period, the CON continued to evolve and take shape. The advanced economies of Australia, Canada, New Zealand, UK amongst others were well placed to leverage the Bretton Woods framework to strengthen their respective trade and investment relations.

In 1961, the UK applied to join the European Community, now known as the European Union (EU), and more than a decade later in 1973 the UK along with Denmark, Ireland and Norway acceded to the EU.[29] Article 24, provided that 'the United Kingdom shall be added to the Member States specified in the first sentence of Article 131 of the EEC Treaty'.[30] Put another way, 'from about 1960, the UK government was in negotiations with the then member states of the EEC with a view to the United Kingdom joining the EEC and associated European organisations. In October 1971, when it had become apparent that those negotiations were likely to be successful, and following debates in each House, the House of Lords and the House of Commons each resolved to "approve ... Her Majesty's Government's decision of principle to join the European Communities on the basis of the arrangements which have been negotiated. However, nearly 20 years later the UK would leave the EU".[31]

A significant milestone took place in 1971 with the the first Commonwealth Heads of Government Meeting (CHOGM) taking place.[32] Ever since there have been meetings every two years. This forum brings together the leaders of all Commonwealth countries where:

---

[26] Michael Bordo, *The operation and demise of the Bretton Woods system: 1958 to 1971*, The State University New Jersey, https://cepr.org/voxeu/columns/operation-and-demise-bretton-woods-system-1958-1971.

[27] Declaration Priministers 1951, p. 5, https://production-new-commonwealth-files.s3.eu-west-2.amazonaws.com/s3fs-public/2022-01/London-Declaration%202.pdf?VersionId=dHJPLBExX Kr2.HTm6rRivGwUwdTtRt9E.

[28] Michael Bordo, *The operation and demise of the Bretton Woods system: 1958 to 1971*, The State University New Jersey, https://cepr.org/voxeu/columns/operation-and-demise-bretton-woods-system-1958-1971.

[29] Council Decision of the European Communities, of 1 January 1973 adjusting the instruments concerning the accession of new Member States to the European Communities, Official Journal of the European Communities, L2/1. https://eur-lex.europa.eu/legal-content/EN/TXT/PDF/?uri=OJ:L:1973:002:FULL&from=EN.

[30] Ibid., Article 24.

[31] Hilary Term [2017] UKSC 5, para 13. https://www.supremecourt.uk/cases/docs/uksc-2016-0196-judgment.pdf.

[32] Commonwealth Heads of Government Meetings. https://www.commonwealthofnations.org/commonwealth/commonwealth-heads-of-government-meetings/.

> the Commonwealth summits are private and, by design, frank and informal. Each summit includes a 'retreat' held away from the conference room and in relaxing surroundings, intended to enhance understanding by allowing leaders to meet as friends. From these retreats have come agreements about Commonwealth action over some difficult issues.[33]

As a collective, the member states that make up the Commonwealth is the largest forum outside of the United Nations. On 22 January 1972, ministers signed a Treaty of Accession which provided that the United Kingdom would become a member of the EEC on 1 January 1973 and would accordingly be bound by the 1957 Treaty of Rome, which was then the main treaty in relation to the EEC, and by certain other connected treaties. As with most international treaties, the 1972 Accession Treaty was not binding unless and until it was formally ratified by the United Kingdom.[34] While the UK never adopted the single market currency of the EU—the Euro, its membership would dilute its ability to engage with the Commonwealth, for instance on trade and investment. On the positive side, it could be argued that with the UK exiting the EU in 2021, it opened the door for better trade and investment relations with the CON. On the other hand, by having the UK a member of the EU, it enabled the CON to have more efficient access to EU markets. However, the UK were subject to EU Commission rules in relation to negotiating trade and investment agreements. That is, when the UK was a member of the EU, they could not go it alone and negotiate trade or investment agreements. They were obliged to negotiate under the rules of the EU. Nonetheless, in the short term, it is difficult to predict whether the UK's exit from the EU has been beneficial to the CON.

Against the backdrop of the above and the UK entering and exiting the EU, it was in 1971 that the Singapore Declaration of Commonwealth Principles were established.[35] The Principles aim to improve equality and minimised discrimination. It extended to include peoples of different races, languages and religions, and display every stage of economic development from poor developing nations to wealthy industrialised nations.[36] There was a concerted effort to recognise the rich diversity of languages, culture, race and religions that made up the Commonwealth of nations. Again in 1979, the Lusaka Declaration of the Commonwealth on Racism and Racial Prejudice Zambia further reinforced the Singapore Declaration, stating the:

> Commonwealth is an institution devoted to the promotion of international understanding and world peace, and to the achievement of equal rights for all citizens regardless of race, colour, sex, creed or political belief, and is committed to the eradication of the dangerous evils of racism and racial prejudice.[37]

---

[33] Ibid.

[34] Hilary Term [2017] UKSC 5, para 13. https://www.supremecourt.uk/cases/docs/uksc-2016-0196-judgment.pdf.

[35] Singapore Declaration of Commonwealth Principles 1971, https://web.archive.org/web/20131202223804/http:/thecommonwealth.org/sites/default/files/history-items/documents/Singapore%20Declaration.pdf.

[36] Ibid.

[37] Commonwealth Declarations, p. 10, https://production-new-commonwealth-files.s3.eu-west-2.amazonaws.com/s3fs-public/2022-01/London-Declaration%202.pdf?VersionId=dHJPLBExXKr2.HTm6rRivGwUwdTtRt9E.

In 1981 the Melbourne Declaration continued to acknowledge the gross inequality of wealth and opportunity currently existing in the world, and to find ways to reduce that inequality,[38] amongst other matters. Two years later, in Goa, India, it was declared that international security would be placed front and centre of member states' minds. The 1983 Goa Declaration identified the increase in 'disregard for the moral and legal principles which should govern the conduct of states; by the degree to which the ethic of peaceful settlement of disputes is being eroded and by the readiness of nations to resort to the illegal use of force'.[39] From 1983 until 2022 another 18 declarations were made around the world in relation to a number of important issues pertaining to peace, stability, young people, discrimination, equality, and the environment, amongst others.

Of significance to this book is the 2018 Declaration on Cyber (DoC), which addresses the 'economic, social, cultural and political life of the Commonwealth, from the impact of cyber (the new digital economy)'.[40] The DoC, made the point of the 'critical role of cyberspace in connecting all Commonwealth member countries, in particular small island developing states, to global value chains in the context of an increasingly globalised economy'.[41] This new found connection, today, has enabled the smaller and more isolated states to more efficiently with other commonwealth members. Moreover, the DoC highlighted the 'shared interest in protecting the security of our networks, security of data, the people that use them, and the services that run on them'.[42] The security of networks and data are underscored by the rule of law. As this book will explain, there are many common themes in relation to the data laws being examined. On the other hand, there is also evidence of significant gaps in the law. As it will be demonstrated, this is also the case with the cyber laws of each nation state. The establishment of a robust legal framework for both cybersecurity and data will make a significant contribution to each state's economic and social development. In addition to the economic and social benefits, there are also environmental advantages. In addressing the need for nation states to deliver on the Sustainable Development Goals, the DoC states nine core principles, these include:

1. ***Recognise and support*** cyberspace as an enabling environment to promote investment and intra-Commonwealth trade in goods and services through open markets, the free flow of information, innovation, and fair competition.
2. ***Commit to*** promote interoperable and global technical standards, through appropriate consultative processes involving industry, academia, governments and other relevant stakeholders, recognising that standards should be open, foster security and trust and not act as barriers to trade, competition or innovation.

---

[38] Ibid., p. 10.

[39] Ibid., p. 15.

[40] Ibid., p. 91.

[41] Ibid.

[42] Ibid.

3. ***Highlight*** the importance of common standards and the strengthening of data protection and security frameworks, in order to promote public trust in the internet, confidence for trade and commerce, and the free flow of data.
4. ***Acknowledge*** the importance of tolerance, respect for diversity, and understanding in cyberspace.
5. ***Affirm*** that the same rights that citizens have offline must also be protected online.
6. ***Commit*** to limit the circumstances in which communication networks may be intentionally disrupted, consistent with applicable international and domestic law.
7. ***Recognise*** that without cybersecurity citizens are at risk of crime or exploitation, and *commit* to strengthening legislative, social and educational measures that protect the vulnerable.
8. ***Recognise*** that access to information and digital literacy can be a powerful catalyst for economic empowerment and inclusion, and *commit* to take steps towards expanding digital access and digital inclusion for all communities without discrimination and regardless of gender, race, ethnicity, age, geographic location or language.
9. ***Emphasise*** that enhanced digital inclusion of young people in the Commonwealth can contribute in a positive way to their education, social engagement and entrepreneurship.[43]

On the backdrop of the above, I posit that the principles promote a deeper level of harmonisation among Commonwealth states. Most noteworthy is the reference to international and domestic law, and the need for states to strengthen their domestic laws. Significant too, is how the Commonwealth is using the DoC to promote the developing digital economy through the 'intra-Commonwealth trade in goods and services through open markets, the free flow of information, innovation, and fair competition'.[44] This is highly relevant to this book which examines the digital economy across the Commonwealth. It will also be relevant to international arbitration, because arbitration is a well-understood legal mechanism and framework that can resolve investment and commercial disputes.

Moreover, the DoC goes further and promotes the need for states to establish frameworks to effectively respond to cyber intrusions. However, it must be understood that this alone, without considering data, is complex in and of itself. Thus, it calls for states to undertake strategic planning and establish incident response capabilities, supported by appropriate legislation and a law enforcement and criminal justice system capable of addressing cybercrime. It is this law that will be examined in the book (see Part III). In addition, the DoC makes the case for international cooperation. I maintain that, by doing so according to the 9 principles described, states will be given the opportunity to be actively involved at the international level when

[43] Ibid., p. 92.

[44] Ibid.

establishing rules and transnational law. These include committing to the following 4 actions:

1. the establishment of effective and proportionate domestic cybercrime and cybersecurity frameworks that take into account principles in existing international instruments, acknowledging the evolving tactics of cybercriminals and the transnational nature of cybercrime, and use national contact points and other practical measures to enable cross-border access to digital evidence through mutually agreed channels to improve international cooperation to tackle cybercrime;
2. working towards common standards, harmonised legal approaches and improved interoperability, including through the use of Commonwealth model laws; and consider the potential for further Commonwealth cooperation in this regard, including the possible coordination of common positions in international fora;
3. promoting frameworks for cyberspace, including the applicability of international law, agreed voluntary norms of responsible state behaviour, and the development and implementation of confidence building measures to encourage trust, cooperation and transparency, consistent with the 2015 Report of the United Nations Group of Governmental Experts on Developments in the Field of Information and Telecommunications in the Context of International security (UNGGE); and
4. moving forward discussions on how existing international law, including the Charter of the United Nations, and applicable international humanitarian law, applies in cyberspace in all its aspects.[45]

A common theme that has emerged is the need for harmonised laws and standards to manage and govern cybersecurity. It also emphasises the importance of international law that is urgently needed for both cybersecurity and data. This book will make the case that, as a collective, the member states of the Commonwealth are in a unique position to come together and set, shape and influence the international law for both cybersecurity and data.

In 2018, the United Kingdom, Declaration on the Commonwealth Connectivity Agenda for Trade and Investment (CCTI), underscores the need for this book, stating:

> …11th WTO [World Trade Organisation] Ministerial Conference and we affirm our commitment to free trade in a transparent, inclusive, fair, and open rules-based multilateral trading system as a foundation for economic development and growth. We encourage member countries to work collectively towards strengthening the system and on trade issues which will lead to more prosperity in the world economy.[46]

Arguably, it affirms the commitment to free trade under the open rules-based multilateral trading system of the WTO trading rules. The GATS [General Agreement on Trade in Services], a multilateral agreement covering global trade in services,

[45] Ibid., p. 94.

[46] Ibid., p. 95.

defines trade in services.[47] That said, the GATS applies to the service sector, with two exceptions. According to Article I:2, services supplied include:

(a) from the territory of one Member in to the territory of any other Member (Mode 1—Cross-border trade);
(b) in the territory of one Member to the service consumer of any other Member (Mode 2—Consumption abroad);
(c) by a service supplier of one Member, through commercial presence, in the territory of any other Member (Mode 3—Commercial presence); and
(d) by a service supplier of one Member, through the presence of natural persons of a Member in the territory of any other Member (Mode 4—Presence of natural persons).[48]

Article I (3) of the GATS excludes 'services supplied in the exercise of governmental authority'.[49] These are services that are supplied neither on a commercial basis nor in competition with other suppliers, such as social security schemes and health services that are provided under non-market conditions. Additionally, Air Transport Services are exempted from coverage measures affecting air traffic rights. Under the WTO-GATS rules, both data and cybersecurity pertain to trade and investment, and fall within four categories. First, during cross-border activity, users in one state receive services from a third country through a telecommunications or postal network. The data used in these activities can be international and the cybersecurity rules protect that data during point-to-point transmission. These services include, but are not limited to, consultancy or market research reports, tele-medical advice, distance training, or architectural drawings.[50] Second, there is the consumption of data abroad, in cases where nationals of Australia, relocate to the UK, for personal or business reasons. The ensuing question is: what cybersecurity laws are in place to protect this activity from fraud, theft and ransom? The monetisation of data that is currently being conducted through illegal cyber intrusions by ransom requests was, as of 2022, on the increase. In November 2022, an Australian entity, Medibank, was subject to a significant cyber breach that affected both personal data and exposed significant shortfalls in cybersecurity prevention, detection and response. It involved a:

> Ransomware group has threatened to release Medibank customer data as Australia's largest health insurer faces a possible class action after the data of 9.7 million current and

---

[47] World Trade Organisation, Trade Services Division, The General Agreement on Trade in Services, 2013, https://www.wto.org/english/tratop_e/serv_e/gsintr_e.pdf, Article I.1. Also see, General Agreement on Trade in Services, Article I.1, https://www.wto.org/english/docs_e/legal_e/26-gats_01_e.htm. This section draws on the work in Robert Walters, *The Digital Economy and International Trade:* Regulation of Transnational Data Flows, Kluwer Law (2022), Chapter 1.

[48] Ibid., Definition of Services Trade and Modes of Supply, Article I.2.

[49] Ibid., Article I(3).

[50] Ibid., p. 3.

former customers was hacked, in what the health insurer has described as a distressing development'.[51]

It is this health data that is considered the most sensitive data of any individual. Third, 'there is a commercial presence, whereby a service is provided in the United Kingdom, with an office or subsidiary in Singapore, Australia, United States, India or another country'.[52] These services are usually provided by banks, financial institutions, legal firms, hotel groups, and construction companies, amongst others. Fourth, a foreign national of Indonesia provides a service from his/her home state to an organisation based in another state such as Japan.[53] Twelve services areas have been established by members of the WTO[54]:

- Business (including professional services and computer services);
- Communication;
- Construction and related engineering;
- Distribution;
- Educational;
- Environmental;
- Financial (including insurance and banking);
- Health-related and social;
- Tourism and travel-related;
- Recreational, cultural and sporting;
- Transport; and
- Other services not included elsewhere.[55]

That said, the WTO defines electronic commerce as 'the production, distribution, marketing, sale or delivery of goods and services by electronic means'.[56] Article III[57] of the WTO promotes the concept of transparency amongst member states. On the one hand, the general understanding is that the obligations imposed by Article III in regard to transparency apply to all laws and regulations affecting the supply

[51] Josh Taylor, *Medibank says ransomware group's threat to release customer information a 'distressing developme*nt', November 2022, https://www.theguardian.com/technology/2022/nov/08/medibank-data-hack-ransomware-group-threatens-to-release-customer-information.

[52] Robert Walters, *The Digital Economy and International Trade:* Regulation of Transnational Data Flows, Kluwer Law (2022), Chapter 1.

[53] World trade Organisation, Trade Services Division, The General Agreement on Trade in Services, 2013, https://www.wto.org/english/tratop_e/serv_e/gsintr_e.pdf, Article I.1. Also see, General Agreement on Trade in Services, Article I.1, https://www.wto.org/english/docs_e/legal_e/26-gats_01_e.htm This section draws on the work in Robert Walters, *The Digital Economy and International Trade:* Regulation of Transnational Data Flows, Kluwer Law (2022), Chapter 1.

[54] World Trade Organisation, as of 2016, there were 164 members.

[55] World Trade Organisation, Trade Services Division, The General Agreement on Trade in Services, 2013, https://www.wto.org/english/tratop_e/serv_e/gsintr_e.pdf, Article I.1., p. 4, document, MTN.GNS/W/120. See also Robert Walters, Cross Border Data Flows – An Evolving Multilayered Regulatory Approach Required! *Global Privacy Law Review, WoltersKluwer, 2022.*

[56] WTO, (1998), Work Program on Electronic Commerce, WT/L/247.

[57] WTO, Analytical Index, GATS—Article III (Practice) https://www.wto.org/english/res_e/publications_e/ai17_e/gats_art3_oth.pdf.

of a service by electronic means.[58] On the other hand, Article III.3, requires that each member shall promptly and at least annually inform the Council for Trade in Services of the introduction of any new, or any changes to existing, laws, regulations or administrative guidelines which significantly affect trade in services covered by its specific commitments under this Agreement. This has not been fully realised in terms of cross-border data flows, data protection or cybersecurity although most countries have established or are in the process of developing laws for these areas. However, the WTO has the right to request information from other members in relation to the general application or international agreements, such as Free Trade Agreements (FTA) and their implementation of specific provisions. Article III.4 allows a member country to respond to a request from another member country for specific information in relation to an FTA.[59] Article IV encourages the participation of developing countries, a number of which are members of the Commonwealth. Article V goes further by promoting the concept of economic integration. Arguably, this has been difficult to achieve as countries are at different stages of economic development.[60] Article VI requires that each member ensure that all measures of general application affecting trade in services be administered in a reasonable, objective and impartial manner.[61] On this basis, the ensuing and continued development of the digital economy all fall within the WTO-GAT rules, and data along with cybersecurity will form an important part of that economic activity.

Centrally, there are six key areas of engagement across the digital economy. These include clusters:

1. *Physical Connectivity*,[62]
2. *Digital Connectivity*,[63]
3. *Regulatory Connectivity*,[64]

---

[58] World Trade Organisation, Trade in Services, S/L/74, 27 July 1999 (99-3194), Work Programme on Electronic Commerce, Progress Report to the General Council, Adopted by the Council for Trade in Services on 19 July 1999.

[59] Ibid., also see Article III.5, 5. Any Member may notify to the Council for Trade in Services any measure, taken by any other Member, which it considers affects the operation of this Agreement.

[60] Robert Walters, *The Digital Economy and International Trade: Regulation of Transnational Data Flows*, Kluwer Law (2022), Chapter 1.

[61] World Trade Organisation, Analytical Index, GATS – Article VI, Domestic Regulation, https://www.wto.org/english/res_e/publications_e/ai17_e/gats_art3_oth.pdf.

[62] Commonwealth Declarations, p. 97, https://production-new-commonwealth-files.s3.eu-west-2.amazonaws.com/s3fs-public/2022-01/London-Declaration%202.pdf?VersionId=dHJPLBExXKr2.HTm6rRivGwUwdTtRt9E, engaging on trade facilitation, identifying and facilitating implementation issues, infrastructure development including multi-sectoral connectivity and the sharing of trade information, in order to reduce the physical barriers to trade.

[63] Ibid., assisting member countries in expanding ICT capabilities, identifying areas for developing their national digital economies, improving their regulatory framework and building digital infrastructure, inter alia through capacity building and promoting investments, to enable all members to take advantage of the opportunities presented by digital trade.

[64] Ibid., improving understanding of various regulatory regimes, increasing the ease of doing business, promoting good regulatory practice including regulatory cooperation among member countries

4. *Business-to-Business Connectivity*,[65]
5. *Supply Side Connectivity*,[66] and
6. *Inclusive and Sustainable Trade*.[67]

By engaging in these areas, member countries will mainstream as a cross-cutting issue. These connectivity principles and concepts are important in bringing together the member countries of the Commonwealth and strengthening their engagement. Most noteworthy is the development of the concept of regulatory connectivity (Table 1.1).

Arguably, regulatory connectivity is achieving different things. First, it is argued that, the promotion of regulatory cooperation implies that legal harmonisation is to be achieved where possible. Second, any regulation should not impose unnecessary trade barriers, which would ensure the WTO-GAT rules are fully implemented. Third, the attainment of mutual recognition goes some way to achieving the harmonisation of standards as well as the law. Noteworthy, is how states should work towards improving data collection. To achieve this, cooperation needs to be strengthened in order to achieve legal harmonisation. It also requires these states to work together to develop, shape and influence the international data and cybersecurity agenda. Although this goal may appear to be elusive, this book makes the case that Commonwealth members, having established an agreed set of values, is in a very unique position to consolidate this relationship. The potential for strong partnerships extends far beyond the Commonwealth itself; it can reach out to other nation states that have similar values and standards of governance. This book is not calling for any sovereignty to be acceded to the Commonwealth. Such a proposition would never be accepted by all the members. By far, the current process for managing relationships has been through the use of Declarations which have had the most effect to date.

Significantly, declarations are considered a soft law[68] tool, the value of which is highlighted by Oliver:

---

to reduce non-tariff barriers, improving services data collection, and mutual recognition, in order to reduce regulatory barriers, address the capacity deficit and improve the regulatory environment for business, especially micro, small and medium enterprises and consumers.

[65] Ibid., supporting dialogue between the public and private sectors and between businesses, assisting member countries to attract investment through capacity building, facilitating the needs of the micro, small and medium enterprises to access finance, and reflecting on how domestic regimes could facilitate business-to-business connectivity, particularly with the aim of enhancing the private sector's role in promoting the blue and green economy.

[66] Ibid., encouraging the participation of all members in global value chains, fostering global value chains (GVC) linkages and sharing knowledge among members and harnessing them for economic growth, as well as the creation of export diversification opportunities for micro, small and medium enterprises, and exploring possibilities to collaborate on national trade portals.

[67] The Commonwealth, Commonwealth Connectivity Agenda: Action Plan, Responding to Future Trends Through a Connected Commonwealth, p. 19. https://production-new-commonwealth-files.s3.eu-west-2.amazonaws.com/s3fs-public/2022-01/D16991_TRD_Connectivity_Action_Plan_All_0.pdf?VersionId=xuGALxsJ8iSP067MZOQvoMZ5rrjEWlxD.

[68] Michèle Olivier, *The relevance of 'soft law' as a source of international human rights*, The Comparative and International Law Journal of Southern Africa, Vol. 35, No. 3 (2002), pp. 289–295. Also see, Mauro Barelli, "The Role of Soft Law in the International Legal System: The Case

Table 1.1 Commonwealth connectivity (see Footnote 66)

Business-to-business connectivity			
Support public–private dialogue on connectivity			
Digital connectivity	Physical connectivity	Regulatory connectivity	Supply-side connectivity
Objective: Supporting the development of national digital economies	Objective: Supporting best practice in digital infrastructure development	Objective: Improving regulatory regimes across the Commonwealth	Objective: Encouraging the participation of all members in global value chains
Initial Initiatives: 1. Promote understanding of the impact of digital transformation 2. Assist capacity-constrained members to create a strong environment for digital trade and industry 3. Develop evidence-based policies that enable digital skills development, digital trade and digital industrial development 4. Develop principles to support digital connectivity in the Commonwealth	*Initial Initiatives*: 1. Share experiences on how digital technologies can enhance the operation and capacity of infrastructure 2. Engage on how countries can develop digital infrastructure 3. Develop principles of sustainable investment in digital infrastructure for Commonwealth members 4. Explore how countries can improve access to digital infrastructure to bridge digital divides and promote inclusive growth	*Initial Initiatives*: 1. Facilitate and exchange views and experiences to enhance international regulatory cooperation 2. Establish common understanding of regulatory practices and how to go about developing Commonwealth Good Regulatory Practices 3. Develop best practice for good regulatory practice and regulatory impact assessments 4. Build capacity for Commonwealth members to design and implement good regulatory practices	*Initial Initiatives*: 1. Facilitate and exchange views and experiences on the agriculture and fisheries sector, with a particular focus on smart agriculture and smart fisheries 2. Explore how countries can enhance the role of MSMEs through specific policies 3. Explore how the Commonwealth can promote inclusive and sustainable growth 4. Seek technical assistance to support members' agriculture and fisheries exports
Inclusive—sustainable trade			
Mainstream gender, youth, green and blue economy considerations into commonwealth cooperation			

'Soft law' lies on the moral and political level. Soft law further plays an important role in facilitating and mobilising the consent of states required to establish binding international law. 'Soft law', though not a source of law, remains legally relevant and is therefore a matter governed by international law. Customary international law is suggested as an alternative method to account for the status of international human rights resolutions. International authority is referred to, suggesting that a non-conventional approach to the traditional requirements of *usus and opinio iuris* is justified in order to lend legal status to human resolution.[69]

---

of the United Nations Declaration on the Rights of Indigenous Peoples." *The International and Comparative Law Quarterly* 58, no. 4 (2009): 957–83.

[69] Ibid.

According to Simon Chesterman, David Malone, and Santiago Villalpando, from a 'lawmaking perspective, soft law is simply a convenient description for a variety of non-binding normatively worded instruments used in contemporary international relations by states and international organisations'.[70] There is no better example of where declarations have been widely supported and agreed upon by the international community, than the area of human rights. The Declaration of Human Rights 1948, established in the aftermath of WWII, is a shining example of the international community coming together to ensure the peoples of the world have a level of protection from other people and the nation state. Simon Chesterman makes the important that point:

> in January 2016, the Singapore Academy of Law convened a major conference on Legal Convergence in an Asian Century. Building on the launch of the ASEAN economic community, the conference also created a new institute to promote convergence. Revealingly, the language of 'convergence' was chosen as opposed to 'harmonization'.[71]

On this basis, the declaration process for the Commonwealth of Nations has worked very well in achieving a stronger level of consensus amongst nation states. However, a lingering question remains: is there a way for the Commonwealth to go beyond the use of Declarations so as to achieve a stronger consensus? A possible model that has been structured based on the framework of consensus is the Association of South East Asian Nations (ASEAN). Chesterman highlights how problematic legal convergence can be when ASEAN, unlike the supranational polity of the European Union (EU), has been afforded a level of sovereignty. That is, ASEAN member states have not afforded any sovereignty to ASEAN itself. Its members are not required to transpose any supranational law into their own national laws. Chesterman further states that:

> Though the chances of a radically different approach to global governance seem remote, the traditional view of sovereignty espoused by many Asian states may slow the expansion of human rights and other norms, although it does not look set to reverse them completely. Nor will any change necessarily be coherent. As this article has been at pains to stress, there is no one 'Asian' view of the world. Greater involvement of Asian states will primarily increase pluralism in the international order.[72]

Therefore, the ensuing question is: can the Commonwealth adopt an approach similar to that of ASEAN to strengthen the engagement and consensus of its member states? The challenge is that some nation states have taken different directions. For instance, Singapore is an integral member of ASEAN and the Commonwealth. As a commonwealth country, Singapore is a good example of how the competing expectations from these forums do not necessarily enable the state to meet their respective agendas. That said, it is argued that the wide interpretation of the Commonwealth Declarations allows each member country to adapt its respective data, cyber and

---

[70] Simon Chesterman David Malone, Santiago Villalpando, *UN Treaty-Making in Practice and in Theory*, Chapter 6 The choice of a Treaty hard law versus soft law, The Oxford Handbook of United Nations Treaties, in Alan Boyle, Oxford Public International Law.

[71] Simon Chesterman, Asia's Ambivalence about International Law and Institutions: Past, Present and Futures, *European Journal of International Law*, Volume 27, Issue 4, 1 (2016), p. 978.

[72] Ibid.

AI programs to align with these priorities. Conversely, the current process is likely to result in such member states adopting the ASEAN position rather than that of the Commonwealth. Furthermore, some members of the Commonwealth are also members states of the EU. For example, Cyprus and Malta are bound by the EU to support the Union's law on data, cybersecurity and AI, before that of the Commonwealth. Yet again, it is my view that these member states can achieve both, because of the wide interpretation of the Commonwealth Declarations. Can the Commonwealth be as effective as the EU and ASEAN in bringing together member countries? This book will attempt to address this issue. I believe that it is on the way to doing so. It has undertaken important legal projects pertaining to data protection and cyber law. Historically, it has also explored international arbitration. These projects need to continue and be improved. This book calls for the Commonwealth to adopt the proposed changes outlined. The next section will briefly explore legal harmonisation versus legal convergence.

1.1 Legal Convergence Versus Legal Harmonisation

The issue of legal harmonisation versus convergence is nothing new. Both concepts have been around for some time. To take this beyond merely the law, arguably, it is prevalent in policy and standards. Simply put, at a government-to-government level there is, and has been, a move towards legal convergence and harmonisation. This has been evident since the 1950s in the area of transnational trade and investment law. However, the 'concepts of convergence, harmonization, and unification seem to be imprecise notions in comparative law'.[73] The question is: apart from a declaration, what can or could be a way forward that could be utilised by the Commonwealth to bring member countries together? Filomena Chirico and Pierre Larouche posit that 'scholarship often assumes that convergence or divergence between legal systems is easily perceptible, in the face of the formal sources of law.

Chirico and Larouche further state that, within the legislation of a legal system, *A* is entitled to the goods sold that pass to the buyer upon the conclusion of a valid contract, whereas the applicable legislation in *B*'s system states that title to the goods sold passes to the buyer upon delivery of the goods to the buyer'.[74] It is this area of transnational sales law that has gone further than converging—to being harmonised. It has seen the integration of sales law between legal families such as the common and civil law. In highlighting the benefits of legal harmonisation, Chirico and Larouche argue that costs associated with business are all but removed, because:

- externalities are addressed and removed;
- transaction costs are eliminated, since cross-border activities will be subject to the same set of rules in all the relevant legal systems;

---

[73] Jan Smits, *A European Private Law as a Mixed Legal System*, Maastricht Journal of European and Comparative Law 5, (1998), pp. 328–40.

[74] Filomena Chirico and Pierre Larouche, *Convergence and Divergence, in Law and Economics and Comparative Law*, https://d1wqtxts1xzle7.cloudfront.net/36770870/9789067048842-c2-libre.pdf?

- information imperfections disappear, since parties can rely on the common legal framework thus established.

As a consequence, cross-border activity would be boosted as would investment, consumption and growth.[75] While harmonisation might not remove all associated costs, such as compliance costs, it narrows the gap between diverging legal frameworks. In other words, harmonisation can go some way to reducing the level of sovereignty imposed over the law by the state. According to Chirico and Larouche, harmonisation provides a level of equilibrium across various areas of the law as they are integrated into the legal system. The authors refer to the top-down approach, whereby harmonisation acts as a break within the legal system, creating a specific "harmonized area" which co-exists with other remaining areas. In an ideal situation, the implementation (incorporation) of harmonised law should be done seamlessly, without distorting the legal system.[76] This approach can be seen in the EU where the European Commission develops laws and member states transpose them into national law. However, this does not occur within ASEAN.

Nonetheless, convergence has been, in part, thrust upon nation states and economies as a result of economic shocks. This has been no more evident than when nation states responded to economic conditions that have had a profound impact on national economies. On the one hand, states responded by offering economic stimulus packages. On the other hand, it forced a deeper level of financial convergence (policy, standards and the law). Anupam Chander and Randall Costa in referring to 'Henry Hansmann and Reinier Kraakman describe a number of mechanisms by which convergence on a regulatory model might occur there are, broadly speaking, three ways in which a model of corporate law can come to be recognized as superior: by force of logic, by force of example, and by force of competition'.[77] Chander and Costa further point out how Hansmann and Kraakman speak of corporate laws as mechanisms that can also have an effect in other areas of law.[78] Therefore, a level of convergence encourages greater cooperation and, more importantly, economic stability and certainty.

Put another way, under the WTO-GATS rules there was a move towards converging trade rules for all nation states. However, as there has been a significant shift towards bilateral and multilateral trade agreements (BITS-MITS), they were originally all about 'cross-border market *access* for goods and services'.[79] David Luff argues that 'GATS, similarly to the GATT, aims at protecting equality of competitive opportunities for companies in domestic markets regardless of their origin and the origin of their services. It further aims to enable WTO Members to

---

[75] Ibid., p. 27.

[76] Ibid., p. 28.

[77] Anupam Chander, Randall Costa, *Clearing Credit Default Swaps: A Case Study in Global Legal Convergence,* Chicago Journal of International Law (2010), p. 672. See also Henry Hansmann and Reinier Kraakman, *The End of Histoy for Corporate Law,* 89 Georgetown L J (2001), pp. 439–445.

[78] Ibid.

[79] Joost Pauwelyn, *The Re-Convergence of International Trade and Investment Law: Causes, Questions, and Reform,* Proceedings of the Annual Meeting, published by the American Society of International Law 255 (2014), pp. 107–110.

regulate them "*in order to meet national policy objectives*'.[80] On the other hand, Joost Pauwelyn, argues that investment treaties have 'traditionally been about *protecting* private investors that had previously been admitted into a foreign country. Governments tie their hands vis-a-vis private actors so as to attract investment. Both trade (access) and investment (protection) were set up as instruments in pursuit of what is essentially the same goal: economic development'.[81] What they do in practice is create a framework and environment for stronger government-to-government, private sector-to-government, and private sector-to-private sector entities engagement. They can be viewed as a first step towards greater legal convergence.

In another example that is highly pertinent to this book is the convergence of arbitration rules.[82] Roger Alford makes the case that:

> international norms reflected in the WTO differ from those guaranteed in BITs. The WTO agreements are concerned with trade liberalization, while BITs are concerned with investment protection. Many WTO norms, such as those addressing tariffs, non-tariff barriers, and unilateral trade remedies have no corollary in BITs. Likewise, BIT protections against unlawful expropriation, denial of justice, and the guarantee of full protection and security have no corollary in the WTO agreements.[83]

On the one hand, BITs are playing an important role in the new digital economy, and the principle of nation treatment will be explored in Part IV (arbitration). They are providing for a level of trade liberalisation. On the other hand, they have a role in investment protection. Thus, convergence from international 'trade law towards international investment law can be identified in the expansion of the epistemic community of interstate commissions/committees consisting of political representatives, along with transnational institutions'.[84]

On the other hand, ASEAN as a bloc has two Commonwealth members: Singapore and Malaysia. ASEAN is based on the core principle of consensus and the rule of law. The Commonwealth under the 2013 Charter also emphasises how essential the rule of law[85] is to its members. Moreover, there are 26 Commonwealth nation states

[80] David Luff, *International Trade Law and Broadband Regulation: Towards Convergence?* Journal of Network Industries (2002), p. 240. See also GATS, World trade Organisation https://www.wto.org/english/res_e/publications_e/ai17_e/gats_art1_jur.pdf, GATTS, World Trade Organisation, https://www.wto.org/english/docs_e/legal_e/gatt47_01_e.htm.

[81] Joost Pauwelyn, *The Re-Convergence of International Trade and Investment Law: Causes, Questions, and Reform*, Proceedings of the Annual Meeting, published by the American Society of International Law 255 (2014), pp. 107–110.

[82] Roger Alford, *The Convergence of International Trade and Investment Arbitration*, Santa Clara Journal of International Law (2013), p. 35.

[83] Ibid., p. 40.

[84] Yuliya Chernykh, *Assessing Convergence between International Investment Law and International Trade Law through Interpretative Commissions/ Committees: A Case of Ambivalence?* Cambridge University Press (2020), pp. 230–240.

[85] The Commonwealth Charter 2013 Article VII states, we believe in the rule of law as an essential protection for the people of the Commonwealth and as an assurance of limited and accountable government. In particular we support an independent, impartial, honest and competent judiciary and recognise that an independent, effective and competent legal system is integral to upholding

that form part of the African Union, which also implements the rule of law.[86] Francis Jacobs makes the point that ASEAN, similar to the EU, relies heavily on the concept of the rule of law for the 'creation of an effective system of dispute settlement as both an integrationist and legitimizing tool vis-a'-vis the international community'.[87] As a concept, it is well understood that the 'rule of law has mainly been developed in western democracies, and is thus strongly influenced by their values, it has some important universal traits'.[88] Its relevance to the overall position taken in this book cannot be underestimated. Jacobs, in referring to EU law which is applicable to Malta and Cyprus (two Commonwealth members) highlights that the concept applies 'not only to public authorities, but also to other 'powerful' bodies, which sometimes seem able to act above the law, taking advantage of their status and mobility to avoid the law, or to evade taxation'.[89]

In further referring to the European Court of Justice (ECJ), Jacobs argues that Directive 95/46/EC on the protection of individuals with regard to the processing of personal data and on the free movement, was interpreted broadly. According to Jacobs, the ECJ 'innovatively attributed an obligation to a private company (Google) on the basis of its "decisive role" in the effective protection of individuals' fundamental rights to privacy and to the protection of personal data'.[90] On this basis, both the European Union and ASEAN have endorsed the rule of law primarily in 'economic' sectors.[91] Arguably, it is the economic basis for the adoption and application of the rule of law that directly relates to data and cybersecurity laws. In reconciling this point, the transnational use of data alone now constitutes its own economic activity. Further, it is argued that cybersecurity underpins and now protects this economic activity by minimising the illegal collection and sale of that data, whether on the open market, or by ransom.

Institutionally, because the WTO rules apply to the digital economy, it has for many years based its trade rules on the application of the rule of law. This is particularly the case for Dispute Settlement Understanding (DSU). Despite the concept being critical to the development and application of data laws, it is also a means of dispute settlement. Again, this book is predicated on dispute resolution, arbitration

---

the rule of law, engendering public confidence and dispensing justice. https://www.mfat.govt.nz/assets/Peace-and-Security/Read-the-full-Charter-of-the-Commonwealth-1.pdf.

[86] Constitutive Act of the African Union, p. 3. Article 4—Principles https://au.int/sites/default/files/pages/34873-file-constitutiveact_en.pdf.

[87] Francis Jacobs, *The Rule of Law as Key to the ASEAN Legal Order: How Can It Be ensured*, p. 205, In Gary Low (Ed.), Convergence and Divergence of Private Law in Asia, Cambridge University Press (2022).

[88] Ibid.

[89] Ibid.

[90] Ibid., see also, Case C-131/*12 Google Spain SL and Google Inc. v. Agencia Española de Protección de Datos* (AEPD) *and Mario Costeja Gonzáleź* [2014] ECLI:EU:C:2014:317.

[91] Ibid., p. 213.

(Part IV) in particular. More specifically, Article 25 of the DSU provides for arbitration.[92] The importance of legal convergence as opposed to legal harmonisation has been embraced by ASEAN for the best part of a decade. This is particularly evident in the area of data laws. As Chief Justice Sundaresh Menon stated in 2016 at the *Doing Business Across Asia: Legal Convergence in an Asian Century*:

> The second project could be aimed at the convergence of data privacy laws. This is an area that is ripe for policy and legal review and reform in this age of the Internet and smart businesses. The number of national data privacy laws in the world has grown exponentially since the first such legislation was passed in Sweden in 1973. Data privacy laws are now a common feature of the legal landscape in many countries but, in Asia, studies suggest that they are neither "universal nor … close to uniform". This has been attributed to our different legal traditions and also to our diverse rates of development, policies and cultures. This could be earmarked as a subject that would benefit greatly from applied study. To that end, we have had preliminary discussions with similar institutes to collaborate in a joint project to draw up global principles on data privacy laws and we have thus far been met with considerable interest.[93]

The speech delivered by the Chief Justice of Singapore came at an important time, not long after the state of Singapore had implemented its 2012 data laws. Arguably, Singapore has shown a high level of leadership in many areas of transnational and national commercial and private law. Arguably, this observation can also apply to cybersecurity laws. The Chief Justice is calling for greater cooperation, which is something the Commonwealth urgently requires. Such an approach also needs to be undertaken in regard to cybersecurity laws. I concur with this view, as there needs to be a lot more cooperation amongst Commonwealth states in this area of the law alone, to ensure that the digital economy grows and improves the economic status of every Commonwealth nation. Three years earlier, another Justice from Australia, argued that:

> Efforts to promote convergence of commercial legal systems provide an important mechanism by which to reduce these legally related transactional costs. By convergence, I am referring to the harmonisation of substantive legal principle and civil procedure amongst nations states, to increasing uniformity in conflict of law rules, and to development of similarity and shared approaches to dispute resolution amongst judicial systems.[94]

Commercial law has been highly successful in gaining traction as a means of converging legal concepts and principles. Arguably, this has been a significant step toward achieving legal harmonisation, which has brought many economic and social benefits to the world. However, it has been a little more difficult for private and criminal law areas of data and cybersecurity. I argue that this is because the interconnectedness of data and cybersecurity has converged to such an extent that the

[92] World Trade Organisation, Dispute Settlement Understanding, Article 25, https://www.wto.org/english/tratop_e/dispu_e/disp_settlement_cbt_e/c8s2p1_e.htm.

[93] Asian Business Law Institute, President of SAL sets out his vision for legal convergence and ABLI, 2016, https://abli.asia/NEWS-EVENTS/Whats-New/ID/7.

[94] The HON TF Bathurst Chief Justice of NSW, The Importance of developing Convergent Commercial Law Systems, Procedurally and Substantively, 15th Conference of chief Justices of Asia and the Pacific, 2013, https://www.supremecourt.justice.nsw.gov.au/Documents/Publications/Speeches/Pre-2015%20Speeches/Bathurst/bathurst_2013.10.28.pdf.

two can no longer be separated from each other. Although this book is calling for the Asian Business Law Institute to expand its legal convergence programs, it also argues that the Commonwealth could take the lead in this area. Therefore, in order to reconcile the differences between data and cybersecurity law, this book argues for a greater level of legal convergence amongst Commonwealth countries.

This convergence will enable the states to influence their respective regional blocs and, over time, help determine the transnational rules for achieving a balance between data flows within the digital economy and ensuring a robust level of protection. The success or otherwise of legal convergence can be indicated by an examination of transnational arbitration. Therefore, this book will highlight the benefits of UNCITRAL's [United Nations Commission on International Trade Law] convergence of arbitration laws, and examine its effect on national laws. That said, the uniform commercial laws that have been successfully implemented by UNCITRAL are well documented. For instance, for a number of years the 'Hague Conference on Private International Law (HCCH), the United Nations Commission on International Trade Law (UNCITRAL) and the International Institute for the Unification of Private Law (UNIDROIT) have been preparing uniform law texts that promote the progressive harmonization and modernization of commercial contract law'.[95] Transnational contract law is a clear indication that the first step to legal harmonisation through legal convergence has been highly successful. That is:

> …the HCCH, UNCITRAL and UNIDROIT have produced a series of texts that are complementary: the United Nations Convention on Contracts for the International Sale of Goods (1980) (CISG); the UNIDROIT Principles of International Commercial Contracts (UPICC); and the HCCH Principles on Choice of Law in International Commercial Contracts (HCCH Principles). In addition, UNCITRAL has prepared treaties, such as the United Nations Convention on the Use of Electronic Communications in International Contracts (2005) (Electronic Communications Convention) and the Convention on the Limitation Period in the International Sale of Goods (1974, amended in 1980) (Limitation Convention), that are closely related to the CISG and complement it with regard to specific 1978 Agency Convention); and the Convention on the Law Applicable to Conmatters. Similarly, the HCCH has historically adopted a number of treaties that deal with choice of law rules in international sales: the Convention on the Law Applicable to International Sales of Goods (1955) (HCCH 1955 Sales of Goods Convention); the Convention on the Law Applicable to Agency (1978) (HCCH 1978 Agency Convention); and the Convention on the Law Applicable to Contracts for the International Sale of Goods (1986) (HCCH 1986 Sales Convention).[96]

Arguably, this is one of the best examples of legal convergence achieving legal harmonisation. Legal harmonisation is a step beyond legal convergence as it involves the full integration of the same laws into national legal frameworks. It is argued that by taking a similar approach to facilitate the legal convergence of data (protection-flows) and cybersecurity laws, this will improve the economic outcomes of the world community. It is important to make the distinction in relation to data protection and data flows. Data flows are supported by provisions within data laws, to facilitate the transnational flows of data. This has become important to the growth of the digital

---

[95] United Nations Commission on International Trade Law, and UNIDROIT Legal Guide to Uniform Instruments in the Area of International Commercial Contracts, with a Focus on Sales, p. 1, https://uncitral.un.org/sites/uncitral.un.org/files/media-documents/uncitral/en/tripartiteguide.pdf.

[96] Ibid., p. 1.

economy. Data protection are those provisions in the data laws that, provide controls and obligation on organisations to protect personal data. Although this position is premised solely on the economic (trade and investment) benefits, any such convergence will need to be weighed against the need to further tighten laws so as to restrict the use of data on the grounds of national security. A more uniform approach to the legal landscape has:

> achieved global set of rules which are international in their origin, formulation and framework of application and interpretation; consequently, uniform law diminishes the legal obstacles to the flow of international trade, levels the playing field among buyers and sellers, strengthens commercial relations among States and generates investment opportunities.[97]

Therefore, the timing is right for the Commonwealth to engage with the aforementioned international institutions not only for the purpose of developing data-protection laws, but also to better understand whether elements of cybersecurity law should also fall within the legal framework of trade and investment as opposed to specifically criminal law. Doing so will provide a strong case indicating how data and cybersecurity laws can follow the same or similar pathway. The economic benefits and outcomes could be significantly substantial to national and the international economy.

Antonios Platsas reinforces the position taken in this book. Platsas has identified five key principles that can facilitate the legal convergence process:

- Fidelity;
- Conferred Powers;
- Subsidiarity;
- Proportionality; and
- Conditionality.[98]

Arguably, in part, some of these principles put forward by Platsas can be found in modern day data laws, and to a lesser extent cyber laws. Platsas goes on to say that:

> Fidelity asks from nation-states to refrain from breaching their international obligations; equally, the extra-national should not intervene in matters of national law, unless it has been conferred the relevant legal powers and authority to do so. Subsidiarity suggests that what can be achieved at the lower level of authority in a circle of convergence (national level) does not have to be the subject matter of legal interference at the higher level of authority (extra-national level) in the same circle. Proportionality requires the extra-national to exercise its administration in a fashion that does not go beyond *vires*, legal expectations and the very requisites of proportionality itself, for example, the acts of the extra-national have to be suitable, necessary and proportionate *per se*. Conditionality deals with the imposition of conditions on the part of the extra-national to the national. The national is asked to implement an extra-national relevant agenda of convergent economic law in exchange for economic benefit.[99] [emphasis added]

---

[97] Ibid., p. 2.

[98] Antonios Platsas, The idea of legal convergence and electronic law, 2011, p. 682, in Bottis Maria, Alexandropoulou Eugenia, Ioannis Iglezakis, *Values and Freedoms in Modern Information Law and Ethics*, Nomiki Bibliothiki Group.

[99] Ibid., pp. 682–683.

These principles can also be found in the supranational laws of the EU, of which Malta and Cyprus are member states. Noneheless, Platsas goes a step further arguing (and I agree) that under the current legal arrangements for technology, this could be further from actual reality. He adds:

> One is at odds, however, when it comes to the very global nature of the internet and the parallel local application of various laws in the matter (mostly at the domestic and regional level). Cyberspace is global - cyberspace regulation is not. The sustainability of this paradox to this day is one that puzzles. In a world that unites in law, the diversification of e-laws is striking, if not alarming. Also, the fact that the internet as a whole is one of the clearest examples of globalisation. In particular, one speaks here of globalisation of information. However, the current legal regimes observed do not point to such finding.[100]

To reconcile this dillema it is argued that the Commonwealth is substantially well placed to strengthen the development and implementation of a full program of data and cyber laws. Although the Commonwealth is developing a Model Law for Data and Cyber Crime,[101] a Model Bill on Privacy and Model Bill on the Protection of Personal Information, this book will demonstrate how a lot more could be done to achieve a greater level of legal convergence. The Model Bills could be raised to a level of Model Law. The accentuating question is whether it is time for the Commonwealth to take more of an international approach to data and cybersecurity law. How can this be done? It is argued that the Commonwealth could engage with the Hague Conference on Private International Law (HCCH), the United Nations Commission on International Trade Law and the International Institute for the Unification of Private Law to advance the need for international law, legal guides, principles and model laws. The next section examines the Commonwealth digital economy.

1.2 The Commonwealth Digital Economy

The digital economy of Commonwealth members has the potential to be significant. In 2020, the Secretariate released a report titled: The State of the Digital Economy in the Commonwealth.[102] It has not been updated for three years and the figures reported are the most recent. However, because this report is, in my view, an important document informing Commonwealth members of the potential benefits of the digital economy, it should remain current. It was reported that in 2015, 'e-commerce in the Commonwealth generated roughly US$354 billion in sales, representing 3.5% of total Commonwealth GDP, but only six Commonwealth countries—the UK, Canada, Australia, India, Singapore and Malaysia—accounted for 85% of all B2C e-commerce sales'.[103] It was argued that by adopting '50% of broadband across all countries, Commonwealth GDP is expected to grow by between US$74

---

[100] Ibid., p. 683.

[101] The commonwealth, Commonwealth Model Law, https://thecommonwealth.org/commonwealth-model-laws.

[102] The State of the Digital Economy in the Commonwealth, 2020, https://production-new-commonwealth-files.s3.eu-west-2.amazonaws.com/s3fs-public/2022-01/Digital%20Connectivity%20Report_low%20res_.pdf?VersionId=ZqZJyDDbskgK_LRyiymHJuPPUAI3UVks.

[103] Ibid., p. 16.

billion and $263 billion'.[104] This alone raises the need for this book to examine the current laws and identify the means by which the Commonwealth can expand and strengthen its legal program. More specifically, the report stated that these 'countries have active legislation in four key categories relevant to data regulation: (a) presence of a legal framework for electronic transactions/e-signature; (b) a legal framework for data protection/privacy online; (c) a legal framework for consumer protection when purchasing online; and (d) a legal framework for cyber-crime prevention'.[105]

The economic benefits that e-commerce can offer to Commonwealth states, the report also emphasised the need for a strong legal framework to support this new economic activity. It makes the case for all Commonwealth members to adopt data privacy and cyber security laws. However, as stated in Part II and Part III, a number of states have yet to implement such laws, the importance of which cannot be underestimated. They do and will support the relevant skills sets that are needed to drive the future digitalised economy. For instance, modelling GDP losses associated with skills gaps, it is posited that GDP losses in South Africa (US$2 billion), Singapore (US$2.74 billion), Malaysia (US$0.394 billion), Australia (US$15.65 billion) and the UK (US$28 billion) have been largely driven by shortages of highly-skilled workers. It is argued that without a robust legal framework, the skills set of personnel in this highly technical economy is significantly diluted.

Nonetheless, internet penetration has been quite subdued. In 2017, 'Commonwealth countries had reached 48% internet penetration. That is, the countries of Brunei, United Kingdom, Canada and New Zealand ranked the highest, with more than 90% of the population having internet access, while more than half (28) of the Commonwealth member states fall below the world average on this measure'.[106] However, it was reported that in 'Kiribati, Malawi, Sierra Leone, Solomon Islands and PNG…less than 15% of the population were connected to the internet'.[107] In addition, and 'according to the GSMA mobile connectivity, Australia ranks the top country in the world, with a MCI score of 88.4 in 2018. Singapore ranks second, with an MCI score of 86.6, and New Zealand is third with an MCI score of 85.2. At the other end of the spectrum, a number of Commonwealth African countries (Eswatini, The Gambia, Malawi, Sierra Leone and Zambia), along with Pakistan and Solomon Islands, perform poorly on the MCI, suggesting key enablers of mobile connectivity are deficient in these countries'.[108] The Commonwealth Digital Connectivity Cluster is focused on supporting inclusive digital transformation across the Commonwealth:

- **Digital Economy**—digital transformation, specifically enabling the digital economy and digital value chains to facilitate trade;

[104] Ibid., p. 15.

[105] Ibid., p. 16.

[106] Ibid., p. 58.

[107] Ibid.

[108] Ibid.

- **Digital Trade**—is working to improve digital connectivity across the Commonwealth, provide an enabling environment for digital trade, and assist capacity-constrained members to take advantage of the opportunities presented by digital trade; and
- **Digital Industrial Policy**—sharing experience and expertise to enhance understanding and capacity in digital industrial policy by developing the evidence-based policies that facilitate the development of digital skills, digital trade, and digital industries across the Commonwealth.[109]

However, one of the major impediments to the digital economy being fully efficient and effective across the Commonwealth is that each country is at a different stage of development in terms of its infrastructure. A report in 2021 noted that a significant 'digital divide exists across the Commonwealth in terms of access, affordability and performance of hard infrastructure and soft infrastructure, which includes knowledge and technical skills'.[110] In determining the level of performance of the various regions that make up the Commonwealth, it was clear that the developed countries far exceeded that of the developing countries. For instance, countries in Europe and Asia performed better than those in other regions such as Africa, the Pacific and the Caribbean.[111] However, i the report did not mention the internal divide between urban and rural/regional areas in regard to the development of and success to the digital infrastructure. For instance, there are a number of Commonwealth countries such as India,[112] Australia and Canada, where digital services are either not available or as reliable as their urban counterparts. This internal national divide continues to be a challenge for many governments. If not addressed, it will impede the economic growth of the digital economy.

In recognising the need for a highly productive and supportive infrastructure framework, the Commonwealth has estimated that there needs to be a significant level of ongoing investment until 2030. Simply put, the level of infrastructure 'can reduce the global infrastructure bill by 40%, equivalent to US$1 trillion annually, creating savings that could boost economic growth by about 3% or more than US$3 trillion by 2030. For developing countries in Asia Pacific, USD$22.6 trillion in infrastructure investment will be needed from 2016 to 2030, equating to USD$1.5 trillion per year, if the region is to maintain growth and eradicate poverty. This figure would increase to US$26 trillion if an additional investment of US$1.7 trillion per year was included for cli-mate change mitigation costs'.[113] In effect, the Commonwealth understands the role and importance of digital trade within and across the wider digital economy.

[109] The Commonwealth, Digital Connectivity, https://thecommonwealth.org/connectivity-agenda/digital.

[110] Radika Kumar, Niels Strazdins, The Digital Infrastructure Divide in the Commonwealth, Trade Competitiveness Briefing Paper, (2021) p. 24.

[111] Ibid.

[112] Robert Walters, Leon Trakman, *Cross Border Data Flows*, 2022, a report for the United Kingdom [unpublished].

[113] Radika Kumar, Niels Strazdins, The Digital Infrastructure Divide in the Commonwealth, Trade Competitiveness Briefing Paper, (2021) p. 4.

For the Commonwealth, digital trade is a key element of digital transactions that are transnational.[114] Central to the proper function of digital trade and investment is personal data and, just as important, cybersecurity. Simon Lacey identifies five key areas of digital trade:

1. *Cross-border trade in ICT goods and services*;
2. *Digital goods*;
3. *Digitally-ordered goods*;
4. *Digitally-ordered services*; *and*
5. *Digitally-delivered services.*[115]

These areas are predominantly related to the online purchase of goods both nationally and internationally. However, Lacey's list does not include elements of the new digital economy such as FinTech; not does it reflect the rapid growth of online access to financial services. Apart from the standard commercial activities between individuals, Lacey notes the scope of e-commerce and digital trade chapters that have recently been included in bilateral, regional and mega-regional Free Trade Agreements (FTA). The Trans-Pacific Partnership (TTP), which became the Comprehensive and Progressive Agreement for Trans-Pacific Partnership (CPTPP), was the first FTA to contain binding treaty provisions for a set of commitments specifically negotiated with a view to addressing the needs of companies and citizens in the global digital economy.[116] This agreement did much to codify the existing status quo to achieve a balance of outcomes between what big digital business was asking for and what governments were willing to acquiesce to in terms of binding constraints on regulatory interventions in the digital economy. This is an important point as later, this book will examine the dispute resolution law of transnational arbitration in investor state and commercial transactions.

Case Study-1

Regional Comprehensive Economic Partnership [RCEP][117]
The RCEP came into force in January 2022.[118] Chapter 12 provides for Electronic Commerce. Online personal information protection is covered in accordance with Article 12.8.1, and ensures each

[114] Simon Lacey, *Digital Reboot: The Case for a Newly Invigorated Aid for Digital Trade Initiative*, International Trade Working Paper (2021), p. 10.

[115] Ibid., p. 10.

[116] Ibid.

[117] Robert Walters, *The Digital Economy and International Trade:* Regulation of Transnational Data Flows, Kluwer Law (2022), pp. 215–218. This case study of a free trade agreement came from earlier work undertake in 2022.

[118] Regional Comprehensive Economic Partnership (RCEP) agreement to enter into force on 1 January 2022, https://asean.org/regional-comprehensive-economic-partnership-rcep-to-enter-into-force-on-1-january-2022/.

'party can adopt or maintain a legal framework which ensures the protection of this important data'.[119] In drawing similarities with the TPP, Article 128.2, requires that 'in the development of its legal framework for the protection of personal information, each Party shall take into account international standards, principles, guidelines, and criteria of relevant international organisations or bodies'.[120] Further, each Party shall publish information on the personal information protection it provides to users of electronic commerce, including how: (a) individuals can pursue remedies; and (b) business can comply with any legal requirements.[121] Article 12.8.4 also requires the Parties 'shall encourage juridical persons to publish, including on the internet, their policies and procedures related to the protection of personal information'.[122] In promoting privacy over the internet, Article 12.8.5, 'encourages Parties to protect personal information transferred from a Party'.[123] While not expressly referring to cross-border transfers, it could mean both domestic and international transfers. While the above take a privacy protection focus, more specifically Section D promotes the idea of cross-border electronic commerce. In that basis, Article 12.14 requires Parties to take particular steps in relation to location of computing facilities. Importantly, it allows a degree of flexibility by the parties to use or locate such facilities in a Party's own territory, and develop their own measures to protect information and confidential communications. Further, Article 12.15 provides for the cross-border transfer of information. According to Article 12.15.1. makes it clear that countries understand that each other will have their own regulatory requirements that need to be met in regards to transferring information. This accords, to the current fragmented approach taken by nation states that are Party to RCEP. It also acknowledges that each member has their own sovereign needs for regulating data flows/transfers. Yet, Article 12.15.2, goes onto say that 'no one should prevent cross-border transfer of information in the conduct of business'.[124] Two matters arise here. First, it is asserted that there is a clear acknowledgement that information (data) is a fundamental requirement of the digital economy. Second, it promotes the idea for states not to place restrictive measures

[119] Ibid., Article 12.8.1.
[120] Ibid., Article 12.8.2.
[121] Ibid., Article 12.8.3.
[122] Ibid., Article 12.8.4.
[123] Ibid., Article 12.8.5.
[124] Ibid., Article 12.15.2.

in place to prevent transfers. In recognition of the importance of the new digital economy, Article 12.5 promotes the adoption of paperless trading as far as possible. Doing so, reinforces how this book has demonstrated that data will only increase as less and less paper is used. It will heighten the growth in data transfers and trade in goods and services that rely on personal data. In my view Chapter 12 of RCEP is very similar to that of the TPP. Surprisingly, countries did not take a broader view and recognise interoperability as a means of enhancing data transfers. Moreover, Chapter 12 makes no reference to regionalisation, internationalisation or harmonisation of cross-border data transfer law. It has by and large retained the status quo, which it is argued was a missed opportunity by all who are participants in RCEP.

A number of Commonwealth countries are party to the RCEP, including Australia, New Zealand, Brunei Darussalam and Singapore. India was originally involved in the negotiations, but withdrew completely in 2019. The point is that these agreement(s) can be subject to investor state disputes which, nevertheless, could be resolved through arbitration. In another development, Singapore has been a leader in the development of digital agreements. This type of agreement is arguably expressing the need to retain and improve the current status of the rule of law, with reference to long-standing international rules for governing data and their transnational flows. These developments highlight how data and cybersecurity will underscore the developing digital economy in the decades to come. Given these developments, it is important to understand the data and cybersecurity laws that will, in part, facilitate the growth of the digital economy.

Case Study-2

Australian and Singapore Digital Economic Agreement[125]

Notably, the Australian and Singapore Digital Agreement was established to amend the broader FTAs between the two countries, specifically Chapter 14 related to the Digital Economy.[126] It defines personal information to mean any information, including data, about an identified or identifiable natural person. Article 17

[125] Robert Walters, *The Digital Economy and International Trade:* Regulation of Transnational Data Flows, Kluwer Law (2022), p. 108. This case study of a free trade agreement came from earlier work undertake in 2022.

[126] Ibid., Australian and Singapore Digital Agreement, https://www.dfat.gov.au/sites/default/files/australia-singapore-digital-economy-agreement.pdf.

deals specifically with personal information and there is a general recognition that there are significant economic and social benefits for protecting the personal information of persons who conduct or engage in electronic transactions and commerce.[127] It calls for both Parties to take into account the principles and guidelines of relevant international bodies, such as the APEC Cross-Border Privacy Rules System[128] and the *OECD Guidelines Governing the Protection of Privacy and Trans-border.* Article 17.3 specifically references the OECD Guidelines requiring each Party to take into account when developing its legal framework include limitation on collection, data quality, purpose specification, use limitation, security safeguards, transparency, individual participation and accountability. Article 17.4 calls for 'non-discriminatory practices to be adopted in order to protect persons who conduct or engage in electronic transactions from personal information protection violations occurring within its jurisdiction'.[129] To provide a higher level of transparency, Article 17.5 requires each 'Party to publish information on the personal information protections along with information on how a data subject can pursue remedies and how businesses can comply with any legal requirements'.[130] In promoting transparency and accountability Article 17.6 'encourages enterprises in its territory to publish, including on the Internet, their policies and procedures related to protection of personal information'.[131] More generally, and not specific to personal information but wider information that is transferred by electronic means, Article 23, makes it clear that either Party has its own regulatory requirements. Every effort should be undertaken to ensure that there is no prohibition or restrictions placed on cross-border transfer of information by electronic means, including personal information, provided the information is in relation to the business of a covered person.[132] However, Article 23.3

[127] Ibid., Article 17.

[128] Articles, 17.8 and 17.9, The Parties recognise that the CBPR System is a valid mechanism to facilitate cross-border information transfers while protecting personal information. The Parties shall endeavour to jointly promote the CBPR System, with the aim to improving awareness of, and participation in, the CBPR System, including by industry.

[129] Ibid., Article 17.4.

[130] Ibid., Article 17.5.

[131] Ibid., Article 17.6.

[132] Ibid., Article 23.2.

allows a level of restrictions to be established to protect from discrimination or not disguised any restriction on trade. Further, any restrictions are not to impede transfers of information greater than are required to achieve the objective. Article 26 promotes the idea of data innovation so as to support the cross-border transfer of information by electronic means and promote data-driven innovation in the digital economy. Article 37, encourages cooperation in areas of capacity building across the Asia region in areas of the 'digital connectivity; small and medium business sector digital transformation; data protection regimes; and mechanisms to facilitate the cross-border transfer of information'.[133]

The evolution of the digital economy has been so rapid that, as stated earlier in this chapter, financial services have also been part of that change. In December, 2022, two Commonwealth countries, Bahamas and Nigeria,[134] were leading the way by experimenting with central bank digital currencies (CBDCs). CBDCs could transform the way that the financial services sector operates in coming years. They can:

- make payments more cost effective;
- increase financial inclusion, particularly rural and regional locations; and
- improve cross-border (transnational) payment by being prompt and more efficient.[135]

However, this new proposed finance operation comes with its own risks. The International Monetary Fund (IMF) note that holding large amounts of CBDCs could have a compression effect on bank margins; possible significant reputational risk; and pose challenges to countries that do not have a sophisticate and mature institutional framework. This includes a robust legal framework for personal data and cybersecurity. To date, it has been difficult to determine the economic benefit of CBDCs. Nonetheless, over the past four years, since 2018, a number of these CBDC assets have appeared on the market. These include:

- *CBOB, Sand Dollar*[136];
- *BOC*[137];

---

[133] Ibid., Article 37.

[134] Tobias Adrian, New Framework for the Digital Economy, International Monetary Fund, 2022, https://www.imf.org/en/News/Articles/2022/04/20/sp042022-new-framework-digital-economy.

[135] Ibid.

[136] Gabriel Soderberg, *Behind the Scenes of Central Bank Digital Currency Emerging Trends, Insights, and Policy Lessons*, International Monetary Fund (2022), p. 2. The Sand Dollar was officially launched in October 2020. In late 2021, there were around 20,000 active Sand Dollar wallets in a population of about 400,000, and functions are continuously being developed.

[137] Ibid., the BOC has not found a pressing case for a digital currency given the present state of the Canadian payments system. However, it continues to build the technical capacity to issue a CBDC, and monitor developments that could increase its urgency.

- *PBOC, e-CNY*[138];
- *ECCB, DCash*[139];
- *Sveriges Riksbank, e-krona*[140]; *and*
- *BCDU, e-peso.*[141]

Problematic though is that as at December 2022, this is an area of the digital economy that is significantly under-regulated. Nevertheless, in September 2022, the IMF [International Monetary Fund] released a synopsis of the challenges that CBDCs pose to personal data and cybersecurity. The IMF is calling for both personal data/ privacy and cybersecurity to be embedded in the CBDC design. The IMF stated 'technology enables central banks to ensure that both cybersecurity and privacy protection are embedded in any CBDC design'.[142] A salutary point to make is that at every point of the digital economy lifecycle, personal data and cyber security should be a key feature of the economic regulatory tool box in order to provide stability and certainty. However, the achievement of this regulatory stability and certainty could be problematic if a country has in place investment conditions/settings to deter investment. If its regulatory design restricts or excludes early entrants, this may lead to a complex investor state dispute.

The formal and functional status of personal data and cybersecurity in and across the digital economy, is only beginning to be fully understood. The United Nations Capital Development Fund (UNCDF) noted that in a small sample of African nations that are also members of the Commonwealth (Ghana, Kenya, Uganda and Zambia), as enterprises in a developing country become increasingly reliant on information and technology assets, that country will face the same cyber and personal data threats

---

[138] Ibid., no formal decision has been taken to launch the e-CNY. The PBOC runs a pilot in parallel in different regions. By October 2021, there were over 123 million e-CNY wallets registered with individuals and about 9.2 million wallets held by firms—a rapid increase from approximately six million active e-CNY wallets in April 2021. In a population of nearly one and a half billion, the share of e-CNY users is now approaching 10%.

[139] Ibid., No decision has been made to formally issue DCash. In March 2021, the ECCB launched a pilot program to successively extend DCash throughout the countries of the Eastern Caribbean Currency Union (ECCU) and run the program for 12 months. Given its rapid adoption, ECCB is now considering transitioning to an official CBDC launch.

[140] Ibid., No decision has been made to issue the e-krona. The Riksbank has developed a proof of concept and is exploring technological and policy angles of CBDC. A government inquiry is investigating the role of the state in the digital payments system, including the potential role of a CBDC.

[141] Ibid. After ending a pilot in 2018, the BCDU has changed leadership and has opted to not pursue a second pilot due to other priorities and a lack of resources. Potentially, a second pilot will be launched in the future.

[142] Giulia Fanti, Josh Lipsky, Ole Moehr, *Central bank digital currencies may pose security risks, but responsible design can turn them into opportunities*, International Monetary Fund, (2022), https://www.imf.org/en/Publications/fandd/issues/2022/09/Central-bankers-new-cybersecurity-challenge-Fanti-Lipsky-Moehr.

encountered by the developed countries.[143] Globally, cybercrime in 2020 was estimated to have nearly doubled to USD 945 billion from USD 522.5 billion in 2018, while spending on cybersecurity in 2020 was expected to exceed USD 145 billion together comprising 1.3% of global GDP.[144] While there are no specific statistics available for the Commonwealth, which accounts for one third of the world's total population,[145] intra-Commonwealth merchandise trade was estimated at US$433 billion[146] and intra-Commonwealth services exports were valued at US $238 billion in 2019.[147] Arguably, this will increase as the Commonwealth members becomes even more connected through the digital economy. It will also grow significantly due to the increasing population in rural/regional areas outside of the urbanised major cities (Chapter 1, 2018 Declaration on the Commonwealth Connectivity Agenda for Trade and Investment). This book will examine both the data and cybersecurity laws of Commonwealth members. It is anticipated that it will become a valuable reference for practitioners and policy makers. It will demonstrate how there is further work that the Commonwealth can undertake to strengthen the cooperation between member countries.

There is no doubt that the commercial and investment reality of cybersecurity and data in the digital economy will result in disputes. This book makes the case that arbitration can be used effectively to resolve commercial and liability-related issues involving technology that uses data and requires it to be secure. The next section outlines the structure and methodology of this book.

1.3 Structure and Methodology

The methodology adopted in this book involves an analysis of legal developments of the data and cybersecurity laws of all member countries of the Commonwealth. The general purpose of the book is to examine the extent to which data and cybersecurity laws vary from country to country. Part I offers suggestions on ways that the Commonwealth can improve the convergence and harmonisation of these areas of

---

[143] United Nations Capital Development Fund, *Policy Accelerator The role of cybersecurity and data security in the digital economy*, 2021, p. 3, https://static1.squarespace.com/static/5f2d7a54b7f75718fa4d2eef/t/62082f066a25c62651a9ae40/1644703527175/EN-UNCDF-Brief-CyberSecurity-2022.pdf.

[144] Ibid.

[145] The Commonwealth, US$345 billion loss in trade for Commonwealth countries due to pandemic, 2021, https://thecommonwealth.org/press-release/us345-billion-loss-trade-commonwealth-countries-due-pandemic.

[146] The Commonwealth, Chapter 1: Commonwealth Trade and the Pandemic, 2021, https://trade-review.thecommonwealth.org/chapter-one/#ch01_s5.

[147] Ibid.

laws. The Commonwealth has begun to undertake these steps, with the implementation of the Model Privacy Bill[148] and the Model Bill on the Protection of Personal Information.[149] The book contrasts and compares specific provisions of these two important Model Bills to confirm or otherwise the extent to which each member country of the Commonwealth has integrated the concepts and principles into their respective national laws (see research limitations). The comparison will demonstrate how data laws alone have become highly incoherent and significantly fragmented.

On the other side, the Commonwealth has also developed and equivalent Model Bill on Computer Related Crime (Cybersecurity).[150] In Part II, a similar approach has been undertaken to compare the specific provisions of the Model Bill with the national laws of Commonwealth member states. This book will identify a number of differences between the Model Bill and the laws of the nation states being compared. This book is the first of a series, and is a comparative analysis of the current-day legislation. At times, it will be descriptive and, in some cases, the provision(s) of the national laws have been directly transposed. This process has enabled the direct differences within and between the laws to be clearly identified. Generally, however, a conscious effort has been made to identify themes within the laws so as to make comparisons that are not unnecessarily detailed. Otherwise, the book would be double the size. It does not address how each jurisdiction's judiciary has responded to each of the concepts and the offence provisions being compared. Part III of this book compares the national laws of the countries in relation to international arbitration. Arbitration is a necessary inclusion in this book because data and cybersecurity come under the umbrella of commercial disputes. In addition, the book addresses data and cybersecurity in investor-state arbitration. Both commercial and investor-state arbitration will complement the trade and investment discussion due to the potential and likely disputes that will arise in the digital economy and that will include data and cybersecurity. In this part, the core elements of commercial arbitration have been identified, and the ensuing provisions of national law are outlined. Part III presents the key principles and concepts of arbitration that will need to be considered as the number of disputes related to the digital economy increases.

This research adopts the methodology of comparative law. Regarding Malta and Cyprus, because they are current members of the European Union (EU), the relevant EU laws will be considered in this research. Notably, the EU itself as a supranational polity is not a member of the Commonwealth, so the book does not discuss the United Kingdom (UK) and the BREXIT process. At times, it refers to and explains the extent to which the UK continues to retain the EU legal framework.

---

[148] The Commonwealth Model Privacy Bill, Office of Civil and Criminal Justice Reform, https://www.asianlaws.org/gcld/cyberlawdb/COM/P15370_9_ROL_Model_Privacy_Bill_0.pdf.

[149] The Commonwealth Model Bill on the Protection of Personal Information, Office of Civil and Criminal Justice Reform, https://www.asianlaws.org/gcld/cyberlawdb/COM/P15370_6_ROL_Model_Bill_Protection_Personal_Information_2.pdf.

[150] Model Law on Computer and Computer Related Crime, Office of Civil and Criminal Justice Reform, 2017, p. 1 https://production-new-commonwealth-files.s3.eu-west-2.amazonaws.com/migrated/key_reform_pdfs/P15370_11_ROL_Model_Law_Computer_Related_Crime.pdf.

Ibid., sections, 5, 6, 7, 8, 9.

Apropos of the above, Edward Eberle opines that a comparison of applied to laws provides insight into the other law, our own law and, as importantly, our own perceptions and intuitions—a self-reflection that can often yield insight into our view of the law.[151] According to Eberle, any comparative law analysis should address the following questions:

- Do we see law as only rules—commands that channel us along prescribed paths?
- Do we see law as filtered through the lens of our own law—native predispositions associated with our home territory?
- Is this a form of cognitive lock-in which colours or even blinds us?
- This would, of course, be quite natural, as we all reflect our own acculturations.
- Or do we see law as only illusion?
- Do we sense a disjunction between law as written versus law as applied or as practiced within a given culture?
- Is there some operation code or hidden formant we are missing that actually drives the pattern of law?[152]

However, undertaking such an intensive comparison of all Commonwealth countries' laws can be problematic as it requires us to separate ourselves from what Eberle describes as 'our own native culture'. This is because culture, legal families, history and national identify, amongst others, all influence how a person perceives and interpret the law. Therefore, comparative law offers us avenues by which to access other, foreign patterns of thought and organization different from those with which we are familiar.[153] In some cases, this offers us an opportunity to learn about histories and cultures outside our own national boundaries. Eberle maintains that this exposure provides a deeper level of understanding and a sense of 'commonalities in legal systems, such as rules, categories, or patterns of thought or order that resonate across national borders and sit also in our own law'.[154] In other words, comparative law discloses points of 'agreement and difference in the solution which is provided by several legal systems for the same legal problem'.[155] Clive Schmittoff asserts that the function of comparative law finds a system of legal abstractions based on the results of factual comparison, or as a special branch of the science of law. This is because it would be too difficult to discuss the historical beginnings and the cultural, religious, and other influences that have shaped the current day legal frameworks of the respective states.

---

[151] Edward Eberle, *The Methodology of Comparative Law,* Roger Williams University Law Review: Vol. 16: Iss. 1, (2011), pp. 51 53.

[152] Ibid.

[153] Ibid.

[154] Ibid.

[155] Clive Schmittoff, The Science of Comparative Law, The Cambridge Law Journal, 7(1), (1939), p. 94.

Adopting Max Rheinstein's approach,[156] comparative legal research is undertaken in two stages. The first stage requires each comparatist to study his own law. The author of this book has made a comprehensive study of Australia's data and cybersecurity laws. The second phase of Rheinstein's approach involves the study of foreign law, of the legal systems (including legislation and case law), which are currently in force. This is different from the comparative approach suggested by Peter de Cruz who considers the linguistic and terminological problems, and the cultural differences between legal systems.[157]

This book applies Rheinstein's approach by comparing all Commonwealth foreign data and cybersecurity laws. As this book demonstrates, and something that Rheinstein argues, although words may be in the same language, they may have either different or similar meanings even though they pertain to different legal systems. There is no better example than the definition of data and personal data, where the terms are different but, in practice, have the same meaning. However, overall, definitions vary greatly. A major challenge throughout this book is comparing the terminology and terms used by nation states within their respective national laws. Therefore, the extent to which comparisons have been undertaken is limited.

1.3.1 Referencing, Terminology and Limitation to This Research

Referencing throughout the book will be duplicated and be outside convention due to the breadth and depth of law being examined and compared. This is because, due to the nature of the law, the task of comparing the laws of all the different countries/jurisdictions being examined is a complex one. Hence, referencing has been structured in this way to ensure the reader can clearly identify the legal or scholarly source.

Further to the above, references to personal data, personal information or data or information pertain to personal data. The laws being examined do make references to data and information, particularly when defining these terms within the laws as the same. Each chapter will confirm where reference to particular terms, concepts or principles have been used and applied interchangeably. Additionally, the terms *state, nation states, countries* or *jurisdiction* refer to all the countries examined in this book, as well as the supranational polity of the European Union which is not a country.

[156] Max Rheinstein, *Comparative Law - Its Functions, Methods and Usages*, 22 Arkansas Law Review 415 (1968) p. 416.

[157] Peter de Cruz, *Comparative Law in a Changing World*, Cavendish Publishing Limited, (1991).

The terms *personal data, personal information, data* and *information* are all interchangeable and refer to *personal data.* This is because the laws of the respective jurisdictions examined in this book refer to such data as either personal information or personal data. Throughout this book, the terms and terminology used will be compared to indicate to the reader where there are gaps in the law, and clarification from the country is required. This is a complex comparative analysis that cannot be underestimated, because as the digital economy grows, commercial and personal disputes will arise related to the use of personal data and cyber security. Hence, the book does not examine all the rights afforded to data subjects whose personal data has been transferred to a third country.

Research Questions

The research questions have been developed following extensive research on the activities the Commonwealth is undertaking in relation to the evolving developments in data and cybersecurity law. Therefore, the core questions are:

- Is there an alternative way for the Commonwealth to strengthen the relationship amongst member states through data and cybersecurity governance and the law?
- Is legal convergence better than the status quo?
- Is there a need for a greater level of legal harmonisation?
- What further international involvement can the Commonwealth Secretariate advance in order to strengthen the legal norms and frameworks for data and cybersecurity in the new digital economy?
- Can international arbitration be an effective tool for resolving disputes related to data and cybersecurity?
- Is it time for Ethics to be included into the regulatory frameworks for data and cybersecurity?

Research Limitations

In this book, all member countries of the Commonwealth are analysed and compared. That said, there are limitations to this research. One of the overall dillemas is the competing policy objectives that data laws alone aim to achieve.

On the one hand the data laws have been developed to provide for a level of privacy protection over the internet, and protection-control for the data subject of their personal data. On the other hand, the dat laws provide for the flow of data nationally and internationally. These competing objectives alone are complex and have different economic outcomes. Data flows aims to build the digital economy. Data protection restricts the economic benefits from data flows, by placing a level of regulatory burden on an organisayion that trades in data. In comparing the data laws of the Commonwealth, the focus will be on the following principles and concepts:

- definitions;
- application to public and private sectors;
- controller, consent and processor;
- storage retention;

- localisation;
- international data transfer;
- data rights;
- data portability; and
- right to be forgotten.

An individual chapter will be devoted to each of the above concepts. Each chapter will be descriptive in that it will present the actual and specific provisions of the laws. This will be followed by an analysis that will indicate the differences in the approaches taken by Commonwealth states. For example, the definition of personal data varies significantly across all Commonwealth countries. Some states have included the term 'biometric' in the general definition, while other states have defined the term separately. In adopting this approach, the book aims to provide a comprehensive comparison of the key themes within the respective national laws.

The same approach has been adopted when considering the cybersecurity laws. That is, the comparative analysis has been limited to the concepts and principles pertaining to:

- illegal access;
- interference with data;
- interference with computer systems;
- illegal interception of data;
- illegal devices;[158]
- fraud;
- theft; and
- ransom.

The way that cybersecurity laws have been structured can be problematic. Simply put, some countries have adopted provisions from the respective Commonwealth Model Law, but many countries have not. Most chapters do cover instances where the actual provision from the national laws will be replicated. Each chapter will begin with an Abstract that specifies the relevant section/article in the Model Bill/Law.

Given the above, the examination has been confined to determining whether the offence itself exists, and to the key terms and terminology that are used in the provisions of the respective states legislation. By adopting this comparative approach, it is hoped that the reader will obtain an important general overview of the divergences and nuances of the laws. Hence, the reader who is relying on this resource as a practical guide will need to undertake further research to clarify the application of some terms, and their application in that state. Another purpose of the research conducted for this book is to determine whether each country has followed the Commonwealth Model Law.[159] Importantly, this book identifies the intersection of private law and criminal law. That is they are not often compared as a collective. This book further

[158] Commonwealth Secretariate, Model Law on Computer and Computer Related Crime, sections, 5, 6, 7, 8, 9. https://production-new-commonwealth-files.s3.eu-west-2.amazonaws.com/migrated/key_reform_pdfs/P15370_11_ROL_Model_Law_Computer_Related_Crime.pdf.

[159] Ibid.

demonstrates how the inter-connectedness of international trade, investment, criminal and private law will all be important to the new digital economy. Understanding the raft of laws pertaining to the digital economy is going to be highly challenging. One such area is international arbitration, commercial and investor-state arbitration. This is an area that is not often considered in relation to the potential challenges facing the digital economy. Furthemrore, not having access to large IT companies to confirm and analyse an Ethical framework/strategy makes it very challenging to fully understand how entites have responded, if at all.

Because of the extent to which laws will be examined, and the subsequent comparative analysis, the core chapters examining the respective state laws will be, unavoidably, descriptive. There will be limited reference to case law; rather, the focus will be on the current regulatory frameworks that have been established. In addition, because the laws of Commonwealth jurisdictions are being compared, it is outside the scope of this book to provide an analysis of every country's judicial and regulatory decisions on the offences, concepts and principles discussed. Hence, this is the first of a series of books, and it is anticipated that it will be updated every 3–5 years and will include the latest data and cyber laws of the Commonwealth. In addition, there is limited scholarly discussion and analysis in the monograph, as most of the content would be a repetition of what is stated in the book written by Robert Walters, Leon Trakman, Bruno Zeller (*Data Protection Law A Comparative Analysis of Asia–Pacific and European Approaches*, Springer 2019) and that of Robert Walters and Marko Novak (*Cyber Security, Artificial Intelligence, Data Protection & the Law*, Springer 2021). In most of the chapters, the author draws upon a number of judicial decisions in selected states. This is because data and cybersecurity judicial and regulatory decisions are limited and only in the past decade have such decisions been handed down as both areas of law are still evolving. Nieth data or cybersecurity law is fully settled.

1.3.2 Parts and Chapters

The 29 chapters of this book have been divided into **four Parts**. **Part I** is lengthy as it explains to the reader the extent of policy, legal scholarship and the law that need to be addressed when discussing and considering a pathway forward in relation to data, cybersecurity and arbitration in the digital economy. It draws upon the history and evolution of the Commonwealth. The problem definition identified in this book confirms that the data and cybersecurity laws examined are complex, multi-layered and incoherent. **Part II** examines and compares the data laws of all member countries of the Commonwealth. In Part **III,** the cybersecurity laws and responses of Commonwealth states are examined and compared. **Part IV** discusses the growing importance of international arbitration as a means of resolving commercial and investor-state disputes involving data and cybersecurity issues across the digital economy.

Chapter 3 compares all the Commonwealth states' data and privacy laws with the Commonwealth MBP and MBPPI. It shows how difficult it has become to define the term *personal data*, and describes the divergent approaches that have been taken. The definition of data is the starting point to establishing data flow policies, controls and protections of personal data. The terminology used by states will vary. Some will define data as personal data, while others will define it as personal information. The establishment of a Regulator has become very important to the administration and implementation of data law. Chapter 4 confirms whether the respective jurisdictions have required that a Regulator be established. It will demonstrate how jurisdictions have opted to define the Regulator as a Privacy, Information or Data Protection Commissioner.

The concepts of controller and consent, and the processing provisions within data laws have, along with the other concepts and principles, been compared in this book. Chapter 5 addresses these concepts collectively rather than individually. It provides an outline of the extent to which consent applies, and whether there are formal obligations for a controller and/or a processor to be appointed. The retention or storage of data has emerged as an issue in some jurisdictions. Chapter 6 examines how the respective jurisdictions have approached the governance of this concept. It confirms or otherwise whether there are time limits placed on the storage or data.

Data localisation is another important concept that is a recent addition to data law. Chapter 7 examines how data localisation requires entities in both the private sector and government sector to store the personal data of its citizens. Chapter 8 is a comprehensive examination of the law related to data flows. It highlights the importance of data flows to the digital economy, and demonstrates how the developments in this area of the law are significantly divergent.

Another recent development has been the introduction of the concept of data portability. Chapter 9 explains that people in most jurisdictions can request that their personal data be transferred to another organization within the state. The concept itself creates a level of competition, in that one single entity will not have a monopoly on the data being held.

The Right to be Forgotten has become a strongly acknowledged right, one which was initiated by the EU. Chapter 10 addresses this concept and confirms that neither the Commonwealth MBP nor the MBPPI provides for a specific right to be forgotten or erasure. This is problematic and is another area that the Commonwealth should consider in any review of these Model Laws. A formal and functional requirement of law administration is its application. Therefore, Chap. 11 determines whether or not the data laws of all jurisdictions apply to both the public and private sectors. It will be demonstrated that there is significant divergence in approaches. Finally, Chap. 12 summarises the overall the adoption of data rights.

Part III addresses the issues pertaining to cybersecurity law in Commonwealth member states. There is little doubt that both data and cybersecurity laws have an increasing level of interconnectedness. Chapter 14 begins by examining the offence of illegal access by a person who intentionally, without lawful excuse or justification, accesses the whole or any part of a computer system, thereby committing an offence punishable, on conviction, by imprisonment for a period or a fine, or both. The interference with data is examined in Chap. 15, and is closely aligned with the offence of illegally accessing a computer and its systems and infrastructure. Chapter 16 examines the responses by the respective jurisdictions to the offence of interfering with a computer system.

In addition to the aforementioned offences, the interception of data is another important offence provision that the Commonwealth Model law has developed. Therefore, Chap. 17 will examine the approach taken by the Commonwealth members in regard to this offence. It is argued that the interception of data is closely related to the use of devices to commit such offences. This chapter does not deal with the interception of data by government for enforcement purposes. In an equally important development, there are a plethora of devices on the market today that can access data both legally and illegally with ease. Thus, Chap. 18 compares the responses to addressing the use of illegal devices. Noteworthy is that the above offences have been addressed by the Commonwealth Model Law. However, the remaining offences below are not. It is argued that there is an urgent need for a review of the Commonwealth Model Law to consider the inclusion offence provisions for fraud (discussed in Chap. 19), identity theft (Chap. 20) and ransom-extortion (Chap. 21).

Part IV discusses the increasing importance of arbitration to the digital economy, and in particular data and cybersecurity. It makes the case that both commercial and investor-state arbitration are being considered as viable options to litigation when resolving disputes involving these areas. Chapter 22 introduces arbitration and highlights the work undertaken by the Commonwealth. Finally, as a pathway forward, ethics that now forms part of cybersecurity has been highlighted to confirm or otherwise whether further work is needed to address this concept with in the law. Doing so, may assist in strengthening future trade and investment relations between countries bilaterally so as to set themselves apart from other trading and investment guidelines across the world.

Similar to Part I and Part II, Chap. 23 gives the key definitions of terms such as *arbitration; international commercial arbitration; arbitration agreement; foreign arbitral award; arbitration award*, and examines whether they have been expressed by the respective national laws. In regard to the United Nations Commission on International Trade Law [UNCITRAL] Model Law on Arbitration (Model Law), Chap. 24 reveals the member countries of the Commonwealth that have adopted the Model Law, and confirms whether it has been addressed within the national laws.

On the one hand, Chap. 25 deals with the appointment of an arbitrator(s) under the relevant laws. It does not address a party's ability to challenge the appointment. One of the key areas of arbitration in the digital economy will be the use of experts. Therefore, Chap. 26 explores the role of this position because there will be specialists from the fields of law and technology who will need to be called upon to provide expert information and advice on data and cybersecurity, as well as emerging technologies and artificial intelligence.

Chapter 27 emphasizes the importance of enforcing an arbitral award. It draws upon the UNCITRAL Model Law on Arbitration which has served international commercial arbitration well. Once an arbitral award has been handed down by a

Tribunal, the decision is final and enforceable on the parties. Arguably, both international commercial arbitration and investor-state arbitration can be applied to both data and cybersecurity. Therefore, Chap. 28 presents and examines a recent example of an investor-state arbitration that included data and, to a lesser extent, the security of that data.

Finally, Chap. 29 confirms that data and cybersecurity law are important to the international digital economy. While they are separate in terms of law, in practice they are significantly connected. It briefly discusses the increasing attention that *Ethics* is having in the governance of data and cybersecurity. It call for further research and collalloration with the technology sector to better understand what and how ethics has been included into an organisations operations. Secondly, the chapter reveals the significant divergences in the national laws. Thirdly, it demonstrates that the Commonwealth has the opportunity to take a great role in developing international cooperation to enhance the digital economy via data and cyber law. Lastly, international arbitration is an important mechanism for resolving investor-state disputes and transnational commercial disputes that involve data and cybersecurity issues. It is envisaged that the Commonwealth and its members can collaborate and undertake the reforms suggested in this book. Doing so will strengthen the rule of law, the current values-based system of the Commonwealth according to the rules-based system. It will help to promulgate democratic values around the world, and ensure the digital economy is strengthened by a greater level of legal harmonisation and convergence.

Part II
Data Laws

Chapter 2
Data Flows and Data Protection Law

2.1 Introduction

This book is the first of its kind to offer an analysis of the data and cybersecurity laws of all nation states that make up the Commonwealth of Nations. This book makes the case and calls for greater integration of the Commonwealth of Nations. This is not a call for imperialism or a return to colonisation. The book argues that now that the United Kingdom is no longer a member of the European Union, there is an opportunity for the Commonwealth of Nations (CON) to reinvigorate its trade and investment relations, building on the current rule of law, within the digital economy. The Commonwealth of Nations has a collective population of more than 2.5 billion people, comprising all CON countries.[1] In November 2022, it was estimated that the world population had reached 8 billion.[2]

Data Protection and Privacy over the Internet

Although the concept of privacy is a multi-dimensional one, scholars over time and space have attempted to confine it to a single definition.[3] It can present in many different forms, such as within the home or over the Internet. Famously, Warren and Brandeis enunciated that the right to privacy was based on a principle of "inviolate personality",[4] thus laying the foundation for a concept of privacy which can be

---

[1] The Commonwealth, November 2022 https://thecommonwealth.org.

[2] United Nations, November 2022, https://www.un.org/en/dayof8billion.

[3] Shraddha Kulhari, "Data Protection, Privacy and Identity: A Complex Triad." *Building-Blocks of a Data Protection Revolution: The Uneasy Case for Blockchain Technology to Secure Privacy and Identity*, 1st ed., Nomos Verlagsgesellschaft mbH, (2018), p. 23.

[4] Samuel Warren and Louis Brandeis, *'The Right to Privacy' (1890) 4 Harvard Law Review 193*, as cited in Judith DeCew, 'Privacy', The Stanford Encyclopedia of Philosophy, 2015 https://plato.stanford.edu/archives/spr2015/entries/privacy/ In Shraddha Kulhari, "Data Protection, Privacy and Identity: A Complex Triad." *Building-Blocks of a Data Protection Revolution: The Uneasy Case for*

R. Walters, *Cybersecurity and Data Laws of the Commonwealth*,
https://doi.org/10.1007/978-981-99-3935-0_2

understood to be the control over one's own information. Westin defined privacy as a 'claim of individuals, groups or institutions to determine for themselves when, how and to what extent information about them is communicated to others'.[5] Kalhari in referring to Roger Clarke's work, identifies four categories of privacy: privacy of the person; of behaviour; of data; and of communication. Yet, in examining Clarke's analysis, the four areas of privacy extend to:

> **Privacy of the Person**, sometimes referred to as 'bodily privacy', is concerned with the integrity of the individual's body. In its broadest sense, it could be interpreted as extending to freedom from torture and right to medical treatment, although these are more commonly seen as human rights rather than as aspects of privacy.
> **Privacy of Personal Behaviour** includes what is sometimes referred to as 'media privacy'. However, the notion of 'private space' is vital to all aspects of behaviour, pertains to 'private places' such as the home and toilet cubicle, and is also relevant to public places, where casual observation by a few people in the vicinity is very different from systematic observation and the recording of images and sounds.
> **Privacy of Personal Communications**, includes what is sometimes referred to as 'interception privacy'. Individuals desire the freedom to communicate among themselves, using various media, without the routine monitoring of their communications by other persons or organisations.
> **Privacy of Personal Data** is sometimes referred to as 'data privacy and information privacy. Individuals claim that data about themselves should not be automatically available to other individuals and organisations, and that, even where data is possessed by another party, the individual must be able to exercise a substantial degree of control over that data and its use. The last five decades have seen the application of information technologies to a vast array of abuses of data privacy.[6]

It is this last point raised by Clarke that is most pertinent to this book as it relates to the protection and privacy of personal data, along with its security in a time of increasing cyber intrusions. It is the personal data that has been defined by national and supranational laws, and gives rise to the operation of the other concepts and principles compared in this book.

Blockchain Technology to Secure Privacy and Identity, 1st ed., Nomos Verlagsgesellschaft mbH, (2018), p. 23.

[5] Alan F. Westin, 'Privacy and Freedom', Washington and Lee Law Review, Vol. 25 Issue 1 (1967) 7, http://scholarlycommons.law.wlu.edu/cgi/viewcontent.cgi?article=3659&context=wlulr In Shraddha Kulhari, "Data Protection, Privacy and Identity: A Complex Triad." *Building-Blocks of a Data Protection Revolution: The Uneasy Case for Blockchain Technology to Secure Privacy and Identity*, 1st ed., Nomos Verlagsgesellschaft mbH, (2018), p. 23.

[6] Roger Clarke, *What's Privacy?* Workshop at the Australian Law Reform Commission, (2006), http://www.rogerclarke.com/DV/Privacy.html.

Against the backdrop above, is the need to consider how culture, geographic location and linguistics have shaped and influenced the development of data and privacy law. It is beyond the scope of this book to describe the cultural backgrounds of all the countries of interest.

Thompson et al. have proposed models to explain and understand how members of a society share beliefs and values.[7] It is these beliefs and values that have shaped the way that nation states respond to the protection of data transmitted via the Internet. The authors describe a national culture in terms of six dimensions; in this model, culture is defined as "the collective programming of the mind that distinguishes the members of one group or category of people from others". This forms a national identity, which shapes the national laws for data protection, cross-border data flows, and privacy. Thompson et al. go on to say that:

> Although every collective is comprised of individuals, in aggregate the members of a collective often exhibit similar patterns along the six dimensions. Differences in cultural dimensions are associated with differences in privacy concerns in some domains. For example, high power distance has been shown to be related to higher levels of concerns over social network services privacy, and higher levels of individualism have been found to be related to lower levels of privacy concerns. Differences in these dimensions may also have implications for how members of a society accept government surveillance or how they enact measures to protect their privacy.[8]

From Australia to Singapore, to India, to Canada to Malta, to the UK and the other 51 Commonwealth members, all have their own unique national identities, culture and language that have shaped their respective development of data laws. Furthermore, their responses have been influenced by their geographic location, and economic, social and environmental needs. Thompson et al. go further, stating that:

> Those in high power distance cultures are accustomed to an unequal distribution of authority. Hence, they are more likely to tolerate governmental interferences with privacy than those in low power distance cultures. In the consumer space, there is relationship between privacy concerns and acceptance of information collection is moderated by power distance. Individuals in countries high on the power distance index have lower levels of interpersonal trust. As a consequence, individuals in those countries may not only accept but even desire greater government involvement, which is seen as a means to protect them. Moreover, as those from high power distance cultures are used to a hierarchical social structure they may be more accepting of information gathering from those in a position of authority and the influence of any personal concerns may be weaker.[9]

A further examination of the individualistic or collectivist calculus, and its determinative influence.

> confirmed that those nations with a higher level of collectivism did place a greater emphasis on privacy protections, presumably in order to safeguard their collective. Culture moderates

---

[7] Thompson, N. and McGill, T. and Bunn, A. and Alexander, R. 2020. *Cultural Factors and the Role of Privacy Concerns in Acceptance of Government Surveillance.* Journal of the Association for Information Science and Technology. 71: (2020) pp. 1129– 1135.

[8] Ibid.

[9] Ibid.

> the intentions to use protective technology; a finding which is associated with the cultural influence on perceptions about privacy.[10] [emphasis added]

Subsequently, we see many of the data laws coming into existence only in the past decade. It is in the more mature jurisdictions of Australia, New Zealand, Canada, Malta, Cyprus and UK (subject to EU GDPR upon membership), that data and privacy law dates back more than three decades. Put another way:

> Privacy and data protection are intimately related. The emergence of the first data protection legislations in the early 1970s, as well as their subsequent developments, were and have been aimed at tackling problems generated by new technologies. Within the broad spectrum of problems to be resolved, the application of those data protection regulatory schemes were – to a great extent – motivated by privacy concerns. In fact, one can say that the incessant development and sophistication of data protection legal frameworks across the last decades has taken place as a result of the fact that individuals' privacy is continuously under threat via increasingly novel means. This process of distinguishing a series of different generations of data protection legislations, characterizing them as progressive extensions of the legal protection of privacy.[11]

This book will demonstrate the above: that those states which have recently added data laws to their respective legal frameworks have been influenced not only by their own identities and culture, but also by the broader international approach to this complex area of law and policy.

Table 2.1 lists the current member countries that make up the Commonwealth of Nations as of 1 January 2023. It is outside the scope of this book to specify when each of the member countries was accepted as a full member of the Commonwealth.

Commonwealth member states are dispersed widely across the globe and comprise both developed and developing countries. Some states such as Malta and Cyprus are members of the European Union, a supranational polity. Other states, notably the United Kingdom, have recently exited the EU. Member countries are located in the Americas the Caribbean, and the Indo Pacific region. The table above will be duplicated in this book to provide an up-to-date table of current data, cyber-security and arbitration laws.

2.1.1 Regional Influences

There are a number of regional influences that have both a direct and indirect impact on the way Commonwealth members engage with other members. Hence, this section will discuss only the African Union (AU), the Association of South East Asian Nations, the Organisation for Economic Cooperation and Development, Organisation for Economic Cooperation and Development, and the South Asian Association for Regional Cooperation.

---

[10] Ibid.

[11] Norberto Andrade, *Data Protection, Privacy and Identity: Distinguishing Concepts and Articulating Rights.* 6th International Summer School, (2010), Helsingborg, Sweden. pp. 90–92.

Table 2.1 Members of the commonwealth

Africa	Asia	Caribbean and Americas	Europe	Pacific
Botswana	Bangladesh	Antigua and Barbuda	Cyprus	Australia
Cameroon	Brunei Darussalam	Bahamas	Malta	Fiji
Gabon	India	Barbados	United Kingdom	Kiribati
Gambia	Malaysia	Belize		Nauru
Ghana	Maldives	Canada		New Zealand
Kenya	Pakistan	Dominica		Papua New Guinea
Kingdom of Eswatini	Singapore	Grenada		Samoa
Lesotho	Sri Lanka	Guyana		Solomon Islands
Malawi		Jamaica		Tonga
Mauritius		Saint Lucia		
Mozambique		Saint Kitts and Nevis		
Namibia		Saint Vincent and The Grenadines		
Nigeria		Trinidad and Tobago		
Rwanda				
Seychelles				
Sierra Leone				
South Africa				
Togo				
Uganda				
United Republic of Tanzania				
Zambia				

African Union [AU]

Twenty-six African countries are members of both the Commonwealth (see Table 1.1) and the AU. The latter was launched in 2002, in Durban, South Africa, following a decision in September 1999 by its predecessor, the Organisation of African Unity (OAU), to create a new continental organisation to build on its work.[12] Similar to its ASEAN counterpart, the AU prides itself on consensus. Of importance is Article 3, because unlike the EU member states, AU members do not relinquish any of their sovereignty to the AU. Article 3 states that the Union's purpose shall be to defend the sovereignty, territorial integrity and independence of its member states.[13] Via Article 5, the AU has created a number of institutions that include:

(a) The Assembly of the Union;
(b) The Executive Council;
(c) The Pan-African Parliament;
(d) The Court of Justice;
(e) The Commission;

[12] African Union, https://au.int/en/overview.

[13] The Constitutive Act https://au.int/sites/default/files/pages/34873-file-constitutiveact_en.pdf.

(f) The Permanent Representatives Committee;
(g) The Specialized Technical Committees;
(h) The Economic, Social and Cultural Council;
(i) The Financial Institutions.[14]

In terms of the institutional framework, these institutions are very similar to those established by the EU. On the other hand, the framework is significantly different from that of ASEAN. Within ASEAN, the institutional framework does not contain a Court, and is represented by individuals from each of the member states. It is out of scope to discuss and compare the differences between each of the regional organisations. Arguably, they each have their own level of influence regarding the development and implementation of data and cybersecurity laws.

A major point of difference between ASEAN and AU is that across Africa there is a move towards strengthening their respective relationships by taking a common approach to the governing of data and cybersecurity. The African Union Convention on Cyber Security and Personal Data Protection, adopted in 2014[15] and guided by the Constitutive Act 2000, sets a high-level framework for the governing of data and cybersecurity. The Preamble states that Member States of the African Union be Guided by the Constitutive Act of the African Union adopted in 2000, considering that this Convention on the Establishment of a Legal Framework for Cyber-security and Personal Data Protection embodies the existing commitments of African Union Member States at sub-regional, regional and international levels to build an information society. The importance of this early convention cannot be underestimated. It is a reflection of the understanding the member countries have of the impending digital economy, and how data and cybersecurity will form an integral part of trade and investment. As will be demonstrated throughout this book, the data protection laws of African nations that are also members of the Commonwealth have, by and large, been established only recently.

Furthermore, the Southern African Development Community (SADC) was established in1980, its main aim being to coordinate development projects in order to lessen economic dependence on the then-apartheid South Africa. A number of Commonwealth members are founding members, including Botswana, Lesotho, Malawi, Mozambique, United Republic of Tanzania, Zambia and Zimbabwe'.[16] Most

[14] Ibid., Article 5.

[15] The African Union Convention on Cyber Security and Personal Data Protection 2014, https://au.int/sites/default/files/treaties/29560-treaty-0048_-_african_union_convention_on_cyber_security_and_personal_data_protection_e.pdf.

[16] African Union, Southern African Development Community, https://au.int/en/recs/sadc.

noteworthy is that in 2013, the SADC developed a Model Law on Data Protection,[17] which provides for:

- Data Protection Authority;
- Quality of the Data;
- General Rules on the Processing of Personal Data;
- Duties of the Data Controller and Data Processor;
- Rights of the Data Subject; and
- Recourse to the Judicial Authority.[18]

While it is beyond the scope of this book to examine the Model Law in full, it is another demonstration of the regional approach being taken by countries when developing their respective data laws. Arguably, the above high-level concepts governing the data are also shaping and influencing the governance of data. These concepts can be found in the current data laws of other members of the Commonwealth. Furthermore, the Economic Community of West African States (ECOWAS) passed the Personal Data Protection Act 2010.[19] It encourages member countries to 'establish a legal framework of protection for privacy of data relating to the collection, processing, transmission, storage, and use of personal data without prejudice to the general interest of the State'.[20] When read in conjunction with the current data laws and the 2013 Model Law of SADC, of African member states of the Commonwealth, this early 2010 Act, arguably established a robust framework to follow. Both set out many of the core principles and concepts that had been established by the OECD.

In reconciling the differences in cyber laws and government responses to cyber breaches, in 2008, the East African Community (EAC)[21] adopted the Framework for Cyber Laws.[22] When developing these laws, the Task Force examined the work undertaken by the Commonwealth,[23] amongst other institutions. One of the key recommendations is the critical importance of data rotection and privacy to ensure that:

(a) the privacy of citizens is not eroded through the Internet;
(b) the legislation allowing access to official information is appropriately taken into account;

[17] Southern African Development Community, Model Law Data Protection, https://www.itu.int/en/ITU-D/Projects/ITU-EC-ACP/HIPSSA/Documents/FINAL%20DOCUMENTS/FINAL%20DOCS%20ENGLISH/sadc_model_law_data_protection.pdf.

[18] Ibid.

[19] The Economic Community of West African States, Data Protection Act 2010, https://www.statewatch.org/media/documents/news/2013/mar/ecowas-dp-act.pdf.

[20] Ibid., p. 4.

[21] United Nations, Harmonising Cyberlaws and regulations: The Experience of the East African Community, https://au.int/sites/default/files/newsevents/workingdocuments/27223-wd-harmonizing_cyberlaws_regulations_the_experience_of_eac1.pdf.

[22] East African Community Legal Framework for Cyber Laws, 2008, http://repository.eac.int:8080/bitstream/handle/11671/1815/EAC%20Framework%20for%20Cyberlaws.pdf?seq.

[23] Ibid., p. 4.

(c) the institutional implications of such reforms; and
(d) international best practice in the area is fully taken into account.[24]

However, according to the East African Community, these were draft laws and have not been updated. The importance of their work lies in its giving an outline of the interconnectedness between data and cybersecurity laws. There is a general recognition that while they pose a regulatory burden (cost) to trade and investment, such laws are becoming increasingly more important to the stability of the digital economy.

More recently, in November 2022, the Commission of the AU along with the African Development Bank established a grant that would deliver the Digital Market Development project.[25] The project will assist in the 'implementation of digital economy projects to enhance a continental single digital market. It also supports the implementation of the African Continental Free Trade Area and the Digital Transformation Strategy for Africa'.[26] This is against the backdrop of recent estimates that Africa's digital economy has expanded and is continually growing, with a market size of USD$115 billion which is expected to reach USD $712 billion by 2050.[27] Judging by this timeframe, it is also anticipated that Africa will be home to a third of the world's youngest people, who will be urbanising and accounting for 1 in 6 of the world's internet users. Given these trends, African member countries of the Commonwealth will provide a strong and valuable pathway to data and cyber governance, as they will encounter a number of challenges along the way. It remains to be seen whether, under the current AU structure, there will be a push towards legal convergence. Furthermore, a major sector in the economy will be financial services, which is worth over $165 bn and growing.[28] As this sector alone continues to grow, many people in rural and regional areas will have unprecedented access to financial services. In addition, commerce alone in the small and medium business sector accounts for 83% of private-sector employment.[29] As this sector also transitions to the online world, the digital economy will expand. This will generate an increasing amount of personal data which could be compromised by unauthorised breaches of systems and infrastructure.

---

[24] Ibid., p. 18.

[25] African Development Bank Group, African Development Bank and African Union Commission sign $9.73 million grant agreement to drive digital market development in Africa, https://www.afdb.org/en/news-and-events/press-releases/africa-development-bank-and-african-union-commission-sign-973-million-grant-agreement-drive-digital-market-development-africa-56615.

[26] Ibid.

[27] European Business Council of Africa, 2022, https://www.ebcam.eu/publications/reference-reports-and-documents/2989-the-inflection-point-africa-s-digital-economy-is-poised-to-take-off Also see Endeavour, 2022, https://endeavornigeria.org/wp-content/uploads/2022/06/Endeavor_The-Inflection_Point_June-2022.pdf.

[28] Endeavour, 2022, p. 36, https://endeavornigeria.org/wp-content/uploads/2022/06/Endeavor_The-Inflection_Point_June-2022.pdf.

[29] Ibid.

ASEAN [Association of South East Asian Nations]

Notably, Singapore and Malaysia are members of ASEAN. The ASEAN[30] has released a number of strategic documents that guide the development of cross-border data flows throughout South East Asia. The 2021 ASEAN Master Digital Plan (Digital Plan)[31] is intended to achieve three desirable outcomes:

(1) to extend current efforts and ensure connectivity to the Internet throughout ASEAN;
(2) to ensure that any connectivity is safe and relevant to the needs of end users; and
(3) to provide the platform for existing barries to be removed to ensure business and consumers can operate in a coherent and efficient environment.[32]

These three outcomes, while aspirational within a five-year period, are underpinned by a number of desirable actions. Notably, the achievement of these desired outcomes will deliver a 'trusted digital service and prevent consumer harm. A key part of this is ensuring that cybersecurity and digital data governance best practices are adopted as widely as possible, both to mitigate the direct impact of a breach on business and consumers and to build'.[33] As detailed below, a core element of the development and implementation of data policy and law within the digital economy is the assurance that there will be a high level of trust. Establishing this level of trust will support system certainty, infrastructure, and frameworks. One of the main enabling actions of DO3 is to 'identify improvements in legal and regulatory measures on the management of protection of data and other data-related activities that could be harmful'.[34]

The 2022 draft ASEAN Cybersecurity Cooperation Strategy[35] makes an important point in relation to the interconnection between economic certainty and protecting data, systems and infrastructure. It states how 'cybersecurity is a key enabler of the economic progress and betterment of living standards in the digital economy'.[36] The point is that cybersecurity is integral to the digital economy (trade and investment),

---

[30] Association of South East Asian Nations [ASEAN], a Regional Bloc that is made of member countries including, Brunei, Cambodia, Indonesia, Laos, Malaysia, Myanmar, the Philippines, Singapore, Thailand, and Vietnam, https://asean.org/about-asean/member-states/ This section draws on the work in Robert Walters, *The Digital Economy and International Trade:* Regulation of Transnational Data Flows, Kluwer Law (2022), Chapter 1.

[31] ASEAN Master Digital Plan 2021–2025, https://asean.org/book/asean-digital-masterplan-2025/ A DO is an action or an aim that directs the future governance of digital regulation.

[32] Ibid.

[33] Ibid., p. 6.

[34] Ibid., p. 16.

[35] Association of South East Nations, Cybersecurity Cooperation Strategy, 2022, https://asean.org/wp-content/uploads/2022/02/01-ASEAN-Cybersecurity-Cooperation-Paper-2021-2025_final-23-0122.pdf.

[36] Ibid., p. 2.

and follows the ASEAN Cybersecurity Cooperation Strategy 2017–2020, which was a roadmap for regional cooperation intending to achieve the objective of a safe and secure ASEAN cyberspace. It further highlights the interrelationship between cyber and data. It makes the point that:

> traditional cyber and digital risks issues are no longer as straightforward as they used to be as these domains have evolved to be more cross-cutting and complex. International and domestic conversations on the correlation between cyber and digital issues such as data security, misinformation and disinformation, influence operations and fake news, to name a few, are gradually gaining more traction in cybersecurity discussions.[37]

In addition, it follows key areas of work that include:

(1) Advancing Cyber Readiness Cooperation;
(2) Strengthening Regional Cyber Policy Coordination;
(3) Enhancing Trust in Cyberspace;
(4) Regional Capacity Building; and
(5) International Cooperation.[38]

The above is premised on the growth in the digitalisation of the trade and investment economy. Furthermore, it is premised on the sophistication of cyber-attacks and the increase in these attacks that have emerged over the past decade. That said, 'networks are more interconnected today, with supply chains of computer products and services being complex and varied. In this context, a sophisticated exploit such as the recent high-profile cyberattacks have indiscriminately impacted many unsuspecting victims beyond the prime targets and potentially create consequences that disrupt regional and international stability'.[39] Importantly, and unlike the EU, ASEAN takes a strategic consensus approach, rather than a top-down approach, by offering a platform for cooperation to build capacity.[40] This approach, intended to secure the cyber world, will become increasingly important to securing the digital economy.

However, 'the digitization of Asian economies is generating a vast pool of data, and companies in the region appear to be in a good position to monetize the value of this data'.[41] As the technology landscape continues to change, entities will need 'to strengthen the capabilities they need in order to manage digital transformations, and also strike a balance between reaping the economic benefits of using exploding data pools, while being sensitive to risks and concerns'.[42] Significantly,

[37] Ibid., p. 6.

[38] Ibid., p. 6.

[39] Ibid., p. 6.

[40] Ibid.

[41] Mckinsey Company, Harnessing the power of data and technology to win in the Asian century, 2022, https://www.mckinsey.com/featured-insights/future-of-asia/videos/harnessing-the-power-of-data-and-technology-to-win-in-the-asian-century.

[42] Ibid.

the 'digital economy is on track to grow to $1 trillion by 2030, as millions of new internet users fuel online businesses in fields including e-commerce and virtual finance'.[43] Although this projected new activity will bring significant benefits to ASEAN economies, potentially, it may pose many challenges to cybersecurity.

Organisation for Economic Cooperation and Development [OECD]

Vincenzo Spiezia and Jan Tscheke maintain that the OECD acknowledges the progress that the international community has made towards the development of international and regional legal frameworks.[44] While not specifically citing Commonwealth member states, it is argued that the work undertaken by the OECD has been pivotal to the development of data laws, whether in Africa, Europe, UK, Pacific, Central or South East Asia.

In 1980, the OECD developed the Guidelines on the Protection of Privacy and Transborder Flows of Personal Data (updated in 2013). Five years later, this was followed by the Declaration on Transborder Data Flows 1985. Both the Guidelines and the Declaration have been instrumental in establishing the policy platform for nation states to develop their respective data protection laws that, in part, provide for cross-border data flows. Later in 2016, in the OECD Ministerial Declaration on the Digital Economy, ministers and high-level representatives from 41 countries and the European Union declared that they would support the free flow of information via policies that reinforce the Internet's openness, while respecting applicable frameworks for privacy and data protection, and strengthening digital security.[45] Specifically, they believe that, given a particular level of data protection, international data agreements will aim to increase the interoperability between (or even harmonise) different frameworks across national jurisdictions.[46] This can reduce regulatory burdens and foster cross-border data flows for participating countries, particularly those with similar levels of data protection but incompatible regulatory approaches. The preamble to the original OECD (1980) Privacy Guidelines explicitly states that disparities in national legislations threaten to hamper the free flow of personal data across frontiers, causing potentially serious disruptions to important sectors of the economy. The preamble also states that this potential risk has been the

---

[43] ASEAN's digital economy projected to hit $1tn by 2030, https://asia.nikkei.com/Business/Business-trends/ASEAN-s-digital-economy-projected-to-hit-1tn-by-2030.

[44] Vincenzo Spiezia, Jan Tscheke, International agreements on cross-border data flows and international trade: A statistical analysis, Organisation for Economic Cooperation and Development, OECD Science, Technology and Industry Working Papers 2020/09, p. 16. Note, that this section regarding the draws on the earlier work from Robert Walters highlighted above in chapter I. *The Digital Economy and International Trade:* Regulation of Transnational Data Flows, Kluwer Law (2022), Chapter 1. The reason for this duplication of work is because the OECD Guidelines are, and have been, the most influential framework in providing a roadmap for countries across the Commonwealth to establish national data laws.

[45] Ibid., p. 6.

[46] Ibid.

reason that 'OECD member countries considered it necessary to develop guidelines which would help to harmonise national privacy legislation and, while upholding such human rights [data privacy], would at the same time prevent interruptions in international flows of data'.[47]

Pertinent to the above, Part II of the 2013 Guidelines on the Protection of Privacy and Transborder Flows of Personal Data sets out the most recognisable principles and concepts governing data internationally. These are:

- **Collection Limitation**—There should be limits to the collection of personal data and any such data should be obtained by lawful and fair means and, where appropriate, with the knowledge or consent of the data subject.[48]
- **Data Quality**—Personal data should be relevant to the purposes for which they are to be used, and, to the extent necessary for those purposes, should be accurate, complete and kept up-to-date.[49]
- **Purpose Specification**—The purposes for which personal data are collected should be specified not later than at the time of data collection and the subsequent use limited to the fulfilment of those purposes or such others as are not incompatible with those purposes and as are specified on each occasion of change of purpose.[50]
- **Use Limitation**—Personal data should not be disclosed, made available or otherwise used for purposes other than those specified, with the consent of the data subject; or (b) by the authority of law.[51]
- **Security Safeguards**—Personal data should be protected by reasonable security safeguards against such risks as loss or unauthorised access, destruction, use, modification or disclosure of data.[52]
- **Openness**—There should be a general policy of openness about developments, practices and policies with respect to personal data. Means should be readily

---

[47] Ibid.

[48] OECD Guidelines on the Protection of Privacy and Transborder Flows of Personal Data, 2013, https://www.oecd.org/sti/ieconomy/oecdguidelinesontheprotectionofprivacyandtransborderflowsofpersonaldata.htm. The OCED's 38 member include: Austria, Australia, Belgium, Canada, Chile, Colombia, Costa Rica, Czech Republic, Denmark, Estonia, Finland, France, Germany, Greece, Hungary, Iceland, Ireland, Israel, Italy, Japan, Korea, Latvia, Lithuania, Luxembourg, Mexico, the Netherlands, New Zealand, Norway, Poland, Portugal, Slovak, Slovenia, Spain, Sweden, Switzerland, Turkey, the United Kingdom and the United States.

[49] Ibid. See also, Professor Graham Greenleaf Asia–Pacific developments in information privacy law and its interpretation, 2006, pp. 3–11. https://www.google.com/search?q=Greenleaf+oecd+pRINSIPLES, Graham Greenleaf, "APEC privacy principles Version 2: not quite so Lite, and NZ wants OECD full strength" [2003] PrivLawPRpr 30; (2003) 10(3) Privacy Law and Policy Reporter 45. Graham Greenleaf, It's Nearly 2020, so What Fate Awaits the 1980 OECD Privacy Guidelines? (A Background Paper for the 2019 OECD Privacy Guidelines Review) (2019) 159 Privacy Laws & Business International Report 18–21, pp. 3–6.

[50] Ibid., pp. 3–11.

[51] Ibid., pp. 3–11.

[52] Ibid., pp. 3–11.

available of establishing the existence and nature of personal data, and the main purposes of their use, as well as the identity and usual residence of the data controller.[53]

- **Individual Participation**—An individual should have the right (a) to obtain from a data controller, or otherwise, confirmation of whether or not the data controller has data relating to him; (b) to have communicated to him, data relating to him within a reasonable time; at a charge, if any, that is not excessive;
- in a reasonable manner; and in a form that is readily intelligible to him; (c) to be given reasons if a request made under subparagraphs (a) and (b) is denied, and to be able to challenge such denial; and (d) to challenge data relating to him and, if the challenge is successful to have the data erased, rectified, completed or amended.[54]
- **Accountability**—A data controller should be accountable for complying with measures which give effect to the principles stated above.[55]

Since the 2013 review of the Guidelines, the OECD has acknowledged that personal data has come to play an even more important role in all economies, societies and people's everyday lives. These trends in data collection, analysis and use are transforming business models and organisational practice across all sectors of our economies.[56] In 2021, the OECD undertook a review of the Guidelines,[57] which confirmed the importance of privacy as an international reference on minimum standards for privacy and personal data protection that adherents implement in practice through legislation, enforcement and policy measures. Graham Greenleaf[58] argued that the Guidelines should be left as they are.[59] However, Greenleaf did put forward the need to retain Part II of the 2013 version as it:

> … add(s) a considerable range of new rights and obligations reflecting some of the content of the GDPR and Convention 108+, thus positioning the OECD Guidelines as a more credible contender to be a moderate minimum standard of data privacy protections, and as a candidate for what convergence (or even 'interoperability') initiatives could aim to implement.[60]

---

[53] Ibid., pp. 3–11.

[54] Ibid., pp. 3–11.

[55] Ibid.

[56] Ibid. See Robert Walters, *The Digital Economy and International Trade:* Regulation of Transnational Data Flows, Kluwer Law (2022), Chapter 1.

[57] OECD, Report on the Implementation of the Recommendation of the Council Concerning Guidelines Governing the Protection of Privacy and Transborder Flows of Personal Data, JT03473010, (2021), pp. 4–6.

[58] Graham Greenleaf, *It's Nearly 2020, so What Fate Awaits the 1980 OECD Privacy Guidelines?* (A Background Paper for the 2019 OECD Privacy Guidelines Review) (2019) 159 Privacy Laws & Business International Report 18-2, UNSW Law Research Paper No. 19-42, Graham Greenleaf AM, Professor of Law & Information Systems, UNSW, Australia, and a member of the OECD's Privacy Guidelines Expert Group (PGEG). Also in Robert Walters, *The Digital Economy and International Trade:* Regulation of Transnational Data Flows, Kluwer Law (2022), Chapter 1.

[59] Ibid.

[60] Ibid.

On the one hand, the Guidelines themselves only recommend that member countries adhere to the Principles in order to achieve a minimum standard; they do not specifically call for legal convergence.[61] On the other hand, the OECD itself has acknowledged that a number of member countries have recommended the establishment of an international binding convention.[62] Having written extensively on the OECD Principles, and drawing on the work of Greenleaf, Chesterman and Trakman, they have, in my view, been the most instrumental influence in shaping and directing the way that not only Commonwealth countries, but also, the world, have established data laws. They were originally developed in 1981 and to this day they provide the foundation for laws governing data protection, and the use of data in trade and investment. Arguably, they have been used by regional institutions such as ASEAN, African Union, APEC, and the EU to develop laws and policy directions for data governance. It is imperative that they be reviewed and, where required, updated to ensure their relevance to and across the digital economy.

Asia–Pacific Economic Cooperation [APEC]

A number of Commonwealth countries are members of both the OECD and APEC, including but not limited to Australia, Brunei, Malaysia, Papua New Guinea, Singapore, Canada and New Zealand.[63] The APEC[64] privacy framework has set the course for member countries to consider the following principles as core elements of their respective legal frameworks:

- Prevention of harm: information must not be misused;
- Notice: individuals have the right to know what information is collected about them and for what purpose(s);
- Collection limitations: only the personal information that is relevant to the intended purpose(s) should be collected;
- Data usage: data should be used only for the purpose(s) of the collection;
- Choice: individuals must be given a choice in relation to the collection, use, transfer, and disclosure of their personal information;
- Integrity: personal information must be accurate, complete, and kept up to date;
- Security: personal information must not be used in any way that will compromise the individual to whom the data applies;
- Access and Correction: individuals must be able to access and change their personal information for whatever reason;

[61] OECD Guidelines on the Protection of Privacy and Transborder Flows of Personal Data, https://www.oecd.org/sti/ieconomy/oecdguidelinesontheprotectionofprivacyandtransborderflowsofpersonaldata.htm.

[62] Ibid., at 30.

[63] Asia–Pacific Economic Cooperation, 2021, https://www.apec.org/about-us/about-apec Note, that this section regarding the draws on the earlier work from Robert Walters highlighted above in chapter I.

[64] Asia–Pacific Economic Cooperation, https://www.apec.org/Groups/Committee-on-Trade-and-Investment/Electronic-Commerce-Steering-Group.

- Accountability: organizations and individuals must be held accountable for the manner in which they handle and use personal data.[65]

The principles and concepts above come from the OECD data framework, and today can be found in the data laws of Commonwealth countries. That is, the countries that are members of both the Commonwealth and APEC have, by and large, adopted most, if not all, of the aforementioned principles and concepts. Additionally, the APEC Cross-Border Privacy Rules (CBPR)[66] is a government-backed data privacy certification system that companies can join to demonstrate compliance with internationally-recognized data privacy protections. The CBPR established the following principles:

- enforceable standards;
- accountability;
- risk-based protections;
- consumer-friendly complaint handling;
- consumer empowerment;
- consistent protections; and
- cross-border enforcement cooperation.[67]

Graham Greenleaf states that 'APEC is unusual in being an organization of states which does not have a constitution or a treaty to establish it (unlike ASEAN), operates by consensus, and undertakes commitments on a voluntary basis. It claims to be 'the only inter-governmental grouping in the world'.[68] Greenleaf goes on to explain how 'the APEC Cross-border Privacy Enforcement Arrangement (CPEA) in which '[a]ny Privacy Enforcement Authority in an APEC economy may participate in cross-border co-operation, enforcement and information sharing'.[69] The regional influence on the governance of data is becoming increasingly complex. It is multilayered and has seen the adoption of similar principles and concepts that can be found in the OECD Guidelines. However, they do diverge from each other and, to some extent, continue to move in different directions.

South Asian Association for Regional Cooperation [SAARC]

The SAARC comprises several notable Commonwealth countries, namely, India, Pakistan and Sri Lanka. Combined, they have the largest population of any of the other Commonwealth member countries. Greenleaf notes that the 'development of

---

65 Asia–Pacific Economic Cooperation, Privacy Framework 2015, https://cbprs.blob.core.windows.net/files/2015%20APEC%20Privacy%20Framework.pdf.

66 Asia–Pacific Economic Cooperation, Cross-Border Privacy Rules https://www.apec.org/about us/about-apec/fact-sheets/what-is-the-cross-border-privacy-rules-system.

67 Ibid.

68 Graham Greenleaf, 'International Structures Affecting Data Privacy in Asia', *Asian Data Privacy Laws: Trade & Human Rights Perspectives* Oxford, (2014), p. 33.

69 Ibid., p. 48.

privacy protection in South Asia has been stalled by many factors'.[70] This remains the case to date, with India yet to establish specific data laws. Moreover, the SAARC is yet to formally establish any cybersecurity strategy.

In this section, a brief outline has been given of the regional influences of several Commonwealth countries on the development and implementation of both data and cyber laws. While it is outside the scope of this book to comprehensively address the gaps and similarities in the approaches taken by these countries, it can be argued that this is an area meriting further research. It is also argued that the Commonwealth should engage with these institutions in order to achieve a level of consistency and certainty for trade and investment. It calls for more work to be undertaken to understand the differences in cybersecurity laws so as to reconcile them and achieve some harmonisation. Is it time for the OECD Guidelines to be reviewed to better address breaches in cyber systems that see large quantities of data being illegally extracted and used as ransom or for other nefarious purposes?

Organization of Eastern Caribbean States [OECS]

Saint Kitts, Saint Vincent, and Antigua and Barbuda[71] in 2022 had sought a consultancy[72] to undertake a project to harmonise the data laws of member countries. This is something the Commonwealth could be involved with to ensure that the proposed harmonised model meets the model laws of the Commonwealth, and addresses those gaps in the laws identified in this book. It will be interesting to see the impact that the work of the OECS will have in terms of results and recommendations. The ensuing question is whether the project can achieve a deeper level of legal harmonisation.

International Telecommunication Union [ITU]

Founded in 1865, the ITU, is one of the oldest international organisations.[73] The ITU has recognised that there is an increasingly strengthening connection between data and cybersecurity. It also notes that there is a 'need to redefine policy priorities, the roles of stakeholders, and to identify new tools has never been more pressing. Tensions, nevertheless, persist between established and emerging approaches to

---

[70] Graham Greenleaf, Privacy in South Asian (SAARC) States, Reasons for Optimism, *Privacy Laws & Business International Report* 18 *UNSWLRS* 11 (2018) p. 1.

[71] Organisation of Eastern Caribbean States, https://oecs.org/en/who-we-are/member-states.

Antigua and Barbuda, Saint Kitts and Nevis, Montserrat, Anguilla and the British Virgin Islands, and the Windward Islands: Dominica, Saint Lucia, Saint Vincent and the Grenadines and Grenada, Martinique and Guadeloupe.

[72] Ibid., https://www.eccb-centralbank.org/files/TORs%20and%20RFPs/REOI%20and%20TOR%20-%20Drafting%20the%20Harmonized%20Data%20Protection%20Legislation%20in%20the%20ECCU%20(LEGOP_CLEARED).pdf.

[73] International Telecommunication Union, https://www.itu.int/en/about/Pages/default.aspx.

policy and regulation and new strategies will need to prove themselves'.[74] In reconciling this tension, the Commonwealth should engage with the ITU in the development of future policy and law related to data and cybersecurity. The ITU also notes that:

> Data are vital for achieving universal and meaningful digital connectivity. Data help us understand our world. They tell us where we were, where we are, what works and what does not. They are a key element in empirical research for identifying trends, patterns and good practices. Data help policy-makers design better, more targeted and more effective policy interventions.[75]

This acknowledges that data is the future of the digital economy, and that regulation has to be responsive, agile, pragmatic and consistent to avoid future ambiguities or uncertainties. This will be difficult to achieve and getting the balance right is vitally important to the economic deliverables offered by the digital economy. However, it must be accompanied by adequate cybersecurity. Bodies such as the Commonwealth and its members can play a pivotal role in the ongoing development of these domains. Furthermore, the ITU states:

> Privacy and data protection regulations are important in determining how personal data is used and protected. On the other hand, countries have to enable official access for law enforcement to counter terrorism and to prevent money laundering. This tension generates difficult policy discussions on the use of encryption and access to data stored in other countries.[76]

Essentially, what the ITU is saying is that data and cybersecurity law are now so interconnected that they cannot be separated. However, it is recognised that the legal frameworks of cybersecurity and data are very different and have been designed to achieve different outcomes. Nonetheless, the ITU has developed a large body of standards that are assisting sectors to address the tension between data and cybersecurity. Overall, the organisation and its standards[77] are having a positive influence on the governance and intersection of data and cybersecurity.

Commonwealth Data Law

In the ensuing chapters, the data laws of all Commonwealth states will be compared with those in the Commonwealth Model Bill on the Protection of Personal Information (MBPPI) 2017, and the Model Bill for Privacy (MBP) 2017.[78] The MBPPI, addresses the core element of this book by underscoring the need for appropriate data laws for the data-driven economy. Put another way, 'personal information is a significant component of trade and business in today's data-driven economy. Adequate

[74] International Telecommunication Union, Development Sector, Global Connectivity Report (2022), p. xix.

[75] Ibid., p. 153.

[76] Ibid., p. 9.

[77] International Telecommunication Union, Standards, https://www.itu.int/pub/T-FG/e There are a large number of standards that have been developed to support data and cybersecurity governance.

[78] Model Bill for Privacy 2017, https://www.asianlaws.org/gcld/cyberlawdb/COM/P15370_9_ROL_Model_Privacy_Bill_0.pdf.

laws and policies for data protection, and in particular, cross-border flow of personal data are critical to participation in global value chains'.[79] Likewise, the MBP makes the point that 'personal information is a significant component of trade and business in today's data-driven economy. Adequate laws and policies for data protection, and in particular, cross-border flow of personal data are critical to participation in global value chains'.[80]

Further, the MBP emphasises the interconnectedness of regional entities and the influence that this has had on the development of data laws in some of the Commonwealth member states. For instance, the MBP states that 'Australia, Canada, New Zealand and the United Kingdom, as members of the Organization for Economic Cooperation and Development (OECD), have developed advanced data protection regimes in line with the OECD Guidelines on the Protection of Privacy and Transborder Flows of Personal Data'.[81] In addition, the 'data protection laws in Cyprus, Malta and the United Kingdom have also been driven by European Union law'.[82] However, it must be noted that the MBP was developed in 2017 when the UK was still a member of the EU, exiting the supranational Union in 2021. Nonetheless, as of December 2022, the UK has by and large retained most of the data laws it inherited under the EU's legal framework. Moreover, it notes that 'Commonwealth member countries in Asia and Pacific regions have been influenced by the Asia–Pacific Economic Cooperation (APEC) privacy framework, and Commonwealth jurisdictions in Africa and the Americas benefit from a number of regional regimes and guidelines'.[83] The MBPPI also acknowledges the same regional influences. Prior to presenting a comparative analysis of the data laws of all Commonwealth countries (Table 2.1), this chapter begins with a discussion of the similarities and differences between the MBP and the MBPPI. It will identify key themes, and limit the comparative analysis to the following main concepts and principles, each of which will be the subject of a separate chapter: Definitions;

- Controller, Consent and Processor;
- Storage Retention;
- Localisation;
- International Transfer;
- Data Portability;
- Right to be Forgotten;
- Application to Public and Private Sectors; and
- Data Rights.

[79] Commonwealth Model Bill on the Protection of Personal Information 2017, https://production-new-commonwealth-files.s3.eu-west-2.amazonaws.com/migrated/key_reform_pdfs/P15370_6_ROL_Model_Bill_Protection_Personal_Information_2.pdf.

[80] Model Bill for Privacy 2017, p. 1.

[81] Ibid., p. 1.

[82] Ibid.

[83] Ibid.

Firstly, Table 2.2 provides an outline of the current day data laws established by each of the Commonwealth countries. Importantly, there are a number of countries who are yet to establish specific data laws. The ensuing chapters will demonstrate the fragmentation within and across the national data laws of Commonwealth countries. It points out that the developed countries of Australia, Canada, UK, and New Zealand, amongst others have had data laws in place for a number of decades. Whereas, the developing countries, and countries in Asia have only recently adopted such laws.

There are significant differences between the Model Bills of the Commonwealth. The MBPPI[84] focuses on the processing of personal information, the duties of organisations, and access to personal data. On the other hand, the MBP emphasises the need for national laws to address data security issues. First the collection of personal information needs to be defined. However, there does not seem to be common agreement on a definition of the term 'collection of personal information'. Nonetheless, any laws should provide for not only the collection, but also for the source and accuracy of the personal information obtained to ensure that an individual is not wrongly identified. The second issue is the accuracy of that information at the time of collection. Sometimes, this can be problematic since personal information can change over time, such as when a person changes his or her place of residence. Thus, there is a need to place a limit on the use and disclosure of that data. However, the MBP does not provide any details about what constitutes the use and disclosure of personal information. Neither does it provide conditions for the use or disclosure of the data. Third, is the storage and retention of data. This has become increasingly important due to the vast quantities of data that have been acquired and will continue to be acquired over the coming decades. Arguably, the retention of data is encouraging states to set a maximum level of data-storage time. This begs the question: once disposed of, is the data really deleted from the technology systems? The MBP emphasises the need for people to be able to correct their data when it has been stored in error and that each state should establish a Regulator.[85]

On the other hand, the MBPPI extends the MBP by providing for a greater level of controls for personal data that prot4ects a personon's [privacy online. This section will focus on only three key distinct areas: first, Processing of Personal Information; second, Duties of Organisations with Respect to Records of Personal Information; and third, Access to that Information. In addition to the principles set out by the MBP, the MBPPI calls for collection, source, limitations, accuracy and security. Moreover, it takes these concepts a step further. For instance, under Processing of Personal Information, the following are stipulated:

- Appropriate purpose;
- Requirement of knowledge and consent;
- Collection of personal information;

[84] The Commonwealth, Model Bill on the Protection of Personal Information https://www.asianlaws.org/gcld/cyberlawdb/COM/P15370_6_ROL_Model_Bill_Protection_Personal_Information_2.pdf.

[85] The Commonwealth, Model Privacy Bill, Office of Civil and Criminal Justice Reform, 2017, https://www.asianlaws.org/gcld/cyberlawdb/COM/P15370_9_ROL_Model_Privacy_Bill_0.pdf.

Table 2.2 Data laws of commonwealth member countries as at December 2022

Africa & Europe	Data Law	Indo Pacific	Data law	Caribbean and Americas	Data law
Botswana	Data Protection Act—Act No. 32 of 2018[86]	Bangladesh	Proposed Data Protection Act, 2022[87]	Antigua and Barbuda	Data Protection Act 2013[88]
Cameroon	No law. Preparing Privacy Bill[89]	Brunei Darussalam	Draft law: Personal Data Protection Order[90]	Bahamas	Data Protection Act 2008[91]
Gabon	Law No. 001/2011 on the Protection of Personal Data[92]	India	Information Technology Act 2000[93]	Barbados	Data Protection Act 2019[94]
Gambia	No specific laws	Malaysia	Personal Data Protection Act 2010[95]	Belize	Data Protection Act, 45 of 2021[96]

(continued)

[86] Data Protection Act, No. 32 of 2018, https://www.bocra.org.bw/sites/default/files/documents/DataProtectionAct.pdf.

[87] Proposed Data Protection Act, 2022, https://ictd.portal.gov.bd/sites/default/files/files/ictd.portal.gov.bd/page/6c9773a2_7556_4395_bbec_f132b9d819f0/Data%20Protection%20Bill%20en%20V13%20Unofficial%20Working%20Draft%2016.07.22.pdf.

[88] Data Protection Act 2013, http://laws.gov.ag/wp-content/uploads/2019/02/a2013-10.pdf.

[89] Cameroon, November 2022, https://www.dataguidance.com/notes/cameroon-data-protection-overview.

[90] Draft law: Personal Data Protection Order, https://info.ushijima-law.gr.jp/hubfs/pi_legislation/Brunei(English).pdf and https://www.aiti.gov.bn/media/jc4mhify/pcp personaldataprotectionprivatesector_20052021_final3.pdf.

[91] Data Protection Act 2008, http://laws.bahamas.gov.bs/cms/images/LEGISLATION/PRINCIPAL/2003/2003-0003/DataProtectionPrivacyofPersonalInformationAct_1.pdf.

[92] Law No. 001/2011 on the Protection of Personal Data, https://www.dataguidance.com/notes/gabon-data-protection-overview.

[93] Information Technology Act 2000, http://www.dot.gov.in/sites/default/files/itbill2000_0.pdf.

[94] Data Protection Act 2019, https://gisbarbados.gov.bb/download/data-protection-act-2019/.

[95] Personal Data Protection Act 2010, https://www.kkmm.gov.my/pdf/Personal%20Data%20Protection%20Act%202010.pdf.

[96] Data Protection Act, 45 of 2021, https://www.nationalassembly.gov.bz/wp-content/uploads/2021/07/Data-Protection-Bill-2021-updated.pdf.

Table 2.2 (continued)

Africa & Europe	Data Law	Indo Pacific	Data law	Caribbean and Americas	Data law
Ghana	No specific laws. Draft Data Protection and Privacy Policy Strategy 2019[97] Data Protection Act 2012[98]	Maldives	No specific laws	Canada	Consumer Privacy Protection Act[99]
Kenya	*Data Protection Act, 2019*[100]	Pakistan	No specific laws	Dominica	No specific laws
Kingdom of Eswatini	Data Protection Act 2022[101]	Singapore	Personal Data Protection Act 2012[102]	Grenada	No specific laws
Lesotho	*Data Protection Act, 2013*[103]	Sri Lanka	Personal Data Protection Act No. 9 of 2022[104]	Guyana	No specific laws

(continued)

[97] Draft Data Protection and Privacy Policy Strategy 2019, November 2022, https://www.dataguidance.com/sites/default/files/data-protection-and-privacy-draft-policy-and-strategy-august-2019.pdf.

[98] Data Protection Act 2012, https://nita.gov.gh/theevooc/2017/12/Data-Protection-Act-2012-Act-843.pdf.

[99] Personal Information Protection and Electronic Documents Act (S.C. 2000, c. 5).
https://laws-lois.justice.gc.ca/eng/acts/P-8.6/index.html Personal Information Protection and Electronic Documents Act Note also: Digital Charter Implementation Act, 2022 Consumer Privacy Protection Act, Personal Information and Data Protection Tribunal Act, Artificial Intelligence and Data Act.

[100] Data Protection Act, 2019.

[101] Data Protection Act 2022, https://www.esccom.org.sz/legislation/DATA%20PROTECTION%20ACT.pdf.

[102] Personal Data Protection Act 2012, https://sso.agc.gov.sg/Act/PDPA2012.

[103] Data Protection Act 2013, http://www.nic.ls/lsnic/community/policies/Data_Protection_Act_2011_Lesotho.pdf.

[104] Personal Data Protection Act No. 9 of 2022, https://www.parliament.lk/uploads/acts/gbills/english/6242.pdf.

Table 2.2 (continued)

Africa & Europe	Data Law	Indo Pacific	Data law	Caribbean and Americas	Data law
Malawi	No specific law. Data Protection Bill 2021[105]	Australia	Privacy Act 1988 (Cth)[106]	Jamaica	Data Protection Act, 2020[107]
Mauritius	Data Protection Act 2017[108] Data Protection (Fees) Regulations 2020	Fiji	No specific laws	Saint Lucia	Privacy and Data Protection Act 2009[109]
Mozambique	No specific laws	Kiribati	Data Protection Act 1998 and Policy—not accessible	Saint Kitts and Nevis	Data Protection Act, 5 of 2018[110]

(continued)

[105] Data Protection Bill 2021, https://digmap.pppc.mw/wp-content/uploads/2022/03/Malawi-Data-Protection-Bill-final-draft-210630-.pdf.

[106] Privacy Act 1988, November 2022, https://www.legislation.gov.au/Details/C2014C00076/Download.

The States and Territories of Australia have each established their own laws, they include and not limited to: Australian Capital Territory – *Information Privacy Act 2014*. New South Wales, *Privacy and Personal Information Protection Act 1998* and *Health Records and Information Privacy Act 2002*. Northern Territory, *Information Act*, in force at 12 April 2017. Queensland, *Information Privacy Act 2009*. South Australia, South Australia has issued an administrative instruction requiring its government agencies to generally comply with a set of Information. Tasmania, *Personal Information and Protection Act 2004*. Victoria, *Privacy and data Protection 2014* and *Freedom of Information Act 1992*.

[107] Data Protection Act, *2020*, https://japarliament.gov.jm/attachments/article/339/The%20Data%20Protection%20Act,%202020.pdf.

[108] Data Protection Act 2017, Data Protection Bill 2020, https://japarliament.gov.jm/attachments/article/339/The%20Data%20Protection%20Act,%202020.pdf https://dataprotection.govmu.org/Documents/DPA_2017_updated.pdf?csf=1&e=0rlrff and https://inecnigeria.org/wp-content/uploads/2020/08/DATA-PROTECTION-Bill-2020.pdf.

[109] Privacy and Data Protection Act 2009, https://www.govt.lc/media.govt.lc/www/resources/legislation/PrivacyAndDataProtectionBill.pdf.

[110] Data Protection Act, 5 of 2018, https://www.theinformationcollective.com/dpl/st-kitts-data-protection-act.

Table 2.2 (continued)

Africa & Europe	Data Law	Indo Pacific	Data law	Caribbean and Americas	Data law
Namibia	No specific laws. Have had a draft Bill since 2020	Nauru	No specific laws	Saint Vincent and The Grenadines	Privacy Act 2003[111]
Nigeria	Data Protection Regulation 2019[112] Draft Data Protection Bill	New Zealand	Privacy Act 2020[113]	Trinidad and Tobago	Data Protection Act 2011[114]
Rwanda	Law n°058/2021 of 13/10/2021 relating to the protection of personal data and privacy (the "Data Protection Law")[115]	Papua New Guinea	No specific laws		
Seychelles	Data Protection Act 2003[116] Not enforced	Samoa	No specific laws		
Sierra Leone	No specific laws. National Cybersecurity and Data Protection Strategy[117]	Solomon Islands	No Specific laws		
South Africa	*Protection of Personal Information Act, 2013*[118]	Tonga	No Specific laws		

(continued)

[111] Privacy Act 2003, https://www.theinformationcollective.com/dpl/st-vincent-and-the-grenadines-the-privacy-act.

[112] Data Protection Regulation 2022, https://ndpb.gov.ng/Files/Nigeria_Data_Protection_Bill.pdf.

[113] Privacy Act 2020, https://www.privacy.org.nz/privacy-act-2020/privacy-principles/.

[114] Data Protection Act 2011, https://rgd.legalaffairs.gov.tt/laws2/Alphabetical_List/lawspdfs/22.04.pdf.

[115] Law n°058/2021 of 13/10/2021 relating to the protection of personal data and privacy (the Data Protection Law), https://www.minijust.gov.rw/fileadmin/user_upload/Minijust/Publications/Official_Gazette/_2021_Official_Gazettes/October/OG_Special_of_15.10.2021_Amakuru_bwite.pdf.

[116] Data Protection Act 2003, https://assets.contentstack.io/v3/assets/blt5775cc69c999c255/bltdf6549c2c030f7a7/seychelles-data-protection-act.pdf.

[117] National Cybersecurity and Data Protection Strategy, https://www.itu.int/en/ITU-D/Cybersecurity/Documents/National_Strategies_Repository/00090_03_Sierra%20Leone%20national-cyber-security-strategy-2017-final-draft.pdf.

[118] Protection of Personal Information Act, 2013, https://www.gov.za/sites/default/files/gcis_document/201409/3706726-11act4of2013protectionofpersonalinforcorrect.pdf.

Table 2.2 (continued)

Africa & Europe	Data Law	Indo Pacific	Data law	Caribbean and Americas	Data law
Togo	Law No. 2019-014 Relating to the Protection of Personal Data[119] French only had to rely on other material				
Uganda	Data Protection and Privacy Act 2019[120]				
United Republic of Tanzania	Personal Data Protection Bill 2022[121]				
Zambia	Data Protection Act 2021[122]				
Cyprus	General Data Protection Region—Member of the European Union				
Malta	General Data Protection Region—Member of the European Union				
United Kingdom	General Data Protection Region[123] Data Protection and Digital Information Bill 2023[124] Thus, UK to meet EU Adequacy arrangements has retained most laws				

- Source of personal information;
- Collection without knowledge or consent;
- Limits on use of personal information;
- Limits on disclosure of personal information;
- Condition for use or disclosure of personal information;

[119] Law No. 2019–014 Relating to the Protection of Personal Data, French only, https://jo.gouv.tg/sites/default/files/JO/JOS_29_10_2019-64E%20ANNEE-N°26%20TER.pdf#page=1.

[120] Data Protection and Privacy Act 2019, https://ict.go.ug/wp-content/uploads/2019/03/Data-Protection-and-Privacy-Act-2019.pdf.

[121] Personal Data Protection Act 2022, passed Parliament November 2022, https://abcattorneys.co.tz/wp-content/uploads/2022/10/TANZANIA-DATA-PROTECTION-BILL-2022.pdf.

[122] Data Protection Act 2021, https://www.parliament.gov.zm/sites/default/files/documents/acts/Act%20No.%203%20The%20Data%20Protection%20Act%202021_0.pdf.

[123] General Data Protection Regulation (GDPR) (Regulation 2016/679 Of the European Parliament and the European Council, on the protection of natural persons with regard to the processing of personal data and on the free movement of such data and repealing Directive 95/46/EC (General Data Protection Regulation), Official Journal of the European Union L 119/1. https://eur-lex.europa.eu/eli/reg/2016/679/oj.

[124] Data Protection and Digital Information Bill 2023, https://commonslibrary.parliament.uk/research-briefings/cbp-9606/ and https://www.shlegal.com/insights/data-protection-update---july-2022.

- Use of personal information outside *[name of country]; and*
- Disclosure of personal information outside *[name of country].*[125]

Second, there is a greater call for organisations to ensure that the governance of personal data is undertaken to ensure that it is accurate and secure, and that there is disclosure of its uses, retention and practices. Third, another layer of processes pertains to the access to personal information, such as the right of a person to gain access, the procedures enabling the access, any fees, a copy or record, and correction of the personal information. Importantly, the Model Laws refer specifically to personal information rather than personal data. They are a valuable tool that can be used by Commonwealth states to achieve a level of legal convergence. However, they are not compulsory, and nation states are not required to follow the MLs. As stated earlier in this book, a member of the Commonwealth does not have to relinquish any of its sovereignty to the Commonwealth Secretariate. The MLs do provide a valuable platform for member countries that have yet to establish data laws. They do have a separate and distinct focus by ensuring the MBP is about information privacy (privacy over the internet), whereas the MBPPI has a focus on data protection. They are distinct features because data protection is viewed as a tool of privacy. Robert Walters, Leon Trakman, and Bruno Zeller reinforce this point of privacy being a tool for data protection.[126]

On the other side, Paul De Hert and Serg Gutwirth see data protection as a tool of transparency.[127] It is my view that the national laws for data and privacy have converged, albeit not fully or to the point of harmonisation. When there is some convergence, it becomes very difficult for governments and regulators to balance the economic benefits with the assurance of a high level of protection. Put another way, this book is calling on governments to ensure there is an adequate level of protection of the data being transmitted over the Internet. On the other hand, for every protection or control afforded to data subjects, there is equally a level of regulation that allows for the transnational use of that data. This book will examine the way that transnational data provisions of the respective national laws provide for a high level of controls and rights afforded to data subjects. At the same time, there are provisions that enable data to flow transnationally and with relative ease. Both MLs are based on the OECD Guidelines on the Protection of Privacy and Transborder Flows of Personal Data. This indicates the importance of these Guidelines in providing a platform for nation states to develop national laws. However, in my view they should and could be reviewed to extend their reach. The next section will compare the data laws of all countries of the Commonwealth.

---

125 Robert Walters, Leon Trakman, Bruno Zeller, Data Protection Law: A comparative Analysis of Asia–Pacific European Approaches, Springer (2019), pp. 14–15.

126 Ibid.

127 Ibid., De Hert P, Gutwirth S, (2009) *Privacy, Data Protection and Law Enforcement. Opacity of the Individual and Transparency of Power*. in E. Claes, A. Duff & S. Gutwirth (Eds.), *Privacy and the Criminal Law*, pp. 61–104.

2.2 Conclusion

The Commonwealth has established a framework for members to develop and strengthen their respective data protection laws. The challenge will be whether all members adopt the framework. This is because that there are a number of member states that have had privacy and data laws in place for a number of decades, well before the MPPI and MPI were established.

Nonetheless, in regard to the laws of Commonwealth members, at the time of writing, Cameroon is undertaking preparations in relation to data laws. Similarly, Brunei Darussalam had prepared drafts laws. These will not be compared and discussed in this book which is concerned with examining and comparing only those data laws that are currently implemented. That said, Dominica, Fiji, Gambia, Grenada, Guyana, Maldives, Mozambique, Namibia, Nauru, Pakistan, Papua New Guinea, Samoa, Solomon Islands, Sierra Leone, and Tonga do not have any specific data laws. Note that several attempts to obtain the data laws from Kiribati were unsuccessful.

Although the Seychelles established its data laws in 2003, these have not been implemented and therefore will not be included in the comparison. Also, although Tanzania established the Personal Information Protection Act 2022 in November 2022, at the time of writing, no English version was available. However, Tanzania has been included since that country's law firms have provided brief introductions in the English language. Due to the sectorial approach taken in Canada, only the Personal Information Protection and Electronic Documents Act (S.C. 2000, c. 5) is used for comparison. In the ensuing chapters, the aforementioned concepts and principles are compared, beginning with the definition of personal data.

In this chapter, an overview was provided in relation to the data laws that will be compared in the following chapters. It reveals that there are a number of international and regional organisations that are influencing and shaping the development of data laws. At a regional level, the influence is addressing local needs. At the international level, it is taking a global view of the issues related to data and cybersecurity. However, it is my view that the approaches taken by these organisations lack coherence and consistency. Understandably, they are all pulling in different directions.

One of the major developments has been the Commonwealth's establishment of the MBP and the MBPPI, which are providing a large number of member countries with guidelines for the adoption of a similar approach to data law. However, the Commonwealth is a voluntary organisation and states are under no obligation to adopt the Bills. This book is not calling for the Commonwealth to go down the same road as the European Union which required member countries to relinquish some of their sovereignty. This will never happen. However, the Commonwealth is in a good position to leverage from this work, and engage more closely with the international and regional organisations to develop future data and cyber law. The following chapters compare the data laws of Commonwealth members.

Chapter 3
Definitions Personal Data—Information

3.1 Introduction

This chapter compares the data and privacy laws of Commonwealth states with those of the Commonwealth's MBP and MBPPI. It highlights the difficulty of finding a common definition of personal data, and discusses the divergent approaches that have been taken. The MBP defined personal data as information about an identifiable individual that is recorded in any form including:

(a) information relating to the race, national or the origin, religion, age or marital status of the individual;
(b) information relating to the education or the medical, criminal or employment history of the individual or information relating to financial transactions in which the individual has been involved;
(c) any identifying number, symbol or other particular assigned to the individual;
(d) the address, finger prints or blood type of the individual;
(e) thenameoftheindividualwhereitappearswithotherpersonalinformation relating to the individual or where the disclosure of the name itself would reveal information about the individual;
(f) correspondence sent to a public authority by the individual that is explicitly or implicitly of a private or confidential nature, and replies to such correspondence that would reveal the contents of the original correspondence; or
(g) the views or opinion so any other person about the individual.[1]

[1] The Commonwealth, Model Privacy Bill, Office of Civil and Criminal Justice Reform, 2017, https://www.asianlaws.org/gcld/cyberlawdb/COM/P15370_9_ROL_Model_Privacy_Bill_0.pdf.

R. Walters, *Cybersecurity and Data Laws of the Commonwealth*,
https://doi.org/10.1007/978-981-99-3935-0_3

The MPPI defines personal information as:

(a) information relating to the race, national or ethnic origin, religion, age or marital status of the individual;
(b) information relating to the education or the medical, criminal or employment history of the individual or information relating to financial transactions in which the individual has been involved;
(c) any identifying number, symbol or other particular assigned to the individual;
(d) the address, fingerprints or blood type of the individual;
(e) the name of the individual where it appears with other personal information relating to the individual or where the disclosure of the name itself would reveal information about the individual;
(f) correspondence sent by the individual that is explicitly or implicitly of a private or confidential nature, and replies to such correspondence that would reveal the contents of the original correspondence;
(g) the views or opinions of any other person about the individual;
(h) information that can be manipulated by a reasonably foreseeable method to identify the individual; or
(i) information that can be linked by a reasonably foreseeable method to other information that identifies the individual or that can be manipulated by a reasonably foreseeable method to identify the individual.[2]

There are notable differences between the Commonwealth MBP and MBPPI, in particular regarding the personal information that can be manipulated or linked to technology that can manipulate such data. Generally, this chapter will show how the definitions above have, by and large, been incorporated within the national laws of the Commonwealth states. However, it will be argued that there remain complex and significant issues that need to be addressed by laws that are convergent and harmonised. This chapter poses the question: are the definitions above adequate for future decades which will see the development of new critical and artificial intelligent technologies? This, along with the other chapters, will be descriptive to highlight the actual specifics of each definition of personal data. Notably, general data and sensitive data have taken on special meanings that, in part, can be found in both the MBP and MBPPI.

To fully understand data law, as a starting point is the definition of personal data or personal information. Having such a legal definition is important so as society understands how a person's identifying information has been defined. This chapter will demonstrate how the data laws of the Commonwealth member states being examined vary significantly, specifically in their definitions of personal data. This is evident when comparing the nation states' laws with the Commonwealth MBP and MBPPI.

[2] The Commonwealth, Model Bill on the Protection of Personal Information https://www.asianlaws.org/gcld/cyberlawdb/COM/P15370_6_ROL_Model_Bill_Protection_Personal_Information_2.pdf.

Lee Bygrave makes the point that a problem with the terms 'data' and 'information' is that although they appear in such definitions, they have rarely been analysed systematically, either by legislators or (other) jurists. While much effort has been directed at delineating the nature of the link between data/ information and persons, the precise meanings of the terms 'data' and 'information' have been largely taken for granted.[3] This dillema has been further pronounced because as this chapter demonstrates, some states refer to personal 'data', while other states refer to personal 'information'. Further, Bygrave argues that:

> In the fields of informatics and computer science, however, there has been—naturally enough—relatively systematic explication of information concepts. In these fields, the notion of 'data' usually denotes signs, patterns, characters or symbols which potentially represent something (a process or object) from the 'real world' and, through this representation, may communicate information about that thing. Thus, the 'information' as such denotes the semantic content of the data communicated to a person. In the terminology of semiotics, data have a primarily sigmatic (representational) function while information has primarily semantic and cognitive elements. Another characteristic typically ascribed to data is that they are more or less consciously shaped with the intention of communicating or otherwise processing information.[4]

What Bygrave is arguing is that within the technology domain, data and information are sometimes going to be used synonymously. Today this is an inevitable part of collecting and using personal data in the realms of informatics, science, biotech and, now, artificial intelligence.

Notwithstanding the above, four years following his first article, Bygraves posits that legislators have taken the neutral approach in relation to defining personal data.[5] He argues that personal data or personal information can be linked, directly or in individual persons by easily identifying the individual when they are online. He believes that the precise meaning of the terms in definitions have been taken for granted, with most effort directed at elucidating the link between data or information and persons. The architects of data protection law have generally intended to give the terms a broad ambit and to draft the legal provisions that are technology neutral.[6] It is this broad ambit that can been seen to varying degrees across all the Commonwealth countries examined in this book. Some nation states will define data in general terms and then define personal data more specifically. Other states will define biometric, genetic, health and sensitive data separately, although some states such as the UK, Malta and Cyprus that follow the EU GDPR[7] have what I describe as an 'all-in'

---

[3] Lee Bygrave, *The Body as Data? Biobank Regulation via the "Back Door" of Data Protection Law*. Law, Innovation and Technology 2(1), (2010), p. 13.

[4] Ibid., p. 14.

[5] Lee Bygrave, *Information Concepts in Law: Generic Dreams and Definitional Daylight*, Oxford Journal of Legal Studies (2014), p. 96.

[6] Ibid.

[7] Regulation 2016/679 Of the European Parliament and the European Council, on the protection of natural persons with regard to the processing of personal data and on the free movement of such data and repealing Directive 95/46/EC (General Data Protection Regulation), Official Journal of the European Union L 119/1.

definition. It arguably captures nearly every element of how a person can be identified over the Internet. When examining the various definitions, this chapter will be quite descriptive to ensure the reader fully understands the extent of the meaning of personal and other data.

Starting with **Antigua** and **Barbuda**, in Section 2 of their data laws, personal data is defined to mean any information in respect of commercial transactions, which: is being processed wholly or partly by means of equipment operating automatically in response to instructions given for that purpose; is recorded with the intention that it should wholly or partly be processed by means of such equipment; or is recorded as part of a relevant filing system or with the intention that it should form part of a relevant filing system, that relates directly or indirectly to a data subject, who is identified or identifiable from that information or from that and other information in the possession of a data user, including any sensitive personal data and expression of opinion about the data subject.[8] Additionally, sensitive personal data consists of 'information as to the physical or mental health or condition of a data subject, his or her sexual orientation, his or her political opinions, his or her religious beliefs or other beliefs of a similar nature, the commission or alleged commission by him or her of any offence or any other personal data as the Minister may determine by Order published in the Gazette'.[9]

Australia has developed a long-standing law that is 'multilayered and includes regulation by government (primary legislation, regulations and codes), and industry self-regulation'.[10] The national *Privacy Act 1988* is the principal legislation that regulates privacy, personal data and personal information throughout Australia. This book only deals with the national privacy law and not those privacy laws of the states and territories such as Vicvtoria or Queensland. Section 6 of this Act defines 'personal information to mean information or an opinion about an identified individual, or an individual who is reasonably identifiable whether the information or opinion is true or not, and whether the information or opinion is recorded in a material form or not'.[11] On the one hand, a unique feature of Australia's privacy laws is the Australian Privacy Principles,[12] which are binding on individuals and entities. On the other hand, they do not define personal information. The major difference between Australia's definition and those of the other nation states, is the use of the word 'information' and not 'data'. Moreover, Section 6 goes further to define sensitive information to mean: information or an opinion, racial or ethnic origin; political opinions; membership of a political association; religious beliefs or affiliations; or philosophical beliefs; membership of a professional, trade association or trade union;

[8] Data Protection Act 2013, section 2 http://laws.gov.ag/wp-content/uploads/2019/02/a2013-10.pdf.

[9] Ibid.

[10] Robert Walters, Leon Trakman, Bruno Zeller, *Data Protection Law: A comparative Analysis of Asia–Pacific European Approaches*, Springer (2019), p. 115.

[11] Privacy Act 1988, section 6. C2014C00076.

[12] Privacy Act 1988, schedule 1.

sexual orientation or practices; criminal record; health information; genetic information; biometric information-templates. Notably, Australia's definition of sensitive data includes genetic and biometric information, whereas most other nation states have separated this data, and defined each element specifically.

The interconnectedness between the data law and cybercrime was demonstrated by the Court in the case of *Brown.*[13] In this case, the appellant pleaded guilty to 57 crimes of dishonesty, most of which concerned identity fraud.[14] The Court stated that:

> On 26 June 2006, the appellant received the computer, knowing it to be stolen, from an accomplice. Using the computer, she accessed the householder's bank account, altered personal information relating to it, changed the online banking facility to telephone banking, and, with intent to defraud, transferred $9,000 from the account into an account in her own name with another bank. At the same time, she arranged electronically for a further $9,000 to be transferred in the same way on 5 July 2006.[15]

The identity theft/fraud resulted from the theft of a wallet containing the victim's personal information and her credit union card.[16] In actuality, this personal identifying information would contain the person's name, credit card details, and specific number (union-financial) and possibly her address. **While out of scope of this book, comparing the definition of personal information under the Privacy Act 1988, and Part 9.5 of the Criminal Code Act 1995 (Cth), elements of the above personal information fall within both definitions. However there is no specific offence of identity fraud or theft under privacy law in Australia**. It would also provide information about the financial provider. There was enough information for the defendant to make a number of withdrawals, and gain access to a quantity of cash. Importantly, as argued in this book, data laws are directly applicable to some of the cybersecurity-cybercrime offences although, despite the privacy of the person being compromised, this is not the main issue resolved by the court. Therefore, it could be argued that over time, there investigation and response to these offences by law enforcement and the judiciary need to be more wholistic.

On the other hand, Section 2 of the **Bahamas** data laws provides three distinct definitions of data, personal data and sensitive data. Data constitutes, 'information in a form in which it can be processed'.[17] Personal data relates 'to a living individual who can be identified either from the data or from the data in conjunction with other information in the possession of the data controller'.[18] Sensitive personal data is defined more specifically as it includes: racial origin; political opinions or religious or other beliefs; physical or mental health (other than any such data reasonably

---

[13] *Brown v Tasmania* [2008] TASSC 33.

[14] Ibid., para 2.

[15] Ibid., para 3.

[16] Ibid., para 12.

[17] Data Protection Act 2008, section 2, http://laws.bahamas.gov.bs/cms/images/LEGISLATION/PRINCIPAL/2003/2003-0003/DataProtectionPrivacyofPersonalInformationAct_1.pdf.

[18] Data Protection Act 2008, section 2, http://laws.bahamas.gov.bs/cms/images/LEGISLATION/PRINCIPAL/2003/2003-0003/DataProtectionPrivacyofPersonalInformationAct_1.pdf.

kept by them in relation to the physical or mental health of their employees in the ordinary course of personnel administration and not used or disclosed for any other purpose); trade union involvement or activities; sexual life or criminal convictions, the commission or alleged commission of any offence, or any proceedings for any offence committed, the disposal of such proceedings or the sentence of any court in such proceedings'.[19]

For **Belize**, 'data' generally refers to data that is processed by means of 'equipment operating automatically in response to instructions given for that purpose; is recorded with the intention that it should be processed by equipment or as part of a relevant filing system or with the intention that it should form part of a relevant filing system'.[20] In going further, the data laws define 'personal data that relates to an individual who can be identified, from that data together with other information in the possession of the data controller'.[21] Sensitive data has also been given a distinct definition, and constitutes 'racial, ethnic origin, political opinions, religious belief, membership of a political body or trade union. It also includes genetic, biometric data, sexual orientation or sexual life, financial record or position; criminal record; or proceedings for any offence committed or alleged to have been committed'.[22] Health records have been defined, but not as health data.

On the one hand, **Barbados** has developed a broad definition of personal data. Personal data constitutes 'data which relates to an individual who can be identified from that data; or from that data together with other information which is in the possession of or is likely to come into the possession of the data controller'.[23] On the other hand, data has been defined to mean information that is processed by means of equipment operating automatically in response to instructions; is recorded with the intention that it should be processed by means of such equipment; or part of a relevant filing system. Health and genetic data have also been given their own specific definitions.[24] Arguably, this is very general. On the other hand, in **Botswana**, personal data refers to any information relating to an identified or identifiable individual, which individual can be identified directly or indirectly, in particular by reference to an identification number, or to one or more factors specific to the individuals' physical, physiological, mental, economic, cultural or social identity; and data shall

[19] Data Protection Act 2008, section 2, http://laws.bahamas.gov.bs/cms/images/LEGISLATION/PRINCIPAL/2003/2003-0003/DataProtectionPrivacyofPersonalInformationAct_1.pdf.

[20] Data Protection Act, 45 of 2021, section 2 https://www.nationalassembly.gov.bz/wp-content/uploads/2021/07/Data-Protection-Bill-2021-updated.pdf.

[21] Data Protection Act, 45 of 2021, section 2 https://www.nationalassembly.gov.bz/wp-content/uploads/2021/07/Data-Protection-Bill-2021-updated.pdf.

[22] Data Protection Act, 45 of 2021, section 2 https://www.nationalassembly.gov.bz/wp-content/uploads/2021/07/Data-Protection-Bill-2021-updated.pdf.

[23] Data Protection Act 2019, section 2, https://gisbarbados.gov.bb/download/data-protection-act-2019/.

[24] Data Protection Act 2019, section 2, https://gisbarbados.gov.bb/download/data-protection-act-2019/.

be construed accordingly. In addition, sensitive personal data that reveals a personals racial or ethnic origin, political opinion, religious belief or philosophical belief, physical or mental health or condition, sexual life, personal financial information, sexual life, filiation, or any alleged of commissionable offence, genetic, biometric and personal data of minors. While outside the scope of this section, biometric, genetic, and minors' personal data have been defined separately.[25]

Unfortunately, **Bangladesh** currently has a fragmented legal landscape for data protection and data flows (*Digital Security Act 2018*). Hence, this section will focus on the data laws proposed in 2022. If implemented unchanged, data has been defined as a 'representation of any information, knowledge, fact, concepts or instructions which are being prepared or have been prepared in a formalized manner and is intended to be processed, is being processed, or has been processed in a computer system or computer network, and may be in any form including computer printout, magnetic or optical storage media, punch cards, punched tapes or stored internally in the memory of the computer, and includes the personal data for that purpose: provided that, the anonymized, encrypted or pseudonymized data which is incapable of identifying any individual shall not be included within the purview of personal data'.[26] Unlike Botswana and a number of other states, Bangladesh is proposing to define health data to mean 'data related to the state of physical or mental health of the data subject, and includes records regarding the past, present or future state of the health of such data subject, data collected in the course of registration for, or provision of health services, data associating the data subject to the provision of specific health services'.[27] Moreover, compared to other states, sensitive data is somewhat limited to financial, commercial, health data (both physical or mental including medical records), genetic data (has been defined separately) and biometric data. Genetic and biometric data is under the umbrella of sensitive data whereas, in Botswana, it has been defined separately. **Canada's** Personal Information Protection and Electronic Documents Act (PIPED) has, in my view, taken a minimalist approach to defining personal information as 'information about an identifiable individual'.[28] Genetic and biometric data have not been defined, unlike the approach taken by many other nation states. On the other hand, personal health information is defined to comprise physical mental health, service provided body part or any bodily substance of the individual or information derived from the testing.[29]

---

[25] Data Protection Act, No. 32 of 2018, section 2, https://www.bocra.org.bw/sites/default/files/documents/DataProtectionAct.pdf.

[26] Proposed Data Protection Act, 2022, section 2. https://ictd.portal.gov.bd/sites/default/files/files/ictd.portal.gov.bd/page/6c9773a2_7556_4395_bbec_f132b9d819f0/Data%20Protection%20Bill%20en%20V13%20Unofficial%20Working%20Draft%2016.07.22.pdf.

[27] Proposed Data Protection Act, 2022, section 2. https://ictd.portal.gov.bd/sites/default/files/files/ictd.portal.gov.bd/page/6c9773a2_7556_4395_bbec_f132b9d819f0/Data%20Protection%20Bill%20en%20V13%20Unofficial%20Working%20Draft%2016.07.22.pdf.

[28] Personal Information Protection and Electronic Documents Act (S.C. 2000, c. 5), section 2, https://laws-lois.justice.gc.ca/eng/acts/P-8.6/index.html.

[29] Personal Information Protection and Electronic Documents Act (S.C. 2000, c. 5), section 2, https://laws-lois.justice.gc.ca/eng/acts/P-8.6/index.html.

As members of the EU, **Cyprus** and **Malta** are subject to the data protection legal framework (Regulation 2016/679 - GDPR) of the Union.[30] In one of the most broadly applied definitions, personal data 'means any information relating to an identified or identifiable natural person ('data subject'); an identifiable natural person is one who can be identified, directly or indirectly, in particular by reference to an identifier such as a name, an identification number, location data, an online identifier or to one or more factors specific to the physical, physiological, genetic, mental, economic, cultural or social identity of that natural person'.[31] It is an all-encompassing definition that makes no distinction between sensitive personal data and general personal data. In a very recent case before the Court of Justice of the European Union,[32] the Grand Chamber ruled that:

> Article 7(c) of Directive 95/46/EC of the European Parliament and of the Council of 24 October 1995 on the protection of individuals with regard to the processing of personal data and on the free movement of such data and point (c) of the first subparagraph of Article 6(1) and Article 6(3) of Regulation (EU) 2016/679 of the European Parliament and of the Council of 27 April 2016 on the protection of natural persons with regard to the processing of personal data and on the free movement of such data, and repealing Directive 95/46/EC (General Data Protection Regulation), read in the light of Articles 7, 8 and 52(1) of the Charter of Fundamental Rights of the European Union, must be interpreted as precluding national legislation that provides for the publication online of the declaration of private interests that any head of an establishment receiving public funds is required to lodge, in so far as, in particular, that publication concerns name-specific data relating to his or her spouse, cohabitee or partner, or to persons who are close relatives of the declarant, or are known by him or her, liable to give rise to a conflict of interests, or concerns any transaction concluded during the last 12 calendar months the value of which exceeds EUR 3 000. Article 8(1) of Directive 95/46 and Article 9(1) of Regulation 2016/679 must be interpreted as meaning that the publication, on the website of the public authority responsible for collecting and checking the content of declarations of private interests, of personal data that are liable to disclose indirectly the sexual orientation of a natural person constitutes processing of special categories of personal data, for the purpose of those provisions.[33]

In ruling the above, the Court also highlighted how it was easy to determine a person's sexual orientation from the publication of a partner they cohabitate with.[34] This is one example amongst many others where European courts have confirmed the definition of personal data, and how people can be identified from the definition in practice.

---

[30] Regulation 2016/679 Of the European Parliament and the European Council, on the protection of natural persons with regard to the processing of personal data and on the free movement of such data and repealing Directive 95/46/EC (General Data Protection Regulation), Official Journal of the European Union L 119/1.

[31] Regulation 2016/679 Of the European Parliament and the European Council, on the protection of natural persons with regard to the processing of personal data and on the free movement of such data and repealing Directive 95/46/EC (General Data Protection Regulation), Official Journal of the European Union L 119/1. Article 4.

[32] Case C-184/20, *OT v Vyriausioji tarnybinės etikos komisija*, https://curia.europa.eu/juris/document/document.jsf?text=&docid=263721&pageIndex=0&doclang=EN&mode=req&dir=&occ=first&part=1&cid=878732.

[33] Ibid.

[34] Ibid., para 119.

Significantly, upon leaving the EU, the **United Kingdom** obtained an adequacy decision[35] within months. Generally, the UK has continued to follow the EU framework, in the same way as **Malta** and **Cyprus**. Section 3 of the UK **GDPR** broadly defines personal data to mean any information relating to an identified or identifiable living individual. That is, personal data is defined under the Article 4(1) of UK [GDPR] as: "Any information relating to an identified or identifiable natural person ('data subject'); an identifiable natural person is one who can be identified, directly or indirectly, in particular by reference to an identifier such as a name, an identification number, location data, an online identifier or to one or more factors specific to the physical, physiological, genetic, mental, economic, cultural or social identity of that natural person." Further, Article 4(1) has four primary elements: (1) any information, (2) relating to, (3) identified or identifiable, and (4) natural person. The interpretation of these four elements under the (EU) GDPR is provided in Article 29 Working Party as follows:

1. *Any Information*, Under Article 29 Working Party it is clarified that the wordings call for a wide interpretation. The nature of information can be objective i.e., pertaining to a substance in one's blood or subjective, like assessments made by insurance companies, Banks etc.
2. *Relating to*—the information must relate to an individual.
3. *Identified or Identifiable*—An individual can be considered identified or identifiable when that individual can be distinguished from all other members of the group.
4. *Natural Person*—The individual being identified or identifiable are supposed to be living individual in principle.[36]

At the time of writing, the UK was undertaking a review of its data protection laws. Thus, there are elements of the Data Protection Act 2018 that will change over time. However, the extent to which those changes will depart from the current framework that is similar to the EU GDPR, and the 2021 Adequacy decision, is far from settled.[37] In the case of *Kelway*[38] the court was required to confirm the definition of personal data as it related to the UK national laws which at the time had transposed/replicated the definition given in the EU GDPR. Notably, the Court provided a level of guidance on the interpretation of personal data. It stated that three concepts were identified: purpose, concept and result. The Court noted that the result concept is of particular significance in this case. In drawing on work from the World Intellectual Property Organisation, it stated that:

---

[35] European Commission, Data protection: Commission adopts adequacy decisions for the UK, June 2021, https://ec.europa.eu/commission/presscorner/detail/en/ip_21_3183.

[36] Ibid.

[37] Data Protection Act 2021, https://www.parliament.gov.zm/sites/default/files/documents/acts/Act%20No.%203%20The%20Data%20Protection%20Act%202021_0.pdf.

[38] (*R (Kelway) v The Upper Tribunal (Administrative Appeals Chamber) and Northumbria Police and R (Kelway) v Independent Police Complaints Commission [2013] EWHC 2575 (Admin), 20 August 2013.*) https://www.bailii.org/ew/cases/EWHC/Admin/2013/2575.html#para49.

> The Working Party has already paid attention to the issue of when the information may be considered as "relating" to a person. In the context of discussions on the data protection issues raised by RFID tags, the Working Party noted that "data relates to an individual if it refers to the identity, characteristics or behaviour of an individual or if such information is used to determine or influence the way in which that person is treated or evaluated. In view of the cases mentioned above, and along the same lines, it could be pointed out that, in order to consider that the data "relate" to an individual, a "content" element OR a "purpose" element OR a "result" element should be present.[39]

Secondly, the Court referenced the content element connecting the personal data with that of the role of the controller. Third, the information relates to that person, and this has to be assessed in the light of all circumstances surrounding the case. For example, the results of medical analysis clearly relate to the patient, or the information contained in a company's folder under the name of a certain client clearly relates to him.[40] This information would constitute personal data. On this basis, the Court noted that the data can be considered to relate to an individual because their use is likely to have an impact on a certain person's rights and interests, taking into account all the circumstances surrounding the precise case.[41] In applying a technology-based example, the Court noted that:

> monitoring of taxis' position to optimize service having an impact on drivers. A system of satellite location is set up by a taxi company which makes it possible to determine the position of available taxis in real time. The purpose of the processing is to provide better service and save fuel, by assigning to each client ordering a cab the car that is closest to the client's address. Strictly speaking the data needed for that system is data relating to cars, not about the drivers. The purpose of the processing is not to evaluate the performance of taxi drivers, for instance through the optimization of their itineraries. Yet, the system does allow monitoring the performance of taxi drivers and checking whether they respect speed limits, seek appropriate itineraries, are at the steering wheel or are resting outside, etc. It can therefore have a considerable impact on these individuals, and as such the data may be considered to also relate to natural persons. The processing should be subject to data protection rules.[42]

Most notably, the Court made the point of connecting technology with for example, the use of a satellite for collecting and using personal data. This will undoubtedly be amplified when AI and devices in the home and office are connected to the Internet 24 h a day. Regarding purpose, the Court argued that it related to a certain person. Apart from dissecting the definition of personal data, the Court highlighted the connection between technology and personal data as defined by the law. As this chapter has highlighted, and the information below demonstrates, the definition of personal data is broad and complex. Within the digital economy, elements of personal data can emerge from anywhere.

---

[39] Ibid., para 51.

[40] Ibid.

[41] Ibid.

[42] Ibid.

Moving to Central Asia, section 2 of the **Indian** SPDI Rules, defines personal information[43] as any information that relates to a natural person, which, either directly or indirectly, in combination with other information available or likely to be available with a body corporate, is capable of identifying such person. On the other hand, sensitive personal data or information is any personal information pertaining to (i) password; (ii) financial information such as Bank account or credit card or debit card or other payment instrument details; (iii) physical, physiological and mental health condition; (iv) sexual orientation; (v) medical records and history; (vi) biometric information; (vii) any detail relating to the above clauses as provided to body corporate for providing service; and (viii) any of the information received under the above clauses by body corporate for processing, stored or processed under lawful contract or otherwise: provided that, any information that is freely available or accessible in the public domain or furnished under the Right to Information Act 2005, or any other law being in force at the time shall not be regarded as sensitive personal data or information for the purposes of these rules.

Among the African nations, **Gabon** defines personal data as any 'natural, legal, public or private person, any organisation or association which, alone or with others, makes the decision to collect and process personal data and determines the purposes thereof'.[44] Unlike other jurisdictions, Gabon does not have a catch-all definition. For instance, sensitive data constitutes any 'natural, legal, public or private person, any organisation or association that processes data on behalf of the data controller'.[45] Further, health data has also been given a separate definition to include 'data concerning the physical and mental condition of a data subject, including the genetic data'.[46] This is a different approach from that of those nation states that have amalgamated all three definitions into one single definition. The alternative has seen nation states separate all or part of the above definitions. On the other side, **Ghana** defines personal data as that data which consists of information that relates to the 'race, colour, ethnic or tribal origin of the data subject; the political opinion of the data subject; the religious beliefs or other beliefs of a similar nature, of the data subject; the physical, medical, mental health or mental condition or DNA of the data subject; the sexual orientation of the data subject; the commission or alleged commission of an offence by the individual; or proceedings for an offence committed or alleged to have been committed by the individual, the disposal of such proceedings or the

43 Ministry of Communications and Information Technology, 2011, https://www.meity.gov.in/writereaddata/files/GSR313E_10511%281%29_0.pdf.

44 Law No. 001/2011 on the Protection of Personal Data, https://www.dataguidance.com/notes/gabon-data-protection-overview Note that the law is in French, and utilised https://caseguard.com/articles/promoting-data-privacy-and-protection-in-gabon/ and DLA Piper, https://www.dlapiperdataprotection.com/index.html?t=law&c=GA.

45 Ibid.

46 Ibid.

sentence of any court in the proceedings'.[47] This is a single definition that includes health and other elements of sensitive data that have been defined separately by other nation states.

In section 2 of **Jamaica's** data laws, personal data has been defined to be a 'living individual; or an individual who has been deceased for less than thirty years, who can be identified from that information alone or from that information and other information in the possession of, or likely to come into the possession of, the data controller. It also includes 'any expression of opinion about that individual and any indication of the intentions of the data controller or any other person in respect of that individual'.[48] An important observation compared to the other state is that, a minor has been defined to be a person under the age of 18. Health records, biometric data has been defined separately. On the other hand, sensitive data has its own definition to include genetic, biometric data, filiation, racial, ethnic origin, political opinions, philosophical—religious beliefs, membership in any trade union, physical, mental health, sex life and the alleged commission of any offence(s).[49] Those state that define sensitive data separately from general personal data have done so, with commonality of including health data generally. Nevertheless, there still remain several differences that will need to be reconciled when interpreting and applying the law.

Back to Africa, in section 2 of its data laws, **Kenya** provides for '*personal data* to mean any information relating to an identified or identifiable natural person. *Biometric data*, health data, personal data and sensitive personal data have all been defined separately under the Kenya law. Additionally, data means information which (a) is processed by means of equipment operating automatically in response to instructions given for that purpose; (b) is recorded with intention that it should be processed by means of such equipment; (c) is recorded as part of a relevant filing system; (d) otherwise forms part of an accessible record; (e) recorded information which is held by a public entity'.[50] Further, *health data* means data related to the state of physical or mental health of the data subject and includes records regarding the past, present or future state of the health, data collected in the course of registration for, or provision of health services, or data which associates the data subject to the provision of specific health services. *Sensitive personal data* constitutes data revealing the natural person's race, health status, ethnic social origin, conscience, belief, genetic data, biometric data, property details, marital status, family details including names of the person's children, parents, spouse or spouses, sex or the sexual orientation of the data subject.[51]

---

[47] Data Protection Act 2012, section 96, https://nita.gov.gh/theevooc/2017/12/Data-Protection-Act-2012-Act-843.pdf.

[48] Data Protection Act, 2020, section 2, https://japarliament.gov.jm/attachments/article/339/The%20Data%20Protection%20Act,%202020.pdf.

[49] Data Protection Act, 2020, section 2, https://japarliament.gov.jm/attachments/article/339/The%20Data%20Protection%20Act,%202020.pdf.

[50] Data Protection Act 2019, https://www.odpc.go.ke/dpa-act/.

[51] Data Protection Act 2019, https://www.odpc.go.ke/dpa-act/.

Section 2 of the data laws of **The Kingdom of Eswatini** defines data generally as all representations of information no matter the format or medium.[52] Personal data or information is that information which can identify anyone. It is a broad definition that also includes race, religion, age, sex, ethnicity, address, identity number, finger prints, blood type and name, amongst other identifying data. It has captured health and biometric data, where other states have defined it separately.[53] On the other hand, unlike other jurisdictions, **Lesotho** law has separate definitions for data and personal data: data constitutes, 'an unidentified data record, anonymised personal data or a fact about an unidentified individual. Further, personal data is any data that relates to a living individual who can be identified from that data, and be identified for data that is in the control and possession of a controller'.[54]

Thus far, this chapter has demonstrated how the states being examined have adopted very different approaches to defining personal data. Most, if not all, definitions have certain elements in common relating to an individual's name, date of birth, age, race, religion, sex, ethnicity, identity number, finger prints and blood type. However, it is argued that before the emergence of technology, information such as name, address, race and age have been standard identifiable data since time immemorial. Technology has changed the extent and level of data that can be captured. Today, the capture of identity numbers (which some nation states have enshrined in law) is a recent addition. Moreover, IP addresses and biometric identifiers, are more recent because without technology, these identity-related data could not be captured. Most noteworthy is how some states are now protecting people's opinions and gender as these constitute personal data. Also of significance is the separation of sensitive data from general data while it can be argued that in some circumstances where this occurs, this data has been afforded a greater level of protection. However, unlike the EU members, it may diminish this data's overall protection. Having a single definition that captures all the data mentioned in this chapter can be achieved, and it is my view that the consolidation of a single approach will offer greater protection and better economic outcomes.

Malawi defines personal data as any information relating to an 'individual who can be identified or is identifiable, directly or indirectly by reference to an identifier such as a name, an identification number, location data, an online identifier or one or more factors specific to the physical, physiological, genetic, psychological, cultural, social or economic identity of that individual'.[55] In addition, sensitive personal data

[52] Data Protection Act 2022, section 2, https://www.esccom.org.sz/legislation/DATA%20PROTECTION%20ACT.pdf.

[53] Data Protection Act 2022, section 2, https://www.esccom.org.sz/legislation/DATA%20PROTECTION%20ACT.pdf.

[54] Data Protection Act 2013, section 2. http://www.nic.ls/lsnic/community/policies/Data_Protection_Act_2011_Lesotho.pdf.

[55] Data Protection Bill 2021, section 2 https://digmap.pppc.mw/wp-content/uploads/2022/03/Malawi-Data-Protection-Bill-final-draft-210630-.pdf.

relates to 'biometric data, race or ethnic origin; religious or similar beliefs, conscience or philosophy, health status, sex life or sexual orientation and political opinions'.[56]

In South East Asia, **Malaysia's** Personal Data Protection Act 2010,[57] has defined personal data as information that forms part of a commercial transaction that: (a) is being processed wholly or partly by means of equipment operating automatically in response to instructions given for that purpose; (b) is recorded with the intention that it should wholly or partly be processed by means of such equipment; or, (c) is recorded as part of a relevant filing system or with the intention that it should form part of a relevant filing system that relates directly or indirectly to a data subject who is identified or identifiable from that information or from that and other information in the possession of a data user, including any sensitive personal data and expression of opinion about the data subject, but does not include any information that is processed for the purpose of a credit reporting business carried on by a credit reporting agency under the Credit Reporting Agencies Act 2010.[58] In addition, sensitive personal data has been separated from general personal data. Sensitive personal data is 'any personal data consisting of information as to the physical or mental health or condition of a data subject, his political opinions, his religious beliefs or other beliefs of a similar nature, the commission or alleged commission by him of any offence or any other personal data as the Minister may determine by order published in the *Gazette*'.[59]

In **Mauritius**, rather than having a general definition of personal data, data has been specifically categorised as biometric, genetic, physical or mental health, or, special categories of personal data.[60] Most noteworthy is how the state has defined special categories of personal data, in a similar way to other states that have defined the same data as sensitive data. In other words, special categories of personal data pertain to data which identifies racial or ethnic origin; political opinion or adherence; religious or philosophical beliefs or membership of a trade union. It can also identify a person's physical or mental health or condition, and sexual orientation, practices or preferences along with their genetic, biometric or alleged offences committed.[61] In another example of how this state digresses from other states, the transmission of traffic data has been defined as 'communication by means of a computer system and generated by the system that form part in the chain of communication, indicating

---

[56] Data Protection Bill 2021, section 2 https://digmap.pppc.mw/wp-content/uploads/2022/03/Malawi-Data-Protection-Bill-final-draft-210630-.pdf.

[57] Personal Data Protection Act 2010, https://www.kkmm.gov.my/pdf/Personal%20Data%20Protection%20Act%202010.pdf.

[58] Personal Data Protection Act 2010, section 4, https://www.kkmm.gov.my/pdf/Personal%20Data%20Protection%20Act%202010.pdf.

[59] Personal Data Protection Act 2010, section 4, https://www.kkmm.gov.my/pdf/Personal%20Data%20Protection%20Act%202010.pdf.

[60] Data Protection Act 2017, section 2 https://dataprotection.govmu.org/Documents/DPA_2017_updated.pdf?csf=1&e=0rlrff.

[61] Data Protection Act 2017, section 2 https://dataprotection.govmu.org/Documents/DPA_2017_updated.pdf?csf=1&e=0rlrff.

the communication's origin, destination, route, time, date, size, duration, or type of underlying service'.[62]

Section 7 of **New Zealand's** data laws has a very broad definition of personal information which constitutes any information that can identify[63] a person. The definition captures all the other definitions that this book has identified. It includes biometric, genetic, health and sensitive data, and has many similarities to its larger neighbour, Australia. On the other hand, in **Nigeria**, personal data is any information relating to an individual who can be identified or is identifiable, directly or indirectly by reference to an identifier such as a name, an identification number, location data, an online identifier or one or more factors specific to the physical, physiological, genetic, psychological, cultural, social or economic identity of that individual.[64] Apart from defining biometric data, the law has not defined health data itself. On the other side, sensitive personal data in Nigeria constitutes that data which identifies an individual through genetic, biometric data, race or ethnic origin; religious or reflective conscience or philosophy; health status; sex life; political opinions or affiliations; trade union memberships; or any other personal data prescribed by the Commission.[65]

However, **Rwanda**, under Article 3 defines personal data as 'any information relating to an identified or identifiable natural person who can be identified, directly or indirectly, in particular by reference to an identifier such as a name, an identification number, location data, an online identifier or to one or more factors specific to the physical, psychological, genetic, mental, economic, cultural or social identity of that natural person'.[66] Similarly, sensitive personal data having been defined separately includes, race, health status, criminal records, medical records, social origin, religious or philosophical beliefs, political opinion, genetic or biometric information, gender preference or family details.[67]

Importantly, in South East Asia, **Singapore** defines personal data very broadly to mean whether true or not an individual can be identified from that data, or from that data together with other information to which an organisation has access.[68] It can best be described as an all-in definition, meaning that neither health nor sensitive

---

[62] Data Protection Act 2017, section 2 https://dataprotection.govmu.org/Documents/DPA_2017_updated.pdf?csf=1&e=0rlrff.

[63] Privacy Act 2020, section 7 https://www.privacy.org.nz/privacy-act-2020/privacy-principles/.

[64] Data Protection Regulation 2022, section 65 https://ndpb.gov.ng/Files/Nigeria_Data_Protection_Bill.pdf.

[65] Data Protection Regulation 2022, section 65 https://ndpb.gov.ng/Files/Nigeria_Data_Protection_Bill.pdf.

[66] Law n°058/2021 of 13/10/2021 relating to the protection of personal data and privacy (the Data Protection Law), Article 3, https://www.minijust.gov.rw/fileadmin/user_upload/Minijust/Publications/Official_Gazette/_2021_Official_Gazettes/October/OG_Special_of_15.10.2021_Amakuru_bwite.pdf.

[67] Law n°058/2021 of 13/10/2021 relating to the protection of personal data and privacy (the Data Protection Law), https://www.minijust.gov.rw/fileadmin/user_upload/Minijust/Publications/Official_Gazette/_2021_Official_Gazettes/October/OG_Special_of_15.10.2021_Amakuru_bwite.pdf.

[68] Personal Data Protection Act 2012, section 2 https://sso.agc.gov.sg/Act/PDPA2012.

data has been defined separately. The Commission[69] pointed out that sensitive data would constitute:

> NRIC/Passport numbers; personal data of a financial nature such as bank account details, Central Depository account details, securities holdings, transaction and payment summaries; names of the policyholder's dependants or beneficiaries, the sum insured under the insurance policy, the premium amount and type of coverage; an individual's personal history involving drug use and infidelity; sensitive medical conditions; and personal data of minors.[70]

It is evident from the above, that the various elements constituting sensitive personal data have been reflected in the laws of those nation states that have defined sensitive data in similar ways. The major difference is the terminology used such as NRIC, amongst others.

In the 2022 Singapore case of *Reed, Michael v Bellingham, Alex* (*Attorney-General, intervener*)[71] the Court was required to determine whether the 'appellant's emotional distress and the loss of control of his personal data fall within the meaning of "loss or damage", and that he is therefore entitled to claim injunctive relief under s 32'.[72] Firstly, section 32 of the PDPA provides that:

(1) Any person who suffers loss or damage directly as a result of a contravention of any provision in Part IV, V or VI by an organisation shall have a right of action for relief in civil proceedings in a court.
(2) If the Commission has made a decision under this Act in respect of a contravention specified in subsection (1), no action accruing under subsection (1) may be brought in respect of that contravention until after the decision has become final as a result of there being no further right of appeal.
(3) The court may grant to the plaintiff in an action under subsection (1) all or any of the following:

    (a) relief by way of injunction or declaration;
    (b) damages;
    (c) such other relief as the court thinks fit.[73]

The Court, when conducting a comprehensive discussion of a number of the PDPA provisions, ruled that the appellant's emotional distress was a form of "loss or damage" according to the meaning of s 32(1). Even though the Court did not confirm or draw upon the definition of personal data, the case reinforces the argument put forward in this chapter: that a definition of personal data must exist in order for any loss or damage to be considered under section 32.

---

[69] Case No DP-1611-B0323 Aviva Ltd [2017] SGPDPC 14.

[70] Ibid., para 17. Note discussion from para 14 to 20. Also see Warren B Chik, Pang Keep Ying Joey, The Meaning and Scope Of Personal Data Under The Singapore Personal Data Protection Act, Singapore Academy of Law Journal, SAcLJ (2014), pp. 354–357.

[71] [2022] SGCA 60.

[72] Ibid., para 1.

[73] Ibid., para 2.

According to the data laws of **South Africa**, personal information is that which applies to an 'identifiable, living, natural person, and where it is applicable, an identifiable, existing juristic person, including, but not limited to—(a) information relating to the race, gender, sex, pregnancy, marital status, national, ethnic or social origin, colour, sexual orientation, age, physical or mental health, well-being, disability, religion, conscience, belief, culture, language and birth of the person; (b) information relating to the education or the medical, financial, criminal or employment history of the person; (c) any identifying number, symbol, e-mail address, physical address, telephone number, location information, online identifier or other particular assignment to the person; (d) the biometric information of the person; (e) the personal opinions, views or preferences of the person; (f) correspondence sent by the person that is implicitly or explicitly of a private or confidential nature or further correspondence that would reveal the contents of the original correspondence; (g) the views or opinions of another individual about the person; and (h) the name of the person if it appears with other personal information relating to the person or if the disclosure of the name itself would reveal information about the person'.[74]

Section 56 of the data laws of **Sri Lanka**, located in Central Asia, defined various elements of data such as, financial, health, biometric and genetic data. This section relates to data, personal data concerning health, and personal data revealing specific information. The three separate definitions are unlike any other of the laws being compared. First, data concerning health is 'personal data related to the physical or psychological health of a natural person, which includes any information that indicates his health situation or status'. Second, personal data revealing racial or ethnic origin constitutes personal data such as photographs that may indicate or be related to the race or ethnicity of a natural person.[75] Third, personal data is any information that can identify a data subject directly or indirectly, and includes identifiers such as a name, an identification number, financial data, location data or an online identity; or one or more factors specific to 'the physical, physiological, genetic, psychological, economic, cultural or social identity of that individual or natural person'.[76]

In the Americas, **Saint Lucia** gives a general definition of data that includes 'facts, information or concepts that are being prepared or have been prepared in a form suitable for use in an electronic system including computer programme, text, images, sound, video and information within a database or electronic system'.[77] The definition of personal data is quite detailed and includes sensitive and health-related data. Personal data is defined as any information such as race, national or ethnic origin, religion, age, sexual orientation, sexual life or marital status that can

---

74 Protection of Personal Information Act 2013, section 1 https://www.gov.za/documents/protection-personal-information-act.

75 Personal Data Protection Act No. 9 of 2022, section 2 https://www.parliament.lk/uploads/acts/gbills/english/6242.pdf.

76 Personal Data Protection Act No. 9 of 2022, section 2 https://www.parliament.lk/uploads/acts/gbills/english/6242.pdf.

77 Privacy and Data Protection Act 2009, section 2, https://www.govt.lc/media.govt.lc/www/resources/legislation/PrivacyAndDataProtectionBill.pdf.

identify a data subject. It also includes information relating to the education, medical, criminal or employment history of the data subject or information relating to financial transactions, any identifying number, symbol or the address, fingerprints, DNA, or blood type, and the views or opinions of any other person about the data subject.[78] Other states have gone into more specific detail when defining personal data. Saint Luca has adopted a quite broad approach to include most if not all the data that has been defined by other jurisdictions. On the other hand, **Saint Kitts and Nevis**, defines personal data as any information in respect of commercial transactions, which is being processed wholly or partly by means of 'equipment operating automatically in response to instructions given for that purpose. It also constitutes data that is recorded with the intention that it should wholly or partly be processed by means of such equipment; or as part of a relevant filing system or with the intention that it should form part of a relevant filing system. The data can directly or indirectly relate to a data subject, including any sensitive personal data and expression of opinion about the data subject'.[79] Even though biometric, genetic and health data have not been defined, sensitive data pertains to 'physical or mental health or condition, sexual orientation, political opinions, religious beliefs, and the commission or alleged commission of any offence'.[80] This is a subtle but important difference compared to the laws of many other jurisdictions which have grouped political and religious information together.

Saint Vincent and The Grenadines has a less comprehensive definition of personal information. Section 4 states that personal information is that information which is recorded in any form, and includes race, gender, national or ethnic origin, religion, age or marital status of the individual.[81] It also relates to identifying information such as education or the medical, criminal or employment history of the data subject. The definition has also been broadened to include any 'identifying number, symbol, address, fingerprints, 'Deoxyribo Nucleic Acid' or blood type, name that appears on correspondence sent to a public authority along with the views or opinions of any other person about the individual'.[82] Moreover, the blood type is not often personal data that has been defined in specific terms.

Formally, **Tanzania** has defined personal data. However, at the time of writing, the new 2022 laws were not available in English. **Togo**, on the one hand, defines personal data broadly, and separates general data from health and genetic personal data. On the other hand, 'personal data refers to any information relating to an identified or identifiable natural person directly or indirectly, by reference to one or more identification elements, specific to his physical, physiological, genetic, psychic,

[78] Privacy and Data Protection Act 2009, section 2, https://www.govt.lc/media.govt.lc/www/resources/legislation/PrivacyAndDataProtectionBill.pdf.

[79] Data Protection Act, 5 of 2018, section 2 https://www.theinformationcollective.com/dpl/st-kitts-data-protection-act Also see https://aglcskn.info/wp-content/documents/Annual-Laws/2018/ACTs/Act-5-of-2018-Data-Protection-Act-2018.pdf.

[80] Data Protection Act, 5 of 2018, section 2 https://www.theinformationcollective.com/dpl/st-kitts-data-protection-act.

[81] Privacy Act 2003, section 4 https://www.theinformationcollective.com/dpl/st-vincent-and-the-grenadines-the-privacy-act.

[82] Ibid.

cultural, social or economic identity'.[83] It also constitutes, genetic data that pertains to the hereditary characteristics of an individual or groups of individuals who are related. Sensitive data has been specified to include all 'personal data relating to racial or ethnic origin, opinions or religious affiliations, political activities, union, sex life, health, prosecution and criminal or administrative sanctions'.[84] Moreover, personal data also includes health data, which is 'any information concerning the physical and mental state of a person concerned, including genetic data'.[85]

In one of the most comprehensive definitions of personal data, **Trinidad-Tobago** adopted a three-stage approach by referring to personal data and personal information. First, data has been defined to mean 'any document, correspondence, memorandum, book, plan, map, drawing, pictorial or graphic work, photograph, film, microfilm, sound recording, videotape, machine-readable record and any other documentary material, regardless of form or characteristics, and any copy of those things'.[86] Second, and most noteworthy, personal information is anything that can identify a data subject, including his or her 'race, nationality or ethnic origin, religion, age or marital status of the individual, education or the medical, criminal, employment history, financial transactions, identifying number, symbol, address, telephone number, correspondence, views, opinions, fingerprints, deoxyribonucleic acid, blood type or the biometric characteristics'.[87] Third, the comprehensive approach taken by **Trinidad-Tobago** is illustrated by the reference to sensitive personal information as 'political affiliations or trade union membership, religious or other beliefs, physical or mental health, sexual orientation or sexual life, or criminal or financial record'.[88]

In defining data, **Uganda** has taken a similar approach to that of the other Commonwealth states. Section 2 defines data as any information that is processed by means of equipment operating automatically. This would be a form of artificial intelligence whereby the information is inputted by an individual or organisation. Data is also that information that has been processed by equipment including all technology, and recorded in a relevant filing system. On the other hand, personal

[83] Tshepiso Hadebe Togolese Republic, 2020, https://dataprotection.africa/wp-content/uploads/2020/03/Togolese-Republic-Factsheet-update-20200331.pdf.

[84] Ibid.

[85] Law No. 2019-014 Relating to the Protection of Personal Data, French only, https://jo.gouv.tg/sites/default/files/JO/JOS_29_10_2019-64E%20ANNEE-N°26%20TER.pdf#page=1 and, Tshepiso Hadebe Togolese Republic. https://dataprotection.africa/wp-content/uploads/2020/03/Togolese-Republic-Factsheet-update-20200331.pdf.

[86] Data Protection Act 2011, section 1, https://rgd.legalaffairs.gov.tt/laws2/Alphabetical_List/lawspdfs/22.04.pdf.

[87] Data Protection Act 2011, section 1, https://rgd.legalaffairs.gov.tt/laws2/Alphabetical_List/lawspdfs/22.04.pdf.

[88] Data Protection Act 2011, section 1, https://rgd.legalaffairs.gov.tt/laws2/Alphabetical_List/lawspdfs/22.04.pdf.

data comprises any information that can identify a data subject, including nationality, age marital status, educational level, occupation, identification number-data and any other information a controller may possess.[89]

Finally, in **Zambia**, data has been given a number of separate definitions. A distinctive feature is the meaning of meta data which is data that describes other data. This is arguably, all other data that has not been defined by the data laws. Most significantly, data constitutes 'numbers, letters, alphabetic or numeric strings, symbols or codes in any form'.[90] Nonetheless, personal data and sensitive personal data have distinct meanings to ensure they capture the key elements of identifying data subjects. That is, personal data 'relates to an individual who can be directly or indirectly identified from that data which includes a name, an identification number, location data, an online identifier, or one or more factors specific to the physical, physiological, genetic, mental, economic, cultural or social identity of that natural person'. On the other hand, sensitive personal data comprises any data that suppresses a data subject's fundamental rights and freedoms, such as race, marital status, ethnic origin or sex, genetic, biometric, child abuse political opinions, religious or other beliefs, trade union, and mental health, or physical or mental condition'.[91] A key addition to the definition of sensitive personal data is child abuse.[92] There is no other definition that includes this protective mechanism. The Commonwealth should consider adding this to the Model law and ensuring its adoption by other nation states. Health data has not been defined.

A number of states have defined biometric data either within the general meaning of personal data, or separately. Simon Chesterman makes the point that defining personal data has brought about a number of benefits. For example, other benefits more explicitly link convenience and security, such as trusted-traveller programmes that allow approved individuals expedited clearance through border procedures. 'Approval' involves an interview and background check, as well as the storing of biometric identification data.[93] Chesterman asserts that today, governments possess more information about their citizens than at any point in history. Though difficult to measure, much of this information does improve security and simplify daily communications and transactions. It also increases the possibility of abuse leading to the loss

[89] Data Protection and Privacy Act 2019, section 2 https://media.ulii.org/files/legislation/akn-ug-act-2019-9-eng-2019-05-03.pdf.

[90] Data Protection Act 2021, section 2, https://www.parliament.gov.zm/sites/default/files/documents/acts/Act%20No.%203%20The%20Data%20Protection%20Act%202021_0.pdf.

[91] Data Protection Act 2021, section 2 https://www.parliament.gov.zm/sites/default/files/documents/acts/Act%20No.%203%20The%20Data%20Protection%20Act%202021_0.pdf Note that "child" has the meaning assigned to the word in the Constitution;, and "child abuse" includes physical and emotional neglect, physical injury, other than accidental injury, ill treatment and sexual abuse of a child; "child abuse data" means personal data consisting of information as to whether the child data subject is or has been the subject of, or may be at risk of, child abuse.

[92] Data Protection Act 2021, section 2 https://www.parliament.gov.zm/sites/default/files/documents/acts/Act%20No.%203%20The%20Data%20Protection%20Act%202021_0.pdf.

[93] Simon Chesterman, *Privacy and Surveillance in the Age of Terror*, Global Politics Strategy, (2010), p. 34.

or misuse of data, especially in regard to the discriminatory treatment of particular groups.[94] Whether used for surveillance, law enforcement, national security or some other public interest, this information, when coupled with data-privacy laws, is the personal data that has been defined.

Despite this, and as indicated above, a number of the laws of Commonwealth countries do include biometric data in their respective definitions of personal data. As the digital economy grows, the amount of biometric data will also increase. In other words, 'biometric data such as fingerprints and iris scans have a prominent place in identity verification and identification. For example, biometric passports have become a standard tool for a variety of states. Another example is India's Aadhaar programme, which uses biometric technology to record fingerprints and iris scans in addition to personal information such as name, date of birth and domicile. Biometric technology is also used for border control and migration management in Australia, UK, Singapore, and most other Commonwealth states'.[95] Anna Bedusch confirms 'the emergence of solutions combining biometrics and blockchain technologies for digital identification'.[96] Further, Bedusch explains:

> Blockchain uses decentralised distributed ledger technology which can be an advantage for digital identity providers as data is not stored in a single central database. Instead, the data is encrypted and recorded in the different blocks of the chain, making it challenging to delete or tamper with the information. However, this also means that any personal information directly stored in the chain cannot be easily removed (, creating challenges for data protection. Similarly, blockchain is not exempt from security concerns, as for example, private keys may be stolen by hackers or lost. Still, blockchain enthusiasts maintain that this technology could contribute to building a self-sovereign identity, or in other words, a digital identity owned and controlled by the user – who can then decide with whom and when to share information contained in their 'digital wallet'.[97]

Two critical issues are emerging here. Firstly, the definition of personal data is so divergent that there are many situations to which the definition does not apply, or needs to be applied separately, or cannot be applied at all. In addition, the security concerns associated with new technologies are far from being adequately addressed and personal data can, at times, be increasingly vulnerable to illegal use. Additionally, striking a balance between security and economic outcomes will continue to challenge governments, regulators and businesses.

On the other hand, Collin Bennett, in referring to Ian Lawson, maintains that the economic implications for the data subject are not fully understood from the use of their defined personal data. That is:

---

[94] Ibid.

[95] Ana Bedusch, *Digital identity: Contemporary challenges for data protection, privacy and non-discrimination rights*, Big Data & Society (2019), p. 2.

[96] Ibid.

[97] Ibid.

> To the extent that business obtains and uses personal information without a market mechanism to govern the exchange, business is a classic free rider in the economy. It consumes a common property resource without covering the externalities related to its extraction and use.[98]

Bennett goes further, stating that when an organization benefits from the use of the personal information, either itself or by trading that information to third parties, the original information provider—the data subject—receives no benefits. Furthermore:

> That situation has perpetuated because of the reluctance of many businesses to be transparent about their practices and to establish mechanisms to obtain informed consent when they wish to use personal information for secondary uses. Business remains a free-rider as long as individuals are kept in the dark about how their information is being used and disclosed. Classic economic theorizing would contend that an imperfect market place can be rectified by two mechanisms. First, one can give a value to personal information so that the costs and benefits of transactions are allocated more appropriately.[99]

Most noteworthy is that Bennett was writing during the 1990s, well before the implementation of the EU GDPR, and most of the states compared in this book had yet to implement data-privacy laws. Notable exceptions were the EU, UK, Australia, Canada and New Zealand. Most of the other nation states began to develop their respective data-privacy laws only in the mid- to late 2000s. Thus, the question arises: what has changed today in 2023? Not much, as personal data is still being used for economic benefit by a few. The notable difference has been that with the increase in the number of data laws being established and implemented, the definition of personal data has been given a lot more emphasis due to its legal status. Consequently, our personal data defined by the law has become even more vulnerable. Increasingly, there are publicised breaches of personal data that is held by large organisation across the Commonwealth. However, a detailed discussion about the extent of data privacy breaches is outside the scope of this chapter.

Put another way, the 'advances in technology have made us as a society think more about cyber security and privacy, particularly how we consider and protect personal information'.[100] The consequences of these developments have 'introduced a temporal dimension to the definition of personal information and we have also witnessed new types of data emerging (e.g., phone sensor data, stress level measurements). These rapid technological changes introduce several challenges as legislation is often inadequate, and therefore questions regularly arise pertaining to whether information should be considered personal or sensitive and thereby better protected'.[101] This is challenging issue for regulators and governments. As emphasises above, the disparate and highly fragmented approaches to defining personal

---

[98] Ian Lawson, *Privacy and the Information Highway: Regulatory Options for Canada*. Ottawa: Industry Canada. (1995), in Colin J. Bennett, Adequate Data Protection by the Year 2000: The Prospects for Privacy in Canada, International Review of Law, Computers & Technology, 11:1, (1997) p. 84.

[99] Ibid.

[100] Rahime Belen Saglam, Jason R.C. Nurse, Duncan Hodges, Personal information: Perceptions, types and evolution, Journal of Information Security and Applications, Volume 66, (2022), p. 1.

[101] Ibid.

data today, has resulted in an inconsistent and less coherent approach across nation states. This will be exacerbated when AI technology becomes even more entrenched in our daily lives (work and home).

3.2 Conclusion

This chapter has illustrated the significant differences in the ways that states define their respective personal data or personal information. It is argued that the definition of personal data is the starting point to determining not only the level of breach possible under the respective laws, but also where there is criminal activity involved by using that data. In some cases, the various definitions are simple; however, most definitions are highly complex and difficult for a lay person to fully navigate. Put simply, when dealing with one country, the definition of personal data is all but straightforward. Moreover, when having to deal with multiple countries, and the more countries involved the more complex it will become to interpret and understand the various components of the definition(s). Most noteworthy is the issue of terminology. Often, different terms are used for the same identifiable data. For instance, where a state has included a person's opinion in the definition, it could include reflective conscience or philosophy. This is just one example amongst many where terminology further complicates the layman's ability to interpret the many laws. Most states have adopted either a single or a two-stage approach. Some states such as Trinidad-Tobago have taken a three-stage approach, establishing what is arguably one of the most comprehensive definitions to date. The highly detailed definition includes, but is not limited to any document, correspondence, memorandum, book, plan, map, drawing, pictorial or graphic work, photograph, film, microfilm, sound recording, videotape, machine-readable record and any other documentary material, regardless of form or characteristics, and any copy of those things'.[102] Second is that personal information is anything that can identify a data subject, including their 'race, nationality or ethnic origin, religion, age or marital status of the individual, education or the medical, criminal, employment history, financial transactions, identifying number, symbol, address, telephone number, correspondence, views, opinions, fingerprints, deoxyribonucleic acid, blood type or the biometric characteristics'.[103] Third approach, whereby, sensitive personal information is 'political affiliations or trade union membership, religious or other beliefs, physical or mental health, sexual orientation or sexual life, or criminal or financial record'.[104]

[102] Data Protection Act 2011, section 1, https://rgd.legalaffairs.gov.tt/laws2/Alphabetical_List/lawspdfs/22.04.pdf.

[103] Data Protection Act 2011, section 1, https://rgd.legalaffairs.gov.tt/laws2/Alphabetical_List/lawspdfs/22.04.pdf.

[104] Data Protection Act 2011, section 1, https://rgd.legalaffairs.gov.tt/laws2/Alphabetical_List/lawspdfs/22.04.pdf.

The definition above, when analysed, comprises everything covered by the EU. Importantly, it includes those areas of technology that can identify a person, including artificial intelligence that provides a machine-readable record. Although the definition is exhaustive, and considers technology more-so than is done by many other states, the terminology is an issue. In comparing this definition with that of the EU GDPR, the latter states that any 'identifier' is information that could include all of the above. Essentially, the terms and terminology used within the respective laws will need to be carefully considered and made consistent across all definitions.

Today, that which has been defined by the law can easily be changed as it becomes 'anonymous to re-identifiable as more diverse data sets (e.g., aggregated from multiple sources) become collectable from the public domain. Purchasing habits, which may not seem to be sensitive at first glance, may reveal highly sensitive data through data-driven inferences, for example, they may be used to reveal an unhealthy life style, location data, financial difficulties and even illegal activity when processed over time'.[105] Furthermore, IP addresses are being targeted in cybersecurity breaches, even though they are now considered to be personal information. This is particularly the case for transnational data flows.[106] This position has been reinforced in the earlier Case-582/14 where the Court pointed out that:

> personal data is defined as information relating to an identified or an identifiable natural person. Also, an identifiable person is one who can be identified directly or indirectly by reference to an identification number or to one or more factors that are specific to the person's physical, physiological, mental, economic, cultural or social identity. The court also noted that it was held in Scarlet Extended (C-70/10), IP addresses of internet users were protected as personal data because they allowed users to be identified even though this case was concerning collection and identification of IP addresses by internet service providers. In answering this question, the court observed that a dynamic IP address alone doesn't amount to information of an identified person but for it to fall under the definition in Article 2(1)(a) Directive 96/45 there must be additional data that can lead to the identification of a natural person.[107]

The Court also referred to Recital 26 Directive 95/46 which states that:

> to determine whether a person is identifiable, account should be taken of all the means likely reasonably to be used either by the controller or by any other person to identify the said person. The referring court highlighted that German law doesn't allow internet service providers to transmit data necessary for the identification of a data subject directly to online media services providers except in the event of cyber attacks when the online media services provider can contact a competent authority who can contact the internet service provider for such information that may help bring criminal proceedings. In light of this, the court held that an IP dynamic address is personal data where an online media services provider has legal means that enable them to identify natural persons.[108]

---

[105] Ibid. pp. 1–3.

[106] Robert Walters, *Digital Economy and International Trade: Transnational Data Flows*, Wolters Kluwer Law (2022), Chpt 14.

[107] Case C-582/14, *Patrick Breyer v Bundesrepublik Deutschland*, paras 31 to 50, https://curia.europa.eu/juris/document/document.jsf?text=&docid=184668&pageIndex=0&doclang=EN&mode=lst&dir=&occ=first&part=1&cid=9280641.

[108] Ibid.

The above reinforces the importance of this book. In other words, today, data and cybersecurity are intertwined significantly in practical technology terms, yet, through and by the law, they are very different, and achieve different things. The case cited above is important because three states included in this comparative examination—the UK, Malta and Cyprus—were all member states of the EU when this case was decided. As stated earlier, although the UK exited the EU in 2021, it has retained to date most, if not all, of the EU legal framework for data. It reinforces that in the definitions of personal data, there are references to an identification number or to one or more factors that are specific to the person's physical, physiological, mental, economic, cultural or social identity—all of which contribute in some way to making personal data vulnerable to cybercrime activity.

Moreover, as this book demonstrates, there is a close relationship between personal data and criminal online-computer activity. This chapter has also highlighted that the fragmented approach to defining personal data is widespread. Some states and jurisdictions have a catch-all definition which includes anything that can identify an individual. On the other side, there are states that have separated out the definition to cover general, health, sensitive, and biometric data, amongst others. This should be an area that can easily be addressed by all countries. A way to resolve this is for the MBP and the MPPI to be revised and for a consistent definition of personal information to be established. This will provide greater certainty of protection for this data, but also, when it is traded and transferred internationally. Practitioners and the business community will benefit significantly because compliance costs will decrease just by not having to know the different definitions of data when undertaking international transfers. While the EU is not part of the Commonwealth, it should be an observer. Currently, two EU member countries—Malt and Cyprus—are also members of the Commonwealth. Additionally, the UK at this stage has retained the EU's definition of personal data within their national law. Thus, finally, it is argued that the Commonwealth MBP and MPPI should reflect the catch-all definition of the EU GDPR.

Chapter 4
Regulator

4.1 Introduction

The creation of an independent Regulator is an important step to ensuring the promotion and implementation of data laws within a country. Generally, the Regulator has the title of Privacy, Information or Data Protection Commissioner who has been afforded legal powers to investigate and make decisions on breaches of the law. In Commonwealth countries, the specific title of the Commissioner will vary from nation to nation. Commissioners also have some responsibility for educating stakeholders and raising the awareness of data protection and data flows within their respective nation state, and for collaborating and cooperating with other Commissioners.

The MBPPI refers to the Regulator as the Privacy Commissioner. Section 4 defines a Privacy Commissioner to mean the personal appointed under section 16 of the Privacy Act, *[year of enactment]*.[1] It sets out the powers, role and responsibility of the Commissioner when dealing with data/privacy matters. The MBPPI outlines the role of a Commissioner, which includes:

> The role of a Privacy Commissioner is also set out, including the requirement to make an annual report to Parliament. In light of the fact that some developing Commonwealth countries may face challenges in securing adequate resources for an independent body or authority to deal with complaints under the legislation, the Model Bill makes provision for a Privacy Commissioner appointed under the Model Privacy Bill (dealing with the protection of personal information in the public sector) to also deal with complaints under this Model Bill.[2]

---

[1] The Commonwealth, Model Bill on the Protection of Personal Information https://www.asianlaws.org/gcld/cyberlawdb/COM/P15370_6_ROL_Model_Bill_Protection_Personal_Information_2.pdf.

[2] Ibid., p. 3.

R. Walters, *Cybersecurity and Data Laws of the Commonwealth*,
https://doi.org/10.1007/978-981-99-3935-0_4

On the other hand, the MBP creates the office of Privacy Commissioner and provides for investigation of complaints and accountability to Parliament.[3] The Privacy Commissioner provisions may be omitted in the case of a country with insufficient resources to create an additional public officer position. In such cases, the enacting country may designate an existing officer to perform certain critical functions related to the protection of personal privacy. Furthermore, many of the Commissioners who have been appointed are young. They have not held the position for long enough to report on completed investigations and the ensuing outcome(s). It is the view of the Commonwealth Secretariat that, provided such person has adequate independence in the exercise of his or her duties under the Model Bill, the integrity of the legislation would not be jeopardised.[4] Independence is an important feature because it ensures the Commissioner will be free of government and political interference.

This chapter determines whether Commonwealth members through their respective data laws have established an independent Regulator according to the MBP and MBPPI. It does not compare the formal and functional arrangements of each Regulator.

Most, if not all, Commonwealth members are required by law to establish a Regulator, or some other kind of supervisory body. While some aspects of their role may be different depending on the respective nation state, they have similar responsibilities to undertake investigations into the breach of data laws. Various terms have been used to describe the Regulator, one of which is 'supervisory authority'. By and large, they all undertake the same task of overseeing the data laws of the nation.

However, what is questionable is the extent to which they can practise independently of the government. It been put forward that the:

> guarantee of the independence of national supervisory authorities is intended to ensure the effectiveness and reliability of the monitoring of compliance with the provisions concerning protection of individuals with regard to the processing of personal data. The guarantee of 'complete independence' was established not to grant a special status to those authorities themselves as well as their agents, but in order to strengthen the protection of individuals and bodies affected by their decisions.[5]

Thomas Zerdick stated the above in the context of the EU, of which Malta and Cyprus are members. In my view, the EU framework is, understandably, the most advanced. It is multi-layered from the Commission to Member States and requires a Regulator at each level. This is further supported by the appointment of controllers and processors within private and government organisations that provide valuable information to the Commission level. In many countries, they have taken on the role of a court. This chapter determine only whether each country of the Commonwealth is required, under the data laws, to establish a Regulator. It will briefly examine decisions handed down by the Regulator s from the UK and Singapore.

[3] The Commonwealth, Model Privacy Bill, Office of Civil and Criminal Justice Reform, 2017, https://www.asianlaws.org/gcld/cyberlawdb/COM/P15370_9_ROL_Model_Privacy_Bill_0.pdf.

[4] Ibid.

[5] Thomas Zerdick, *Article 52. Independence*, In: The EU General Data Protection Regulation (GDPR). Edited by: Christopher Kuner, Lee A. Bygrave and Christopher Docksey, Oxford University Press (2020) p. 875.

In 2022, the UK Information Commission Office (IOC) issued a fine of £85,000 to Allapplianceservices UK Ltd (AUKL), based in Brighton. The entity made 99,313 unsolicited direct marketing calls to people registered with the TPS between 1 January 2021 and 28 June 2021. AUKL came to the attention of the ICO via the Financial Conduct Authority. The ICO's investigation found AUKL appeared to use pressure tactics during the calls insisting that card details be given, with one person saying they "just wanted AUKL to go away" and so handed over their payment details. The ICO concluded the company contravened electronic marketing law in order to maximise turnover and profit. One of the complainants had reduced capacity as a result of a stroke, and a second had dementia.[6] The penalty was issued under section SSA of the UK Data Protection Act 1998. The penalty is in relation to a serious contravention of regulation 21 of the Privacy and Electronic Communications (EC Directive) Regulations 2003.[7] In its investigation, the IOC noted that:

> On 30 March 2021, the Commissioner received a referral from the Financial Conduct Authority ("FCA"). The FCA Complainant reported that on 1 February 2021 they had received an unsolicited call from a company regarding the renewal of a washing machine insurance policy. The FCA Complainant suggested that during the call they were misled by the company, which claimed that it was in fact the individual's current policy provider, when it was later discovered that it was not. During the call, the caller took a sum of money from the FCA Complainant after taking their debit card details, but did not provide a payment reference number. Later, on 10 February 2021, having received insurance paperwork from this company, and upon realising that they were insured by another company already, the FCA Complainant attempted to cancel the policy and seek a refund. They called the company back using the number detailed on the insurance documents - 0203 4413093. Those documents named the company as 'All Appliance UK', with a footnote stating that "*All Appliance UK is a trading style of ALLAPPLIANCESERVICES UK Ltd*". The FCA Complainant was told that his policy would be cancelled, however despite numerous follow-up calls and letters from the FCA Complainant, by the time of their complaint to the FCA, their money had not been refunded. Following this referral, the Commissioner conducted research to see whether any complaints had been logged with the TPS which identified AUKL or its trading style. Two such complaints were located, with one providing the Calling Line Identifier ("CLI") of 0203 4413093, and the second identifying a CLI of 0333 4438517.[8]

The importance of the above cannot be underestimated. The role and responsibility of the Regulator has taken on a judicial function. It is argued that the UK is one of, if not the most advanced[9] Regulator in relation to data. It demonstrated the broad role that these organisations have to ensure a high level of governance and administration of data laws. It also demonstrates the connection between data protection, data security and the commercial benefits derived from having access to that data. In the example above, the organisation would have had access potentially to thousands of numbers that could have disclosed the personal data of individuals. In confirming the above, the IOC noted that:

---

[6] Information Commissioner Office, Allapplianceservices UK Ltd, 2022, https://ico.org.uk/media/action-weve-taken/mpns/4023200/allapplianceservices-mpn-20221128.pdf.

[7] Ibid., para 1.

[8] Ibid., paras 16–17.

[9] This position is based on the consulting work the author of this book has undertaken on behalf of the UK Government in relation to data and cybersecurity.

> together with details for the volume of calls made/connected over a particular period; details of how data used for those calls was sourced; copies of any data protection policies and contractual arrangements with third-party data providers; evidence that the recipients of its calls had provided valid notification (i.e., consent) to receive those calls, etc.[10]

Most notably, the IOC confirmed the referenced direct elements of the data laws of the UK. While not stating the actual provisions of the DPA, by determining that personal data was involved, the IOC confirmed that the data fell within the definition of personal data. Noteworthy too, the reference to consent, which has been discussed in this book, was an important element of the investigation as it helped to confirm a breach of the relevant laws. The extent of the personal data and lack of consideration of the data laws was significant. The IOC noted that:

> between 1 January 2021 and 28 June 2021, AUKL made 211,487 connected unsolicited direct marketing calls, of which 99,313 were to individuals who had been registered with the TPS for not less than 28 days. AUKL had relied on verbal assurances from its third-party data provider that the data it had purchased had been screened against the TPS register.[11]

The aforementioned investigation and outcome further confirm the importance of this book. It is argued that a Regulator's functions and responsibilities are significantly important to the future governance of data and indirectly to cybersecurity. It is vital for the protection of the data in commercial activities, and is only going to become more complex. As repeated throughout this book, data and its security within and across technology are connected and difficult to separate.

In relation to the above, **Australia** has a dedicated Regulator: the Office of the Australian Information Commissioner (the Commissioner). The Commissioner has the power to monitor, audit, advise, educate, report and provide guidance to the community on all privacy-related issues.[12] The Commissioner also has the power to monitor and report on the adequacy of equipment and user safeguards.[13] In addition, the broad-based powers of the Commissioner extend to assessing the Australian Privacy Principles to determine their adequacy. However, Australia has not achieved an Adequacy decision with the EU (Malta-Cyprus). The Commissioner can issue enforcement undertakings, conduct investigations, review complaints, and exempt certain documents from freedom of information. The Commissioner can also undertake enforcement proceedings in the Federal Court or Federal Circuit Court of Australia. Moreover, the Commissioner plays a key role in reviewing and determining enforcement for and of Commonwealth government agencies in privacy-related matters.[14] Furthermore, the Commissioner can issue guidelines to ensure

---

[10] Ibid., para 18.

[11] Ibid., para 34.

[12] Privacy Act 1988, section 27, 28. C2014C00076. In Robert Walters, Leon Trakman, Bruno Zeller, *Data Protection Law: A comparative Analysis of Asia–Pacific European Approaches,* Springer (2019), p. 131.

[13] Ibid., Privacy Act 1988, section 27–33. C2014C00076.

[14] Ibid., Privacy Act 1988, section 35–70. C2014C00076.

compliance with the APPs. These guidelines have been in place for more than a decade. With the Australian laws being in place since the late 1980s, it is my view that the Regulator, laws, Australian Privacy Principles and Guidelines are quite mature in comparison with those of many of the other Commonwealth members.

Antigua and Barbuda requires a Regulator, according to section 21, whereby the Information Commissioner has the powers, functions and duties, conferred on it by the data laws, and through 'the Information Commissioner pursuant to the Freedom of Information Act 2004, particularly under Parts V, VI and VII, shall be applicable as relevant for carrying out and enforcing the protection of data pursuant to the provisions of this Act'.[15] **The Bahamas** have regulated for a Data Protection Commissioner.[16] Interestingly, it is set up as a corporation that is responsible for investigations, enforcement where the data controller or processor has breached the laws, managing complaints, and ensuring overall compliance with the Act. A Regulator in the form of a Data Protection Commissioner is a legislative requirement in **Barbados.**[17] In order to qualify for the position, the individual has to be an 'attorney-at- law and has so practised for a period of not less than 7 years, or for periods amounting in the aggregate to not less than 7 years'.[18] The functional responsibilities of the Commissioner are very similar to those of other countries that also regulate for the same position. That said, the Commissioner is responsible for monitoring, enforcing, promoting awareness of the rules and controller, and conducting investigations and audits to ensure compliance with the data laws.

In **Belize**, section 68 of the data laws requires that a Data Protection Commissioner be established.[19] Again, and similar to the other jurisdictions examined, the functions of the Commissioner extend to monitoring, enforcing, promote awareness and understanding of the risks, undertake investigations and audits to ensure compliance with the laws.[20] In, **Botswana** in accordance with sections 4 and 5, the Act requires that a Commission be established. The Commission is afforded the 'power to do all such things as are necessary to protect the personal rights of individuals with regard to their personal data, and shall ensure the effective application of and compliance with this Act, in particular, to the right to protection of personal data, access, rectification, objection and cancellation of such data. Its overarching responsibility is to ensure there is a high level of compliance with the Act, by issuing instructions

---

[15] Data Protection Act 2013, section 21 http://laws.gov.ag/wp-content/uploads/2019/02/a2013-10.pdf.

[16] Data Protection Act 2008, section 14, http://laws.bahamas.gov.bs/cms/images/LEGISLATION/PRINCIPAL/2003/2003-0003/DataProtectionPrivacyofPersonalInformationAct_1.pdf.

[17] Data Protection Act 2019, section 70, https://gisbarbados.gov.bb/download/data-protection-act-2019/.

[18] Data Protection Act 2019, section 70, https://gisbarbados.gov.bb/download/data-protection-act-2019/.

[19] Data Protection Act, 45 of 2021, section 68 https://www.nationalassembly.gov.bz/wp-content/uploads/2021/07/Data-Protection-Bill-2021-updated.pdf.

[20] Data Protection Act, 45 of 2021, section 68 https://www.nationalassembly.gov.bz/wp-content/uploads/2021/07/Data-Protection-Bill-2021-updated.pdf.

and opinions to ensure the security and safety of the data'.[21] Section 41 enables the Regulator to undertake investigations to ensure the protection of data according to the Act. The Commission can receive complaints from the community that may lead to an investigation; however, any complaint is to be in writing. In **Bangladesh**, the proposed data laws could require a Data Protection Office[22] to be established.

The **Canadian** Commission has been given an extensive role and obligations under the PIPEDA. Apart from the confidentiality requirements related to the disclosure of information,[23] the responsibility afforded to the Commissioner is far reaching and includes investigations, enforcement (entering and searching premises), and the examination of records.[24] The Commission has played a vital role in promoting Canada's data laws and educating its citizens accordingly. The formal and functional responsibilities of Commissioners go beyond what the national laws require. A good example has been the work undertaken in Canada, where the Commissioner has been actively involved in developing a pathway for Privacy by Design in the context of Big Data.[25] Specifically, in 2012, Canada identified the role of artificial intelligence in privacy by design. In response to the evolution and application of algorithms, Canada noted that:

> algorithms can now automatically infer that different digital transactions in different systems are in fact related to the activity of a single person or household. A bank that wants to better serve its customers will be eager to know if a specific customer has three relationships with the bank and has an enormous Twitter following. In the past, identifying the difference between six people each with one fact versus one person with six facts was expensive and difficult — something only the larger organizations could accomplish. Today, the advanced analytics needed to reconcile like entities over diverse data sets (commonly called Entity Resolution) on a Big Data scale are becoming available to organizations of all sizes.[26]

The impact on personal data and the potential breach of privacy over the Internet is significant. This vulnerability is becoming increasingly evident in the escalation of cyber intrusions. In response, in 2012, the Canadian Commissioner suggested that privacy by design can be supported by a number of principles whereby privacy practices are embedded in the procedures implemented by organisations.[27] Fast forward to 2022, and a number of jurisdictions, in addition to members of the Commonwealth, have adopted the concept of privacy by design. Most notable of these are the EU, UK,

---

[21] Data Protection Act, No. 32 of 2018, section 14. https://www.bocra.org.bw/sites/default/files/documents/DataProtectionAct.pdf.

[22] Proposed Data Protection Act, 2022, chapter IX. https://ictd.portal.gov.bd/sites/default/files/files/ictd.portal.gov.bd/page/6c9773a2_7556_4395_bbec_f132b9d819f0/Data%20Protection%20Bill%20en%20V13%20Unofficial%20Working%20Draft%2016.07.22.pdf.

[23] Personal Information Protection and Electronic Documents Act (S.C. 2000, c. 5), section 20, https://laws-lois.justice.gc.ca/eng/acts/P-8.6/index.html.

[24] Personal Information Protection and Electronic Documents Act (S.C. 2000, c. 5), section 12.1, https://laws-lois.justice.gc.ca/eng/acts/P-8.6/index.html.

[25] Privacy by Design, from Rhetric to Reality, 2012, https://www.ipc.on.ca/wp-content/uploads/Resources/PbDBook-From-Rhetoric-to-Reality.pdf.

[26] Ibid., p. 8.

[27] Ibid., p. 13.

Cyprus, Malta, Australia, Singapore and Malaysia. What this means is that privacy by design has emerged to encourage organizations to both drive and demonstrate their commitment to privacy more so than some strict technical compliance definition.[28] This is one such response amongst many others that the Commissioner has over the past decade implemented in Canada alone. By setting standards, industry sectors can adopt them to suit their own particular needs. Similar actions are being undertaken in other states.

Notwithstanding the above, **Cyprus** and **Malta** are subject to a multilayered approach under the EU legal framework for the supervision of data. Simply put, they are required to establish a Supervisory Authority (SA)—Data Protection Authority.[29] At the supranational level, the Union has appointed a European Data Protection Supervisor (EDPS) and is responsible for monitoring the protection of personal data that has been processed by EU institutions.[30] Currently, the UK implements the same framework. It is argued that the **UK** has a mature Regulator which has been in place for a number of years—the Information Commissioner Section 114, DPA.[31] The Information Commissioner has undertaken a number of high-profile investigations regarding the breach of the local data laws. In November 2022, the Commissioner issued a strong reprimand to the Department of Education of the UK, for the misuse of the data of 28 million children across the country. The Commissioner, in issuing this reprimand, stated that:

> No-one needs persuading that a database of pupils' learning records being used to help gambling companies is unacceptable. Our investigation found that the process put in place by the Department of Education were woeful. Data was being misused, and the Department was unaware there was even a problem until a national newspaper informed them. We all have an absolute right to expect that our central government departments treat the data they hold on us with the utmost respect and security. Even more so when it comes to the information of 28 million children.[32]

In the example above, most notable is the quantity of data the Commissioner's office was able to uncover, and the extent to which it had been used, and may be potentially used in future. More importantly, it was the data of children, who are by far one of the most vulnerable in the community. The role of an independent Regulator cannot be underestimated. For every investigation and audit undertaken, it raises

---

[28] Ibid., p. 14.

[29] Regulation 2016/679 Of the European Parliament and the European Council, on the protection of natural persons with regard to the processing of personal data and on the free movement of such data and repealing Directive 95/46/EC (General Data Protection Regulation), Official Journal of the European Union L 119/1. Article 51. Recitals (117) to (123). Article 29 Working Party Guidelines on the Lead Supervisory Authority, WP 244.

[30] European Data Protection Supervisor, https://edps.europa.eu/_en.

[31] Data Protection Act 2018, section 114, https://www.legislation.gov.uk/ukpga/2018/12/pdfs/ukpga_20180012_en.pdf.

[32] Information Commissioner's Office, Department for Education warned after gambling companies benefit from learning recirds database, 2022, https://ico.org.uk/about-the-ico/media-centre/news-and-blogs/2022/11/department-for-education-warned-after-gambling-companies-benefit-from-learning-records-database/.

the level of awareness of the importance for organisations to ensure they have robust systems in place to govern the collection, storage and use of data. When publicised in the way the UK Commissioner's office does, it also informs the broader community of the seriousness of protecting personal data. It raises the level of accountability and transparency of organisations and their respective data governance practices. The resulting effect is that over time, this form of privacy by design will become entrenched in the everyday thinking and practice of individuals and entities, thus raising the standard of data protection.

However, in some cases such as **India** which does not have a dedicated Regulator, in the same way as other nation states have for the governance of data use, they are limited in their response to protecting data in data flows. This is something that India needs to address, as the digital economy is developing rapidly in this country. **Gabon** has established a Regulator, which is the CNPDCP[33] [French—Commission Nationale pour la Protection des Donnees a Caractere Personel] that is responsible for ensuring that the processing of personal data is undertaken according to Chapter III of the data law. The powers afforded to the Regulator include, but are not limited to, overseeing the activities of 'controllers and processors authorising processing operations that involve a high risk to rights and liberties of individuals; establishing and publishing standards; receiving complaints, petitions, and claims; advising public authorities; informing the Public Prosecutor; carrying out inspections and audits; and proposing legislative reform'.[34] **Ghana**, also has the power to establish a dedicated Regulator. Section 1 of the data laws establishes a Commission which has the responsibility to 'implement and monitor compliance with the Act, and make the administrative arrangements it considers appropriate for the discharge of its duties. Additionally, the Commission will investigate complaints, along with keeping and maintaining the Data Protection Register'.[35] In **Jamacia**, a similar approach is required for an Information Commissioner[36] to be established. Similar to other Regulators, the responsibilities extend to 'monitoring compliance, providing advice to the relevant Minister, promote awareness of the laws, and consult trade associations or data controllers'.[37] A notable difference is that the trade associations are to be consulted and must provide information to the Regulator on request. This Regulator is different from others compared in this book in that it does not specifically call for investigations and audits to be carried out. However, by way of responsibility to

[33] Law No. 001/2011 on the Protection of Personal Data, https://www.dataguidance.com/notes/gabon-data-protection-overview Note that the law is in French, and utilised https://caseguard.com/articles/promoting-data-privacy-and-protection-in-gabon/ and DLA Piper, https://www.dlapiperdataprotection.com/index.html?t=law&c=GA.

[34] Ibid.

[35] Data Protection Act 2012, Sections 1, 2, 3, 4, 5 https://nita.gov.gh/theevooc/2017/12/Data-Protection-Act-2012-Act-843.pdf.

[36] Data Protection Act, 2020, section 4, https://japarliament.gov.jm/attachments/article/339/The%20Data%20Protection%20Act,%202020.pdf.

[37] Data Protection Act, 2020, section 4, https://japarliament.gov.jm/attachments/article/339/The%20Data%20Protection%20Act,%202020.pdf.

monitor the implementation of the laws, could extend to audits and wider investigations. According to schedule 3, a Judge may intervene where the Commissioner may have contravened the data laws. This specific provision is not reflected anywhere else, and provides a further level of oversight. Other states could implement similar, although it would be prudent for such to be specified ion the data laws.

In the **Kingdom of Eswatini**, section 5 establishes a Commission for the management and governance of personal data across the state. It has full responsibility for enforcement, compliance, auditing and promoting to the private sector the importance of data management.[38] In **Kenya**, the Office of the Data Protection Commissioner was established under Part II of the Act. The Commissioner was appointed in November 2020. At the time of writing, the Commissioner was in the process of setting up operations. In accordance with section 8 of the Act,[39] the Commissioner's powers, duties, and responsibilities include enforcement of the provisions of the Act; the maintenance of the register of data controllers and data processors; oversight and assessment on data processing to ensure it is in accordance with the Act either on its own motion or on request by a data subject or on request of a private or public body; the promotion of self-regulation among data controllers and processors; investigation of complaints by any person on infringement of rights under the Act. In addition, the Data Commissioner shall prescribe thresholds required for mandatory registration of data controllers and data processors, and in making such determination, the Data Commissioner shall consider (a) the nature of industry; (b) the volumes of data processed; (c) whether sensitive personal data is being processed; and (d) any other criteria the Data Commissioner may specify. Further, a data controller or data processor is required to register under section 18 shall apply to the Data Commissioner. There are is specific information required that includes: (a) a description of the personal data to be processed by the data controller or data processor; (b) a description of the purpose for which the personal data is to be processed; (c) the category of data subjects, to which the personal data relates; (d) contact details of the data controller or data processor; (e) a general description of the risks, safeguards, security measures and mechanisms to ensure the protection of personal data; (f) any measures to indemnify the data subject from unlawful use of data by the data processor or data controller.[40] Arguably, the position of Commissioner is still relatively new, and it is likely that the guidance and assistance of other nation states will be sought for the implementation of data programs and investigations.

Similar to the other Commonwealth member countries, **Lesotho**, has regulated for the establishment of a Commission. Section 6 of the data laws achieves this. Section 7 outlines the functions of the Commission, which are similar to most other nation states: to promote education and awareness, enforce the law, conduct investigations and audits. Furthermore, the Commission also is required to report to the Parliament

---

[38] Data Protection Act 2022, sections 5, 6. https://www.esccom.org.sz/legislation/DATA%20PROTECTION%20ACT.pdf.

[39] Data Protection Act 2019, https://www.odpc.go.ke/dpa-act/, section 8.

[40] Ibid.

on its operations and annual outcomes.[41] In **Malawi**, 'the Malawi Communications Regulatory Authority as the Authority to regulate and monitor personal data protection and digital privacy in Malawi and oversee the implementation of and be responsible for the enforcement of the Bill. A Data Protection Office is established within the Authority responsible for the activities relating to data protection under the Bill. Part II also describes various administrative processes relating to the Authority's data protection duties, functions and powers'.[42]

Malaysia has appointed a Personal Data Protection Commissioner (the Commissioner).[43] The Commissioner is responsible for implementing and enforcing the data protection laws, and overseeing the development of operational policies and procedures and to promote associations or bodies representing data users to prepare codes of practice.[44] The Commissioner is appointed for three years, and t a Deputy Commissioner and Assistant Commissioners may be appointed where necessary.[45] Importantly, according to section 59, the Commissioner reports directly to the relevant Minister. One of the first cases to emerge in relation to competing interests regarding personal data was decided by the High Court of Malaya at Kuala Lumpur in 2022. In *Genting*[46] the Court confirmed that the Director General of the Inland Revenue office cannot rely on the Income Tax Act 1967 to override the provisions of the protections under the Personal Data Protection Act 2010. In November 2018, the Inland Revenue Office (the Revenue) requested information pertaining to the name, Malaysian Identity Card number, passport number, company registration number, address and postcode of members of the Applicant's associations, society or club for the years 2016 and 2017 as well as the amount of any annual membership fee.[47] Essentially, the Revenue wanted to access the data base of the Applicant so as to retrieve the personal data of customers for investigations into tax evasion. The Court noted that the Revenue was essentially asking for the Personal Data of the Applicant's customer. The Revenue argued that such information would assist the Revenue to enlarge its tax base and increase tax collection.[48] In coming to this position, the Court noted that the Revenue relied on section 81 of the Income Tax Act 1967 and section 39 of the Personal Data Protection Act 2010.[49] The Court also noted:

---

[41] Data Protection Act 2013, section 6, 7, http://www.nic.ls/lsnic/community/policies/Data_Protection_Act_2011_Lesotho.pdf.

[42] Data Protection Bill 2021, Part II, https://digmap.pppc.mw/wp-content/uploads/2022/03/Malawi-Data-Protection-Bill-final-draft-210630-.pdf.

[43] Personal Data Protection Act 2010, section 47, https://www.kkmm.gov.my/pdf/Personal%20Data%20Protection%20Act%202010.pdf.

[44] Personal Data Protection Act 2010, section 47 & 48, https://www.kkmm.gov.my/pdf/Personal%20Data%20Protection%20Act%202010.pdf.

[45] Personal Data Protection Act 2010, section 50, https://www.kkmm.gov.my/pdf/Personal%20Data%20Protection%20Act%202010.pdf.

[46] *Genting* Malaysia Bhd v Pesuruhjaya *Perlindungan Data Peribadi & Ors*, 2022 CLJ 399.

[47] Ibid., para 9.

[48] Ibid.

[49] Ibid.

> Revenue informed that in the event the personal data is not provided, they would be able to conduct the tax audits and investigations on the companies within Genting Group, and obtain the necessary personal data and personal data forms, part of the transactional data their tax audits and investigations. In response the Application it could not disclose the personal data to the Revenue due to contravening the data laws.[50]

The outcome of this case depended on the court's interpretation and application of the provisions of the tax laws versus the data laws. The Court ruled that section 81 of the Income Tax Act 1967 does not give to the Revenue the power to force individuals and entities to provide personal data, and that privacy over the Internet is protected under the national constitution.[51] It demonstrates that while there will be legislation providing the power to undertake certain activities that will require access to personal data, such power should not be used to exceed the requirements and protections under national data laws. Moreover, it is argued that this is potentially an area of further research and vigilance to determine whether other states are having to grapple with the same, or similar, competing legislative issues/requirements. Thus far, this is the first case of its kind found in the Commonwealth.

Section 4 of the data laws of **Mauritius** establishes a Data Protection Office, although the terminology is different from that of other states. It establishes a Commissioner who is responsible for the implementation of the data laws. Section 5 describes the Commissioner's functions to ensure compliance, approve Codes of Practice or Guidelines, maintain a register of controllers and processors; exercise control over all data processing operations, promote self-regulation, undertake investigations and address community complaints.[52]

A Privacy Commissioner has long been established in **New Zealand**.[53] The Commissioner, according to section 17, is responsible for monitoring compliance with the Act, advising the relevant Minister, undertaking research, raising awareness and educating the community, amongst other functions. Generally, these functions are similar to those of other Commissioners or Commissions, and must be implemented under the law. A notable difference is that there is no need for a register. Similar to Australia, New Zealand has established a total of 13 binding Privacy Principles[54] that govern how personal information should be collected, handled and used. Likewise, **Nigeria** does require a Regulator in the form of a Data Protection Commission (the Commission). The Commission itself has broad powers and functions to promote

---

[50] Ibid. para 14.

[51] Ibid., para 154.

[52] Data Protection Act 2017, section 5, 6, https://dataprotection.govmu.org/Documents/DPA_2017_updated.pdf?csf=1&e=0rlrff.

[53] Privacy Act 2020, sections 13, 17 https://www.privacy.org.nz/privacy-act-2020/privacy-principles/.

[54] Privacy Act 2020, section 22 https://www.privacy.org.nz/privacy-act-2020/privacy-principles/, also see Privacy Principles, https://www.privacy.org.nz/assets/New-order/Your-responsibilities/Privacy-resources-for-organisations/2020-A-quick-tour-of-the-privacy-principles-Oct-2020.pdf.

public and general awareness of data law, deploy technology, receive complaints, and conduct investigations, particularly in relation to to cross-border data transfers.[55]

In **Rwanda,** the Regulator is established by different laws. Law No. 26/2017 of 31 May 2017 Establishing the National Cyber Security Authority and Determining its Mission, Organisation and Functioning (the Authority)[56] outlines the formal and functional arrangements of the Regulator. While predominantly applying to cyber security, Articles 9 and 10[57] outline the functional arrangements and powers of the Authority to establish strategies and guidelines, and undertake intelligence activities (investigations and audits) to determine the threat of cyber intrusions that may compromise data.

The Personal Data Protection Commission (the Commission),[58] according to section 5, ensures that there is a Regulator in **Singapore**. Under section 6, the Commission has specific functions: to promote awareness of data; consultancy, advisory, technical, managerial or other specialist service; advise and represent government; conduct research and studies; manage technical cooperation; administer and enforce the data laws, and undertake other functions. The Regulator has been very active in responding to organisational breaches of the national data laws. A recent example involving the Thompson Health[59] medical clinic demonstrated a clear link between cybersecurity and data. Most noteworthy is that the issue related to the direct access to the personal health data of Singapore citizens. The background of the case is:

> On 26 October 2020, the Personal Data Protection Commission (the "Commission") was notified that the Thomson Medical Pty. Ltd. (the "Organisation") Health Declaration Portal was not secure, enabling public access to the personal data of visitors (the "Incident") stored in a CSV (comma separated values) file. Visitor data collected on the Organisation's Health Declaration Portal had been stored concurrently in a publicly-accessible CSV file as well as a secured database from 16 April 2020, when the health declaration portal was first used by the Organisation to 8 September 2020, when the storage of the visitor data was changed to only the secured database instead of the CSV file. The CSV file was hosted on the Organisation's web server.[60]

---

[55] Data Protection Regulation 2022, section 7 https://ndpb.gov.ng/Files/Nigeria_Data_Protection_Bill.pdf.

[56] Law No. 26/2017 of 31 May 2017 Establishing the National Cyber Security Authority and Determining its Mission, Organisation and Functioning, https://www.risa.rw/index.php?eID=dumpFile&t=f&f=200&token=879db39536c789b880aac104dd7fe369ed2cd8ec.

[57] Law n°058/2021 of 13/10/2021 relating to the protection of personal data and privacy (the Data Protection Law), Article 9 and 10, https://www.minijust.gov.rw/fileadmin/user_upload/Minijust/Publications/Official_Gazette/_2021_Official_Gazettes/October/OG_Special_of_15.10.2021_Amakuru_bwite.pdf.

[58] Personal Data Protection Act 2012, section 5, https://sso.agc.gov.sg/Act/PDPA2012?ProvIds=P12-#P12-.

[59] Case No. DP-2010-B7246 Thomson Medical Pte. Ltd. [2022] SGPDPCS 15.

[60] Ibid., paras 1 and 2.

Problematic was that Thompson Health had breached section 50 of the Personal Data Protection Act 2012. In so doing, Thompson Health:

> admitted that, contrary to the instructions given to the employee to switch the data storage from the CSV file to secured database exclusively, and the organisation's protocols, its in-house developer had omitted to remove a software code, causing the visitor data to be stored in the CSV file and the same in-house developer had omitted to change the default web server configuration, thereby allowing public access to the hosted CSV file. The switch to storage in a secured database would have ensured access controls by requiring user login ID and secure password protection, as well as encryption of data transfers using SSL certificates. The access controls would ensure that only authorized users would be able to access the data.[61]

Regarding the extent of the personal data that was accessible, the Regulator concluded:

> the affected CSV file contained the personal data of 44,679 of the Organisation's visitors, including the date and time of visit, temperature, type of visitor (purpose of visit), name of visitor, name of newborn, contact number, NRIC/FIN/passport number, doctor/clinic name or room visiting, and answers to a health declaration questionnaire (which included a declaration by the visitor that he/she did not have any symptoms or recent exposure to the Covid-19 virus).[62]

Significantly, the Regulator confirmed that 'the Organisation failed to conduct reasonable pre-launch testing before the Health Declaration Portal went live. While acceptance testing and some technical tests were conducted, there had been no security testing to verify that there were access controls to the visitor data collected'.[63] Although the Regulator did not issue a fine, Thompson Medical was required to undertake a number of directive actions, and ensure that the intended measures include the development and implementation of a data retention policy to meet the Retention Limitation Obligation under section 25 of the data laws.[64] The regulatory action demonstrates that personal data can be highly vulnerable, and requires protection. Arguably, health data is considered the most personal data that an individual has. It can reveal information about a person that, in the wrong hands, could be used for extortion purposes.

At the time of writing, **South Africa** was in the process of establishing a dedicated Regulator. Section 39 provides for an Information Regulator 'who have been afforded similar investigative and governance powers to that of other countries, specifically the UK'.[65] Although **Sri Lanka** introduced data laws as recently as 2022, it was quick to ensure there is a Data Protection Authority. Section 28 requires that such an Authority be established, and be responsible for the governance of data in the

61 Ibid., para 3.

62 Ibid., para 4.

63 Ibid., para 7.

64 Ibid., para 16 ii.

65 Protection of Personal Information 2013, section 39, https://www.gov.za/documents/protection-personal-information-act.

state.[66] The responsibility also extends to safe guarding privacy, protection of data, and compliance of the data laws themselves. Section 32 ensures that the Authority oversees what data controllers and processors do when collecting, using and storing data. It also allows the Authority to undertake investigations, make inquiries, and receive complaints.

In the Americas, section 6 of the data laws of **Saint Lucia** establish a Data Protection Commissioner, whose function it is to ensure compliance with the Act, undertake investigations, and establish a register of data controllers.[67] The Commissioner's responsibilities extend to the control of processors, instructing controllers, investigating reports and claims, and issuing directions or statements to ensure the promotion of the laws, and educating citizens about them. In its advisory capacity, the Commissioner can advise the relevant Minister,[68] amongst other things. The common thread here is that all Commissioners have functions related to overseeing the implementation of data laws by the public and private sectors in most nation states. This may differ from state to state, whereby the public sector could be exempted or have different data obligations to that of the private sector. Similarly, **Saint Kitts and Nevis** requires the appointment of an Information Commissioner.[69] Accordingly, section 24 outlines the formal and functional arrangements which are generally the same as those of other states: to monitor compliance, provide advice to public and private entities, and report on community complaints. The Commissioner is to also investigate[70] complaints to ensure an entity is not in breach of the data laws. In maintaining the consistent approach in this region of the world, in **Saint Vincent and The Grenadines,** data laws establish a Privacy Commissioner who is responsible for investigating breaches of the data laws. The Commissioner is also responsible for promoting privacy over the Internet, making public statements, undertake research, law reform, and report to the relevant Minister on its operations.[71]

---

[66] Personal Data Protection Act No. 9 of 2022, section 31 https://www.parliament.lk/uploads/acts/gbills/english/6242.pdf.

[67] Privacy and Data Protection Act 2009, section 15, 16, https://www.govt.lc/media.govt.lc/www/resources/legislation/PrivacyAndDataProtectionBill.pdf.

[68] Privacy and Data Protection Act 2009, section 12, 41 to 50, https://www.govt.lc/media.govt.lc/www/resources/legislation/PrivacyAndDataProtectionBill.pdf.

[69] Data Protection Act, 5 of 2018, section 23 https://www.theinformationcollective.com/dpl/st-kitts-data-protection-act.

[70] Data Protection Act, 5 of 2018, sections 25 to 30 https://www.theinformationcollective.com/dpl/st-kitts-data-protection-act.

[71] Privacy Act 2003, section 16 to 19 https://www.theinformationcollective.com/dpl/st-vincent-and-the-grenadines-the-privacy-act.

Tanzania's 2022 data laws establish the Personal Data Protection Commission, which is responsible for conducting investigations and research, monitoring technology developments, and overseeing the implementation of the new laws.[72] At this preliminary stage, the proposed Commission, when operational, will undertake activities similar to those of the other African Commissions. **Togo** has established the Personal Data Protection Authority,[73] however, there is little information available as to its roles, responsibilities and functions. Section 7 of the data laws establishes the Office of the Information Commission in **Trinidad-Tobago**. Further, section 8 appoints a Commissioner, and section 9 specifies the functions which are: conducting audits, investigations, ensuring compliance, and providing advice on the collection, use and storage of data.[74]

Uganda has established the National Information Technology Authority[75] (the Authority) which is responsible for data governance. Accordingly, section 3 obliges the Authority to ensure that the controller, processors and collectors implement the principles established for data collection, use and processing. Further, section 28 requires that the Authority investigate every complaint received by a controller, processor or collector. In addition, section 29 requires the Authority to have a register listing 'every person, institution or public body collecting or processing personal data'.[76] There are limited expressed powers in the primary laws. A Data Protection Commissioner is established under section 4 of the **Zambian** data laws. The Commissioner's primary functions is to register controllers, data processors, licence(d) data auditors, disseminate information and promote the laws. It is also responsible for advising Government and representing the state at international forums.[77] A major difference between Zambia and the other states is the role of the Civil Service Commissioner in appointing the Data Commissioner. The Civil Service Commission is responsible for appointing an inspector who is responsible for carrying out investigations and audits[78] to ensure compliance with the laws, and ensure the controllers and processors are acting lawfully

[72] Fatma Songoro, Brief Highlight and Analysis of the Tanzania Data Protection Bill, 2002, October 2022, https://victoryattorneys.co.tz/insights-brief-highlight-and-analysis-of-the-tanzania-data-protection-bill-2022/.

[73] Republic of Togo and the United Nations Economic Commission for Africa sign a Memorandum of Understanding to Establish the African Cybersecurity Center, 2022, https://www.uneca.org/stories/republic-of-togo-and-the-united-nations-economic-commission-for-africa-sign-a-memorandum-of.

[74] Data Protection Act 2011, section 7, 8, 9, https://rgd.legalaffairs.gov.tt/laws2/Alphabetical_List/lawspdfs/22.04.pdf.

[75] Data Protection and Privacy Act 2019, section 2 https://media.ulii.org/files/legislation/akn-ug-act-2019-9-eng-2019-05-03.pdf Also see National Information Technology Authority, https://www.nita.go.ug.

[76] Data Protection and Privacy Act 2019, section 29 https://media.ulii.org/files/legislation/akn-ug-act-2019-9-eng-2019-05-03.pdf.

[77] Data Protection Act 2021, sections 4, 5, https://www.parliament.gov.zm/sites/default/files/documents/acts/Act%20No.%203%20The%20Data%20Protection%20Act%202021_0.pdf.

[78] Data Protection Act 2021, sections 7, 8 https://www.parliament.gov.zm/sites/default/files/documents/acts/Act%20No.%203%20The%20Data%20Protection%20Act%202021_0.pdf.

A particular challenge in this short comparison of the data laws was deciding the amount of detail required to give a comprehensive view of the powers of each Regulator and his/her specific responsibilities. The general theme emerging is that each Regulator that has been established has the power to audit and investigate breaches of data laws. They also have responsibility to educate the public and raise their awareness of data law. This is particularly important for those states that have only recently (i.e., in the past five years) implemented these laws. Further research could be undertaken to better understand the investigative powers and competencies of the Regulator, to ensure a consistent response to breaches of the law. Additionally, research could also be needed to ensure that penalties are consistent. These issues were not addressed above. The Regulators established in the nation states discussed above have a number of tools at their disposal to ensuring compliance with data laws, such as fines, reprimands, warnings, and show cause, amongst others.

4.2 Conclusion

The regulation for and of an independent body that oversees the governance and administration of data laws, has in my view, proven to be one of the most important features of the legal framework. While it is not clear whether all states have ensured that a Regulator is totally independent from political influence. It is argued that for this reason, having a Regulator is far better than not having one.

This chapter has examined the Commonwealth members' respective data laws to determine whether these laws provided for the establishment of a Regulator. Consistent with the preceding chapters, it has demonstrated that while there is by and large a consistent response to and the need for a Regulator to be established by the national laws of the respective states the 'Regulator' is often referred to in different terms such as: Commissioner, Commission, Information Commissioner Office, Privacy Commissioner or Authority, amongst others.

Generally, the large majority of Regulators established are independent of the government and free of political interference. However, in practice, this might not be the case in some of the developing countries. What has become evident is that those member countries such as the UK, Canada and Australia that have had a Regulator and their respective data laws in place for more than a decade are well advanced in terms of establishing the Regulator's role and responsibility. As mentioned above, today these countries influence the development of policy and standards to enhance and strengthen the concept of privacy by design.

The prevailing view is that Regulators have a significant responsibility in the current and future development of the digital economy. They will be required to undertake reviews of the laws to ensure the data laws remain current in light of the constant technology changes. They are required to strike a balance between ensuring data protection while enabling it to benefit the state economically, particularly with the increase of transnational data flows. The countries who have only recently established their data laws are continuing to grapple with the roles and responsibilities of the Regulator. While outside the scope of this chapter, it can be argued that many developing nations are going to struggle to manage this transition.

In response to the above, and to strengthen the role and function of the respective Regulators, the Commonwealth could undertake to establish guidelines indicating the roles and responsibilities of Regulators. It should investigate the viability of an exchange program for the respective staff of these Regulators to share knowledge, resources and information. This would strengthen collaboration and enable a greater level of consistency in approach to educating the general public and business sectors, and undertaking investigations of breaches of the data laws.

Chapter 5
Controller, Consent, Processing

5.1 Introduction

The concepts of controller, consent, and processing provisions within data laws have, along with the other concepts and principles compared in this book, also emerged as important to the economic development of the digital economy. Put another way, as the world deals with the rapid development of technology, systems and infrastructure are able to process ever-increasing quantities of personal data. In some of the jurisdictions compared, a multi-layered approach to the requirement for the appointment of a controller and processor is a mandatory obligation. On the other hand, other jurisdictions have adopted a minimalist approach, requiring only a controller and no other officers, or no controller. Governments, organizations, individuals, and other entities around the world now realise the benefits—economic, social and environmental—associated with the collection of personal data. However, in order for data subjects to have a level of control over their data, the law has generally responded by ensuring a controller is responsible for collecting and using the data, and ensuring that data subject have consented to their data being used.

Neither the MBP nor the MBPPI specify the requirements for the appointment and function of a controller. However, the national laws of many Commonwealth countries provide for the appointment and responsibilities of a controller or processor.[1] The MBPPI, according to section 8, establishes the requirement of knowledge and consent. Thus, personal data should not be collected or used without the consent of the data subject.[2] The MBP requires a level of consent (express or implied) under section 11, only in relation to the disclosure of data. On the other hand, according

---

[1] The Commonwealth, Model Privacy Bill, Office of Civil and Criminal Justice Reform, 2017, https://www.asianlaws.org/gcld/cyberlawdb/COM/P15370_9_ROL_Model_Privacy_Bill_0.pdf.

[2] The Commonwealth, Model Bill on the Protection of Personal Information https://www.asianlaws.org/gcld/cyberlawdb/COM/P15370_6_ROL_Model_Bill_Protection_Personal_Information_2.pdf.

R. Walters, *Cybersecurity and Data Laws of the Commonwealth*,
https://doi.org/10.1007/978-981-99-3935-0_5

to Part II, the MBPPI creates a number of requirements pertaining to the collection, consent, use limits, disclosure limits, and use of personal data.[3]

The concept of consent has emerged as another important area of data law because it provides data subjects with control over the collection and use of their data. However, as this chapter demonstrates, jurisdictions have taken different approaches to the administration of consent. Due to the extent of the laws compared in this chapter, the analysis is limited to the data laws. It does not extensively discuss scholars' opinions or judicial decisions, and has been limited to the concept of consent. While this chapter could be separated into three to examine and compare the concepts of (i) controller, (ii) consent and (iii) processing individually, in this first book, it was decided to treat these as a group since they are interconnected. Simply put, a controller is needed to obtain from data subjects their consent to process their personal data. The chapter examines in detail the provisions of the respective data laws.

The concepts of controller, consent and processing are all important to the overall governance of data. Generally, they are separated at law into distinct concepts with specific legal requirements. In this section, they have been grouped together to demonstrate how they interact with each other, albeit differently across member countries. Collectively, they contribute to enabling data flows across international borders, and offer a level of protection to data subjects.[4] Thus, these concepts significantly contribute to the economic development of the digital economy, while balancing this activity with protecting user privacy over the Internet.

Apart from the above, the rationale behind consent has a two-fold outcome. First, it gives the data subject greater control over his/her personal data. Second, it restricts what a controller or processor can do with that data. At law, the concept itself comes in different forms. The formal and functional arrangements of consent are either express or implied. This chapter will examine the national laws of the Commonwealth to determine how the concept of consent has been addressed. Here, the definition of personal data includes health data. Arguably, this is a component of data that comes either with or without a level of consent for it to be used.

The, overarching safeguards that secure the rights and interests of individuals in protecting personal data and its processing is grounded in the concept of consent. Scholars have argued that such 'a system of data protection arranges for specific safeguards when it is necessary and proportional to derogate from consent requirements or certain individual rights'.[5] Mostert and others make the point that:

---

[3] Ibid.

[4] Robert Walters, Leon Trakman, Bruno Zeller, *Data Protection Law: A comparative Analysis of Asia–Pacific European Approaches,* Springer (2019), p. 128. Also see Simon Chesterman, Data Protection Law in Singapore – Privacy and Sovereignty in an Interconnected World, SAL Academy Publishing, 2nd Edit (2018), chapter 2–3.

[5] Menno Mostert, Annelien L. Bredenoord, Bart van der Slooth, Johannes J.M. van Delden, From Privacy to Data Protection in the EU: Implications for Big Data Health Research, European Journal of Health Law, (2018) p. 54.

> These specific safeguards are also essential to allow for the re-use of personal data, without taking heed of the principle of purpose limitation. The overarching safeguards should, amongst other things, include requirements of accountability subject to independent oversight, transparency towards data subjects and the public, ensure that data subjects can invoke their rights and data security. The issue of which specific safeguards should be provided for by law. After all, these specific safeguards should compensate for the loss of individual control as a result of the exceptions from individual rights and consent requirements.[6]

The authors make an important point. They have carefully considered the concept of consent and its role in meeting the broader objective principles of accountability, purpose and transparency under the OECD Principles (see Chap. 1). They confirm that consent is a control mechanism offered to data subjects, and is one of the overall safeguards provided by the law. It is argued that such safeguards ensure that consent can be applied to data flows within the digital economy. This enables data subjects to understand where and how their data is being used. However, further examination of this issue is outside the scope of this book.

Regarding the above, in **Australia**, consent comes in different forms and can be either expressly stated or inferred (implied),[7] written, verbal or silent. The definition of consent constitutes an individual being adequately informed of the issues and obligations before giving consent (express or implied). Consent must be current and specific, or voluntary; more importantly, the person must have the capacity to understand and communicate that consent.[8] In particular, 'express consent is given explicitly, either orally or in writing. This could be a handwritten signature, oral statement, or use of an electronic or voice signature. Generally, it cannot be assumed a person has provided consent on the basis they did not object in the first place to allow their data to be processed or transferred to a third party'.[9] Moreover, there are specific requirements for children. That is, the Australian Privacy Principle (APP) entity will need to determine on a case-by-case basis whether an individual under the age of 18 has the capacity to give consent.[10] An individual under the age of 18 can give consent when they have sufficient understanding and maturity to understand what is being proposed. In some circumstances, it may be appropriate for a parent or guardian to consent on behalf of a young person when a child does not meet the age requirements or lacks the maturity or understanding to do so themselves. If it is not practicable or reasonable for an APP entity to assess the capacity of individuals under the age of 18, the entity may presume that an individual aged 15[11] or over has capacity to consent unless there is something to suggest otherwise. There is no regulated requirement for a controller, processor or data officer in Australia. For the collection of data, an organization cannot undertake this task unless that information

---

[6] Ibid.

[7] *Giller v Procopets* (2008) 24 VR 1, para 394–395.

[8] Privacy Act 1988, section 6. C2014C00076. Also note Australian Privacy Principles 5 and 7.

[9] Robert Walters, Leon Trakman, Bruno Zeller, *Data Protection Law: A comparative Analysis of Asia–Pacific European Approaches*, Springer (2019), p. 128.

[10] Australian Privacy Principles Guidelines, Chapter B: Key concepts, B56, 57, 58, https://www.oaic.gov.au/privacy/australian-privacy-principles-guidelines/chapter-b-key-concepts.

[11] Ibid.

directly relates to one or more of the organization's functions.[12] Personal information cannot be collected unless the person provides consent and the information is required under Australian law, by a court or tribunal order. Collection of personal data can be undertaken by a government agency or a private entity. The processing of personal data can result in information about individuals and entities being modified. In the Western Australian case of *Larkin*,[13] an individual was found guilty of conspiring to cause an unauthorised modification (processing) of data held on a computer, by not engaging a controller or processor, and not having the consent of a data subject to access the data. This offence, involving the modification of data, demonstrates the link between data and cybersecurity. The Court noted that:

> The sole count in an indictment alleged that, from on or about 12 October 2010 to on or about 4 November 2010, the appellants conspired to cause an unauthorised modification of data held in a computer, knowing that the modification would be unauthorised, and being reckless as to whether the modification would impair access to that or any other data held in any computer and/or the reliability, security or operation of any such data, and the modification of the data would impair access to, or the reliability, security or operation of other data by means of a carriage service, contrary to s 11.5(i) and s 477.2(i) of the Criminal Code Act (Cth).[14]

Importantly, the offence covered by the Australian Criminal Code Act has been addressed later in this book (see Pat III). The question in this case is: was the accessed data considered as personal data under the privacy laws of Australia? The Court did not refer to or discuss the issues of the definition of personal data. The case itself was an appeal on sentencing. Importantly, the Court highlighted the importance of section 477.2(i) of the Criminal Code in that it refers to data 13 times and provides: A person is guilty of an offence if:

(a) the person causes any unauthorised modification of data held in a computer; and
(b) the person knows the modification is unauthorised; and
(c) the person is reckless as to whether the modification impairs or will impair:
  (i) access to that or any other data held in any computer; or
  (ii) the reliability, security or operation, of any such data; and
(d) one or more of the following applies:
  (i) the data that is modified is held in a Commonwealth computer;
  (ii) the data that is modified is held on behalf of the Commonwealth in a computer;
  (iii) the modification of the data is caused by means of a carriage service;
  (iv) the modification of the data is caused by means of a Commonwealth computer;
  (v) the modification of the data impairs access to, or the reliability, security or operation of, other data held in a Commonwealth computer;
  (vi) the modification of the data impairs access to, or the reliability, security or operation of, other data held on behalf of the Commonwealth in a computer;
  (vii) the modification of the data impairs access to, or the reliability, security or operation of, other data by means of a carriage service.

Penalty: 10 years imprisonment. Need a FT.

---

[12] Privacy Act 1988, section 16A, 16B, 20C, 80p, C2014C00076. Australian Privacy Principles 3.

[13] *Larkin R* [2012] WASCA 238.

[14] Ibid., para 3, https://www.legislation.gov.au/Details/C2019C00043.

The reference to data in the above provision could be any data. The important point here is that section 477 of the Criminal Code Act pertains directly to computer crime offences. Thus, indirectly, the data in section 477 can constitute personal data that has been defined under the Privacy Act 1988. In taking this position, it is argued that the definition of data (information) is wide enough to comprise anything that is held on a computer that can be modified by a person on another computer. In the case, the government department involved was the Department of Health, which holds vast quantities of personal data, and possibly health data. Health data is considered the most personal data an individual has, and in many Commonwealth states it has been afforded a greater level of protection.

Rather than regulate for the need of a controller, processor, or officer, according to section 2, **Antigua and Barbuda** defines a data user as 'a person who either alone or jointly or in common with other persons processes any personal data or has control over or authorizes the processing of any personal data, but does not include a data processor'.[15] Throughout the legislation, there is reference to the data user only except under section 8 where, if a data processor has been engaged to replace a data user, they can be responsible for protecting the personal data in the same way as a data user. Consent is required for the processing and disclosure of data. However, it is not specified whether such consent is to be explicit or implied. This would need to be reconciled in practice.

Section 2 of the **Bahama's** data laws define a data controller as 'a person who, either alone or with others, determines the purposes for which and the manner in which any personal data are, or are to be, processed'.[16] Further, it defines a data processor as 'a person who processes personal data on behalf of a data controller but does not include an employee of a data controller who processes such data in the course of his employment'.[17] Additionally, section 12 provides for controller duties to ensure any personal data is collected accurately and is up to date. Additionally, to ensure there is a high level of protection for the data collected, the controller can specify controls and protections by either contract or other means. Those other means could be a code or memorandum of understanding. However, this may need further clarification to ensure there that a legal obligation is conferred. The laws provide for a data processor who is also responsible for complying[18] with the data laws. By and large, the obligations of a data processor extend to the unauthorised disclosure[19] of data where there has been no approval provided by the data controller. The data laws do not go beyond a controller or processor. It is a two-tiered responsibility. Sections 6, 13, 17(8) provide for a level of consent to the governance of personal data when it

[15] Data Protection Act 2013, section 2, http://laws.gov.ag/wp-content/uploads/2019/02/a2013-10.pdf.

[16] Data Protection Act 2008, section 2, http://laws.bahamas.gov.bs/cms/images/LEGISLATION/PRINCIPAL/2003/2003-0003/DataProtectionPrivacyofPersonalInformationAct_1.pdf.

[17] Ibid.

[18] Data Protection Act 2008, section 6(3), http://laws.bahamas.gov.bs/cms/images/LEGISLATION/PRINCIPAL/2003/2003-0003/DataProtectionPrivacyofPersonalInformationAct_1.pdf.

[19] Data Protection Act 2008, section 22, http://laws.bahamas.gov.bs/cms/images/LEGISLATION/PRINCIPAL/2003/2003-0003/DataProtectionPrivacyofPersonalInformationAct_1.pdf.

is transferred out of the country. However, the laws do not define consent or specify how it would operate. Nor do the laws contain any reference to express or implied consent. This should be addressed.

The data controller and the data processor are to be registered.[20] Section 53 requires a data controller to implement the 'appropriate technical and organisational measures to ensure that processing is performed in accordance with this Act taking into consideration the nature, scope, context and purposes of processing as well as the risks of varying likelihood and severity to the rights and freedoms of individuals'.[21] This designated responsibility is very broad and, unlike other Commonwealth member countries, **Barbados** does not provide details about the functions of the controller. The formal and functional responsibilities of a data processor are delegated by the controller. The processor and controller are required to protect as far a possible the rights of data subjects,[22] either through a contract or some other formal arrangement. A data processor may engage another processor provided that this is in accordance with the same formal arrangements under the controller. The processing of data has to include the 'name and contact details of the data controller and purposes of the processing; a description of the categories of data subjects; the categories of recipients; transfers of personal data to another country or an international organisation; and time limits for erasure of the different categories of data'.[23] Sections 7 and 8[24] specify that for adult data subjects, consent is to be in written form. Moreover, consent must be given freely, and it can be withdrawn. It is not clearly articulated whether consent is both express and/or implied. Furthermore, section 8 provides that in the case of children, actual consent is to be given by a parent or guardian.

Section 14 of the **Batswana** data law gives a controller the responsibility for ensuring that personal data is processed fairly and accurately, and that data subjects consent to having their data processed. The controller can only collect and use the data for the purpose for which it is going to be processed. Also, the controller is to ensure that the data is secure from any illegal access, destruction or modification. The data should not be stored for longer than necessary, and can be deleted or corrected to ensure accuracy. Consent is to be in writing, and the processing is subject to contractual arrangements.[25] Upon consent being provided, the processing of data is to be undertaken in a manner that protects the interests of the data subject, along

---

[20] Data Protection Act 2019, section 50, 55, https://gisbarbados.gov.bb/download/data-protection-act-2019/.

[21] Data Protection Act 2019, section 51, https://gisbarbados.gov.bb/download/data-protection-act-2019/.

[22] Data Protection Act 2019, section 50, 58, https://gisbarbados.gov.bb/download/data-protection-act-2019/.

[23] Data Protection Act 2019, section 60, https://gisbarbados.gov.bb/download/data-protection-act-2019/.

[24] Data Protection Act 2019, section 7, 8, https://gisbarbados.gov.bb/download/data-protection-act-2019/.

[25] Data Protection Act, No. 32 of 2018, section 15.

with the legitimate interests of the controller or third party.[26] Section 17 relates to cybersecurity since the controller is obliged to ensure that the data has an adequate level of safeguards to ensure its security. However, it does not specify how that data is to be secured or the length of time necessary. Nonetheless, section 20 provides that sensitive data is to be processed in accordance with a greater level of controls. Firstly, consent is required, and the data is that required for national security or any employment obligation the controller has (contractual or otherwise).[27] However, under section 21, a union or some other non-commercial entity can process sensitive personal data related only to political, philosophical, religious or trade union objects. This allows specific sensitive data to be used. As sensitive data includes most, if not all, of the health data, a health professional has specific powers to process that data for health care, hospital, medical diagnosis or preventive medicine, or scientific or legal purposes and specific areas of government.[28] Also, the controller can be assisted by another controller, processor or data protection representative[29] when undertaking specific tasks. It is outside the scope of the book to identify these tasks.

Similar to Botswana, **Bangladesh's** proposed data laws require that processing be undertaken with the consent of the data subject. Consent must be 'free, specific, clear, and capable of being withdrawn'.[30] Responsibility for obtaining consent rests with the data controller. However, where the data controller withdraws consent for processing data under any contractual arrangements, any legal consequences arising from the withdrawal of consent will expire. Nevertheless, processing of data can be undertaken without consent if the controller determines it is necessary for the fulfilment of a contract, compliance with any legal obligations, or to protect the vital interests of the data subject.[31] The principle of vital interest has been given a specific definition: 'life, death or security of a data subject that, pertains to the treatment, public health, medical or research purposes or to respond any medical emergency involving a threat to the life or to the health of a data subject or any other individual; for compliance with any order of the court of competent jurisdiction; for exercise of any functions conferred under any law; for the exercise of any function of the Government authorised by law for the provision of any service or benefit, or the

[26] Ibid., section 16.

[27] Ibid., sections 20 & 21. Data Protection Act, No. 32 of 2018, https://www.bocra.org.bw/sites/default/files/documents/DataProtectionAct.pdf.

[28] Ibid., sections 23, 24, 26, 27. Data Protection Act, No. 32 of 2018, https://www.bocra.org.bw/sites/default/files/documents/DataProtectionAct.pdf.

[29] Ibid., sections 36. Data Protection Act, No. 32 of 2018, https://www.bocra.org.bw/sites/default/files/documents/DataProtectionAct.pdf.

[30] Proposed Data Protection Act, 2022, Sections 6 & 7. https://ictd.portal.gov.bd/sites/default/files/files/ictd.portal.gov.bd/page/6c9773a2_7556_4395_bbec_f132b9d819f0/Data%20Protection%20Bill%20en%20V13%20Unofficial%20Working%20Draft%2016.07.22.pdf.

[31] Proposed Data Protection Act, 2022, section 7. https://ictd.portal.gov.bd/sites/default/files/files/ictd.portal.gov.bd/page/6c9773a2_7556_4395_bbec_f132b9d819f0/Data%20Protection%20Bill%20en%20V13%20Unofficial%20Working%20Draft%2016.07.22.pdf.

issuance of any certification, license or permit'.[32] The protection of privacy over the Internet is not only the controller's responsibility; it extends to the data processor and data collector. Section 9 introduced the term 'data collector', which has not been referenced in any of the other laws being compared. In addition, section 11 goes a step further by including specific provisions for the processing of sensitive personal data. However, this can be undertaken only with the explicit consent of the data subject. Moreover, children's data is afforded a special level of protection. Section 12 specifies that children's data can be processed only after a parent or guardian has given consent. Apart from the above, under section 24, the controller is responsible for ensuring that data security is a priority. In accordance with section 25, data can be retained only for as long as is necessary for the entity to fulfill obligations such as contracts. However, no time period has been established specifying when the data should be fully deleted. Unlike Botswana, it is proposed that integrity of data, keeping of records and reporting of a data breach and audits are additional responsibilities of the controller.[33] These tools are highly significant in the overall governance of data. A data protection officer can be appointed according to section 31. Rather than having a Commission, it is proposed that a Data Protection Office be established,[34] that will have the role of undertaking investigations into the illegal collection, use and storage of data.

In **Belize**, there are two levels of consent: one for the general population, and the other is for children. Section 8 provides for a level of consent to be obtained by a controller for the processing of personal data. It is silent on whether that consent is expressed or implied. However, section 8(2) does extend to a data subject proving consent in the form of a written declaration. Data subjects can withdraw their consent at any time, and this can be undertaken in accordance with any contractual obligations. Section 9[35] specifies that a child's consent is valid only when a parent or guardian has provided for such. A data controller can be appointed and is responsible for specifying the purpose of processing personal data.[36] A processor can also process data provided that this is undertaken according to the requirements set out by the

[32] Proposed Data Protection Act, 2022, section 7. https://ictd.portal.gov.bd/sites/default/files/files/ictd.portal.gov.bd/page/6c9773a2_7556_4395_bbec_f132b9d819f0/Data%20Protection%20Bill%20en%20V13%20Unofficial%20Working%20Draft%2016.07.22.pdf.

[33] Proposed Data Protection Act, 2022, sections 26, 27, 28, 29. https://ictd.portal.gov.bd/sites/default/files/files/ictd.portal.gov.bd/page/6c9773a2_7556_4395_bbec_f132b9d819f0/Data%20Protection%20Bill%20en%20V13%20Unofficial%20Working%20Draft%2016.07.22.pdf.

[34] Proposed Data Protection Act, 2022, sections 35. https://ictd.portal.gov.bd/sites/default/files/files/ictd.portal.gov.bd/page/6c9773a2_7556_4395_bbec_f132b9d819f0/Data%20Protection%20Bill%20en%20V13%20Unofficial%20Working%20Draft%2016.07.22.pdf.

[35] Data Protection Act, 45 of 2021, section 8, 9 https://www.nationalassembly.gov.bz/wp-content/uploads/2021/07/Data-Protection-Bill-2021-updated.pdf.

[36] Data Protection Act, 45 of 2021, section 5 https://www.nationalassembly.gov.bz/wp-content/uploads/2021/07/Data-Protection-Bill-2021-updated.pdf.

controller. Put another way, on behalf of a controller, the processor will be required to process[37] data lawfully under contractual arrangements.

In **Canada**, consent under the PIPEDA is similar to other data protection laws around the world. Section 6.1 states that 'consent of an individual is only valid if it is reasonable to expect that an individual to whom the organization's activities are directed would understand the nature, purpose and consequences of the collection, use or disclosure of the personal information to which they are consenting'.[38] The knowledge and consent of the individual are required for the collection, use, or disclosure of personal information, except where this is inappropriate. The PIPEDA goes on to say that:

> in certain circumstances personal information can be collected, used, or disclosed without the knowledge and consent of the individual. Legal, medical, or security reasons may make it impossible or impractical to seek consent. Consent is required for the collection of personal information and the subsequent use or disclosure of this information. The principle requires "knowledge and consent". Organisations shall make a reasonable effort to ensure that the individual is advised of the purposes for which the information will be used. The form of the consent sought by the organization may vary, depending upon the circumstances and the type of information.[39]

The question arises: can the collection of data be undertaken without consent? Section 7 addresses this situation by stipulating that this is possible when it is in the interest of the individual. In certain circumstances, personal information can be collected, used, or disclosed without the knowledge and consent of the individual.[40] There is no requirement for a controller, processor or officer to be registered, or established for any reason to process data within an organisation.

In regard to **Cyprus** and **Malta**, Article 7 of the EU GDPR sets out the general conditions for consent and requires that a data subject give consent freely. That is, that consent cannot be used as a tool of coercion or otherwise for data to be used. This section is limited to the general requirements of consent. Article 4.11, states that 'consent of the data subject means any freely given, specific, informed and unambiguous indication of the data subject's wishes by which he or she, by a statement or by a clear affirmative action, signifies agreement to the processing of personal data relating to him or her. This takes away any ambiguity surrounding what an agreement might constitute'.[41] Additionally, on the one hand, Article 6(1)(a),

[37] Data Protection Act, 45 of 2021, section 7 https://www.nationalassembly.gov.bz/wp-content/uploads/2021/07/Data-Protection-Bill-2021-updated.pdf.

[38] Personal Information Protection and Electronic Documents Act (S.C. 2000, c. 5), section 4, https://laws-lois.justice.gc.ca/eng/acts/P-8.6/index.html.

[39] Personal Information Protection and Electronic Documents Act (S.C. 2000, c. 5), 4.3, https://laws-lois.justice.gc.ca/eng/acts/P-8.6/index.html.

[40] Personal Information Protection and Electronic Documents Act (S.C. 2000, c. 5), schedule 1, https://laws-lois.justice.gc.ca/eng/acts/P-8.6/index.html.

[41] Regulation 2016/679 Of the European Parliament and the European Council, on the protection of natural persons with regard to the processing of personal data and on the free movement of such data and repealing Directive 95/46/EC (General Data Protection Regulation), Official Journal of the European Union L 119/1. Articles 7 & 4.11. Note Recital 32 requires consent should be given by a

requires that in order for data to be processed, the individual 'has given consent to the processing of his or her personal data for one or more specific purposes'. On the other hand, Article 9 requires that 'explicit consent' be obtained in order to process 'special categories' of personal data, and Article 7(3) ensures that businesses must inform individuals about this right to withdraw consent. There are specific requirements for children's consent. Consent must be obtained from a parent or guardian of a child under 16 years of age. However, children aged 16 years or more may give consent for the processing of data related to themselves. However, member states may introduce domestic laws to lower this age to not less than 13 years.[42] A reoccurring theme under the EU legal data framework is the multilayered approach towards several of the concepts and principles. The data controller and processors are no exception. Having a regulated point of reference within an organisation that is responsible for the collection, use and storage of data provides greater transparency and accountability. The point is that the GDPR regulates the user of the data. It is the controller[43] (joint controllers)[44] processor[45] and data officer[46] who collect, use, and/or store the data. The responsibilities of each will differ although, generally, the controller has a high level of responsibility through agreements.

In **Gabon**, Article 46 of the data laws establishes the framework for the processing of personal data whereby, 'a data controller must receive consent of the data subject or meet any of the following legal bases as established below'.[47] Put another way, consent for the processing of personal data of a data subject is required, and there are

clear affirmative act establishing a freely given, specific, informed and unambiguous indication of the data subject's agreement to the processing of personal data.

[42] Regulation 2016/679 Of the European Parliament and the European Council, on the protection of natural persons with regard to the processing of personal data and on the free movement of such data and repealing Directive 95/46/EC (General Data Protection Regulation), Official Journal of the European Union L 119/1. Article 8.

[43] Regulation 2016/679 Of the European Parliament and the European Council, on the protection of natural persons with regard to the processing of personal data and on the free movement of such data and repealing Directive 95/46/EC (General Data Protection Regulation), Official Journal of the European Union L 119/1. Article 24.

[44] Regulation 2016/679 Of the European Parliament and the European Council, on the protection of natural persons with regard to the processing of personal data and on the free movement of such data and repealing Directive 95/46/EC (General Data Protection Regulation), Official Journal of the European Union L 119/1. Article 25.

[45] Regulation 2016/679 Of the European Parliament and the European Council, on the protection of natural persons with regard to the processing of personal data and on the free movement of such data and repealing Directive 95/46/EC (General Data Protection Regulation), Official Journal of the European Union L 119/1. Article 28.

[46] Regulation 2016/679 Of the European Parliament and the European Council, on the protection of natural persons with regard to the processing of personal data and on the free movement of such data and repealing Directive 95/46/EC (General Data Protection Regulation), Official Journal of the European Union L 119/1. Article 37, 39.

[47] Law No. 001/2011 on the Protection of Personal Data, https://www.dataguidance.com/notes/gabon-data-protection-overview Note that the law is in French, and utilised https://caseguard.com/articles/promoting-data-privacy-and-protection-in-gabon/ and DLA Piper, https://www.dlapiperdataprotection.com/index.html?t=law&c=GA.

'obligations to do so under Article 46; to safe guard the privacy of the data subject; it is in the public interest; and there is a legitimate requirement for the data subject'.[48] However, the controller would need to consider any impact or otherwise of the infringement of other data rights when implementing this procedure. Furthermore, it appears that a controller and processor have certain responsibilities under the laws. While the laws do not reflect the multilayered approach of the EU, with the added requirement, if needed, to appoint a data officer, a:

> data processor must present sufficient guarantees to ensure the security and confidentiality of personal data. This requirement does not relieve the data controller of its obligation to ensure compliance with the measure concerning security and confidentiality displayed in Chapter V of the Data Protection Law.[49]

Nonetheless, there is a formal requirement to be undertaken according to the CNPDCP[50] that includes:

- automatic or non-automatic processing of data regarding criminal convictions, except for processing carried out by Justice officials to ensure the security of affected persons;
- automatic processing of genetic data;
- automatic processing which, considering the nature of the data or of the underlying purpose of processing, may exclude an individual from rights, benefits, contributions, or contract(s), without a legal or regulatory basis;
- automatic processing aimed at interconnection by one or more entities in the context of public service aimed at different public interests, or interconnection between different entities, for different purposes;
- processing which concerns a person's registration number in a national identification database;
- automatic processing of data containing comments, observations, and analysis of social difficulties; and
- automatic processing of biometric data.[51]

Notwithstanding the above, the specific processing of data will require Ministerial approval in situations related to state security, defence, or public safety (e.g., terrorist incidents). Moreover, 'state security' is another term for 'national security', and each nation will have its own priorities in this area.

While there is no requirement for the appointment of a controller or processor in **Ghana**, the data laws do specifically outline essential roles and responsibilities associated with these positions. Put simply, according to section 27, any controller is to be registered with the Regulator. Once registered and carrying out the duties of a controller, they are to ensure that the data subject is aware of the nature of the data being collected; the name and address of the person responsible for the

---

[48] Ibid.

[49] Ibid.

[50] Ibid., and CNPDCP https://www.cnpdcp.ga.

[51] Ibid.

collection; and the purpose of collection. They must determine whether the data is discretionary or mandatory, and the consequences of failure to provide the data'.[52] Noteworthy too, according to section 28, a data controller is responsible for taking appropriate steps to secure the integrity of that data from loss, damage or unauthorised destruction or processing. Accordingly, if a processor is required to process data on behalf of a controller, they can process that data only after receiving approval from the controller.[53] To formalise the responsibilities of the 'controller and processor, a contract is required'.[54] Essentially, consent is required for the processing of data.[55] However, it does not state how the consent is to be provided.

Australia's neighbour, **New Zealand**, has adopted similar data laws. The concept of consent in New Zealand has been captured in schedule 8[56] of the Privacy Act 2020. That is, the collection and use of personal data should be undertaken only with the consent of the data subject. However, there is no definition of consent and it is not clear whether any level of consent is to be expressed or implied or both. Put another way, consent is considered the default basis for collecting personal data under the privacy principles, which must be necessary for a lawful purpose connected with a function or an activity of the agency.[57] Noteworthy too, is how the Act adopts the term 'authorisation' rather than 'consent' when referring to the use of data. However, authorization is generally understood to be something slightly more than consent as it implies a level of informed decision making (i.e., a positive and conscious act) by the individual, whereas consent tends to convey a more passive position on the part of the individual.[58] Additionally, 'the Act does not define the scope of authorization or refer to different forms of it. However, privacy principle 12, which relates to disclosures to foreign entities, requires a stronger form of authorization than appears to be required in other parts of the Act. Privacy principle 12(1)(a) requires that an individual must have been expressly informed of the risks before authorizing an overseas transfer. The Act does not expressly provide for withdrawal of consent'.[59] There is no requirement for a controller or processor to be established or registered. The New Zealand case of *Powell*[60] resulted in an issue regarding the personal data and information of an individual who was involved in an accident:

---

[52] Data Protection Act 2012, sections 27, 28 https://nita.gov.gh/theevooc/2017/12/Data-Protection-Act-2012-Act-843.pdf.

[53] Ibid., section 29 and 30.

[54] Ibid., section 30.

[55] Ibid., section 20.

[56] Privacy Act 2020, schedule 8 https://www.privacy.org.nz/privacy-act-2020/privacy-principles/.

[57] Asian business Law Institute, New Zealand, Status of Consent for Processing Personal Data, 2022, pp. 3–5.

https://fpf.org/wp-content/uploads/2022/06/ABLI-FPF-Consent-Project-New-Zealand-Jurisdiction-Report-1.pdf.

[58] Ibid.

[59] Ibid.

[60] *Powell v Accident Compensation Corporation* [2014] NZACC 89 (4 April 2014).

> …the appellant was injured in 1989. While in receipt of weekly compensation the appellant has maintained a level of part time work since that time. There is no dispute that over the years since her injury the appellant has had and has raised concerns with various actions taken by the respondent with regard to both the collection and release of information about her. As a result, the appellant placed restrictions on the extent of any authority given to the respondent to access records relating to the appellant. This included advising that the appellant's prior written permission was required before the respondent contacted her employers. Over time the appellant developed a supplementary form that she added to the ACC 18 medical certificate which specified various conditions on the collection and release of information relating to the appellant. This approach does not appear to have been objected to by the respondent. In June 2007 the appellant was asked to sign an ACC 2 consent form (which appears to be the precursor to the ACC167 form).[61]

In relation to consent by the data subject to complete the relevant form, the Court noted that:

> Some clients continue to submit 'amended' consent forms, and to request that ACC ask their permission each time any information is released to a third party. Staff should be aware that clients have power to limit ACC's ability to collect and release their information, but only within the provisions of the Privacy Act 1993; and the Health Information Privacy Code 1994. Some aspects of the 'amended' consent forms go beyond the limits of those provisions.[62]

The Court went further in outlining the formal and functional arrangements pertaining to the concept of consent under the Privacy Act. It stated:

> The Privacy Act 1993 allows ACC to release particular information, without further consent, if that release *was* one of the purposes for which the information was gathered. If clients request to be advised when ACC is seeking particular information, then they can be offered notification when ACC is releasing material to a third party. The notification could include a copy of the letter to the third party, and a copy of the documentation involved. Taking the client's view into account is in keeping with Right Z of the Code of ACC Claimant's Rights. The process of simultaneous notification will ensure that the client is kept fully informed, but that no unnecessary delays are incurred.[63]

The Court concluded that whatever option is ultimately adopted, there is nothing in the Act that precludes specific agreements on consent being reached between individual claimants and the respondent, as long as these are consistent with s 72(1)(e).[64] While the case never gave the definition of personal data under the Privacy Act, it clearly attributed the personal data-information from the Act. It highlighted how the formal and functional arrangements of consent can vary, and must be applied according to the law of the state. Further, it highlights how the law, in part, can be extended to the parties making an agreement on how consent can be used and applied. However, in order for this to occur, the data subject needs to have given consent in

[61] Ibid., para 2–5.

[62] Ibid., para 10.

[63] Ibid.

[64] Ibid., para 50.

the first instance. The remainder of this chapter will provide a detailed account of the provisions each state has established in relation to the concepts of consent, controller and/or processor.

The sector-based approach in **India** has resulted in section 5 of the SPD Rules requiring that prior to the collection of information, a body corporate or any person on its behalf shall obtain consent in writing through letter or Fax or email from the provider of the sensitive personal data or information regarding the purpose of usage. Note that in section (7), the provider of information shall, at any time while availing the services or otherwise, also have an option to withdraw its consent given earlier to the body corporate. Such withdrawal of the consent shall be sent in writing to the body corporate. In the case of the provider of information not providing or later on withdrawing his consent, the body corporate shall have the option not to provide goods or services for which the said information was sought.[65] At the time of writing, there was no regulatory requirement for the appointment of a designated controller or processor. **India** does not require an organisation to establish a controller, processor or data protection officer. Rather, in section 5 of the SPD Rules, it established Grievance Officers (GOs)who have a limited role and deal with complaints in relation to sensitive information. Also, a GO must respond to data subjects' requests to access and correct their personal information.[66] It is a restricted role. Their function and responsibilities are different from those of controllers and processors under the UK laws, for instance. That said, in this regard, no doubt there will be a number of other differences between India and other jurisdictions.

Data controllers and their representatives, such as a processor or officer need to be registered in **Jamacia.**[67] Only upon registration will the controller be able to process personal data by notice according to sections 11 and 12. A data processor is a 'person, other than an employee of the data controller, who processes the data on behalf of the data controller'.[68] However, a processor is under the direction of a controller and the seventh standard, which is an 'appropriate technical and organisational measure to ensure there is no unlawful processing undertaken, and that the Commissioner is notified of any breach'.[69] A further unique feature of Jamacia's laws is the eight standards[70] that have been established, with which a controller must comply. Also,

[65] Ministry of Communications and Information Technology, 2011, https://www.meity.gov.in/writereaddata/files/GSR313E_10511%281%29_0.pdf.

[66] Ministry of Communications and Information Technology, 2011, https://www.meity.gov.in/writereaddata/files/GSR313E_10511%281%29_0.pdf.

[67] Data Protection Act, 2020, section 14, https://japarliament.gov.jm/attachments/article/339/The%20Data%20Protection%20Act,%202020.pdf.

[68] Data Protection Act, 2020, section 2, https://japarliament.gov.jm/attachments/article/339/The%20Data%20Protection%20Act,%202020.pdf.

[69] Data Protection Act, 2020, section 30, https://japarliament.gov.jm/attachments/article/339/The%20Data%20Protection%20Act,%202020.pdf.

[70] Data Protection Act, 2020, sections 22 to 31, https://japarliament.gov.jm/attachments/article/339/The%20Data%20Protection%20Act,%202020.pdf.

there are a number of exemptions under Part V that will not be discussed in this section. It is argued that the eight standards are very similar to the overall principles of data governance established by the OECD. For instance,

- first standard is that personal data shall be processed fairly and lawfully[71]
- second standard is that personal data shall be obtained only for one or more specified and lawful purposes[72]
- third standard is that personal data shall be adequate, relevant, and limited to what is necessary for the purposes for which they are processed[73]
- fourth standard is that personal data shall be accurate[74]
- fifth standard requires personal data to be processed for any purpose shall not be kept for longer than is necessary[75]
- sixth standard is that personal data shall be processed in accordance with the rights of data subjects[76]
- seventh standard is that appropriate technical and organisational measures[77]
- eighth standard is that personal data shall not be transferred to a State or territory outside of Jamaica unless that State or territory ensures an adequate level of protection for the rights and freedoms of data subjects in relation to the processing of personal data.[78]

Essentially, these standards are a combination of data rights, controls and protection that are adhered to when a processing activity is to be undertaken. On the other hand, section 9 specifically states that the processing of personal data can be done only with the consent of the data subject. Further, consent is 'informed, specific, unequivocal, freely given, expression of will by which the data subject agrees to the processing of that data subject's personal data'.[79] Any such consent can be withdrawn.

---

[71] Data Protection Act, 2020, sections 22, https://japarliament.gov.jm/attachments/article/339/The%20Data%20Protection%20Act,%202020.pdf.

[72] Data Protection Act, 2020, sections 25, https://japarliament.gov.jm/attachments/article/339/The%20Data%20Protection%20Act,%202020.pdf.

[73] Data Protection Act, 2020, sections 26, https://japarliament.gov.jm/attachments/article/339/The%20Data%20Protection%20Act,%202020.pdf.

[74] Data Protection Act, 2020, sections 27, https://japarliament.gov.jm/attachments/article/339/The%20Data%20Protection%20Act,%202020.pdf.

[75] Data Protection Act, 2020, sections 28, https://japarliament.gov.jm/attachments/article/339/The%20Data%20Protection%20Act,%202020.pdf.

[76] Data Protection Act, 2020, sections 29, https://japarliament.gov.jm/attachments/article/339/The%20Data%20Protection%20Act,%202020.pdf.

[77] Data Protection Act, 2020, sections 30, https://japarliament.gov.jm/attachments/article/339/The%20Data%20Protection%20Act,%202020.pdf.

[78] Data Protection Act, 2020, sections 31, https://japarliament.gov.jm/attachments/article/339/The%20Data%20Protection%20Act,%202020.pdf.

[79] Data Protection Act, 2020, sections 9, https://japarliament.gov.jm/attachments/article/339/The%20Data%20Protection%20Act,%202020.pdf.

Explicit and implicit consent have been defined under section 2 of the data laws of the **Kingdom of Eswatini.** According to sections 9 and 10,[80] explicit consent is required from the data subject for the collection and processing of their personal data. While there are no formal arrangements for the appointment of a controller or processor, the laws according to sections 11, 15 and 21 impose a level of obligation on a controller when collecting and processing data. Likewise, under sections 15 and 16, a processor is required to undertake certain functions to ensure the security of personal data. Again, it is the terms and terminology that generally will mean the same. The important element will be understanding the extent of the reach of the terms.

Kenya, in section 2 of the data laws, defines consent as any 'manifestation of express, unequivocal, free, specific and informed indication of the data subject's wishes by a statement or by a clear affirmative action, signifying agreement to the processing of personal data relating to the data subject'.[81] Additionally, section 32 contains specific circumstances where consent is required. That is, section 32(1), provides that a 'data controller or data processor shall bear the burden of proof for establishing a data subject's consent to the processing of their personal data for a specified purpose. Unless otherwise provided under this Act, a data subject shall have the right to withdraw consent at any time. The withdrawal of consent under subsection 32 (2) shall not affect the lawfulness of processing based on prior consent before its withdrawal. In determining whether consent was freely given, account shall be taken of whether, among others, the performance of a contract, including the provision of a service, is conditional on consent to the processing of personal data that is not necessary for the performance of that contract'.[82] In addition, and as is widely understood, children are and have been the most vulnerable cohort in terms of Internet activity. Thus, section 33 is specific in this regard: '…children and requires a controller or data processor shall not process personal data relating to a child unless (a) consent is given by the child's parent or guardian; and (b) the processing is in such a manner that protects and advances the rights and best interests of the child. A data controller or data processor shall incorporate appropriate mechanisms for age verification and consent in order to process personal data of a child'.[83] Further section 33(4) excludes a 'data controller or data processor that exclusively provides counselling or child protection services to a child from the need for consent from a child's parent or guardian'.[84] In addition, PART III of the DPA provides for controllers and processors. Thus, section 18, requires a controller or processor to be registered with the Data Commissioner.

[80] Data Protection Act 2022, sections 2, 9, 10. https://www.esccom.org.sz/legislation/DATA%20PROTECTION%20ACT.pdf.

[81] Data Protection Act 2019, section 2, https://www.odpc.go.ke/dpa-act/.

[82] Data Protection Act 2019, section 32, https://www.odpc.go.ke/dpa-act/.

[83] Data Protection Act 2019, section 33, https://www.odpc.go.ke/dpa-act/.

[84] Data Protection Act 2019, section 33, https://www.odpc.go.ke/dpa-act/.

Firstly, section 2 of the data laws of **Lesotho** defines of the various forms of consent. For instance, explicit consent is any voluntary, specific and informed consent communicated expressly by spoken or written words. Additionally, implicit consent is that which has been inferred from signs or other actions, while opt-in or opt-out consent constitute express and implied consent respectively.[85] Functionally, most other nation states have made provision for express or implied consent or both. For instance, the 'processing of personal information is to be undertaken with the explicit consent of the data subject'.[86] General consent is required for the collection of data under sections 17 and 18, along with the retention of data records under section 19. Secondly, while not specifying whether a controller is required, the concept has been defined to mean a public or private body that processes personal data.[87] The data laws do not specify the need for, or define, a processor or data officer. The processing of personal data can be undertaken only with the explicit consent of the data subject, for the performance of a contract, obligations of a data controller or public body.[88]

Malawi data laws provide for the 'principles governing the processing of personal data. It requires a data controller or data processor to process data fairly and in a transparent manner and only where (a) the data subject has given and not withdrawn his consent, and (b) the data are required for legitimate purposes outlined in the Bill. The Bill further limits the processing of sensitive personal data'.[89] An important component of these laws is the requirement that the controller and processor be registered.[90] This requirement is not a common theme in the laws that have been examined. Additionally, a data controller or data processor is required 'to obtain the consent of a parent or legal guardian where the processing of personal data relates to a person below the age of eighteen years of age. Further, Part III requires a data controller and data processor to carry out a data protection impact assessment where processing is likely to result in high risk to the rights and freedoms of a data subject and to notify the Malawi Communication Regulatory Authority of the results'.[91] In **Malaysia**, consent has also emerged as standard practice when controller or processor collects or uses personal data.[92] Section 6(3) is important because it requires that personal data not be processed unless this is for a lawful purpose directly related to an activity of the data user. In addition, the 'processing of the personal data is necessary for or directly related to that purpose; and the processing of that personal

---

[85] Data Protection Act 2013, section 2, http://www.nic.ls/lsnic/community/policies/Data_Protection_Act_2011_Lesotho.pdf.

[86] Ibid., section 15.

[87] Ibid., section 2.

[88] Ibid., section 15.

[89] Data Protection Bill 2021, Part III, https://digmap.pppc.mw/wp-content/uploads/2022/03/Malawi-Data-Protection-Bill-final-draft-210630-.pdf.

[90] Data Protection Bill 2021, Part VII, https://digmap.pppc.mw/wp-content/uploads/2022/03/Malawi-Data-Protection-Bill-final-draft-210630-.pdf.

[91] Data Protection Bill 2021, Part III, https://digmap.pppc.mw/wp-content/uploads/2022/03/Malawi-Data-Protection-Bill-final-draft-210630-.pdf.

[92] Personal Data Protection Act 2010, section 6, https://www.kkmm.gov.my/pdf/Personal%20Data%20Protection%20Act%202010.pdf.

data is adequate but not excessive in relation to that purpose. The data user is able to process the data without any consent where the performance of a contract to which an individual is a party, or when complying with an existing contract. Consent is also required to ensure the best interests of the per- son are protected such as life, death or security'.[93] Generally, the principle of consent prohibits the processing of any data, unless it is for a lawful purpose directly related to the activity of the data user. On the other hand, for sensitive personal data in relation to physical, mental health or condition, political opinions or religious beliefs, explicit consent has to be obtained.[94] To date, there is no requirement for data users to appoint a data protection officer in Malaysia, often referred to as a data control officer (controller). Section 14 of the PDPA allows the Minister to register a class of data users. The data user is responsible for a number of security matters in accordance with sections 9 and 2.5 of the Personal Data Protection Code of Practice.[95] Data users are responsible for safeguarding the confidentiality, integrity and availability of personal data. The data user is also required to implement security measures to protect personal data from loss, misuse, modification, unauthorized access, disclosure and alteration or destruction.[96]

According to the data laws of **Mauritius**, controllers and processors are to be registered[97] with the Commissioner. Unless registered, no one is allowed to process personal data. Section 21 establishes the obligations of processors and controllers when using personal data. They must ensure that data is processed lawfully, fairly and in a transparent manner. Data collection is done for explicit, specified and legitimate purposes, and it must be adequate, relevant and limited to what is necessary. Further, the data can be collected and used only provided the controller or processor maintains a high level of accuracy, keeps the data up to date, and in a form which permits identification of data subjects for no longer than is necessary (a form of retention). These activities must be undertaken in accordance with the controller's policies and procedures. Further, section 23 requires that upon collection of data, a data subject be informed of the controller's details, purpose, intended recipients, and right to withdraw consent, amongst other things. Again, consent appears to have been similarly replicated in Mauritius and, under section 24, it is to be given 'freely given, account shall be taken of whether, inter alia, the performance of a contract, including the provision of a service, is conditional on consent to the processing of

[93] Personal Data Protection Act 2010, section 6, https://www.kkmm.gov.my/pdf/Personal%20Data%20Protection%20Act%202010.pdf.

[94] Personal Data Protection Act 2010, sections 6 and 40, https://www.kkmm.gov.my/pdf/Personal%20Data%20Protection%20Act%202010.pdf.

[95] Personal Data Protection Act 2010, sections 9, 2.5, https://www.kkmm.gov.my/pdf/Personal%20Data%20Protection%20Act%202010.pdf.

[96] Ibid., Personal Data Protection Act 2010, https://www.kkmm.gov.my/pdf/Personal%20Data%20Protection%20Act%202010.pdf.

[97] Data Protection Act 2017, section 14, 15, https://dataprotection.govmu.org/Documents/DPA_2017_updated.pdf?csf=1&e=0rlrff.

personal data that is not necessary for the performance of that contract'.[98] Consent can be withdrawn at any time.

In **Nigeria**, the controller is responsible for obtaining the data subjects' consent. This specific requirement places an onus on a controller[99] Who is charged with 'determining whether consent was freely and intentionally given, account shall be taken of whether, *inter alia*, the performance of a contract, including the provision of a service, is conditional on consent to the processing of personal data that is not necessary for the performance of that contract'.[100] Significantly too, silence or 'inactivity by the data subject shall not constitute consent'.[101] Withdrawal of consent can be undertaken at the discretion of the data subject. Any form of consent can be in 'writing, orally, or through electronic means'.[102] Thus, a major difference in Nigeria is the extent to which implied consent can apply. In reconciling this, the data laws have defined consent as:

> freely given, specific, informed, and unambiguous indication, whether by a written or oral statement or an affirmative action, of an individual's agreement to the processing of personal data relating to him or to another individual on whose behalf he has the Commission to provide such consent.[103]

The point in relation to affirmative action is unlikely to constitute an implied level of consent. This is because the action would affirm the consent. On the other hand, if an action rather than words affirms a level of consent, implied consent could be indicated. Section 32 affords children their own type of consent, via a parent or legal guardian. Notwithstanding the above, the controller while not regulated as having to be placed within an organisation, has a great obligation to data subjects. This includes, but is not limited to, informing a data subject of 'the identity, residence or place of establishment of, and means of communication'.[104] The data subjects must be informed about purpose of the data processing, their general rights, and their right to lodge a complaint. Finally, according to section 30, a processor has similar obligations, although they are different from those of a controller,. Essentially, both the controller and processor are required to manage data according to the principles set out in section 25, such as processing the data fairly, lawfully and in a transparent manner. Additionally, the data is to be only collected for a specific purpose, and

---

98 Data Protection Act 2017, section 24, https://dataprotection.govmu.org/Documents/DPA_2017_updated.pdf?csf=1&e=0rlrff.

99 Data Protection Regulation 2022, section 26 https://ndpb.gov.ng/Files/Nigeria_Data_Protection_Bill.pdf.

100 Data Protection Regulation 2022, section 26 https://ndpb.gov.ng/Files/Nigeria_Data_Protection_Bill.pdf.

101 Data Protection Regulation 2022, section 27 https://ndpb.gov.ng/Files/Nigeria_Data_Protection_Bill.pdf.

102 Data Protection Regulation 2022, section 27 https://ndpb.gov.ng/Files/Nigeria_Data_Protection_Bill.pdf.

103 Data Protection Regulation 2022, section 65 https://ndpb.gov.ng/Files/Nigeria_Data_Protection_Bill.pdf.

104 Data Protection Regulation 2022, section 28 https://ndpb.gov.ng/Files/Nigeria_Data_Protection_Bill.pdf.

retained for no longer than is necessary. However, there is no specified time. The data must also be accurate, complete, not misleading and secure. Even though there is no mention of cybersecurity, the reference to 'secure' is, in part, indicating a connection between data and cybersecurity law.

In **Rwanda**, a controller or processor has a level of responsibility and is to be registered and recorded on the states register.[105] Upon the issue of a registration certificate by the Authority, the controller or processor[106] can undertake the collection, use, disclosure and storage of data. For the collection and use of personal data, Article 3 ensures that consent is a freely given, specific, informed, and unambiguous indication of the data subject's wishes by which they, by an oral, written, or electronic statement, or by a clear affirmative action, signify agreement to the processing of personal data relating to them. Therefore, express and implied consent is required.

Singapore regards it as a matter of great importance that data subjects consent to the processing or otherwise of their personal data.[107] The threshold test for consent commenced after 2 July 2014, according to section 13 related to the collection, use or disclosure of data unless the data subject has consented to the issue of that data. Section 14 specifies what constitutes consent. Section 15 provides for deemed consent which requires additional steps to be taken to ensure that the data usage has no adverse effect on the data subject. On the one hand, data subjects have the right to withdraw their consent.[108] On the other hand, according to section 17, data can be collected, used or disclosed without consent although this relates only to the vital interests of the individual,[109] or for reasons such as the public interest, business improvement or research.[110] In the 2020 matter of *Majesty*,[111] the Singapore Regulator was required to examine the concept of consent in relation to debt collection by means of a video recording. The Regulator commented that the case 'concerns a debt collection company's posting of a video recording on social media as a tactic to shame a debtor. The recordings in question captured exchanges between the company's representative and staff of the debtor company'.[112] The background of the case is as follows:

---

[105] Law n°058/2021 of 13/10/2021 relating to the protection of personal data and privacy (the Data Protection Law), Article 29, https://www.minijust.gov.rw/fileadmin/user_upload/Minijust/Publications/Official_Gazette/_2021_Official_Gazettes/October/OG_Special_of_15.10.2021_Amakuru_bwite.pdf.

[106] Law n°058/2021 of 13/10/2021 relating to the protection of personal data and privacy (the Data Protection Law), Article 30, 31, https://www.minijust.gov.rw/fileadmin/user_upload/Minijust/Publications/Official_Gazette/_2021_Official_Gazettes/October/OG_Special_of_15.10.2021_Amakuru_bwite.pdf.

[107] Personal Data Protection Act 2012, section 13, https://sso.agc.gov.sg/Act/PDPA2012.

[108] Personal Data Protection Act 2012, section 15, https://sso.agc.gov.sg/Act/PDPA2012.

[109] Personal Data Protection Act 2012, schedule 1, https://sso.agc.gov.sg/Act/PDPA2012.

[110] Personal Data Protection Act 2012, schedule 2, https://sso.agc.gov.sg/Act/PDPA2012.

[111] *Majestic Debt Recovery Pte Ltd* [2020] SGPDPC 7.

[112] Ibid., para 1.

> Majestic Debt Recovery Pte Ltd a company in the business of collecting debts on the behalf of its clients. On 22 March 2019, the Personal Data Protection Commission received a complaint from the managing director of a debtor company stating that the Organisation had been engaged by the Company's sub-contractor to recover debts from the Company. The Complainant stated that on or around 21 March 2019, the Organisation's representatives visited the Company's premises to collect a debt on behalf of its client. Not surprisingly, heated words were exchanged with the Company's personnel when the Representatives attempted to recover the debt. The Representatives recorded video footage of the exchanges with the Company's personnel, including the Complainant, on a tablet device. The Complainant and the Company's personnel could be identified from the images and audio captured by the Recording. According to the Complainant, he "*protested against the taking of [the Recording and] posting it [on] social media but [the Representative] said he would do it*". The Representatives nonetheless took the Recording and subsequently posted it on the Organisation's official public Facebook page.[113]

Subsequently, the Regulator found video recordings on the Facebook Page. These videos also captured images and voices of other individuals who appeared to be either individual debtors or representatives of corporate debtors of the Organisation's clients. However, the Organisation did not have any knowledge of the Personal Data Protection Act 2012 prior to this incident, and had not developed any data protection policies or practices.[114] On the question of consent, the Regulator noted that:

> section 13 of the PDPA [Personal Data Protection Act 2012] prohibits organisations from collecting, using or disclosing personal data about an individual unless the individual's consent is obtained (either actual or deemed) or such collection, use or disclosure is required or authorised under the PDPA or any written law.[115]

The Regulator, when interpreting section 13, emphasised the importance and application of consent to the collection and use of personal data. The Regulator further stated:

> In relation to the Organisation's assurance that it would in future obtain consent from individuals concerned, it seems unlikely or even unconceivable that an individual who owed a debt would willingly *consent* to be filmed by the debt collecting agency calling on him, and for such recordings to be posted on social media. If such consent were obtained *ex ante* by an organisation, for example at the time when the loan was first given, and the purpose for posting the recording on social media is to shame the debtor, there is a real risk that this purpose may not be one which a reasonable person would consider appropriate under section 18 of the PDPA; or that consent thus obtained is vitiated under section 14(3), as having been obtained through unfair, or deceptive or misleading practices.[116]

In assessing the formal and functional application of consent, the Regulator went on to say:

> Even if consent had been obtained previously, section 16(1) of the PDPA provides that on giving reasonable notice to the organisation, an individual may at any time withdraw any consent given, or deemed to have been given in respect of the collection, use or disclosure

---

[113] Ibid., para 2.

[114] Ibid., paras 3–4.

[115] Ibid., para 6.

[116] Ibid., para 7.

> by that organisation of personal data about the individual for any purpose. As mentioned, the Complainant had expressly objected to the video recording and the subsequent posting of the video on the Facebook Page. In the circumstances, I find that even if consent was given previously as asserted by the Organisation, it had been withdrawn by virtue of the Complainant's express objections at the material time. Accordingly, the Organisation did not have consent to post the Recording on its Facebook Page; and (c) Furthermore, even if consent had been obtained to post the video recording on social media to shame the debtor, I have grave doubts if the consent will stand up to scrutiny under section 14(2) of the PDPA, which vitiates consent obtained through unfair, and deceptive or misleading practices. For example, if consent to post video recordings made during debt recovery attempts was made *a condition* of obtaining the loan, it could possibly go beyond what is reasonable in order to provide the loan: see section 14(2)(a). Consent obtained through such unfair practice is vitiated by section 14(3). Neither would such a purpose be one which a reasonable person — on an objective standard — would likely consider to be appropriate under section 18 of the PDPA.[117]

This demonstrates that the Singapore data laws stipulate that data subjects' consent must be given and that such consent can be withdrawn at any time. It further stipulates how consent is to be obtained and whether that process was or can be justified. However, such consent should not be used to recover debt. Even though the application of consent in this situation was not appropriate, the Regulator confirmed that the organisation involved was cooperative and no further action was taken. However, this indicates that the importance of consent cannot be underestimated. Today, it is a fundamentally important concept of data law as it ensures that data subjects have some control over personal data.

Even though there are no specific provisions for a data controller or processor to be appointed in **Sri Lanka**, controllers and processors have been described by the laws as having a central role in the governance of data.[118] For instance, sections7 and 8 ensure that a controller processes data adequately and that the processing is relevant and proportionate to the intended purpose. The law also requires the controller to ensure the data is kept up to date and that data subjects can have their data erased or amended without undue delay. Section 12 contains a unique feature in that the controller is to implement a Data Protection Management Programme designed to establish and maintain a catalogue of data records to demonstrate the manner in which the data protection obligations referred to in sections 5, 6, 7, 8, 9, 10 and 11 have been implemented. This programme is also designed to ensure there are safeguards for data protection impact assessments, and is part of the overall governance structure for controllers. Section 20 provides for the appointment of a Data Protection Officer (DPO). However, only those with the appropriate qualifications can be appointed as DPOs.[119] This is something not specified in most of the other laws being compared. According to sections 21 and 22, the controller has responsibility for the functions of a controller. These obligations are generally required to be in writing, for instance,

---

[117] Ibid., para 13.

[118] Personal Data Protection Act No. 9 of 2022, sections 6, 7, 8, 9, 10, 11, 12 https://www.parliament.lk/uploads/acts/gbills/english/6242.pdf.

[119] Personal Data Protection Act No. 9 of 2022, sections 20 https://www.parliament.lk/uploads/acts/gbills/english/6242.pdf.

through a contract. A controller or processor may use personal data only with the consent of the data subject. Section 14 gives data subjects the right to withdraw their consent at any time. Consent must be explicit and 'freely given, specific, informed and unambiguous indication by way of a written declaration or an affirmative action signifying a data subject's agreement to the processing of personal data'.[120] Further, schedule 1 provides that any processing of personal data is to be undertaken upon consent of the data subject.

South Africa (SA) does not regulate for a controller or processor. On the other hand, **SA** gives data subjects a level of consent. While predominantly pertaining to the processing of personal information under section 11, a data subject can provide voluntary, express, and informed consent. Also, 'a data subject may withdraw consent to processing of personal information at any time. This withdrawal of consent does not affect processing of personal information in accordance with other processing rules, such as where the processing complies with an obligation imposed by law on the responsible party'.[121] An important feature of the SA data laws is that section 1 defines a 'competent person' as any 'person who is legally competent to consent to any action or decision being taken in respect of any matter concerning a child. Additionally, 'child" means a natural person under the age of 18 years who is not legally competent'.[122] In **Tanzania**, the 2022 data laws do not give many details about the responsibilities of the controller or processor, nor about the application of consent.

Saint Lucia's data laws place significant obligations on a controller. That is, section 21 requires a controller to collect data based on fact, purpose and intended recipients while, under section 22, there are constraints on the processing of personal data. There are no specific provisions related to a processor or other officers.[123] On the one hand, according to section 22, consent relates to express consent, on which there is greater reliance. The concept of consent is limited as it has not been defined and does not include children. **Saint Kitts and Nevis** provides for a general principle of consent.[124] Generally, consent is not defined and can be either expressed or implied. Importantly, for sensitive personal data, consent must be explicit and cannot be given by a third party. Arguably, and unlike other states, there are no rigorous requirements for consent. Section 11of the data laws of **Saint Vincent and The Grenadines**

---

[120] Personal Data Protection Act No. 9 of 2022, sections 2, 14, https://www.parliament.lk/uploads/acts/gbills/english/6242.pdf.

[121] Protection of Personal Information 2013, section 11, https://www.gov.za/documents/protection-personal-information-act.

[122] Protection of Personal Information 2013, section 1, https://www.gov.za/documents/protection-personal-information-act.

[123] Privacy and Data Protection Act 2009, section 12, https://www.govt.lc/media.govt.lc/www/resources/legislation/PrivacyAndDataProtectionBill.pdf.

[124] Data Protection Act, 5 of 2018, Principles 7, 9, sections 16, 19, 20, https://www.theinformationcollective.com/dpl/st-kitts-data-protection-act.

provides for the disclosure of personal data by either expressed or implied consent.[125] There are no other guidelines specifying how and to what consent applies. There is no requirement for a controller or processor to be established within an entity, or for them to be registered.

For **Tanzania,** the 2022 laws from sections 14 to 21 deal with the conditions for the registration of data collectors and data processors. They also specify the conditions for registration certificates, an inspection of registered information and the registration period.[126] Sections 22 to 30 set out the procedures for the collection, use, security and storage of personal data. There has been limited commentary on the extent to which consent will apply. Unlike many other states, consent has not been included as a requirement for the transfer of data outside[127] of the state. On the other hand, consent does not generally include data that is used in research, statistics or where data is anonymized. Similarly, in **Togo**, the processing of personal data is considered legitimate if the data subject gives his consent. However, 'this requirement may be waived when the treatment is necessary for compliance with a legal obligation; execution of a public interest; performance of a contract to which the person concerned is a party or the execution of pre-contractual measures taken at his request; or to safeguard the interest or fundamental rights and freedoms of the data subject'.[128] On the other hand, the collection and processing of data is prohibited if it is likely to reveal 'racial, ethnic origin, parentage, political opinions, religious or philosophical convictions, union membership, sex life, genetic data and data relating to the health condition of the data subject concerned'.[129]

Even though consent has not been defined, the concept is reflected throughout the **Trinidad-Tobago** data laws, in relation to the processing of personal data. Sections 6, 30, 40 and 45[130] while applying to public bodies, requires that the collection, retention or disclosure of personal information be undertaken only provided that authorisation has been given by a data subject. A specific feature of these laws is that section 72 requires that a code of conduct be prepared by organisations that requires consent to be clearly articulated. There is no definition of consent, and only limited direction of express or implied consent being applicable. There is no requirement for the appointment of a controller, processor or officer.

Uganda, under section 9 of its data laws, allows a data collector, processor and controller to collect or process personal data, provided the data subject has provided consent, or for non-profit purposes, political, philosophical, religious or

[125] Privacy Act 2003, section 11 https://www.theinformationcollective.com/dpl/st-vincent-and-the-grenadines-the-privacy-act.

[126] Fatma Songoro, Brief Highlight and Analysis of the Tanzania Data Protection Bill, 2002, October 2022, https://victoryattorneys.co.tz/insights-brief-highlight-and-analysis-of-the-tanzania-data-protection-bill-2022/.

[127] Ibid.

[128] Tshepiso Hadebe Togolese Republic, 2020, p. 2, https://dataprotection.africa/wp-content/uploads/2020/03/Togolese-Republic-Factsheet-update-20200331.pdf.

[129] Ibid.

[130] Data Protection Act 2011, section 6, 30,40, 45, https://rgd.legalaffairs.gov.tt/laws2/Alphabetical_List/lawspdfs/22.04.pdf.

trade union.[131] The point to make is that consent must be given by a data subject as a 'freely, specific, informed, unambiguous indication of the data subject's wish which he or she, by a statement or by a clear affirmative action',[132] through an agreement. In regard to children, section 8 specifies that parental or guardian consent is required in order for children's data to be processed. However, no age limit is specified. Therefore, other laws of the state need to be examined to confirm the age requirement for children in Uganda. Significantly, it sets out the principles that are to be implemented by a controller, processor or officer-collector of personal data. The principles align with those of the OECD: accountability, collect and process data fairly and lawfully; collect, process, use or hold adequate, relevant and not excessive or unnecessary personal data, retain personal data for the period authorised by law or for which the data is required, quality, transparency and observe security[133] safeguards. Again, the link between data laws and cybersecurity is clearly evident in Uganda.

As mentioned earlier, although the **UK** is no longer a member of the EU, at the time of writing, it had retained the EU legal framework. The UK, in adopting the multi-layered approach of the EU, Malta and Cyprus (see above), the appointment of a controller, processor and officer to govern the collection, use and storage of data is similar. That said, the processing of personal data should be undertaken only after obtaining the free, specific, informed and unambiguous consent of the individuals concerned, or for a legitimate reason laid down in law.[134] In the *Planet49* case, it was clarified by the Court of Justice of the European Union that failing to obtain consent via a 'clear affirmative action' given by the users could lead to a breach of the GDPR.[135] For instance, according to the court, it would appear impossible in practice to determine objectively whether users had actually given their consent by not deselecting a pre-ticked checkbox that is required for continuing their primary activity on the website visited.[136]

Consent is defined under Article 4(11) of UK, GDPR as freely given, specific, informed and unambiguous indication of the data subject's wishes by which he or she, by a statement or by a clear affirmative action, signifies agreement to the processing of personal data relating to him or her. Article 6(1)(a) of UK, GDPR clarifies that processing is lawful only if consent is provided for those specific purposes. Additionally, under Article 7, UK, GDPR, the controller must be able demonstrate that

[131] Data Protection and Privacy Act 2019, section 9 https://media.ulii.org/files/legislation/akn-ug-act-2019-9-eng-2019-05-03.pdf.

[132] Data Protection and Privacy Act 2019, section 2 https://media.ulii.org/files/legislation/akn-ug-act-2019-9-eng-2019-05-03.pdf.

[133] Data Protection and Privacy Act 2019, section 20, 21 https://media.ulii.org/files/legislation/akn-ug-act-2019-9-eng-2019-05-03.pdf.

[134] Article 5 (2) of the modernised Convention for the Protection of Individuals with regard to Automatic Processing of Personal Data.

[135] C673/17 Planet49 GmbH [2019] ECLI:EU: C:2019:801, 61.

[136] Ibid., 55.

the data subject consented to the processing of his or her personal data,[137] additionally, the subject's consent must be given in plain language with the requisite of consent being in distinguishable format, the data subject should furthermore, have the right to withdraw this consent at any given time and the free consent given should be of such nature that performance of contract is conditional on consent.[138] The data subject's consent to the processing of his or her data is of paramount importance under section 2(1)(a) unless otherwise specified under the Data Protection Act. The importance of consent is enunciated as the first data protection principle under section 86 which qualifies it as lawful and fair. However, consent is not required for processing personal data under the ambit of "law enforcement purposes" which include the prevention, investigation, detection or prosecution of criminal offences or the execution of criminal penalties, including the safeguarding against and the prevention of threats to public security.[139] Also, consent is not required for personal data interception and processing by the intelligence agencies of the UK.[140] The same is governed under Part IV of Data Protection Act and Investigatory Powers Act (IP Act). The aim of the IP Act is to consolidate the UK's patchwork of surveillance laws and provide a transparent, legally grounded legitimacy to interception of communication to prevent serious crimes.[141] Initially, the IP Act was challenged for violating the Human Rights Act, 1998 incorporated under the aegis of the European Convention on Human Rights. However, the High Court reviewed the Act and held that the IP Act was not incompatible with the Human Rights Act. The formation of the Investigatory Powers Commission, an independent body responsible for preventing abuse, guarantees that there are safeguards to prevent potential abuse of the Act.[142] Noteworthy was that this occurred before the UK had left the EU.

In **Zambia**, the data laws define consent as any written, freely given, specific, informed and unambiguous indication of the data subject's wishes by which such data subject, by a statement or by a clear affirmative action, signifies agreement to the processing of personal data relating to that data subject.[143] Consent is to be obtained prior to the processing of personal data,[144] and it may be withdrawn. As mentioned earlier, data controllers and processors are to be registered. Generally, a

---

[137] Article 7(1), UKGDPR, https://www.legislation.gov.uk/ukpga/2018/12/pdfs/ukpga_20180012_en.pdf.

[138] Article 7, UKGDPR. https://www.legislation.gov.uk/ukpga/2018/12/pdfs/ukpga_20180012_en.pdf.

[139] Sections 31, 35(2), Data Protection Act, 2018; Article 2(2)(b) UKGDPR. https://www.legislation.gov.uk/ukpga/2018/12/pdfs/ukpga_20180012_en.pdf.

[140] 2(2)(c) UKGDPR. https://www.legislation.gov.uk/ukpga/2018/12/pdfs/ukpga_20180012_en.pdf.

[141] S McKay, *Blackstone's Guide to the Investigatory Powers Act 2016* (Oxford, OUP, 2017).

[142] Carey, Scott (27 April 2018). "The Snoopers' Charter: Everything you need to know about the Investigatory Powers Act". *Computerworld UK*. IDG UK.

[143] Data Protection Act 2021, section 2 https://www.parliament.gov.zm/sites/default/files/documents/acts/Act%20No.%203%20The%20Data%20Protection%20Act%202021_0.pdf.

[144] Data Protection Act 2021, section 15, 16, https://www.parliament.gov.zm/sites/default/files/documents/acts/Act%20No.%203%20The%20Data%20Protection%20Act%202021_0.pdf.

data controller and processor use personal data that it is collected lawfully, fairly and transparently. It must be collected for explicit, specified and legitimate purposes, and must be accurate and kept up to date. Any collected data is to be stored in a manner that ensures its security and enables it to be identified later. The three-tiered approach in Zambia similar to that of Malta and Cyprus. Put simply, in Zambia a data auditor, processor and controller are to be registered.[145] Children and an additional concept of vulnerable persons have been afforded separate rights, whereby a parent or legal guardian is responsible for giving consent. However, an age limit for a child and a definition of 'vulnerable persons' have not been provided. This is not to say that these concepts are not defined elsewhere in national law.

A central issue concerns the wide approach that the respective jurisdictions have taken to defining the concepts of controller, consent and processor. Some jurisdictions have taken a comprehensive approach to these three concepts, while some jurisdictions have not adopted any of these concepts. Further research is needed to fully understand the three concepts individually. This is because the above comparison does not consider children specifically.

5.2 Conclusion

The concepts of consent, controller and processor compared in this chapter are important features of current data laws. This chapter has shown that a highly fragmented approach has been taken by nation states when including these concepts in their respective laws. Some jurisdictions have opted for a multi-layered approach to the concept of controller and processor, requiring organisations to establish these positions. This is particularly the case for Cyprus and Malta.

Essentially, accountability and transparency are fundamental to the operation of data law. Put another way, in order for data to be collected, stored and processed, an individual within an organisation will have responsibility for that function. Thus, generally, the laws oblige an organisation to formally establish these positions. The EU takes it a step further and provides that a third data office can be established. In practice, what this means is that the level of obligations placed on a controller or processor enable that person to be audited or investigated when there is a breach of the respective data laws. It underscores the principle of accountability.

Arguably, in terms of the entire life cycle of the collection, use and storage of data, the importance of allocating a formal level of responsibility indirectly forces organisations to develop internal policies and practices to ensure compliance with the laws. The resulting effect is that, over time, people place trust in the laws and their application. However, the fragmentation makes it a highly complex area of law.

[145] Data Protection Act 2021, section 19 https://www.parliament.gov.zm/sites/default/files/documents/acts/Act%20No.%203%20The%20Data%20Protection%20Act%202021_0.pdf.

In comparing Australia and the EU alone, Australian law on the one hand does not specifically address data control; instead, the APPs require a level of accountability from an organisation. On the other hand, the EU has applied three levels, holding all positions accountable.

On the other hand, consent has given more control and value to data subjects. The essential feature of consent is whether it is implied or expressed. Does the state provide for one or both? This needs to be confirmed, because it will vary from state to state. Further, in reconciling the differences, there will need to be a common understanding of what constitutes express consent. Is it in writing and how is that to be undertaken? Likewise, is silence merely an implied type of consent?

Another area that needs to be reconciled is the age limit and requirements for consent in relation to children. This is highly variable. Some states require consent from a parent or guardian, and others do not. Moreover, the age limits will differ significantly from state to state. Overall, consent is required for a legitimate purpose. It is argued that the Commonwealth can undertake further work to reconcile the differences in the adoption of these concepts within the MBP and MBPPI.

Finally, this chapter has demonstrated the direct link between cybersecurity and data governance. While it has mentioned only one judicial decision made in Australia, this demonstrated that when access to a computer and modification to data has been undertaken without engaging a controller or processor or obtaining the consent of a data subject, an offence has been committed, not necessarily under the data laws.

Chapter 6
Storage Retention

6.1 Introduction

As the amount of data being generated continues to increase, that data is being retained at a rate that was unimaginable only a decade ago. The digital economy will certainly increase the amount of data being stored. This trend will continue given the rapid development of technology, particularly with artificial intelligence becoming mainstream in many sectors. The extent of data storage is not fully understood. The ability of data subjects to have their personal data deleted outright from the Internet is also not fully understood by the lay person due to a lack of information being available to the community.

More transparency is needed. This chapter examines the storage retention provisions established by Commonwealth countries. The retention of data is directly related to its security. In other words, it directly relates to cybersecurity because when computer systems and infrastructure are breached, the stored data is vulnerable to illegal use. The resulting effect is a potential compromise of an individual's privacy over the Internet.

The MBP[1] does not provide requirements for the retention of records. On the other hand, section 20 of the MPPI states that an organisation shall not retain a record of personal information after the purpose for which the organisation collected the information has been fulfilled unless:

(a)Another law requires the organisation to retain the record;
(b)The organisation reasonably requires the record for purposes related to its operation; or
(c)The regulations authorise the organisation to retain it.

[1] The Commonwealth, Model Privacy Bill, Office of Civil and Criminal Justice Reform, 2017, https://www.asianlaws.org/gcld/cyberlawdb/COM/P15370_9_ROL_Model_Privacy_Bill_0.pdf.

R. Walters, *Cybersecurity and Data Laws of the Commonwealth*,
https://doi.org/10.1007/978-981-99-3935-0_6

In addition, an organisation that has used a record of personal information about an individual in order to make a decision about the individual shall retain the record for such period of time as may be prescribed after making the decision, to allow the individual a reasonable opportunity to request access to the information.[2] This chapter begins by examining the laws of Australia.

The retention of data is another concept that is complex. On the surface, it appears to be straightforward: a company collects data and retains it for a period of time and then deletes it. However, this begs the question: what is a suitable period of time for data to be retained? Also: should the laws specify a time limit for the retention of data, after which it is to be deleted from the records of the entity which has stored the data? This issue is discussed because, as this chapter demonstrates, most if not all of the laws compared do not specify a time limit for the retention of personal data.

Regarding the above, the approach taken by nation states has been very broad as they use terminology such as—'retained for a period' (or words to that effect). Some states have limited the retention time to certain sectors such as health or financial credit, while other sectors are more or less free to do what they like, as long as they comply with the data laws of the state. Much has been written about the policy and practices of organisations in regard to implementing good strategies for data retention and storage requirements. Thus, a cycle of data retention needs to be embedded in the practices of an organisation to ensure the data is disposed of in a way that ensures it cannot be retrieved. In practice, this may be difficult to achieve, and the laws do not necessarily oblige entities to ensure data cannot be retrieved once it has been deleted (Fig. 6.1).

The diagram above depicts the data lifecycle from creation to deletion. Data can be used for a variety of purposes including international trade. Generally, following its use, the data is archived and after a period of time, it is deleted. However, it is understood by the technology profession that the retention of data poses a number of challenges since it comprises:

- Email and other electronic communications;

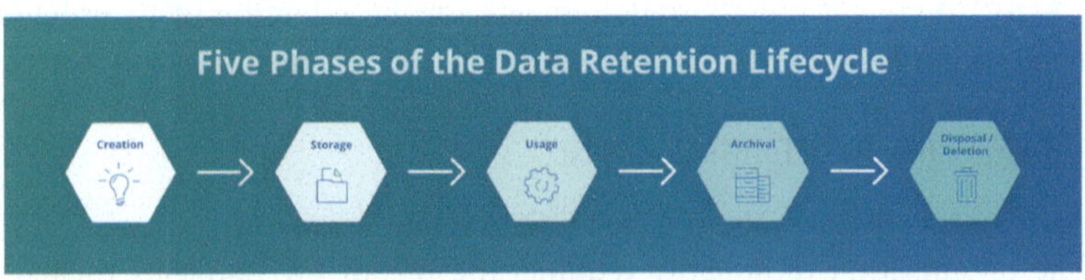

Fig. 6.1 Five phases of the data retention lifecycle[3]

---

[2] The Commonwealth, Model Bill on the Protection of Personal Information https://www.asianlaws.org/gcld/cyberlawdb/COM/P15370_6_ROL_Model_Bill_Protection_Personal_Information_2.pdf.

[3] Data Retention 1010: Policies and Practices, https://www.egnyte.com/guides/governance/data-retention.

- Office files, such as documents, presentations, spreadsheets;
- Databases;
- Customer, partner, and supplier records;
- Employee documentation;
- Transactional data;
- Contracts and billing information;
- Invoices and receipts; and
- Accounting, banking, finance, and tax documents and data.[4]

The various sectors that collect data (banking-finance, health, education, agriculture, environment, tourism, power and water utilities, government and non-government) are very different in nature. For instance, data sets used in scientific research on health will likely have little or no relevance to the banking and finance sector. Thus, this chapter demonstrates the minimalist approach that has been taken towards data retention. However, in my view, this is going to be an emerging issue in the future, since some entities simply hold onto data for extended periods. While there are no unauthorised breaches or intrusions of computers or systems, the data is safe. However, when a serious breach occurs, that is when governments may be forced to respond. It is argued that the Commonwealth should do more in this area and needs to undertake a comprehensive research project to confirm or otherwise the need for data-retention time limits to be established within member country laws.

In **Australia,** the retention of data under the Privacy Act 1988 is somewhat limited to only credit reporting. Credit reporting information must be deleted following the retention period.[5] Section 20W describes the type of credit information and the period for which it is to be retained. Generally, the period ranges between 2, 5, 7 years for credit, repayment and payment information, bankruptcy and insolvency. APP 11 requires organisations to de-identify or destroy personal data and information when it is no longer required. At the time of writing, the *Privacy Legislation Amendment (Enforcement and Other Measures) Bill 2022*[6] had been introduced and passed by the Australian Parliament. However, there were no additions specifying any further requirement for the retention of personal information. Section 9 of the data laws of **Antigua and Barbuda** specifies that data can be retained for a period no longer than that required for the purpose for which that data is to be processed.[7] There is no set time limit. There are no specific retention requirements under the data laws of the **Bahamas**. However, there are sectorial retention requirements for health, finance

---

[4] Ibid.

[5] Privacy Act 1988, section 20W, C2014C00076.

[6] Australian Parliament, https://www.aph.gov.au/Parliamentary_Business/Bills_Legislation/Bills_Search_Results/Result?bId=r6940.

[7] Data Protection Act 2013, section 9 http://laws.gov.ag/wp-content/uploads/2019/02/a2013-10.pdf.

and telecommunications records of data.[8] **Barbados,** does not specify data retention[9] provisions nor time limits for the storage of data. **Saint Lucia** does not have laws pertaining to data retention.

There are no retention requirements in the data laws of **Botswana**, other than very broad provisions where necessary (see section on controller, consent, processor). That is, there is no timeframe specified for the retention of data. **Belize** has no data-retention retention laws. Similarly, **Malta** and **Cyprus** have no specific timeframe for the retention of data. Any retention requirements provide a flexible approach according to Article 5(1)(e).[10] Note that there is other EU law that deals with data retention such as that related to telecommunications data, although this is not examined here. The **UK** and **Gabon**[11] have the same approach; that is, a timeframe has not been specified**. Ghana,** according to section 24 of the data laws,[12] require that the controller not retain data records for any length of time greater than is necessary. However, there is not specified time period for the retention to expire, and the data records to be destroyed. Significant too, the controller can destroy or delete the data records. The controller can also de-identify the records. This must be undertaken to ensure the data is no longer accessible or intelligible. In **Canada,** section 37 requires records to be retained,[13] although no specific timeframe is articulated. In **India**, a body corporate or person holding sensitive personal data cannot retain that information for longer than is required. However, it is for the judiciary to determine what is meant by 'no longer required'. Arguably, entities will need to prove that they are either not using or still using the required data. Section 7 of the IT Act clarifies ways of retaining electronic documents, records and information.[14] The electronic record is to be retained in the format it was originally generated. The regulatory requirements setting out the retention for data is sporadic and there is no consistent

---

[8] Sean McWeeny, *Data Protection and Privacy 2022: The Bahamas*, https://practiceguides.chambers.com/practice-guides/data-protection-privacy-2022/the-bahamas.

[9] *Data Protection Act 2019*, https://gisbarbados.gov.bb/download/data-protection-act-2019/.

[10] Regulation 2016/679 Of the European Parliament and the European Council, on the protection of natural persons with regard to the processing of personal data and on the free movement of such data and repealing Directive 95/46/EC (General Data Protection Regulation), Official Journal of the European Union L 119/1. Article 5(1)(e) of the GDPR states that data kept in a form which permits identification of data subjects for no longer than is necessary for the purposes for which the personal data are processed; personal data may be stored for longer periods insofar as the personal data will be processed solely for archiving purposes in the public interest, scientific or historical research purposes or statistical purposes in accordance with Article 89(1) subject to implementation of the appropriate.

[11] Law No. 001/2011 on the Protection of Personal Data, https://www.dataguidance.com/notes/gabon-data-protection-overview Note that the law is in French, and utilised https://caseguard.com/articles/promoting-data-privacy-and-protection-in-gabon/ and DLA Piper, https://www.dlapiperdataprotection.com/index.html?t=law&c=GA.

[12] Data Protection Act 2012, sections 24 https://nita.gov.gh/theevooc/2017/12/Data-Protection-Act-2012-Act-843.pdf.

[13] Personal Information Protection and Electronic Documents Act (S.C. 2000, c. 5), section 37, https://laws-lois.justice.gc.ca/eng/acts/P-8.6/index.html.

[14] Information and Technology Act, 2008, section 7.

approach due to the sectorial laws. The retention requirements for ISPs and UASL licenses must comply with the Telegraph Act 1885. However, the current law and position adopted throughout India is arguably contrary to the current review of data protection. In **Jamacia,** data retention is subject only to a minimal standard of not to be kept for longer than is necessary.[15] While this section does not examine any data regulation pertaining to retention, a prescribed period of retention by the Minister through Regulations[16] can be implemented.

Data retention is an exercise in risk management. In other words, there is the potential for significant risk to individuals and entities when data is retained for extended periods of time. Thus, one of the most pronounced common themes that has emerged is that while there are retention requirements within the respective laws, no time frame has been specified. Furthermore, the terminology used such as 'retain that information for longer than is required, or 'retain that information for longer than is necessary' is broad enough to give entities some flexibility in terms of using the data for business needs.

Section 39 of the **Kenya** data laws provides for 'retention of data under various circumstances which are as long as is reasonably necessary to satisfy the purpose for which the data is collected and processed; as required or authorised by law including sectoral laws; as consented to by the data subject; or for historical, statistical, journalistic, literature, art, or research purposes'.[17] Under the Kenya Information and Communications Act, the data retention procedures must ensure confidentiality, accuracy, and security. Call data records must be retained for a minimum of three years. There is no specified time limit for the retention of subscriber information. Under the National Payment System Act, financial information must be retained for a minimum of seven years. In the **Kingdom of Eswatini**, section 13[18] ensures that any retention of data is done so with the consent of the data subject. Any retention of records of data is for as long as the controller thinks fit. This could be problematic, as there is no specific timeframe limiting the data-storage period.

In **Lesotho**, the retention of personal data has also emerged as an important feature of this country's data laws. Section 19 requires that data records be retained by a controller, or where a contract obliges it to be done. Data subjects are to consent to the retention of their personal data. However, the law does not specify a retention period. This time period for retention could be stipulated in a code of conduct, after which the data is to be destroyed or deleted.[19] As stated earlier, the ensuing question is: has the deleted data really been deleted? Can it ever be retrieved? These are questions for IT experts. However, the concept of consent, while not often addressed by other

---

[15] *Data Protection Act*, 2020, sections 28, https://japarliament.gov.jm/attachments/article/339/The%20Data%20Protection%20Act,%202020.pdf.

[16] *Data Protection Act*, 2020, sections 74, https://japarliament.gov.jm/attachments/article/339/The%20Data%20Protection%20Act,%202020.pdf.

[17] Data Protection Act 2019, https://www.odpc.go.ke/dpa-act/, section 39.

[18] Data Protection Act 2022, section 13. https://www.esccom.org.sz/legislation/DATA%20PROTECTION%20ACT.pdf.

[19] Data Protection Act 2013, section 19, http://www.nic.ls/lsnic/community/policies/Data_Protection_Act_2011_Lesotho.pdf.

states, is another addition to the retention laws. In practice though, what does the consent fully constitute? Does it allow an organisation to retain the data indefinitely? Has the organisation communicated to the data subject what consent will ultimately mean?

On examining the retention laws of **Malawi**, it appears that a limited approach has been taken to address the issue of data storage. Although sections 23 and 30[20] require data to be retained for a period, no specific length of time is mentioned. This is in and of itself a reoccurring theme in the laws that have been examined. It is argued that this issue alone merits further attention and research. More can be done to provide timelines for data to be retained. In my view, sensitive data could have a limited retention period attached. The respective states all have defined what constitutes data. Some jurisdictions have gone further and provided a clear definition of sensitive personal data, while others have a general catch-all definition. In **Malaysia,** section 10 of the PDPA requires that personal data shall not be kept for longer than is necessary.[21] The PDPA does not stipulate the time frame allowed for storage of the personal data, but leaves it to the discretion of the data user. Once the data is no longer required, it must be destroyed or permanently deleted. The data user is required to take all reasonable steps to ensure that all personal data is destroyed permanently. In addition, the *Personal Data Protection Regulations 2013* and *Personal Data Protection Standards 2015,* require personal data collection forms to be destroyed within a period of 14 days, unless such forms have "legal value" in connection with the commercial transaction.[22] Data users are also required to dispose of personal data when it has been inactive for a period of 24 months. Generally, the under the revenue laws of Malaysia, legal documents must be destroyed after six years and seven years, depending on the nature of the data.[23]

Mauritius provides for storage retention under section 21. In this case, data is to be kept for no longer than is necessary. In regressing the retention of data, section 39(7) requires that a controller ensure there are time limits not only established for the rectification, erasure or restriction of processing of personal data, but also or for a periodic review of the need for the storage of the personal data.[24] However, the time limits are not specified. On the other hand, **New Zealand,** under privacy principle 9, requires that an organisationnot keep personal information for longer than it is required for the purpose for which it may lawfully be used.[25] Similar to all other jurisdiction examined, there is no specified time for data retention. **Nigeria** has

[20] Data Protection Bill 2021, section 23, 30, https://digmap.pppc.mw/wp-content/uploads/2022/03/Malawi-Data-Protection-Bill-final-draft-210630-.pdf.

[21] Personal Data Protection Act 2010, section 10, https://www.kkmm.gov.my/pdf/Personal%20Data%20Protection%20Act%202010.pdf.

[22] Malaysia, Personal Data Protection Regulations 2013 and Personal Data Protection Standards 2015.

[23] Malaysia, Personal Data Protection Regulations 2013 and Personal Data Protection Standards 2015.

[24] Data Protection Act 2017, section 39(7), https://dataprotection.govmu.org/Documents/DPA_2017_updated.pdf?csf=1&e=0rlrff.

[25] Privacy Act 2020, Principle 9 https://www.privacy.org.nz/privacy-act-2020/privacy-principles/

no retention provisions apart from that in section 39, which requires the controller or processor to ensure that the stored data has safeguards for security, integrity and confidentiality.[26] However, there is no timeframe specified for the retention of data. In the African nation of **Rwanda**, Article 52[27] requires a level of data storage retention although no retention period is specified. Similar to the other nation states examined in this section**, Singapore** under section 25 pf the PDPA expresses a level of retention for personal data. There is no timeframe specifying the retention period, and it is quite open to allow businesses to retain the data for as long as is necessary.[28] This is intended for business or legal purposes. The other nation states examined do not specify the level of retention pertaining to legal or business purposes. It is, by and large, open to interpretation and in this country, clarification is required.

In a recent development, the retention of data has been hotly debated. For instance, proponents indicate that the storage of data is necessary in order to offer high-quality searches to users. Critics allege that any benefits from these "network effects" in searches are minimal and are outweighed by a loss of privacy and data security.[29] In reinforcing the argument put forward by this book, it is noted that 'data retention is deeply intertwined with legal developments in privacy and data security'.[30] Lesley Chiou and Catherine Tucker discuss the above in the context of antitrust issues associated with the commercial activity that data is generating. Importantly, the position taken by Chiou and Tucker further confirms the commercial relationship between the digital economy and data, and its security. Therefore, cyber security has great commercial value. On that basis, making the case for international arbitration further underscores the research this book provides. Further, they point out that 'when establishing the legal framework for data retention, policymakers must weigh the benefits and costs of data retention to firms, private citizens, and society, so it is important to establish first whether and how much benefit exists from the practice of data retention'.[31]

Centrally, the retention laws do not provide a time period. Arguably, this is not by accident. It gives an organisation the flexibility to determine it stores and re-uses the data. However, with the continuing increase in the number of data breaches, a time period should be imposed. However, more evidence is needed to determine when or where the data is most vulnerable? During transmission or during storage? Once determined, the laws can respond accordingly.

---

[26] Data Protection Regulation 2022, section 39 https://ndpb.gov.ng/Files/Nigeria_Data_Protection_Bill.pdf.

[27] Law n°058/2021 of 13/10/2021 relating to the protection of personal data and privacy (the Data Protection Law), Article 52, https://www.minijust.gov.rw/fileadmin/user_upload/Minijust/Publications/Official_Gazette/_2021_Official_Gazettes/October/OG_Special_of_15.10.2021_Amakuru_bwite.pdf.

[28] Personal Data Protection Act 2012, section 25, https://sso.agc.gov.sg/Act/PDPA2012?ProvIds=P16-#pr26-.

[29] sley Chiou, Catherine Tucker, Search Engines and Data Retention: Implication for Privacy and Antitrust, Working Paper 23815, National Bureau of Economic Research, (2017) p 2.

[30] Ibid.

[31] Ibid.

Moreover, Chiou and Tucker in their study found that:

> restrictions to data retention provoked by privacy concerns may impose fewer costs if directed at limits on the recency of data (right to be forgotten-policies). More generally, the length of data retention has become an issue in this debate over privacy. The question is whether the benefits of privacy (less data retention) for consumers outweigh any potential costs to consumers (lower quality search results). Our study suggests that retaining data for shorter periods of time does not lead to lower quality searches; in other words, we do not find a cost to privacy in our setting.[32]

Significantly, although this study was completed in 2017, it is excellent and continues to be relevant. However, further study is needed to understand the implications of AI and other emerging technologies for both the retention of data and its susceptibility to illegal access and misuse.

For **Sri Lanka**, section 9 requires every controller to ensure that personal data that is being processed is retained in a form which permits identification of data subjects only for such period as may be necessary or required for the purposes for which such personal data is processed. Yet again, no timeframe has been established. In **South Africa's** data laws, section 14 states that records of 'personal information must not be retained any longer than is necessary for achieving the purpose for which the information was collected or subsequently processed'.[33] However, there are exceptions that include, 'retention of the record is required or authorised by law; the responsible party reasonably requires the record for lawful purposes related to its functions or activities; retention of the record is required by a contract between the parties thereto; or the data subject or a competent person where the data subject is a child has consented to the retention of the record'.[34]

Various approaches are taken by Commonwealth nations in the Americas. For example, **Saint Kitts and Nevis** provides for data retention according to Principle 11 which deals with the processing of data. On the other side, this is based on the premise that the data not be kept for longer than is necessary.[35] Again, this is a very broad application of this principle. This begs the question: after what period of time is the retention of data no longer necessary? None of the laws examined have established a time after which data must be destroyed. This, in my view, is an area that needs to be reconciled. With the increased sophistication of security breaches and ransomware intended to force organisations or businesses to pay for the return or destruction of stolen data, there is a need for time limits to be imposed on the retention of data. In **Saint Vincent and The Grenadines,** section 14[36] enables the Minister to make regulations or establish guidelines for data retention, although there are no specific provisions within the data laws for the retention of data.

[32] Ibid, p. 19.

[33] Protection of Personal Information 2013, section 14, https://www.gov.za/documents/protection-personal-information-act.

[34] Ibid.

[35] Data Protection Act, 5 of 2018, Principles 11 https://www.theinformationcollective.com/dpl/st-kitts-data-protection-act.

[36] Privacy Act 2003, section 14 https://www.theinformationcollective.com/dpl/st-vincent-and-the-grenadines-the-privacy-act.

Noteworthy is that in **Tanzania,** sections 22 to 33 of the 2022 laws specify the requirements for data storage. More clarification is needed on the Tanzanian laws. However, there is no timeframe specified.[37] In the country of **Togo**, although there are data-storage requirements, there is little governance in respect to retention. Moreover, in **Trinidad-Tobago,** data can be retained by a public body for a set period of time. This time will be established by the relevant Minister,[38] and will allow data subjects to obtain access to their data. While in **Uganda,** it is asserted that they have developed a strong level of retention laws. Centrally, section 18 requires that retention can be specified by contract, or a data subject's consent, and where required by other laws of the state. However, there is no specified time limit for such data retention.

Moreover, there are a number of exemptions pertaining to data retention; these are usually associated with national security, public revenue, or a court or tribunal. In the **UK**'s the *Watson* case, the Court found that the scope of the UK's data retention laws was too wide and incompatible with European Union law.[39] The UK Court stated that:

> The claimants in three separately issued claims, which we heard together, apply for judicial review of the data retention powers in section 1 of the Data Retention and Investigatory Powers Act 2014 (IP Act). Mr Brice and Mr Lewis, the claimants for whom Mr Drabble QC appeared, are concerned about the width of the powers to retain and gain access to their data on a number of grounds, including (but not limited to) the confidentiality of communications with solicitors. Mr Davis and Mr Watson, who are joint claimants in case CO/3794/2014, do so as members of the House of Commons who share those general concerns but also in addition have particular concerns about the confidentiality of communications to and from constituents. Mr Davis is Conservative MP for Haltemprice and Howden; Mr Watson is Labour MP for West Bromwich East.[40]

This matter was before the court when the UK was still a member of the EU, and therefore the EU data laws were applied. While at the time of enacting the IP Act in 2016, the government maintained that the IP Act was compatible with the ECHR,[41] the UK government following the *Watson* case made changes to the IP Act and introduced the Data Retention and Acquisition Regulations 2018. These regulations increased the threshold for accessing communications data only for the purposes of serious crimes defined as offences for which an offender can be sentenced to imprisonment for a term of 12 months or more, and required that authorities consult an independent Investigatory Powers Commissioner before requesting data. After

---

[37] Fatma Songoro, Brief Highlight and Analysis of the Tanzania Data Protection Bill, 2002, October 2022, https://victoryattorneys.co.tz/insights-brief-highlight-and-analysis-of-the-tanzania-data-protection-bill-2022/.

[38] Data Protection Act 2011, section 6, 30, 40, 45, https://rgd.legalaffairs.gov.tt/laws2/Alphabetical_List/lawspdfs/22.04.pdf.

[39] *Tele2 Sverige AB v Post- ochtelestyrelsen and Secretary of State for the Home Department v. Watson* (C 203/15; C-698/15).

[40] [2015] EWHC 2092 (Admin), para 1.

[41] Home Office, 'Investigatory Powers Bill European Convention On Human Rights Memorandum' (2015) https://www.gov.uk/government/uploads/system/uploads/attachment_data/file/473763/European_Convention_on_Human_Rights_Memorandum.pdf.

this case (but not because of it), the UK left the EU, although in 2022 it received an Adequacy Decision[42] from the EU confirming that its national data laws had adequacy. This is because the data laws had not been changed, and EU data laws were retained and fully integrated in UK's national law. Finally, in **Zambia,** data retention refers to a process of retention of personal data for a specified purpose for a defined period.[43] Yet again, the length of the data-retention period has not been specified.

6.2 Conclusion

The issue of data retention has become another complex area of laws, when viewed transnationally. This chapter has limited its comparison to the legislative provisions of the respective states rather than embarking on a scholarly discussion of the topic. This is because, by and large, data retention is a matter of practicality, and a large number of organisations have addressed the legal concerns through their own policies and procedures.

Notwithstanding the above, the brief comparison has demonstrated how common themes of terminology have emerged. Some states have placed a greater focus on the retention of sensitive data, where it has been defined by that state. This would not work in a jurisdiction that has not defined sensitive data. On the other hand, in some states, retention has been restricted to data that is stored for business or legal purposes, while others have specified a public body (e.g., government).

Essentially, states vary in regard to the terminology they use to the retention period. For example, some states use the term 'no longer than is necessary' as the general requirement. On the other side, other states use the term 'longer than is required'. While it is argued that these are similar, and it is left open for the court to decide what constitutes a period of time, it does leave the period of retention open to interpretation.

Nonetheless, it is argued that as the issue of retention becomes more important as cyber intrusions continue to rise, entities may be forced to retain the data for as short a period as possible. This is against the backdrop of fully understanding the life cycle of data retention, from the time it is collected to the time is it either destroyed or deleted. Organisations need to fully understand this cycle in order to make good decisions about data that should and should not be retained for extended periods of time.

---

[42] Information Commissioner Office, Adequacy, https://ico.org.uk/for-organisations/dp-at-the-end-of-the-transition-period/data-protection-and-the-eu-in-detail/adequacy/.

[43] Data Protection Act 2021, section 2 https://www.parliament.gov.zm/sites/default/files/documents/acts/Act%20No.%203%20The%20Data%20Protection%20Act%202021_0.pdf.

Given all of the above, it is argued that the Commonwealth should undertake a specific research project on data retention and the future issues that might arise from technology advancements such as artificial intelligence. A research project needs to determine whether there should be a time limit for the retention for data. If taken up and there is legislative reform, it would provide another layer of trust in data laws. If data retention is subject to a definite time restriction, this will constrain cyber-attacks and the illegal collection and use of data.

Chapter 7
Localisation

7.1 Introduction

Data localisation has been a new addition to the data laws over the past decade. It is a sovereign response by nation states to ensure that their citizens' data is stored on the territory of the state. Put another way, data localisation requires entities in both the private sector and government sector to store the personal data of its citizen in country. However, to date, the localisation laws are restricted and have not been widely adopted throughout the world. In 2022, it was reported that.

> …75 percent of all countries have implemented some level of data localization rules. These have major implications for the IT footprints, data governance, and data architectures of companies, as well as their interactions with local regulators. Localization rules are generally intended to prevent cybercrimes (such as identify theft), to promote local economies (for instance, by creating jobs), and, perhaps most significantly, to address rising concerns about privacy. That is often the most contentious issue, and different jurisdictions are reaching different conclusions about how to balance it against the desire of companies to leverage data for their own commercial interest.[1]

Hence, governments and regulators are facing a potential significant dilemma in relation to the localisation of data storage versus the free flow of data to strengthen the digital economy and promote national economic growth. This chapter demonstrates how members of the Commonwealth have taken a very restrictive approach to responding to the growing call by some countries for data to be stored locally. Neither the MBP or the MBPPI[2] contain requirements for data localisation. I believe

[1] Mckinsey & Company, Localization of data privacy regulations creates competitive opportunities, 2022, https://www.mckinsey.com/capabilities/risk-and-resilience/our-insights/localization-of-data-privacy-regulations-creates-competitive-opportunities.

[2] The Commonwealth, Model Privacy Bill, Office of Civil and Criminal Justice Reform, 2017, https://www.asianlaws.org/gcld/cyberlawdb/COM/P15370_9_ROL_Model_Privacy_Bill_0.pdf.

R. Walters, *Cybersecurity and Data Laws of the Commonwealth*,
https://doi.org/10.1007/978-981-99-3935-0_7

that this issue should be reconciled, and the Commonwealth should include data localisation provisions in both the MBP and MBPPI.

The OECD highlights how the concept of data localisation has increasingly become a tool of control for nation states. As it develops, it is contrary to the Open Data concept espoused by nation states such as the UK. The OECD notes that with the 'growing cross-border data flows, governments have been updating and adapting their data policies, leading to a rising number of cross-border data regulations. To date, much of the work in this area has focused on measures that condition the movement of data across borders, with less analysis on policies that mandate that data be stored locally—also known as local storage requirements or data localisation'.[3] To date, across the Commonwealth, relatively few nation states have specified localisation requirements in their data laws. Most states have chosen not to establish these laws.

Niether, **Australia, Bahamas, Barbados, Belize, Botswana, Canada, Cyprus, Gabon, Jamacia, Lesotho, Malaysia, Malta, Mauritius, New Zealand, Nigeria, Singapore, Sri Lanka, South Africa, Saint Luca, Saint Kitts** and **Nevis, Saint Vincent and The Grenadines, The Kingdom of Eswatini, Togo, Trinidad-Tobago, Uganda,** and the **United Kingdom** provide for the right to data localisation. It is not clear whether **Tanzania** will establish localisation requirements. However, **Australia** does require health and income tax data to be stored within the territory of the nation state.[4] An emerging trend is that indigenous populations are using data localisation rules to strengthen their own position and opportunities within their own states. For example, the data sovereignty rights are exercised by the Mauri indigenous people of New Zealand over any Mauri data recognised in New Zealand municipal law and international law.[5] The developments are another extension of the rights of data subjects in terms of protecting local indigenous communities. Whether this will extend to other Commonwealth states is yet to be seen. On the other hand, there are current data localisation provisions specific to the finance sector in **Bangladesh**. However, it is outside the scope of this book to examine these. It is expected that localisation provisions will be included in the proposed new data laws. It is not clear whether **Ghana's** law requires data to be stored locally. **Antigua and Barbuda** do not have any data localisation requirements. Nonetheless, the development of data localization laws 'usually comes in the form of requirements to store data domestically or restrictions on cross-border data flows, acts as a barrier to digital trade. For

The Commonwealth, Model Bill on the Protection of Personal Information https://www.asianlaws.org/gcld/cyberlawdb/COM/P15370_6_ROL_Model_Bill_Protection_Personal_Information_2.pdf.

[3] Organisation for Economic Co-operatiin and Development, A Preliminary Mapping of Data Localisation Measures, 2022, p. 4. https://www.oecd-ilibrary.org/docserver/c5ca3fed-en.pdf?expires=1670982521&id=id&accname=guest&checksum=FBF12C508653813FF2BB48E0859E0C1B.

[4] My Health Records Act 2012, section 77. Privacy Act 1988, section 20Q(3). C2014C00076.

[5] Nwachukwu T. Obi II The Balkanisation of the Internet: Data Nationalism in the European Union and its Effects on the Development of Technology, 2022, p. 10, http://arno.uvt.nl/show.cgi?fid=157767 The United Nations, Declaration on the Rights of Indigenous Peoples of the General Assembly, A/RES/61/295, Articles; 1, 2, 3, 7, 8, 9, 11, 12, 15, 16, 21, 25, 27, 31, 39.

example, data localisation requirements have hampered the development of mobile money- enabled remittance services, resulting in added costs for migrant workers and their families. Since modern data protection laws often put in place safeguards for the transfer of personal data beyond national borders, they can effectively operate as data localization requirements'.[6]

The geopolitical influences on the development of localisation laws have attracted great attention over the last 5 years. To underscore this position, in 2020, Jennifer Daskal and Justin Sherman summarised the evolving developments of data localisation thus:

> Put simply, once-forceful calls for a "free and open" internet are increasingly being replaced by efforts to protect, control, and manage the internet and its related risks, often in a geographically bordered way. These and many other measures are all classifiable as forms of data nationalism—defined loosely as the effort by nation-states to ensure control over data for a range of security, privacy, normative, and economic-based reasons. The measures are being initiated by countries both democratic and authoritarian; by countries with both advanced economies and emerging market economies; by countries located in the north and south, east and west. And the costs are potentially many: to the economy, to security, to privacy, and to the balance of powers geopolitically.[7]

The concept of data localisation is challenging the notion of the free flow of transnational data. It is placing government control at the centre of data governance, particularly in regard to having data stored within the country. Daskal and Sherman further note that:

> The purpose, nature, and implications of these moves toward data nationalism vary significantly. Some are done in pursuit of national security and law enforcement objectives. Others are motivated by data privacy and consumer protection concerns. Several are a response to perceived foreign interference threats and flows of unwanted information. Many look to bolster domestic innovation and local industry. In the majority of cases, a combination of motivations overlaps in difficult- to-disentangle ways. The nature and effect of the measures vary significantly as well. Even data localization efforts are not all the same. Some require copies of particular data to be stored locally; others mandate that data cannot leave the jurisdiction at all. Both have costs, but the nature of the costs differs.[8]

Arguably, this chapter confirms the position taken by Daskal and Sherman in that the different approaches taken by Commonwealth nations is significant. Data localisation, in part, dilutes the ability for data to provide its full economic benefit in and across the digital economy. This is because there are restrictions on where it can be stored.

---

[6] Amelia Bleeker, Data Protection in The Caribbean, 2020, p. 8, https://repositorio.cepal.org/bitstream/handle/11362/47155/1/FOCUSIssue1Jan-Mar2020.pdf.

[7] Jennifer Daskal, Justin Sherman data Nationalism on the Rise: The Global push for State Controlled Data, 2020, p. 3, https://datacatalyst.org/wp-content/uploads/2020/06/Data-Nationalism-on-the-Rise.pdf.

[8] Ibid.

In **India**, data localisation, also referred to as Data Nationalism, is posing a challenge to the free flow of data across international borders.[9] It enables nation states to significantly restrict the storage of data in country. However, although it is fast becoming an international issue, it is very much in its infancy and should not be viewed as a barrier to achieving data adequacy between two countries. In India, no firm decision has been made about the data localisation rules that may be established. The impact on large, medium and small businesses from the use of data transnationally is not fully understood in India. It remains to be seen whether India has included a localisation requirement in its specific data laws when they are implemented. The **Kenyan** Data Protection (General) Regulations 2021 were established to provide for general enforcement of the Act and cover the rights of a 'data subject, obligations to uphold these rights by data controllers and processors, and specifics on how to implement these rights are detailed. Importantly, they also provide for a level of data localisation limited to processing'.[10] That is, the Regulations require the localisation of processing in Kenya by controllers and processors who are processing data for the public good.[11] Furthermore, localisation requires that processing be done through a server in Kenya and that a copy of the data be stored in a server located in Kenya. However, **Rwanda** has no direct provisions for data localisation, although under Article 50, a data controller or processor must store personal data in Rwanda. This localisation rule also extends to include a registration that has been approved by the Authority to enable that storage outside[12] the state. Similarly, **Zambia** has no broad

---

[9] Reserve Bank of India (RBI), Storage of Payment System Data, (RBI, April 6, 2018) https://rbi.org.in/scripts/NotificationUser.aspx?Mode=0&Id=11244: Reserve Bank of India (RBI), Statement on Developmental and Regulatory Policies, (RBI, April 5, 2018), https://rbi.org.in/Scripts/BS_PressReleaseDisplay.aspx?prid=43574: Reserve Bank of India (RBI), First Bi-monthly Monetary Policy Statement, 2018–2019, (RBI, April 10, 2018), https://rbi.org.in/scripts/BS_ViewBulletin.aspx?Id=17479; Reserve Bank of India (RBI), Storage of Payment System Data, (RBI, April 6, 2018), https://m.rbi.org.in/Scripts/FAQView.aspx?Id=130 (https://rbi.org.in/scripts/NotificationUser.aspx?Mode=0&Id=11244) (https://rbi.org.in/Scripts/BS_PressReleaseDisplay.aspx?prid=43574) (https://rbi.org.in/scripts/BS_ViewBulletin.aspx?Id=17479) (https://m.rbi.org.in/Scripts/FAQView.aspx?Id=130) These laws will need to be considered when undertaking an process of assessment for cross-border transfers and adequacy, Public Records Act, 1993; United Access License for Telecom Service Providers, 2004; National Data Sharing and Accessibility Policy (NDSAP), 2012; The Companies Act, 2013; MeghRaj Initiative; National Telecom MDM Roadmap, 2015; FDI Policy, 2017; The IRDAI (Outsourcing of Activities by Indian Insurers) Regulation, 2017; Reserve Bank of India Storage of Payment System Data, 2018 and 2019; and Draft National E-Commerce Policy.

[10] Kenyan Data Protection (General) Regulations 2021, https://www.odpc.go.ke/regulations/data-protection-general-regulations-2021/.

[11] Kenyan Data Protection (General) Regulations 2021, regulation 25, https://www.odpc.go.ke/regulations/data-protection-general-regulations-2021/.

[12] Law n°058/2021 of 13/10/2021 relating to the protection of personal data and privacy (the Data Protection Law), Article 50, https://www.minijust.gov.rw/fileadmin/user_upload/Minijust/Publications/Official_Gazette/_2021_Official_Gazettes/October/OG_Special_of_15.10.2021_Amakuru_bwite.pdf.

data localisation requirements, although section 70(3)[13] takes a narrow approach to ensuring that any sensitive data is stored locally.

Nevertheless, while there are a number of nation states that have no data localisation laws at a national level, what has emerged over the past eight years is the inclusion of such provisions in multilateral and bilateral trade agreements.

Table 7.1 shows the current trade, economic, digital agreements that Commonwealth member states have established with other members of the Commonwealth and with non-members. It does not include investment agreements.

This new development regarding data localisation is an important means of controlling data about which little has been written. On the other hand, and while data localisation rules are being included in the agreements listed above, they may not necessarily reflect the localisation rules within the respective states data laws. Singapore is a case in point as it takes a very open approach to data governance and has no localisation rules. Singapore has a digital strategy[14] that ensures its growth as a regional technology hub in South East Asia. This is an area requiring further research to compare the current provisions of each agreement. This could be a priority project for the Commonwealth. It would enable the Commonwealth to develop model principles or law to ensure that future trade, economic and investment agreements are addressing data localisation needs appropriately. This is more important than ever in a highly contested economic, security and geopolitical time of tension.

Essentially, the OECD has placed data localisation laws under three categories. First is the flow of data with no restrictions applied by localisation laws. Second is storage conditions, pertaining only to the storage of data. This narrow category is in contrast to the third category requiring that storage and processing be coupled together and requiring a level of localisation. Additionally, the OECD notes that (Fig. 7.1):

> Data localisation measures that are in place today vary widely, often in relation to their underlying policy objectives; the sectors or types of data targeted; and the wider legal and policy environment. In addition, even within a particular country, or regions within countries, different types of data localisation measures can apply to different types of data (personal data, health data, telecommunication data, banking or payment processing data; insurance data; or satellite and mapping data to name but a few). There are also cases where data localisation requirements are aimed at less well- defined data categories such as "important data" or "critical data" and operators such as "critical information infrastructure operators" or "network operators".[15]

[13] Data Protection Act 2021, section 70(3) https://www.parliament.gov.zm/sites/default/files/documents/acts/Act%20No.%203%20The%20Data%20Protection%20Act%202021_0.pdf.

[14] Singapore, Digital Strategy, https://www.smartnation.gov.sg/about-smart-nation/digital-government/.

[15] Organisation for Economic Development and Cooperation, A Preliminary Mapping of Data Localisation Measures, 2022, p. 6, https://www.oecd-ilibrary.org/docserver/c5ca3fed-en.pdf?expires=1671421638&id=id&accname=guest&checksum=450EE555D293F4242A5AA6BDB3B69A17.

Table 7.1 Trade, economic and digital agreements[16] with data localisation provisions of commonwealth countries

Name	Type	Parties	Year
Comprehensive and progressive trans-pacific partnership agreement	Free trade agreement	Australia, Brunei Canada, New Zealand, Singapore Note: there are other nation states party to this agreement that are not members of the Commonwealth	2016
Updated Singapore–Australia free trade agreement	Free trade agreement	Australia–Singapore	2016
Free trade agreement between the democratic socialist republic of Sri Lanka and the Republic of Singapore	Free trade agreement	Singapore–Sri Lanka	2018
Australia–Peru free trade agreement	Free trade agreement	Australia–Peru	2018
Comprehensive and progressive agreement for trans-pacific partnership	Free trade agreement	Australia, Brunei, Canada, New Zealand, Singapore Note: there are other nation states that are not members of the Commonwealth that are party to this agreement	2018
United States–Mexico–Canada agreement	Free trade agreement	Canada Note: there are other nation states that are not members of the Commonwealth that are party to this agreement	2018
Indonesia–Australia comprehensive economic partnership agreement	Economic partnership agreement	Australia Note: Indonesia is not a member of the Commonwealth	2019
Australia–Singapore digital economy agreement	Economic partnership agreement	Australia, Singapore	2020
Digital economy partnership agreement ("DEPA") between Singapore, Chile and New Zealand	Economic partnership agreement	Singapore New Zealand Note: Chile is not a member of the Commonwealth	2020
Regional comprehensive economic partnership ("RCEP")	Economic partnership agreement	Australia, Brunei, India, Malaysia, Singapore Note: the other parties to this agreement are not members of the Commonwealth	2020
Trade and cooperation agreement between the European Union and the European Atomic Energy Community, of the One Part, and the United Kingdom of Great Britain and Northern Ireland, of the other part	Free Trade Agreement	European Union (Malta–Cyprus), United Kingdom	2020

(continued)

[16] Organisation for Economic Development and Cooperation, A Preliminary Mapping of Data Localisation Measures, 2022, https://www.oecd-ilibrary.org/docserver/c5ca3fed-en.pdf?expires=1671421638&id=id&accname=guest&checksum=450EE555D293F4242A5AA6BDB3B69A17.

Table 7.1 (continued)

Name	Type	Parties	Year
United Kingdom–Australia	Free trade agreement	United Kingdom Australia	2021
Korea–Singapore digital partnership agreement	Digital economic agreement	Singapore Note: Korea is not a member of the Commonwealth	2021
United Kingdom–New Zealand free trade agreement	Free trade agreement	United Kingdom New Zealand	2022
United Kingdom–Singapore digital economy agreement	Free trade agreement	United Kingdom–Singapore	2022

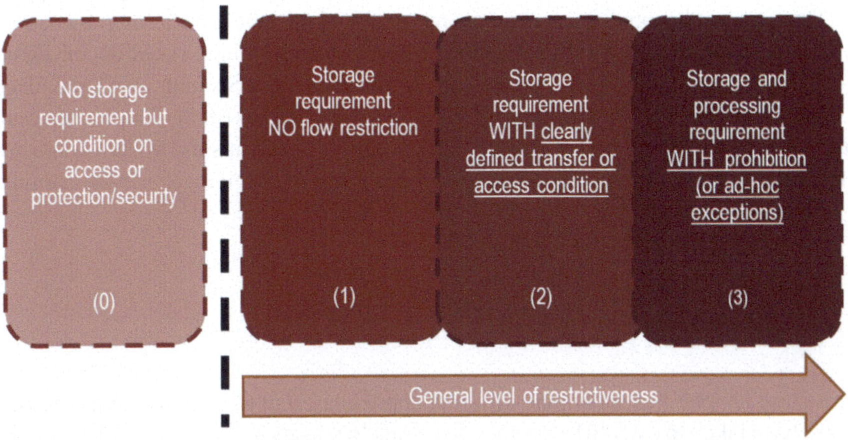

Fig. 7.1 OECD typology[17] and three categories of data localisation measures and requirements for data flows

Notwithstanding the above, data localisation laws are often seen as a barrier to data flows and the expansion of the digital economy. However, it is argued that they should be viewed as a set of rules that are part of the overall world trading mechanisms. Simply put, data localization measures are subject to rules under international trade agreements, particularly the *General Agreement on Trade in Services* (GATS) as they affect the 'production, distribution, marketing, sale and delivery' of various internet and internet-enabled services.[18] Neha Mishra makes the following important point:

> Applying GATS to data localisation measures raises several questions such as the general exception (GATS Art. XIV) and the national security exception (GATS Art. XIV bis). The absence of international consensus on internet governance issues coupled with the dated

[17] Organisation for Economic Development and Cooperation, A Preliminary Mapping of Data Localisation Measures, 2022, p. 7, https://www.oecd-ilibrary.org/docserver/c5ca3fed-en.pdf?expires=1671421638&id=id&accname=guest&checksum=450EE555D293F4242A5AA6BDB3B69A17.

[18] Neha Mishra, Privacy, Cybersecurity, and GATS Article XIV: A New Frontier for Trade and Internet Regulation? World Trade Review, 19(3) (2020), p. 343.

> nature of GATS will pose complex problems if disputes on data localization measures are brought before the WTO. To a certain extent, GATS Art. XIV can be creatively and thoughtfully applied to reduce protectionist data localization barriers while preserving a country's right to regulate on grounds of cybersecurity and privacy. However, the application of GATS Art. XIV entails extensive assessment of complex technical issues to balance free flow of data with legitimate public policy concerns. In assessing such issues, WTO tribunals can consider a range of technical and factual evidence to assess the technical efficacy of data localization measures in achieving privacy and cybersecurity. However, as the broader internet regulatory framework is deeply divided between multistakeholder—transnational internet governance norms and domestic public policy, this assessment is not always straightforward. Ultimately, the role of international trade law in data flow regulation is circumscribed by the lack of binding norms in internet governance.[19]

Thus, as data becomes even more economically viable as a means whereby nation states can grow their respective economies, one of three things could occur. First, the current approach to data localisation remains the same. Second, over time, data localisation laws are diluted and ultimately become non-existent. Third, they and strengthened and more nation states establish similar mechanisms. Mishra confirms the commercial importance of data. This needs a level of vigilance over the coming decades.

7.2 Conclusion

This short chapter has shown the different approaches that Commonwealth member states have taken to establish (or otherwise) data localisation provisions. The concept of data localisation is new and has been formulated for geopolitical purposes: that is, to ensure that their citizens' personal data remains within the territory. As demonstrated, the large majority of Commonwealth states have not adopted any localisation laws.

Data localisation does restrict the movement of data, which ultimately can have an impact on the growth and development of the digital economy. That is because the digital economy needs data to flow freely across all international borders. On the other hand, localisation rules may be of some benefit, particularly in enforcement situations where the unauthorised access to data is in breach of cybersecurity law.

Arguably, the more transnational the data becomes, the more complex and difficult it is for regulators to track and investigate the data breaches. As demonstrated later in this book, the criminal laws pertaining to cybersecurity are also significantly fragmented, and differ across the Commonwealth member states.

Broadly speaking, data localisation mandates that the storage of data be undertaken within a certain territory or geographical location. In other situations, there might be specific elements of data, such as health data, that must be stored on the territory of the state.

[19] Neha Mishra, Privacy, Cybersecurity, and GATS Article XIV: A New Frontier for Trade and Internet Regulation? World Trade Review, 19(3) (2020), p. 343.

Moreover, there are various interests involved in localisation, apart from geopolitics, that include data protection, privacy, the digital economy, crypto assets, patents, intellectual property, health, education and, more broadly, general trade. Thus, having a clear definition of personal data does help to provide stronger control over that data. It also enables states to stipulate more appropriate localisation restrictions.

Hence, it is argued that the Commonwealth could develop a project on data localisation, and ensure that countries fully understand the economic and social benefits associated with localisation restrictions, as well as their drawbacks. Such a project could and should also include the benefits of protecting this type of data for local indigenous peoples. Finally, the number of digital economic agreements is increasing and they are establishing data localisation rules, outside of the national laws. Therefore, this area of research is highly important to the future digital economy.

Chapter 8
Data Flows: International Transfer

8.1 Introduction

In regard to cross-border data flows, while not an emerging area in practice, nation states have begun to take more notice of their beneficial impact on the economy. Essentially, this chapter reveals that a number of Commonwealth member countries have not included in their laws any specific provisions for cross-border data flows. This chapter will draw on earlier work undertaken in relation to transnational data flows.[1] Put another way:

> the ubiquitous exchange of data across borders has given rise to concerns by governments and citizens about some of the negative side effects of so much information – in particular personal data or personally identifiable information – being collected, transferred and used, often without the knowledge of those individuals to whom the data refer. For some countries, concerns related to privacy – but also in some cases, national security – have led to growing calls for deeper and more widespread regulation of the Internet and its underlying data flows. As a result, governments are updating data-related regulations and increasingly conditioning the transfer of data across borders or requiring that data be stored locally.[2]

---

[1] Robert Walters, *The Digital Economy and International Trade: Transnational Data Flows Regulation,* WoltersKluwer (2022), Chap. 1.

[2] Francesca Casalini, Javier López González (2019), *"Trade and Cross-Border Data Flows",* OECD Trade Policy Papers, No. 220, (2019) OECD Publishing, Paris. http://dx.doi.org/10.1787/b2023a47-en.

R. Walters, *Cybersecurity and Data Laws of the Commonwealth*,
https://doi.org/10.1007/978-981-99-3935-0_8

The amount of transnational flow of personal data cannot be underestimated. It has been prolific in banking and finance for decades, and in the tourism industry, among many other sectors. However, today, technology makes it possible for this data to be transferred to most places in the world within seconds. The MBPPI takes a limited approach to the use or disclosure of personal information outside its country of origin, according to sections 15 and 16. On the other hand, the MBP[3] makes no mention of cross-border data flows.

In my view, this chapter is one of the most important in this book. It relates directly to international trade, and it is the provisions and responses embedded in the national laws of Commonwealth countries that unlock investment opportunities in the future. Data flows have to be secure transnationally because they can be subject to significant cyber breaches. While this chapter briefly considers the international rules of trade that benefit data flows, it does not provide a comprehensive account of these rules. Rather, the chapter demonstrate how the states being examined have dealt with the issue of data flows within their respective data laws. It is my view that this is another area where the Commonwealth should expand its work by, at least, including these important provisions in the MBPPI. A limitation of this chapter is that it lacks judicial decisions related to international data transfers. Nonetheless, cross-border data flows are connected to cybersecurity issues and are vulnerable to cybercrime.

Today, the global mobility of data has exceeded all expectations and has become a central element of the digital economy. Simply put, they 'do not recognise geographical borders, and these data flows have made us more interconnected than ever before'.[4] However, governing or regulating the cross-border transfer of data has become very challenging. This chapter will reveal that some nation states do not have any provisions whatsoever, while other jurisdictions have comprehensively regulated this activity. Sam Sacks and Justin Sherman summarise the interconnectedness of data governance under three key regulatory areas:

1. *Economic growth/innovation:* objectives to create and access large databases of data for research and development of data-intensive technologies like machine learning/artificial intelligence, as well as for cross-border transactions and ecommerce;
2. *National security/law enforcement:* a government's interest in ensuring access to data for purposes of domestic and international security; other governments' converse concerns about misuse of that data; and desires to protect data against foreign collection; and

---

[3] The Commonwealth, Model Privacy Bill, Office of Civil and Criminal Justice Reform, 2017, https://www.asianlaws.org/gcld/cyberlawdb/COM/P15370_9_ROL_Model_Privacy_Bill_0.pdf The Commonwealth, Model Bill on the Protection of Personal Information https://www.asianlaws.org/gcld/cyberlawdb/COM/P15370_6_ROL_Model_Bill_Protection_Personal_Information_2.pdf.

[4] Australian Government, Office of the Australian Information Commissioner, https://www.oaic.gov.au/privacy/the-privacy-act/review-of-the-privacy-act/privacy-act-review-issues-paper-submission/part-8.

3. *Content moderation policies and practices:* competing demands on what is and is not permissible content, and possible ways to manage that conflict while also ensuring the free flow of data.[5]

Sacks and Sherman assert that these three areas utilise 'tools or "levers" that set the terms around how data is collected, used, transferred, and stored'.[6] More specifically, in regard to cross-border data flows, the authors state that on the one hand, governments support data flows across borders—or conversely, how governments restrict those flows—is a major focal point across each of the three aforementioned areas of data governance. For example, the term "data localization", appears frequently in policy discussions in reference to restrictions on the ability of firms to transfer data from domestic sources to foreign countries—in other words, the opposite of free data flow.[7] Essentially, this chapter reveals that a number of Commonwealth member countries have not included specific cross-border data flows provisions within the law.

Beginning in the 1970s in Europe, trans-border data flow regulation has spread around the world.[8] A number of instruments regulating trans-border data flows have been enacted on an international scale, some legally binding, and others not. Christopher Kuner notes that the variety of instruments, the diversity of international organizations that have enacted them, and the failure to agree on a global standard for data protection have meant that there is a lack of overall global harmonisation.[9] In 2023, very little has changed. Governments have taken a cautious approach to opening up the digital economy. The limited regulation in this area is, in my view, not achieving a strong enough level of legal harmonisation. On the one hand, some governments are establishing legal mechanisms to restrict the flow of data internationally. On the other hand, some governments have developed legal mechanisms to open up data flows in order to strengthen the digital economy.

Data flows are subject to the rules of the current-day WTO [World Trade Organisation] and GATs [General Agreement on Trade in Services], the multilateral agreement covering global trade in services, defines trade in services.[10] The GATS applies in principle to all service sectors, with two exceptions. According to Article I:2, the GATS covers services supplied (a) from the territory of one Member into the territory of any other Member (Mode 1—Cross-border trade); (b) in the territory of

[5] Sam Sacks, Justin Sherman, "Defining Data Governance." *Global Data Governance: Concepts, Obstacles, and Prospects*, New America, 2019, pp. 7–8.

[6] Ibid.

[7] Ibid.

[8] Christopher Kuner, *Transborder Data Flows and Privacy Law*, Oxford University Press (2013), p 25. In Robert Walters, The Digital Economy and International Trade: *Transnational Data Flows Regulation,* WoltersKluwer (2022), Chap. 1.

[9] Ibid, p. 26.

[10] World trade Organisation, Trade Services Division, The General Agreement on Trade in Services, 2013, https://www.wto.org/english/tratop_e/serv_e/gsintr_e.pdf, Article I.1. Also see, General Agreement on Trade in Services, Article I.1, https://www.wto.org/english/docs_e/legal_e/26-gats_01_e.htm In Robert Walters, *The Digital Economy and International Trade:* Regulation of Transnational Data Flows, Kluwer Law (2022*)*, Chap. 1.

one Member to the service consumer of any other Member (Mode 2—Consumption abroad); (c) by a service supplier of one Member, through commercial presence, in the territory of any other Member (Mode 3—Commercial presence); and (d) by a service supplier of one Member, through the presence of natural persons of a Member in the territory of any other Member (Mode 4—Presence of natural persons).[11] Moreover, Article I (3) of the GATS excludes "services supplied in the exercise of governmental authority". These are services that are supplied neither on a commercial basis nor in competition with other suppliers. Cases in point are social security schemes and any other public service, such as health or education, that is provided under non-market conditions. Furthermore, Air Transport Services are exempted from coverage measures affecting air traffic rights and services directly related to the exercise of such rights. However, today, all the other areas of trade collect and use to varying degrees personal data that is defined by the respective data protection and privacy laws compared throughout this book.

The GATS treatment of data can be summarised as:

> under cross border activity users in one state receive services from a third country, through the telecommunications or postal network. These services include, but not limited to, consultancy or market research reports, tele-medical advice, distance training, or architectural drawings.[12]

The ensuing dilemma for nation states is this: how to enable the flows of data to expand and benefit the digital economy, and at the same time ensure that the personal data of data subjects is protected and that their privacy over the Internet is secure? Data transfers in **Australia** are allowed in accordance with the Australian Privacy Principles (APP 8), and section 5B of the Privacy Act[13] which applies to acts or practices engaged in outside Australia and the external Territories. To date, Australia has taken a hands-off approach to data transfers. Australia does not have a data adequacy program, nor has it received a data adequacy decision from the EU. Arguably, this is an area requiring improvement in light of the number of data breaches occurring in Australia in 2022[14] alone. In **Antigua and Barbuda** data

[11] Ibid, Definition of Services Trade and Modes of Supply, Article I.2.

[12] Ibid, p. 3.

[13] Privacy Act 1988, section 5B, C2014C00076. Also see Australian Government, Data Transfers, Guidelines for Data Transfers, https://www.cyber.gov.au/sites/default/files/2022-12/24.%20ISM%20-%20Guidelines%20for%20Data%20Transfers%20%28December%202022%29.pdf.

[14] Optus affected an estimated 9.8 million individual records, with data now reportedly in the hands of hackers. Australia loses over $242 M to Crypto scams in 2022. Australian Bureau of Statistics, has revealed it has fended off close to a billion cyber-attacks against the census. Australia's No. 1 health insurer says hacker stole patient details Woolworths—personal details of 2.2 million customers. Telstra 300,000 former employers data breach. Costa Group tax, banking, financial passports.

Sources: https://thecommonwealth.org/news/commonwealth-experts-meet-singapore-explore-solutions-increasing-cyber-risks-asia and https://www.techbusinessnews.com.au/australian-cyber-security-concerns-continue-to-rise-in-2022/ and https://www.theguardian.com/technology/2022/oct/20/census-website-struck-by-a-billion-attempted-cyber-attacks-australian-bureau-of-statistics-reveals and https://www.reuters.com/technology/after-telco-hack-australia-faces-wave-data-breaches-2022-10-20/ and https://www.itnews.com.au/news/large-australian-education-data-leak-traced-to-third-party-service-552781.

laws, there are no specific data transfer provisions that facilitate data flows. The only reference is found in section 8, stipulating that 'security measures are required to be in place for data to be transferred'.[15]

To expand the digital economy of the **Bahamas,** surprisingly, the country has taken a limited approach. The Commissioner has responsibility for prohibiting the transfer of data outside of the state, 'where there is a failure to provide protection either by contract or otherwise equivalent to that provided under this Act'.[16] However, when determining whether to prohibit a transfer of personal data outside of the country, the Commissioner is to consider whether the transfer would be likely to cause damage or distress to any person. Thus, the prohibition will remain in place until such time that the person specifies the time when it is to take effect; the grounds for the prohibition; and fulfill the any requirements of a notice issued.[17] The notice can be cancelled at the discretion of the Commissioner. The international transfer of data from **Barbados** to a third country cannot be undertaken unless there is an adequate level of protection in the receiving state.[18] Barbados has gone further by describing what an adequacy level of protection would look like. Under section 23, an adequate level of protection is one which is adequate in all the circumstances of the case, having regard in particular to the 'nature of the personal data; the country or territory of origin of the information contained in the data; and the country or territory of final destination of that information; the purpose and law in force'.[19] To further complement the adequacy requirements, section 24 provides safeguards that constitute a legally binding and enforceable instrument to be used by public authorities; binding corporate rules in accordance with section 25; standard data protection clauses prescribed by the Commissioner with the approval of the Minister; contractual clauses; or provisions, authorised by the Commissioner'.[20] The African nation of **Botswana,** defines trans-border flow as the international flow of personal data[21] which can be transmitted by either electronic or other forms of transmission, including satellite. The level of protection (adequacy) is to be assessed by the Commissioner.[22] Importantly, according to section 49, the Commissioner is to establish that the criteria of adequacy is based on the nature of the data, purpose, duration, processing, country of origin

[15] Data Protection Act 2013, section 8 http://laws.gov.ag/wp-content/uploads/2019/02/a2013-10.pdf.

[16] Data Protection Act 2008, section 17, http://laws.bahamas.gov.bs/cms/images/LEGISLATION/PRINCIPAL/2003/2003-0003/DataProtectionPrivacyofPersonalInformationAct_1.pdf.

[17] Ibid.

[18] *Data Protection Act 2019*, section 22 https://gisbarbados.gov.bb/download/data-protection-act-2019/.

[19] *Data Protection Act 2019*, section 23 https://gisbarbados.gov.bb/download/data-protection-act-2019/.

[20] *Data Protection Act 2019*, section 24 https://gisbarbados.gov.bb/download/data-protection-act-2019/ According to section 25, data controllers and processors can develop binding corporate rules.

[21] Data Protection Act, No. 32 of 2018, section 48. https://www.bocra.org.bw/sites/default/files/documents/DataProtectionAct.pdf.

[22] Data Protection Act, No. 32 of 2018, section 49.

and final destination, rule of law, rules and safeguards. Even though there are similarities with the EU adequacy framework, a comparison is outside the scope of this book. The reference to the rule of law, rules and safeguards are fundamental values of democracy, which the Commonwealth promotes. However, the safeguards that are expected by the Commissioner may not be applicable if the third country does not provide a level of adequacy required—where the data subject has provided consent for the transfer to occur. This could be achieved through an appropriate contractual arrangement made by the controller.[23]

In **Bangladesh**, the proposal for data flows is limited. According to section 42, sensitive data, user-created or generated data and classified data shall be stored in Bangladesh, and shall remain beyond the jurisdiction of any court and law enforcers other than Bangladesh. Section 43 also[24] stipulates that any classified data specified by the Government, from time to time, by general or special order, may not be transferred to a place or system outside Bangladesh if it is not authorized so by the Government. Nonetheless, where a data subject provides consent for the transfer of data, that can be undertaken. In another example, in **Belize,** section 23 requires that when personal data is transferred to a third country, the receiving state must provide an adequate level of protection.[25] An adequate level of protection must take into account the nature of the personal data, country or territory of origin of the information contained in the data.[26] Additionally, an adequate level of protection needs to consider the final destination country, its purpose, the period for processing the data, the extent of local data laws, and any international obligations. Interestingly, the **Canadian** PIPEDA contains no provisions for cross-border data transfers.

Unlike some of the states mentioned above, **Malta** and **Cyprus** [EU members] have established some of the most comprehensive rules in relation to cross-border data transfers.[27] Data transfers are to be undertaken according Article 44 of the GDPR which provides that:

---

[23] Data Protection Act, No. 32 of 2018, section 49.

[24] Proposed Data Protection Act, 2022, section 42, 43. https://ictd.portal.gov.bd/sites/default/files/files/ictd.portal.gov.bd/page/6c9773a2_7556_4395_bbec_f132b9d819f0/Data%20Protection%20Bill%20en%20V13%20Unofficial%20Working%20Draft%2016.07.22.pdf.

[25] Data Protection Act, 45 of 2021, section 23 https://www.nationalassembly.gov.bz/wp-content/uploads/2021/07/Data-Protection-Bill-2021-updated.pdf.

[26] Data Protection Act, 45 of 2021, section 24 https://www.nationalassembly.gov.bz/wp-content/uploads/2021/07/Data-Protection-Bill-2021-updated.pdf.

[27] Regulation 2016/679 Of the European Parliament and the European Council, on the protection of natural persons with regard to the processing of personal data and on the free movement of such data and repealing Directive 95/46/EC (General Data Protection Regulation), Official Journal of the European Union L 119/1. Article 4 (23), defines, cross-border processing to be the processing of personal data which takes place in the context of the activities of establishments in more than one Member State of a controller or processor in the Union where the controller or processor is established in more than one Member State; or processing of personal data which takes place in the context of the activities of a single establishment of a controller or processor in the Union but which substantially affects or is likely to substantially affect data subjects in more than one Member State.

> Any transfer of personal data which are undergoing processing or are intended for processing after transfer to a third country or to an international organization shall take place only if, subject to the other provisions of this Regulation, the conditions laid down in this Chapter are complied with by the controller and processor, including for onward transfers of personal data from the third country or an international organization to another third country or to another international organization. All provisions in this Chapter shall be applied in order to ensure that the level of protection of natural persons guaranteed by this Regulation is not undermined.[28]

Unique to the EU is the adequacy framework under Article 45 of the GDPR. After the UK left the EU in 2021, it quickly sought to obtain data adequacy certification from the Union.[29] Essentially, the EU decision acknowledged that the **UK** data laws have been assessed as having controls similar to those of the EU. The only other two Commonwealth countries[30] that have obtained adequacy certification are Canada and New Zealand. The ensuing question is: will other Commonwealth countries seek to obtain adequacy certification from the EU? This will be up to individual Commonwealth states. However, it is my view that the Commonwealth could: 1) develop its own Commonwealth adequacy program/framework, and 2) undertake a study or survey to confirm or otherwise the need for the Secretariate to work with member countries and help them to obtain adequacy certification if they choose to do so. At the time of writing, the UK had retained the EU framework for data flows. In fact, the UK are proponents of the Open Data[31] concept. Put another way, the UK advocates the opening up of data transfers so that data can flow freely across international borders. This would bring significant economic benefits to the UK and those countries that adopt the same approach.

The formal and functional arrangements in **India** are found in section 7 of the SPD Rules which allow the transfer of information to, or by, a body corporate or any person on its behalf who may transfer sensitive personal data or any other information, to any other body corporate or a person in India, or located in any other country that ensures the same level of data protection that is adhered to by the body corporate as provided for under these Rules.[32] The transfer may be allowed only if it is necessary

[28] Regulation 2016/679 Of the European Parliament and the European Council, on the protection of natural persons with regard to the processing of personal data and on the free movement of such data and repealing Directive 95/46/EC (General Data Protection Regulation), Official Journal of the European Union L 119/1. Article 44. Also see Recital 101 and 102.

[29] European Commission, Data protection: Commission adopts adequacy decisions for the UK, https://ec.europa.eu/commission/presscorner/detail/en/ip_21_3183.

[30] European Commission, Adequacy decisions, How the EU determines if a non-EU country has an adequate level of data protection. https://ec.europa.eu/info/law/law-topic/data-protection/international-dimension-data-protection/adequacy-decisions_en.

[31] United Kingdom, UK and World Economic Forum to lead regulation revolution to foster industries of the future, 2019, https://www.gov.uk/government/news/uk-and-world-economic-forum-to-lead-regulation-revolution-to-foster-industries-of-the-future.

[32] Ministry of Communications and Information Technology, 2011, https://www.meity.gov.in/writereaddata/files/GSR313E_10511%281%29_0.pdf.

for the performance of a lawful contract between the body corporate or any person on its behalf and provider of information or where such person has consented to the data transfer.

In **Gabon**, the transfer of personal data to a third country can be undertaken provided that the receiving country has an adequate level of protection.[33] However, where adequacy cannot be obtained, a data controller can still transfer the data provided: the data subject has provided consent; the transfer is necessary to save that person's life; safeguard a public interest; ensure the right of defence in a court of law; or for the performance of a contract between the data subject and the data controller.[34] On the other hand, **Ghana** has no specific provisions within its data laws that govern the way in which international data transfers are to be governed., **Jamacia**, under the 8th standard, personal data in accordance with section 31 can be transferred beyond the state provided that there is an adequate level of 'protection for the rights and freedoms of data subjects in relation to the processing of personal data'.[35] The threshold test for achieving adequacy is the nature of the personal data; the State or territory of origin and destination of that information. Furthermore, adequacy will also be based on the purpose for which the data is being processed,, the laws in force in the receiving state, and any international obligations (trade agreements).

In the **Kingdom of Eswatini,** the trans-border flow of data can be undertaken in accordance with section 32 of the data laws.[36] Notably, there are separate requirements for the transfer of data within SADC (Southern African Development Community—African Union) member states, as opposed to non-SADC[37] members. It is outside the scope of this book to examine these differences any further. Basically, individuals and entities need to exercise vigilance to ensure that the transfer of data to third countries is undertaken correctly. On the other hand, sections 48 and 49 of **Kenya's** data laws require a controller/processor as the entity transferring the personal data, to ensure that the recipient is bound by a standard of protection comparable to that provided in Kenya. Additionally, section 50 allows the Cabinet Secretary to prescribe, based on grounds of strategic interests of the state or protection of revenue, a certain type of processing that shall only be effected 'through a server or a data centre located in Kenya'.[38] The extent to which this provision has been utilised needs to be clarified at the time of an adequacy assessment. There is a requirement for an organisation to retain a copy of any data transferred outside of Kenya. The

---

[33] Law No. 001/2011 on the Protection of Personal Data, https://www.dataguidance.com/notes/gabon-data-protection-overview Note that the law is in French, and utilised https://caseguard.com/articles/promoting-data-privacy-and-protection-in-gabon/ and DLA Piper, https://www.dlapiperdataprotection.com/index.html?t=law&c=GA.

[34] Ibid.

[35] *Data Protection Act*, 2020, section 31, https://japarliament.gov.jm/attachments/article/339/The%20Data%20Protection%20Act,%202020.pdf.

[36] Data Protection Act 2022, sections 32, 33. https://www.esccom.org.sz/legislation/DATA%20PROTECTION%20ACT.pdf.

[37] Data Protection Act 2022, section 33. https://www.esccom.org.sz/legislation/DATA%20PROTECTION%20ACT.pdf.

[38] Data Protection Act 2019, https://www.odpc.go.ke/dpa-act/, sections 48, 49, 50.

Data Protection (General) Regulations 2021 (DPGR), Regulations 39 to 48, also regulate the 'transfer of data outside of Kenya. Specifically, Regulation 39 defines data in transit to mean 'personal data transferred through Kenya in the course of onward transportation to a country or territory outside Kenya, without the personal data being accessed or used by, or disclosed to, any entity while in Kenya, except for the purpose of such transportation'.[39] This is a unique feature of the DPGR. Regulation 40 stipulates that a 'data controller or data processor who is a transferring entity shall before transferring personal data out of Kenya ascertain that the transfer is based on appropriate data protection safeguards; an adequacy decision made by the Data Commissioner; transfer as a necessity; or consent of the data subject. Further Regulation 41 (1), goes onto say that a transfer of personal data to a another country or a relevant international organisation is based on the existence of appropriate safeguards where a legal instrument containing appropriate safeguards for the protection of personal data binding the intended recipient that is essentially equivalent to the protection under the Act and these Regulations; or the data controller, having assessed all the circumstances surrounding transfers of that type of personal data to another country or relevant international organisation, concludes that appropriate safeguards exist to protect the data'.[40] Regulation 43 specifies the rules for corporate entities.

The international transfer of data outside of **Lesotho** is to be governed by a code or some other appropriate mechanism such as a contract.[41] Data subjects are required to give their consent for their personal data to be transferred to another country, and the receiving country must adhere to the principles of reasonable processing. This approach departs from that of many other countries. The formal and functional arrangements set by Lesotho do not seek to ensure that theire is a level of adequate protection or similar controls in the receiving country. This could be problematic. It is recommended that these laws be reviewed to bring them into line with the standard requirement of adequacy.

In **Malawi,** Part VI restricts a 'data controller or data processor from transferring personal data from Malawi to another country except in the circumstances outlined therein'.[42] Thus, section 34 allows a data controller or processor to transfer data outside of Malawi only if, in the recipient state, 'data is subject to a law, binding corporate rules, contractual clauses, code of conduct or certification mechanism that affords an adequate level of protection'.[43] The adequacy of protection is determined according to section 35 that includes, but is not limited to, the availability of 'enforceable data subject rights, ability of data subjects to enforce their rights through administrative or judicial redress, and the rule of law generally. It is also

---

[39] Data Protection (General) Regulations 2021 Kenya.

[40] Data Protection (General) Regulations 2021 Kenya, R 40, 41.

[41] Data Protection Act 2013, section 52, http://www.nic.ls/lsnic/community/policies/Data_Protection_Act_2011_Lesotho.pdf.

[42] Data Protection Bill 2021, Part VI, https://digmap.pppc.mw/wp-content/uploads/2022/03/Malawi-Data-Protection-Bill-final-draft-210630-.pdf.

[43] Data Protection Bill 2021, section 34, https://digmap.pppc.mw/wp-content/uploads/2022/03/Malawi-Data-Protection-Bill-final-draft-210630-.pdf.

assessed by any binding instruments such as contracts, and functioning of an independent, competent data protection or similar supervisory authority with adequate enforcement powers; and any international binding agreements'.[44] This could be a convention or trade-investment agreement.

In order to transfer personal data to places outside **Malaysia**, according to section 129, 'a data user shall not transfer any personal data of a data subject to a place outside Malaysia unless to such place as specified by the Minister, upon the recommendation of the Commissioner, by notification published in the *Gazette'*.[45] The Malaysian law also stipulates that the Minister can intervene by specifying where the data can be transferred, as long as the legislation in the state to which the data is being transferred has a similar level of protection.[46] Moreover, any data transfer must have the consent of the data subject, or be part of an enabling contract. Moreover, the Commissioner can also intervene, according to section 129(4), where there is the belief that the receiving state does not have appropriate data laws. Also, the Commissioner is to make recommendations to the relevant Minister as to whether or not the data is to be transferred.

Data flows are also an integral part of the economy of **Mauritius**. Hence, section 36 extensively governs the flows of data outside of the state. Such data can be transferred only after the Commissioner has been informed that there are appropriate safeguards in place to protect the data. It is argued that this is one of the most important developments in this area of the law. It provides for a tracing mechanism, and organisations are obliged to show how the data is being managed. Additionally, explicit consent is required. It is the required level of consent that varies across the states examined. Data transfers can be undertaken according to a contract, although there is no reference to a level of adequacy. In addition, there is no reference to ensuring the same level of protection in the third country receiving the data. It is argued that the approach adopted by Mauritius is more flexible than that of the other states being compared. On the other hand, section 23 makes the Commissioner responsible for ensuring that any data transfer is done with suitable protection. This requires further clarification of what constitutes a level of suitable protection.

New Zealand promotes the need for international data transfers. Section 7 defines a foreign entity or person as an individual who is neither present nor incorporated on the territory of the state. According to Privacy Principle 12, an agency may disclose personal information to a foreign person or entity only if the agency can meet one or more of the following requirements:

- The individual concerned authorises disclosure after being expressly informed that the foreign person/entity may not be required to protect the information in a way that provides comparable safeguards to those under the Privacy Act;

---

[44] Data Protection Bill 2021, section 35, https://digmap.pppc.mw/wp-content/uploads/2022/03/Malawi-Data-Protection-Bill-final-draft-210630-.pdf.

[45] Personal Data Protection Act 2010, section 129, https://www.kkmm.gov.my/pdf/Personal%20Data%20Protection%20Act%202010.pdf.

[46] Personal Data Protection Act 2010, section 129(1), https://www.kkmm.gov.my/pdf/Personal%20Data%20Protection%20Act%202010.pdf.

- The foreign person/entity is carrying on business in New Zealand and is subject to the Privacy Act;
- The disclosing agency believes on reasonable grounds that the foreign person/entity is subject to laws that provide comparable safeguards to those under the Privacy Act;
- The disclosing agency believes on reasonable grounds that the recipient is a participant in a prescribed binding scheme;
- The disclosing agency believes on reasonable grounds that the recipient is subject to privacy laws of a prescribed country; or
- The disclosing agency believes on reasonable grounds that the foreign person/entity is required to protect the information in a way that provides comparable safeguards to those under the Privacy Act, e.g. pursuant to an agreement between the disclosing agency and the foreign person/entity (noting that the Privacy Commissioner has provided Model Clauses for small/medium enterprises to use).
- Under the Privacy Act: prescribed binding scheme means a binding scheme specified in regulations made under section 213 of the Privacy Act. Currently, no such regulations have been made and prescribed country means a country specified in regulations made under section 214. Currently, no such regulations have been made.[47]

However, according to section 193 of the Privacy Act, the Commissioner can prohibit a transfer of personal information from New Zealand to another State, if:

> the information has been, or will be received in New Zealand from another country and is likely to be transferred to a third country that will not be subject to a law providing comparable safeguards to the Privacy Act; and the transfer would be likely to lead to a contravention of the basic principles of national application set out in Part Two of the OECD Guidelines and set out in Schedule 8 of the Privacy Act.[48]

Most significant and similar to the UK, in 2012, New Zealand received an adequacy decision[49] from the European Commission. This decision recognizes that New Zealand's data protection laws provide an adequate level of data protection compared with the European GDPR, for cross-border data transfers. Thus far, the chapter has examined some of the differences in the approaches taken by the respective states when regulating international data transfers. Some, in my view, have described extensively what needs to occur, while others have taken a limited approach. Yet others have not regulated this activity. Importantly, some states require that the Commissioner be informed of data transfer, and it is my position that this initiative should be widely adopted.

---

[47] Privacy Act 2020, Principle 12 https://www.privacy.org.nz/privacy-act-2020/privacy-principles/

[48] Privacy Act 2020, section 193 https://www.privacy.org.nz/privacy-act-2020/privacy-principles/.

[49] European Commission, 2013/65/EU: Commission Implementing Decision of 19 December 2012 pursuant to Directive 95/46/EC of the European Parliament and of the Council on the adequate protection of personal data by New Zealand (notified under document (2012) (9557) Text with EEA relevance, *OJ L 28*.

On the one hand, **Nigeria** has developed specific provisions to govern the cross-border transfer of data. Of the jurisdictions compared, section 42 of the Nigerian data laws contains some of the most comprehensive provisions for the transnational movement of data. Section 42 places a significant level of obligation on the controller and processor not to transfer any data outside of Nigeria unless, there are 'binding corporate rules, contractual clauses, code of conduct or certification mechanism that affords an adequate level of protection'.[50] Problematic, though, is the lack of context in regard to the application of 'adequate'. This needs further clarification in the law. On the other hand, **Rwanda's** Article 48 allows for the transfer of personal data to a third country. Data subjects are required to consent to this transfer. Generally, the transfer of data is limited to cases where a contract has been established or the transfer is in the public interest. Article 49 requires that any contract enabling data transfers set out clearly the roles and responsibilities of each party.[51] However, the law does not specify a threshold level for the protection of data being transferred. There is no reference to equivalence or adequacy.

The transfer of data outside the small island nation of **Singapore** is emerging as a key economic activity. That said, according to section 26, any transfer of data can be undertaken only if the receiving state has a standard of protection comparable to that of Singapore. This is another example where there is some convergence. However, it is my view that this broad provision offers a substantial amount of flexibility. Additionally, it provides for an exemptions: the Commission can decide that even though the receiving states laws are not fully comparable, the systems, protections and processes in place are enough to warrant comparability. For the international transfer of data, **Sri Lanka** has developed its own data adequacy program. According to section 26(2), when 'making an "adequacy decision", the Minister shall, in consultation with the Authority take into consideration the relevant written law and enforcement mechanisms relating to the protection of personal data in a third country and the application of the provisions of Part I, Part II and sections 20, 21, 22, 23, 24 and 25 of Part III of this Act, and such other prescribed criteria relating to the processing of personal data, in a third country for the purpose of cross border data flow'.[52] Section 2, defines cross-border data flow 'to be the movement of personal data out of the territory of Sri Lanka for the purpose of processing personal data in a third country.

Section 72 of **South Africa's** Protection of Personal Information Act 2013, provides the platform for 'data transfers outside the country cannot be undertaken unless, the third party who is the recipient of the information is subject to a law, binding corporate rules or binding agreement which provide an adequate level of

---

[50] Data Protection Regulation 2022, section 42 https://ndpb.gov.ng/Files/Nigeria_Data_Protection_Bill.pdf.

[51] Law n°058/2021 of 13/10/2021 relating to the protection of personal data and privacy (the Data Protection Law), Article 49, https://www.minijust.gov.rw/fileadmin/user_upload/Minijust/Publications/Official_Gazette/_2021_Official_Gazettes/October/OG_Special_of_15.10.2021_Amakuru_bwite.pdf.

[52] Personal Data Protection Act No. 9 of 2022, sections 26 https://www.parliament.lk/uploads/acts/gbills/english/6242.pdf.

protection that effectively upholds principles for reasonable processing of the information that are substantially similar to the conditions for the lawful processing of personal information relating to a data subject who is a 50 natural person and, where applicable, a juristic person'.[53] Transfers require a data subject's consent, or data may be transferred for the fulfilment or conclusion of a contract. The transfer can take place if it is beneficial for the data subject.

In **Saint Lucia,** according to section 28, personal data can be transferred outside the state. However, any transfer is restricted and must have the written consent of the Commissioner, and specify the country and its level of adequate protections where a contract applies.[54] The adequacy safeguards of the third country are to stipulate the 'nature of the personal data; purpose and duration of the proposed processing; the country or territory of origin and country of final destination; the rules of law in force in the country or territory in question; and any relevant codes of conduct or other rules and security measures which are complied with in that country or territory'. Across the Americas, **Saint Kitts and Nevis** has no transnational transfer provisions; nor does **Saint Vincent** and **The Grenadines.** In **Tanzania,** sections 31 and 32 of the new 2022 data laws establish the conditions for cross-border data transfer where the concept of adequacy is used as a criterion for countries that can receive personal data from Tanzania. However, the Commission has a high level of responsibility and is able to prohibit the transfer of personal data outside the country.[55] Adequacy of protection in the receiving country will suffice provided that an assessment is undertaken to determine any gaps in the law. Thus, the processor is responsible for ensuring that the operation of the laws is adequate in the receiving country.

The cross-border transfer of data is allowed in **Togo**, and this requires a level of protection similar to those of other Commonwealth nations. The adequacy level of protection extends to the 'protection of life, privacy, fundamental rights and freedoms of individuals with regard to the processing of the data'.[56] Before any transfer of personal data to a third country is undertaken, the controller must first inform the Regulator.[57] There are no specific provisions for the international transfer of data outside of **Trinidad-Tobago.**[58] However, 'where personal information under the custody and control of an organisation is to be disclosed to a party residing in another jurisdiction, the organisation shall inform the individual to whom it relates of the

---

[53] Protection of Personal Information Act 2013, section 72, South Africa.

[54] *Privacy and Data Protection Act 2009*, section 28, https://www.govt.lc/media.govt.lc/www/resources/legislation/PrivacyAndDataProtectionBill.pdf.

[55] Fatma Songoro, Brief Highlight and Analysis of the Tanzania Data Protection Bill, 2002, October 2022, https://victoryattorneys.co.tz/insights-brief-highlight-and-analysis-of-the-tanzania-data-protection-bill-2022/.

[56] Tshepiso Hadebe Togolese Republic, 2020, p3, https://dataprotection.africa/wp-content/uploads/2020/03/Togolese-Republic-Factsheet-update-20200331.pdf.

[57] Tshepiso Hadebe Togolese Republic, 2020, p. 3, https://dataprotection.africa/wp-content/uploads/2020/03/Togolese-Republic-Factsheet-update-20200331.pdf.

[58] Data Protection Regulation 2022, https://ndpb.gov.ng/Files/Nigeria_Data_Protection_Bill.pdf.

purpose for which the information is being collected once that purpose is known to the organisation, the relevant public body with responsibility for Data Protection in the other jurisdiction, and obtain his consent before disclosing the information'.[59] In **Uganda,** data being transferred outside of the state has been captured by processing data in a third country. The state has taken a minimal approach to prescribing the process for data transfers. According to section 19, a controller or processor who stores data outside the state is to ensure that there is an equivalent level of protection. The data subject is to provide consent.[60] Importantly, the term 'equivalent' is used rather than 'adequate'. This is based on the argument that equivalent has a higher threshold than that of adequacy. Essentially, Uganda focuses more on the processing of the data rather than on its transfer to a third country. The transfer of data from **Zambia** to a third country can be undertaken according to section 70. However, section 71 requires that are data subject has consented to any transfer and, where the data forms part of a contract, the Commissioner approves the transfer. Alternatively, the Minister can approve the transfer. There are, however, a number of exemptions that do not require the Commissioner's approval. These apply to sectors such as health and emergency services.[61] However, there are no details about what constitutes an emergency situation. It also extends to where consent has been provided explicitly or the transfer is necessary.

8.2 Conclusion

A central theme of this book is the digital economy and the many benefits that the free flow of data will bring to the Commonwealth. There has been a steady increase in the amount of transnational flow of personal data, and the implications of this relatively new economy activity are only beginning to be fully understood. Today, personal data can be found in and across every sector. The international transfer of this data offers significant economic and social benefits. This chapter has not considered the transfer rules for law enforcement or national security.

This chapter has demonstrated how data transfers fall within the WTO-GATT rules and, therefore, will play an increasingly important role in international trade. It has also highlighted how the data laws pertaining to transnational transfers are significantly different across the Commonwealth states. That said, data transfers are an important component of the 4th Industrial Revolution. Yet, the security issues

[59] Data Protection Regulation 2022, section 72, https://ndpb.gov.ng/Files/Nigeria_Data_Protection_Bill.pdf.

[60] Data Protection and Privacy Act 2019, sections 19 https://media.ulii.org/files/legislation/akn-ug-act-2019-9-eng-2019-05-03.pdf.

[61] Data Protection Act 2021, sections 70, 71. https://www.parliament.gov.zm/sites/default/files/documents/acts/Act%20No.%203%20The%20Data%20Protection%20Act%202021_0.pdf.

related to this data operation are not fully understood, and it is argued that there are vulnerabilities in computers and supporting systems that will enable easy access to personal data.

This chapter has deliberately provided a more detailed account of data transfer provisions in order to demonstrate the differences in the approaches taken by nations when developing their laws in this regard. It is asserted that some countries, such as Australia, have taken a hands-off approach whereby the standard is that the receiving country is assessed to have a similar level of protection.

Arguably, this can be viewed in two ways. Firstly, the laws of the receiving state are to show that they ensure approximately the same level of protection for that data. Secondly, the adequacy framework for Cyprus and Malta under the EU laws ensures that there is a level of adequate protection. Neither of these approaches ensures strong legal harmonisation. Rather, it can be argued that the EU Adequacy framework provides a level of legal convergence and harmonisation, but it has shortcomings in terms of specifying the level of protection required.

Problematic too, is that this adequacy program is currently limited to a few countries. Moreover, it appears that other countries are reluctant to adopt a similar Adequacy Decision Program. Additionally, the application of consent by the data subject for the international transfer of their data will need to be considered. It must be noted that the EU Adequacy Program is different from the national laws that require a level of adequacy. While they achieve a similar outcome, it needs to be confirmed on a country-by-country basis that, once adequacy has been determined, that determination is indefinite. Or, is it applicable only to a one-off transfer?

In regard to the above, some states will require explicit consent, whereas other will not require any consent. One of the main functions of the adequacy rules is to ensure that a data subject's rights in the EU or Australia have the same level of protection when that data is transferred to Malaysia or Kenya. Another important development has been that in some jurisdictions the controller and/or processor are obliged to undertake certain activities before the data is transferred. For instance, and while not examined in this book, impact assessment(s) may be required in some states.

Most noteworthy is that some states do not require the receiving state to have a level of protection or similar controls. This, in my view, is highly problematic. Here, the important question is: how can data subjects be confident about how and where their personal data is collected, stored, and used? Furthermore, to which country will the data be transferred without their knowledge?

Nonetheless, in many states, the Regulator is responsible for restricting or prohibiting the transfer of data to a third country. Yet again, this is another area of inconsistency. In other states, the Regulator is to prescribe the requirements for data transfers. Additionally, those states that are obliged to appoint a controller generally assign to that controller the responsibility for data transfers.

Significantly, most of the laws allow data transfers to be undertaken by legal mechanisms such as contracts and binding corporate rules. The requirements for data transfers to and from public organisations, such as government, should be considered. In this regard, some states do have specific requirements.

The MBP and MBPPI demonstrate the different approaches taken to deal with the transfer of data to third countries. This is another area that needs to be reconciled. The MBPPI is specific and relates only to the use and disclosure of data. Whereas, the MBP does not address international data transfers. There is, in some cases the requirement for data transfers to be reported to the national Regulator.

Arguably, this requirement should be further explored and adopted more widely across the Commonwealth. This will provide greater transparency and accountability for data transfers, and will ensure that any transfer can be tracked and traced from its original sources to its final destination. Thus, should the Commonwealth take the step to develop an office for the recording and reporting of all data transfers? Or, should an international organisation be established to undertake this task?

Chapter 9
Data Portability

9.1 Introduction

Data portability is another recent addition to the data legal framework. It places data subjects in a commanding position, allowing them to have greater control over their personal data. For instance, it allows data subjects to request that an organisation transfer their personal data to another organisation that may be totally unrelated. For instance, a person residing in Canada may have his or her medical records at hospital A. Under the concept of portability, the individual can request that Hospital A transfer his or her personal data to Hospital B. However, neither the MBP nor the MBPPI[1] provides specifically for data portability. This chapter reveals that a large number of Commonwealth states do not provide for the right to data portability. Therefore, it is argued that, as a starting point, the Commonwealth Secretariate should amend the MBP and MBPPI to include data portability.

Another view is that data portability is an extension of data law, and places stronger focus on the consumer. Hence, the laws that have included this concept also make the controllers responsible for the management of personal data according to the request of a data subject. The respective laws will direct the controller or processor to undertake certain tasks. For instance, there will be a requirement or otherwise for the data to be transferred from one entity to another, within the country. In my view, it accords with the right to data access. This is an extension of the principle of access. That is, the right of access allows data subjects, just that: access to their data information so that they can request that it be transferred to another entity. However, access to data is distinct from portability; with access, data subject only obtains a copy of the data held by the entity. This right to access will depend on the laws and practices of the state and entity involved.

[1] The Commonwealth, Model Privacy Bill, Office of Civil and Criminal Justice Reform, 2017, https://www.asianlaws.org/gcld/cyberlawdb/COM/P15370_9_ROL_Model_Privacy_Bill_0.pdf The Commonwealth, Model Bill on the Protection of Personal Information https://www.asianlaws.org/gcld/cyberlawdb/COM/P15370_6_ROL_Model_Bill_Protection_Personal_Information_2.pdf.

R. Walters, *Cybersecurity and Data Laws of the Commonwealth*,
https://doi.org/10.1007/978-981-99-3935-0_9

Data portability regulation has been described as a remedy against the concentration of power in the control and use of data, in too few hands.[2] Arguably, it places greater control of personal data in the hands of data subjects. It allows an individual to move this or her personal data from one organisation to another. While this chapter focuses on the law of data portability, rather than discussing what the concept actually means in practice, it can be summarised in the following way:

> First, data portability can give users more control over their information. At a basic level, data portability ensures that consumers always have the option to gain full control over their data by obtaining a complete copy of their information. Data portability ensures that consumers can independently backup their data, without relying on a third party. For example, data portability allows consumers to archive a copy of personal photos that they may have created and shared using a mobile app, ensuring that even if they stop using the app, they still have a copy of their data. Data portability is especially useful in this context when a company ends a service, changes a free service to a paid one, modifies its terms of service, or goes out of business, as it ensures users do not lose their data.[3]

This consumer-led approach helps open up the data and gives it additional value. In other words:

> Second, data portability can allow users to unlock more value from their data. A prerequisite for data-driven innovation is the ability of organisations to access data. When data is tied to a single service, its value is limited to how that service can use the information. Data portability allows users to share their data with additional services, creating more opportunities for data-driven innovation because of greater efficiency, more data availability, and the ability to reuse data for secondary purposes. For example, consumers might use data portability to quickly transfer a digital copy of their credit card spending to an online budgeting app. Not only does this ability to transfer data create greater value for consumers, by giving them greater insights on their personal finances, but it also enables a whole new class of financial planning apps that would not otherwise exist without access to this data. Similarly, consumers without much of a credit history may struggle to get access to credit; data portability allows them to show their cash flow on prepaid card accounts, opening up new possibilities for underwriting.[4]

It is the sharing of data between organisations that will drive services and create opportunities in the new digital economy. At a personal level, where data subjects in the modern world are largely accountable for some debt, portability can demonstrate the spending habits of a person, particularly when obtaining credit might be difficult. Daniel Castro posits that data portability strengthens competition in four ways:

> First, data portability fosters competition by reducing the opportunity for companies to artificially lock in customers by making it prohibitively expensive or cumbersome to move to another provider. Second, data portability can promote competition by creating more transparency about fees and alternatives. For example, consumers might use an app to analyse their home energy usage data to discover if they would pay less with an alternative energy provider, or review their bank fees to see if they would save money by switching to a different

---

[2] Inge Graef, Jeroen Verschakelen, Peggy Valcke. Putting the right to data portability into a competition law perspective. *Law: The Journal of the Higher School of Economics*, (2013) pp. 53–63.

[3] Daniel Castro, *Improving Consumer Welfare with Data Portability*, Centre for Data Innovation (2021) pp. 2–4.

[4] Ibid.

> financial institution. Third, data portability has pro-competitive effects by encouraging businesses to retain customers by offering better services. For example, when consumers can easily switch music streaming services, these services may invest in new ways to keep their users engaged on their platform, such as developing better recommendation algorithms. Fourth, data portability allows new entrants to better compete with incumbents who may have collected data under less restrictive data protection laws and regulations. Without data portability and allowances for secondary uses of data, data protection rules can have anti-competitive effects, thus hurting consumer welfare and limiting innovation.[5]

These four features are, in my view, are important for the development of the digital economy. More competitiveness can result in more data being moveable across the economy. Thus, one argument could be that the more data in the system travels around a country, the more difficult it is for that data to be collected and used illegally. Conversely, it could result in data being accessed and used in ways that compromise the data subject. This is, as I have stated repeatedly, a major challenge: a balance has to be struck between the free movement of data, enabling data subjects to move their data around, and ensuring a high level of cybersecurity and protection for that data.

In regard to data portability, neither the **Bahamas, Botswana, Canada, India, Ghana, Jamacia, Lesotho, Mauritius, New Zealand, Saint Lucia, Singapore, Sri Lanka, South Africa, Saint Kitts and Nevis, Saint Vincent and The Grenadines, The Kingdom of Eswatini, Togo, Trinidad-Tobago,** and **Uganda** provide for the right to data portability, as of 2023.

Bangladesh provides for data portability according to section 13. In **Australia**, data portability has been provided for consumers under the *Competition and Consumer Act 2010*.[6] It has taken a consumer-led approach to allow individuals to transfer their personal data between businesses. **Antigua** and **Barbuda** have no provision for data portability. According to **section 15,** data subjects in **Barbados** can exercise their right to data portability.[7] However, there are conditions related to the portability of that data, under the oversight of a controller. In **Belize,** the right to data portability has become an important feature of their national laws. Section 16, allows data subjects to transfer[8] their data from one organisation to another. **Malawi** does provide for data portability,[9] allowing data subjects to receive their data and have it transmitted to another controller in another organisation. **Nigeria** does provide for

---

[5] Ibid.

[6] Australian Government, Office of the Australian Information Commissioner, Compliance and Enforcement Policy, Consumer Right Data, https://www.oaic.gov.au/consumer-data-right/compliance-and-enforcement-policy.

[7] *Data Protection Act 2019*, section 15, https://gisbarbados.gov.bb/download/data-protection-act-2019/.

[8] Data Protection Act, 45 of 2021, sections 16 https://www.nationalassembly.gov.bz/wp-content/uploads/2021/07/Data-Protection-Bill-2021-updated.pdf.

[9] Data Protection Bill 2021, section 30, https://digmap.pppc.mw/wp-content/uploads/2022/03/Malawi-Data-Protection-Bill-final-draft-210630-.pdf.

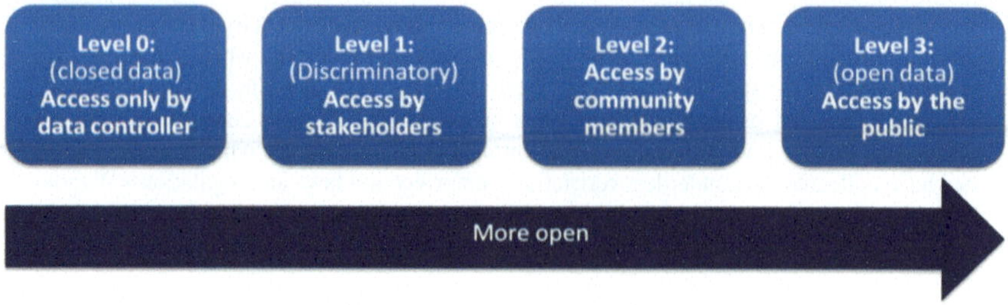

Fig. 9.1 OECD highlight the degrees of data openness and access[13]

the right to data portability under section 39. In so doing, it is subject to the Commission for this right to be operative. That said, once the right becomes operational, data subjects are entitled to receive their data without delay. This allows one controller to transmit the data to another controller.[10]

The OECD makes this important point:

> …data portability has become an essential tool for enhancing access to and sharing of data across digital services and platforms. This report explores to what extent data portability can empower users (natural and legal persons) to play a more active role in the re-use of their data across digital services and platforms. It also examines how data portability can help increase interoperability and data flows and thus enhance competition and innovation by reducing switching costs and lock-in effects.[11]

While most of the laws contain additional, stricter protections for sensitive personal data, the categories of sensitive data included in the EU—GDPR (implemented by Malta and Cyprus) are not always reflected, including personal data relating to sexual orientation and ethnic origin.[12] Data portability improves data flows which, in turn, strengthen the economic outcomes of the digital economy (Fig. 9.1).

The OECD goes on to say that:

> under data portability, data holders are required to provide conditioned access to data, in a commonly used, machine-readable structured format, either to the user, whose data are concerned, or to a third party chosen by the user. The provision of data in this format is, however, not specific to data portability. This kind of format is a technical minimal requirement of all EASD approaches, including open data.[14]

---

[10] Data Protection Regulation 2022, section 35 https://ndpb.gov.ng/Files/Nigeria_Data_Protection_Bill.pdf.

[11] Organisation for Economic Cooperation and Development, 2021, p. 2, https://www.oecd-ilibrary.org/docserver/a6edfab2-en.pdf?expires=1671056625&id=id&accname=guest&checksum=053C9901C9D207D9C6018E58CD25E455.

[12] Amelia Bleeker, Data Protection in The Caribbean, 2020, p. 6, https://repositorio.cepal.org/bitstream/handle/11362/47155/1/FOCUSIssue1Jan-Mar2020.pdf.

[13] It isOrganisation for Economic Cooperation and Development, 2021, p. 9, https://www.oecd-ilibrary.org/docserver/a6edfab2-en.pdf?expires=1671056625&id=id&accname=guest&checksum=053C9901C9D207D9C6018E58CD25E455.

[14] Ibid, p. 9.

Arguably, the OECD is saying that data portability will enhance the economic and social outcomes of countries as part of the evolving digital economy. Apart from the economic and social benefits, it gives data subjects more control over their personal data, and strengthens business' competitiveness. The Singapore Government noted that:

> From a competition perspective, data portability could lead to efficiencies for organisations, as organisations may find it easier to gain access to more varied data sets. This could, in turn, improve their ability to develop and improve product offerings which are better targeted to their customer base, by deriving more insights from an expanded data set. Data portability could also lead to a reduction of switching costs, as a customer can request for his/her data to be transferred to a competitor, without having to re-enter that information. This allows consumers to switch to the supplier with the most attractive offer, thus enhancing competition. Furthermore, in certain circumstances, organisations rely on data as an important, or even essential, input in the creation of comparable products. The inability of an organisation to gain access to such data could thus hinder its ability to effectively enter the market or expand its presence. A data portability requirement could facilitate access to this critical input, and lower the barriers to entry and expansion, thereby enhancing competition.[15]

If fully realised, competition is one of the major outcomes of the implementation of this concept, and offers significant benefits to the community by reducing costs to the customer and organisations. The economic benefits are far from fully realised because of the limited number of nation states that have adopted the concept.

The EU was one of the leaders in developing the concept of data portability. According to Article 20 of the GDPR,[16] the citizens of Cyprus and Malta, members of the Commonwealth as well as the EU, have the right to data portability. As of December 2022, the right to data portability is recognised under Article 20 of the **UK** GDPR.[17] Under the UK legislative framework, data subjects have the right to transmit their data to another controller without hindrance from the controller to which the personal data was initially provided. As mentioned in other chapters, the UK has thus far retained most of the EU legal framework. **Gabon** provides for data portability,[18] while **Ghana** does not have specific provisions for data portability.

---

[15] Singapore, Discussion paper on Data Portability Personal Data Protection Commission In collaboration with Competition and Consumer Commission of Singapore, 2019, p. 3, https://www.pdpc.gov.sg/-/media/Files/PDPC/PDF-Files/Resource-for-Organisation/Data-Portability/PDPC-CCCS-Data-Portability-Discussion-Paper---250219.pdf.

[16] Regulation 2016/679 Of the European Parliament and the European Council, on the protection of natural persons with regard to the processing of personal data and on the free movement of such data and repealing Directive 95/46/EC (General Data Protection Regulation), Official Journal of the European Union L 119/1. Articles 20.

[17] Data Protection Act, 2018. Schedule 2, https://www.legislation.gov.uk/ukpga/2018/12/pdfs/ukpga_20180012_en.pdf.

[18] Law No. 001/2011 on the Protection of Personal Data, https://www.dataguidance.com/notes/gabon-data-protection-overview Note that the law is in French, and utilised https://caseguard.com/articles/promoting-data-privacy-and-protection-in-gabon/ and DLA Piper, https://www.dlapiperdataprotection.com/index.html?t=law&c=GA.

In **Kenya,** similar to Cyprus and Malta (EU-GDPR), data subjects have the right to 'receive their data in a structured, commonly used, machine-readable format, to transmit this ported data to another data controller or processor, or to request the transfer to another data controller or processor where possible'.[19] The right to portability is limited to the extent that processing may be necessary for the performance of a public-interest task, the exercise of official authority, or portability may adversely affect the rights and freedoms of others. That is, section 38 provides for '(1) A data subject has the right to receive personal data concerning them in a structured, commonly used and machine-readable format. (2) A data subject has the right to transmit the data obtained under sub-section, to another data controller or data processor without any hindrance. (3) Where technically possible, the data subject shall have the right to have the personal data transmitted directly from one data controller or processor to another. (4) Where data controller or data processor declines to comply with a request under sub-section, the Data Commissioner may make a determination on the technical capacity of the data controller or data processor. (5) The right under this section shall not apply in circumstances where (a) processing may be necessary for the performance of a task carried out in the public interest or in the exercise of an official authority; or (b) it may adversely affect the rights and freedoms of others. (6) A data controller or data processor shall comply with data portability requests, at reasonable cost and within a period of thirty days. (7) Where the portability request is complex or numerous, the period under sub-section 6 may be extended for a further period as may be determined in consultation with the Data Commissioner'.[20]

At the time of writing, **Malaysia** was undertaking a review of its data laws that had been tabled in the national Parliament in October 2022. The proposal, if accepted, will introduce a number of new obligations pertaining to data portability, as well obligations for both data users and data processors.[21] However, vigilance will be needed to determine the outcome of these new proposals in 2023 and beyond. Article 20 of the **Rwandan** data laws allows a data subject to request that the data controller, in writing or electronically, resend the personal data concerning them as it was provided to the data controller, in a structured and readable format.[22] **Tanzania,**

[19] Data Protection Act 2019, https://www.odpc.go.ke/dpa-act/.

[20] Data Protection Act 2019, section 38 https://www.odpc.go.ke/dpa-act/.

[21] Kerk Ying Chew, Chun Hau Ng, *Malaysia: Proposed amendments to the Personal Data Protection Act 2010 expected to be tabled at Parliament*, https://www.globalcompliancenews.com/2022/08/20/https-insightplus-bakermckenzie-com-bm-data-technology-malaysia-proposed-amendments-to-the-personal-data-protection-act-2010-expected-to-be-tabled-at-parliament_1_08082022/.

[22] Law n°058/2021 of 13/10/2021 relating to the protection of personal data and privacy (the Data Protection Law), Articles 20, https://www.minijust.gov.rw/fileadmin/user_upload/Minijust/Publications/Official_Gazette/_2021_Official_Gazettes/October/OG_Special_of_15.10.2021_Amakuru_bwite.pdf.

provides for the right to data portability.[23] The ability for a data subject to request that their data be transferred[24] between data controllers of different organisations also exists in **Zambia.**

9.2 Conclusion

Relatively few Commonwealth countries have adopted the concept of data portability, as demonstrated in this brief chapter.

Data portability is a consumer-oriented concept as it gives data subjects greater control over their personal data. It enables a data subject to request of an organisation that has collected their personal data to transfer that same data to another organisation. It is not an international transfer, and pertains only to domestic transfers. It creates a level of competition in the market by preventing a single organisation from being the sole collector, user and storer of personal data. Thus, the concept serves to promote the digital economy and create additional opportunities for data transactions.

It is asserted that data portability law overlaps with competition law. However, a problem arises when personal data is transferred from an organisation with a system that is well-protected against cyber intrusions to one that offers less protection. This has the potential to make the data more vulnerable to cybercrime. More research is needed to better understand the vulnerability and exposure of portable data.

Essentially, this had been confirmed by the OECD, whereby, under data portability, data holders are required to provide data subjects access to that data, so as it can be transferred from one organisations to another. When the data is transferred to another organisation where its access is easier, the data becomes vulnerable to cyber-attacks. However, any level of vulnerability will need to be offset by the benefits offered by the portability of data

Finally, it has been confirmed that neither the MBP nor the MBPPI has accounted for data portability. To enhance the digital economy, the Commonwealth should, as a matter of urgency, revise both instruments and include model provisions for data portability. More work is needed to understand the competing effect that data portability may have on data flows, and whether it will dilute the economic benefits of data collection and use across the digital economy.

---

[23] Fatma Songoro, Brief Highlight and Analysis of the Tanzania Data Protection Bill, 2002, October 2022, https://victoryattorneys.co.tz/insights-brief-highlight-and-analysis-of-the-tanzania-data-protection-bill-2022/.

[24] Data Protection Act 2021, section 65. https://www.parliament.gov.zm/sites/default/files/documents/acts/Act%20No.%203%20The%20Data%20Protection%20Act%202021_0.pdf.

Chapter 10
Right to Be Forgotten [RTBF]: Erasure

10.1 Introduction

Arguably, the Right to be Forgotten [RTBF] or the right to erasure was established by the EU as a formidable mechanism allowing data subjects to control when and how their personal data can be removed from the Internet. Put another way, 'the championing of a right to be forgotten in response to the explosive dissemination of personal data on the internet has often been seen as the near exclusive preserve of EU data regulators'.[1] Furthermore, the RTBF has been viewed by some as being difficult to achieve. It has been summarised thus: Even more reason to consider the passage of a legal right to be forgotten and erasure is the substantial difficulty of removing, or even being aware of, all tracking devices and specialized HTTP packets. ""Zombie cookies," also known as "Flash cookies," are larger collections of information relying on the Adobe software and preventing users from blocking them through web browsers' privacy controls[2]. While, this chapter does not confirm whether the current day laws have addressed the above concerns, it demonstrates how most Commonwealth member states have in some form provided for the RTBF. That is, various forms of the right to data deletion and erasure have emerged. Today, Erdos notes that 15 G20 countries with data protection legislation support a version of this right. This is a small portion of the countries examined in this book that generally do not support the RTBF. The RTBF has been described as:

---

[1] David Erdos, *The 'right to be forgotten' beyond the EU: an analysis of wider G20 regulatory action and potential next steps,* Journal of Media Law, 13:1, (2021), pp. 33–35.

[2] Ryan Singel, *PrivacyLawsuit Targets Net Giantsover 'Zombie' Cookies,* (2010), http://www.wired.com/threatlevel WIRED /2010/07/zombie-cookies-lawsuit/. In Tsesis, Alexander, The Right to Erasure: Privacy, Data Brokers, and the Indefinite Retention of Data, 49 Wake Forest L. Rev. 433 (2014), p. 438.

R. Walters, *Cybersecurity and Data Laws of the Commonwealth*,
https://doi.org/10.1007/978-981-99-3935-0_10

> is a privacy ruling that enables Europeans to delist certain URLs appearing in search results related to their name. In order to illuminate the effect this ruling has on information access, we conducted a retrospective measurement study of 3.2 million URLs that were requested for delisting from Google Search over five years. Analysis reveals the countries and anonymized parties generating the largest volume of requests (just 1,000 requesters generated 16% of requests); the news, government, social media, and directory sites most frequently targeted for delisting (17% of removals relate to a requester's legal history including crimes and wrongdoing); and the prevalence of extraterritorial requests. The results dramatically increase transparency around the Right to be Forgotten and reveal the complexity of weighing personal privacy against public interest when resolving multi-party privacy conflicts that occur across the Internet.[3]

While many laws provide for the right itself, in practice it is not another area requiring regulatory balance between personal privacy over the Internet and the broader public interest. In addition, and something that is not often associated with the right, is its potential impact on data flows and the economic benefits these flows provide. That is, a data subject could request that their data be deleted, invoking the RTBF, before the entity can on-sell the data. In May 2014, the Court of Justice of the European Union in the case of *Google Spain* established a RTBF.[4] A data subject can request that their personal data be delisted, as information must be "inaccurate, inadequate, irrelevant or no longer relevant, or excessive in relation to those purposes and in the light of the time that has elapsed".[5] As a result, it found its way into the EU General Data Protection Regulation 2016/679.[6] Since then, countries around the world have followed the EU and established the right within their national data laws. This chapter examines how the Commonwealth member states have responded to the issue of RTBF.

---

[3] Theo Bertram, Elie Bursztein, Stephanie Caro, Hubert Chao, Rutledge Chin Feman, Peter Fleischer, Albin Gustafsson, Jess Hemerly, Chris Hibbert, Luca Invernizzi, Lanah Kammourieh Donnelly, Jason Ketover, Jay Laefer, Paul Nicholas, Yuan Niu, Harjinder Obhi, David Price, Andrew Strait, Kurt Thomas, Al Verney. 2019. Five Years of the Right to be Forgotten. In 2019 ACM SIGSAC Conference on Computer and Communications Security (CCS'19), November 11–15, 2019, London, United Kingdom. ACM, New York, NY, USA, p. 14. https://doi.org/10.1145/3319535.3354208.

[4] *Google Spain SL and Google Inc. v Agencia Española de Protección de Datos (AEPD) and Mario Costeja González*. http://eur-lex.europa.eu/legal-content/EN/TXT/?uri=CELEX%3A62012CJ0131.

[5] Ibid.

[6] Regulation 2016/679 Of the European Parliament and the European Council, on the protection of natural persons with regard to the processing of personal data and on the free movement of such data and repealing Directive 95/46/EC (General Data Protection Regulation), Official Journal of the European Union L 119/1. Article 17. Note, subject to Articles 6, 8, 9, and 21.

Beginning with **Botswana**, this country only allows personal data to be corrected, and there is no right to be forgotten. Yet, this is being considered in **Bangladesh,**[7]at the time of writing this book. **Antigua and Barbuda** provide for limited erasure of personal data. It has no specific provisions, but is part of the definition of processing.[8] There is a limited right to erasure in the **Bahamas.** In accordance with section 10, it is combined with the right to rectification. A data subject can request of a data controller that their personal data be erased[9] within forty days of the request according to section 6 that pertains to data being recorded accurately, amongst other things. In **Barbados,** section 12 allows data subjects to erase their personal data.[10] It is a comprehensive requirement and obligation is placed on the controller to respond to any request for erasure, and that this should take no longer than is necessary. It is argued that this could be tightened up to ensure that a prompt and effective response is provided to data subjects. **Belize** has included the right to erasure so that data subjects can obtain from a data controller a commitment to erase[11] their data from the Internet. In **Canada,** although there is no direct and clear RTBF, according to section 4.5.3, personal information that is no longer required to fulfil the identified purposes should be destroyed, erased, or made anonymous. Organisations are required to develop guidelines and implement procedures for the destruction of personal information.[12] However, this does not extend to data subjects requesting that their data be erased.

The right to erasure in **Cyprus and Malta,** otherwise referred to as the right to be forgotten (RTBF) has been established by the EU. In my view, it has been a corner stone of the EU data framework, and enables data subjects to have greater control over their data and its use. It enables a data subject to request that their data be removed from the Internet. Article 17 of the GDPR provides that a 'data subject shall have the right to obtain from the controller the erasure of personal data concerning him or her without undue delay and the controller shall have the obligation to erase personal data without undue delay'.[13] The RTBF can be applied when the personal data is no longer required, consent has been withdrawn, there has been an objection to the data being processed, the data has been unlawfully processed, or there are some

[7] Proposed Data Protection Act, 2022, section 18. https://ictd.portal.gov.bd/sites/default/files/files/ictd.portal.gov.bd/page/6c9773a2_7556_4395_bbec_f132b9d819f0/Data%20Protection%20Bill%20en%20V13%20Unofficial%20Working%20Draft%2016.07.22.pdf.

[8] Data Protection Act 2013, section 2 http://laws.gov.ag/wp-content/uploads/2019/02/a2013-10.pdf.

[9] Data Protection Act 2008, section 10 and 6, http://laws.bahamas.gov.bs/cms/images/LEGISLATION/PRINCIPAL/2003/2003-0003/DataProtectionPrivacyofPersonalInformationAct_1.pdf.

[10] *Data Protection Act 2019*, section 12 https://gisbarbados.gov.bb/download/data-protection-act-2019/.

[11] Data Protection Act, 45 of 2021, sections 13 https://www.nationalassembly.gov.bz/wp-content/uploads/2021/07/Data-Protection-Bill-2021-updated.pdf.

[12] Personal Information Protection and Electronic Documents Act (S.C. 2000, c. 5), section 4.5.3, https://laws-lois.justice.gc.ca/eng/acts/P-8.6/index.html.

[13] Regulation 2016/679 Of the European Parliament and the European Council, on the protection of natural persons with regard to the processing of personal data and on the free movement of such data and repealing Directive 95/46/EC (General Data Protection Regulation), Official Journal of the European Union L 119/1. Article 17. Note, subject to Articles 6, 8, 9, and 21.

other obligations required by the law. This also accords with the **UK**, although the right is not absolute and applies only to certain circumstances.[14] The UK GDPR does not specify how a data subject can submit a valid request. Therefore, an individual can submit a request for erasure either verbally or in writing. A request can also be submitted to any section of an organisation and does not have to be to a specific person or contact point.[15] However, requests made for such erasure can be refused by the controller for law enforcement agencies (except intelligence services) with reason for such refusal.[16] However, disclosure of the reason for refusal may be restricted in a proportionate manner.[17] The right to erasure exists in regards to personal data processed by intelligence agencies under section 100(2) of Data Protection Act, if in the eyes of the court such processing personal data infringe any of sections 86 to 91. The important judgment of *NT1 and NT2 v Google LLC*[18] handed down by the High Court in 2018 established and clarified under which circumstances a person can successfully 'erase' unwanted information from the digital landscape under UK law. Holding that "the specific rights asserted by the individual concerned will still need to be evaluated, and weighed against any competing free speech or freedom of information considerations, or other relevant factors, that may arise in the particular case".[19] Thus the RTBF:

> allows citizens to ask search engines not to display specific URLs linked to their name if the information contained on those webpages is inadequate, irrelevant or no longer relevant, or excessive in relation to the purposes for which they were processed.[20]

Therefore, it is the search engines and other infrastructure that is capturing and storing the data of millions of individuals. For instance, in undertaking this research, a number of search engines to locate various books, journals and reports. In this case, every search would result in the author's personal details being recorded by the search engine provider.

[14] Article 17, UKGDPR.

[15] Right to erasure, Information Commissioner's Office, Accessed from: <https://ico.org.uk/for-organisations/guide-to-data-protection/guide-to-the-general-data-protection-regulation-gdpr/individual-rights/right-to-erasure/#ib10>.

[16] Section 48(1)(b)(i), Data Protection Act, 2018.

[17] Section 48(3), Data Protection Act, 2018.

[18] [2018] EWHC 799 (QB).

[19] [2018] EWHC 799 (QB) 166.

[20] Google wins landmark case: Right to be forgotten only applies in EU, https://nakedsecurity.sophos.com/2019/09/25/google-wins-landmark-case-right-to-be-forgotten-only-applies-in-eu/.

on the one side, **Gabon,** a general right of erasure[21] is available to data subjects. While for **Ghana,** the right to erasure is restricted. Section 44 of the data laws limit the erasure of data to when the Commission is satisfied, upon a complaint from a data subject, that the data is to be erased.[22] The small state of **Togo** does allow data subjects to request the erasure of their personal data.[23] On the other hand, in the **Kingdom of Eswatini,** section 20 provides for enabling data to be deleted; however, this does not mean that it is fully erased.[24] Additionally, **Lesotho,** according to section 27, allows data subjects to request that a controller either correct or delete their personal data.[25] It is a limited right to erasure, and would not extend to the full right to be forgotten. There is no specific RTBF in **Malawi.** However, according to section 2, erasure has been captured under the definition of processing.[26] Therefore, further clarification is needed as to specify the extent to which this would, or could, extend. There is no specific RTBF in **Mauritius**, although section 39[27] does provide a limited right to erasure. However, there are exceptions to any data being erased where data retention is in the public interest, for historical statistics, or for a legal claim. Some, but not all, states have these exceptions, and clarification is required to confirm the extent of any exception(s).

On the other side, **New Zealand,** the RTBF is not guaranteed. Significantly though, Privacy Principle 7 allows data subjects to request that their personal data be corrected, although it is a lower level of this right. However, it does not provide for the deletion or complete erasure of the data. It is argued that New Zealand could and should amend this right so that it is aligned with the EU provisions. Interestingly, the Adequacy Decision given by the EC does not mention the RTFG, erasure or deletion of personal data. However, the Harmful Digital Communications Act 2015 established the right of individuals to apply to the District Court for a take-down order. It allows a person who alleges that he or she has suffered or will suffer harm as a result of a digital communication can submit a complaint to Netsafe and request that the material be taken down or corrected. While not fully applicable in **Nigeria,** the right

[21] Law No. 001/2011 on the Protection of Personal Data, https://www.dataguidance.com/notes/gabon-data-protection-overview Note that the law is in French, and utilised https://caseguard.com/articles/promoting-data-privacy-and-protection-in-gabon/ and DLA Piper, https://www.dlapiperdataprotection.com/index.html?t=law&c=GA.

[22] Data Protection Act 2012, sections 44 https://nita.gov.gh/theevooc/2017/12/Data-Protection-Act-2012-Act-843.pdf.

[23] Tshepiso Hadebe Togolese Republic, 2020, p. 1, https://dataprotection.africa/wp-content/uploads/2020/03/Togolese-Republic-Factsheet-update-20200331.pdf.

[24] Data Protection Act 2022, sections 2, 20. https://www.esccom.org.sz/legislation/DATA%20PROTECTION%20ACT.pdf.

[25] Data Protection Act 2013, section 27, http://www.nic.ls/lsnic/community/policies/Data_Protection_Act_2011_Lesotho.pdf.

[26] Data Protection Bill 2021, section 2, https://digmap.pppc.mw/wp-content/uploads/2022/03/Malawi-Data-Protection-Bill-final-draft-210630-.pdf.

[27] Data Protection Act 2017, sections 39, https://dataprotection.govmu.org/Documents/DPA_2017_updated.pdf?csf=1&e=0rlrff.

to erasure[28] can be granted upon request by a data subject. It is not as comprehensive as the right stipulated in the laws of Cyprus, Malta, or the UK. In **Saint Lucia**, there is no specific RTBF. Section 32 provides for the right to rectification, which includes erasure.[29] However, this is limited to the commissioner requesting such. Introduced in 2022, section 16 allows all data subjects in **Sri Lanka** to request that their personal data be erased, particularly in relation to its processing.[30] In **Rwanda,** there are no specific provisions for the RTBF. Yet, Article 36 allows a data subject to request that their personal data be erased from the states register.[31] This is a narrow version of the right to erasure as it only pertains to that data which is recorded on the register. Tanzania, is to provide for the right of erasure.[32] A similar approach has been taken by **Uganda,** which has no specific RTBF. However, according to the right to rectification,[33] there is a general right that allows people to have their data erased. In **Zambia,** the right to erasure allows data subjects to request that their personal data be erased[34] by a controller from the Internet. Finally, **Australia, India, Jamacia, Malaysia, Singapore**, **South Africa, Saint Kitts and Nevis, Saint Vincent and The Grenadines,** and **Trinidad-Tobago** do not provide for the right to be forgotten. However, the judiciary in India has considered the right to be forgotten in both cases of *Sri Vasunathan v The Registrar General*, 2017 SCC Online Kar 424. *Justice K.S. Puttaswamy (Retd.) and Anr v Union of India and Ors.*, (2017) 10 SCALE 1. To date, however, that consideration has not resulted in a common law right to RTBF. **Kenya** also provides for "anonymization" that allows data subjects to have their personal identifiers removed from personal data, making them no longer identifiable. More specifically, section 26 gives a data subject the right to have false or misleading personal data deleted. However, to date, Kenya has not fully recognised the RTBF.

---

28 Data Protection Regulation 2022, sections 35 and 2 https://ndpb.gov.ng/Files/Nigeria_Data_Protection_Bill.pdf.

29 *Privacy and Data Protection Act 2009*, section 32, https://www.govt.lc/media.govt.lc/www/resources/legislation/PrivacyAndDataProtectionBill.pdf.

30 Personal Data Protection Act No. 9 of 2022, sections 16 https://www.parliament.lk/uploads/acts/gbills/english/6242.pdf.

31 Law n°058/2021 of 13/10/2021 relating to the protection of personal data and privacy (the Data Protection Law), Articles 36, https://www.minijust.gov.rw/fileadmin/user_upload/Minijust/Publications/Official_Gazette/_2021_Official_Gazettes/October/OG_Special_of_15.10.2021_Amakuru_bwite.pdf.

32 Fatma Songoro, Brief Highlight and Analysis of the Tanzania Data Protection Bill, 2002, October 2022, https://victoryattorneys.co.tz/insights-brief-highlight-and-analysis-of-the-tanzania-data-protection-bill-2022/.

33 Data Protection and Privacy Act 2019, section 28 https://media.ulii.org/files/legislation/akn-ug-act-2019-9-eng-2019-05-03.pdf.

34 Data Protection Act 2021, section 60. https://www.parliament.gov.zm/sites/default/files/documents/acts/Act%20No.%203%20The%20Data%20Protection%20Act%202021_0.pdf.

10.2 Conclusion

The RTBF is another concept that emerged from the EU and, arguably, has transformed the way individuals, entities and countries respond to the protection of data. This chapter has confirmed that neither the MBP nor the MBPPI provides specifically for for erasure or right to be forgotten. This, in my view, is another area for the Commonwealth to consider in any review of these Model Laws.

What this chapter has revealed is that the terminology and the interpretation of laws vary from state to state within the Commonwealth. For instance, some states refer to 'deleting data' or 'erasing data' while other states have partially responded by imposing rules for the rectification of that data. Arguably, rectification is distinct from the formal and functional process of completely deleting and removing that data from the Internet. Another approach has been the anonymisation of the data of a data subject, meaning that the data subject cannot by identified over the Internet as any identifying data has, supposedly, been removed.

However, it is yet to be fully realised whether this means that RTBF has been fully achieved. It is slowly emerging and being accepted in states that have yet to include the concept within their national laws. For instance, India's judiciary has recognised that there is a common law right to RTBF. This is a major step for India. On the other hands, in some states such as New Zealand, the right is not fully guaranteed. This can be problematic and leaves data subjects with some uncertainty, exacerbated by the highly fragmented approach taken by Commonwealth members.

Surprisingly, some of the countries compared in this chapter have had data-privacy laws for more than a decade, yet have not provided for the RTBF. This right gives data subjects greater over their personal data. Thus, what has emerged is not only a highly contested area of the laws; it is also inconsistent and significantly multi-layered when evaluated against the other rights that data subjects have been afforded.

In conclusion, with the constant evolution of technology, the breadth and depth of data that has been captured and retained by organisations has both a positive and negative impact on data subjects. For instance, people who uploads personal videos of themselves in their early adulthood, and a decade or so later want to remove that information which contains person identifiable information and data, cannot do so. The RTBF enables data subjects to have that information and data removed, which is for their benefit. Thus, it is my view that this concept and right alone needs to be available regardless of the Commonwealth country where the data subject resides.

Chapter 11
Public and Private Sectors

11.1 Introduction

The application of data laws to either the public or private sectors, or both, will vary from nation state to nation state. Section 5 of the MBPPI provides a framework indicates how it should apply. That is, the national laws should apply only to all private sector organisations, and not to public authorities.[1] On the other hand, section 6 of the MPB makes the case that legislation should bind the Crown.[2]

It is my view that this needs to be reconciled by the Commonwealth. The Commonwealth separates the application of the Model Bills into two categories: the MBP applies only to the Crown, and the MBPPI tapplies to the private sector. This is possibly sending conflicting messages to member countries.

This chapter demonstrates that member countries of the Commonwealth have not adopted a consistent or coherent approach to the application of their respective data laws to the public and private sectors. As stated earlier in the book, data protection is a tool ensuring privacy. In order for the laws to be meaningful, and provide a balanced framework that protects data-privacy while strengthening economic growth, they need to be applied consistently to government and the private sector.

This will engender a greater level of trust, confidence and certainty in the legal frameworks established for data. It will also improve the security of personal data. This brief chapter begins by examining Australia's data laws. It is quite descriptive, revealing the provisions in the laws of various Commonwealth nation states. This is because there is little scholarly discussion on the issue, and no decisions have been handed down by any judiciary or regulator.

---

[1] The Commonwealth, Model Bill on the Protection of Personal Information, section 5, https://www.asianlaws.org/gcld/cyberlawdb/COM/P15370_6_ROL_Model_Bill_Protection_Personal_Information_2.pdf.

[2] The Commonwealth, Model Privacy Bill, Office of Civil and Criminal Justice Reform, 2017, section 6,https://www.asianlaws.org/gcld/cyberlawdb/COM/P15370_9_ROL_Model_Privacy_Bill_0.pdf.

R. Walters, *Cybersecurity and Data Laws of the Commonwealth*,
https://doi.org/10.1007/978-981-99-3935-0_11

Arguably, it is important to apply the data laws to both the public and private sectors in order to ensure that the community has a high level of trust in data governance. Not doing so dilutes the application of data laws across the community. It is asserted that by not applying the data laws to both sectors, trust and accountability are eroded. It is these principles and concepts that are at the very heart of the OECD Guidelines Governing the protection of privacy and Transborder Flows of Personal Data.[3] It states:

> These Guidelines apply to personal data, whether in the public or private sectors, which, because of the manner in which they are processed, or because of their nature or the context in which they are used, pose a risk to privacy and individual liberties.[4]

The Guidelines go further and provide the Accountability Principle requiring an organisation to have in place a privacy management programme. In **Australia,** section 4 of the *Privacy Act 1988* states that the Act applies to the Commonwealth, states and territories and extended territories of Australia. By binding the Crown, the federal government and all federal government agencies must also comply with the Act. Neither the Act nor the APPs apply to State and Territory governments. An APP entity includes government agencies, and private sector and not-for-profit organisations with an annual turnover of more than AU $3 million. That is, those small businesses with an annual turnover of less than $3 million have fewer obligations.[5] The Data Protection Act 2013 of **Antigua and Barbuda** applies to both the public and private sectors.[6] In the **Bahamas,** the data laws in section 3[7] bind both the public and private sectors. This approach is consistent with that of most of the other Commonwealth countries.

While the law of **Barbados** do not specifically state that the data laws apply to both the public and private sector, it defines a public authority as 'a public office or a ministry, department, agency, unit other authority of the Government including a statutory body'.[8] In **Belize**[9] the data laws are applicable to the private sector.

---

[3] OECD Guidelines Governing the protection of privacy and Transborder Flows of Personal Data, https://legalinstruments.oecd.org/en/instruments/OECD-LEGAL-0188.

[4] Ibid, p. 6.

[5] Privacy Act 1988, section 6D. C2014C00076.

[6] Data Protection Act 2013, section 3 http://laws.gov.ag/wp-content/uploads/2019/02/a2013-10.pdf. The objectives of this Act are to safeguard personal data processed by public bodies and private bodies.

[7] Data Protection Act 2008, section 3, http://laws.bahamas.gov.bs/cms/images/LEGISLATION/PRINCIPAL/2003/2003-0003/DataProtectionPrivacyofPersonalInformationAct_1.pdf.

[8] *Data Protection Act 2019*, section 2, https://gisbarbados.gov.bb/download/data-protection-act-2019/.

[9] Data Protection Act, 45 of 2021, https://www.nationalassembly.gov.bz/wp-content/uploads/2021/07/Data-Protection-Bill-2021-updated.pdf.

Botswana's data laws have limited application and do not apply to 'personal or household activity, national security, defence, public safety, prevention, investigation or proof of offences, the prosecution of offenders or the execution of sentences or security measures, amongst other things'.[10] In the proposed laws of **Bangladesh,**[11] it is not clear whether they will apply to both the public and private sectors. The **Canadian** PIPED applies only to the private sector.[12] In **Cyprus** and **Malta,** the GDPR applies to both public and private organisations. Importantly, Article 4 specifies and includes public authorities in the definitions of controllers and processors, and Article 37 requires that all public authorities appoint a data protection officer. The courts are exempt from this rule.[13] The UK has retained the EU framework since leaving the Union in 2021. In **Gabon**, the data laws apply to both the public and private sectors, for the collection, transmission, use, and storage of data by a natural, legal, public, or private person.[14] The same position is taken in **Ghana** where the data laws apply to both the private and public sectors.[15]

For India their current sectorial approach relies on the judiciary for a determination of what constitutes privacy over the Internet, and how it will apply to the public and private sectors. The proposed Digital Data Protection Bill[16] is likely to change this significantly. At the time of writing, in December 2022, the Indian Government was still revising the draft proposal. The **Jamaican** data[17] laws apply to both the public and private sectors. The Data Protection Act 2019[18] applies to all processing of personal data by any data controller or data processor established or residing in **Kenya,** and who processes personal data while in Kenya, or not established or residing in Kenya but processing personal data of data subjects located in

---

[10] Data Protection Act, No. 32 of 2018, section 3, https://www.bocra.org.bw/sites/default/files/documents/DataProtectionAct.pdf.

[11] Proposed Data Protection Act, 2022, sections. 4. https://ictd.portal.gov.bd/sites/default/files/files/ictd.portal.gov.bd/page/6c9773a2_7556_4395_bbec_f132b9d819f0/Data%20Protection%20Bill%20en%20V13%20Unofficial%20Working%20Draft%2016.07.22.pdf.

[12] Personal Information Protection and Electronic Documents Act (S.C. 2000, c. 5), section 4, https://laws-lois.justice.gc.ca/eng/acts/P-8.6/index.html.

[13] Regulation 2016/679 Of the European Parliament and the European Council, on the protection of natural persons with regard to the processing of personal data and on the free movement of such data and repealing Directive 95/46/EC (General Data Protection Regulation), Official Journal of the European Union L 119/1. Article 4 and 37.

[14] Law No. 001/2011 on the Protection of Personal Data, https://www.dataguidance.com/notes/gabon-data-protection-overview Note that the law is in French, and utilised https://caseguard.com/articles/promoting-data-privacy-and-protection-in-gabon/ and DLA Piper, https://www.dlapiperdataprotection.com/index.html?t=law&c=GA.

[15] Data Protection Act 2012, sections. 45 and 91 and https://nita.gov.gh/theevooc/2017/12/Data-Protection-Act-2012-Act-843.pdf.

[16] India Digital Data Protection Bill, https://www.meity.gov.in/writereaddata/files/The%20Digital%20Personal%20Data%20Potection%20Bill%2C%202022_0.pdf.

[17] *Data Protection Act*, 2020, section 2, see definition of public authority, https://japarliament.gov.jm/attachments/article/339/The%20Data%20Protection%20Act,%202020.pdf.

[18] Data Protection Act 2019, https://www.odpc.go.ke/dpa-act/ Supported by the Data Protection (General) Regulations 2021.

Kenya. The Kenya Information and Communications Act applies to telecommunication service providers that have been granted an operating licence by the Communications Authority. In the **Kingdom of Eswatini,** it is not clear whether the data laws apply to both the public and private sectors. Section 4 exempts the Act from applying to data processed on behalf of the state on national security or defence grounds.[19]

Unlike the other jurisdictions examined, **Lesotho** has taken a different pathway when applying its data laws. Section 3 clearly states that the laws apply when the principal place of business is on the territory of Lesotho. However, if the place of business is outside the Lesotho territory, but the business uses automated or non-automated technology within the territory, the laws apply.[20] Even though it is silent regarding the law's application to the public or private sector, section 4 exempts personal or household activity; de-identified personal information; national security, or journalistic purpose. However, in section 2, there is a definition of controller and public body,[21] and it states that the laws apply to both public and private entities. In **Malawi, t**he data laws do not 'apply to the collection or processing of personal data for personal, recreational or household purposes, or for security, law enforcement or public health purposes'.[22] Hence, the laws apply to both the public and private sectors. In **Malaysia,** the PDPA applies to any person who has control over, or authorizes the processing of, any personal data in respect of commercial transactions.[23] It applies to any person who is not physically located in Malaysia, but uses equipment in Malaysia for processing data. Section 3 provides an exemption to all Federal and State Governments.[24] The PDPA does not apply to any personal data that is processed outside Malaysia, unless that data is to undergo further in Malaysia.

Generally, the data laws apply to both the public and private sectors in **Mauritius.** However, there are exemptions since the Act does not apply when personal data is to be exchanged between Ministries, Government departments and public sector agencies where such exchange is required on a need-to-know basis.[25] The data laws of **New Zealand**[26] apply to both the public and private sectors, while in **Nigeria,** the Act is specific in its application. Section 2 is quite specific when explaining the application of the data laws. It applies to a data controller or processor domiciled, ordinarily resident or operating in Nigeria. It also applies to personal data that is

[19] Data Protection Act 2022, https://www.esccom.org.sz/legislation/DATA%20PROTECTION%20ACT.pdf.

[20] Data Protection Act 2013, section 3, http://www.nic.ls/lsnic/community/policies/Data_Protection_Act_2011_Lesotho.pdf.

[21] Ibid, section 2.

[22] Data Protection Bill 2021, p. 3, https://digmap.pppc.mw/wp-content/uploads/2022/03/Malawi-Data-Protection-Bill-final-draft-210630-.pdf.

[23] Personal Data Protection Act 2010, section 2, https://www.kkmm.gov.my/pdf/Personal%20Data%20Protection%20Act%202010.pdf.

[24] Personal Data Protection Act 2010, section 3, https://www.kkmm.gov.my/pdf/Personal%20Data%20Protection%20Act%202010.pdf.

[25] Data Protection Act 2017, section 3 https://dataprotection.govmu.org/Documents/DPA_2017_updated.pdf?csf=1&e=0rlrff.

[26] Privacy Act 2020, section 6 https://www.privacy.org.nz/privacy-act-2020/privacy-principles/.

processed in Nigerian territory. However, it is worth noting that when the controller or processor is not domiciled, resident or operating in the territory, but the data subject is, the laws remain applicable. This provides a level of extra-territorial reach. What is not clear is whether it applies to government. Based on section 2, it could be argued that it does apply to both the public and private sectors if a controller or processor is in Nigeria.[27]

While it is not clear whether **Rwanda's** data laws apply to both public and private organisations, Article 2 provides that 'data controllers, processors, or third parties that are established or ordinarily residing in Rwanda and processing personal data while in Rwanda, as well as, those not residing in Rwanda, however the processing of data and data subjects are located in the state'.[28] Similarly, the **Singapore** PDPA applies to private sectors.[29] By and large, the PDPA does not apply to public agencies. Specifically, Parts 3, 4, 5, 6, 6A and 6B do not impose any obligation on a public agency, individual acting in a personal or domestic capacity, employee acting in the course of their employment, or, other organisations.[30] Part 3 relates to overall compliance with the PDAPA, whereas Part 4 deals with collection, use and disclosure. On the other hand, Part 5 deals with rights of a data subject to access and correct his or her personal data. Part 6 and 6A deal with the notification of data breaches.

South African data laws[31] apply to both the public and private sectors. Section 2 of the **Sri Lankan** data laws applies to the processing of data within the state, or by a controller or processor where they are resident, incorporated, offers goods or services to data subjects, and specifically monitors the behaviour of data subjects in Sri Lanka.[32] Section 5 of the **Saint Lucia**[33] data laws clearly apply to both the public and private sectors. **St Kitts and Nevis** data laws[34] apply to both the public and private sectors. In **St Vincent and The Grenadines,** data laws apply to public authorities[35] as they do for the private sector. In **Tanzania,** it is not clear from the non-English version whether the 2022 laws pertain to both the public and private

[27] Data Protection Regulation 2022, section 2 https://ndpb.gov.ng/Files/Nigeria_Data_Protection_Bill.pdf Note the exceptions in section 3.

[28] Law n°058/2021 of 13/10/2021 relating to the protection of personal data and privacy (the Data Protection Law), Article 2, https://www.minijust.gov.rw/fileadmin/user_upload/Minijust/Publications/Official_Gazette/_2021_Official_Gazettes/October/OG_Special_of_15.10.2021_Amakuru_bwite.pdf.

[29] Personal Data Protection Act 2012, section 4, https://sso.agc.gov.sg/Act/PDPA2012.

[30] Personal Data Protection Act 2012, section 4, https://sso.agc.gov.sg/Act/PDPA2012.

[31] Protection of Personal Information Act 2013, https://www.gov.za/sites/default/files/gcis_document/201409/3706726-11act4of2013popi.pdf.

[32] Personal Data Protection Act No. 9 of 2022, section 2 https://www.parliament.lk/uploads/acts/gbills/english/6242.pdf.

[33] *Privacy and Data Protection Act 2009*, section 5, https://www.govt.lc/media.govt.lc/www/resources/legislation/PrivacyAndDataProtectionBill.pdf.

[34] Data Protection Act, 5 of 2018, section 4 https://www.theinformationcollective.com/dpl/st-kitts-data-protection-act.

[35] Privacy Act 2003, section 6 https://www.theinformationcollective.com/dpl/st-vincent-and-the-grenadines-the-privacy-act.

sectors. The data laws of **Trinidad-Tobago** apply to both the public and private sectors.[36] In **Uganda,** the data law applies to both the public and private sectors, and also stipulates whether an organisation collects, processes, uses, or discloses data within or outside of Uganda.[37] Thus, the Ugandan laws have some extraterritorial effect. Finally, the data laws of **Zambia** apply to both the public and private[38] sectors. From the above, it is clear that nation states need to be more specific about the sectors to which their respective legislation applies.

11.2 Conclusion

This brief chapter has demonstrated that the Commonwealth has taken very different approaches to the application of the Model Laws, when establishing a framework for member countries to follow. It is argued that this separation of the application of the MBP to only the Crown and the MBPPI to the private sector needs to be amended. I argue that they should apply equally to both the public and private sectors.

Doing so will engender a greater level of trust in and certainty about data protection, while providing a pathway for investment across the digital economy, because investors will have greater clarity. The current incoherence creates a highly fractured approach to ensuring that both the public and private sectors are accountable for and transparent about their use of data.

Arguably, to optimise the level of public trust, data laws should apply to government as they do for the private sector. Not doing so will create an environment where individuals may not confident in government handling their personal data, and ensuring that it is protected. If data laws are not applied to the public sector, this will erode the accountability and transparency of government entities. Furthermore, by not applying the law equally to both the public and private sectors, this demonstrates that a state is not fully meeting the objectives of the OECD Guidelines governing the protection of privacy and Transborder Flows of Personal Data.[39] Some states such as Canada have specific and separate laws for the private and public sectors.

However, most other states have consolidated their data laws under a single piece of legislation that applies to either the public or private sectors, or both. This is increasingly important as more and more states regulate for the establishment of a Commissioner. Thus, the Regulator has a role to ensure that government is fulfilling its obligations under the data laws.

[36] Data Protection Act 2011, section 1, https://rgd.legalaffairs.gov.tt/laws2/Alphabetical_List/lawspdfs/22.04.pdf.

[37] Data Protection and Privacy Act 2019, section1 https://media.ulii.org/files/legislation/akn-ug-act-2019-9-eng-2019-05-03.pdf.

[38] Data Protection Act 2021, https://www.parliament.gov.zm/sites/default/files/documents/acts/Act%20No.%203%20The%20Data%20Protection%20Act%202021_0.pdf.

[39] OECD Guidelines Governing the protection of privacy and Transborder Flows of Personal Data, https://legalinstruments.oecd.org/en/instruments/OECD-LEGAL-0188.

Finally, it is argued that data laws have to apply to all public organisations that are under the direct or indirect control of government. There should be under no circumstances a separation at law for the application of data obligations, in facilitating transnational data flows or protecting the data. In regressing the formal and functional arrangements surrounding the operation of data across the community and government, there needs to be a consistent approach applied across all nation states. It has been briefly identified the potential risks for not doing so. Moreover, as governments adopt new technology capable of capturing more data, the laws should be applicable to the public sector.

Chapter 12
Data Rights

12.1 Introduction

This chapter brings together the overall rights that states have adopted. It provides a general overview and includes the rights discussed in previous chapters. This concluding chapter is short and confirms whether a state has clearly expressed the rights that a data subject has within the national laws. Having now studied this area of transnational law since 2018, I can conclude that the aforementioned rights have been established mainly by the EU. Its laws have been the most influential, as evident across the world and in the laws of Commonwealth nations.

This chapter confirms the overall problem defined in this book: that there are many inconsistencies in the data laws of Commonwealth countries in the Commonwealth. The book demonstrates that this area of the law is significantly fragmented. Of the laws compared in this book, the concepts and principles espoused by the Commonwealth MBP and MBPPI have been addressed in the national laws. Yet, there is a considerable level of additional work that the Commonwealth Secretariate should and could undertake to enhance and strengthen the MBP and MBBPI. The ensuing question is whether the two Model Laws could be combined into a single Model Law.

The Commonwealth supports this view:

> The state of data protection laws across the Commonwealth varies from state to state. Jurisdictions such as Australia, Canada, New Zealand and the United Kingdom, as members of the Organization for Economic Cooperation and Development, have developed advanced data protection regimes in line with the OECD Guidelines on the Protection of Privacy and Transborder Flows of Personal Data. Data protection laws in Cyprus, Malta and the United Kingdom have also been driven by European Union law. Commonwealth member countries in Asia and Pacific regions have been influenced by the Asia-Pacific Economic Cooperation (APEC) privacy framework, and Commonwealth jurisdictions in Africa and the Americas

R. Walters, *Cybersecurity and Data Laws of the Commonwealth*,
https://doi.org/10.1007/978-981-99-3935-0_12

> benefit from a number of regional regimes and guidelines. Many Commonwealth countries, however, have not yet enacted comprehensive data protection laws.[1]

The above has been reinforced by the MBP. Most notable is that both the MBP and the MBPI were established six years ago in 2017. This book is calling for a review of these Model Laws. Such a review will be timely, as Commonwealth nation states increasingly make use of technologies such as AI and Quantum. Finally, this chapter begins by examining the overall rights of the countries compared.

The rights of data subjects that have been afforded by the current day data laws of Commonwealth nation states have been in response to the growing need to protect individuals' privacy over the Internet. Put simply:

> It is clear that privacy, itself a fundamental right, is a value that the right to data protection seeks to protect. There are different formulations of what the right to privacy entails, spanning from the rather limited idea of privacy only attaching to those intimate matters to which a 'reasonable expectation of privacy' might attach (*Campbell*, 2004), to a wider notion of 'the right to be left alone', to an even broader, more recent, idea that the right to privacy is closely related to the protection of one's identity. Data protection clearly fits closest within this third sphere – while some data (such as medical information) might be of the sort to which a reasonable expectation of privacy attaches, other data (e.g. identifying data such as one's address and phone number) falls outside of that scope. Equally, the idea of the right to be left alone presupposes some intrusion into one's day-to-day life, yet the data leaks showed that a great deal of surveillance happens in the background, unbeknownst to those whose data is being collected for those purposes.[2]

Thus, data is increasingly interconnected with cybersecurity. It is the systems and infrastructure that support a computer that, when compromised, allow the illegal access to and use of personal data. In response to the data breaches, and the vulnerability of data over the Internet, a multilayered approach has been undertaken by governments around the world to develop rights and controls to protect the data by means of the law. It has been identified only a limited number of rights that have been provided to data subjects. In comparing these rights with the Commonwealth MBP and MBPPI, there are significant gaps. This is problematic as it has created a lot of unnecessary complexity in reconciling the differences between the laws. It is argued that the rights afforded all come back to the starting point of this chapter. That is the definition of data, which confirms where, how and why the specific right will apply. Therefore:

> Data protection is one of the essential fundamental rights and has to be preserved in a digital world as in the former analogue society. There must be an open eye for threats to society, internal and external, but fundamental rights such as privacy must be considered of great value for a society and must be available for all persons on an equal basis.[3]

---

[1] The Commonwealth, Model Bill on the Protection of Personal Information, 2017, https://www.asianlaws.org/gcld/cyberlawdb/COM/P15370_6_ROL_Model_Bill_Protection_Personal_Information_2.pdf.

[2] Yvonne McDermott, (2017). Conceptualising the right to data protection in an era of Big Data. *Big Data & Society*, *4*(1). (2017), pp. 1–2, https://doi.org/10.1177/2053951716686994.

[3] Rob van den Hoven van Genderen, Cybercrime investigation and the protection of personal data and privacy, Council of Europe, 2008, p. 6. https://rm.coe.int/16802fa3a3.

In supporting this proposition:

> The right to access information guarantees protection of basic rights by adhering to basic management principles such as implementing the principle of advertising that excludes disclosure of public confidential information, the use of means of communication, and the promotion of IT services. Companies and governments have many chances to protect the personal information collected from individuals and their online habits to meet customer needs in a modern way.[4]

Put another way:

> The Internet is escalating cybercrime and increasing the amount of material available, its distribution efficiency, and its accessibility to a certain level that shows the ease of access and utilisation of excessive use. Privacy and the law protects the basic right of citizens to protect their data whenever government authorities use their personal data. In particular, the personal data of victims, witnesses, and suspected crimes will be adequately protected and cross-border cooperation in the fight against cybercrime, however, service providers should increase their privacy-related activities respectively [emphasis added].[5]

Data protection laws, when combined with cybersecurity, provide a robust level of protection for all individuals. However, as will be demonstrated in Part 2 of this book, the cases discussed rarely, if ever, examine the data laws in combination with the criminal offences being decided by the judiciary. Generally, this chapter will bring together the rights that have been afforded to individuals by the respective Commonwealth states.

Data subjects in **Antigua and Barbuda** are afforded the right of 'access, notice and time, denial of access, form of access, rectification, disclosure and processing of sensitive data'.[6] While many of these rights have been addressed in this book, the most important is the processing of sensitive data. Section 18 places a number of restrictions on the processing of sensitive data that will need to be considered such as the application of express consent. Nonetheless, note the exemption according to section 19 related to criminal offences. Australia has also provided for a similar set of rights. In the **Bahamas**, data subjects have the right to access, rectify, erase, and prohibit the use of their data for purposes of direct marketing. Further, according to section 8, a data subject can submit a request to a data controller to access their data. Accordingly, the data controller has 40 days to provide a response and inform the data subject of the data kept by the controller, supply the data or provide an explanation of the data where said data may be unintelligible.[7] In addition, sections 10 and 11 provide that a data subject can also make a written request for the rectification or

---

[4] Muharman Lubis, Dini Oktarina D. Handayani, *The relationship of personal data protection towards internet addiction: Cyber crimes, pornography and reduced physical activity*, Procedia Computer Science,Volume 197, (2022), pp. 151–153.

[5] Ibid, p. 159.

[6] Data Protection Act 2013, sections 12, 13, 14, 15, 16, 17, 18 http://laws.gov.ag/wp-content/uploads/2019/02/a2013-10.pdf.

[7] Data Protection Act 2008, sections 8, http://laws.bahamas.gov.bs/cms/images/LEGISLATION/PRINCIPAL/2003/2003-0003/DataProtectionPrivacyofPersonalInformationAct_1.pdf.

erasure of data under section 6. In **Barbados,** data rights include access, rectification, erasure, restriction, portability and protection from direct marketing.[8]

Botswana has a limited level of explicit rights (see above controller, consent, processing). On the other hand, **Bangladesh** goes beyond Botswana and, according to section 13, a data subject has specific rights to access their data, data correction, withdrawal consent, and importantly rights of foreign data subjects. This provision is a standout compared to many other states. It provides that any citizen of the Commonwealth resident in Bangladesh has the same rights[9] as those of a local Bangladeshi. In addition, data subjects can prevent their personal data being processed. The request for the execution of any of these rights, is to be undertaken in writing.[10] In **Belize,** a number of rights are afforded to data subjects that include access, rectification, erasure, restriction, portability, protection from damage and loss, and from direct marketing.[11] In **Canada**, the rights are not clearly specified. On the other side, what has been expressed as rights in most other jurisdictions, has been established as a set of Principles. Thus, the principles extend to:

- Access;
- Accountability;
- Purposes;
- Consent;
- Limiting Collection;
- Limiting Use, Disclosure, and Retention;
- Accuracy;
- Safeguards;
- Openness; and
- Individual Access;
- Challenging Compliance.[12]

While a lengthy discussion of these principles is beyond the scope of this book, they have assisted nation states to develop their data laws. The principles help to promote certainty and trust in the law. They all go some way to underpinning and supporting the expansion of the new digital economy. **Cyprus** and **Malta** have what can be argued as the most comprehensive set of rights afforded to a data subject. The laws ensure that transparent communication and information are provided, data

---

[8] *Data Protection Act 2019*, sections 10, 11, 12, 13, 14, 15, 16, 17, https://gisbarbados.gov.bb/download/data-protection-act-2019/.

[9] Proposed Data Protection Act, 2022, sections 17. https://ictd.portal.gov.bd/sites/default/files/files/ictd.portal.gov.bd/page/6c9773a2_7556_4395_bbec_f132b9d819f0/Data%20Protection%20Bill%20en%20V13%20Unofficial%20Working%20Draft%2016.07.22.pdf.

[10] Proposed Data Protection Act, 2022, sections 20. https://ictd.portal.gov.bd/sites/default/files/files/ictd.portal.gov.bd/page/6c9773a2_7556_4395_bbec_f132b9d819f0/Data%20Protection%20Bill%20en%20V13%20Unofficial%20Working%20Draft%2016.07.22.pdf.

[11] Data Protection Act, 45 of 2021, sections 11 to 18 https://www.nationalassembly.gov.bz/wp-content/uploads/2021/07/Data-Protection-Bill-2021-updated.pdf.

[12] Personal Information Protection and Electronic Documents Act (S.C. 2000, c. 5), schedule 1, 4.1 to 4.10,https://laws-lois.justice.gc.ca/eng/acts/P-8.6/index.html.

subjects have access to their data, and have the right to amend their data or have it erased (see below right to be forgotten). In addition, a data subject has the right to restrict the use of their data, and object to its being used in a certain way.[13] The **UK** continues to follow the EU legal framework, which is also that of Malta and Cyprus.

For **Gabon,** according to the Law No. 001/2011 on the Protection of Personal Data,[14] data subjects have the following rights: data protection and personal privacy, right of access, and to rectification, erasure, objection, and data portability. Moreover, data subjects have the right to not be subject to data processing decisions made solely on the basis of automated processing, if said processing will lead to adverse consequences. There are a number of rights afforded to data subjects under the data laws of **Ghana.** These include access, correction, and the manner of access to personal data.[15]

In Central Asia, **India** does not provide for an extensive level of rights similar to those of the other Commonwealth countries. The proposed Digital Data Protection Bill[16] is likely to change this significantly. At the time of writing in December 2022, the Indian Government was still revising the draft proposal. In **Jamacia,** data rights comprise access, consent and rectification.[17] The rights of data subjects in the **Kingdom of Eswatini,** are limited to access and correction.[18] Erasure is mentioned only under the definition of processing in section 2, and data subjects can request their data be deleted under section 20. On the one hand, Kenya is specific under section 26[19] which provides access, and the right to be informed, object to processing, correction, and deletion. On the other hand, in **South Africa**, there are a limited number of rights that have been addressed throughout this chapter.

In the country of **Lesotho,** the rights afforded to data subject are access and correction of data. It is a somewhat limited set of data rights.[20] **Malawi** 'grants a data subject individual rights with respect to personal data, including the right to freely (a) obtain from a data controller or data processor copies of his personal data

---

[13] Regulation 2016/679 Of the European Parliament and the European Council, on the protection of natural persons with regard to the processing of personal data and on the free movement of such data and repealing Directive 95/46/EC (General Data Protection Regulation), Official Journal of the European Union L 119/1. Articles 12, 13, 14, 15, 16, 17, 18, 19, 21 and 22.

[14] Law No. 001/2011 on the Protection of Personal Data, https://www.dataguidance.com/notes/gabon-data-protection-overview Note that the law is in French, and utilised https://caseguard.com/articles/promoting-data-privacy-and-protection-in-gabon/ and DLA Piper, https://www.dlapiperdataprotection.com/index.html?t=law&c=GA.

[15] Data Protection Act 2012, sections 32 to 36 https://nita.gov.gh/theevooc/2017/12/Data-Protection-Act-2012-Act-843.pdf.

[16] India Digital Data Protection Bill, https://www.meity.gov.in/writereaddata/files/The%20Digital%20Personal%20Data%20Potection%20Bill%2C%202022_0.pdf.

[17] *Data Protection Act*, 2020, sections 6 to 13, https://japarliament.gov.jm/attachments/article/339/The%20Data%20Protection%20Act,%202020.pdf.

[18] Data Protection Act 2022, sections 2, 20. https://www.esccom.org.sz/legislation/DATA%20PROTECTION%20ACT.pdf.

[19] Data Protection Act 2019, https://www.odpc.go.ke/dpa-act/.

[20] Data Protection Act 2013, section 26, 27, http://www.nic.ls/lsnic/community/policies/Data_Protection_Act_2011_Lesotho.pdf.

in a commonly used electronic format and demand correction of any inaccurate information or deletion of inaccurate, incomplete or misleading information, and (b) object, or withdraw his consent previously given, to the processing of his personal data'.[21] In **Malaysia**, data subjects are afforded several rights and some control over their personal data. While the rights are limited in comparison to those of other nation states, a data subject can obtain access to their personal data to[22] correct,[23] withdraw consent,[24] and prevent the processing of data if it is determined that it can cause distress or is associated with direct marketing.[25]–**Mauritius** has limited the rights of data subjects to: access, automated decision making, rectification, erasure, restriction and objection.[26]

New Zealand affords a limited set of rights to a data subject compared to the number of rights established by other states. That is, the purpose of data collection must be communicated to the data subject, in addition to granting access and ensuring the data is secure. Also, a data subject has the right to object to direct marketing.[27] In addition, the correction of personal data can be requested by a data subject. **Nigeria** does provide a number of rights for data subjects. Most notable is the right for data subjects to confirm whether their data is being stored or processed. These rights extend to the purpose of processing, the categories of data that are involved, the end recipient, and the period for which the data will be stored. Further to this is this ability of the data subject to obtain rectification, and lodge a complaint, amongst others. Section 36 provides the right to withdrawal consent,[28] and section 37 allows the data subject to make an objection.[29] Finally, section 38 enables a data subject to obtain information regarding the automated decision-making that has been undertaken in relation to their data.[30] The final right is expressed in section 39, whereby data subjects can request that their data be transferred from one organisation to another (data portability—see below).

[21] Data Protection Bill 2021, Part IV, https://digmap.pppc.mw/wp-content/uploads/2022/03/Malawi-Data-Protection-Bill-final-draft-210630-.pdf.

[22] Personal Data Protection Act 2010, section 12, 30, https://www.kkmm.gov.my/pdf/Personal%20Data%20Protection%20Act%202010.pdf.

[23] Personal Data Protection Act 2010, section 12, 34, https://www.kkmm.gov.my/pdf/Personal%20Data%20Protection%20Act%202010.pdf.

[24] Personal Data Protection Act 2010, section 38, https://www.kkmm.gov.my/pdf/Personal%20Data%20Protection%20Act%202010.pdf.

[25] Personal Data Protection Act 2010, section 42, 43, https://www.kkmm.gov.my/pdf/Personal%20Data%20Protection%20Act%202010.pdf.

[26] Data Protection Act 2017, section 34, 35, 36, 37, https://dataprotection.govmu.org/Documents/DPA_2017_updated.pdf?csf=1&e=0rlrff.

[27] Privacy Act 2020, Principles 1 to 12 https://www.privacy.org.nz/privacy-act-2020/privacy-principles/.

[28] Data Protection Regulation 2022, section 36 https://ndpb.gov.ng/Files/Nigeria_Data_Protection_Bill.pdf.

[29] Data Protection Regulation 2022, section 37 https://ndpb.gov.ng/Files/Nigeria_Data_Protection_Bill.pdf.

[30] Data Protection Regulation 2022, section 38 https://ndpb.gov.ng/Files/Nigeria_Data_Protection_Bill.pdf.

Rwanda, similar to many of the other states on the African continent, provides for the right to be informed, access, rectification, erasure, opt-out, portability, and decisions by automated technology.[31] **Saint Lucia** affords specific rights to data subjects. Sections 29–33 stipulate that a data subject has the right to access his or her personal data, rectify such data,[32] and prohibit data processing. **St Kitts and Nevis,** have stablished a number of rights for data subjects, including access, denial and form of access, rectification and processing of personal data.[33] Compared to many other states, the rights are somewhat limited. The data laws of **St Vincent and The Grenadines** do not clearly specify the rights of data subjects. This needs to be reconciled. **Singapore** affords a limited set of rights to data subjects; they are: access, correction, consent, preservation and care under the PDPA.[34] In **Sri Lanka,** the rights of data subjects include access, withdrawal of consent and objection, rectification and completion, erasure, and automated individual decision making.[35] However, this is subject to the business and consumer approach that Singapore generally takes to ensure that it is competitive in the region.

In **South Africa**, the data laws afford a number of rights to data subjects, intended to increase the control that data subjects have over their personal data. These rights include the data subject participation rights stipulated in sections 23–25, which give 'the right to access personal data, correct it, or even destroy it if certain conditions are met. In addition, section 5 of POPIA outlines broader data subject rights, such as rights to object to different forms of processing, and to submit a complaint to the IRSA, or take civil claims on the basis of interference with their data'.[36] **Tanzania's** 2022 data laws, according to sections 33–38, will provide a set of rights to data subjects, such as the right to 'access personal data, the right to restrict processing, the right to object to the processing of their personal data for commercial advertisement, the right to rectification, the right to not be subjected to Automated individual decision making that may affect the data subject. Data subjects will also be entitled to compensation for damage suffered due to the unlawful processing or collection of

---

[31] Law n°058/2021 of 13/10/2021 relating to the protection of personal data and privacy (the Data Protection Law), Articles 3, 6, 45, 36, 37, 8, 20, 21, https://www.minijust.gov.rw/fileadmin/user_upload/Minijust/Publications/Official_Gazette/_2021_Official_Gazettes/October/OG_Special_of_15.10.2021_Amakuru_bwite.pdf.

[32] *Privacy and Data Protection Act 2009*, section 32, https://www.govt.lc/media.govt.lc/www/resources/legislation/PrivacyAndDataProtectionBill.pdf.

[33] Data Protection Act, 5 of 2018, sections 14 to 19 https://www.theinformationcollective.com/dpl/st-kitts-data-protection-act.

[34] Personal Data Protection Act 2012, sections Parts 4, 5 & 6 https://sso.agc.gov.sg/Act/PDPA2012?ProvIds=Sc2-#Sc2.

[35] Personal Data Protection Act No. 9 of 2022, sections 13 to 18 https://www.parliament.lk/uploads/acts/gbills/english/6242.pdf.

[36] Protection of Personal Information 2013, section 23 to 25, https://www.gov.za/documents/protection-personal-information-act. Also see Privacy and personal data protection in Africa: A rights-based survey of legislation in eight countries, p 248, https://www.apc.org/sites/default/files/PrivacyDataProtectionAfrica_CountryReports.pdf.

their personal data'.[37] **Togo,** according to Law No. 2019-014, provides data subjects with a set of rights comprising access to information, objection, rectification, deletion and erasure.[38] A data subject in **Trinidad-Tobago**[39] has the right to access, correct, and disclose personal information.[40]

In **Uganda,** the rights of data subject include access, knowing the purpose for which the information is collected, and preventing processing and direct marketing, along with decisions affecting data subjects based on processing by automatic means.[41] Additionally, data subjects are afforded the right to rectification and to opt-out. Finally, **Zambia** provides data subjects with a number of rights that have been extended to include, right to be informed, access, rectification, erasure, object/opt-out, portability and not to be subject to automated decision-making.[42] This last right is an addition that has not been fully accepted or adopted by other jurisdictions. Put another way, where technology can intervene and make decisions in an automated way, it prevents person-to-person intervention. This technology is rapidly gaining traction through artificial intelligence. It will require vigilance, and it is argued that this is another area that should be researched by the Commonwealth.

12.2 Conclusion

The chapter has demonstrated the fragmented approach that has been taken by Commonwealth members not only when implementing the MBP and MBPPI, but also in terms of data laws in general. There is a significant level of inconsistency and incoherence. Data protection and data flow laws are a recent addition to the overall legal framework of many Commonwealth nation states.

Essentially, it has shown that Australia, the UK, Cyprus, Malta, New Zealand and Canada have a mature legal framework, having had their respective laws operational for more than 15 years. For most of the remaining Commonwealth states, data law has been developed and implemented only in the last decade. Also, although India of all the Commonwealth states has the largest population, it has yet to adopt specific

[37] Fatma Songoro, Brief Highlight and Analysis of the Tanzania Data Protection Bill, 2002, October 2022, https://victoryattorneys.co.tz/insights-brief-highlight-and-analysis-of-the-tanzania-data-protection-bill-2022/.

[38] Tshepiso Hadebe Togolese Republic, 2020, p1, https://dataprotection.africa/wp-content/uploads/2020/03/Togolese-Republic-Factsheet-update-20200331.pdf.

[39] Data Protection Regulation 2022, https://ndpb.gov.ng/Files/Nigeria_Data_Protection_Bill.pdf.

[40] Data Protection Regulation 2022, section 36, 44, 45, 46, 52, 56, 75 https://ndpb.gov.ng/Files/Nigeria_Data_Protection_Bill.pdf.

[41] Data Protection and Privacy Act 2019, sections 24 to 28 https://media.ulii.org/files/legislation/akn-ug-act-2019-9-eng-2019-05-03.pdf.

[42] Data Protection Act 2021, sections 58 to 69. https://www.parliament.gov.zm/sites/default/files/documents/acts/Act%20No.%203%20The%20Data%20Protection%20Act%202021_0.pdf.

data laws. It is likely that India will implement its new laws in late 2023 or 2024. This will be a watershed moment for India, who is one of the largest technology economies in the world.

A comparison of the rights afforded to data subjects in the respective nation states has demonstrated that further work is needed by the Commonwealth, should it genuinely want to see greater cooperation and integration of all its member states. A starting point has to be a revision of the MBP and MBPPI to eliminate inconsistencies. Doing so will have a number of benefits. First, it will extend the use of data in the digital economy. It will provide greater certainty. It will reduce the regulatory burden on organisations that operate across multiple jurisdictions. Further, it will make the respective data laws easier to understand. In each of the previous chapters, recommendations are made regarding the projects that the Commonwealth should undertake to ensure that the data laws are current and consistent.

More importantly, it has been demonstrated that there is an increasing convergence of data and cybersecurity. This this interconnectedness will be confirmed in subsequent chapters. Today, technology is connecting people and organisations with ease via Internet. As a consequence, an increasing amount of data is being generated, collected, used and stored online. It is argued that as electronic devices continue to penetrate the home and office, people will become increasingly dependent on the Internet and cyberspace for social, political and economic engagement. This will continue to grow, and we do not know where it will end.

The emergence of artificial intelligence will further add to and strengthen this connectedness. Thus, everybody needs to feel safe, and have a high level of trust in the technological systems and infrastructure that are being utilised by organisations. While not often discussed by government, unless there is a serious cyber breach and large numbers of people's data compromised, the digital economy has the potential to surpass the traditional industrial economy in the forthcoming decades.

Notwithstanding the above, the ensuing challenge for governments and regulators is to maintain vigilance and ensure the laws keep pace with technology. This will be highly complex and difficult to achieve as data and cybersecurity become more interconnected. As will be demonstrated later in this book, the sophistication of cyber intrusions has only begun to be fully understood. They are performed by state and non-state actors, and arguably can pose the most significant threat to the future economy. Those risks are further heightened by the mobility of people today as they take their computer devices from one country to the next. It is those risks that can easily escalate to illegal capture and use of personal data.

Finally, this book demonstrates that data law begins with a well-defined definition, supported by specific and various concepts such as, Controller, Consent & Processor; Storage Retention; Data Localisation; International Transfer; Data Portability; Right to be Forgotten; the application to Public and Private Sectors; and Data Rights. Because this book does not address all the concepts now found in data laws, further research is required.

Part III
Cyber Security Legal Concepts

Chapter 13
Cyber Security Laws

Data and cybersecurity are interconnected through a computer, systems and infrastructure that collect and use the information. However, at law, they have been separated. The ensuing chapters will be based on the foundational work undertaken by the Commonwealth through its Model Law on Computer and Computer Related Crime, which has defined cybersecurity categories comprising: (a) offences aimed at computers, computer or communications systems, their users or the data they contain; and (b) more traditional offences committed using these systems, especially if technologies have significant effects on how the crime is committed or investigated.[1] The comparative analysis extends to the detail of the provisions stipulated in the laws. This is because the terms and terminology used by the various states is significantly different.

In relation to the above, Curtis and Oxburgh draw a connection between a recent addition to the technology space and its functional arrangements. In addition, without naming a fundamental offence provision (compared in this Part) that has emerged in cybersecurity law, the authors posit that 'simply by providing an online pool of shared resources, facilitating access to "off the shelf attack" software and processing resources such as botnets to perform and automate attacks, the cloud presents an online environment in which offenders can hunt, operate and distribute spoils with relative ease and anonymity'.[2] Further, in drawing a connection between the systems that capture and use the data and data itself, the authors argue that:

[1] Model Law on Computer and Computer Related Crime, Office of Civil and Criminal Justice Reform, 2017, p. 1 https://production-new-commonwealth-files.s3.eu-west-2.amazonaws.com/migrated/key_reform_pdfs/P15370_11_ROL_Model_Law_Computer_Related_Crime.pdf.

[2] Curtis, J Oxburgh, G. (2022). Understanding cybercrime in 'real world' policing and law enforcement. The Police Journal (2022), p. 1.

R. Walters, *Cybersecurity and Data Laws of the Commonwealth*,
https://doi.org/10.1007/978-981-99-3935-0_13

> By its very nature as a shared data centre, cloud technology increases the number of devices that can be accessed through an Internet connection and thus the number of opportunities for offenders to exploit. The effect of the cloud as a force multiplier not only results in a greater yield to perpetrator efforts but also further reduces the risk of prosecution. Thus, the Internet and cloud computing offer a spectrum of criminal options, from the influence of a networked computer on traditional crime, to crimes that are automated and occur entirely within a virtual environment.[3]

The connection to the Internet gives individuals immediate access to platforms and systems, that can be used for both legal and illegal purposes. The illegal access or intrusion by the deliberate actions of people has required governments around the world to respond by establishing cybersecurity or cybercrime laws. These terms will be used interchangeably throughout this Part.

The Model Law that is otherwise referred to as the *Computer and Computer Related Crimes Act (CCRA)*, goes some way to bringing about a synergy or convergence of data and cyber law. Similar to the Model Law on data governance discussed in Part II of this book, it will be argued that the CCRA should also be reviewed to include additional cybercrime offence provisions related to theft, ransom and fraud. This is because these offences are increasingly appearing as criminal activity. More specifically, it has identified five key areas of importance to cybersecurity over the Internet:

- Illegal access;
- Interfering with data;
- Interfering with computer system;
- Illegal interception of data; and
- Illegal devices.[4]

This book will not discuss the offences or related issue regarding child pornography as outlined in section 10. Further, section 3, draws a connection between data and its security. It defines specific data terms, such as

- *computer data*: any representation of facts, information or concepts in a form suitable for processing in a computer system, including a program suitable to cause a computer system to perform a function;
- *computer data storage medium*: any article or material (for example, a disk) from which information is capable of being reproduced, with or without the aid of any other article or device;
- *traffic data*: computer data (a) that relates to a communication by means of a computer system; and (b) is generated by a computer system that is part of the chain of communication; and (c) shows the communication's origin, destination, route, time-date, size, duration or the type of underlying services.[5]

---

[3] Ibid.

[4] Ibid, sections, 5,6,7,8,9.

[5] Ibid, section 3.

Section 5 of the CCRA outlines what illegal access constitutes, whereby, a person who intentionally, without lawful excuse or justification, accesses the whole or any part of a computer system commits an offence punishable, on conviction, by imprisonment for a period not exceeding, or a fine not exceeding, or both.[6] Section 6 concerns the interference with data, whereby a person who, intentionally or recklessly, without lawful excuse or justification, takes any of the following actions:

1. destroys or alters data;
2. renders data meaningless, useless or ineffective;
3. obstructs, interrupts or interferes with the lawful use of data; or
4. obstructs, interrupts or interferes with any person in the lawful use of data; or
5. denies access to data to any person entitled to it; commits an offence punishable, on conviction, by imprisonment for a period not exceeding [*period*], or a fine not exceeding [*amount*], or both. Subsection (1) applies whether the person's act is of temporary or permanent effect.[7]

One of the most important areas of cyber intrusions that has emerged concerns individuals or entities gaining illegal access to a computer system. Section 7 deals with the issue of interference with a computer system, whereby a person who intentionally or recklessly, without lawful excuse or justification (a) hinders or interferes with the functioning of a computer system; or (b) hinders or interferes with a person who is lawfully using or operating a computer system; commits an offence punishable, on conviction, by imprisonment for a period not exceeding, or a fine not exceeding, or both.[8]

In another sign that data has taken a specific role in the CCRA, section 8 governs the illegal interception of data. That is, a person who, intentionally without lawful excuse or justification, intercepts by technical means (a) any non-public transmission to, from or within a computer system; or (b) electromagnetic emissions from a computer system that are carrying computer data; commits an offence punishable, on conviction, by imprisonment for a period not exceeding, or a fine not exceeding, or both.[9] On the other hand, section 9 deals with illegal devices. It prohibits a person from producing, selling or procuring a device to enable the access to a computer system, amongst others things. Section 9 states that a person commits an offence if that person (a) intentionally or recklessly, without lawful excuse or justification, produces, sells, procures for use, imports, exports, distributes or otherwise makes available: (i) a device, including a computer program, that is designed or adapted for the purpose of committing an offence against section 5, 6, 7 or 8; or (ii) a computer password, access code or similar data by which the whole or any part of a computer

[6] Ibid, section 5.

[7] Ibid, section 6.

[8] Ibid, section 7. In subsection (1) "hinder", in relation to a computer system, includes but is not limited to: (a) cutting the electricity supply to a computer system; (b) causing electro-magnetic interference to a computer system; (c) corrupting a computer system by any means; and (d) in putting, deleting or altering computer data.

[9] Ibid, section 8.

system is capable of being accessed; with the intent that it be used by any person for the purpose of committing an offence against section 5, 6, 7 or 8; or (b) has an item mentioned in subparagraph (a)(i) or (a)(ii) in his or her possession with the intent that it be used by any person for the purpose of committing an offence against section 5, 6, 7 or 8.[10] The CCRA goes further by setting out a number of procedural powers. Powers in criminal law are related to the state having the ability to take certain actions so that investigations can be conducted to determine the illegal collection, use, storage and/or dissemination of data. The standard areas of evidence include, search and seizure, record of and access to seized data,[11] and production of data,[12] disclosure of stored traffic data,[13] preservation of data,[14] and the illegal interception of traffic data.[15] On this basis, this chapter will examine and compare the laws of all commonwealth countries, with the above principles and concepts provided under the Model Law, and also:

- Fraud;
- Theft; and
- Ransom.

Therefore, the ensuing chapters will confirm whether the relevant cyber laws of all Commonwealth countries address the key areas of illegal access; interfering with data; interfering with a computer system; illegal interception of data; illegal devices; fraud; identity theft; and ransom. Cybersecurity law underpi, supports and protection international trade and investment. It is an important feature of the economy. Wihtout robust cyber law, the economic foundation and fabrication of society will be significantly compromised.

Table 13.1 shows the extent to which member countries of the Commonwealth have adopted cybersecurity laws.

A notable difference between all member countries is the way that the cybersecurity laws have been structured. A number of countries have opted for a single piece of legislation. That is, they have adopted a single Act, such as the Cybersecurity Act that regulates some or all of the core issues identified in the CCRA. On the other hand, some countries have adopted the approach of amending existing criminal laws. What has emerged is an inconsistent and incoherent approach. It has created, and

[10] Ibid, section 9. A person found guilty of an offence against this section is liable to a penalty of imprisonment for a period not exceeding, or a fine not exceeding, or both. Where a person possesses more than item(s) mentioned in subparagraph (1)(a)(i) or (1)(a)(ii), a court may, having regard to all the circumstances, infer that the person possesses the item with the intent that it be used by any person for the purpose of committing an offence against section 5, 6, 7 or 8. Subsection 3 is an optional provision. For some countries such a presumption may prove very useful while for others, it may not add much value, in the context of this particular offence. Countries need to consider whether the addition would be useful within the particular legal context.

[11] Ibid, section 14.

[12] Ibid, section 15.

[13] Ibid, section 16.

[14] Ibid, Sect. 17.

[15] Ibid, Sect. 19.

Table 13.1 Cyber security laws as at December 2022

Africa and Europe	Cyber law	Indo Pacific	Cyber law	Caribbean and Americas	Cyber law
Botswana	Cybercrime and related Crimes Act 2018[16]	Bangladesh	*Digital Security Act, 2018*[17]	Antigua and Barbuda	Electronic Crimes Act 2013[18]
Cameroon	Law No 2010-12 of 21 December relating to cybersecurity and cybercriminality in Cameroon[19]	Brunei Darussalam	Computer Misuse act 2007[20]	Bahamas	Computer Misuse Act 2006[21]
Gabon	Ordinance No 15/PR/2018 23 February 2018 on Cybersecurity and Cybercrime[22] French only version	India	Information Technology Act (2000)[23]	Barbados	Computer Misuse Act, 2005[24]
Gambia	Information and Communication Act 2009[25] Criminal Procedure Code 1933	Malaysia	Computer Crimes Act 1997[26]	Belize	Cybercrime Act 2020[27]

(continued)

16 Cybercrime and related Crimes Act 2018, https://www.bocra.org.bw/cybercrime-and-computer-related-crimes-act-2018.

17 Digital Security Act 2018, https://www.cirt.gov.bd/wp-content/uploads/2020/02/Digital-Security-Act-2020.pdf.

18 Electronic Crimes Act 2013, http://laws.gov.ag/wp-content/uploads/2019/02/a2013-14.pdf.

19 Law No 2010-12 of 21 December relating to cybersecurity and cybercriminality in Cameroon, http://www.minjustice.gov.cm/index.php/en/instruments-and-laws/laws/302-law-no-2010-12-of-21-december-relating-to-cybersecurity-and-cybercriminality-in-cameroon.

20 Computer Misuse Act 2007, https://www.agc.gov.bn/AGC%20Images/LAWS/ACT_PDF/C/CHAPTER%20194.pdf.

21 Computer Misuse Act 2006, http://laws.bahamas.gov.bs/cms/images/LEGISLATION/PRINCIPAL/2003/2003-0002/ComputerMisuseAct_1.pdf.

22 Ordinance No 15/PR/2018 23 February 2018 on Cybersecurity and Cybercrime, http://www.droit-afrique.com/uploads/Gabon-Ordonnance-2018-15-cybersecurite-cybercriminalite.pdf.

23 Information Technology Act (2000), https://thelawreviews.co.uk/title/the-privacy-data-protection-and-cybersecurity-law-review/india, and https://www.indiacode.nic.in/handle/123456789/1999.

24 Computer Misuse Act, 2005, http://www.oas.org/juridico/spanish/cyb_bbs_computer_misuse_2005.pdf.

25 Information and Communication Act 2009, https://ictpolicyafrica.org/en/document/2by2f59p583?page=1 Criminal Procedure Code, https://static1.squarespace.com/static/5a7c2ca18a02c7a46149331c/t/5f025f49fb7f38664f1ed2f3/1593991003326/Criminal+Code+%2C+Act+No.+25+of+1933.pdf.

26 Computer Crimes Act 1997, https://www.nacsa.gov.my/legal.php.

27 Cybercrime Act 2020, https://www.nationalassembly.gov.bz/wp-content/uploads/2020/10/Act-No.-32-of-2020-Cybercrime.pdf.

Table 13.1 (continued)

Africa and Europe	Cyber law	Indo Pacific	Cyber law	Caribbean and Americas	Cyber law
Ghana	Cybersecurity Act 2020[28]	Maldives	No specific laws	Canada	Criminal Code 1985[29]
Kenya	The Kenya Information and Communications Act, 1998 Computer Misuse and Cyber Crimes Act of 2018[30]	Pakistan	The Prevention of Electronic Crimes 2016[31]	Dominica	No specific laws
Kingdom of Eswatini	*Computer Crime and Cybercrime Act No.6 of 2022*[32]	Singapore	Cybersecurity Act 2018[33]	Grenada	Electronic Crimes Bill 2013[34]
Lesotho	The Computer Crimes and Cyber Security Bill, 2022[35]	Sri Lanka	Cyber Security Act, No. of 2019[36]	Guyana	Cyber Crime Act 2018[37]
Malawi	Electronic Transactions and Cyber Security Act 2017[38]	Australia	Crimes Act 1914 (Cth), note state-based laws also[39]	Jamaica	The Cyber Crimes Act 2015[40]

(continued)

[28] Cybersecurity Act 2020, https://csdsafrica.org/wp-content/uploads/2021/08/Cybersecurity-Act-2020-Act-1038.pdf.

[29] Criminal Code 1985, https://laws-lois.justice.gc.ca/pdf/c-46.pdf.

[30] Kenya, various legislation exist, https://www.ca.go.ke/industry/cyber-security/overview/ and https://ictpolicyafrica.org/en/document/pb8w26fcso?page=2.

[31] The Prevention of Electronic Crimes 2016, https://na.gov.pk/uploads/documents/1470910659_707.pdf.

[32] *Computer Crime and Cybercrime Act No.6 of 2022*, https://www.esccom.org.sz/legislation/COMPUTER%20CRIME%20&%20CYBERCRIME%20ACT.pdf.

[33] Cybersecurity Act 2018, https://sso.agc.gov.sg/Acts-Supp/9-2018/.

[34] Electronic Crimes Bill 2013, https://ecagrenada.com/Grenada-Electronic-Crimes-Act-2013.pdf.

[35] The Computer Crimes and Cyber Security Bill, 2022, https://senate.parliament.ls/2022/05/19/computer-crime-and-cyber-security-bill-2022/.

[36] Cyber Security Act, No. of 2019, https://cert.gov.lk/documents/Cyber%20Security%20Bill.pdf.

[37] Cyber Crime Act 2018, https://parliament.gov.gy/publications/acts-of-parliament/cyber-crime-act-2018.

[38] Electronic Transactions and Cyber Security Act 2017, https://media.malawilii.org/files/legislation/akn-mw-act-2016-33-eng-2017-12-31.pdf.

[39] Crimes Act 1914, https://www.legislation.gov.au/Details/C2021C00127.

[40] The Cyber Crimes Act 2015, https://www.japarliament.gov.jm/attachments/339_The%20Cybercrimes%20Acts,%202015.pdf.

Table 13.1 (continued)

Africa and Europe	Cyber law	Indo Pacific	Cyber law	Caribbean and Americas	Cyber law
Mauritius	Cybersecurity and Cybercrime Act 2021[41]	Fiji	Cybercrime Act 2021 (Act No. 3 of 2021)[42]	Saint Lucia	Electronic Crimes Bill 2009[43]
Mozambique	No specific law. Resolution no. 5/2019, Mozambique ratified the African Union Convention on Cybersecurity and the Protection of Personal Data. In addition, significant reforms to the criminal code, approved by Law no. 24/2019, covering matters of cybercrime	Kiribati	Cybercrime Act 2021[44]	St Kitts and Nevis	Electronic Crimes Bill 2017[45]
Namibia	The *Cybercrime* Bill (2019)[46] Under review 2022	Nauru	Cybercrime Act 2015[47]	St Vincent and The Grenadines	Cybercrime Act 2016[48]
Nigeria	Cyber Crime Act 2015[49]	New Zealand	Crimes Act 1961[50]	Trinidad and Tobago	The Cybercrimes Bill 2017[51]

(continued)

[41] Cybersecurity and Cybercrime Act 2021, https://ncb.govmu.org/ncb/legislations/THE%20CYBERSECURITY%20AND%20CYBERCRIME%20ACT%202021.pdf.

[42] Cybercrime Act 2021 (Act No. 3 of 2021), https://www.ilo.org/dyn/natlex/natlex4.detail?p_lang=en&p_isn=111060&p_classification=01.

[43] Electronic Crimes Bill 2009, https://www.govt.lc/media.govt.lc/www/resources/legislation/ElectronicCrimesBill.pdf.

[44] Cybercrime Act 2021, https://www.mict.gov.ki/download/file/fid/320.

[45] Electronic Crimes Bill 2017, https://aglcskn.info/wp-content/documents/Act17TOC/Ch-04_41-Electronic-Crimes-Act.pdf.

[46] The *Cybercrime* Bill (2019), https://economist.com.na/70910/general-news/government-in-the-midst-of-finalising-the-cyber-crime-bill-and-consolidated-national-ict-policy/.

[47] Cybercrime Act 2015, http://ronlaw.gov.nr/nauru_lpms/files/acts/a59d9691f5a195412b877493a2a95e8b.pdf.

[48] Cybercrime Act 2016, https://www.gov.vc/images/PoliciesActsAndBills/SVG_Cybercrime_Act_2016.pdf.

[49] Cyber Crime Act 2015, https://lawpadi.com/wp-content/uploads/2015/08/CyberCrime_ProhibitionPreventionetc_Act_2015.pdf.

[50] Crimes Act 1961, https://www.legislation.govt.nz/act/public/1961/0043/latest/DLM330422.html.

[51] The Cybercrimes Bill 2017, https://ttcsirt.gov.tt/wp-content/uploads/2022/04/Cyber_Crime_Bill_DRAFT_2017.pdf.

Table 13.1 (continued)

Africa and Europe	Cyber law	Indo Pacific	Cyber law	Caribbean and Americas	Cyber law
Rwanda	Law N° 60/2018 OF 22/8/2018 on prevention and punishment of cyber crimes[52]	Papua New Guinea	*Cybercrime Code Act 2016*[53]		
Seychelles	Computer Misuse act 1998[54]	Samoa	No specific laws. 2022 Ratified the Budapest Convention on Cybercrime[55]		
Sierra Leone	Cyber Crime Act 2020[56]	Solomon Islands	No specific laws		
South Africa	Cybercrimes Act 2021[57]	Tonga	Computer Crimes Act 2003[58]		
Togo	*The Law on Cybersecurity and Fight against Cybercrime of 2018*[59]				
Uganda	*Computer Misuse Act, 2011*[60]				
United Republic of Tanzania	*Cybercrimes Act, 2015*[61]				
Zambia	The Cyber Security and Cyber Crimes Act, 2021[62]				

(continued)

[52] Law N° 60/2018 OF 22/8/2018 on prevention and punishment of cyber crimes, https://www.risa.rw/fileadmin/user_upload/Others%20documents/Cyber_Crimes_Law.pdf.

[53] *Cybercrime Code Act 2016*, https://www.parliament.gov.pg/uploads/acts/16A_35.pdf.

[54] Computer Misuse Act 1998, https://seylii.org/akn/sc/act/1998/17/eng%402015-12-31.

[55] No specific laws, https://www.samoaobserver.ws/category/samoa/100397.

[56] Cyber Crime Act 2020, http://www.sierra-leone.org/Laws/2020-Cybercrime%20Act.pdf.

[57] Cybercrimes Act 2021, https://cybercrimesact.co.za.

[58] Computer crimes Act 2003, https://ago.gov.to/cms/images/LEGISLATION/PRINCIPAL/2003/2003-0014/ComputerCrimesAct2003_1.pdf.

[59] *The Law on Cybersecurity and Fight against Cybercrime of 2018*, https://ictpolicyafrica.org/en/document/g3nbf9okuht?raw=true&page=2.

[60] *Computer Misuse Act, 2011*, https://ulii.org/akn/ug/act/2011/2/eng@2011-02-14.

[61] *Cybercrimes Act, 2015* https://rsf.org/sites/default/files/the_cyber_crime_act_2015.pdf.

[62] The Cyber Security and Cyber Crimes Act, 2021, https://www.parliament.gov.zm/sites/default/files/documents/acts/Act%20No.%202%20of%202021The%20Cyber%20Security%20and%20Cyber%20Crimes.pdf.

Table 13.1 (continued)

Africa and Europe	Cyber law	Indo Pacific	Cyber law	Caribbean and Americas	Cyber law
Cyprus	Cybersecurity Act 2019[63] Cyber Resilience Act[64] However, this does not form part of the book comparison				
Malta	Cybersecurity Act 2019[65]				
United Kingdom	Computer Misuse Act 1990[66]				

will continue to create, a complex legal environment for individuals and entities to navigate. Furthermore, the ensuing chapters will highlight how fragmented the laws have become. In other words, some countries have adopted all of the Commonwealth core legal issues on cybersecurity, while others have not. For example, and this is a good indicator, the titles of the laws vary significantly. It is recommended that a standard approach be taken when naming the laws, so that the general public and businesses can easily identify their legal requirements for future cyber-related matters. Countries such as Australia should have specific legislation on cybercrime. Most noteworthy, is that the laws have been developed and implemented only in the last decade from 2010 onwards.

The ensuing chapters will not examine the jurisdictions of **Maldives, Dominica, Mozambique, Samoa,** and the **Solomon Islands** as they do not have any specific cybersecurity laws. The cyber laws of **Gabon** and **Togo** cannot be compared as they are currently available only in French.[67] In **Gambia**, the cyber laws are covered by both the Information and Communication Act 2009 (ICA) and the Criminal Procedure Code. However, the following chapters will examine only the Information and Communication Act 2009. Doing so has determined that there are no related offences in the ICA. Thus, Gambia will not be discussed in any of the chapters. The country of **Cameroon** will not be used for comparison as the laws are structured very differently, and generally pertain to an organisation and electronic communications networks. The laws place obligations on the person who provides access to the systems and

[63] Regulation (EU) 2019/881 of the European Parliament and of the Council of 17 April 2019 on ENISA (the European Union Agency for Cybersecurity) and on information and communications technology cybersecurity certification and repealing Regulation (EU) No 526/2013 (Cybersecurity Act) OJL 151. https://eur-lex.europa.eu/eli/reg/2019/881/oj.

[64] Cyber Resilience Act, https://digital-strategy.ec.europa.eu/en/library/cyber-resilience-act.

[65] Regulation (EU) 2019/881 of the European Parliament and of the Council of 17 April 2019 on ENISA (the European Union Agency for Cybersecurity) and on information and communications technology cybersecurity certification and repealing Regulation (EU) No 526/2013 (Cybersecurity Act) OJL 151. https://eur-lex.europa.eu/eli/reg/2019/881/oj.

[66] Computer Misuse Act 1990, https://www.legislation.gov.uk/ukpga/1990/18/contents.

[67] The author of this book is not conversant in French.

infrastructure, rather than the illegal intrusion of those systems. Although are specific privacy provisions, it is the network provider that is obliged to inform and protect data. Most, if not all of the offences are covered by the Criminal Procedure Code. **Sri Lanka** has adopted the approach of regulating for an Agency that is responsible for the development and oversight of cybersecurity matters according to the Cyber Security Act 2019.[68] It is beyond the scope of this book to examine the other criminal laws **of Sri Lanka** to confirm or otherwise the offences addressed in this Part. On the other hand, **Australia** has state and national laws within their respective Crime laws. **New Zealand** does not have specific cyber laws, in the same way as most of the jurisdictions compared. Both Australia and New Zealand have incorporated their respective cybercrime laws into their respective criminal laws. It is my view that this is an area that needs to be changed as a matter of urgency to emphasise to the community the importance of protection against computer-based crime. Having specific laws consistent with many other Commonwealth nation states will raise the profile of the importance of cybersecurity to protect economic activity aling with data, and make it a lot simpler to access the offence provisions.

At the time of writing, **Namibia** was undertaking a review of their cyber laws; hence, it has not been included in the overall comparison. Thus, based on this, the book will examine and compare only those states laws that are specific to cybersecurity-crime. **Cyprus** and **Malta**, as members of the EU, have implemented Regulation 2019/881[69] that establishes the European Union Agency for Cybersecurity. This Regulation does not set the standards for offences related to cybersecurity but, instead, invokes a set of standards through a certification scheme. Therefore, it will not form part of the overall comparison. Hence, the national laws of **Cyprus and Malta** will not be examined in this book. Moreover, there are a number of provisions that will be duplicated in each chapter, because the provision(s) themselves overlap and relate to offences that are not separated. To address this overlap, the provision(s) will be reflected in each chapter throughout this part.

When comparing the respective Commonwealth nation states' laws with the CCRA, it quickly became apparent that Botswana has structured its Cybercrime Act as a model for other states to replicate. Under each section of the Act, there is a note highlighting, for example, where the provision or provisions align with the CCRA (Interfering with Computer System). Many other states have followed this approach. However, there is a large number who have not. It is out of scope to identity those states individually. The Commonwealth could put out a communique requesting that the same approach be taken. Other jurisdictions should follow this structure, so that individuals and entities can quickly identify the relevant provisions. The following chapters do not compare the penalties provided for each offence. More generally, the ensuring chapters will demonstrate that further and urgent research is

---

[68] Cyber Security Act, No. of 2019, https://cert.gov.lk/documents/Cyber%20Security%20Bill.pdf.

[69] Regulation (EU) 2019/881 of the European Parliament and of the Council of 17 April 2019 on ENISA (the European Union Agency for Cybersecurity) and on information and communications technology cybersecurity certification and repealing Regulation (EU) No 526/2013 (Cybersecurity Act) OJL 151. https://eur-lex.europa.eu/eli/reg/2019/881/oj.

needed to reconcile the differences in approaches taken by countries when developing their respective cybersecurity laws. Due to the breadth and depth of laws compared, there is limited scholarly discussion. Instead, there is a great focus on examining the offence provisions themselves and the recent judicial decisions from selected countries. However, there is an emerging issue of importance to set the scene: directors and officers of companies will have a high level of responsibility to manage the risk posed by cybersecurity.

Commercial Risk and the evolving Fiduciary Duty

Increasingly, the judiciary is holding individuals and corporate entities to account for failure to adequately address the risk of cybersecurity risk. There now appears to be a fiduciary obligation attached to directors' duties to ensure that adequate measures to mitigate cybersecurity risk have been implemented by organisations.

The formal and functional arrangements for the future management of cybersecurity risk by entities was summarised by the Australian Federal Court in 2022. In the case of *Australian Securities and Investments Commission v RI Advice Group Pty Ltd*,[70] the Court stated that:

> RI Advice contravened ss 912A(1)(a) and (h) of the Corporations Act from 15 May 2018 to 5 August 2021 as a result of its failure to have documentation and controls in respect of cybersecurity and cyber resilience in place that were adequate to manage risk in respect of cybersecurity and cyber resilience across its AR network, and as a result of this conduct, it a) failed to do all things necessary to ensure the financial services covered by the Licence were provided efficiently and fairly, in contravention of s 912A(1)(a) of the Corporations Act; and b) failed to have adequate risk management systems, in contravention of s 912A(1)(h) of the Corporations Act.[71]

The case is important because it highlights and reinforces the above: that directors and officers of a company have a duty of care.[72] In addressing section 92(1)(a) and (h) of the Corporations Act, the Court went on to say that:

> Cyberspace, and cyber-attacks, concern digital or computer technology or networks, and involve attacks directed at computers, computer systems or other information communication technologies. Cybersecurity is the ability of an organisation to protect and defend the use of cyberspace from attacks. Cyber resilience is the ability to anticipate, withstand, recover from and adapt to adverse conditions, stresses, attacks or compromises on systems that use or are enabled by cyber sources. Risks relating to cybersecurity, and the controls that can be deployed to address such risks evolve over time. As financial services are increasingly conducted using digital and computer technology, cybersecurity risk has also increased. Cybersecurity risk forms a significant risk connected with the conduct of the business and provision of financial services. It is not possible to reduce cybersecurity risk to zero,

---

70 *Australian Securities and Investments Commission v RI Advice Group Pty Ltd* [2022] FCA 496.

71 Ibid, para 2.

72 Ian Ramsay, Miranda Webster, '*An analysis of the use of stepping stones liability against company directors and officers*' (2021) 50(1) *Australian Bar Review* 1.

> but it is possible to materially reduce cybersecurity risk through adequate cybersecurity documentation and controls to an acceptable level.[73]

While the Court focused on the risks posed to an entity by cyber-attacks, it went further by emphasising the interconnectedness of cybersecurity and personal data. The Court argued that cybercrime by malicious actors targets personal information.[74] Thus, the reference to personal information constitutes personal data, as defined by the data protection and privacy laws, outlined earlier in this book. Moreover, the level of cybersecurity governance implemented within the organisation, the Court considered the practices adopted. In so doing, the Court noted that:

> The Cyber Resilience Initiative, designed by IOOF and implemented across 2020 and 2021 directly with the AR Practices (and by 6 August 2021 with the majority of AR Practices) had implemented, and been approved as being implemented, the majority of all the 11 best practices in the RI Advice Cyber Security Support Guide, to a good level. However, RI Advice acknowledges that whilst the measures it assessed and developed across the period 15 May 2018 to 5 August 2021 in order to improve cybersecurity and cyber resilience for the ARs were designed so as to meet RI Advice's understanding of its obligations, it took too long to implement and ensure such measures were in place across its AR Practices. RI Advice accepts that it should have had a more robust implementation of its program so that the measures were more quickly in place at each of the AR Practices and the majority of the AR network was confirmed as operating pursuant to such cybersecurity and resilience measures earlier than 6 August 2021.[75]

The Court in conclusion noted that from 15 May 2018 to 5 August 2021, RI Advice contravened s 912A(1)(a) of the Act in that it failed to do all things necessary to ensure that the financial services covered by its Licence were provided efficiently and fairly, by failing to ensure that adequate cybersecurity measures were in place and/or adequately implemented across its Authorised Representatives. Additionally, from the above date, the Court also noted RI Advice failed to have adequate risk management systems, by failing to implement adequate cybersecurity and cyber resilience measures and exposing its Authorised Representatives' clients to an unacceptable level of risk.[76]

13.1 Conclusion

Even though this is only one example from a single Commonwealth country, it demonstrates that under the common law, there will be an increasing need for directors and officers of commercial corporations to be vigilant. It will require them to undertake and implement sound risk management frameworks and practices to minimize as far as possible the exposure of the organization to cybersecurity incursions.

---

[73] *Australian Securities and Investments Commission v RI Advice Group Pty Ltd* [2022] FCA 496, paras 57–58.

[74] Ibid, para 59.

[75] Ibid, paras, 63–64.

[76] Ibid, paras, 65–66.

Further, and most importantly, it highlights how personal data is closely aligned and interconnected with cybersecurity in the new digital economy. The point to note in this case, is the need for organisations, whether large or small, to develop and implement sound cybersecurity policies, procedures and practices, and ensure that staff within the organisation know how the systems and infrastructure need to be protected from cyber-incursions.

Similarly, in Canada the above position has been expressed and includes:

> Directors and officers owe statutory and common law duties to exercise reasonable care and diligence in running the company, including exercising appropriate oversight over the company's cybersecurity program. Investors or other stakeholders could pursue such claims against directors and officers through a derivative action, on behalf of the company, to seek to remedy the harms suffered by the company as a result of director or officer negligence. Under securities law, directors and officers can be held liable for omissions or misrepresentations in the company's public disclosure, which could include disclosures about the status of cybersecurity incidents, risks and preventative measures.[77]

However, there have been no judicial decisions addressing this matter. While the above is only a brief outline of the issue associated with directors and officers being responsible for cybersecurity to protect data and other information, there is a need for additional research in this area. Company officers will need to be aware of and implement practices within the organization to prevent cyber intrusions. This is going to be challenging for the small and medium-sized business community. Government and regulators will need to support this sector. Although similar developments have also appeared in the United States,[78] they will not be discussed since the US is not a Commonwealth country.

[77] TORYS, Director and officer liability for cybersecurity breaches in Canada and the US, https://www.torys.com/our-latest-thinking/publications/2022/04/director-and-officer-liability-for-cybersecurity-breaches-in-canada-and-the-us.

[78] Securities and exchange Commission, Cybersecurity Risk Management, Strategy, Governance, and Incident Disclosure, https://www.sec.gov/rules/proposed/2022/33-11038.pdf.

Chapter 14
Illegal Access

14.1 Introduction

This chapter will examine how the countries of the Commonwealth (apart from the aforementioned exceptions) have included or otherwise the concept of illegal access in their respective cyber laws. It will draw upon section 5 of the Model Law, which provides for illegal access where:

> a person who intentionally, without lawful excuse or justification, accesses the whole or any part of a computer system commits an offence punishable, on conviction, by imprisonment for a period not exceeding, or a fine not exceeding, or both.[1]

This chapter does not provide a word-by-word comparison of the laws. Due to the fragmented approach of the laws across all of the countries compared, a high-level approach has been taken to confirm where the offence provision has been adopted. Generally, where there is an offence provision, this demonstrates consistency with other jurisdictions. Where there is reference to a general offence provision, this means that the state has a provision similar those of the other states compared. Overall, there is a need for further research to detail the subtle but significant differences. Importantly, in reconciling the differences between the states, subtle themes will emerge. It will be important for regulators, practitioners and policy makers to reconcile the differences in approach in regard to cross-border offences. This first chapter demonstrates that effective cybersecurity can have a positive economic impact. Put another away, cybersecurity can be viewed as an enabler.

[1] Model Law on Computer and Computer Related Crime, Office of Civil and Criminal Justice Reform, 2017, section 5, https://production-new-commonwealth-files.s3.eu-west-2.amazonaws.com/migrated/key_reform_pdfs/P15370_11_ROL_Model_Law_Computer_Related_Crime.pdf.

R. Walters, *Cybersecurity and Data Laws of the Commonwealth*,
https://doi.org/10.1007/978-981-99-3935-0_14

Overall, the African states and some of the Pacific countries have generally followed the CCRA. However, countries such as Australia have included the offences in their respective criminal laws. This has, in my view, created a higher level of fragmentation. It will be complex and difficult for the general practitioner to locate the relevant offence provisions. That said, and while this does not translate where those states have not addressed the offences described by the CCRA, it does demonstrate the inconsistencies across countries.

The digital economy is providing huge benefits to consumers around the world and to entities that are servicing them. However, like any commercial activity, there are challenges arising from this new, technology-driven activity. A major challenge is the potential for illegal access to computers and their systems that collect large quantities of personal data. This alone has resulted in a greater interconnectivity between cybersecurity and data. David Wicki-Berchler reaffirms this point, arguing that:

> The phenomenon of cybercrime is strongly tied to the rise of computers in both personal and commercial use. This is because the new opportunities of data processing and data exchange, which are the very strength of computers, can be meaningfully used as much as they can be abused unethically and criminally.[2]

This has produced a significant impact on the world economy and, while not specifically stated, is hampering the development of the digital economy. That is because, as cybersecurity threats and breaches increase, the resulting effect is that organisation have to spend more money to protect their data. Wicki-Berchler further makes the point that:

> Society is paying a high price for the amenities of the Internet, as the cost of cybercrime was estimated to have reached US$2 trillion dollars in 2019. Some of the weakest links is the safety and security measures such as human error, and taking shortcuts in operating a computer.[3]

Based on the above, the cost will only increase as the sophistication of technology further enables and facilitates ease of access to computer systems and data. When people discuss and think about cybersecurity, it is generally from the perspective of the offences individuals commit to access a computer and data, and the cost to business and the community. However, he broader economic development, it can be viewed as an economic enabler. For instance:

> A small number of new technologies (such as big data, mobile computing and cloud) are revolutionising IT markets and enabling new trends in the IT market. Whilst these trends can rightly be seen as economic enablers they also present significant cybersecurity challenges. From a microeconomic perspective, cybersecurity maturity of large companies are typically more concerned about cyber security related risks than rest of world. The rapid development

[2] David Wicki-Birchler, *The Budapest Convention and the General Data Protection Regulation: acting in concert to curb cybercrime?*. Int. Cybersecur. Law Rev. 1, (2020) p. 63.

[3] Ibid, p. 64.

> of new technologies however has made it clear that traditional approaches to Cyber Security are insufficient. Security concerns are slowing adoption of some technologies, especially mobile and cloud, which is preventing the EU from making the most of innovation to boost its economic efficiency.[4]

The treatment of cybersecurity as an economic enabler will provide jobs across the Commonwealth. This can be seen in the education sector, where cybersecurity courses today are mainstream. On the other hand, the economic impacts of cyber intrusions will continue to be problematic and cost the community.

In **Antigua and Barbuda**, section 2 defines access to mean that the context of an electronic system means to communicate with, store data in, retrieve data from, or otherwise make use of any of the resources of the electronic system.[5] More specifically, section 3 provides that no person without lawful authority can have access to an electronic system or network.[6]

According to section 476.2 of the Criminal Code Act 1995 **Australia,** there is a single offence for a number of different issues such as access to a computer. Section 477.1 is similar and applies to more serious computer-related offences comprising:

(a) access to data held in a computer; or
(b) modification of data held in a computer; or
(c) the impairment of electronic communication to or from a computer; or
(d) the impairment of the reliability, security or operation of any data held on a computer disk, credit card or other device used to store data by electronic means; by a person is unauthorised if the person is not entitled to cause that access, modification or impairment.[7]

Arguably, the above provision covers multiple offences in addition to unauthorised access to a computer, and will be addressed later in this book. It is further argued that accessing a computer and its systems is the starting point for the collection and extraction of data. In the case of *Soyke*[8] there was an appeal on sentencing, whereby the 'applicant pleaded guilty to four computer related offences under s 477 of the *Criminal Code Act 1995* (Cth), which each carry a maximum penalty of 10 years imprisonment. The appeal was dismissed. However, 17 offences of attempt to cause unauthorised access to restricted data under ss 478.1(1) and 11.1(1) of the Code, which each carried maximum penalties of 2 years imprisonment, were also taken into account on sentencing, in accordance with s 16BA of the *Crimes Act 1914* (Cth)'.[9] More specifically, the case demonstrated the interconnectedness of

---

[4] Enisa, Cybersecurity as and Enabler, 2016, https://www.enisa.europa.eu/publications/enisa-position-papers-and-opinions/cybersecurity-as-an-economic-enabler.

[5] Electronic Crimes Act 2013, section 2, http://laws.gov.ag/wp-content/uploads/2019/02/a2013-14.pdf.

[6] Ibid, section 3.

[7] *Australian Criminal Code Act 1995*, section 476.2. Note sections 477.1, 477.2, 477.3, creates the same offence for serious computer access, modification or impairment. Note also Division 478.

[8] *Soyke v R* [2016] NSWCCA 112.

[9] Ibid, para 2.

cybercrime and data-related issues. However, the Court did not consider data in the context of privacy and its definition under the *Privacy Act 1988* (Cth). The individual offences for which the appellant entered his pleas were:

- **Sequence 1**: Cause unauthorised modification of computer data, contrary to s 477.2(1) *Criminal Code Act 1995* (Cth); imprisonment for 18 months to commence on the date of sentence (15 October 2015), expiring on 14 April 2017.
- **Sequence 3**: Attempt cause unauthorised modification of data contrary to s 477.2(1) and 11.1(1); imprisonment for 12 months to commence on the date of sentence (15 October 2015) expiring 14 October 2016.
- **Sequence 6**: Unauthorised access to data with intent to commit serious indictable offence, contrary to s 477.1(1)(a)(i); imprisonment for 2.5 years, to commence on 15 April 2016 expiring on 14 October 2016.
- **Sequence 7**: Unauthorised access to data with intent to commit serious offence, contrary to s 477.1(1)(a)(i); imprisonment for 18 months to commence on 15 August 2016, expiring on 14 February 2018.[10]

The case not only involved the access to a computer and data, but also the modification of or interference with that data. The case also demonstrated how complex the forensics of cyber intrusions (hacking) have become. The sophistication cannot be underestimated and the case also highlighted the devices (see chapter xx) used to access data and material online. The Court noted that:

> The agreed facts were lengthy and complex; a chart setting out the details of the offences, prepared by the applicant's solicitor advocate, was attached to the sentencing judgment. In summary, the applicant came to police attention after unauthorised access by an unknown person, using an identified moniker, to the system of an internet service provider, Netspeed Communications. The applicant was identified as having used Vodafone Telecommunication Services held in both his own and his mother's name to gain that access. He pursued a variety of steps which it is unnecessary to describe, to hide his own Internal Protocol address, but used his laptop to access his personal email and Facebook accounts, where traces of these measures were left behind.[11]

Generally, offences that involve illegal access to a computer and its systems and infrastructure, will involve other direct and indirect offences such as illegal access to or use of devices, fraud, theft, interfering, intrusion, amongst others. Not all of these offences have been addressed by the CCRA.

In the **Bahamas**, any person who, without authority, knowingly causes a computer to perform any function for the purpose of securing access to any program or data held in any computer shall be guilty of an offence.[12] In addition, section 4 goes further whereby a person commits an offence if he causes a computer to perform any function for the purpose of securing access to any program or data held in any computer with intent to commit an offence.[13]

---

[10] Ibid, para 4.

[11] Ibid, para 42.

[12] Computer Misuse Act 2006, section 3 http://laws.bahamas.gov.bs/cms/images/LEGISLATION/PRINCIPAL/2003/2003-0002/ComputerMisuseAct_1.pdf.

[13] Ibid, section 4.

On the other hand, **Bangladesh** does not define access in the same way as **Botswana** (see below). Sections 17 and 18 provide for offences related to illegal computer and systems access. Section 17 protects illegal access to any critical information infrastructure. If any person, intentionally or knowingly engages in illegal access to any critical information infrastructure; or by means of illegal access, causes or tries to cause harm or damage to it, or makes or tries to make it inactive, then such act of the person shall be an offence.[14] Additionally, section 18 minimises the illegal access to computer, digital device, computer system, where any person intentionally makes or abets to make illegal access to any computer, computer system or computer network; or makes or abets to make illegal access with intent to commit an offence, then such act of the person shall be an offence.[15] Similar to Botswana, **Barbados** has neatly set out the relevant provisions addressing the need to ensure a high standard of cybersecurity. This is not to say that the other states compared have not undertaken the same. Rather, their laws vary clearly reflect what is in the CCRA. Yet, this approach is far from consistent across all the members of the Commonwealth. Section 4 of the Barbados laws data regulates the lawful access to a computer, programmes and its systems. It also protects the access and movement of data, by creating an offence for the unlawful access to both.[16]

Belize also has adopted a well-structured legal framework, whereby an offence for illegal access to a computer and its systems and infrastructure are strongly protected.[17] In **Botswana,** access relates to any computer or computer system used to instruct, communicate with, store data in, retrieve data from, or otherwise make use of any of the resources of the computer or computer system.[18] Section 4, provides that any person who (*a*) intentionally accesses or attempts to access the whole or any part of a computer or computer system knowing that the access he or she intends to secure is unauthorised; or (*b*) causes a computer or computer system to perform any function as a result of unauthorised access to such system, commits an offence and is liable to a fine not exceeding P20 000 or to imprisonment for a term not exceeding one year, or to both.[19]

---

[14] Digital Security Act 2018, section 17, https://www.cirt.gov.bd/wp-content/uploads/2020/02/Digital-Security-Act-2020.pdf.

[15] Digital Security Act 2018, section 18 https://www.cirt.gov.bd/wp-content/uploads/2020/02/Digital-Security-Act-2020.pdf.

[16] Computer Misuse Act, 2005, sections 4, 7, 9 and 10 http://www.oas.org/juridico/spanish/cyb_bbs_computer_misuse_2005.pdf.

[17] Cybercrime Act 2020, section 3 https://www.nationalassembly.gov.bz/wp-content/uploads/2020/10/Act-No.-32-of-2020-Cybercrime.pdf.

[18] Cybercrime and related Crimes Act 2018, section 2, https://www.bocra.org.bw/cybercrime-and-computer-related-crimes-act-2018.

[19] Ibid, section 5, places obligations on a person who commits an offence where such person knowingly and by any means, without authorisation or exceeding the authorisation he or she is given (*a*) secures access or intends to secure access to any computer or computer system for the purpose of obtaining, directly or indirectly, any computer service; or (*b*) intercepts, intends to access or causes to be intercepted, directly or indirectly, any function of, or any data within, a computer or computer system.

Similarly in **Brunei,** any person who knowingly causes a computer to perform any function for the purpose of securing access without authority to any program or data held in any computer is guilty of an offence.[20] **Canada** has adopted an approach similar that of Australia in accounting for computer protection laws. Simply put, Canada has no specific legislation for cyber-related crimes. Any offences have been captured by the Criminal Code. On that basis, section 342.1 is multidimensional and indirectly could create an offence for unlawful access to a computer or data.[21]

On the one hand, **Eswatini**, like many of the other African nations, has adopted an approach that appears to have followed the CCRA. On that basis, section 3 provides that unlawful access to a computer system is an offence.[22]

On the other hand, in **Fiji**, section 5 makes it an offence for unauthorised access to computer systems.[23] In **Ghana**, the laws by and large pertain to critical infrastructure and not generally to computers, systems and infrastructure. Section 40 creates an offence for unauthorised access to critical information infrastructure (defined in section 97).[24] This position is a subtle but important departure from the other states, and what constitutes critical infrastructure within the states needs to be carefully considered. While the definition has not been analysed, it is likely to be different from that of other states that have adopted the same approach. **Grenada** has adopted another approach and, according to section 5, arguably has one of the most comprehensive provisions related to an unlawful access to or interference with electronic systems or networks for the purpose of downloading or extracting data or information.[25] Section 5 also extends to damage of the systems or networks for the extraction of data and information. Similar to the other states examined, section 3 of the data laws of **Guyana**'s has a general offence for illegal access to a computer system.[26]

In **India**, in section 29, while predominantly related to data offences, there is an indirect connection to cyber security. That is, this section provides for access to computers whereby a controller or any person authorised by him shall, if he has reasonable cause to suspect that [any contravention of the provisions of this Chapter] has been committed, have access to any computer system, any apparatus, data or any other material connected with such system, for the purpose of searching or causing a

[20] Computer Misuse Act 2007, section 3/4, https://www.agc.gov.bn/AGC%20Images/LAWS/ACT_PDF/C/CHAPTER%20194.pdf.

[21] Criminal Code 1985, https://laws-lois.justice.gc.ca/pdf/c-46.pdf.

[22] *Computer Crime and Cybercrime Act No.6 of 2022, section 3* https://www.esccom.org.sz/legislation/COMPUTER%20CRIME%20&%20CYBERCRIME%20ACT.pdf.

[23] Cybersecurity and Cybercrime Act 2021, https://ncb.govmu.org/ncb/legislations/THE%20CYBERSECURITY%20AND%20CYBERCRIME%20ACT%202021.pdf.

Cybercrime Act 2021 (Act No. 3 of 2021), https://www.ilo.org/dyn/natlex/natlex4.detail?p_lang=en&p_isn=111060&p_classification=01.

[24] Cybersecurity Act 2020, section 40 https://csdsafrica.org/wp-content/uploads/2021/08/Cybersecurity-Act-2020-Act-1038.pdf.

[25] Electronic Crimes Bill 2013, section https://ecagrenada.com/Grenada-Electronic-Crimes-Act-2013.pdf.

[26] Cyber Crime Act 2018, https://parliament.gov.gy/publications/acts-of-parliament/cyber-crime-act-2018.

search to be made for obtaining any information or data contained in or available to such computer system.[27] This is a direct example of the interconnectedness between data and cyber-related crime.

In relation to the above, in 2022, the OECD, released the Framework on Digital Security: Cybersecurity for Prosperity that recognises 'the economic and social dimension of cybersecurity is becoming a public policy priority as governments realise that market forces alone are insufficient to incentivise businesses, public sector organisations and individuals to better manage digital security risk, according to their role'.[28] In regard to regulation, the OECD is referring to market regulation where 'policy intervention is needed because market forces are insufficient to create an optimal level of digital security'.[29] It addresses and emphasises the importance of digital security (that includes personal and commercial data) to 'financial, health or energy services, the disruption or destruction of which would affect the functioning of the economy and society, human lives, as well as national security'.[30] Important is the 'digital security of the products that contain (computer) code and associated services (Icloud) on which all stakeholders depend to carry out their economic and social activities'.[31] It is these systems and infrastructure that all contribute to the collection, use, processing and storage of data across the Commonwealth. More importantly, in late 2022, in response to the overall global cybersecurity threats, the United Nations (UN) began developing a cybercrime treaty.[32] While the preliminary process of determining what might constitute a structure was deliberated, during the 2022 meeting the 'representative of the European Union, in its capacity as observer, made a statement on behalf of the European Union and its member States'.[33] Further it states that the representative of the Holy See made a statement in its capacity as a non-member observer State. While a Commonwealth member can approach and offer input to the process as an individual country alone, in the same way as the EU, the Commonwealth Secretariate should engage in this process as a collective as well

[27] Information Technology Act (2000), https://thelawreviews.co.uk/title/the-privacy-data-protection-and-cybersecurity-law-review/india, and https://www.indiacode.nic.in/handle/123456789/1999, section 29.

[28] Organisation for Economic Development Co-operation, Policy Framework on Digital Security, https://www.oecd-ilibrary.org/docserver/a69df866-en.pdf?expires=1674008200&id=id&accname=guest&checksum=FDDE07F8DBF0FE4FB1D7E8D20D7A5853.

[29] Ibid.

[30] Ibid.

[31] Ibid.

[32] United Nations, Ad Hoc Committee to Elaborate on a Comprehensive International Convention on countering the Information and Communications Technologies for Criminal Purposes, 2022, https://www.unodc.org/unodc/en/cybercrime/ad_hoc_committee/home.

[33] United Nations General Assembly, Report of the Ad Hoc Committee to Elaborate a Comprehensive International Convention on Countering the Use of Information and Communications Technologies for Criminal Purposes on its first session (2022) p 2, A/AC.291/7.https://documents-dds-ny.un.org/doc/UNDOC/GEN/V22/016/71/PDF/V2201671.pdf?OpenElement.

as an observer. The proposed Convention or Treaty structure preamble is purported to contain the following:

1. General provisions;
2. Criminalisation;
3. Procedural measures and law enforcement;
4. International cooperation;
5. Technical assistance, including exchange of experience;
6. Preventive measures;
7. Mechanism of implementation; and
8. Final provisions.[34]

The work is expected to proceed throughout 2023 and into 2024 and beyond. It will take some time for such an international legal instrument to be fully agreed to and established. The details, at the time of writing were not available for the sections listed above. Overall, it is my view that the Commonwealth can play an important role in this process. The CCRA can provide a better understanding and knowledge of the issues that need to be addressed. It is argued that the concepts and principles covered by the CCRA and the additional concepts of fraud, theft and ransom should be included under the area of criminalisation.

Moreover, 'the most influential and important international cybercrime treaty is the *Council of Europe Convention on Cybercrime*, more commonly referred to as the Budapest Convention'.[35] Interestingly, the 'Convention was the first international cybercrime treaty and has been adopted by 68 countries,[36] including Commonwealth members Australia, Canada, Mauritius, UK, the Council of Europe (which includes the European Union as well as other countries), Japan, the U.K., and the US'.[37] New Zealand, Trinidad and Tobago and South Africa were observers at the Budapest Convention. Further, the Budapest Convention was developed to 'establish a global approach to cybercrime that would involve harmonising national law, improving investigative abilities, and enabling international cooperation'.[38] While out of scope to compare the Budapest Convention with the CCRA, it can be confirmed that in section 1, Article 1 to Article 8 of the BC replicates section 5 to section 9 of the CCRA, in terms of the concepts that have been compared in Part III of this book.

In its formal and functional arrangements, **Jamaica,** consistent with other African states, has adopted a similar approach in that its laws reflect what is in the CCRA. Section 3 provides that a person who knowingly obtains, for himself or another

---

[34] Ibid, p 7.

[35] Christian Ohanian, The UN Cybersecurity Treaty has a Cybersecurity problem in it, Just Security, October 2022,https://www.justsecurity.org/83582/the-un-cybercrime-treaty-has-a-cybers ecurity-problem-in-it/.

[36] Council of Europe, Parties/Observers to the Budapest Convention and Observer Organisations to the T-CY,https://www.coe.int/en/web/cybercrime/parties-observers.

[37] Christian Ohanian, The UN Cybersecurity Treaty has a Cybersecurity problem in it, Just Security, October 2022,https://www.justsecurity.org/83582/the-un-cybercrime-treaty-has-a-cybers ecurity-problem-in-it/.

[38] Ibid.

person, any unauthorised access to any program or data held in a computer, commits an offence.[39] In **Kenya,** sections 14 and 15 establish a strict offence for illegal access to a computer. It states that a person who causes, whether temporarily or permanently, a computer system to perform a function, by infringing security measures, with intent to gain access, and knowing such access is unauthorised, commits an offence and is liable.[40] On the other hand, in **Kiribati** section 7 stipulates that access of any kind by any person to any computer program or computer data held in a computer system is illegal or unauthorised if that person is not entitled to control access of the kind in question to the computer program or computer data; and does not have consent to access by him of the kind in question to the computer program or computer data from any person who is so entitled.[41] In **Lesotho**, it is an offence to access the whole or any part of a computer system without the appropriate authority.[42]

In further evaluating Commonwealth members' responses to cybersecurity **Malawi** has an all-in offence under section 84, whereby a person cannot gain unauthorized access to, or intercept, or interfere with data or a computer.[43] On the other hand, **Malaysia**, defines data as representations of information or of concepts that are being prepared or have been prepared in a form suitable for use in a computer.[44] This is not to say that other states' laws do not define data or computer data; however, it is beyond the scope of this book to compare definitions of data in terms of relevant cyber laws. This is an area for further research. Those states that define data, in whatever form, arguably are making a connection with the data protection laws they have established in that it is an offence to unlawfully access[45] a computer and its related systems and infrastructure.

Mauritius defines access to mean gaining entry to a program or computer data stored in a computer system.[46] Thus, any person any person who gains unauthorised access to any program or data held in a computer system shall commit an offence.[47] Thus, some states have defined the process of access, although most do not. The chapter thus far has shown that most states do have an offence for the illegal access to a computer and its systems and infrastructure. What differs amongst most states

---

[39] The Cyber Crimes Act 2015, section 3 https://www.japarliament.gov.jm/attachments/339_The%20Cybercrimes%20Acts,%202015.pdf.

[40] Computer Misuse and Cybercrimes Act 2018, section 14 and 15 https://ictpolicyafrica.org/en/document/pb8w26fcso?page=2.

[41] Cybercrime Act 2021, section 7 https://www.mict.gov.ki/download/file/fid/320.

[42] The Computer Crimes and Cyber Security Bill, 2022, https://senate.parliament.ls/2022/05/19/computer-crime-and-cyber-security-bill-2022/.

[43] Electronic Transactions and Cyber Security Act 2017, section 84 https://media.malawilii.org/files/legislation/akn-mw-act-2016-33-eng-2017-12-31.pdf.

[44] Computer Crimes Act 1997, section 2 https://www.nacsa.gov.my/legal.php Also see section 8 Presumptions.

[45] Ibid, section 3.

[46] Cybersecurity and Cybercrime Act 2021, section 2 https://ncb.govmu.org/ncb/legislations/THE%20CYBERSECURITY%20AND%20CYBERCRIME%20ACT%202021.pdf.

[47] Ibid, section 7.

is the terminology used to describe the offences. This difference in terminology will need to be reconciled, particularly for cross-border offences.

Further, in **Nauru,** section 6, similar to most other Commonwealth members, has clearly outlined the offences pertaining to the illegal access to computer systems and data. Section 4 includes a person, who wilfully, without lawful excuse, accesses the whole or any part of a protected computer, commits an offence. Note that a Protected computer is a general computer.[48] In **New Zealand,** section 249 establishes that everyone is liable to imprisonment for a term not exceeding seven years who, directly or indirectly, accesses any computer system and thereby, dishonestly or by deception, and without claim of right, obtains any property, privilege, service, pecuniary advantage, benefit, or valuable consideration; or causes loss to any other person.[49] Additionally, section 252 makes it an offence to access a computer without the appropriate authority.

On the one hand, in **Nigeria**, it is considered an offence for any person, without authorization, to intentionally accesses in whole or in part, a computer system or network for fraudulent purposes and obtain data that are vital to national security or commercial or industrial secrets.[50] On the other hand, **Pakistan** has defined access to data and access to information systems as important features of its laws.[51] This demonstrates the alignment between data and cybersecurity. Section 3 makes it an offence to access either an information system or data. Section 6, makes it an offence to access the information system or data of a critical infrastructure. **Papua New Guinea** is another member country that has adopted a similar approach to that of the African nations and structured its current day laws to reflect the CCRA. However, Section 4 extends the offence of general unauthorised access to include hacking.[52]

In **Rwanda**, a person cannot without authorisation access a computer or its data.[53] Similarly, **Seychelles** has an offence for illegal access to a computer and its system, although it goes a step further and includes that such an activity occur with criminal intent.[54] Likewise for **Sierra Leone** who have a dual offence for access and access

[48] Cybercrime Act 2015, section 6 http://ronlaw.gov.nr/nauru_lpms/files/acts/a59d9691f5a195412b877493a2a95e8b.pdf.

[49] Crimes Act 1961, section 249, https://www.legislation.govt.nz/act/public/1961/0043/latest/DLM330422.html.

[50] Cyber Crime Act 2015, section 6, https://lawpadi.com/wp-content/uploads/2015/08/CyberCrime_ProhibitionPreventionetc_Act_2015.pdf.

[51] The Prevention of Electronic Crimes 2016, section 2, 3, 6 https://na.gov.pk/uploads/documents/1470910659_707.pdf. Critical infrastructure information system or data means an information system program or data that supports or performs a function with respect to a critical infrastructure.

[52] *Cybercrime Code Act 2016, section 4* https://www.parliament.gov.pg/uploads/acts/16A_35.pdf.

[53] Law N° 60/2018 OF 22/8/2018 on prevention and punishment of cyber crimes, Article 16 https://www.risa.rw/fileadmin/user_upload/Others%20documents/Cyber_Crimes_Law.pdf Note there are other offences relates to accessing a computer and data.

[54] Computer Misuse Act 1998, sections 3, 4, https://seylii.org/akn/sc/act/1998/17/eng%402015-12-31.

to a protected system.[55] **South Africa** also makes it an offence to access a computer system and computer storage, which is not often mentioned by other states.[56] In **Saint Lucia,** rather than be restricted specifically to a computer and its systems, section 5 makes it an offence to access the whole or any part of an electronic system.[57] Electronic system constitutes any electronic device or a group of interconnected or related devices.[58] In **Saint Kitts and Nevis**, section 4 invokes an offence of illegal access. It states that a person who, without lawful excuse or justification or in excess of a lawful excuse or justification, knowingly accesses the whole or any part of a computer system, commits an offence.[59] However, it is unclear what is meant by 'remaining'. However, for **Singapore,** there is no specific offence for illegal access to a computer. Rather, there is an offence for failing to provide access to an authorised person exercising their powers to conduct an investigation.[60] Nonetheless, **St Vincent and The Grenadines** has a general offence of illegal access to computer systems.[61]

Finally, **Tonga** is another country located in the Pacific that has by and large adopted the approach that reflects the CCRA. Section 4 provides that a person who wilfully, without lawful excuse, accesses any computer system commits an offence. This includes public and private computer infrastructure.[62] Similarly, **Trinidad and Tobago,** have the same offence and extended it to include remaining in a computer system.[63] Remaining in a computer could be referring to the length of time that a person has access to the system or its infrastructure. In **Uganda** and the **United Kingdom,**[64] access to a computer and data is unlawful where it is unauthorised.[65] The **United Republic of Tanzania** provides for the same offence.[66] In **Zambia** the same offence extends to interference with a computer and data.[67]

---

[55] Cyber Crime Act 2020, section 25, 26 http://www.sierra-leone.org/Laws/2020-Cybercrime%20Act.pdf.

[56] Cybercrimes Act 2021, section 2 https://cybercrimesact.co.za.

[57] Electronic Crimes Bill 2009, section 5 https://www.govt.lc/media.govt.lc/www/resources/legislation/ElectronicCrimesBill.pdf.

[58] Ibid, section 2.

[59] Electronic Crimes Bill 2017, section 4 https://aglcskn.info/wp-content/documents/Act17TOC/Ch-04_41-Electronic-Crimes-Act.pdf.

[60] Cybersecurity Act 2018, https://sso.agc.gov.sg/Acts-Supp/9-2018/.

[61] Cybercrime Act 2016, section 3 https://www.gov.vc/images/PoliciesActsAndBills/SVG_Cybercrime_Act_2016.pdf.

[62] Computer crimes Act 2003, section 4 https://ago.gov.to/cms/images/LEGISLATION/PRINCIPAL/2003/2003-0014/ComputerCrimesAct2003_1.pdf.

[63] The Cybercrimes Bill 2017, section 5,6 https://ttcsirt.gov.tt/wp-content/uploads/2022/04/Cyber_Crime_Bill_DRAFT_2017.pdf.

[64] Computer Misuse Act 1990, section 1 https://www.legislation.gov.uk/ukpga/1990/18/contents.

[65] *Computer Misuse Act, 2011, section 12* https://ulii.org/akn/ug/act/2011/2/eng@2011-02-14.

[66] *Cybercrimes Act, 2015, section 4* https://rsf.org/sites/default/files/the_cyber_crime_act_2015.pdf.

[67] The Cyber Security and Cyber Crimes Act, 2021, *section* 49 https://www.parliament.gov.zm/sites/default/files/documents/acts/Act%20No.%202%20of%202021The%20Cyber%20Security%20and%20Cyber%20Crimes.pdf.

14.2 Conclusion

This chapter has briefly mentioned the economic cost and enabling benefits that are being derived from cybersecurity. Today, cybersecurity is a core part of government and private sector business, and has been supported by comprehensive laws. However, as shown above, when comparing the responses of governments of Commonwealth states, the approaches are different. This is a complex area of law, and in my view, will become increasingly transnational.

In reconciling the difference between the states compared above, what it apparent is the use and application of terminology within the law. Some states define the concept of access, yet many do not. A definition can be a starting point to better understanding and applying the concept of access as an offence within the law. Many states have a general and broad offence provision. The Commonwealth CCRA has provided for the concept of access; however, across the member countries it has become highly fragmented. Some states have specifically focused on critical infrastructure. In addition, states have gone into more detail and stipulate that access includes a computer system and its infrastructure, adding further behavioural elements to the offence such as a person acting dishonestly or by deception, and without claim of right, obtains any property, privilege, service, pecuniary advantage, benefit, or valuable consideration, or causes loss.

This approach does depart from that taken by many other states; however, it provides a clear message and deterrence to individuals who contemplate engaging in this illegal activity. Furthermore, another approach has focused on accessing information systems. Again, this is another example of terminology used in reference to all computer systems. Another formal and functional response has been to attach specific provisions whereby others assist in the commission of such offences by instructing, communicating, storing data, retrieving data and using devices to assist in the commission of the offence.

Relevant to the above, the connection between cybersecurity and data governance is also being considered in more detail by some states. For example, some states have gone further to include within the offence provision both computer programs and computer data. Arguably, this development highlights how data can be on any computer. However, all the laws compared stop short of making a distinct connection with the relevant national data protection laws. This alignment has been confirmed by the OECD.

Problematic though is that some states have not developed specific laws for computer-related crime. Most of the states that have developed their respective laws over the past 15 years, have specific laws that align with the Commonwealth CCRA, while other states have chosen to include these offence provisions in their criminal laws. This should be reconciled, because it makes it highly confusing and complex for the lay person to find and understand the offences provided. The ensuing chapters will also demonstrate how many of the offences within the CCRA are connected to each other.

Chapter 15
Interfering with Data

15.1 Introduction

Central to the interference of data is the access to and interference with computers, their systems and networks. The interference with data can involve both commercial and personal data. This chapter compares the Commonwealth states' laws with the CCRA which, in section, provides that a person who, intentionally or recklessly, without lawful excuse or justification, engages in any of the following acts:

(a) destroys or alters data;
(b) renders data meaningless, useless or in effective;
(c) obstructs, interrupts or interferes with the lawful use of data; or
(d) obstructs, interrupts or interferes with any person in the lawful use of data; or
(e) denies access to data to any person entitled to it; commits an offence punishable, on conviction, by imprisonment for a period not exceeding [period], or a fine not exceeding [amount], or both. Subsection (1) applies whether the person's act is of temporary or permanent effect.[1]

This chapter will demonstrate the significant cross-over or alignment of cybersecurity and data. This chapter does not provide a word-by-word comparison of the laws. Due to the fragmented approach of the laws across all of the countries compared, a high-level approach has been taken to confirm where the offence provision has been adopted. The different approaches taken by the nation states being compared is significant, and practitioners who are dealing with cross-border cybersecurity matters will need to navigate carefully the laws of the respective states.

[1] Model Law on Computer and Computer Related Crime, Office of Civil and Criminal Justice Reform, 2017, https://production-new-commonwealth-files.s3.eu-west-2.amazonaws.com/migrated/key_reform_pdfs/P15370_11_ROL_Model_Law_Computer_Related_Crime.pdf.

R. Walters, *Cybersecurity and Data Laws of the Commonwealth*,
https://doi.org/10.1007/978-981-99-3935-0_15

The interference with data has significant economic consequences for organisations and the digital economy. However, the economic impacts are not fully understood or widely reported. Arguably, it is a growing area of research, and it is an area where the Commonwealth could do further work to improve the protection of data across the digital economy.

Interference with data can be accomplished by various means. It can be done directly by humans who have accessed a computer system or by devices being used by individuals. Simply put:

> Digital technology and cybercrime are pervasive features of modern life. Approximately 60% of the world's population are internet users and the global adoption of digital technology is rapidly increasing; global internet penetration increased by approximately 7% over the course of one year (from January 2020 to January 2021). The increased adoption of digital technology has caused an evolution in criminal behavior, resulting in the increased occurrence of 'cybercrime'.[2]

With this level of connectivity, the potential for interfering with data becomes even more complex. With more than half of the world's population using the Internet, there will be state and non-state actors attempting to access technology systems and infrastructure to obtain personal and commercial data. Once collected, that data can be modified and returned to the Internet or an organisation's system. This, in and of itself poses significant challenges to the digital economy. While it is difficult to calculate the financial impact that the interference with or modification of data has on businesses, a 2018 study determined the level of victimisation was significant in that:

> Two third of the businesses in our sample (66.5% or 181 businesses) have been victims of one of the five cybercrime types, at least once in the last 12 months. Specifically, illegal access and data/system interference are much more prevalent than the other types: 50% of the businesses report illegal access and 44% data/system interference. Less than a quarter admit cyber extortion (24.1%), and still fewer internet fraud (12.9%) and cyber espionage (3.6%). In the case of cyber extortion, 59 of the 66 victimized businesses report having been requested ransom money and seven protection money. None admits receiving a hush money request. As for fraud, internet banking fraud—with 22 businesses admitting victimization—is reported more frequently than advance fee fraud (8) and auction fraud (1). The majority of the businesses have suffered repeated attacks: 83.2% of the victims report repeated incidents of illegal access, 72.7% of data/system interference, 62.9% of internet fraud and 57.4% of cyber extortion. Only for cyber espionage, the number of repeat victims is lower than half.[3]

Together with access, data interference ranked very high, with half of the survey respondents saying that therir data had been modified in some way. Although the overall sample size was small, comprising only 181 entities in Europe, the study revealed that:

---

[2] Kirsty Phillips, Julia C. Davidson, Ruby R. Farr, Christine Burkhardt, Stefano Caneppele, Mary P. Aiken Conceptualizing Cybercrime: Definitions, Typologies and Taxonomies, Forensic Sciences, (2022), p. 379, https://doi.org/10.3390/forensicsci2020028.

[3] Letizia Paoli, Jonas Visschers, Cedric Verstraete, *The impact of cybercrime on businesses: A novel conceptual framework and its application to Belgium* Crime, Law and Social Change (2018), p. 16.

> between 11.3% and 24.2% of the businesses estimate losing between €1 and €9,000, because of one of these three cybercrime types. Much smaller percentages of businesses confronted with illegal access (last/only: 3.3%; all: 3.2%) and data/system interference (last/only: 5.8%; most serious: 6.3%) admit to suffering losses of €10,000 or more.[4]

While this estimated loss is not considered significant, when taking into account that this is only a very small sample of businesses, an increase in cyber intrusions will inevitably see greater financial losses. The above estimate is based on the actual direct loss to a business; however, the indirect losses, such as reputation, will be more difficult to determine. Noteworthy too, measuring this indirect loss will be more challenging.

Data and system interference are:

> most frequently provoked by malware infections, but they can also result from malicious actions of persons or groups who have first gained illegal access. System interference, in addition, can also be caused by (D)DOS (i.e., (Distributed) Denial of Service) attacks or by spamming. In this case, the IT-system becomes overloaded by the massive quantity of data (requests) sent to the system.[5]

Given the above, it can be concluded that one offence can and usually does lead to another offence. Arguably the offences compared in this book are connected. Interference with data relates directly to the wider offences related to computer access and interference with the systems and infrastructure. Problematic though, is that the level of, and how the data is interfered with is not fully understood by the general public. It is well understood by the technology practitioners. This is because interference can occur at any stage during the data life cycle comprising data collection, use and storage—all of which stages are vulnerable to attack. This chapter will demonstrate how the various states have approached this important issue. It will also reveal that in some states, there is no specific offence for interference with data. A point to note is that this chapter does not include references to or any analysis of interference with the privacy of an individual.

Some Commonwealth states have adopted the concept of data interference and computer interference directly from the European Convention on Cyber-Crime[6] and Article 4—Data Interference, which provides that.

- Each Party shall adopt such legislative and other measures as may be necessary to establish as criminal offences under its domestic law, when committed intentionally, the damaging, deletion, deterioration, alteration or suppression of computer data without right.
- A Party may reserve the right to require that the conduct described in paragraph 1 result in serious harm.[7]

---

[4] Ibid, p. 21.

[5] Ibid, p. 9.

[6] Organisation of American States Secretariate for Legal Affairs, http://www.oas.org/juridico/english/cyber_legis.htm This website makes a distinction between a number of Commonwealth states having adopted the principles and concepts of the European Convention on Cyber-Crime 2006.

[7] Ibid.

Notably, these Commonwealth states include Antigua and Barbuda, Bahamas, Barbados, St. Vincent and the Grenadines, and Trinidad and Tobago. In **Antigua and Barbuda** section 3[8] provides that no person without lawful authority can interfere (damage, disrupt, destroy, delete or alter information) within an electronic system or network.[9] Nevertheless, it has been widely recognised that it generally constitutes a company's data or information that is unlawfully modified, destroyed, removed or deteriorated in a computer, computer system and internet data.[10] It can also include electronic manuscripts, data messages, diffusion of malware and viruses. Arguably, with technological advancements such as artificial intelligence, other practices will emerge that will potentially interfere with data. Interestingly, there has been little scholarly discussion on data interference as a major cyber offence.

In **Australia**, section 476.2 of the Criminal Code Act 1995, stipulates a single offence covering a number of different issues such as access, modification or impairment of a computer or data. It states that: (a) access to data held in a computer; or (b) modification of data held in a computer; or (c) the impairment of electronic communication to or from a computer; or (d) the impairment of the reliability, security or operation of any data held on a computer disk, credit card or other device used to store data by electronic means; by a person is unauthorised if the person is not entitled to cause that access, modification or impairment.[11] In support of this provision, there has been a study undertaken by Australia. On the other hand, regarding the Australian law, the Council of Europe observed that substantive offences appear to have been already covered:

> ...although – perhaps due to the specifities of the Australian legal system – a different approach seems to have been followed for some of them. For example, in some Australian legal provisions different types of conduct listed in the Convention have been combined (e.g. illegal access, data interference, system interference) or individual provisions of the Convention are reflected in several different provisions in Australia. This is compatible with the Convention but may create difficulties in international cooperation when applying dual criminality.[12]

---

[8] Electronic Crimes Act 2013, section 2, http://laws.gov.ag/wp-content/uploads/2019/02/a2013-14.pdf.

[9] Ibid, section 3.

[10] European Innovation, Technology, and Science Center Foundation, Protecting Yourself from Cybercrime, https://eitsc.com/blog/protecting-yourself-from-cybercrime/.

[11] *Australian Criminal Code Act 1995*, section 476.2.

[12] Australian Parliament, Chapter 6, Criminal and Law Enforcement Framework, https://www.aph.gov.au/parliamentary_business/committees/house_of_representatives_committees?url=coms/cybercrime/report/chapter6.htm The chapter discusses the existing criminal law framework intended to combat cybercrime and canvasses Australia's possible accession to the Council of Europe Convention on Cybercrime. The chapter concludes that Australian criminal law (substantive and procedural) is well developed but that legal policy in this field must ensure an appropriate focus on the transnational nature of cybercrime and particular challenges of digital evidence. There is also a strong case for a more strategic focus on the disruption of botnets and prosecution of botherders that will require intense international cooperation.

A common theme has emerged in some but not all Commonwealth countries, in that the Council of Europe Convention on Cybercrime has arguably been a major influence on the development of cybersecurity law. It follows that the data protections laws of the EU have also had a major influence on the way that countries, not only those in the Commonwealth, but also across the world, have developed their respective data laws.

Moreover, the Australian Parliament noted that there was a strong alignment of Australia's current cybercrime framework with the Convention's 'core offences' of data interference; computer related forgery and fraud offences; and corporate criminal liability for cybercrime.[13] However, it found that there is scope to strengthen provisions for illegal access, system interference and misuse of device offences. Specifically, Microsoft Australia said:

> The Code's unauthorised access offence only applies in respect of data that is protected by an access control system (this qualification is permitted by the Convention). The Code's data interference offence is likely to regulate a broader range of conduct than its Convention counterpart due to its application to reckless data interference as well as that caused intentionally. The Code does not contain an equivalent to the Convention's system interference offence, but its unauthorised impairment of electronic communications offence is targeted at denial-of-service attacks in the same way that the Convention system interference offence is (at least in part).[14]

Thus, the concept of data interference, which is not a well-settled criminal offence, is closely connected to other offences such as fraud, theft, and possibly ransom. Arguably, it is my view the CCRA should be revised to include additional offence provisions for theft, fraud and ransom/extortion/inducement.

On the one hand, in the **Bahamas**, section 4 refers to any person who causes a computer to perform any function for the purpose of securing access to any program or *data* held in any computer with intent to commit an offence.[15] On the other hand, in **Bangladesh**, section 19 specifically relates directly to interference with data. It can be described as one of the most comprehensive offence provisions related to interference with data. Section 19 provides that it is an offence to damage a computer, computer system, whereby any person that collects any data, data-storage, information or any extract of it from any computer, computer system or computer network, or collects information with moveable stored data-information of such computer, computer system or computer network, or collects copy or extract of any data; or (b) intentionally inserts or tries to insert any virus or malware or harmful software into any computer or computer system or computer network; or (c) willingly causes or tries to cause harm to data or data-storage of any computer, computer system, computer network, or causes or tries to cause harm to any programme saved in the computer, computer system, or computer network; or (d) obstructs or tries to obstruct a valid or authorized person to access into any computer, computer system

---

[13] Ibid, 6.70.

[14] Ibid, 6.70.

[15] Computer Misuse Act 2007, section 4, https://www.agc.gov.bn/AGC%20Images/LAWS/ACT_PDF/C/CHAPTER%20194.pdf.

or computer network by any means; or (e) willingly creates or sells or tries to create or sell spam or sends unsolicited electronic mails without permission of the sender or receiver, for marketing any product or service; or (f) takes service of any person, or deposits or tries to credit the charge fixed for the service to the account of any other person fraudulently or by means of unfair interference to any computer, computer system or computer network, then such act of the person shall be an offence.[16]

Notwithstanding the above, some states have opted to broaden this offence to include destroy, obstruct, interrupts or interferrs with commercial or personal data. In **Barbados,** section 5 adds another layer of protection to data, whereby it is an offence to destroy alter, obstructs, interrupts or interferes with data.[17] Similarly, in **Belize** it is an offence for a persona to interfere with and access data unlawfully.[18] In **Botswana,** section 2 defines data to mean any representation of facts, information or concepts in a form suitable for processing in a computer or computer system; any information recorded in a form in which it can be processed by equipment operating automatically in response to instructions given for that purpose; or any programme suitable to cause a computer or computer system to perform a function, and includes traffic data and subscriber information.[19] Moreover, section 7 provides that a person who intentionally and without lawful excuse or justification, does or attempts to do any of the following (*a*) damages, deteriorates, deletes, alters or modifies computer data; (*b*) renders computer data meaningless, useless or ineffective; (*c*) obstructs, interrupts or interferes with the lawful use of computer data, is committing an offence.[20]

In **Brunei** a person who causes a computer to perform any function for the purpose of securing access without authority to any program or data held in any computer is guilty of an offence.[21] On the other hand, as aforementioned, **Canada** has no specific legislation for cyber-related crimes. Cyber-related offences are included in the Criminal Code. Hence, section 342.1(C) is multidimensional and indirectly could create an offence for unlawful interference with data.[22] Canada needs to provide further clarification of this offence.

---

[16] Digital Security Act 2018, section 19 https://www.cirt.gov.bd/wp-content/uploads/2020/02/Digital-Security-Act-2020.pdf.

[17] Computer Misuse Act, 2005, section 5 and 7 http://www.oas.org/juridico/spanish/cyb_bbs_computer_misuse_2005.pdf.

[18] Cybercrime Act 2020, sections 4 and 5 https://www.nationalassembly.gov.bz/wp-content/uploads/2020/10/Act-No.-32-of-2020-Cybercrime.pdf.

[19] Cybercrime and related Crimes Act 2018, section 3, https://www.bocra.org.bw/cybercrime-and-computer-related-crimes-act-2018.

[20] Ibid, section 7.

[21] Computer Misuse Act 2007, section 3, https://www.agc.gov.bn/AGC%20Images/LAWS/ACT_PDF/C/CHAPTER%20194.pdf.

[22] Criminal Code 1985, https://laws-lois.justice.gc.ca/pdf/c-46.pdf.

In **Eswatini**, section 6 makes it an offence where a person has interfered with data.[23] However, **Fiji** does not create an offence for unauthorised interference to data.[24] Interestingly, **Ghana**, does not have provisions to address the interference with data in the same way as the other states being compared. Sections 71 to 75 give officers the power to obtain access to data.[25] In **Grenada**, section 5 stipulates that it is an offence to unlawfully interfere with electronic systems or networks in order to download or extract data or information.[26]

Generally, most states have developed an offence provision addressing the interference with data. However, as mentioned above, the country of Ghana does not. In **Guyana,** similar to the other states examined, section 6 has an offence for illegal interference with data.[27] **India** does not have a specific offence for interference of data under the Information Technology Act 2000. The difference in terminology could be problematic and vigilance will be required by practitioners when interpreting and applying the respective laws.

Jamaica, while not creating a specific offence for interference with a computer, takes a narrower approach to the unauthorised modification of the contents of any computer that would have an impact on and to data.[28] On the other hand, **Kenya,** similar to many of the other Africa countries compared in this book, have established an offence for interference with data.[29] **Kiribati** under section 9 is more specific than most of the other states, specifying that the unauthorised data interference, where a person who, knowingly or recklessly, and without authority damages or deteriorates, deletes, alters, obstructs, interrupts, interferes with computer data is an offence.[30] The same can be said of **Lesotho** which makes it an offence to interfere with data.[31]

In an important development, the states of **Malawi, Malaysia, Mauritius, Nauru, New Zealand** all provide for the same offence. That is, **Malawi,** has an all-in offence under section 84, whereby, a person cannot gain unauthorized access to, or intercept,

---

[23] *Computer Crime and Cybercrime Act No.6 of 2022, section 3* https://www.esccom.org.sz/legislation/COMPUTER%20CRIME%20&%20CYBERCRIME%20ACT.pdf.

[24] Cybersecurity and Cybercrime Act 2021, section 6 https://ncb.govmu.org/ncb/legislations/THE%20CYBERSECURITY%20AND%20CYBERCRIME%20ACT%202021.pdf.

Cybercrime Act 2021 (Act No. 3 of 2021), https://www.ilo.org/dyn/natlex/natlex4.detail?p_lang=en&p_isn=111060&p_classification=01.

[25] Cybersecurity Act 2020, section 71, 72, 73.74, 75 https://csdsafrica.org/wp-content/uploads/2021/08/Cybersecurity-Act-2020-Act-1038.pdf.

[26] Electronic Crimes Bill 2013, section https://ecagrenada.com/Grenada-Electronic-Crimes-Act-2013.pdf.

[27] Cyber Crime Act 2018, https://parliament.gov.gy/publications/acts-of-parliament/cyber-crime-act-2018.

[28] The Cyber Crimes Act 2015, section 5 https://www.japarliament.gov.jm/attachments/339_The%20Cybercrimes%20Acts,%202015.pdf.

[29] Computer Misuse and Cybercrimes Act 2018, section 16 https://ictpolicyafrica.org/en/document/pb8w26fcso?page=2.

[30] Cybercrime Act 2021, section 7 https://www.mict.gov.ki/download/file/fid/320.

[31] The Computer Crimes and Cyber Security Bill, 2022, https://senate.parliament.ls/2022/05/19/computer-crime-and-cyber-security-bill-2022/.

or interfere with data or a computer.[32] In **Malaysia,** section 5 establishes an offence for interference with data, via interference with (modification of)[33] a computer. **Mauritius** has taken a different approach, and sees interference as hindering the functioning of a computer system by inputting, transmitting, damaging, deleting, deteriorating, altering or suppressing a computer, including data.[34] **Nauru,** section 8 restricts a person being able to interfere with data.[35]**New Zealand**'s section 250 stipulates that it is an offence for any individual to damage, delete, modify, or otherwise interfer with or impair any data in any computer system.[36]

In **Nigeria** any person who interferes with a computer unlawfully will have committed an offence.[37] In **Pakistan**, section 5 makes it an offence to interfere with or damage an information system or data.[38] However, **Singapore** does not provide for the same. On the other hand, **Papua New Guinea** ensures that a person cannot interfere with data.[39] In **Rwanda**, a person without authorisation cannot access a computer or its data in order to interfere with it.[40] **Seychelles** has adopted a different approach by creating an offence for the modification of computer material (including data).[41] **Sierra Leone** makes it a dual offence to interfere with data.[42] **South Africa** has also an offence for the illegal interference with data.[43] **Saint Lucia** law focuses on the to a system that results in a compromise of data. Section 20 states that a person is not to cause damage to the public or any person, interfere with, interrupt or obstruct the functioning, reliability or usefulness of an electronic system by inputting, transmitting, damaging or deteriorating any data.[44] In **Saint Kitts and Nevis,** section 5

32 Electronic Transactions and Cyber Security Act 2017, section 84 https://media.malawilii.org/files/legislation/akn-mw-act-2016-33-eng-2017-12-31.pdf.

33 Computer Crimes Act 1997, section 5 https://www.nacsa.gov.my/legal.php.

34 Cybersecurity and Cybercrime Act 2021, section 9 https://ncb.govmu.org/ncb/legislations/THE%20CYBERSECURITY%20AND%20CYBERCRIME%20ACT%202021.pdf.

35 Cybercrime Act 2015, section 8 http://ronlaw.gov.nr/nauru_lpms/files/acts/a59d9691f5a195412b877493a2a95e8b.pdf.

36 Crimes Act 1961, section 249, https://www.legislation.govt.nz/act/public/1961/0043/latest/DLM330422.html.

37 Cyber Crime Act 2015, section 8, https://lawpadi.com/wp-content/uploads/2015/08/CyberCrime_ProhibitionPreventionetc_Act_2015.pdf.

38 The Prevention of Electronic Crimes 2016, section 5 https://na.gov.pk/uploads/documents/1470910659_707.pdf. Critical infrastructure information system or data" means an information system program or data that supports or performs a function with respect to a critical infrastructure.

39 *Cybercrime Code Act 2016, section 4* https://www.parliament.gov.pg/uploads/acts/16A_35.pdf.

40 Law N° 60/2018 OF 22/8/2018 on prevention and punishment of cyber crimes, Article 16 https://www.risa.rw/fileadmin/user_upload/Others%20documents/Cyber_Crimes_Law.pdf Note there are other offences relates to accessing a computer and data.

41 Computer Misuse Act 1998, sections 6, https://seylii.org/akn/sc/act/1998/17/eng%402015-12-31.

42 Cyber Crime Act 2020, section 25, 26 http://www.sierra-leone.org/Laws/2020-Cybercrime%20Act.pdf.

43 Cybercrimes Act 2021, section 2 https://cybercrimesact.co.za.

44 Electronic Crimes Bill 2009, section 20 https://www.govt.lc/media.govt.lc/www/resources/legislation/ElectronicCrimesBill.pdf.

considers it an offence when a person, knowingly and without lawful excuse or justification interferes with data by destroying, altering, and/or obstructing the computer data.[45]

In concluding this chapter, the laws of **St Vincent and The Grenadines** include the offence of illegal interference with data.[46]**Tonga** also has an offence for interference with data.[47] Similarly, **Trinidad and Tobago,** have the same offence.[48] A unique feature of Trinidad and Tobago is the offence created for the acquisition of data under section 8. In **Uganda,** accessing a computer in order to interfere with data is unlawful.[49] The **United Republic of Tanzania** has a similar offence.[50] **Zambia**, however, has the same offence, although it is termed 'misrepresentation' according to section 51.[51] Surprisingly, the **United Kingdom** does not provide for the same offence.[52]

15.2 Conclusion

This chapter has demonstrated the close alignment between cybersecurity and data protection. As revealed, most Commonwealth countries have provisions within their respective cyber laws that restrict or totally prohibit the interference with data. That is, data which may be personal, commercial or scientific.

While the chapter has not confirmed or otherwise a definition of data within the respective laws, generally, data comprises any data that a computer system can collect, use and store. This is an area of further research, and practitioners will need to determine whether a specific definition has been provided, so as to ensure that the term 'data' does not apply only to specific areas.

[45] Electronic Crimes Bill 2017, section 5 https://aglcskn.info/wp-content/documents/Act17TOC/Ch-04_41-Electronic-Crimes-Act.pdf.

[46] Cybercrime Act 2016, section 7 https://www.gov.vc/images/PoliciesActsAndBills/SVG_Cybercrime_Act_2016.pdf.

[47] Computer crimes Act 2003, section 5 https://ago.gov.to/cms/images/LEGISLATION/PRINCIPAL/2003/2003-0014/ComputerCrimesAct2003_1.pdf.

[48] The Cybercrimes Bill 2017, sections 7 https://ttcsirt.gov.tt/wp-content/uploads/2022/04/Cyber_Crime_Bill_DRAFT_2017.pdf.

[49] *Computer Misuse Act, 2011, section 12* https://ulii.org/akn/ug/act/2011/2/eng@2011-02-14.

[50] *Cybercrimes Act, 2015, section 7* https://rsf.org/sites/default/files/the_cyber_crime_act_2015.pdf.

[51] The Cyber Security and Cyber Crimes Act, 2021, section 51 https://www.parliament.gov.zm/sites/default/files/documents/acts/Act%20No.%202%20of%202021The%20Cyber%20Security%20and%20Cyber%20Crimes.pdf.

[52] Computer Misuse Act 1990, https://www.legislation.gov.uk/ukpga/1990/18/contents.

A further development has been the terminology used by the states. For instance, some states make direct reference to interference with data, while other states refer to the modification of data. Some states define data and many do not. Thus, the elements that constitute data will need to be clarified. On the other hand, some states have coupled the interference provision with that of damaging an information system.

Another important observation is that rather than using the term 'interference with data', states have also either included or directly relied on the term 'impaired the data'. This needs to be clarified to specify the point at which impairment becomes interference. In reconciling the varied approaches, some states have also used terms such as 'compromising' or 'tampering' with data. Thus, it is argued that while this limited comparative analysis is highly useful and demonstrates the different terminologies, further clarification would be needed to ensure they all refer to a level of interference with data.

In one of the most detailed offence provisions related to data interference, **Bangladesh** has taken the view that connecting data with the computer is important. It also connects the storage of data with its extraction from a computer, its system or network. Further, it provides that interference can comprise collecting, copying, inserting a virus or malware, and harming where the data is stored. Obstructing a computer and its systems or networks, or even selling spam and sending unsolicited mails that are not authorised for marketing also constitute a form of interference.

Finally, a person who fraudulently or unfairly interferes with data through a computer has committed an offence. Arguably, there are many similarities between interference with data and interfering with a computer. Interfering with a computer will, in most situations, occur before the data is interfered with. That is, unless the offence occurs via some hand-held device such as an Iphone. The ability to interfere with data compromises not only the economic benefits it brings, but also the privacy of data subjects. It can easily be used to extort benefits from entities and individuals.

Chapter 16
Interfering with a Computer System

16.1 Introduction

The interference with computer systems by state and non-state actors in not new. It has been occurring since the computer became mainstream equipment within government and the business sector. Today, wherever one travels, human activity will invariably be supported by a computer. For instance, there are computer systems throughout airports and in aeroplanes, and people travelling are likely to carry a device that can connect to the Internet.

This chapter compares the approaches taken by countries to deal with interference with a computer or computer system. Section 7 of the CCRA, provides that an offence is committed by any person who intentionally or recklessly, without lawful excuse or justification:

1. (a) Hinders or interferes with the functioning of a computer system; or
2. (b) Hinders or interferes with a person who is lawfully using or operating a computer system; commits an offence punishable, on conviction, by imprisonment for a period not exceeding [period], or a fine not exceeding [amount], or both.

In subsection (1) "hinder", in relation to a computer system, includes but is not limited to (a) cutting the electricity supply to a computer system; (b) causing electromagnetic interference to a computer system; (c) corrupting a computer system by any means; and (d) inputting, deleting or altering computer data.[1] Similar to the other chapters in Part III, this chapter does not provide a word-by-word comparison of the laws. Due to the fragmented approach to the laws by all of the countries compared, a high-level approach has been taken to confirm those countries where the offence has been included in the law.

[1] Model Law on Computer and Computer Related Crime, Office of Civil and Criminal Justice Reform, 2017, https://production-new-commonwealth-files.s3.eu-west-2.amazonaws.com/migrated/key_reform_pdfs/P15370_11_ROL_Model_Law_Computer_Related_Crime.pdf.

R. Walters, *Cybersecurity and Data Laws of the Commonwealth*,
https://doi.org/10.1007/978-981-99-3935-0_16

The approach taken in this chapter highlights the limited scholarly discussion on the interference with a computer system as a single topic. Generally, it has been discussed in conjunction with other related offences.

Interference with computer systems is not new. It has been taking place since the humble computer became part of mainstream society. Malik and Choudhury summarise interference with a computer system thus:

> System interference aims at criminalising acts of computer sabotage and the resultant loss of availability of the information service. The offence covers intentional hindering of a lawful use of computer systems, including telecommunication facilities, by using or influencing computer data. Such legal regulations may criminalize various forms of denial-of-service attacks that may stop, for instance, a website from communication with other computers.[2]

Apart from the potential to sabotage the computer itself, interference can also extend to the sabotage to data. It can be linked to the illegal use of devices, which is covered later in this Part. Problematic though, is that individuals and entities are able to interfere with computers and compromise them without ever being detected. In some nation states, constant surveillance of individuals' online activities is undertaken every day by illegal means. In reaffirming this proposition, Malik and Choudhury go further, stating that:

> Criminals are increasingly utilizing a variety of technical communication methods for the facilitation of offences and also for the purpose of criminal communications. Tracing the source of communications is essential to discovering offender identity and as intelligence.[3]

Put another way, the ability to trace any interference with a computer system is increasingly being able to be done with ease. However, as this practice continues to develop and evolve, the people undertaking the criminal activity are able to find new ways to interfere with computer systems. Thus, there are two types of interference with computer systems. First is the illegal interference by people. Second is the authorised interference by government and regulators when investigating offences of fraud, identity theft, money laundering, and extortion, amongst others. This chapter examines only the provisions of the respective laws in relation to the illegal interference with computer systems, dealt with in section 7 of the CCRA.

In **Antigua and Barbuda,** section 3[4] provides that no person without lawful authority can have interfere with an electronic system or network.[5] As mentioned in the two preceding chapters, **Australia,** in section 476.2 of the Criminal Code Act 1995, provides a single offence for the modification or impairment of a computer or data. It states that: (a) access to data held in a computer; or (b) modification of data held in a computer; or (c) the impairment of electronic communication to or from a computer; or (d) the impairment of the reliability, security or operation of

---

[2] Jitender Malik, Sanjaya Choudhury, Illegal access to a computer system: The dark truth of our society, Journal of information and Computer Science, Vol 9, Iss 12, (2019), p. 434.

[3] Ibid, p. 443.

[4] Electronic Crimes Act 2013, section 2, http://laws.gov.ag/wp-content/uploads/2019/02/a2013-14.pdf.

[5] Ibid, section 3.

any data held on a computer disk, credit card or other device used to store data by electronic means; by a person is unauthorised if the person is not entitled to cause that access, modification or impairment.[6] **In addition and more importantly, Part 9.5 of the Criminal Code Act 1995 (Cth) provides for the offence of identify crime, whereby there is an offences for dealing with and being in possession of identification information.**

The treatment of this offence by the **Bahamas** can be found under section 7 that refers to any person who interferes with or interrupts or obstructs the lawful use of, a computer.[7] In addition, section 6 and 6(3) makes it an offence for a person to secure access to a computer without authority. In **Bangladesh,** section 19, mentioned in the previous chapter, deals with interference with a computer system. Also, interference with a computer system and its functions is an offence in **Barbados.**[8] In **Belize** a person who obstructs, damages or denies access to a computer and its related systems and infrastructure will be committing an offence.[9]

In **Botswana,** under section 8, a person who intentionally, without lawful excuse or justification—(*a*) hinders or interferes with the functioning of a computer or computer system; or (*b*) hinders or interferes with a person who is lawfully using or operating a computer or computer system, commits an offence. Further, a person who intentionally, without lawful excuse or justification, commits an act which causes, directly or indirectly (*a*) a denial, including a partial denial, of access to a computer or computer system; or (*b*) an impairment of any programme or data stored in a computer or computer system, commits an offence.[10] **Brunei, Canada, Eswatini, Ghana** and **Grenada** have all adopted the offence provision, although there are subtle but important variations. **Brunei,** under section 7,[11] considers it an offence when a person interferes with, or interrupts or obstructs the lawful use of a computer. Also, section 4 creates an offence where a person causes a computer to perform any function for the purpose of securing access to any program or data held in a computer with intent to engage in a criminal activity. In **Canada,** as highlighted in the previous chapter, there is no specific legislation for cyber-related crimes. Any offences have been captured by the Criminal Code. On that basis, section 342.1(a) is multidimensional and indirectly could create and offence for unlawful interference of a computer.[12] **Eswatini**, according to section 8, makes it an offence to illegally interfere with

---

[6] *Australian Criminal Code Act 1995*, section 476.2.

[7] Computer Misuse Act 2007, section 3/4, https://www.agc.gov.bn/AGC%20Images/LAWS/ACT_PDF/C/CHAPTER%20194.pdf.

[8] Computer Misuse Act, 2005, section 6 http://www.oas.org/juridico/spanish/cyb_bbs_computer_misuse_2005.pdf.

[9] Cybercrime Act 2020, section 5 and 6 https://www.nationalassembly.gov.bz/wp-content/uploads/2020/10/Act-No.-32-of-2020-Cybercrime.pdf.

[10] Cybercrime and related Crimes Act 2018, section 8, https://www.bocra.org.bw/cybercrime-and-computer-related-crimes-act-2018.

[11] Computer Misuse Act 2007, section 7, https://www.agc.gov.bn/AGC%20Images/LAWS/ACT_PDF/C/CHAPTER%20194.pdf.

[12] Criminal Code 1985, https://laws-lois.justice.gc.ca/pdf/c-46.pdf.

the functioning of a computer.[13] This also extends to destroying computer storage systems. In **Ghana**, according to section 40, it is an offence to interfere with critical information infrastructure.[14] On the one hand, **Grenada,** in section 5 provides for and offence for the unlawful interference to electronic systems or networks to download or extract data or information.[15] On the other hand, in **Guyana,** similar to the other states examined, section 7 stipulates an offence for illegal interference with a computer system.[16] The notable exclusion, thus far, when comparing the above with the CCRA, is that the states have generally used the term 'interfere' rather than 'hinder'. On further examining the respective states' responses, generally, any interference would need to be intentional. That said, it is important for those who are applying these laws to clarify the terminology so as to ensure that intent is the threshold test for confirming or otherwise that an offence has been committed.

Fiji does not have a direct offence for the interference with a computer.[17] Arguably, it is problematic for any country not to have specific offences for these types of activities. However, in **India,** section 65 of the Information Technology Act, 2000 establishes the offence of tampering:

> Whoever knowingly or intentionally conceals, destroys or alters or intentionally or knowingly causes another to conceal, destroy, or alter any computer source code used for a computer, computer programme, computer system or computer network, when the computer source code is required to be kept or maintained by law for the time being in force, shall be punishable with imprisonment up to three years, or with fine which may extend up to two lakh rupees, or with both.[18]

In addition, section 43 provides the penalty and compensation for damages to a computer and computer system needs a replacement. For instance, 43 (h) stipulates that there will be charges for the services availed of by a person to the account of another person for tampering with or manipulating any computer, computer system, or computer network. Importantly, computer resource has been defined under the IT Act as constituting a computer, computer system, computer network, data, computer

[13] *Computer Crime and Cybercrime Act No.6 of 2022, section 8* https://www.esccom.org.sz/legislation/COMPUTER%20CRIME%20&%20CYBERCRIME%20ACT.pdf.

[14] Cybersecurity Act 2020, section 40 https://csdsafrica.org/wp-content/uploads/2021/08/Cybersecurity-Act-2020-Act-1038.pdf.

[15] Electronic Crimes Bill 2013, section https://ecagrenada.com/Grenada-Electronic-Crimes-Act-2013.pdf.

[16] Cyber Crime Act 2018, https://parliament.gov.gy/publications/acts-of-parliament/cyber-crime-act-2018.

[17] Cybersecurity and Cybercrime Act 2021, section 6 https://ncb.govmu.org/ncb/legislations/THE%20CYBERSECURITY%20AND%20CYBERCRIME%20ACT%202021.pdf.

Cybercrime Act 2021 (Act No. 3 of 2021), https://www.ilo.org/dyn/natlex/natlex4.detail?p_lang=en&p_isn=111060&p_classification=01.

[18] Information Technology Act 2000, section 65. Explanation. For the purposes of this section, computer source code means the listing of programmes, computer commands, design and layout and programme analysis of computer resource in any form.

data base or software.[19] However, in regard to tampering, neither 'computer source document' nor 'document' has been defined. Thus, and while it is for the local judiciary to define computer source document and whether it constitutes a computer system, it could be argued that it does. In reinforcing the above point, the difference is the terminology used by the various states to describe or define interference. Some states use 'interfere', others use 'modification' or 'tampering'. Yet, it can be argued that interfering or tampering with a computer automatically implies interference with an element of data and information, even if that data was never extracted. By making it an offence to tamper with or modify a computer or system, it is made clear that the accessed data must have been interfered with tampered with in some way, usually by means of an electronic device.

In the case of *Syed Asifuddin and Ors. v. State of Andhra Pradesh and Anr*[20] the Court dismissed the criminal petitions. The case highlighted how the Indian laws are relevant to current-day cybersecurity matters, and in particular interference (manipulation-tampering) with a computer and its systems. The Court noted that:

> The learned Additional Public Prosecutor, Sri H. Prahlad Reddy and the learned counsel for the second respondent, Sri D. Seshadri Naidu, submit that when a cognizable offence under various provisions of different statutes is registered and investigation is pending, this Court cannot quash the F. I. R., at the stage of investigation. After conducting appropriate preliminary investigation and examining witnesses the police have come to the conclusion that the petitioners have committed offences involving highly technical aspects, and therefore unless and until proper evidence is let in before the criminal Court, on mere assertions of the accused a crime cannot be quashed. They would contend that the cell phone handsets with CDMA technology supplied by the second respondent to its subscribers are dedicated to Reliance Indicomm Limited and by *interfering* with the computer programme and converting the handsets to be responsive to the technology adopted by TTSL is itself an offence and therefore these petitions are not maintainable.[21]

On this basis, the reference to 'interfere' would be considered in light of the manipulation of data. Although this related to commercial data, the Court stated that:

> The main allegation against the petitioners is that the MIN of Reliance phone is irreversibly integrated with ESN and the petitioners hacked ESN so as to wean away RIM customers to TATA Indicom service. The question is whether the manipulation of this electronic 32-bit number (ESN) programmed into Samsung N191 and LG-2030 cell phone instrument exclusively franchised to second respondent amounts to altering source code used by these computer handsets i.e., cell phone instruments. In the background facts, a question would also arise whether such alteration amounts to hacking with computer system? If the query answered in the affirmative, it is always open to the police to alter the F. I. R., or it is always open to the criminal Court to frame a charge specifically with regard to hacking with computer system, which is an offence under section 66 of the IT Act. At this stage, we may read section 65 and 66 of the IT Act.[22]

---

[19] Information Technology Act (2000), https://thelawreviews.co.uk/title/the-privacy-data-protection-and-cybersecurity-law-review/india, and https://www.indiacode.nic.in/handle/123456789/1999, section 29.

[20] 2005 CriLJ 4314. https://indiankanoon.org/doc/1459676/.

[21] Ibid, para 8.

[22] Ibid, para 40.

Put another way, the interference could also be construed as tampering with a computer or its data. The Court reaffirmed this position, arguing that:

> Tampering with computer source documents - Whoever knowingly or intentionally conceals, destroys or alters or intentionally or knowingly causes another to conceal, destroy, or alter any computer source code used for a computer, computer programme, computer system or computer network, when the computer source code is required to be kept or maintained by law for the time being in force, shall be punishable with imprisonment up to three years, or with fine which may extend up to two lakh rupees, or with both.[23]

Thus, the form and functional definition of tampering with a computer will constitute a level of interference. It can occur in a number of different forms depending on the activity being undertaken by an individual or other entity. Nonetheless, what needs to be understood is the level of difference between cybersecurity and the security of information and data. They can be distinctly separated at law, even though they are aligned together in practice.

Difference Between Information Security and Cybersecurity.[24]

Patrick McClanahan and San Joaquin make the point below that the terms 'cybersecurity' and 'information security' are often used interchangeably.[25] The authors also point out that both are 'responsible for security and protecting the computer system from threats and information breaches and often cybersecurity and information security are so closely linked that they may seem synonymous and unfortunately, they are used synonymously'.[26] The authors have demonstrated this separation of cyber security and information (data) security in the following the table. It also indicates how the systems and infrastructure are used and needed for the transmission of data around the world. It also shows how the interconnectedness, while being differentiated as shown below, is going to challenge individuals and organisations in practice, as well as regulators since the laws may need to be reviewed and updated regularly. Furthermore, it demonstrates that the principles and concepts of the CCRA, although well-placed, they could be expanded upon to include fraud, theft and ransom.

Cyber security	Information (data) security
It is the practice of protecting the data from outside the resource on the internet	It is all about protecting information from unauthorized user, access and data modification or removal in order to provide confidentiality, integrity, and availability
Cybersecurity to protect anything in the cyber realm	Information security is for information irrespective of the realm

(continued)

[23] Ibid, para 65.

[24] Patrick McClanahan, San Joaquin, Information Security, p. 1https://eng.libretexts.org/Courses/Delta_College/Information_Security/01%3A_Information_Security_Defined/1.4_-_Attacks_Types_of_Attacks.

[25] Ibid.

[26] Ibid.

(continued)

Cyber security	Information (data) security
Cybersecurity strikes against cybercrimes, cyber frauds and law enforcement	Information security strives against unauthorized access, disclosure modification and disruption
It deals with threats that may or may not exist in the cyber realm such as a protecting your social media account, personal information, etc	It deals with information assets and integrity confidentiality and availability
	It is about the ability to protect the use of cyberspace from It deals with protection of data from any form of threat. Cyber-attacks

The concepts of cybersecurity and information can c be separated. Although they are dealt with under data law and cybercrime law, they are becoming increasingly intertwined. The security of information (personal data) depends on the systems and infrastructure being as secure as possible. It is argued that fraud and theft of personal data can occur only when an individual or entity has gained illegal access to a computer and its systems or infrastructure.

Jamaica, while not creating a specific offence for the interference with a computer, takes a narrower approach to the unauthorised modification of the contents of any computer.[27] On the other hand, **Kenya,** similar to many of the other Africa countries compared in this book, has established an offence for interference with a computer.[28] In **Kiribati,** section 10 states that a person who, knowingly or recklessly, and without authority hinders or interferes with the functioning of a computer system by inputting, transmitting, damaging, deleting, deteriorating, altering or suppressing.[29] While in **Lesotho,** a general offence exists for the interference with a computer system.[30] Clearly, some states have adopted the terminology of the CCRA, while other have not. In reaffirming the point above, the exclusion of the term 'hinder' from most national laws, could become challenging in the future, since 'hinder' could be analogous to 'modification' and, more broadly, 'interference'.

As mentioned in the previous chapter**, Malawis** has an all-in offence under section 84, whereby, a person cannot not gain unauthorised access to, or intercept, or interfere with data or a computer.[31] In **Malaysia** a similar offence also exists, with section 5 establishing an offence for interference with a computer and its related systems.[32] **Mauritius** has taken a different approach, under section 9 and defined interference as being the hindering of the functioning of a computer system by

[27] The Cyber Crimes Act 2015, section 5 https://www.japarliament.gov.jm/attachments/339_The%20Cybercrimes%20Acts,%202015.pdf.

[28] Computer Misuse and Cybercrimes Act 2018, section 16 https://ictpolicyafrica.org/en/document/pb8w26fcso?page=2.

[29] Cybercrime Act 2021, section 7 https://www.mict.gov.ki/download/file/fid/320.

[30] The Computer Crimes and Cyber Security Bill, 2022, https://senate.parliament.ls/2022/05/19/computer-crime-and-cyber-security-bill-2022/.

[31] Electronic Transactions and Cyber Security Act 2017, section 84 https://media.malawilii.org/files/legislation/akn-mw-act-2016-33-eng-2017-12-31.pdf.

[32] Computer Crimes Act 1997, section 5 https://www.nacsa.gov.my/legal.php.

inputting, transmitting, damaging, deleting, deteriorating, altering or suppressing a computer.[33] **Nauru**'s section 10 restricts a person being able to interfere with an information system such as a computer.[34] In **New Zealand**, an offence is committed when a person intentionally or recklessly destroys, damages, or alters any computer system.[35] This subtle but important divergence from the other states is important. There is an element of intention involved, which is distinct from recklessness. Simply put, they are different things. Most noteworthy is that the term 'interference' is not used and the provision is quite specific in that the conduct is limited to destroying, damaging or altering a computer.

In **Pakistan**, section 5 makes it an offence to interfere with or damage an information system (computer).[36] One of Australia's closest neighbours, **Papua New Guinea,** has made it an offence, according to section 9, to interfere with an electronic device, which includes a computer system.[37] Again, the notable difference that has emerged is the terminology being used by nation states to mean the same thing. The addition by Pakistan has been 'information system'. It is argued that this would include a computer system. In **Rwanda**, a person cannot without authorisation, access a computer or its data.[38] Similarly, **Seychelles** has an offence for illegal modification of a computer system.[39] Likewise, **Sierra Leone,** in section 29 stipulates the offence of unauthorised system interference.[40] **South Africa** also has a general offence of interfering with a computer system and computer storage.[41]

Finally, **Singapore** does not provide for the same, while **Saint Lucia,** has focused on the damage done to a system. Hence, section 20 states that a person is not to cause damage to the public or any person, interfere with, interrupt or obstruct the functioning, reliability or usefulness of an electronic system (computer system).[42] On the other, **Saint Kitts and Nevis** takes a similar approach, and under section 6 considers it an offence when a person, knowingly and without lawful excuse or justification,

---

[33] Cybersecurity and Cybercrime Act 2021, section 9 https://ncb.govmu.org/ncb/legislations/THE%20CYBERSECURITY%20AND%20CYBERCRIME%20ACT%202021.pdf.

[34] Cybercrime Act 2015, section 10 http://ronlaw.gov.nr/nauru_lpms/files/acts/a59d9691f5a195412b877493a2a95e8b.pdf.

[35] Crimes Act 1961, section 250, https://www.legislation.govt.nz/act/public/1961/0043/latest/DLM330422.html.

[36] The Prevention of Electronic Crimes 2016, section 5 https://na.gov.pk/uploads/documents/1470910659_707.pdf. Critical infrastructure information system or data" means an information system program or data that supports or performs a function with respect to a critical infrastructure.

[37] *Cybercrime Code Act 2016, section 9* https://www.parliament.gov.pg/uploads/acts/16A_35.pdf.

[38] Law N° 60/2018 OF 22/8/2018 on prevention and punishment of cyber crimes, Article 16 https://www.risa.rw/fileadmin/user_upload/Others%20documents/Cyber_Crimes_Law.pdf Note there are other offences relates to accessing a computer and data.

[39] Computer Misuse Act 1998, sections 3,4, https://seylii.org/akn/sc/act/1998/17/eng%402015-12-31.

[40] Cyber Crime Act 2020, section 29 http://www.sierra-leone.org/Laws/2020-Cybercrime%20Act.pdf.

[41] Cybercrimes Act 2021, section 6 https://cybercrimesact.co.za.

[42] Electronic Crimes Bill 2009, section 20 https://www.govt.lc/media.govt.lc/www/resources/legislation/ElectronicCrimesBill.pdf.

interferes with a computer system.[43] Likewise, **St Vincent and The Grenadines** has an offence of illegal access to computer systems.[44] **Tonga,** has an offence for interference with a computer system.[45] Similarly, **Trinidad and Tobago** address the same offence.[46] **Uganda,** establishes an offence for obstruction of a computer, which has the same effect as interference.[47] The **United Republic of Tanzania** has a similar offence.[48] However, in **Zambia** it is not clear whether provision is made for such offence. It could fall within section 51(2), where messages are sent via a computer.[49] However, it is my view that this needs to be clarified by local authorities. Significantly, the **United Kingdom** does not provide for the same offence.[50]

The development of the offence provision for interference with a computer system has emerged as a significant contribution to the overall response to cybersecurity. Problematic with the above comparison is the general similarities when coupled with the subtle differences in the use and application of terms.

16.2 Conclusion

This chapter has confirmed the importance of making it an offence to interfere with a computer system. Computers are the fundamental backbone of the digital economy. They are integral to systems and infrastructure that transfer data nationally and internationally. The computer system itself facilitates international trade in the digital economy. Thus, as technology advances, it is of paramount importance that computer systems have the highest level of protection.

The CCRA had identified that the terms 'interfere' and 'hinder' are pertinent to any offence associated with interference with a computer system. However, this chapter has confirmed that very few states apply the term 'hinder'. A salient point is that states have used different terminology to provide for the offence. However, in

[43] Electronic Crimes Bill 2017, section 5 https://aglcskn.info/wp-content/documents/Act17TOC/Ch-04_41-Electronic-Crimes-Act.pdf.

[44] Cybercrime Act 2016, section 8 https://www.gov.vc/images/PoliciesActsAndBills/SVG_Cybercrime_Act_2016.pdf.

[45] Computer crimes Act 2003, section 6 https://ago.gov.to/cms/images/LEGISLATION/PRINCIPAL/2003/2003-0014/ComputerCrimesAct2003_1.pdf.

[46] The Cybercrimes Bill 2017, section 9 https://ttcsirt.gov.tt/wp-content/uploads/2022/04/Cyber_Crime_Bill_DRAFT_2017.pdf.

[47] *Computer Misuse Act, 2011, section 16* https://ulii.org/akn/ug/act/2011/2/eng@2011-02-14.

[48] *Cybercrimes Act, 2015, section 9* https://rsf.org/sites/default/files/the_cyber_crime_act_2015.pdf.

[49] The Cyber Security and Cyber Crimes Act, 2021, section 51 https://www.parliament.gov.zm/sites/default/files/documents/acts/Act%20No.%202%20of%202021The%20Cyber%20Security%20and%20Cyber%20Crimes.pdf.

[50] Computer Misuse Act 1990, https://www.legislation.gov.uk/ukpga/1990/18/contents.

some circumstances, clarification would be required to ensure that the same terms are used in reference to interference. The use of different terminology for this offence is another example of the divergent approaches taken by member countries of the Commonwealth.

The divergence in terminology cannot be ignored. The chapter commenced with a statement that it would not provide a word-by-word account of divergence in the offence provisions being compared, The brief comparison of laws demonstrates that the divergence in approaches can have significant practical outcomes when applying and interpreting the laws, particularly in cross-border related offences. That is, and while the law of the offence will usually apply where the offence has been committed, in transnational breaches, there may be the possibility of multiple offences (interference) in different states. The following duplicates some of the provisions compared above. On that basis, the subtle but important divergences in terminology from the above relate to the way that states have referred to the following:

- Modification of the contents of any computer; or
- Interference of computer and its related systems; or
- Hindering the functioning of a computer system (inputting, transmitting, damaging, deleting, deteriorating, altering or suppressing a computer); or
- Information system such as a computer; or
- [Intentionally or recklessly destroys, damages, or alters] any computer system; or
- Interfere with an electronic device (a computer);
- An electronic system or network; or
- Modification or impairment of a computer or data; or
- Interrupts or obstructs the lawful use of, a computer; or
- Interfere with the functioning of a computer, or
- Tampering with a computer.

This comparison reveals the divergence of terminology adopted by the respective states. The formal and functional arrangements all appear to directly or indirectly relate to the offence of interference with a computer system. However, the judiciary in each state may apply and different interpretation. Further research is needed. It is recommended that the Commonwealth work with its members to reduce the divergence in order to obtain a more consistent approach to the use of terminology. Notable also, is that some states require there to be an intentional element attached to the offence, or to show that the actual interference was reckless, while other states are all but silent on this point of the offences compared, this is arguably one of the most important, as it is the interface between humans and data. Finally, there was very little alignment with data (reference to data within the offence provision). This could be strengthened.

Chapter 17
Illegal Interception of Data

17.1 Introduction

The interception of data is closely related to the use of devices to commit such offences. There are two forms of data interception. First is the legal interception of data by government and regulators for the purposes of law enforcement, national security and other related matters. Second is the illegal interception by individuals and entities attempting to gain a personal or commercial advantage over another. This type of activity is not new. In this chapter, the focus is on illegal interception; therefore, interception of data by government for law enforcement purposes will not be discussed.

There is no doubt that digitisation of technology has, in some cases, made it easier for people to illegally intercept data and information, both personal and commercial. The impacts of this activity can be enormous, both financially and personally. Furthermore, it can result in threat, fraud and extortion (via ransomware) being used against individuals and entities (see later chapters).

This chapter, similar to the preceding chapters examines the illegal interception of data according to section 8 of the CCRA. Section 8 provides that a person who, intentionally without lawful excuse or justification, intercepts by technical means such as any non-public transmission to, from or within a computer system; or electromagnetic emissions from a computer system that a recarrying computer data; commits an offence punishable, on conviction, by imprisonment for a period not exceeding [*period*], or a fine not exceeding [*amount*], or both.[1] This chapter takes a high-level approach to determine where the offence has been adopted. It will demonstrate how devices are emerging as a sophisticated tool used for the interference with

[1] Model Law on Computer and Computer Related Crime, Office of Civil and Criminal Justice Reform, 2017, https://production-new-commonwealth-files.s3.eu-west-2.amazonaws.com/migrated/key_reform_pdfs/P15370_11_ROL_Model_Law_Computer_Related_Crime.pdf.

R. Walters, *Cybersecurity and Data Laws of the Commonwealth*,
https://doi.org/10.1007/978-981-99-3935-0_17

and interception of data, which in turn has the potential to significantly disrupt the digital economy. The chapter does not discuss any court decisions in relation to this offence.

The illegal interception of personal data is closely connected with the illegal processing of personal data, which is regulated by data protection laws. On the other hand, the interception of commercial data is regulated by other laws such as intellectual property or patent law, including contract laws. This chapter examines the offence provisions of Commonwealth countries to ascertain the extent to which their laws protect the illegal interception of data generally. It does not make a distinction between the interception laws and the provisions for processing of data in the states' data protection laws.

Essentially, attacks associated with the interception of data and information result in the unauthorised collection, use and storage of data. They can also extend to the interception of files that contain highly sensitive commercial information related to national security, such as the construction of military equipment. Amongst this and other commercial data, personal data, such as the names of military personnel, will also be intercepted. This chapter deals only with the illegal interception of data, as described in section 8 of the CCRA. It does not include a discussion of the legal interception of data used by government and regulators for law enforcement or national security. Mathew Zakaras[2] made the point back in 2001 that hacking was a form of internet intrusion that was commonly being used to intercept data being transmitted across the Internet. He states:

> One method of attacking computer networks is eavesdropping or the passive interception of network traffic. The eavesdropper observes patterns of traffic (sources and destinations) on a network using a packet sniffer in order to determine the relationships among organizations and individuals. In this process, the information is only observed, not changed. A packet sniffer is a program that monitors network packets flowing through a computer.[3]

This network traffic is generating large quantities of data that can be intercepted with ease in some cases. Individuals and entities that have no connection to government are becoming increasingly more sophisticated in the way they use technology to intercept data traffic. An important category of illegal interception has been modelled on the violation of privacy, such as tapping and recording of oral telephone conversations, and this principle applies to all forms of electronic data transfer, whether by telephone, fax, e-mail or file transfer.[4] This breach of privacy by means of interception is now deemed an offence under both data and criminal law. Peter Csonka asserts that data interference seeks to provide computer data and computer programs with

[2] Matthew Zakaras, *International computer crimes General Report*, Revue internationale de droit pénal, (Vol. 72), (2001), pp. 813–815.

[3] Ibid.

[4] Peter Csonka, *The Council of Europe's Convention on Cyber-crime and Other European Initiatives*, Revue internationale de droit pénal Volume 77, Issue 3, 2006, p. 484.

protection similar to that which is enjoyed by physical objects against intentional damage. This chapter briefly compares states' laws to determine whether such an offence has been included in the laws of Commonwealth states. Is the comparison is descriptive in nature. Series two of this book will go into a lot more detail.

Antigua and Barbuda, in section 3,[5] provides that no person without lawful authority may steal, conceal, destroy or alter or cause a person to steal, conceal, destroy or alter any source code used for an electronic system with an intention to cause damage.[6] However, under the **Australian** Criminal Code Act 1995, due to the fragmented approach of cybercrime law in this country, there is a deeming provision in section 5F of the *Telecommunications (Interception and Access) Act 1979* (Cth) which provides that for the purposes of this Act, a communication is taken to start passing over a telecommunications system when it is sent or transmitted by the person sending the communication; and is taken to continue to pass over the system until it becomes accessible to the intended recipient of the communication.[7] Thus, the provision operates when the data recipient has been contacted (the beginning, during and conclusion) of the transmission. However, in practice, the data that falls under this provision needs to be clarified. It could relate to telecommunication data only. Nonetheless, telecommunications data, at times, will include personal data being transmitted.

The **Bahamas** considers thay interception, in relation to a function of a computer, includes listening to or recording a function of a computer, or acquiring the substance.[8] In addition, section 6 and 6(3) makes the interception of data an offence. In **Bangladesh**, section 19 goes some way to minimising the illegal interception of data. A person commits an offence when s/he engages in interception for the collection of data, or data storage, or willingly causes or tries to cause harm to data or data-storage of any computer, computer system, computer network, or causes or tries to cause harm to any programme saved in the computer, computer system, or computer network.[9] It is the software systems and computer infrastructure that support the collection, use and storage of data.

Furthermore, in **Barbados**, according to section 7, it is an offence to illegally intercept[10] the transmission of information to or from a computer. However, in the laws of a number of states such as **Belize, Grenada, and Malaysia** there is no mention of a specific offence in regard to the unlawful interception of data. In the contemporary world, this is somewhat problematic. On the other hand, according to **Botswana**'s section 9, an offence is committed by any person who intentionally, without lawful

[5] Electronic Crimes Act 2013, section 6, http://laws.gov.ag/wp-content/uploads/2019/02/a2013-14.pdf.

[6] Ibid, section 3.

[7] Telecommunications (Interception and Access) Act 1979, section 5.

[8] Computer Misuse Act 2007, section 2, https://www.agc.gov.bn/AGC%20Images/LAWS/ACT_PDF/C/CHAPTER%20194.pdf.

[9] Digital Security Act 2018, section 19 https://www.cirt.gov.bd/wp-content/uploads/2020/02/Digital-Security-Act-2020.pdf.

[10] Computer Misuse Act, 2005, section 7 http://www.oas.org/juridico/spanish/cyb_bbs_computer_misuse_2005.pdf.

excuse or justification, and by technical means, intercepts—(*a*) any non-public transmission to, from or within a computer or computer system; or (*b*) any electromagnetic emissions that are carrying data from a computer or computer system, commits an offence.[11] In **Brunei**, although broad, section 6 creates an offence for unauthorised intercept or causing(s) any function of a computer to be intercepted,[12] which includes the transmission of data. In **Canada**, section 342.1(c) could create an offence for unlawful interference for of the purpose of intercepting data.[13] However, this needs to be read in conjunction with section 430 related to the destruction of property. **Eswatini,** according to section 5, makes it an offence to illegally intercept data or information stored or transmitted via a computer.[14] In **Ghana**, sections 71 to 75 give officers the power to intercept data.[15] Furthermore, **Guyana**, similar to the other states examined, has an offence for illegal interception of data and obtaining information from a computer or computer system.[16] **India,** rather than creating an offence for interception, has adopted a different approach allowing for a direction to be issued authorising the interception or monitoring or decryption of any information through any computer resource.[17] This is enabling regulators to undertake investigations. A more specific offence for the interception of data should be established. However, this is for India to decide.

The Interception Process

Patrick McClanahan and San Joaquin,[18] depict the interception process in the following diagram. It shows an interception that took place in 2013. The authors state that the standard interception processes include but are not limited to eavesdropping, wiretapping, copying of files and programs, accessing and copying messages, packet sniffing and key logging to capture data from the computer or network.[19] This process is still relevant today. The exception is the emergence and use of artificial intelligence (AI), which potentially poses greater challenges to data protection (Fig. 17.1).

---

[11] Cybercrime and related Crimes Act 2018, Section 9, https://www.bocra.org.bw/cybercrime-and-computer-related-crimes-act-2018.

[12] Computer Misuse Act 2007, Section 6, https://www.agc.gov.bn/AGC%20Images/LAWS/ACT_PDF/C/CHAPTER%20194.pdf.

[13] Criminal Code 1985, https://laws-lois.justice.gc.ca/pdf/c-46.pdf.

[14] *Computer Crime and Cybercrime Act No.6 of 2022, Section 8* https://www.esccom.org.sz/legislation/COMPUTER%20CRIME%20&%20CYBERCRIME%20ACT.pdf.

[15] Cybersecurity Act 2020, Section 71, 72, 73.74, 75 https://csdsafrica.org/wp-content/uploads/2021/08/Cybersecurity-Act-2020-Act-1038.pdf.

[16] Cyber Crime Act 2018, https://parliament.gov.gy/publications/acts-of-parliament/cyber-crime-act-2018.

[17] Information Technology Act (2000), https://thelawreviews.co.uk/title/the-privacy-data-protection-and-cybersecurity-law-review/india, and https://www.indiacode.nic.in/handle/123456789/1999 Section 69.

[18] Ibid.

[19] Ibid.

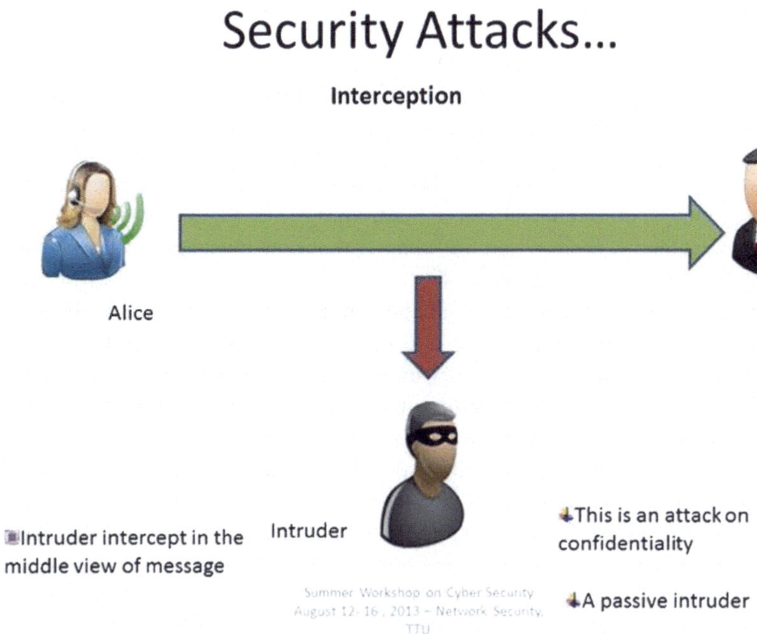

Fig. 17.1 Data vulnerable to illegal interception

The interception of data is here to stay. The sophistication of technology is likely to enable individuals and entities to undertake and gain access to data in the future more easily and more readily. The question is whether the laws are adequate enough to act as a deterrent to this activity.

Jamaica established as an offence the unauthorised interception of computer function or service.[20] In **Kenya**, section 17 makes it clear that it is illegal to intercept data or other information without the appropriate authority.[21] **Kiribati**, under section 8, has made it an offence to intercept data via a computer. On the other hand, section 28 gives police the authority to intercept data where required.[22] **Lesotho** makes it an offence to intercept data and information from a computer or computer system.[23] **Malawi**, has an all-in offence under section 84, whereby, a person cannot not gain unauthorised access to, or intercept, or interfere with data or a computer.[24] In **Mauritius**, according to section 8, a person cannot wilfully intercept or cause to

---

[20] The Cyber Crimes Act 2015, Section 6 https://www.japarliament.gov.jm/attachments/339_The%20Cybercrimes%20Acts,%202015.pdf.

[21] Computer Misuse and Cybercrimes Act 2018, Section 17 https://ictpolicyafrica.org/en/document/pb8w26fcso?page=2.

[22] Cybercrime Act 2021, Sections 8 and 28 https://www.mict.gov.ki/download/file/fid/320.

[23] The Computer Crimes and Cyber Security Bill, 2022, https://senate.parliament.ls/2022/05/19/computer-crime-and-cyber-security-bill-2022/

[24] Electronic Transactions and Cyber Security Act 2017, Section 84 https://media.malawilii.org/files/legislation/akn-mw-act-2016-33-eng-2017-12-31.pdf.

be intercepted without authorisation, any computer data, or electromagnetic emissions carrying computer data.[25] In **Nauru**, section 7 creates an offence that restricts a person being able to intercept data.[26] In **New Zealand,** an offence is committed when a person intentionally intercepts any private communication by means of an interception device.[27] However, there are exceptions that apply to law enforcement personnel, similar to the exceptions in the laws of other Commonwealth states. Unlike the laws examined in other chapters, here, terminology has not emerged as an issue of divergence. Rather, it is shown in this chapter that how most states have applied the terms ‘intercept’ or ‘interception’.

Nigeria has made it an offence to illegally intercept data and messages.[28] In **Pakistan**, section 17 makes it an offence to intercept data and information unlawfully.[29] **Papua New Guinea**, consistent with other states, has an offence provision for the unauthorised interception of information generally, but goes one step further to mention military and other sensitive data.[30] It is not clear whether this would include sensitive personal data of military personnel. This would need to be clarified. In **Rwanda**, it is an offence to intercept data held in a computer system.[31] Likewise, **Sierra Leone** treats the interception of data as an offence.[32] **South Africa** also has a general offence including electromagnetic emissions from a computer system carrying such data, within or which is transmitted to or from a computer system.[33] However, **Seychelles**, **Singapore** doe not provide for the same. Further research is needed to confirm whether there are other laws in these states that cover this type of offence. In the Americas, **Saint Lucia**, under section 22, requires that a person is not, without lawful authority, to intercept by technical means, non-public transmissions of data to, from or within an electronic system.[34] In **Saint Kitts and Nevis**, section 7 makes it an offence to illegally intercept data.[35] **St Vincent and**

---

[25] Cybersecurity and Cybercrime Act 2021, Section 8 https://ncb.govmu.org/ncb/legislations/THE%20CYBERSECURITY%20AND%20CYBERCRIME%20ACT%202021.pdf.

[26] Cybercrime Act 2015, Section 7 http://ronlaw.gov.nr/nauru_lpms/files/acts/a59d9691f5a1954 12b877493a2a95e8b.pdf.

[27] Crimes Act 1961, Section 216B, https://www.legislation.govt.nz/act/public/1961/0043/latest/DLM330422.html.

[28] Cyber Crime Act 2015, Section 9 and 12, https://lawpadi.com/wp-content/uploads/2015/08/CybErCrime_ProhibitionPreventionetc_Act_2015.pdf.

[29] The Prevention of Electronic Crimes 2016, Section 17 https://na.gov.pk/uploads/documents/1470910659_707.pdf.

[30] *Cybercrime Code Act 2016, Section 4* https://www.parliament.gov.pg/uploads/acts/16A_35.pdf.

[31] Law N° 60/2018 OF 22/8/2018 on prevention and punishment of cyber crimes, Article 19 https://www.risa.rw/fileadmin/user_upload/Others%20documents/Cyber_Crimes_Law.pdf Note there are other offences relates to accessing a computer and data.

[32] Cyber Crime Act 2020, Section 25, 26 http://www.sierra-leone.org/Laws/2020-Cybercrime%20Act.pdf.

[33] Cybercrimes Act 2021, Section 3 https://cybercrimesact.co.za.

[34] Electronic Crimes Bill 2009, Section 22 https://www.govt.lc/media.govt.lc/www/resources/legislation/ElectronicCrimesBill.pdf.

[35] Electronic Crimes Bill 2017, Section 7 https://aglcskn.info/wp-content/documents/Act17TOC/Ch-04_41-Electronic-Crimes-Act.pdf.

The Grenadines prohibits by law the illegal acquisition of data, rather that formally expressing it as interception.[36] However, the laws do not define what 'acquisition' means in this context.

Thus, overall, the Internet intermediaries create, process, and store a range of metadata during the course of their operations, most commonly including information about the source, destination, timing, and location of their users' activities.[37] These intermediaries are able to intercept personal data. However, most if not all of the commentary by scholars has focused on the interception of telecommunications between individuals, and the surveillance activities undertaken by nation states. There is little commentary on the interception of data by the general public. Moreover, today, the unlawful interception of data is accomplished with ease by non-state actors, which in the long term can have a detrimental effect on the digital economy. Importantly, there is the problem that interception can have negative impacts on the economy, the extent of which will be difficult to determine. It is likely that any economic impact would be combined with other similar types of cyber offences such as data theft.

Trinidad and Tobago do not have the equivalent offence.[38]**Tonga**[39] **Uganda**[40] **United Republic of Tanzania**[41] all make it an offence to illegally intercept data via a computer. However, **Zambia**[42] adopted a different approach under Part VI, pertaining to law enforcement activities only. Most noteworthy is how the **United Kingdom** does not provide for the same offence.[43]

While this brief chapter has examined the divergences in the states' laws with regard to interception, these laws have more similarities than differences. Unlike the previous chapter, here there is no extensive description of the offence provisions because, generally, they are quite similar.

---

[36] Cybercrime Act 2016, Section 7 https://www.gov.vc/images/PoliciesActsAndBills/SVG_Cybercrime_Act_2016.pdf.

[37] Jaani Riordan, *The Liability of Internet Intermediaries, Data Retention and Interception,* Oxford University Press (2016) p. 564.

[38] The Cybercrimes Bill 2017, https://ttcsirt.gov.tt/wp-content/uploads/2022/04/Cyber_Crime_Bill_DRAFT_2017.pdf.

[39] Computer crimes Act 2003, Section 7 https://ago.gov.to/cms/images/LEGISLATION/PRINCIPAL/2003/2003-0014/ComputerCrimesAct2003_1.pdf.

[40] *Computer Misuse Act, 2011, Section 15* https://ulii.org/akn/ug/act/2011/2/eng@2011-02-14.

[41] *Cybercrimes Act, 2015, Section 6* https://rsf.org/sites/default/files/the_cyber_crime_act_2015.pdf.

[42] The Cyber Security and Cyber Crimes Act, 2021, Part VI https://www.parliament.gov.zm/sites/default/files/documents/acts/Act%20No.%202%20of%202021The%20Cyber%20Security%20and%20Cyber%20Crimes.pdf.

[43] Computer Misuse Act 1990, https://www.legislation.gov.uk/ukpga/1990/18/contents.

17.2 Conclusion

This brief, but important chapter has demonstrated that most Commonwealth countries consider the interception of data to be a serious offence. As stated above, there is little scholarly discussion on this provision, since research has focused on closely examining government interception of data under surveillance laws.

That said, there are some differences amongst the laws compared. While most states do apply either intercept or interception, the differences include, but are not limited to, its function. For instance, some states are specific in relation to illegal interception, whereas other states are not. Problematic is how some states have chosen not to legislate for this offence under their respective computer laws. However, further research is needed to confirm whether such an offence is provided for in other criminal laws of that state.

In further developments, some states have opted to take the minimalist approach. In so doing those states have an expanded provision that applies the term 'collect' rather than 'intercept'. It is argued that this needs to be clarified with the home country. Thus, in adopting this approach, one state has applied collection to also include data storage and the willingness for the individual to harm the data.

Arguably, this requires the element of intention to be proven in the commission of the offence. In another development, the term 'intercepted' has also been used to describe an offence involving the interception of a computer. While not clear whether this pertains to data, it is argued that by intercepting a computer, the resulting effect is the automatic interception of data, whether intentional or otherwise.

The final development in the different terminology is the application of the term 'acquisition of data'. This approach is a clear departure from the other states because it infers that the data must be acquired in some way. Without a clear definition within the law, there could be confusion about the reach that this term has. The ensuing questions is whether the term refers to the voluntary acquisition or acquisition after monetary exchange, amongst others. This needs to be clarified by St Vincent and the Grenadines.

A pertinent issue at the time of writing is the lack of judicial decisions on this offence in all the countries examined. That is, while there are a number of high-profile decisions in relation to the interception of data by government, they do not extend to the same for the private sector. This is another area of further research that is urgently required. Another issue is the lack of information available to determine the impact that the illegal interception of data will have on the digital economy. The Commonwealth should investigate this. In conclusion, this chapter has again demonstrated that personal data is at the core of these offence provisions. While not specifically stated by the CCRA, it is argued that all data can be intercepted. The next chapter examines offences related to devices, and which are dealt with by the CCRA, and reveals how states have approached this issue.

Chapter 18
Illegal Devices

18.1 Introduction

The use of various devices to access computers, systems and infrastructure along with data, has been on the rise over the past decade. It has become a problem that governments and regulators find difficult to combat given the illegal activities of both state and non-state actors. Devices used for IT services can include but are not limited to storage devices, mobile phones, laptops, Ipads, UBS flash drives, network equipment, and home and office equipment. These can all be used to gain access to data and collect personal and commercial information from individuals and entities.

Section 9 of the CCRA deals with illegal devices. It prohibits a person from producing, selling or procuring a device that enables access to a computer system, amongst others things. Section 9 states that a person commits an offence if that person (a) intentionally or recklessly, without lawful excuse or justification, produces, sells, procures for use, imports, exports, distributes or otherwise makes available: (i) a device, including a computer program, that is designed or adapted for the purpose of committing an offence against Section 5, 6, 7 or 8; or (ii) a computer password, access code or similar data by which the whole or any part of a computer system is capable of being accessed; with the intent that it be used by any person for the purpose of committing an offence against section 5, 6, 7 or 8; or (b) has an item mentioned in subparagraph (a)(i) or (a)(ii)in his or her possession with the intent that it be used by any person for the purpose of committing an offence against section 5, 6, 7 or 8.[1]

[1] Model Law on Computer and Computer Related Crime, Office of Civil and Criminal Justice Reform, 2017, section 9, https://production-new-commonwealth-files.s3.eu-west-2.amazonaws.com/migrated/key_reform_pdfs/P15370_11_ROL_Model_Law_Computer_Related_Crime.pdf.

R. Walters, *Cybersecurity and Data Laws of the Commonwealth*,
https://doi.org/10.1007/978-981-99-3935-0_18

This chapter will compare the laws of relevant jurisdictions to confirm or otherwise their adoption of this concept. However, this chapter does not provide a word-by-word comparison of the laws. Due to the inconsistent approaches taken by the respective states, a high-level comparison has been undertaken to confirm where the offence has been adopted. What this chapter does is further highlight how nation states have taken different approaches to making provisions in their laws for offences associated with the use of devices for the purpose of illegally harvesting data and information.

The Internet of Things (IoT) has profoundly changed the way people think about using technology to assist them in their work and daily activities. Internet-connected devices today can be found in homes, offices, public buildings, hospitals, banks, ships,[2] motor vehicles, and aeroplanes, amongst others.[3] Companies today are increasingly having to incorporate cybersecurity strategies into their daily thinking and responses to protect their business. A common criminal activity used by individuals and entities is to hack into systems and infrastructure to obtain data information they are seeking for commercial, national security or some other gain.

> In the last two decades, we have seen digitisation rise to the top of the agenda of executive boards across the globe. As a result, cybersecurity skills and processes in most companies have also advanced – though at a slower pace. The fast growth of the so-called IoT, however, is changing the game. Cybersecurity is more relevant and challenging than ever, and companies will need to pick up the pace of capability building in this area.[4]

The challenges faced by commercial organisations (small, medium and large) from IoT security-related issues cannot be underestimated. This chapter reveals how the laws examined in this book vary greatly; hence, the level of inconsistency and incoherence makes it a highly technical and complex legal landscape to navigate. That said, as the digital economy continues to evolve, new IoT challenges will emerge. Some of these challenges are explained below:

> IoT, security challenges move from a company's traditional IT infrastructure into its connected products in the field and remain an issue through the entire product lifecycle – long after products have been sold. The industrial IoT, or Industry 4.0, means that security becomes a pervasive issue in production as well. Cyber threats in the world of IoT can have consequences beyond compromised customer privacy. Critical equipment, such as pacemakers and entire manufacturing plants, are now vulnerable, meaning that customer health and a company's total production capability are at risk. As the IoT is connecting these additional "things" – be it products, production systems, or other devices – the sheer number

---

[2] Guidelines on Cyber Security Onboard Ships, https://www.ics-shipping.org/wp-content/uploads/2020/08/guidelines-on-cyber-security-onboard-ships-min.pdf.

[3] Robert Walters, Sinta Dewi Rosadi. *Transnational Flow of Personal Data in Home and Office Devices: Is There a Competitive Advantage?* American Journal of Science, Engineering and Technology. Vol. x, No. x, (2022).

[4] McKinsey & Company, Perspectives on transforming cybersecurity, Digital McKinsey and Global Risk Practice March (2019), p. 106, https://www.mckinsey.com/~/media/McKinsey/McKinsey%20Solutions/Cyber%20Solutions/Perspectives%20on%20transforming%20cybersecurity/Transforming%20cybersecurity_March2019.ashx.

> of cybersecurity attack vectors increases dramatically. While in the past, the number of endpoints in a large corporate network would be somewhere between 50,000 and 500,000, with the IoT, we are talking about millions or tens of millions of endpoints. Unfortunately, many of these consist of legacy devices with either no or very insufficient security.[5]

The shift to the digital economy and the Fourth Industrial Revolution (4IR),[6] will integrate IT systems with physical systems to produce a cyber-physical system that brings the real world in a virtual reality.[7] With this shift, regulators and businesses are only beginning to fully understand the cyber threat. In my view, the risks to commercial activity are enormous. More research is needed. The 4IR is the next wave of globalization, which is well under way. Moreover, 'digitally enabled trade, otherwise referred to as e-commerce, has become the major global trade growth story. As the digital age takes hold, services are growing in importance in international trade, both in their own right and as a support to trade in goods'.[8] Essentially, in order for the competing policy objectives of data protection and the free flow of data to find the right balance, cybersecurity and its laws will also have a role to play. Put another way, some nation states want to provide the highest level of protection to the online personal data of data subjects. On the other hand, other nation states want to implement a policy for free-flowing data where there is a minimum standard of protection so as to boost the growth of the digital economy. In my view, this is one of the most significant challenges facing the economy. How does a state maximise its data protection while enabling that same data flow nationally and internationally? One way to achieve this is through the law. The simple Iphone device today has enabled people around the world to gain access to data and information like never before. Iphones are used for commercial transactions daily, and for criminal activity.

Notwithstanding the above, it is the devices that are being used to improve the free flow of data that can be easily compromised, and threatening the very protections of that data. Commercially, there are additional concerns that there has been an increase in the number of threats to intellectual and private property rights. There are also broader issues emerging from the implementation of artificial intelligence (AI) in devices in cars. The ensuing questions is: when there is the theft of personal and

---

[5] Ibid.

[6] Jane Drake-Brockman, Ingo Borchert, Nigel Cory, Ziyang Fan, Christopher Findlay, Fukunari Kimura, Hildegunn Kyvik-Nordas, Magnus Lodefalk, Shin-Yi Peng, Hein Roelfsema, Yose Damuir, Sherry Stephenson, Tu Xinquan, Erik Van Der Marel, Mustafa Yaggi, Impact of Digital Technologies and the Fourth industrial Revolution on Trade in Services, Task Force 1, Trade, Investment and Growth, T20, 2020, pp. 2–3, https://www.g20-insights.org/wp-content/uploads/2020/11/T20_TF1_PB4.pdf. Also see Klaus Schaub, The Fourth Industrial Revolution: what it means, how to respond, 2021, https://jmss.vic.edu.au/wp-content/uploads/2021/06/The_Fourth_Industrial_Revolution.pdf.

[7] Antonella Petrillo, Fabio De Felice, Raffaele Cioffi and Federico Zomparelli, Fourth Industrial Revolution: Current Practices, Challenges, and Opportunities (2018), https://doi.org/10.5772/intechopen.72304, https://www.intechopen.com/chapters/58010.

[8] Jane Drake-Brockman, Ingo Borchert, Nigel Cory, Ziyang Fan, Christopher Findlay, Fukunari Kimura, Hildegunn Kyvik-Nordas, Magnus Lodefalk, Shin-Yi Peng, Hein Roelfsema, Yose Damuir, Sherry Stephenson, Tu Xinquan, Erik Van Der Marel, Mustafa Yaggi, Impact of Digital Technologies and the Fourth industrial Revolution on Trade in Services, Task Force 1, Trade, Investment and Growth, T20, 2020, pp. 2–3.

commercial data and information from a vehicle under the control of an individual or entity, and that data and information is used to cause an accident, are the currentlaws adequate? In other words, is the offence that of interfering with the computer-system or of selling, exporting, importing, or decrypting information?

Similar to the other chapters, this one begins with **Antigua and Barbuda** which, according to section 3,[9] does not specifically address section 9 of the CCRA, but does address the issue of using a device to decrypt data and information. **Australia** has a similar offence for processing a device for the collection and use of data although it has taken an approach different from those of the other states being compared. Section 478.3 states that a person commits an offence if (a) the person has possession or control of data; and (b) the person has that possession or control with the intention that the data be used, by the person or another person, in: (i) committing an offence against Division 477; or (ii) facilitates the commission of such an offence.[10]

In the **Bahamas**, it is an offence to interfere with a computer and its system by means of a device.[11] However, **Bangladesh** does not have any specific provisions regarding illegal devices. However, section 19[12] partly addresses the issue by creating an offence for the extraction of data, insertion of malware or virus, accessing data or restricting access to the system. However, there is no mention of using a device to facilitate this activity. Similarly, **Kiribati** does not provide for a specific offence related to devices. However, section 2 states that computer systems include devices.[13] Thus, within the laws, other offences that relate to computer systems will indirectly apply to devices. However, **Rwanda, Seychelles, Singapore** do not provide for the same. It must be noted that this offence may be mentioned in other legislation. The home country should be consulted to confirm this. This will constitute part of further research in the next edition of this book.

Barbados has restricted significantly a person's ability to use a device to intercept and interfere with data or a computer system.[14] On the other hand, in **Belize**, section 7 prohibits the use of devices to possess, procure for use, produce, sell, import or export, distribute, disclose or otherwise makes available[15] information on a computer of its systems.

[9] Electronic Crimes Act 2013, section 2, http://laws.gov.ag/wp-content/uploads/2019/02/a2013-14.pdf.

[10] Australian Criminal Code Act 1995, section 478.3.

[11] Computer Misuse Act 2007, section 6, https://www.agc.gov.bn/AGC%20Images/LAWS/ACT_PDF/C/CHAPTER%20194.pdf. There is no definition of device. However, electronic constitutes, acoustic, mechanical or other device" means any device or apparatus that is used or is capable of being used to intercept any function of a computer.

[12] Digital Security Act 2018, section 19 https://www.cirt.gov.bd/wp-content/uploads/2020/02/Digital-Security-Act-2020.pdf.

[13] Cybercrime Act 2021, section 2 https://www.mict.gov.ki/download/file/fid/320.

[14] Computer Misuse Act, 2005, section 8 http://www.oas.org/juridico/spanish/cyb_bbs_computer_misuse_2005.pdf.

[15] Cybercrime Act 2020, section 7 https://www.nationalassembly.gov.bz/wp-content/uploads/2020/10/Act-No.-32-of-2020-Cybercrime.pdf.

The formal functional arrangements for the regulation of devices in **Botswana** apply to a person who intentionally, without lawful excuse or justification, manufactures, sells, procures for use, imports, exports, distributes or otherwise makes available, a computer or computer system or any other device, designed or adapted for the purpose of committing an offence. Additionally, a person who intentionally, without lawful excuse or justification, receives, or is in possession of, one or more of the devices, commits an offence. Further, an offence is committed when a person is found in possession of any data or programme with the intention that the data or programme be used, by the person himself or herself or by another person, to commit or facilitate the commission of an offence.[16]

In **Brunei**, section 6, while broad, creates an offence for the use of any device to intercept, access or otherwise any computer.[17] Similarly, in **Canada**, section 342.2 (1) establishes an offence for the use of a device to access a computer,, and applies to any person who, without lawful excuse, makes, possesses, sells, offers for sale, imports, obtains for use, distributes or makes available a device that is designed or adapted primarily to commit an offence.[18] Yet, this needs to be read in conjunction with section 430 related to the destruction of property. In *R v Reeve*,[19] the Court observed that the police were undertaking investigations and sought to seize a computer device that was jointly owned. What emerged were the reasons for the seizure, in that the police sought to preserve and permit access to the data contained on the device.[20] In order to gain access to any data and information on a computer device, authorities would need to take possession of the device. The case centred on the right to privacy according to the Charter Rights in Canada. Specifically, the police discovered child pornography on a home computer device that the accused, Thomas Reeves, shared with his spouse. His spouse consented to the police entering the home and taking the computer from a shared space. The officer did not have a warrant. Reeves claims that the police obtained the child pornography evidence in a manner that infringed his rights under section 8 of the Canadian Charter of Rights and Freedoms and it should have been excluded under section 24.[21] Arguably, the data retained when evaluated against the definition of personal information would constitute an element of personal data. The case demonstrated a clear link between privacy, data protection and cybercrime. Arguably, these types of offences have been reported

[16] Cybercrime and related Crimes Act 2018, section 10, https://www.bocra.org.bw/cybercrime-and-computer-related-crimes-act-2018.

[17] Computer Misuse Act 2007, section 6, https://www.agc.gov.bn/AGC%20Images/LAWS/ACT_PDF/C/CHAPTER%20194.pdf.

[18] Criminal Code 1985, https://laws-lois.justice.gc.ca/pdf/c-46.pdf.

[19] *R. v. Reeves*, 2018 SCC 56, [2018] 3 https://scc-csc.lexum.com/scc-csc/scc-csc/en/item/17405/index.do.

[20] Ibid, para 31.

[21] Ibid, para 1.

in other Commonwealth states, and the personal data and information related to children is highly problematic. Similar issues will arise in commercial matters where the personal data is exposed and relates to the international transactions of companies and individuals.

The position in **Eswatini** is that according to section 9 a person cannot use a device to access and extract data or information from a computer without the appropriate authorisation to do so.[22] Nevertheless, in **Fiji** according to section 8, a person who intentionally manufactures, sells, procures for use, imports, distributes or otherwise makes available a computer system or any other device, or computer data or computer program designed or adapted primarily for the purpose of committing an offence under this Part, commits an offence.[23] In Central Asia, **India**, in Section 66D, states that any person who by means of any communication *device* or computer resource cheats by personating, shall be punished.[24] Thus, the emerging differences in terms and terminology is not only highly relevant to understanding these offences, but also, significantly divergent.

Furthermore, in **Jamaica,** any person using devices that possesses, receives, manufactures, sells, imports, distributes, discloses or otherwise information from a computer, unless authorised has committed an offence.[25] In **Kenya,** devices cannot be used to access data or a computer.[26] Section 18 is quite extensive and states that a person who knowingly manufactures, adapts, sells, procures for use, imports, offers to supply, distributes or otherwise makes available a device, program, computer password, access code or similar data designed or adapted primarily for the purpose of committing any offence under this section, commits an offence. On the other hand, **Lesotho** makes it an offence to misuse devices to apply and access, sell, procure, export or import data and information.[27]

Malawi, under section 84, goes further than most other jurisdictions by stipulating that an offence is committed when a person unlawfully produces, sells, offers to sell, procures for use, designs, adapts for use, distributes or possesses any device, including a computer program, a component or a phone, which is designed primarily to overcome security measures for the protection of data, or performs any of these

---

[22] *Computer Crime and Cybercrime Act No.6 of 2022, section 9* https://www.esccom.org.sz/legislation/COMPUTER%20CRIME%20&%20CYBERCRIME%20ACT.pdf.

[23] Cybersecurity and Cybercrime Act 2021, section 6 https://ncb.govmu.org/ncb/legislations/THE%20CYBERSECURITY%20AND%20CYBERCRIME%20ACT%202021.pdf.

Cybercrime Act 2021 (Act No. 3 of 2021), section 10 https://www.ilo.org/dyn/natlex/natlex4.detail?p_lang=en&p_isn=111060&p_classification=01.

[24] Information Technology Act (2000), https://thelawreviews.co.uk/title/the-privacy-data-protection-and-cybersecurity-law-review/india, and https://www.indiacode.nic.in/handle/123456789/1999, section 66D.

[25] The Cyber Crimes Act 2015, section 10 https://www.japarliament.gov.jm/attachments/339_The%20Cybercrimes%20Acts,%202015.pdf.

[26] Computer Misuse and Cybercrimes Act 2018, section 18 https://ictpolicyafrica.org/en/document/pb8w26fcso?page=2.

[27] The Computer Crimes and Cyber Security Bill, 2022, https://senate.parliament.ls/2022/05/19/computer-crime-and-cyber-security-bill-2022/.

acts with regard to a password, access code or any other similar kind of data with the intent to unlawfully use it.[28] On the one hand, in **Malaysia,** there are no specific offences related to devices themselves that may interfere with computers and their systems. On the other hand, section 2, in defining a computer, refers to a device that collects data or is interconnected with other devices.[29] However, in **Ghana**, there are no specific laws for offences related to the use of devices. **Grenada** has taken an approach different from that of the other states. Grenada rather than regulate for the offence of using a device(s) to access data and information from a computer, opted to regulate offensive behaviour over electronic systems that can discriminate against or injure a person.[30] **Guyana,** similar to the other states examined, in section 8 stipulates that it is an offence to use a device to gain access to a computer system.[31]

In **Mauritius,** it is an offence for any person to intentionally manufacture, sell, procure for use, import, distribute or otherwise make available, a computer system, computer data or any other device, designed or adapted primarily for the purpose of committing any offence under this Act. This approach has emerged as one of the common themes throughout this chapter. Any person who intentionally and without authorisation, receives or is in possession of devices and computer data is committing an offence.[32] There is a lot of cross-over with protecting data from the unauthorised use of any device. On the other hand, **Nauru**, in section 11 prohibits a person from using a device to access a computer and obtain data and information.[33] In **New Zealand** an offence is committed when a person *intentionally uses a device to intercept private communications.*[34] On the other hand, **Nigeria** any person or organization who by means of false pretence induces any person employed by or under the government of the federal, state or local government of Nigeria or any person in charge of electronic devices to deliver to him any electronic messages which includes but is not limited to E-mail, credit and debit cards information, facsimile messages which is not specifically meant for him or his organization (in the latter case except he is authorized to receive such messages for and on behalf of his organization) commits an offence.[35]

---

[28] Electronic Transactions and Cyber Security Act 2017, https://media.malawilii.org/files/legislation/akn-mw-act-2016-33-eng-2017-12-31.pdf.

[29] Computer Crimes Act 1997, section 2 https://www.nacsa.gov.my/legal.php.

[30] Electronic Crimes Bill 2013, section 6 https://ecagrenada.com/Grenada-Electronic-Crimes-Act-2013.pdf.

[31] Cyber Crime Act 2018, https://parliament.gov.gy/publications/acts-of-parliament/cyber-crime-act-2018.

[32] Cybersecurity and Cybercrime Act 2021, section 13 https://ncb.govmu.org/ncb/legislations/THE%20CYBERSECURITY%20AND%20CYBERCRIME%20ACT%202021.pdf.

[33] Cybercrime Act 2015, section 11 http://ronlaw.gov.nr/nauru_lpms/files/acts/a59d9691f5a1954 12b877493a2a95e8b.pdf.

[34] Crimes Act 1961, section 216B, https://www.legislation.govt.nz/act/public/1961/0043/latest/DLM330422.html.

[35] Cyber Crime Act 2015, section 12.5, https://lawpadi.com/wp-content/uploads/2015/08/CyberCrime_ProhibitionPreventionetc_Act_2015.pdf.

In **Pakistan**, there are no specific offences related to the use of devices for illegally accessing a computer system.[36] However, section 15 makes it an offence where a SIM card is unauthorised to be used to access or connect with digital devices. In **Papua New Guinea,** section 16 states that a person cannot use any device to procure, sell, import, export, distribute or otherwise information.[37] In **Sierra Leone**, section 30 creates a general offence whereby an individual and entity commits an offence when illegally using a device for the sale, procurement, import, offers to supply, distribute codes, and data amongst other information.[38] **South Africa** also has a similar offence according to section 7.[39]

Across the Americas, **Saint Lucia,** section 14 provides that a person cannot produce, possess, sell, procure, import, distribute or otherwise make available a device, including a computer program designed or adapted primarily for a password, access code, or similar data by which the whole or any part of an electronic system is capable of being accessed with the intent that it be used for the purpose of committing an offence.[40] Additionally, **Saint Kitts and Nevis** in section 8 stipulates that it is an offence when a person knowingly, without lawful excuse or justification or in excess of a lawful excuse or justification, produces, sells, procures for use, imports, exports, distributes or otherwise makes available a device, including a computer program, that is designed or adapted for the purpose of illegally accessing a computer or data.[41] Again, the expression of the above is a development that has emerged one of the consistent approaches taken by some states. **St Vincent and The Grenadines** deems it an offence to illegally use devices to extract and use data.[42]

[36] The Prevention of Electronic Crimes 2016, section 5 https://na.gov.pk/uploads/documents/1470910659_707.pdf. Critical infrastructure information system or data" means an information system program or data that supports or performs a function with respect to a critical infrastructure.

[37] *Cybercrime Code Act 2016, section 16* https://www.parliament.gov.pg/uploads/acts/16A_35.pdf.

[38] Cyber Crime Act 2020, section http://www.sierra-leone.org/Laws/2020-Cybercrime%20Act.pdf.

[39] Cybercrimes Act 2021, section 7 https://cybercrimesact.co.za.

[40] Electronic Crimes Bill 2009, section 14 https://www.govt.lc/media.govt.lc/www/resources/legislation/ElectronicCrimesBill.pdf.

[41] Electronic Crimes Bill 2017, section 8 https://aglcskn.info/wp-content/documents/Act17TOC/Ch-04_41-Electronic-Crimes-Act.pdf.

[42] Cybercrime Act 2016, section 10 https://www.gov.vc/images/PoliciesActsAndBills/SVG_Cybercrime_Act_2016.pdf.

Finally, **Tonga,** has an offence for interference for the illegal use of devices to access a computer and/or data.[43] Similarly, **Trinidad and Tobago,** have the same offence.[44] **Uganda,** access to a computer and data is unlawful through or via a device.[45] The **United Republic of Tanzania** includes asimilar offence in its laws.[46] In **Zambia**, the same offence also comprises interference with a computer and data.[47] Finally, the **United Kingdom** makes no provision for this offence.[48]

18.2 Conclusion

This chapter has focused on the provisions for the offence related to the use of devices to extract data, as stipulated by the CCRA. It has briefly demonstrated that again there are a number of different approaches by the respective states to reflect this provision within their national laws. It is argued that computers are devices, and there are a large number of devices on the open market that can collect and use data, whether it be in the home or office. While this chapter has not focussed on devices used by government and enforcement agencies to monitor their citizens, there are many examples around the world where this takes place on a daily basis.

Many states have not followed the CCRA. They have opted to go their own way, and as a result there is divergence in the ways that this offence provision is expressed within the national laws. For instance, it is considered an offence to use a device to decrypt data and information. However, this offence has not been widely adopted in the laws examined. This does not mean that the offence is not covered by other national laws. The other development has been the terminology and terms applied within the respective national laws. There are a number of states that have applied the rule of intention or intentional use of a device to obtain data. On the other hand, some states have applied the concept of possession or control to indicate a level of intention to use a device.

---

[43] Computer crimes Act 2003, section 8 https://ago.gov.to/cms/images/LEGISLATION/PRINCIPAL/2003/2003-0014/ComputerCrimesAct2003_1.pdf.

[44] The Cybercrimes Bill 2017, sections 11 https://ttcsirt.gov.tt/wp-content/uploads/2022/04/Cyber_Crime_Bill_DRAFT_2017.pdf.

[45] *Computer Misuse Act, 2011, section 12* https://ulii.org/akn/ug/act/2011/2/eng@2011-02-14.

[46] *Cybercrimes Act, 2015, section 10* https://rsf.org/sites/default/files/the_cyber_crime_act_2015.pdf.

[47] The Cyber Security and Cyber Crimes Act, 2021, section 37 https://www.parliament.gov.zm/sites/default/files/documents/acts/Act%20No.%202%20of%202021The%20Cyber%20Security%20and%20Cyber%20Crimes.pdf.

[48] Computer Misuse Act 1990, https://www.legislation.gov.uk/ukpga/1990/18/contents.

Notwithstanding the above, a further and important development is that a number of states have aligned the provisions with data and information. Even though it is generally not clear whether the states have or do apply this to personal data, the laws do not mention or define what constitute the said data or information. It is argued that by leaving these terms open, national courts are free to interpret and apply the provision to personal data.

Essentially, one of the most common themes to have emerged is the adoption of the provision whereby an offence is committed if a person intentionally, without lawful excuse or justification, manufactures, sells, procures for use, imports, exports, distributes or otherwise makes available, a computer or computer system or any other device, designed or adapted for the purpose of committing an offence. This provision alone has been applied on a number of occasions. It departs from other provisions applying to devices in that it uses the term without 'lawful excuse', recognising that mistakes can be made by anyone. Further, it has an element of commercial protection attached, minimising the manufacture, sale, procurement, import or export of a device that would hold data.

A further prevailing development has been the link between the offence provisions discussed in this book. Some states have considered that a device could be used to interfere with a computer and its system. On the other hand, there is reference to access to data that can be aligned with accessing a computer and personal data. Moreover, the term 'intercept by use of a device' has also been applied. This is another example where many of these offences are all interlinked with each other, but also with the personal data laws. In another example, rather than using 'access', the term 'extract' has been used. Again, the term(s) have been applied to data or information.

The formal and functional arrangements under the respective laws have also been extended by a state that has departed further from the other states, to include a communications device that cheats by impersonating. This distinctive offence highlights how states are viewing the use of devices, and how widely they can be used by the community to compromise data and have an impact on the digital economy.

In conclusion, 'intention' has also been replaced with the term 'knowingly', and included are terms such as 'making devices available', the 'misuse of a device', or, being able to use a device to access a computer and obtain data and information. There are a number of differences in the terminology used by the countries compared. Importantly, practitioners will need to clearly understand what each nation's laws are stating and how the provisions will apply. Most noteworthy is that practitioners will need to carefully look at how the offence provision applies. Is it intentional or knowingly, or was it a mere accident/mistake? Does it refer to data and information, and is there a direct link to data protection? A further accentuating issue that will need to be considered is how the provision interacts with other offences. Is it singular or broad? That is, does the provision concern the use of a device to interfere with or intercept data? These developments are important in dealing with growth of data trading exchange in the digital economy. States will need to be ever more vigilant regarding the criminal activities involving devices that illegally use personal data. A failure to do so will dilute the economic and social benefits that data offers to the digital economy.

Chapter 19
Fraud

19.1 Introduction

Fraud is an emerging threat to personal data. It has long been an issue in international trade and investment. Therefore, the technology available today has enabled state and non-state actors to engage in highly sophisticated fraudulent activities online.

While the CCRA does not cover fraud as it relates to data and computer systems, it is an area, in my view, of increasing concern. As another area of increasing cybercrime, fraudulent activity can include and come in various forms. For instance, it can involve the extraction of personal data and information from financial systems such as credit cards, banking details, health, residence, property ownership or otherwise, upon access to a computer. One of the most pronounced areas of fraud that has been identified is money laundering. This and other fraudulent activities pose significant risks to individuals and entities no matter where the Commonwealth country is located.

Arguably, with the wide adoption of technology and increasing access to data, fraudulent activity is heightened. This chapter compares the ways that member countries of the Commonwealth have addressed the concept of fraud within their respective laws. It will demonstrate how the current approach taken is not consistent, and that there is a lack of specific offence provisions under some states' laws for computer offences.

Similar to the other chapter, I argue that the Commonwealth should revise the CCRA to ensure that it also covers this concept. This chapter does not provide a word-by-word comparison of the laws, but rather, looks at the emerging themes within the provisions of the national laws.

R. Walters, *Cybersecurity and Data Laws of the Commonwealth*,
https://doi.org/10.1007/978-981-99-3935-0_19

Cyber-crime comprises a number of different activities, as demonstrated throughout this Part of the book. This chapter highlights the different approaches that have been taken to regulate for the offence of fraud in cybercrime activity. Notably that in 2017, fraud and financial crime was a trillion-dollar industry, reporting that private companies spent approximately $8.2 billion on anti–money laundering.[1] Both detected and undetected criminal activity, have become more numerous and costly than ever. It is estimated that, for every dollar of fraud institutions lose nearly three dollars, once associated costs are added to the fraud loss itself.[2] The risk to the banking and financial sectors are enormous. They alone transact billions of dollars daily. That is, 'risks for banks arise from diverse factors, including vulnerabilities to fraud and financial crime inherent in automation and digitization, massive growth in transaction volumes, and the greater integration of financial systems within countries and internationally.

Cyber-crime and malicious hacking have also intensified. In the domain of financial crime, regulators continually revise the rules, having to 'account for illegal trafficking and money laundering, and governments have ratcheted up the use of economic sanctions, targeting countries, public and private entities, and even individuals'.[3] The point here is that personal data in some form or another will be part of financial fraud. This is because banking and financial transactions as consumer functions are increasingly being undertaken over the Internet.

No longer do people have to walk into a physical building to make a local, national or international banking transaction. For instance, a person living in Singapore who has bank accounts in both Australia and Singapore, can do an online transaction to transfer money from the Australian account to their Singapore bank account. Before online banking, the person would have to carry cash or credit card, or transfer the money from the Australian account to the Singapore account, whilst in Australia. Thus, the question arises are the laws of nation states that make up the Commonwealth sufficient to address these circumstances? Sarah Correia in a 2022 study within the United Kingdom (UK) found that:

> fraud and computer misuse constitute a large proportion of crimes experienced by victims, with some evidence suggesting this was aggravated during the COVID pandemic. It was estimated that there were 4.6 million incidents of fraud and 1.7 million incidents of computer misuse in the year ending March 2021, adding up to 53% of the total UK crime estimate. Furthermore, compared to the pre-pandemic period, while the number of incidents of *other* crime decreased by 19%, fraud and computer misuse increased by 24% and 85% respectively. In addition, there was a 28% increase in reports of fraud and a 16% increase in criminal activity reported via the UK's national reporting centre Action Fraud.[4]

---

[1] Salim Hasham, Shoan Joshi, Daniel Mikkelsen, *Financial crime and fraud in the age of cybersecurity*, McKinsey & Company, 2019, https://www.mckinsey.com/capabilities/risk-and-resilience/our-insights/financial-crime-and-fraud-in-the-age-of-cybersecurity.

[2] Ibid.

[3] Ibid.

[4] Sarah Correia, *Making the most of cybercrime and fraud crime report data: a case study of UK Action Fraud*, The International Journal of Population Data Science (2022), 10.23889/ijpds.v7i1.1721.

Despite the incidents being fraud-related, this crime can extend widely to also include personal data that is then later used in financial or insurance criminal activity. It can be local, domestic, national and international. Furthermore, in the UK, it can be demonstrated that there is a direct correlation between cyber-crime and fraudulent activity that indirectly involves personal data. The study confirmed that there was a total of 46 types of fraud including:

- Online shopping—which is attributable to the misrepresentation of a product advertised for sale through an internet auction site or the non-delivery of products purchased through an internet auction site; and
- Dating—where the intended victim is befriended on the Internet and eventually convinced to assist their new love financially by sending them money for a variety of emotive reasons. This was also requested because the Internet plays an essential role in its commission, especially when the typical physical places for meeting a potential partner, such as pubs or nightclubs, are closed or restricted during lockdown; and
- Ticket—where the victim purchasing tickets remotely over the phone or internet. Data is solicited because although often cyber-enabled, the opportunity to commit ticket fraud is created by the desire to carry out activities in the physical world.[5]

Invariably, these activities all contain a level of personal data and information. The fraudulent activity is not restricted to individuals but can also include the corporate sector. While there is no specific data for the Commonwealth itself, globally, a 2022 study found that:

> Phishing/pharming, card testing, identity theft, and first-party misuse remain the most prevalent fraud attacks, each affecting more than 3 in 10 merchants globally. Globally, on average, merchants believe 16% of fraudulent disputes should be attributed to first-party misuse (or "friendly fraud"), with the majority of disputed transactions a result of issues with cardholders aiming to obtain free goods, confusion about transaction descriptors, or issuers incorrectly fling disputed transactions as fraud. In some regions and sectors, merchant estimates for this figure ranged as high as 1 in 5. 9-in-10 merchants have experienced at least one fraud management challenge and merchants are struggling to overcome three challenges, on average. The most pervasive and impactful challenges are identifying & responding to fraud attacks, changing business models because of COVID, & expanding into new sales channels.[6]

Given the above, there are significant challenges facing both personal and corporate-business sectors in combating online fraud (generally in ecommerce) which uses extensive quantities of personal data. This is another area that, in my view, needs to be included in the CCRA.

---

[5] Steven Kemp, David Buil-Gil, Asier Moneva, Fernando Miró-Llinares, Nacho Díaz-Castaño, N. (2021). *Empty Streets, Busy Internet: A Time-Series Analysis of Cybercrime and Fraud Trends During COVID-19*. Journal of Contemporary Criminal Justice, 37(4), (2021), pp. 480–485.

[6] Cybersource, Global Fraud and Payments Report (2022), p. 6 https://www.cybersource.com/content/dam/documents/campaign/fraud-report/global-fraud-report-2022.pdf.

Formally, **Antigua and Barbuda**, according to section 6,[7] ensures that a penalty exists where a person who, with intent to defraud, inputs, alters, deletes, or suppresses computer data, resulting in inauthentic data, whether or not the data is directly readable and intelligible. **Australia** under the Criminal Code Act 1995[8] has a general provision for fraud-related offences. However, there are no specific fraud-related offences pertaining to technology-computers. Australia should be more specific when formulating its computer-related crime laws. Is this a real issue? To most people in Australia, it would not. Although, from a global perspective, it creates a regulatory landscape that is complex and hard to navigate unless one understands Australian law. What should happen to reduce an element of regulatory burden, is that countries such as Australia that have included cyber-crime laws in their criminal laws, should adopt specific computer crime laws, similar to other Commonwealth members.

The functional arrangements in the **Bahamas** show that fraud using computer systems can constitute any person who, without authority, knowingly causes a computer to perform any function for the purpose of securing access to any program or data held in any computer shall be guilty of an offence.[9] In addition, section 4 goes further to include any person who causes a computer to perform any function for the purpose of securing access to any program or data held in any computer with intent to commit an offence.[10] Similarly in **Bangladesh**, section 23 provides for digital or electronic fraud, stipulating that when any person commits fraud by using any digital or electronic medium, then such act of the person shall be an offence.[11] Likewise, in **Barbados,** section 9 provides that an offence is committed by any person who knowingly uses a computer to perform any function in order to secure access to any programme or data held in that computer or in any other computer with the intention to commit an offence involving property, fraud or dishonesty.[12] In **Belize**, a person commits an offence who, with the intent to defraud or deceive another person for the purpose of procuring an economic benefit for the person or another where that individual or entity inputs, alters, deletes or suppresses computer data.[13]

[7] Electronic Crimes Act 2013, section 6, http://laws.gov.ag/wp-content/uploads/2019/02/a2013-14.pdf.

[8] Australian Criminal Code Act 1995.

[9] Computer Misuse Act 2006, section 3 http://laws.bahamas.gov.bs/cms/images/LEGISLATION/PRINCIPAL/2003/2003-0002/ComputerMisuseAct_1.pdf.

[10] Ibid, section 4.

[11] Digital Security Act 2018, section 23 https://www.cirt.gov.bd/wp-content/uploads/2020/02/Digital-Security-Act-2020.pdf. Explanation.For carrying out the purposes of this section, "digital or electric fraud" means to change or delete any information of, or add new information to, or tamper any information of, any computer programme, computer system, computer network, digital device, digital system, digital network or social media by a person, intentionally or knowingly or without permission, and doing so, to diminish the value or utility thereof, or try to get any benefit for himself or any other person, or to cause harm to, or deceive, any other person.

[12] Computer Misuse Act, 2005, section 9 http://www.oas.org/juridico/spanish/cyb_bbs_computer_misuse_2005.pdf.

[13] Cybercrime Act 2020, sections 9 https://www.nationalassembly.gov.bz/wp-content/uploads/2020/10/Act-No.-32-of-2020-Cybercrime.pdf.

In **Botswana,** section 15 states that person who performs any of the acts described under this Part, for purposes of obtaining any unlawful advantage by causing forged data to be produced, with the intent that it be considered or acted upon as if it were authentic, commits an offence and is liable to a fine not exceeding P100 000 or to imprisonment for a term not exceeding seven years, or to both. (2) A person who, with intent to procure any advantage for himself or herself or another person, fraudulently causes loss of property to another person by (*a*) any input, alteration, deletion, delaying transmission or suppression of data; or (*b*) any interference with the functioning of a computer or computer system, commits an offence and is liable to a fine not exceeding P100 000 or to imprisonment for a term not exceeding seven years, or to both.[14]

According to section 4, **Brunei,** it is an offence to unlawfully access a computer to undertake fraudulent activities.[15] Nonetheless, in **Canada**, under the Criminal Code, there are general offences for fraud.[16] Section 403 specifically establishes an offence for fraud. However, it is not clear whether this extends to data or a computer. It is my view that this section could be applied, as it pertains to property, which could be read in conjunction with section 403.

In a further development in **Eswatini** according to section 11, a person is not allowed to alter, delete, suppress computer data that to undertake fraudulent activity.[17] Further, in **Fiji**, section 10 creates an offence for both fraud and extortion benefiting from the illegal intrusion to a computer and its systems.[18] A fraudulent activity in the context of **Ghana** relates only to revoking a licence.[19] In **Grenada,** according to section 9, a person cannot defraud another person without justification for interfering with data or an electronic system.[20]

---

[14] Cybercrime and related Crimes Act 2018, section 15, https://www.bocra.org.bw/cybercrime-and-computer-related-crimes-act-2018.

[15] Computer Misuse Act 2007, section 4, https://www.agc.gov.bn/AGC%20Images/LAWS/ACT_PDF/C/CHAPTER%20194.pdf.

[16] Criminal Code 1985, https://laws-lois.justice.gc.ca/pdf/c-46.pdf.

[17] *Computer Crime and Cybercrime Act No.6 of 2022, section 11* https://www.esccom.org.sz/legislation/COMPUTER%20CRIME%20&%20CYBERCRIME%20ACT.pdf.

[18] Cybersecurity and Cybercrime Act 2021, section 6 https://ncb.govmu.org/ncb/legislations/THE%20CYBERSECURITY%20AND%20CYBERCRIME%20ACT%202021.pdf.

Cybercrime Act 2021 (Act No. 3 of 2021), section 8 https://www.ilo.org/dyn/natlex/natlex4.detail?p_lang=en&p_isn=111060&p_classification=01.

[19] Cybersecurity Act 2020, section 40 https://csdsafrica.org/wp-content/uploads/2021/08/Cybersecurity-Act-2020-Act-1038.pdf.

[20] Electronic Crimes Bill 2013, section 9 https://ecagrenada.com/Grenada-Electronic-Crimes-Act-2013.pdf.

In **Guyana,** similar to the other states examined, section 11 has an offence for computer related fraud.[21]

Importantly, in **India,** section 74, provides for the offence of publication for fraudulent purpose, of anyone who knowingly creates, publishes or otherwise makes available a [electronic signature] certificate for any fraudulent or unlawful purpose shall be punished with imprisonment for a term which may extend to two years.[22]

19.2 Case Study—India[23]

India saw its first cybercrime conviction in 2013. It all began after a complaint was filed by Sony India Private Ltd, which runs a website called www.sony-sambandh.com, targeting Non-Resident Indians. The website enables NRIs to send Sony products to their friends and relatives in India after they pay for it online. The company undertakes to deliver the products to the concerned recipients. In May 2002, according to the cybercrime case study, someone logged onto the website under the identity of Barbara Campa and ordered a Sony Colour Television set and a cordless headphone. She gave her credit card number for payment and requested the products to be delivered to Arif Azim in Noida. The payment was duly cleared by the credit card agency, and the transaction was processed. After following the relevant procedures of due diligence and checking, the company delivered the items to Arif Azim. At the time of delivery, the company took digital photographs showing the delivery being accepted by Arif Azim. The transaction closed at that, but after one and a half months the credit card agency informed the company that this was an unauthorized transaction as the real owner had denied having made the purchase. The company lodged a complaint about online cheating at the Central Bureau of Investigation (CBI) which registered a case under section 418, 419 and 420 of the Indian Penal Code. The matter was investigated, and Arif Azim was arrested. Investigations revealed that Arif Azim while working at a call centre in Noida gained access to the credit card number of an American national which he misused on the company's site. The CBI recovered the colour television and the cordless headphone, in this one-of-a-kind *cyber fraud* case. In this matter, the CBI had evidence to prove their case, and so the accused

[21] Cyber Crime Act 2018, https://parliament.gov.gy/publications/acts-of-parliament/cyber-crime-act-2018.

[22] Information Technology Act (2000), https://thelawreviews.co.uk/title/the-privacy-data-protection-and-cybersecurity-law-review/india, and https://www.indiacode.nic.in/handle/123456789/1999, section66 and 74. Also note, "fraudulently" shall have the meaning assigned to it in section 25 of the Indian Penal Code (45 of 1860).

[23] Cyberlaws and Information Security Advisors, https://www.cyberralegalservices.com/detail-casestudies.php.

admitted his guilt. The court convicted Arif Azim under section 418, 419 and 420 of the Indian Penal Code—this being the first time that cybercrime has been convicted. The court, however, felt that as the accused was a young boy of 24 years and a first-time convict, a lenient view needed to be taken. The court, therefore, released the accused on probation for one year. The judgment is of immense significance for the entire nation. Besides being the first conviction in a cybercrime matter, it has shown that the Indian Penal Code can be effectively applied to certain categories of cybercrimes which are not covered under the Information Technology Act 2000. Secondly, a judgment of this sort sends out a clear message to all that the law cannot be taken for a ride.

The above highlights and reinforces the interconnectedness of personal data and cybercrime activity. When individuals provided their credit card details to make the transaction, that information includes certain personal data defined by the data protection laws. It is able to clearly identify the person and their financial details.

In **Jamaica** a person who benefits fraudulently from access to a computer, system or information, to input, alter, delete or suppress any data ("the original data") with the intention that the data, after such input, alteration, deletion or suppression (whether or not that data is readable or intelligible), be considered or acted upon as if that data were the original data—commits an offence.[24]On the one side, **Kenya**, fraudulent activity cannot be undertaken to gain access to a computer to input, alter, modify, delete, suppress or generate any data, or, interfere, hinder, impair or obstruct the function of a computer system.[25] On the other side, **Kiribati** under section 13 establishes an offence for computer related fraud.[26] **Lesotho** makes it an offence to fraudulently procure a benefit from altering or suppressing data and information.[27] In **Malawi,** section 92 states that any person who uses the internet as a medium for any illegal activity or trade, fraudulent transaction or as a means of procuring any internet related fraud, commits an offence.[28]

In **Malaysia**, section 4 establishes an offence of fraud and dishonesty related to accessing computer systems.[29] This straightforward approach has all but been replicated by other states, with some divergence. Furthermore, **Mauritius** explicitly states that any person who, intentionally and without authorisation, causes loss of property to another person by any input, alteration, deletion or suppression of data;

[24] The Cyber Crimes Act 2015, section 10 https://www.japarliament.gov.jm/attachments/339_The%20Cybercrimes%20Acts,%202015.pdf.

[25] Computer Misuse and Cybercrimes Act 2018, section 26 https://ictpolicyafrica.org/en/document/pb8w26fcso?page=2.

[26] Cybercrime Act 2021, section 13 https://www.mict.gov.ki/download/file/fid/320.

[27] The Computer Crimes and Cyber Security Bill, 2022, https://senate.parliament.ls/2022/05/19/computer-crime-and-cyber-security-bill-2022/.

[28] Electronic Transactions and Cyber Security Act 2017, section 92 https://media.malawilii.org/files/legislation/akn-mw-act-2016-33-eng-2017-12-31.pdf.

[29] Computer Crimes Act 1997, section 5 https://www.nacsa.gov.my/legal.php.

or any interference with the functioning of a computer system, to procure for himself or another person any form of advantage shall commit an offence.[30]

A basic approach has been taken by **Nauru** which, under section 14, establishes an offence of fraud,[31] and likewise **Nigeria.**[32] Under the Crimes Act 1961 of **New Zealand**, there is no general offence of fraud. It has been captured by section 240, but is limited to the concept of deception by use of a fraudulent device.[33] However, computer offences have been captured by this legislation, and there could be a general offence for fraud in other legislation. New Zealand's *Walker* case demonstrates the interconnectedness of a number of computer offences.[34] The Court gave the following background of the case:

> Owen Thor Walker is before the Court today having entered guilty pleas in relation to a range of offending with the general description of computer fraud. He was charged under s 252(1) of the Crimes Act with accessing a computer system without authorisation. There are two such charges, one which relates to a period when Mr Walker was 16 years old, the other to a period when he was 17 and 18 years old. Those offences carry a maximum penalty of two years imprisonment. He has also pleaded guilty to a charge of damaging or interfering with a computer system under s 250(2)(c) of the Crimes Act. That carries a maximum sentence of seven years imprisonment. He has further pleaded guilty to two charges of accessing a computer system for a dishonest purpose under s 249(2)(a) of the Crimes Act, one charge relating to the period when he was aged 16 years, the other to the period when he was aged 17 and 18 years. Those offences carry a maximum penalty of five years imprisonment. Finally, he has entered a guilty plea to possessing software for committing a crime under s 251(2)(a) and (b) of the Crimes Act. That offence carries a maximum penalty of two years imprisonment.[35]

Although Walker was only a teenager, the case highlights the extent to which an individual, regardless of age, can undertake criminal activity if he or she is proficient at using technology. The Court stated that Walker's development and use of the code led to the two charges of accessing computer systems without authorisation. The ways in which Mr Walker used his bot code then led to the other charges of:

- Damaging or interfering with a computer system. This resulted in a DDoS (Distributed Denial of Service) attack on the University of Pennsylvania computer system.
- The two charges of accessing computer system for dishonest purpose: Mr Walker used his botnet to covertly install adware on other computers, for which he was paid by the owners of the adware. Adware perhaps can be described as viral advertising.

---

[30] Cybersecurity and Cybercrime Act 2021, Section 14 https://ncb.govmu.org/ncb/legislations/THE%20CYBERSECURITY%20AND%20CYBERCRIME%20ACT%202021.pdf.

[31] Cybercrime Act 2015, section 14 and 21 http://ronlaw.gov.nr/nauru_lpms/files/acts/a59d9691f5a195412b877493a2a95e8b.pdf.

[32] Cyber Crime Act 2015, section 14, https://lawpadi.com/wp-content/uploads/2015/08/CyberCrime_ProhibitionPreventionetc_Act_2015.pdf.

[33] Crimes Act 1961, section 240, https://www.legislation.govt.nz/act/public/1961/0043/latest/DLM330422.html.

[34] *R V Walker* [2008] NZHC 1114.

[35] Ibid, para 1.

- Possessing software for committing a crime. This resulted from Mr Walker having in his possession software or other information that would enable him to access a computer system without authorisation, intending to use that software or other information to commit a crime.[36]

Given the extent of the criminal offences being committed, the Courts are increasingly having to examine and address multiple issues related to computer crimes. This case involves three issues: access, interference and possessing software/devices that can enable and facilitate intrusion into computers and systems. The ability of individuals to engage in covert intrusions into computer systems and infrastructure has the potential to be significant. Even so, there was no mention or acknowledgment by the Court that personal data had been compromised.

In Central Asia, **Pakistan**, according to section 11, provides for electronic forgery where it is an offence to commit a fraud by any input, alteration, deletion, suppression resulting in unauthentic data being made available.[37] Australia's closest neighbour **Papua New Guinea,** has an offence for the fraudulent use of data.[38]

In **Rwanda**, a person cannot fraudulently process another person's information.[39] On the other hand, **Seychelles** has no equivalent offence.[40] **Sierra Leone**, in section 32, creates the offence of fraudulently procuring for an economic benefit the use of any data or program.[41] **South Africa** also has a general offence for cyber fraud.[42] Most states have adopted this concept as a strict offence. Problematic though are the different approaches taken by all states to determine what constitutes fraud. It has created another area of a highly-fragmented approach. However, **Singapore** does not provide for fraud, and any fraud issues pertain only to a licence according to section 26.[43] Importantly, the practitioner would need to consult other laws within the state to confirm whether the offence of fraud exists. It is argued that such an offence would be provided for under the criminal law.

[36] Ibid, para 5.

[37] The Prevention of Electronic Crimes 2016, section 11 https://na.gov.pk/uploads/documents/1470910659_707.pdf.

[38] *Cybercrime Code Act 2016, section 12* https://www.parliament.gov.pg/uploads/acts/16A_35.pdf.

[39] Law N° 60/2018 OF 22/8/2018 on prevention and punishment of cyber crimes, Article 28 https://www.risa.rw/fileadmin/user_upload/Others%20documents/Cyber_Crimes_Law.pdf Note there are other offences relates to accessing a computer and data.

[40] Computer Misuse Act 1998, sections 3,4, https://seylii.org/akn/sc/act/1998/17/eng%402015-12-31.

[41] Cyber Crime Act 2020, section 32 http://www.sierra-leone.org/Laws/2020-Cybercrime%20Act.pdf.

[42] Cybercrimes Act 2021, section 8 https://cybercrimesact.co.za.

[43] Cybersecurity Act 2018, https://sso.agc.gov.sg/Acts-Supp/9-2018/.

In the Americas, **Saint Lucia** section 12 provides for electronic fraud although this is limited to interference with data or an electronic system to induce any person to enter into a relationship.[44] Likewise **Saint Kitts and Nevis**[45]and **St Vincent and The Grenadines** have a general offence of computer-related fraud.[46]

Tonga has no provisions for the offence for fraud.[47] **Trinidad and Tobago,** on the other hand, have a general offence provisionfor computer-related fraud.[48] Finally, **Uganda,** section 19 establishes an offence of electronic fraud.[49] The **United Republic of Tanzania**[50] and **Zambia** have the similar offence.[51] Surprisingly, the **United Kingdom** does not provide for the same offence.[52] However, this is likely to be covered by the UK's criminal laws. There is a significant level of divergence amongst the Commonwealth states in the adoption of and approach to legislation for computer-related fraud. The next section concludes this chapter, highlighting the general themes and terms that have emerged.

19.3 Conclusion

The proliferation of fraudulent activities over the Internet has risen substantially over the past decade. This is likely to increase as the digital economy continues to expand. Put another way, and as highlighted earlier in this book, the IR4 (Industrial Revolution 4) is changing the way the economy functions. Increasingly, our personal and working lives are connected to the Internet. Commercial activities are also being undertaken online in order to reduce costs and increase productivity.

---

[44] Electronic Crimes Bill 2009, section 12 https://www.govt.lc/media.govt.lc/www/resources/legislation/ElectronicCrimesBill.pdf.

[45] Electronic Crimes Bill 2017, section 8 https://aglcskn.info/wp-content/documents/Act17TOC/Ch-04_41-Electronic-Crimes-Act.pdf.

[46] Cybercrime Act 2016, section 13 https://www.gov.vc/images/PoliciesActsAndBills/SVG_Cybercrime_Act_2016.pdf.

[47] Computer crimes Act 2003, section 5 https://ago.gov.to/cms/images/LEGISLATION/PRINCIPAL/2003/2003-0014/ComputerCrimesAct2003_1.pdf.

[48] The Cybercrimes Bill 2017, sections 14 https://ttcsirt.gov.tt/wp-content/uploads/2022/04/Cyber_Crime_Bill_DRAFT_2017.pdf.

[49] *Computer Misuse Act, 2011, section 19* https://ulii.org/akn/ug/act/2011/2/eng@2011-02-14.

[50] *Cybercrimes Act, 2015, section 12* https://rsf.org/sites/default/files/the_cyber_crime_act_2015.pdf.

[51] The Cyber Security and Cyber Crimes Act, 2021, section 35 https://www.parliament.gov.zm/sites/default/files/documents/acts/Act%20No.%202%20of%202021The%20Cyber%20Security%20and%20Cyber%20Crimes.pdf.

[52] Computer Misuse Act 1990, https://www.legislation.gov.uk/ukpga/1990/18/contents.

However, the challenge for governments across the Commonwealth is to respond to the fraudulent online criminal activities. The use of technology allows fraud to be undertaken with an element of ease. This has a significant personal and economic impact on international trade. In response, the Commonwealth and its member countries have developed offence provisions to minimise the impact of fraud over the Internet and to data. This chapter again highlights the fragmented way in which each state has responded to the offence of fraud related to computers and data within their respective national laws.

Consistent with the other chapters on cybersecurity, themes have been identified within the national laws to highlight the subtle but important differences amongst the nation states compared. First, there has generally been a requirement for the laws to ensure that an element of intent or acting knowingly is proven in order for an offence of fraud to exist. Interestingly, the term 'knowingly' has been also been linked to dishonesty. Second, in understanding the terms and terminology used, individuals and entities will need to be cognisant of these variations in terminology in order to fulfil their obligations. Third, some states do not have a specific offence of fraud within their computer-related national laws.

However, there are examples showing that this offence has been captured by the broader criminal laws that states have in place. This is problematic since it may be difficult to locate these laws. Fourth, the terms 'fraud' and 'defraud' have emerged, and it is argued that they mean one and the same. Fifth, there is significant evidence that the offence in most states directly applies to personal data within the digital economy. Sixth, although most states have adopted the concept, it does, however, diverge from the example provided by the CCRA.

Notwithstanding the above, a salutatory development has been the link to other cyber offences involving computer systems and interference with those systems. It has also been extended to include any computer programme. In addition, in one case, the offence of fraud corresponds with the offence of extortion. That is, a person collects data illegally and attempts to obtain a financial benefit from returning it to the rightful owner. In a rare departure from the general approach, fraud has been restricted to where a licence has been issued allowing a person to undertake a specific function.

Moreover, in one of the most comprehensive provisions, the term 'benefit' is used. That is, a person benefits fraudulently from access to a computer, system or information, to input, alter, delete or suppress any data ("the original data") with the intention that the data, after such input, alteration, deletion or suppression (whether or not that data is readable or intelligible), be considered or acted upon as if that data were the original data—commits an offence. This example, arguably includes personal and commercial data. Here, the reference to data, and the use of 'interfere' and 'hinder' all suggest the interconnectedness that this offence has with the other offences compared.

Finally, in a direct correlation between personal data and the offence of fraud, a state provides for the fraudulent processing of another person's information. Therefore, fraudulently procuring for an economic benefit the use of any data or program, comes under the general offence of cyber fraud. Most states have adopted this concept as a strict offence. In reconciling the highly divergent approaches, individuals and entities will need to further clarify these offence provisions with in-country experts. The Commonwealth should undertake further work to ensure that those states that do not have specific cyber laws, or have not separated these from their criminal laws, undertake a level of reform to develop single laws.

Chapter 20
Theft [Identity]

20.1 Introduction

Personal identity theft is increasing and becoming a global problem. With the rise in online activity, and the amount of personal data being collected, at no other time in history have individuals and entities been able to identify and locate an individual with relative ease. State and non-state actors can illegally acquire and use this data and information. More pervasively, the theft of a personal identity is clearly related to the personal data and information as defined under the respective sates data protection and privacy laws.

This chapter demonstrates how identity theft constitutes the theft of personal data that can identify any individual. The chapter confirms or otherwise such an offence. Generally, most of the states examined do provide for such an offence. However, a number of states do not. This is not to say that such an offence does not exist in criminal laws, an examination of which is beyond the scope of this book. This chapter does not provide a word-by-word comparison of the laws. Due to the fragmented approach of the laws across all of the countries compared, a high-level approach has been taken to determine the countries that have addressed this offence in their legislation.

Noteworthy too, is that the CCRA does not cover identity theft as it relates to data and computer systems although, in my view, this is an area of concern. I argue that the Commonwealth should revise the CCRA to ensure that it covers this concept. It directly aligns with and pertains to strengthening the overall protections of data within transnational data flows. Finally, this chapter will recommend that the Commonwealth develop a research project to better understand the economic and social impacts of identity theft. It will recommend that this project be incorporated into a wider legal research project to develop a Model Law that includes provisions for stolen identity.

R. Walters, *Cybersecurity and Data Laws of the Commonwealth*,
https://doi.org/10.1007/978-981-99-3935-0_20

In the modern world of online Internet activity, cyber threats surround our everyday activities. Mishra et al. make the point that cyber threats are motivated by a variety of factors, including the collection of sensitive information, harm to a country's sovereignty, ideological grounds, or other state-level crimes.[1] Sensitive information could mean all of these things and include personal data and information. As highlighted earlier in this book, one of the most important issues in data protection and data flows law, is the way that personal data is defined. In many cases, states have defined sensitive personal data, which has been afforded a greater level of protection and control. One threat to personal data is identity theft. It is pervading many areas including the financial, business and consumer sectors. Identity theft has been described as:

> the intentional, unauthorised use of a person's identifying information for unlawful purposes. It includes infiltration into a person's existing accounts, using a person's identity to open new accounts, or using personal information to obtain instrumental goods and services such as health care and public benefits. Similar to financial fraud, the vast majority of identity theft victims do not have a pre-existing personal relationship with the perpetrator. Yet unlike fraud, most incidents do not involve a direct exchange of information or payment. Rather, identifying information is taken and used without the victim's knowledge or consent, such as through a data breach or malware attack.[2]

The impact of the theft of people's identity is significant. It can cause reputational damage and financial loss, and gives access to an individual's personal life that, no so long ago was well-protected as it was not on the Internet. Identity theft can be used to extort a financial or other benefit from a data subject. This chapter will demonstrate how nation states have taken the theft of a person's identity very seriously and have established comprehensive offence provisions. However, there are a number of nation states that have not established these offences within their respective cybersecurity laws.

Similar to other chapters, beginning with **Antigua and Barbuda,** section 5[3] creates an offence for the identity theft of a person. It states that a person is not to make fraudulent or dishonest use of an electronic signature, password or other unique identification feature of another person.

On the other hand, in **Australia**, according to section 372.1 of the Criminal Code Act 1995, it is made clear that a person commits an offence if: the first person deals in identification information; and the first person intends that any person (the user) (whether or not the first person) will use the identification information to pretend to be, or to pass the user off as, another person (whether living, dead, real or fictitious) for

[1] Alok Mishra, Yehia Ibrahim, Alzoubi Memoona, Javeria Anwar, Asif QumerGil, Attributes impacting cybersecurity policy development: An evidence from seven nations, Computers and Security 120 (2022), pp. 1–3.

[2] Marguerite DeLiema, PhD, David Burnes, PhD, Lynn Langton, PhD, The Financial and Psychological Impact of Identity Theft Among Older Adults, *Innovation in Aging*, Volume 5, Issue 4, (2021) p. 2. https://doi.org/10.1093/geroni/igab043.

[3] Electronic Crimes Act 2013, section 9, http://laws.gov.ag/wp-content/uploads/2019/02/a2013-14.pdf.

the purpose of committing an offence; or facilitating the commission of an offence.[4] More importantly, section 372.1A deals with identification information that involves use of a carriage service. That is, a person (the first person) commits an offence if the first person deals in identification information; and the first person does so using a carriage service; and the first person intends that any person (the user) (whether or not the first person) will use the identification information to pretend to be, or to pass the user off as, another person (whether living, dead, real or fictitious) for the purpose of committing an offence.[5] A carriage service, while not defined, appears to accord with section 376.1, and pertains to a flight on an aircraft since personal data is used to book a ticket over the Internet. The structure of Australia's cybersecurity laws are highly complex, and it is recommended that they be taken out of existing laws and that a single Cyber Crime Act be established. This will make it a lot more economical and efficient for business to understand their obligations and be able to address cyber risk.

In **Bangladesh,** according to section 24, a person commits an offence when, intentionally or knowingly, by using any computer, computer programme, computer system, computer network, digital device, digital system or digital network holds the identity of another person or exhibits the personal information of another person as his own in order to deceive or cheat; or holds the personal identity of any person, alive or dead, as his own by forgery in order to gain a benefit for themselves is an offence.[6] In addition, section 26 makes it an to collection and use identity information. without lawful authorisation of the data subject.[7] This directly relates to the personal data of an individual.

Concerning though, is that the **Bahamas, Barbados, Botswana, Brunei, Eswatini, Ghana, Jamacia, Kiribati, Malawi, Mauritius, Pakistan, Saint Lucia**, **Seychelles, Singapore**, **South Africa, St Vincent and The Grenadines**, and **Togo** have no specific provisions regarding the theft of data or other information from cyber related systems or infrastructure. However, it must be noted that there are likely to be other laws within the respective jurisdictions that may deal with this cybersecurity challenge. For example, there are likely to be theft offences in the criminal laws of respective states. It is outside the scope of this chapter to identify those other laws. It is argued that this needs to be addressed, as theft of personal information is on the increase. **Belize** makes it an offence for a person to use a computer

[4] Australian Criminal Code Act 1995, section 372.1.

[5] Ibid, section 371.1A.

[6] Digital Security Act 2018, section 23 https://www.cirt.gov.bd/wp-content/uploads/2020/02/Digital-Security-Act-2020.pdf.

[7] Ibid, section 26. For carrying out the purposes of this section, "identity information" means any external, biological or physical information or any other information which singly or jointly can identify a person or a system, such as- name, photograph, address, date of birth, mother's name, father's name, signature, national identity card, birth and death registration number, finger print, passport number, bank account number, driving license, e-TIN number, electronic or digital signature, username, credit or debit card number, voice print, retina image, iris image, DNA profile, security related question or any other identification which are available for advance technology.

to unlawfully obtain the identity of another person.[8] **Eswatini** makes reference to identity theft when defining cyber stalking under section 2 of the *Computer Crime and Cybercrime Act No.6 of 2022.*

In **Canada**, sections 367–368 make broad provisions for theft. On the other hand, and more specifically, section 402.2(1) creates the following that every person commits an offence who obtains or possesses another person's identity information with intent to use it to commit an indictable offence that includes fraud, deceit or falsehood as an element of the offence.[9] In *Kalonji*[10] the Court dealt with multiple issues including fraud and identity theft. The Court noted that:

> Mr. Kalonji, Mr. Simmons-McKenzie, Mr. Henry, Ms. Munyenga, Ms. Robinson and Ms. Galbraith are all charged with a number of offences including criminal organization offences, fraud and conspiracy to commit fraud. The essence of the allegations are that Mr. Kalonji and two other men not presently charged (Mr. Boursiquot and "Ace") were running a criminal organization whose main activity was committing account take over frauds. The essence of the account take over fraud is that perpetrators open accounts (called complicit accounts) that are then linked to victim accounts (the information for this often comes from an inside person) by creating joint accounts between the victim account and the complicit account. Funds are then siphoned out by transferring the funds from the victim account to the joint or complicit account through online transfers. Another person then attends at the bank and withdraws the funds, thus resulting in fraudulent transactions given the transfer of identity documents and account numbers.[11]

In applying the test for trafficking in identification, the Court ruled that:

> The law is clear that were the offence charged conspiracy to traffic in identification, the substantive offence of trafficking in identification is not a lesser or included offence (*R. v. Sheppe,* [1980] 2 S.C.J. No. 39). In *R. v. G.R.,* [2005] S.C.J. No. 45, the Supreme Court of Canada held that an offence is an included offence if "its elements are embraced in the offence charged" or "if it is expressly stated to be an included offence." This is a strict test.[12]

In applying this test, the defendants were found not guilty of the above offences under the Criminal Code. However, and while there was no direct correlation between the criminal law and data laws, identity theft related to financial records will have elements of the definition of personal data under the relevant data laws.

---

[8] Cybercrime Act 2020, sections 10 https://www.nationalassembly.gov.bz/wp-content/uploads/2020/10/Act-No.-32-of-2020-Cybercrime.pdf.

[9] Criminal Code 1985, https://laws-lois.justice.gc.ca/pdf/c-46.pdf.

[10] *R. v. Kalonji,* 2019 ONCJ 341.

[11] Ibid, paras 1, 6, 47.

[12] Ibid, para 104.

The formal and functional arrangement in **Fiji,** according to section 11, state that any person who intentionally and without lawful authority or reasonable excuse transfers, possesses or uses through or by a computer system the identification or means of identification of another person with intent to commit or to aid or abet, or in connection with any unlawful activity that constitutes a crime, commits an offence.[13] In **Grenada**, according to section 7, a person is not to fraudulently or dishonestly use an electronic signature, password or other unique identifying feature of another person.[14] Similar to the other states examined, **Guyana,** in section 13 has an offence provision for the protection of a persons' identity.[15]

In **India,** section 66C stipulates that anybody who fraudulently or dishonestly make use of the electronic signature, password or any other unique identification feature of any other person, shall be punished.[16] In a further development, in **Kenya**, identity theft has been extended to include impersonation or an individual's electronic signature, password or any other unique identification feature of any other person.[17] Arguably, this includes elements of, if not all, personal data defined under the Kenyan data laws.

Noteworthy too, **Lesotho,** makes it an offence to use identifying information of a person via a computer system and transfer the identification data to another person, without their authority.[18] Nonetheless, recent work done in **Malaysia** has stated that this type of activity generally includes:

- Financial—which uses information from another person to gain some advantages, such as goods, services and credit, or to access a bank account. It can take one of two forms; the true identity of the name, or the takeover of the account; and
- Medical—obtaining medical benefits involving products or services, or falsely securing reimbursements for medical goods or services allegedly enjoyed. The outcome can lead to a manipulation of the victim's medical record with potentially fatal consequences when wrongful medical decisions are taken with respect to the victim; and

[13] Cybersecurity and Cybercrime Act 2021, section 6 https://ncb.govmu.org/ncb/legislations/THE%20CYBERSECURITY%20AND%20CYBERCRIME%20ACT%202021.pdf.

Cybercrime Act 2021 (Act No. 3 of 2021), section 8 https://www.ilo.org/dyn/natlex/natlex4.detail?p_lang=en&p_isn=111060&p_classification=01.

[14] Electronic Crimes Bill 2013, section 9 https://ecagrenada.com/Grenada-Electronic-Crimes-Act-2013.pdf.

[15] Cyber Crime Act 2018, https://parliament.gov.gy/publications/acts-of-parliament/cyber-crime-act-2018.

[16] Information Technology Act (2000), https://thelawreviews.co.uk/title/the-privacy-data-protection-and-cybersecurity-law-review/india, and https://www.indiacode.nic.in/handle/123456789/1999, section 66C.

[17] Computer Misuse and Cybercrimes Act 2018, section 29 https://ictpolicyafrica.org/en/document/pb8w26fcso?page=2.

[18] The Computer Crimes and Cyber Security Bill, 2022, https://senate.parliament.ls/2022/05/19/computer-crime-and-cyber-security-bill-2022/.

- Criminal—where an individual falsely claims to be the victim of a crime apprehended by the police. The victim can only know what has happened when called to court to face criminal charges arising out of the offender's action; and
- Synthetic—this occurs when the perpetrator combines all the people's details obtained and creates a new identity. For instance, a social security number can be paired with a name and date of birth that are different from the actual owner of the social security number. It is more difficult to trace the crimes committed with the help of this method of identity theft; and
- Tax—speaks in and of itself where a person has gained access to the tax number and details of another person or entity; and
- Child—where a family member has used a child's identity, for example, to obtain credit.[19]

Thus, the unlawful use of a personal identity can vary greatly. The resulting effect is the increased victimisation[20] of people who have had their identities stolen. It will constitute the personal data of the individual. A study undertaken in 2020 by Australia highlighted that:

> Identity theft carried out by criminals through the compromise and misuse of this credential information has wide reaching effects on individuals, businesses, and government organisations alike. The Commonwealth Attorney-General's Department estimates that the compromise and misuse of a person's identity credentials impact between 4 per cent and 5 per cent of Australians aged fifteen years and older each year. This is estimated to cost the economy around AUD $2.2 billion in response measures and losses per annum, on top of the estimates for preventing such crimes being a further AUD $390 million per annum. In fact, identity theft is said to now impact a higher portion of the Australian population per annum than any other household-theft related crime, such as burglary and related personal property thefts.[21]

The functional impacts when scaled up across all Commonwealth countries will show how significant this issue has become. The financial impact in Australia alone gives a small but important indication of how identity theft has now become so pervasive, although the cost to the broader community is yet to be fully understood. In another study, identity fraud affects as many as 133,000 New Zealanders annually at a cost to the economy of as much as $209 million every year.[22] Moreover, the impacts extend from the personal to the corporate sector. IBM note that:

[19] A/P Sinnathamby Sehgar, S.; Zukarnain, Z.A. Online Identity Theft, Security Issues, and Reputational Damage. *Preprints* (2021), https://doi.org/10.20944/preprints202102.0082.v1. Note this is not peer reviewed paper.

[20] Nicole Leeper Piquero, Alex R. Piquero, Stephen Gies, Brandn Green, Amanda Bobnis, Eva Velasquez Preventing: *Identity Theft: Perspectives on Technological Solutions from Industry Insiders,* Victims & Offenders, Vol. 16, No 3, (2021), p. 444.

[21] Megan Wyre David Lacey Kathy Allan, Australia's Identity Theft Response System: Addressing the Needs of Victims, Report to the Criminology Research Advisory Council Grant: CRG 10/15–16, (2020), p. 5, https://www.aic.gov.au/sites/default/files/2020-05/CRG-1015-16-Final-Report.pdf.

[22] IBM, Identity theft: a personal and organisational threat, 2021, https://www.ibm.com/blogs/ibm-anz/identity-theft-a-personal-and-organisational-threat/.

> identity theft goes beyond the personal – it's also the easiest way for criminals to gain access to networks and data. Once a malicious actor has the identity information of a member of your organisation, they can target it with phishing or ransomware attacks.[23]

The Commonwealth should undertake a research project to better understand the impact of identity fraud across all member countries. Not understanding the challenges and economic impact of the theft of personal data will diminish the public's trust in the law and hinder the development of the digital economy.

In **Nauru**, section 17 has invoked identity-related offence to protect the identity of individuals (personal data) that relate to the intentional transfers, possession, or use of that information.[24] On the other hand, **New Zealand** provides for an offence of general theft under section 2019 that pertains to taking any property with intent to deprive any owner permanently of that property or of any interest in that property. However, identity is not a property right, and therefore, it would be difficult to argue that this section would apply.[25] This requires in-country clarification. Nonetheless, the Court in Hayes noted how the individual was able to:

> assumed the identity of six individuals in order to make 120 purchases at the "buy now" price listed by the seller. Those items were, primarily, computer equipment and clothing. The total cost of those purchases was $40,241. Between 19 November and 24 December 2004, (roughly the same period during which the purchases were made), Mr Hayes accessed eight Internet online banking accounts of seven bank customers. Having entered the relevant computer database, Mr Hayes diverted money from the true owner's account to meet the cost of acquiring the 40 items purchased. In effect, Mr Hayes brought about a direct electronic transfer of funds from the customer to the account of the person selling the goods on "Trade Me". The total amount of the funds transferred in this way was $17,456.50.[26]

In assuming this identity, the individual Hayes conducted himself between 11 November and 23 December 2004, Mr Hayes, then aged 17 years, accessing the Internet on-line auction accounts through the "Trade Me" website. The Court stated:

> Trade Me" is the largest on-line Internet auction site operating out of New Zealand. Anyone wishing to offer something for sale by auction on that site applies for and obtains a trading account. Once an account has been secured, that person can advertise his or her items for sale, either with a reserve price or a "buy now" price. Those who hold accounts with "Trade Me" are provided with "user names" and a password to access the account.[27]

While the initial issues involved access to the computer, the actual theft of the identity of six persons was considerably problematic. In order for identity theft to occur via a computer and its systems, a person would need to have access to such. Therefore, it further demonstrates how the computer-related offences are interconnected, and in turn interconnected with data.

---

[23] Ibid.

[24] Cybercrime Act 2015, section 17 http://ronlaw.gov.nr/nauru_lpms/files/acts/a59d9691f5a1954 12b877493a2a95e8b.pdf.

[25] Crimes Act 1961, section 216B, https://www.legislation.govt.nz/act/public/1961/0043/latest/ DLM330422.html.

[26] *The Queen v Hayes* [2006] NZCA 318, paras 8–10.

[27] Ibid, paras 6–7.

In **Nigeria**, any person who is engaged in the services of any financial institution, and as a result of his special knowledge commits identity theft of its employer, staff, service providers and consultants with the intent to defraud is guilty of an offence.[28] Similarly, in **Papua New Guinea**, according to section 12, a person has committed an offence of identity theft when a device has been used to access, manipulate, use, transfer the identification of a person's identifiable data.[29] Moreover, **Rwanda**'s Article 47 establishes an offence for not reporting the theft of data, while Article 40 states that it is an offence for a person to use the identity of another person over the Internet.[30] **Sierra Leone** has a similar stipulation in section 31.[31] Significantly, in **Saint Kitts and Nevis**, section 16 states that person who knowingly, without lawful excuse or justification or in excess of a lawful excuse or justification, uses a computer system at any stage of an offence to transfer, possess, or use a means of identification of another person with the intent to commit, aid or abet, or in connection with, any unlawful activity that constitutes a crime, commits an offence.[32]

Finally, **Trinidad and Tobago,** have the same legislation whereby a person cannot transfer, possess or use identifying information of a person with the intent of committing any offence,[33] that is, any criminal activity. **Uganda** does not have a specific offence related to theft of an identity.[34] The **United Republic of Tanzania**[35] and **Zambia** provide for a similar offence,[36] unlike the **United Kingdom** that does not provide for the same offence,[37] although it could be addressed in their criminal laws. There are diverging responses to the offence of identity theft. Notably, the CCRA does not provide for this offence.

---

[28] Cyber Crime Act 2015, section 22, https://lawpadi.com/wp-content/uploads/2015/08/CyberCrime_ProhibitionPreventionetc_Act_2015.pdf.

[29] *Cybercrime Code Act 2016, section 12* https://www.parliament.gov.pg/uploads/acts/16A_35.pdf.

[30] Law N° 60/2018 OF 22/8/2018 on prevention and punishment of cyber crimes, Article 40, 47 https://www.risa.rw/fileadmin/user_upload/Others%20documents/Cyber_Crimes_Law.pdf. Note there are other offences relates to accessing a computer and data.

[31] Cyber Crime Act 2020, section 31 http://www.sierra-leone.org/Laws/2020-Cybercrime%20Act.pdf.

[32] Electronic Crimes Bill 2017, section 16 https://aglcskn.info/wp-content/documents/Act17TOC/Ch-04_41-Electronic-Crimes-Act.pdf.

[33] The Cybercrimes Bill 2017, sections 15 https://ttcsirt.gov.tt/wp-content/uploads/2022/04/Cyber_Crime_Bill_DRAFT_2017.pdf.

[34] *Computer Misuse Act, 2011, section 19* https://ulii.org/akn/ug/act/2011/2/eng@2011-02-14.

[35] *Cybercrimes Act, 2015, section 15* https://rsf.org/sites/default/files/the_cyber_crime_act_2015.pdf.

[36] The Cyber Security and Cyber Crimes Act, 2021, section 53 https://www.parliament.gov.zm/sites/default/files/documents/acts/Act%20No.%202%20of%202021The%20Cyber%20Security%20and%20Cyber%20Crimes.pdf.

[37] Computer Misuse Act 1990, https://www.legislation.gov.uk/ukpga/1990/18/contents.

20.2 Conclusion

The theft of personal data and information has significant impacts on transnational trade and the digital economy. The personal implication can be catastrophic, and can result in people losing their personal finances. This chapter has demonstrated that identity theft constitutes a level of personal data defined by the respective data protection laws. It is linked to other offences that relate to cybersecurity.

In keeping with the other chapters compared in this Part, general themes have emerged. However, there are many diverging themes, and there is a lack of coherence across the national laws. Significantly, this chapter has confirmed that there is a lack of specific provisions for identity-theft offences within a number of national laws. This is the case in the Bahamas, Barbados, Botswana, Brunei, Eswatini, Ghana, Jamacia, Kiribati, Malawi, Mauritius, Pakistan, Saint Lucia, Seychelles, Singapore, South Africa, St Vincent and The Grenadines, and Togo. This should be reconciled, and the Commonwealth should work with the respective states to ensure that they include provisions for this offence in their national cyber laws. Likewise, where such an offence is provided for in a state's criminal laws, it should be transposed to the cyber laws. If laws for cybercrime are not distinct from a state's criminal laws, this only complicates the laws at a time when the community needs to fully understand their obligations when engaging in online activities.

Similar to most criminal offences, in identity theft there is an element of intention, intent or knowledge, although this will vary depending on the state. This level of intent or otherwise will need to be clarified when applying the law. Additionally, provisions for the offence are extended to include the unauthorized collection and use of identity information without the lawful authority of the data subject. It is my view that this provision relates to the personal data of a person, even though personal data has not been defined or included within the law itself. This is the same position that other states have taken.

Against the backdrop of the above, other terms and terminology that have emerged include where a person obtains or possesses another person's identity information. This is another example where there is a direct link between the offence and the personal data law. It is the person's information and data that are defined under the data laws of the states. Furthermore, in support of the intentional element, the terms 'lawful authority' and 'reasonable excuse' have been included in the laws of some states. It is argued that 'reasonable excuse' would constitute a genuine mistake made by an individual. While the offence has been further supported by one state which has included in its law the fraudulent or dishonest use of an electronic signature, password or other unique identifying feature of another person.

Significantly too, some states have taken a sectorial approach that includes, but is not limited to, the financial, medical and tax. This approach could be problematic if the provision is restricted to only certain industries and professional sectors. This should be reconciled and a broader approach taken. Importantly, it was demonstrated that the functional impacts when scaled up across all Commonwealth countries will show how significant this issue has become.

The financial impact of the theft of personal data is not fully understood. Further research is urgently needed as this can have enormous implications for the development of the digital economy. Identity theft decreases the community's trust in the law and the governance of data, and people may request that organisations change their practices. The CCRA should be amended to include the offence of identity theft.

Chapter 21
Ransom-Extortion

21.1 Introduction

The proliferation of data and access to the Internet via various devices has resulted in not everyone playing by the accepted rules. That is, there are some in the community who exploit the law for a financial or other benefit. The same issue arises in the technology and data world.

The CCRA does not cover ransom as it relates to data and computer systems, in my view, it is an area of increasing concern. I argue that the Commonwealth should revise the CCRA to ensure that it covers this concept. For the purposes of this chapter, 'ransom' and 'extortion' are synonymous. This is because, generally, extortion- and ransom-related offences involve the element of inducement, amongst other things. This offence occurs when there has been the extraction of personal data and information by an individual or entity, or both, and the offender contacts the data subject or company and demands a financial or some other reward for the safe return of that data and/or information.

This chapter does not compare the penalties given for each offence; nor does it provide a word-by-word comparison of the laws. Due to the fragmented approach that the Commonwealth nations being compared have taken when establishing their cyber-related laws, a high-level approach has been taken to determine where the offence has been adopted. Also, this chapter does not deal with ransomware.

The ransom or extortion of personal and commercial information has been on the rise. It is an activity whereby an individual or entity will illegally obtain personal and/or commercial data, and then attempt to sell it back to the individual or entity. The individuals involved may not necessarily seek to obtain a direct financial gain from the activity; instead, they may attempt to gain some other benefit. It was reported in 2022 that new tactics, techniques and procedures are being used to conduct attacks

R. Walters, *Cybersecurity and Data Laws of the Commonwealth*,
https://doi.org/10.1007/978-981-99-3935-0_21

and commit theft offences via the Internet.[1] There is concern that the types of attacks and predation on individuals and commercial organisations are becoming highly sophisticated.

The intrusions are for the purpose of collecting data and, in order for an organization or individual to have that data returned, the perpetrators are using ransom or extortion tactics. These crimes are disrupting the national and transnational commercial activities of both the traditional and the digital economy. Another disturbing development has been the increase in data theft and extortion without the use of any ransomware, leading to the emergence of new marketplaces dedicated to advertising and selling victims' data. This is the personal data that is defined under the respective data laws of jurisdictions.[2] In a high-profile example, the:

> Australian telecommunication company Optus suffered a devastating data breach on September 22, 2022 that has led to the details of 11 million customers being accessed. The information accessed included customers' names, dates of birth, phone numbers, email and home addresses, driver's license and/or passport numbers and Medicare ID numbers. Files containing this confidential information were posted on a hacking forum after Optus refused to pay a ransom demanded by the hacker. Victims of the breach also said that they were contacted by the supposed hacker demanding they pay AU$2,000 (US$1,300) or their data would be sold to other malicious parties.[3]

Even though the payment expected from each data subject for the return of their personal data may not be considered high, when extracted from 11 million people, the financial gain is considerable. The ransom or extortion comes after several overtures that usually lead to a threat, and 'aim to influence the recipient, to obtain compliance with certain demands, rather than actually engaging on the course of action described. However, threats do have a composite relationship to actual harm'.[4] Put another way, 'cyber threatening and extortionate communications, especially in their severe forms, can have very serious consequences for victims: cause significant social or economic harm; place the victims in a state of fear or distress; disrupt the normal course of activities; influence how people react or interact'.[5] In response to this behaviour, most nation states have established laws that minimise the exposure of data subjects and organisation to such threats. Significantly, these offences have not yet reached the judiciary, and it will be important to know and understand how the courts deal with these offences.

---

[1] CrowdStrike, 2022 Global Threat Report, p. 12, https://go.crowdstrike.com/rs/281-OBQ-266/images/Report2022GTR.pdf.

[2] Ibid, p. 12.

[3] Olivia Powel, The biggest data breaches and leaks of 2022: The data breaches that had the biggest impact in the cyber security world over the past 12 months, 2022, https://www.cshub.com/attacks/articles/the-biggest-data-breaches-and-leaks-of-2022.

[4] Ioana, Lucian Vasiu, *Forms and Consequences of the Cyber Threats and Extortion Phenomenon,* European Journal of Sustainable Development (2020), pp. 296–300.

[5] Ibid, p. 300.

This chapter examines how Commonwealth countries have responded to this growing area of sophisticated criminal activity conducted over the Internet. In **Antigua and Barbuda,** according to section 7,[6] no person intentionally or without lawful excuse or justification, can induce another person to enter into a relationship, with the intent to defraud that person or cause that person to act to his own detriment or suffer loss of property. **Australia** has recently proposed that a similar offence be included the Criminal Code Act 1995. However, at the time of writing, it had yet to be inserted into the Criminal Code.[7] Once, this provision becomes fully operational, Australia's laws will be aligned with those of most of other states compared in this book. However, as stated in an earlier chapter, Australia's cybercrime laws are difficult to find, and should be taken out of the broader criminal laws and established as a single Act to bring Australian law in line with that of other Commonwealth countries.

In the **Bahamas**, the offences are considered criminal offences. That is, section 10 creates an offence provision whereby any person who incites, solicits or abets the commission of or who attempts to commit or does any act preparatory to or in furtherance of the commission of any offence under this Act shall be guilty of that offence.[8]

Bangladesh, Barbados, Ghana, Guyana, Jamacia, Kiribati, Malawi, Nauru, Pakistan, Saint Kitts, Saint Lucia, Rwanda, Seychelles, Sierra Leon, Singapore, St Vincent and The Grenadines, Togo, Uganda, and the **United Republic of Tanzania** have no specific provisions for the offence for ransom. However, in some of these jurisdictions, such as in Bangladesh, there is provision for the offence of hacking, even though it is not related to obtaining a financial or some other gain from the hack.[9] While outside the scope of this chapter, these jurisdictions are likely to deal with the offence of ransom under other laws. This is clearly another area requiring further research. In **Belize**, there is no specific provision related to ransom,

---

[6] Electronic Crimes Act 2013, section 7, http://laws.gov.ag/wp-content/uploads/2019/02/a2013-14.pdf.

[7] Australian Parliament, Crimes Legislation Amendment (Ransomware Action Plan) Bill 2022, Amends the: *Criminal Code Act 1995* to: amend the geographical jurisdiction provision for computer offences; introduce standalone offences for extortive conduct associated with ransomware and dealing with data obtained by unauthorised access or modification; introduce aggravated offences relating to cyber-attacks on critical infrastructure assets and producing, supplying or obtaining data under arrangement for payment; and increase maximum penalties for certain other computer offences; *Proceeds of Crime Act 2002* to ensure that existing information gathering powers and freezing orders in relation to financial institutions can also be exercised in relation to digital currency exchanges; and *Crime Act 1914* and *Proceeds of Crime Act 2002* to ensure that law enforcement agencies can seize digital assets (including cryptocurrency) discovered during the execution of a warrant and suspected to be proceeds of crime.

https://www.aph.gov.au/Parliamentary_Business/Bills_Legislation/Bills_Search_Results/Result?bId=r6910.

[8] Computer Misuse Act 2006, section 10 http://laws.bahamas.gov.bs/cms/images/LEGISLATION/PRINCIPAL/2003/2003-0002/ComputerMisuseAct_1.pdf.

[9] Digital Security Act 2018, section 34 https://www.cirt.gov.bd/wp-content/uploads/2020/02/Digital-Security-Act-2020.pdf.

although section 9 could be seen as indirectly creating such an offence. That is, an offence is committed when, with the intent to defraud or deceive another person for the purpose of procuring an economic benefit for the person or another, an individual or entity inputs, alters, deletes or suppresses computer data.[10] It is the procuring or otherwise for an economic benefit that would constitute the offence of ransom. **Ghana**, under section 66,provides for an offence for sexual extortion.

In **Botswana**, under section 14, a person who performs or threatens to perform any of the acts described under this Part, for the purposes of obtaining any unlawful advantage by (*a*) undertaking to cease or desist from such actions; or (*b*) undertaking to restore any damage caused as a result of those actions, commits an offence.[11] On the other hand, in **Brunei**, there is no specific offence provision pertaining to ransom under Computer Misuse Act 2007. However, this does not mean that this offence is not provided for in some other legislation. In **Canada**, section 346 (1) of the Criminal Code, creates a general offence provision for extortion. It states that 'everyone commits extortion who, without reasonable justification or excuse and with intent to obtain anything, by threats, accusations, menaces or violence induces or attempts to induce any person, whether or not he is the person threatened, accused or menaced or to whom violence is shown, to do anything or cause anything to be done'.[12] Therefore, it is argued that this provision can apply to any events related to computer crime. On the other hand, in 2022, the Canadian Ontario Court in the case of *R. v. Vachon-Desjardins*[13] demonstrated the interconnectedness of the concepts and principles compared in this and other chapters of this book. The Court concluded that the 'defendant pleaded guilty before me to five counts in relation to a complex set of offences involving mischief and theft of computer data, extortion, the payment of cryptocurrency ransoms, and participating in the activities of a criminal organisation. The 17 Canadian victims to which this activity relates suffered losses in the millions of dollars'.[14] The offences committed included access, computer interference, interception of data and extortion. Although the case did not articulate it in this way, the Court stated that 'between May 2020 and January 2021, the Defendant victimised 17 Canadian entities and others throughout the world by breaching private computer networks and systems, hi-jacking their data, holding the stolen data for ransom, and distributing stolen data when ransoms were not paid'.[15] Even though it was not clear whether the data was personal data, it is my view that an element

[10] Cybercrime Act 2020, sections 9 https://www.nationalassembly.gov.bz/wp-content/uploads/2020/10/Act-No.-32-of-2020-Cybercrime.pdf.

[11] Cybercrime and related Crimes Act 2018, section 14, https://www.bocra.org.bw/cybercrime-and-computer-related-crimes-act-2018.

[12] Criminal Code 1985, https://laws-lois.justice.gc.ca/pdf/c-46.pdf.

[13] *R. v. Vachon-Desjardins*, 2022 ONCJ 43. https://www.canlii.org/en/on/oncj/doc/2022/2022oncj43/2022oncj43.html.

[14] Ibid, para 1.

[15] Ibid, para 10.

of personal data would have been compromised. This assessment is based on the 17 individuals who lost their crypto currency. In confirming this assessment, the Court stated that:

> Eventually, based on internet protocol addresses, data gleaned from U.S. investigations into various Apple, Google, Microsoft, and Mega.nz accounts, aliases, email addresses, and personal information revealed on social media platforms, the Defendant was identified by the Canadian authorities.[16]

Thus, personal information such as accounts, email addresses, and social media platforms revealed what, in my view, is personal information and personal data defined by data protection and privacy law. In other evidence received by the Court, 'between 10 and 15 unknown individuals hired the Defendant to teach them his methods. Some of these activities benefitted those interested in securing computer networks from these types of attacks. Some of the Defendant's students were likely other cyber threat actors'.[17] The remainder of the background to this case was:

> In the days leading up to the search warrant for his residence, the Defendant transferred 224 Bitcoins out of his electronic wallet ("e-wallet"). He told investigators that this was a payment made to invest in the NetWalker group and the next generation of malicious code that could be used to infiltrate secure computer systems and steal protected data. The Defendant even improved upon the ransom messages used by NetWalker affiliates and eventually convinced the creator of NetWalker to use "mixing services" to disguise funds paid for ransoms in Bitcoin. Over 1200 Bitcoins related to his NetWalker malware activities passed through his e-wallet and were shared with his unindicted co-conspirators and the developer of the NetWalker ransomware. As well, the Defendant admits that his entire ransomware activities involved over 2000 Bitcoins. The RCMP seized slightly less than 720 Bitcoins from the Defendant's e-wallets and accounts. Defendant converted some of the cryptocurrency into Canadian dollars through unlawful channel, obtaining bags of money ranging from $100,000 to $150,000. Cash seized ($640,040) from the Defendant's home and his bank account balances ($420,941) indicate that the Defendant had liquid assets of over one million dollars in January 2021.[18]

Moreover, the Court ordered the collection of DNA from the defendant, which constitutes personal data under data protection law. The Court stated:

> Extortion and participating in the activities of a criminal organization are both primary designated offences for the provision of a sample of deoxyribonucleic acid ("DNA").[19]

While the outcome of the case was a good settlement with forfeiture of proceeds, the Court commended the parties on their negotiated outcome. Yet again, the case demonstrates the interconnectedness of cybercrime, data flows and data protection, and crypto assets that are all part of the emerging digital economy.

---

[16] Ibid, para 5.

[17] Ibid, para 11.

[18] Ibid, paras 12–15.

[19] Ibid, para 38.

Eswatini has established an offence for extortion where a person uses an email, internet or computer system to obtain a benefit from the access to the information or data held within.[20] In **Grenada,** according to section 9, a person cannot defraud another person without justification to interfere with data or an electronic system, via an electronic fraud that a person can induce another to enter into a relationship.[21]

The formal and functional arrangements for the offence of extortion in **Fiji**, according to section 10, constitutes both fraud and extortion when an entity benefits from the illegal intrusion into a computer and its systems.[22] **India**'s Electronic Technology Act contains no specific provision for extortion. However, such provisions are likely to reside in the Penal Code. Similarly, **Malaysia** does not have specific ransom provisions within its Computer Crimes laws, and the relevant criminal laws would need to be consulted. Essentially, the ability for individuals and entities to extort or hold others to ransom is very problematic. The practice involves:

> the exfiltration of data by the attackers which is then used to extort a ransom. The data is often released by attackers on public or dark web sites. Extracted data could include commercially sensitive corporate and customer data. Often, the victim organisation is unable to determine the data that has been exfiltrated, until it is released by the attacker. This also means that criminals release data to embarrass victims, particularly if they have publicly denied any data being stolen. Victims of ransomware attacks need to be aware that data may be leaked over time onto the dark web and could be viewed by competitors, suppliers and customers. There are secondary and tertiary markets where this data can continue to surface, creating a need for continued management focus.[23]

These practices are leading to different types of attacks that can be summarised as:

> *Hack and leak*—After gaining control of a company's IT systems, cybercriminals search for sensitive files which are stolen before systems can be protected and locked. In the event the ransom is not paid, victims are extorted with threats to publish sensitive information, including on the dark web.

> *Targeting Executive*—Cyber criminals have started to directly target top executives. The techniques include emailing them directly with threats and ransom demands, as well as gaining access to their inboxes, files and computers and stealing their organisation's data which is then used for extortion or blackmail.

---

[20] *Computer Crime and Cybercrime Act No.6 of 2022, section 11* https://www.esccom.org.sz/legislation/COMPUTER%20CRIME%20&%20CYBERCRIME%20ACT.pdf.

[21] Electronic Crimes Bill 2013, section 9 https://ecagrenada.com/Grenada-Electronic-Crimes-Act-2013.pdf.

[22] Cybersecurity and Cybercrime Act 2021, section 10 https://ncb.govmu.org/ncb/legislations/THE%20CYBERSECURITY%20AND%20CYBERCRIME%20ACT%202021.pdf.

Cybercrime Act 2021 (Act No. 3 of 2021), section 8 https://www.ilo.org/dyn/natlex/natlex4.detail?p_lang=en&p_isn=111060&p_classification=01.

[23] Australian Government, Locked Out: Tackling Australia's ransomware threat, Cyber Security Industry Advisory Committee, March 2021, p. 4 https://www.homeaffairs.gov.au/cyber-security-subsite/files/tackling-ransomware-threat.pdf.

Tailored Ransom demands—Cybercriminals trawl through stolen data in preparation for ransomware attacks, often demanding a ransom payment that is the same as the insured amount. By insisting on payment in cryptocurrency, the attacker may remain anonymous and free to attack again.[24]

The above demonstrate the sophistication of attacks and the targeted areas that are the most vulnerable. As this book highlights, as long as there continues to be an inconsistent approach to the legal frameworks being established by nation states, it will be difficult to curtail, let alone stop, this activity. The ensuing question is whether such criminal behaviour can ever be stopped. A response to this question is unlikely. It is similar to the issue of preventing drink driving. It has never been achieved even though governments around the world have established criminal laws to discourage this activity. The cyber laws will, at best, reduce the number of incidents. What needs to occur in conjunction with the laws, if for the private sector to implement a set of internal procedure to prevent their exposure to extortion.

Kenya has adopted a broad approach to this issue. sections 34, 35, 36 make provisions for offences related to the inducement to deliver an electronic message, withholding a message and destruction of an electronic message.[25] Most important is section 34 which states that a person cannot provide an inducement to a person where a message has been received in error. The offence that is committed when a person holds on to data and information for a monetary or other benefit is likely to be covered by other legislation.

A further development has been the approach taken by **Lesotho**, that makes it an offence to extort data and information from the illegal access to this information in order to obtain a benefit (financial or otherwise).[26] Similarly, **Mauritius**, under section 18, takes a broad approach to cyber extortion.[27] Therefore, it is argued that any level of inducement constitutes an extortion for the use of data and information collected from a computer and its systems or infrastructure.

A neighbour of Australia, **New Zealand** has no specific provisions for offences related to ransom, although section 251 makes it an offence to sell, distribute or possess software for the purpose of committing a crime. That is, anyone who invites any other person to acquire from him or her, or offers or exposes for sale or supply to any other person, or agrees to sell or supply or sells or supplies to any other person, or has in his or her possession for the purpose of sale or supply to any other person, any software or other information that would enable another person to access a computer

[24] Australian Government, Ransomware Action Plan, 2021, p. 3 https://www.homeaffairs.gov.au/cyber-security-subsite/files/ransomware-action-plan.pdf.

[25] Computer Misuse and Cybercrimes Act 2018, section 26 https://ictpolicyafrica.org/en/document/pb8w26fcso?page=2.

[26] The Computer Crimes and Cyber Security Bill, 2022, https://senate.parliament.ls/2022/05/19/computer-crime-and-cyber-security-bill-2022/.

[27] Cybersecurity and Cybercrime Act 2021, section 18 https://ncb.govmu.org/ncb/legislations/THE%20CYBERSECURITY%20AND%20CYBERCRIME%20ACT%202021.pdf.

system without authorisation, is committing a crime.[28] On the other hand, in **Nigeria**, any person who knowingly or intentionally sends a message or other matter by means of computer systems for ransom or a level of extortion has committed and offence.[29] This is restricted to messages that constitute cyberstalking.

Papua New Guinea, makes it an offence to cyber extort by threatening to upload information of an individual.[30] The term 'threat' is general, and has not been defined. Thus, it could constitute any level of threat. **South Africa** has a general offence of cyber extortion, that should only apply to and be read according to sections 3(1), 5(1), 6(1) or 7(1)(a) or (d), that relate to obtaining any advantage from another person; or compelling another person to perform or to abstain from performing any act.[31] Similarly, **Trinidad and Tobago,** have provisions for the same offence; that is, a person who uses a computer system to gain a benefit from another person, such as, threatening to publish computer data containing personal or private information which can cause public ridicule, contempt, hatred or embarrassment, commits a crime.[32] In **Zambia**, a person commits an offence if that person, through a computer system, with intent seeks to extort or gain anything from any person,[33] and the **United Kingdom** does not provide for the same offence.[34] There is a lack of adoption of the offence of ransom and/or extortion by the cyber laws of the Commonwealth states. Because this chapter has not analysed the other criminal laws within those states that do not provide for this offence, it is an area for further research. Generally, there are complex nuances in the laws provided for the offences, and compared in this Part, which will pose challenges to organisations and practitioners in a transnational setting. The more states involved, the higher the probability, as demonstrated in this book that the laws will be similar, although they diverge significantly in their use of terms and terminology, along with their application. More work is needed to examine decisions made by the respective judiciaries.

21.2 Conclusion

The overall approach taken by Commonwealth members to adopting the concepts and principles of the CCRA is highly fragmented. Part II of this book has demonstrated the subtle but significant differences in the national laws related to access, interference

[28] Crimes Act 1951, section 251.

[29] Cyber Crime Act 2015, section 24, https://lawpadi.com/wp-content/uploads/2015/08/CyberCrime_ProhibitionPreventionetc_Act_2015.pdf.

[30] *Cybercrime Code Act 2016, section 24* https://www.parliament.gov.pg/uploads/acts/16A_35.pdf.

[31] Cybercrimes Act 2021, section 10 https://cybercrimesact.co.za.

[32] The Cybercrimes Bill 2017, sections 19 https://ttcsirt.gov.tt/wp-content/uploads/2022/04/Cyber_Crime_Bill_DRAFT_2017.pdf.

[33] The Cyber Security and Cyber Crimes Act, 2021, section 52 https://www.parliament.gov.zm/sites/default/files/documents/acts/Act%20No.%202%20of%202021The%20Cyber%20Security%20and%20Cyber%20Crimes.pdf.

[34] Computer Misuse Act 1990, https://www.legislation.gov.uk/ukpga/1990/18/contents.

of data and computer, interception of data, identity theft, fraud and ransom. For the practitioner, this will pose challenges in cross-border criminal offences when representing parties. The highly inconsistent approaches will also provide challenges for the resolution of disputes, particularly those being settled by arbitration.

What has emerged is that most of these concepts and principles are connected, cross over, or are aligned. For instance, access to a computer enables the interference with data and a computer system, along with its infrastructure. Unauthorised access also enables the interception of data, whether personal or commercial. It has been demonstrated that these offences all impact, in some way, on personal data and its protection and flow. The unauthorised access to data will decrease the community's trust in the law and technology, and will hamper the growth of the digital economy.

In conclusion, the Commonwealth has embarked on a number of initiatives to foster international cooperation. However, these focus on regions of Africa, the Caribbean and the Pacific.[35] Arguably, these regions are where the developing countries are located. There is, and I agree, a need for this focus on these regions. However, international cooperation could be expanded to include other countries such as the United States and Japan, as observers since they share and implement many of the same values. They can be consulted when future cybersecurity initiatives and law are being developed.

In addition to the broader deficiencies identified in this Part, this chapter has confirmed the lack of reference by the CCRA to ransom- and/or extortion-related offences. One of the most significant concerns that have emerged from the research conducted for this book, is that many nation states have not made in their laws, provisions for the offence of extortion/ransom. This is the case in Bangladesh, Barbados, Brunei, Ghana, Guyana, India, Jamacia, Kiribati, Malawi, Malaysia, Nauru, Pakistan, Saint Kitts and Nevis, Saint Lucia, Rwanda, Seychelles, Sierra Leon, Singapore, St Vincent and The Grenadines, Togo, Uganda, and the United Republic of Tanzania.

Although the terms 'ransom' and 'extortion' have been used interchangeably in this chapter, most states used the term 'extortion' in their laws. In keeping with the overall comparative analysis of laws in this book, there have been several themes related to terms and terminology used in the national laws. Extortion has been underpinned by the intent, intention or knowledge of the individual to undertake to gain a level of benefit from the illegal collection and storage of personal data. It is generally executed by means of threats, accusations, menaces or violence inducements, amongst other behaviours. Problematic is that the states diverge on this issue, and some do not describe these specific behaviours.

A further prevailing development has been that the offence can be justified or there is an excuse explaining why individuals have conducted themselves so as to extort a benefit from another person's data. Furthermore, in one case, the offence provision has been extended to include the use of email, internet or computer system to obtain a benefit from the access to the information or data. Arguably, this is another example where the offence is directly related to personal data defined by the data protection

[35] The Commonwealth, Commonwealth Cyber Declaration Programme, https://thecommonwealth.org/our-work/commonwealth-cyber-declaration-programme.

laws compared within this book. This is in addition to the cyber laws not defining or referencing what constitutes data or information. Therefore, viewed broadly, and in the absence of any judicial decisions, data and information will include personal data. The concept of inducement has also been used to support the overall offence of extortion. They both derive a benefit from the data being returned to the data subject or business.

Finally, this Part has demonstrated that the Commonwealth could and should expand the CCRA in a number of areas. It has highlighted how the cyber laws of each jurisdiction are complex and cumbersome. Further, it has been demonstrated that those states who do not have specific cyber laws should undertake to develop them in the immediate future. This will reduce the overall economic burden of having to seek the provisions in otherwise complex criminal laws. This Part has identified a number of areas meriting further research. Importantly, it has demonstrated that data is closely related to cybersecurity and the law. It requires a more harmonised approach in order to ensure its long-term protection, which will engender greater trust and boost the digital economy. The next Part discusses data and cybersecurity in terms of international arbitration.

Part IV
Data and Cybersecurity in International Arbitration

Chapter 22
International Arbitration

22.1 Introduction

The ongoing developments in and across the digital economy will result in commercial and investor-state disputes. These disputes are an inevitable feature of a mature and developing economy. Simply put, where there are investments by entities that are promoted and supported by nation states, there can be disputes, which could rely on arbitration to resolve them.

Likewise, when commercial disputes arise between organisations, that do not involve government investment, arbitration has been, for a number of decades, an effective and preferred mechanism for resolving contractual disputes.

This Part will examine the role of international investor-state arbitration and international commercial arbitration in data and cybersecurity. Importantly, the Commonwealth has undertaken considerable work in relation to international arbitration.[1]

This chapter will examine this work in the context of how cybersecurity and data within the digital economy could rely on arbitration to resolve investment and commercial related disputes.

Due to the breadth of law to be compared, this Part will consist of the following Chapters:

- Key definitions of terms
- UNCITRAL Arbitration Model Law
- Appointment of Arbitrator, Seat, Arbitration Agreement

[1] The Commonwealth, A Study of International Commercial Arbitration in the Commonwealth, 2020, https://production-new-commonwealth-files.s3.eu-west-2.amazonaws.com/migrated/key_reform_pdfs/A%2BStudy%2Bof%2BInternational%2BCommercial%2BArbitration_PDF_-compressed.pdf.

R. Walters, *Cybersecurity and Data Laws of the Commonwealth*,
https://doi.org/10.1007/978-981-99-3935-0_22

- Experts
- Enforcement of Arbitration Award
- International Centre for Settlement of Investment Disputes—investor states disputes.

E-commerce and the digital economy have been rapidly evolving as technology develops. There are a number of different and competing developments, both commercially and in government. Through technology such as artificial intelligence, the Internet of Things, critical technologies and quantum, the legal landscape in terms of data protection and cybersecurity is being challenged. While consumers today have access to information that previously they would never have been able to obtain with a click, more commercial and investment decisions and activities are being undertaken online.

The technology is bringing people together more closely. It is pervading all sectors including primary industries, supply chains, health, education and investment. Individuals and entities can, in an instant, establish a global presence. However, amongst these gains, security of data and computer systems have been and continue to be a challenge. Thus, where there is a breach of a contract or law that often results in a dispute, there are options for remedying any loss. On the one hand, litigation can be undertaken. On the other hand, a dispute can be resolved through arbitration. This chapter examines the role of arbitration in regard to both data and cybersecurity.

By exploring the role of arbitration in both investor-state disputes and transnational commercial disputes, it will be demonstrated how it can be used to resolve commercial and investment related disputes. In addition, this chapter will explore the national laws pertaining to commercial arbitration, and confirm or otherwise the level of harmonization that has or has not been taken by Commonwealth nations.

Firstly, investor-state arbitration is not often considered or discussed, although the foreign investment is currently alive and well. However, it has not come without its difficulties. For instance, it has been reported that the international investment climate is marked by two major trends that combine to increase foreign investors' exposure to risk in the digital economy:

> ill-prepared, undefined regulatory frameworks for innovative technological products and services expose investors to policy changes that prevent them from implementing their business models. Second, political shifts toward protectionist policies provide government officials with the political will to implement such regulations.[2]

The resulting effect, in part, can be seen in governments' responses through regulation of data and cybersecurity. As stated throughout this book, there are areas of fragmentation, not well-understood regulation, gaps in the regulation and, in some cases, no regulation. In order for the digital economy to function in the same coherent way as the traditional economy, regulation is vital. Robert Ginsburg opines that:

---

[2] Robert Ginsburg, *Investor-State Dispute Settlement in the Digital Economy: The Case for Structured Proportionality*, 39 North West Journal International Law and Business, 171 (2019), p. 173.

> The regulation of technology investments is a necessary component of the new digital economy. Innovations are creating services and products that provide new threats to the environment, consumer safety, and the well-being of third parties.[3]

Second, when considering arbitration and cybersecurity, what comes to mind is the protection of arbitration process from cyber-attacks. This chapter will examine both investor-state and transnational commercial arbitration as it applies to cybersecurity and data within the digital economy. The ensuing question is: what role, if any, can arbitration have in an investor-state dispute? Further: how can cybersecurity and data within the digital economy constitute an investment?

Given the above, a starting point is the International Convention on the Settlement of Investment Disputes between States and Nationals of Other States.[4] In 2020, the Commonwealth undertook a study in relation to arbitration.[5] This recent study made a series of recommendations for the collection of data and information in order to better understand the arbitration landscape across the Commonwealth. The ensuing question was whether the study called for a Model Law in the same way as Model Laws exist for cybersecurity and data. Also, should a Model Law be developed for Arbitration? The study underscored the importance of international trade across Commonwealth members, stating:

> Commonwealth member countries should be encouraged and supported to modernise their arbitration commercial international arbitration framework by becoming party to the New York Convention, 11 and adopting a modern arbitration law based on the 2006 UNCITRAL Model Law.[6]

While there is no specific reference to data flows, data protection or cybersecurity and how to deal with these matters within arbitration, the report identified more broadly the influence of technology in arbitration. It states that:

> The use of technology also impacts on the uptake and usage of arbitration. Technology plays an important part in modern-day dispute resolution. This can include tools like video conferencing and hearing room technology, artificial intelligence, and cloud-based storage to support the conduct of an arbitration. Technological literacy by users, access to technology, and cybersecurity are important concerns in this regard. Currently, technology is not being used to its full potential by stakeholders to aid the international commercial arbitration process.[7]

---

[3] Ibid, p. 174.

[4] International Convention on the Settlement of Investment Disputes Between States and nationals of Other States, https://icsid.worldbank.org/sites/default/files/ICSID%20Convention%20English.pdf.

[5] The Commonwealth, A Study of International Commercial Arbitration in the Commonwealth, 2020, https://production-new-commonwealth-files.s3.eu-west-2.amazonaws.com/migrated/key_reform_pdfs/A%2BStudy%2Bof%2BInternational%2BCommercial%2BArbitration_PDF_-compressed.pdf.

[6] Ibid, p. ix.

[7] Ibid, p. ix.

Essentially, the Commonwealth is restating the combined benefits to be derived from transnational trade between members. Even though the Commonwealth is not a formal trading bloc, members trading between each other rely on either bilateral or multilateral arrangements. An important observation is that in 2018, it was reported that the 'Commonwealth's global exports of goods and services stood in 2016 at US$3.1 trillion, accounting for about 14.8% of the total global exports of goods and services'.[8] This commercial activity is significant, and would not have come without its disputes. Noteworthy is that, currently, the default position of most member countries is to defer to litigation rather than arbitration to resolve disputes.[9] Arguably, in some member countries such as Australia, Singapore, Canada, New Zealand and particularly the UK, arbitration is well-understood and grounded in the respective national laws. Across Africa, arbitration is also on the rise. It has been stated that:

> A major factor in the rise of arbitration in Africa is the general reluctance of foreign investors to submit disputes to the local courts of an African country. Some of the major concerns foreign investors have with regards to courts in Africa are: lack of impartiality of judges, corruption, political instability and civil unrest, length of proceedings.' The I-ARB goes on to point out that another major reason to support international arbitration is that investors prefer the 'relative ease of enforcement because of the existing mechanism under the Convention on the Recognition and Enforcement of Foreign Arbitral Awards.[10]

Problematic though, are the risks of 'inconsistent or conflicting national laws, lack of requisite experience and expertise, enormous costs and time, parallel proceedings, the lack of confidentiality, and the difficulty of enforceability of judgments'.[11] However, the study stopped short of recommending a Model Law on Arbitration. On the other hand, the study called for the development of an 'online platform consolidating basic arbitration information and sources'.[12] In providing a pathway forward, it also highlighted the need for such a platform to 'provide guidance on model arbitration clauses, choosing the applicable law and the seat of an arbitration, and which characteristics should be taken into account before choosing ad hoc or institutional arbitration'.[13] Arguably, this is an important and necessary initiative. While this Part does not assess whether the Commonwealth has made any progress in this area, in my view, this should be established as a matter of urgency. At the time of writing, in December 2022 and January 2023, there was nothing available on the Commonwealth's website that indicated the above had been implemented.

Undoubtedly too, the need for this Part of the book is timely and reaffirms the work undertaken by the Commonwealth. It noted the issues surrounding regulatory design in the area of arbitration 'even if not directly related to international commercial arbitration, can nevertheless have an undesirable impact on its and the Commonwealth's

[8] Ibid, p. 10.

[9] Ibid, p. 12.

[10] Ibid.

[11] Ibid.

[12] Ibid, p. 95.

[13] Ibid.

international commercial arbitration framework'.[14]Most noteworthy, it is making the connection between arbitration, cybersecurity and data. In anticipation of the digital economy and the challenges in dispute resolution that will follow, UNCITRAL[15]to have begun to consider the issue.

Arbitration in the Digital Economy [data-cybersecurity]

It is well-documented that the outbreak of the global pandemic COVID19, forced the world into isolation. It meant that rather than meet and undertake business face to face, engagement was undertaken online. As the digital economy has evolved to what it is today, there has been a greater focus on the small and medium-sized (SME) business sector. This is particularly important in view of the issues discussed in this book. The rationale for this assumption is that most, if not all, large entities have the financial and other resources to deal with disputes related to technology, data and cybersecurity. It is the SME sector that is vulnerable, not only in relation to cybersecurity threats, but also:

> On the needs of the industry, it was noted that enhancing access to justice for all involved in technology-related disputes should be the objective of the project, which would also be in line with Sustainable Development Goal 16 (Peace, Justice and Strong Institutions). It was said that particular attention could be given to businesses with limited knowledge about dispute resolution and capacity to handle disputes such as SMEs. Yet, businesses of all sizes were experiencing an increase in the number and costs of technology-related disputes, rendering the need all the more pressing. It was further mentioned that the availability of counsel with the expertise to advise the disputing parties was another element to be taken into account to ensure access to justice. In this regard, the importance of continued education and training of the different actors involved in technology-related dispute resolution was highlighted.[16] [emphasis added]

In making the case that dispute resolution will be part of not only the overall digital economy, UNCITRAL noted that at their 2021 meeting, arbitration was going to be an important part of resolving commercial conflict in technology, data and cyber-related issues. UNCITRAL argued that the 'Expedited Arbitration Rules in 2021, be adapted to meet the needs of parties faced with technology-related disputes'.[17] However, generally, the UNCITRAL focused on the data and cybersecurity-related issues pertaining to online arbitration, that is, the use of technology in arbitration. This approach has largely been examined by the many arbitration institutions that have responded by developing guidance and protocols for managing cyber risks as

[14] Ibid, p. 48.

[15] UNCITRAL's Dispute Resolution in the Digital Economy Initiative, https://uncitral.un.org/en/parisarbitrationweekdrde#:~:text=The%20UNCITRAL%20project%20on%20the,information%20with%20a%20view%20

.

[16] United Nations Commission on International Trade Law, Legal issues related to the digital economy—dispute resolution in the digital economy, Fifty-fourth session, Vienna, 28 June–16 July 2021, A/CN.9/1064/Add.4.

[17] Ibid, p. 4.

data.[18] On the other hand, Jacques de Werra notes that this proposition is not new and has been well-understood for some time. De Werra points to the United States when seeking confirmation of the above. De Werra goes on to say that the Federal Insecticide, Fungicide, and Rodenticide Act (FIFRA) provides for an arbitration system for defining the (financial) conditions under which the research data submitted by an applicant for registration of a new pesticide can be relied upon by a subsequent applicant.[19] It was also noted that FIFRA in this respect provides for a compulsory data licensing regime through 7 U.S.C. § 136a(c)(1)(D)(ii) under which subsequent applicants for registration for a particular pesticide may use the original registrant's research data to obtain a so-called "'me-too' registration," provided that "the applicant has made an offer to compensate the original data submitter. If the parties cannot agree on the "amount and terms of compensation," either party "may initiate binding arbitration proceedings.[20] Most noteworthy, de Werra makes the case that data portability is the area that is the most challenging because:

> online activities most frequently imply that clients (be there individuals or business clients) store their personal or non-personal data on data storage infrastructures made available by information service providers. Clients should in this respect have the opportunity to use another service provider and thus to transfer/migrate/port their data from their previous service provider to the new one without being hindered in this process. Different regulatory instruments facilitate the smooth migration and portability of data for the benefit of the clients by granting them certain rights to the portability of their data which depend on the type of data at issue and distinguish between non-personal data and personal data.[21]

As highlighted earlier in this book, the laws pertaining to data portability are highly divergent. There are many states inside and outside of the Commonwealth that have no data portability laws whatsoever. The same can be said of cross-border data flows, which were covered earlier in this book. On this basis, both data portability and cross-border data flows, and the law would constitute an area where arbitration can be used to resolve disputes. It is argued that the flow of data across international borders is one factor that is driving the digital economy. Therefore, in agreement with de Werra, I believe that personal data can be a source of direct and indirect arbitration. In direct arbitration, in my view, the data forms part of the arbitration, but is not the sole reason for the dispute. This will only be heightened as the new digital economy is driven by data because, essentially, it is the use of data that drives economic growth.

On the other hand, and similar to data, cybersecurity is outside of the arbitration process but is increasingly being viewed as crucial to an organisation's risk management response to technology intrusions. Simply put, organisations have had to be

---

[18] Allison Goh, *Digital Readiness Index for Arbitration Institutions: Challenges and Implications for Dispute Resolution Under the Belt and Road Initiative,* Journal of International Arbitration, Vol 38, Iss 2 (2021), pp. 253–255.

[19] Jacques de Werra, Using Arbitration and ADR for Disputes about Personal Dara and Non-Personal Data: What Lessons from recent developments in Europe? The American Review of International Arbitration Vol 30: (2019), p. 195.

[20] Ibid, p. 196.

[21] Ibid, p. 198.

proactive in responding to data and cybersecurity laws. What is not often discussed is the direct commercial disputes involving cybersecurity and data. This section is not concerned with the security of data within an arbitration. The argument put forward is that cybersecurity itself, will become the core of a commercial dispute. In taking this position, as stated earlier in this book, the Australian Federal Court in 2022, ruled[22] that as a result of the failure to have documentation and controls in respect of cybersecurity and cyber resilience in place that were adequate to manage risk in respect of cybersecurity and cyber resilience across its AR network, and as a result of this conduct, it (a) failed to do all things necessary to ensure the financial services covered by the Licence were provided efficiently and fairly, in contravention of s 912A(1)(a) of the Corporations Act 2001.[23] This, I believe, it is a major step forward in the absence of any scholarly writing on this core issue. The matter concerned the licencing of a financial entity (which was providing online services) under Australian law, and that the entity failed to establish standard practices and procedures to manage the cyber risks. Thus, by not managing the cyber risks, it exposed personal data that, while not specifically stated, provided a financial benefit to the entity who contravened the law. Arguably, these matters could be arbitrated instead of being settled in the court. In addition, the commercial reality is also that, in the future, such security might be tied to the contractual arrangement, if it is not already, through the purchase and installation of technology infrastructure and systems. Thus, when a dispute arises concerning the products security readiness and the protection of data flows while in transmission, storage or usage, this could all be resolved through arbitration.

Given the above, it is argued that the definition of cybersecurity itself may help to support the argument that it can be a central element of an arbitration. Centrally, the definition has been linked to both data protection/privacy and the commercial realities of having to deal with technology. For example, Jeff Kosseff defines cybersecurity law to be:

> Cybersecurity law promotes the confidentiality, integrity, and availability of public and private information, systems, and networks, through the use of forward-looking regulations and incentives, with the goal of protecting individual rights and privacy, economic interests, and national security.[24]

While there are other definitions that can also be applied, Kosseff's definition of cybersecurity law underscores the relevance of this book. It connects data and cybersecurity within the broader scope of ensuring that the economic interests of individuals and entities are protected. Further, the definition explains how the network and systems are used to capture, store and use the data in cross-border data flows. A dispute could arise related to investment through contractual arrangements; and therefore, one mechanism available for the resolution of dispute is arbitration. It is argued that the economic loss arising from a contractual dispute because of a lack of risk management or mitigation against cyber threats where data is used as part of a

[22] *Australian Securities and Investments Commission v RI Advice Group Pty Ltd* [2022] FCA 496.

[23] Ibid, para 2.

[24] Jeff Kosseff, *Defining Cybersecurity Law* 103 Iowa Law Review 985 (2018) p. 1010.

commercial exchange. Put another way, personal data will increasingly be combined with commercial data and other commercial information and activities. Therefore, and as Jim Pastore believes, the general 'evidence in international arbitration may involve the disclosure of a client's personal health information, trade secrets, financial information, intellectual property, or corporate strategies'.[25] What Pastore is saying is that cybersecurity and data are directly connected with the commercial activities of many organisations today. Therefore, if and where there are contractual obligations on a party to protect data, and the systems and infrastructure that support the use of data, disputes can arise. This should not be confused with any contractual arrangements between a lawyer and client or the Tribunal to protect data and ensure security of the data. In another example, as the digital economy moves to adopt artificial intelligence (AI), arbitration can be an effective tool for addressing liability issues. Nassar Ali Khasawneh, Maria Mazzawi, and Ricardo Christie make an important point in this emerging and complex area of technology practice and law. They state:

> Continuing with the autonomous vehicle example of AI, because of the complexity of multiple service provider business models, liability for damages resulting from an accident involving an autonomous vehicle can rest, in whole or in part, on the automotive manufacturer, hardware vendor, software licensor, mobile network operator, technology provider, or any number of suppliers used by the technology provider. All of these entities and service providers are together responsible in varying degrees for the provision of the components and services required for operation of the autonomous vehicle, where liability can be even more complex if various issues arise simultaneously, which is often the case with interdependent technologies. This will also involve a number of international party, cross-border transaction, IP protected products and technologies, and trade secrets.[26]

The authors argue that the multiple entities that will be involved in AI technology alone could be significant. It is argued that in applying the above as a practical scenario, data and its security across the entire lifecycle of AI will underpin the technologies' performance. It will likely involve transnational transfer of data that will be coupled with other commercial data. This will also be the case for those other emerging critical technologies that embrace the application of autonomous or human behaviour, to operate. Problematic is the issue of liability. In many cases, it will be difficult to define or identify. Consequently, there may be multiple parties to an arbitration. As this part reveals, one of the central features of arbitration in the digital economy will be the use of experts. Expertise to understand not only the law but also the technology itself will be required in order to determine liability.

Moreover, and as demonstrated in Part I of this book, the definitions of personal data varied approach take to the definition of personal data alone is highly divergent across Commonwealth member states. The national laws of specifically define biometric data, others do not, and in many countries, it is afforded a greater level of protection. Nassar Ali Khasawneh, Maria Mazzawi, Ricardo Christie state:

---

[25] Jim Pastore, *Practical Approaches to Cybersecurity in Arbitration*, Fordham International Law Journal (2017) p. 1023.

[26] Nassar Ali Khasawneh, Maria Mazzawi, Ricardo Christie, *Arbitration and the Advent of New Technologies*, Global Arbitration Review, (2022), https://globalarbitrationreview.com/guide/the-guide-telecoms-arbitrations/first-edition/article/arbitration-and-the-advent-of-new-technologies

> Biotechnology projects and use biometric data in technical, expensive, high-risk and collaborative ways. Often, these projects will involve a number of different parties from various jurisdictions, regarding confidential subject matters and sensitive data, thereby requiring complex technologies and arrangements. The cost, internationality, complexity and need for confidentiality associated with such projects make them well suited to arbitration. On a corporate scale, biometric security is becoming less a feature solely in fields that require additional security, but more a commonplace precaution, such as the scanning of fingerprints. With this enters issues of consent and the lawfulness of such consent. For example, under best-practice regulations, if a real alternative to the collection of biometric data is not offered, consent will not be considered freely given, and thereby illegal. While this may not be the case under some regional data protection regulations, it does highlight a number of complex issues that overlap between employee data privacy rights and corporate cybersecurity and confidentiality interests, where such overlap, if turned contentious, could benefit from arbitration.[27]

In practice, security, commercial reality and biometric data cannot be separated. However, at law, they are distinguishable. The risks faced by organisations dealing with biometric data alone requires highly sophisticated technology to capture the unique features of a person. In addressing the broader risks encountered in regard to this data, the authors argue that the:

> data held by these entities is compromised, knowingly or unknowingly, thus opening various entities up to a number of multi-party based liabilities, data breaches and possibly cybersecurity breaches. A breach of information security and personal data occurs by illegal or unauthorised access, including copying, sending, distributing, exchanging, transmitting, circulating or processing data in a way that leads to disclosure to third parties, or damage or alteration thereof during storage, transmission or processing.[28]

Thus, there are cybersecurity and data laws that a party can breach. Again, it may be difficult to determine liability, particularly since arbitration may involve several parties. A similar issue is emerging in the FinTech sector where

> disputes can arise in connection with the transfer of virtual assets, the enforceability of smart contracts, and other security concerns, but they may also concern ownership. For example, the buyers of a non-fungible token (NFT) do not own the underlying virtual asset, nor the licence thereto; they only own the NFT. However, the platform can unilaterally sever the NFT's link to the underlying asset, thereby making the NFT worthless. This can be done if, for example, the buyer does not comply with the terms and conditions of the platform.[29]

Arguably, arbitration can resolve these types of commercial and liability-related disputes, which will most likely involve a data and cybersecurity. Arbitration offers a neutral and confidential environment within which disputes can be resolved. Therefore, it is argued that the evolving digital economy opens up a number of areas for current and future arbitration. Not only will there be the likelihood of multi parties being involved, arbitration in the digital economy will likely have to address multiple issues.

---

[27] Ibid.

[28] Ibid.

[29] Ibid.

Because cybersecurity and data protection can be the direct dispute to be arbitrated, they are likely to arise in investor-state disputes. It will be demonstrated that a party was in dispute over the access to a database storing the personal data of consumers. As the digital economy continues to grow, and the private sector continues to have commercial investments in a country (foreign investment) governments have an obligation to ensure the investment framework remains consistent and certain. However, this may be difficult to achieve because of the shifting nature and priorities of technology investment. A good example is the push by governments around the world to attract and retain investment in technology in the green economy. This sector alone is linked directly to the Internet and there are data and cyber-related issues that are not fully understood.

Table 22.1 lists the commercial arbitration laws of nations that are members Commonwealth of Nations. It does not show any national laws pertaining to investor-state arbitration. Instead, the legislation for the enforcement of awards will be discussed elsewhere in the chapter.

The table indicates the importance of arbitration in the contemporary world. All members of the Commonwealth have arbitration laws. There is a strong degree of convergence with respect to the titles of the respective arbitration laws. The differences are minimal, in that some states have opted to use the titles of the uniform Arbitration Act. The reason that those states have taken this approach is that some countries in Africa have adopted a uniform, regional law. The notable standout is the Commercial Arbitration Act, although the title still contains the word 'arbitration'. Notably too, some laws have been adopted only recently, with Sierra Leone establishing its law in 2022. However, many countries have had well-established arbitration laws for over decades. A number were enacted post World War 2.

The arbitration process can be traced back to the 1500 s. Alan Redfern and Marcus Hunter note that France led the way in the development of national laws on arbitration. The authors explain that:

> In France, an edict of Francis II promulgated in August 1560 made arbitration compulsory for all merchants in disputes arising from their commercial activity. Later, this edict came to be ignored. During the French Revolution, arbitration came back into favour as 'the most reasonable device for the termination of disputes arising between citizens' and, in 1791, judges were abolished and replaced by 'public arbitrators'. However, this proved to be a step too far and in 1806 the French Code of Civil Procedure effectively turned arbitration into the first stage of a procedure that would lead to the judgment of a court.[30]

Yet France is not, and has never been, a member of the Commonwealth. Since its beginnings, many nation states around the world have seen the benefits of arbitration. It has been successful in achieving a level of legal harmonization to provide for the efficient and cost-effective resolution of disputes. A further development came about 100 years later when the UK adopted its first arbitration laws. In 1698, the Locke

---

[30] Alan Redfern, Marcus Hunter, *International Arbitration*, Oxford University Press 6th Edt, (2015), p. 5.

Table 22.1 Members of the Commonwealth Arbitration Laws as at December 2022

Africa and Europe	Cyber Law	Indo Pacific	Cyber Law	Caribbean and Americas	Cyber Law
Botswana	Arbitration Law[31]	Bangladesh	The Arbitration Act 2001[32]	Antigua and Barbuda	Arbitration Act 1975[33]
Cameroon	Uniform Act on Arbitration[34]	Brunei Darussalam	Arbitration Order 2009—Chapter 173 Arbitration[35] International Arbitration Order	Bahamas	Arbitration Act 2009[36]
Gabon	Uniform Act on Arbitration[37]	India	The Arbitration and Conciliation Act 1996[38]	Barbados	Arbitration (Foreign Arbitral Awards)—Arbitration 1958–23[39]

(continued)

31 Arbitration Law, https://africaarbitration.org/resources/law/Botswana%20Arbitration%20Law.pdf.

32 The Arbitration Act 2001, https://www.newyorkconvention.org/webcore/search?search=Bangladesh.

33 Arbitration Act 1975, https://www.newyorkconvention.org/webcore/search?search=Antigua+and+Barbuda.

34 Uniform Act on Arbitration 1999, https://www.newyorkconvention.org/national+arbitration+law+-+cameroon.

35 Arbitration Order 2009 - Chapter 173 Arbitration, https://www.newyorkconvention.org/national+arbitration+law+-+brunei+darussalam and International Arbitration Order 2009, https://www.agc.gov.bn/AGC%20Images/LAWS/BLUV/INTERNATIONAL%20ARBITRATION%20ORDER,%202009.pdf.

36 Arbitration Act 2009, https://www.newyorkconvention.org/webcore/search?search=Bahamas.

37 Uniform Arbitration Act 1999, https://www.newyorkconvention.org/national+arbitration+law+-+cameroon.

38 Arbitration and Conciliation Act 1996, https://www.indiacode.nic.in/bitstream/123456789/1978/1/AAA1996__26.pdf.

39 Arbitration (Foreign Arbitral Awards) - Arbitration 1958-23 http://barbadosparliament-laws.com/en/ShowPdf/110A.pdf and http://barbadosparliament-laws.com/en/ShowPdf/110.pdf.

Table 22.1 (continued)

Africa and Europe	Cyber Law	Indo Pacific	Cyber Law	Caribbean and Americas	Cyber Law
Gambia	Alternative Dispute Resolution Act 2006[40]	Malaysia	Arbitration act 2005[41]	Belize	Arbitration Act 2000[42]
Ghana	Alternative Dispute Resolution Act 2010[43]	Maldives	Arbitration Act 2013[44]	Canada	Commercial Arbitration Act 1985[45]
Kenya	Arbitration Act 2010[46]	Pakistan	Arbitration Act 1940[47]	Dominica	Arbitration Act 1988[48]

(continued)

[40] Alternative Dispute Resolution Act 2006, https://delosdr.org/wp-content/uploads/2018/06/Gambia-The-Alternative-Dispute-Resolution-2005.pdf

[41] Arbitration Act 2005, http://www.arbiter.com.sg/pdf/laws/Malaysia%20Arbitration%20Act%202005%20(Revised%202011).pdf.

[42] Arbitration Act 2000, https://www.international-arbitration-attorney.com/wp-content/uploads/2013/07/Belize-Arbitration-Law.pdf.

[43] Alternative Dispute Resolution Act 2010, https://lawsghana.com/post-1992-legislation/table-of-content/Acts%20of%20Parliament/ALTERNATIVE%20DISPUTE%20RESOLUTION%20ACT,%202010%20(ACT%20798)/28.

[44] Arbitration Act 2013, https://miac.gov.mv/media/documents/Arbitration%20Act.pdf.

[45] Commercial Arbitration Act 1985, https://laws-lois.justice.gc.ca/eng/acts/c-34.6/fulltext.html.

[46] Arbitration Act 2010, https://ncia.or.ke/wp-content/uploads/2021/02/ArbitrationAct4of1995_2.pdf.

[47] Arbitration Act 1940, https://www.ma-law.org.pk/pdflaw/Arbitration%20Act,%201940.pdf.

[48] Arbitration Act 1988, https://www.newyorkconvention.org/national+arbitration+law+-+dominica.

Table 22.1 (continued)

Africa and Europe	Cyber Law	Indo Pacific	Cyber Law	Caribbean and Americas	Cyber Law
Kingdom of Eswatini	Arbitration Act 1904[49]	Singapore	Arbitration Act 2001[50]	Grenada	Arbitration Act 1989[51]
Lesotho	Arbitration Act 1980[52]	Sri Lanka	Arbitration Act 1995[53]	Guyana	Arbitration Act 1916[54]
Malawi	Arbitration Act 1967[55]	Australia	International Arbitration Act 1974[56]	Jamaica	Arbitration Act 2017[57]

(continued)

[49] Arbitration Act 1904, https://osall.org.za/docs/2011/03/Swaziland-Arbitration-Act-24-of-1904.pdf and https://www.eswatinilii.org/na/judgment/high-court-eswatini/2020/33 Recent high court Case referred to the 1904 Act.

Kingdom of eSwatini, one of the few jurisdictions who still do not apply the New York Convention.

[50] Arbitration Act 2001, https://sso.agc.gov.sg/Act/AA2001.

[51] Arbitration Act 1989, https://laws.gov.gd/index.php?option=com_edocman&view=category&id=613&Itemid=181.

[52] Arbitration Act 1980, https://osall.org.za/docs/2011/03/Lesotho-Arbitration-Act-12-of-1980.pdf.

[53] Arbitration Act 1995, https://www.slnarbcentre.com/pdf/ARBITRATION-ACT.pdf

[54] Arbitration Act 1916, https://mola.gov.gy/sites/default/files/Cap%20703%20Arbitration%20Act.pdf.

[55] Arbitration Act 1967, https://malawilii.org/akn/mw/act/1967/26/eng%402014-12-31.

[56] International Arbitration Act 1974, https://www.legislation.gov.au/Details/C2018C00439.

[57] Arbitration Act 2017, https://japarliament.gov.jm/attachments/article/339/The%20Arbitration%20Act,%202017.pdf.

Table 22.1 (continued)

Africa and Europe	Cyber Law	Indo Pacific	Cyber Law	Caribbean and Americas	Cyber Law
Mauritius	International Arbitration Act 2008[58]	Fiji	Arbitration Act 1965[59] International Arbitration Act 2017	Saint Lucia	Arbitration Act 2001[60]
Mozambique	Law on Arbitration, Conciliation and Mediation Law no. 11/99[61]	Kiribati	Arbitration Act 1990[62]	Saint Kitts and Nevis	Arbitration Act 2002[63]
Namibia	Arbitration Act 1965[64]	Nauru	Limitation Act 2017[65] Contains Arbitration Provisions	Saint Vincent and The Grenadines	Arbitration Act 1952[66]

(continued)

[58] International Arbitration Act 2008, https://miac.mu/wp-content/uploads/2021/04/mauritian-international-arbitration-legislation-handbook-updated-2016-1.pdf.

[59] Arbitration Act 1965, https://www.laws.gov.fj/Acts/DisplayAct/2459 and International Arbitration Act 2017 https://www.fiji.gov.fj/getattachment/d9502667-6491-4592-85b2-eff97f245fed/Act-44---International-Arbitration-Act.aspx.

[60] Arbitration Act 2001, http://www.oas.org/es/sla/ddi/docs/Santa_Lucia_Arbitration_Act.pdf.

[61] Law on Arbitration, Conciliation and Mediation Law no. 11/99, https://www.cacm.org.mz/wp-content/uploads/2017/01/Arbitration-Law-11-99.pdf

[62] Arbitration Act 1990, http://www.paclii.org/ki/legis/num_act/aa1990137/

[63] Arbitration Act 2002, www.oas.org › sla › ddi › docs › Saint_Kitt…

[64] Arbitration act 1956, https://www.lac.org.na/laws/annoSTAT/Arbitration%20Act%2042%20of%201965.pdf.

[65] Limitation Act 2017, http://ronlaw.gov.nr/nauru_lpms/files/acts/665725b31f7ba398592d130b557ecb2d.pdf.

[66] Arbitration Act 1971, Laws of Saint Vincent and The Grenadines - New York Convention.

Table 22.1 (continued)

Africa and Europe	Cyber Law	Indo Pacific	Cyber Law	Caribbean and Americas	Cyber Law
Nigeria	Arbitration and Conciliation Act 1990[67]	New Zealand	Arbitration Act 1996[68]	Trinidad and Tobago	Arbitration Act 1939[69]
Rwanda	No. 005/2008 of 14/02/2008 Law on arbitration and conciliation in commercial matters[70]	Papua New Guinea	*Arbitration 1951*[71]		
Seychelles	Commercial Code Act 1977[72]	Samoa	Arbitration Act 1976[73]		
Sierra Leone	Arbitration Act 2022[74]	Solomon Islands	Arbitration Act 1996[75]		

(continued)

[67] Arbitration and Conciliation Act 1990, http://www.commonlii.org/ng/legis/num_act/aac244/ The Act was reformed in 2022.

[68] Arbitration act 1996, https://www.legislation.govt.nz/act/public/1996/0099/latest/DLM403277.html.

[69] Arbitration Act 1939, https://rgd.legalaffairs.gov.tt/laws2/alphabetical_list/lawspdfs/5.01.pdf.

[70] N° 005/2008 of 14/02/2008 Law on arbitration and conciliation in commercial matters, https://www.international-arbitration-attorney.com/wp-content/uploads/2013/07/Rwanda-Arbitration-Law.pdf

[71] *Arbitration Act 1951*, http://www.paclii.org/pg/legis/consol_act/aa1951137.pdf *Also see*, https://www.allens.com.au/insights-news/insights/2020/02/png-proposes-a-new-regime-for-arbitration/

[72] Commercial Code Act 1977, https://www.acerislaw.com/wp-content/uploads/2021/03/Seychelles-Arbitration-Law.pdf.

[73] Arbitration Act 1976, https://www.regulator.gov.ws/images/2017_CONSOLIDATION_LAWS/A/Arbitration-Act-1976.pdf.

[74] Arbitration Act 2022, https://www.parliament.gov.sl/uploads/acts/THE%20ARBITRATION%20ACT,%202022.pdf.

[75] Arbitration Act 1996,

Table 22.1 (continued)

Africa and Europe	Cyber Law	Indo Pacific	Cyber Law	Caribbean and Americas	Cyber Law
South Africa	Arbitration Act 1965[76]	Tonga	International Arbitration 2020[77]		
Togo	*Uniform Arbitration Act*[78]				
Uganda	*Arbitration and Conciliation Act 2000*[79]				
United Republic of Tanzania	*Arbitration Act 2020*[80]				
Zambia	Arbitration Act[81]				
Cyprus	Arbitration Law 1944[82]				
Malta	Arbitration Act 1998[83]				
United Kingdom	Arbitration Act 1996[84]				

[76] Arbitration Act 1965, https://www.gov.za/documents/arbitration-act-14-apr-1965-0000.

[77] International Arbitration Act 2020, https://ago.gov.to/cms/images/LEGISLATION/PRINCIPAL/2020/2020-0112/InternationalArbitrationAct2020_1.pdf.

[78] *Unifor Arbitration Act,* https://www.acerislaw.com/ohada-arbitration-act/

[79] *Arbitration and Conciliation Act 2000,* https://arbitrationlaw.com/sites/default/files/free_pdfs/Uganda%20Arbitration%20and%20Conciliation%20Act.pdf.

[80] *Arbitration Act 2020,* https://www.osg.go.tz/uploads/publications/sw1599657355-Act%20No.%202%20of%202020%20THE%20ARBITRATION%20ACT,%202020%20Final%20chapa.pdf.

[81] Arbitration Act, https://www.parliament.gov.zm/sites/default/files/documents/acts/Arbitration%20Act.pdf.

[82] Arbitration Law 1944, http://www.cylaw.org/nomoi/arith/1944_1_001.pdf and https://thelawreviews.co.uk/title/the-international-arbitration-review/cyprus.

[83] Arbitration Act 1998, https://legislation.mt/eli/cap/387/eng/pdf.

[84] Arbitration Act 1996, https://www.legislation.gov.uk/ukpga/1996/23/contents.

Act had been adopted by the Parliament, and more laws were established in 1833.[85] Arguably, when noting when the arbitration laws were established by the current members of the Commonwealth, most were developed following the two world wars. Redfern and Hunter make the case that in the contemporary world, arbitration is significantly more complex. They stated:

> The modern arbitral process has lost its early simplicity. It has become more complex, more legalistic, more institutionalised, and more expensive. Yet, it's essential features have not changed: the original element remains of two or more parties, faced with a dispute that they cannot resolve for themselves, agreeing that one or more private individuals will resolve it for them by arbitration, and that, if this arbitration runs its full course (that is, if the dispute is not settled in the course of the proceedings), it will not be resolved by a negotiated settlement or by mediation, or by some other form of compromise, but by a decision that is binding on the parties. That decision will be made by an arbitral tribunal, composed of one or more arbitrators, whose task is to consider the case put forward by each party and to decide the dispute.[86]

Notwithstanding the above, and in addition to the national laws, the past 100 years have seen the the development of international law to facilitate the arbitration of disputes. These include:

- The Geneva Protocol on Arbitration Clauses of 1923[87];
- The Geneva Convention 1927[88];
- The Convention on the Recognition and Enforcement of Foreign Arbitral Awards[89];
- The New York Convention 1958[90];
- The ICSID Convention on the Settlement of Investment Disputes between States and Nationals of Other States[91];
- UNCITRAL Arbitration Rule 1976—revised 2010[92]; and

---

[85] Francis Boorman, *Developments in the history of Arbitration: A past for the present?*, Amicus Curiae, Vol 4, No 1, (2022) p. 111.

[86] Alan Redfern, Marcus Hunter, *International Arbitration*, Oxford University Press 6th Ed.,, (2015), para, 1.93, at https://law.fudan.edu.cn/_upload/article/files/77/16/8ff0afe240e99a627fc2b2dfcac5/b4b6dd2d-19a1-4fc2-8690-3857d32b5cd7.pdf.

[87] Alan Redfern, Marcus Hunter, *International Arbitration*, Oxford University Press 6th Ed., (2015), p. 6, The Geneva Protocol on Arbitration Clauses of 1923 was drawn up on the initiative of the ICC and under the auspices of the League of Nations, and signed at Geneva on 24 September 1923.

[88] This Convention for the Execution of Foreign Arbitral Awards followed on from the Geneva Protocol and was signed at Geneva on 26 September 1927: League of Nations Treaty Series (1929–30), Vol. XCII, p. 302.

[89] Ibid, p. 6, The Convention on the Recognition and Enforcement of Foreign Arbitral Awards, signed in New York on 10 June 1958: United Nations Treaty Series (1959), Vol. 330, p. 38, No. 4739. The text of the Convention is set out in Appendix B.

[90] Ibid, The Convention on the Recognition and Enforcement of Foreign Arbitral Awards, signed in New York on 10 June 1958: United Nations Treaty Series (1959), Vol. 330, p. 38, No. 4739.

[91] Ibid, The ICSID Convention on the Settlement of Investment Disputes between States and Nationals of Other States, signed in Washington DC on 18 March 1965: United Nations Treaty Series (1966), Vol. 575, p. 160, No. 8359.

[92] Ibid, Adopted by Resolution 31/98 of the General Assembly of the United Nations on 15 December 1976, these Rules are set out in Appendix D. At its Thirty-ninth Session (New York,

- UNCITRAL Model Law 1985 and respective revisions 2006.[93]

The following section will compare the respective laws in relation to the key themes which include:

- Key definitions of terms;
- UNCITRAL Arbitration Model Law;
- Appointment of Arbitrator, Seat, Arbitration Agreement;
- Experts;
- New York Convention; and
- International Centre for Settlement of Investment Disputes—Investor State Arbitration.

For the purpose of comparison, a general overview will be given of the concepts listed above, which are the key features of arbitration. It is noted that a more comprehensive comparative study is needed to fully understand the divergent approaches taken by Commonwealth member states in regard to arbitration laws. On that basis, it has been decided that the default in the legislation is that where it is more descriptive, such as the UK versus Australia, Australia has by and large replicated the UNCITRAL Arbitration Model Law under schedule 1. On the other hand, the UK which has not adopted the UNCITRAL Arbitration Model Law has replicated many of the provisions contained in the Arbitration Act. This Part will also build on the work already undertaken by the Commonwealth[94] as part of the above report identifying the national arbitration laws. This Part will compare the national laws and identify the relevant provisions of the UNCITRAL Model Law on International Commercial Arbitration 1985 (with amendments as adopted in 2006). It will draw on key judicial decisions in order to better understand the operation and application of the UNCITRAL Model Law. In addition, the Uniform Arbitration Act (UAA)[95] has emerged as a reference source across Africa. If Togo has been nominated as the seat of arbitration, for example, example, the UAA could apply. Thus, practitioners will need to confirm the UAA's applicability or otherwise. The next chapter examines how each

17–28 June 2002), UNCITRAL agreed that revision of the UNCITRAL Rules should be given priority, and that such revision 'should not alter the structure of the text, its spirit, its drafting style, and should respect the flexibility of the text rather than add to its complexity': see UNCITRAL, *Report of Working Group II (Arbitration and Conciliation) on the Work of its Forty-ninth Session*, Vienna, 15–19 September 2008, Doc. No. A/CN.9/665, para. 3.

[93] Ibid, The Model Law on International Commercial Arbitration, adopted by the United Nations Commission on International Trade Law on 21 June 1985.

[94] The Commonwealth, A Study of International Commercial Arbitration in the Commonwealth, 2020, see pages 151 to 632.

[95] Uniform Arbitration Act, https://www.international-arbitration-attorney.com/ohada-arbitration-act/ Applicable for arbitrations with their seat in Benin, Burkina Faso, Cameroon, Central African Republic, Comoros, the Democratic Republic of Congo (ex-Zaire), the Ivory Coast, Gabon, Guinea, Guinea-Bissau, Equatorial Guinea, Mali, Niger, the Republic of the Congo (Congo-Brazzaville), Senegal, Chad and Togo.

state has defined key terms. Additionally, the ensuing chapter has taken a different approach that has been developed for those that are new to the technology sector, and small and mediums sized business that have not dealt with dispute resolution processes through arbitration. The section in relation to the seat of arbitration and a comparison of arbitration agreements has been restricted to only a small number of member countries. Similarly, in the final chapters regarding the use of experts and the enforcement of awards only a small number of member states are examined.

Chapter 23
Key Definitions of Terms

23.1 Introduction

While not often considered when examining the laws of arbitration, the definition of terms in the national laws can vary at times. For instance, simple terms such as 'arbitration' and 'arbitration agreement' could constitute something different. Hence, this chapter will compare the definitions of:

- Arbitration—International Commercial Arbitration;
- Arbitration Agreement;
- Foreign arbitral award;
- Arbitration Award.

In practice, the different approaches are unlikely to change the way an arbitration proceeding will be conducted, or its outcome. If a country is silent regarding an aforementioned concept, this indicates that the national law of that country does not provide a definition for that concept. Where appropriate, the actual definition has been replicated in this chapter to enable a detailed comparative analysis of the differences.

The purpose of this chapter is to highlight, how in a currently fragmented world, having a high level of certainty that is underscored by national laws is paramount to the future of the digital economy. It is argued that generally, beginning with the definition of terms contained in the national laws, is a good starting point for the building of stronger legal convergence.

R. Walters, *Cybersecurity and Data Laws of the Commonwealth*,
https://doi.org/10.1007/978-981-99-3935-0_23

Antigua and Barbuda have taken a minimalist approach. Section 37 states that an award shall not be deemed final if any proceedings for the purpose of contesting the validity of the award are pending in the country in which it was made.[1] **Australia** according to section 3, an *arbitral award* has the same meaning as in the Convention. An *arbitration agreement* is an agreement in writing of the kind referred to in sub-article 1 of Article II of the Convention.[2] The Convention referred to here is the Convention on the Recognition and Enforcement of Foreign Arbitral Awards adopted in 1958 by the United Nations Conference on International Commercial Arbitration at its twenty-fourth meeting, a copy of the English text of which is set out in Schedule 1. Under the UNCITRAL Model law,[3] the definitions are somewhat limited to Article 2 where 'arbitration' means any arbitration whether or not it is administered by a permanent arbitral institution, and 'arbitral tribunal' is a sole arbitrator or a panel of arbitrators.

Unlike Australia, **Botswana** defines only arbitration and arbitrator, meaning, respectively, any proceedings held pursuant to a submission, and any person acting as such pursuant to a submission.[4] In **Bangladesh** the concept of arbitration constitutes any arbitration whether or not administered by a permanent institution. An arbitration agreement means an agreement by the parties to submit to arbitration all or certain disputes which have arisen or which may arise between them in respect of a defined legal relationship, whether contractual or not. In addition to the general definition of arbitration, Bangladesh has defined 'international commercial arbitration' to mean an arbitration relating to disputes arising out of legal 'relationships, whether contractual or not, considered as commercial under the law in force in Bangladesh and where at least one of the parties is an individual who is a national of or habitually resident in, any country other than Bangladesh; or a body corporate which is incorporated in any country other than Bangladesh; or a company or an association or a body of individuals whose central management and control is exercised in any country other than Bangladesh, or the Government of a foreign country. Moreover, arbitral award means a decision made by the arbitral tribunal on the issue in dispute'.[5]

[1] Arbitration Act 1975, https://www.newyorkconvention.org/webcore/search?search=Antigua+and+Barbuda section 37.

[2] International Arbitration Act 1974, https://www.legislation.gov.au/Details/C2018C00439.

[3] UNCITRAL Model Law on International Commercial Arbitration (As adopted by the United Nations Commission on International Trade Law on 21 June 1985, and as amended by the United Nations Commission on International Trade Law on 7 July 2006).

[4] Arbitration Law, https://africaarbitration.org/resources/law/Botswana%20Arbitration%20Law.pdf, section 2.

[5] The Arbitration Act 2001, https://www.newyorkconvention.org/webcore/search?search=Bangla desh, section 2.

Most notably, **Cameroon**[6] **Gabon, Togo**[7] **and Tonga**[8] have adopted the Uniform Act on Arbitration and this legislation does not define any terms. **Gambia,**[9] **Belize,**[10] **Maldives,**[11] **Canada,**[12] **Kingdom of Eswatini**[13] **Guyana**[14] **Fiji**[15] **Mozambique,**[16] **Nigeria,**[17] **Seychelles,**[18] **Papua New Guinea,**[19] **Sierra Leone,**[20] **Solomon Islands,**[21] **Zambia**[22] do not define the terms discussed in this chapter. Even though these states do not define specific concepts within their national laws, they still provide for arbitration proceedings. The ensuing question is whether the respective laws should be changed to address this possible shortcoming? For the purposes of legal convergence and harmonisation it would be beneficial for the terms to be defined in line with the definitions adopted by the majority of nations. However, in practice, it may not be an issue. This is particularly so for those states that have adopted the UNCITRAL Model Law on Arbitration.

---

[6] Uniform Act on Arbitration 1999, https://www.newyorkconvention.org/national+arbitration+law+-+cameroon.

[7] *Uniform Arbitration Act,* https://www.acerislaw.com/ohada-arbitration-act/.

[8] International Arbitration Act 2020, https://ago.gov.to/cms/images/LEGISLATION/PRINCIPAL/2020/2020-0112/InternationalArbitrationAct2020_1.pdf.

[9] Alternative Dispute Resolution Act 2006, https://delosdr.org/wp-content/uploads/2018/06/Gambia-The-Alternative-Dispute-Resolution-2005.pdf.

[10] Arbitration Act 2000, https://www.international-arbitration-attorney.com/wp-content/uploads/2013/07/Belize-Arbitration-Law.pdf.

[11] Arbitration Act 2013, https://miac.gov.mv/media/documents/Arbitration%20Act.pdf.

[12] Commercial Arbitration Act 1985, https://laws-lois.justice.gc.ca/eng/acts/c-34.6/fulltext.html.

[13] Arbitration Act 1904, https://osall.org.za/docs/2011/03/Swaziland-Arbitration-Act-24-of-1904.pdf and https://www.eswatinilii.org/na/judgment/high-court-eswatini/2020/33 Recent high court Case referred to the 1904 Act.

Kingdom of eSwatini, one of the few jurisdictions who still do not apply the New York Convention.

[14] Arbitration Act 1916, https://mola.gov.gy/sites/default/files/Cap%20703%20Arbitration%20Act.pdf.

[15] Arbitration Act 1965, https://www.laws.gov.fj/Acts/DisplayAct/2459 and International Arbitration Act 2017 https://www.fiji.gov.fj/getattachment/d9502667-6491-4592-85b2-eff97f245fed/Act-44---International-Arbitration-Act.aspx.

[16] Law on Arbitration, Conciliation and Mediation Law no. 11/99, https://www.cacm.org.mz/wp-content/uploads/2017/01/Arbitration-Law-11-99.pdf.

[17] Arbitration and Conciliation Act 1990, http://www.commonlii.org/ng/legis/num_act/aac244/ The Act was reformed in 2022.

[18] Commercial Code Act 1977, https://www.acerislaw.com/wp-content/uploads/2021/03/Seychelles-Arbitration-Law.pdf.

[19] *Arbitration Act 1951,* http://www.paclii.org/pg/legis/consol_act/aa1951137.pdf *Also see,* https://www.allens.com.au/insights-news/insights/2020/02/png-proposes-a-new-regime-for-arbitration/

[20] Arbitration Act 2022, https://www.parliament.gov.sl/uploads/acts/THE%20ARBITRATION%20ACT,%202022.pdf.

[21] Arbitration Act 1996, http://webcache.googleusercontent.com/search?q=cache:rRc_9Ziwe5sJ:www.paclii.org/sb/legis/consol_act/aa137.rtf&cd=1&hl=en&ct=clnk&gl=sg&client=safari.

[22] Arbitration Act, https://www.parliament.gov.zm/sites/default/files/documents/acts/Arbitration%20Act.pdf.

Samoa[23] defines an arbitrator only as a referee or valuer. However, in 2017, Fiji also enacted the International Arbitration Act which, in section 2, defines 'arbitral tribunal' as a sole arbitrator, a panel of arbitrators or an emergency arbitrator appointed pursuant to the rules of arbitration agreed to or adopted by the parties. In addition, arbitration means any arbitration whether or not administered by a permanent arbitration agreement, as defined under section 11.

The importance of an arbitration agreement is based on the common approach to arbitration today. Moreover, an arbitration agreement is central to establishing the process for, and the conduct of arbitration, between the parties. In the **Bahamas**, an arbitration agreement is an agreement by the parties to submit to arbitration all or certain disputes that have arisen or which may arise between them in respect of a defined legal relationship whether contractual or not and may be in the form of an arbitration clause in a contract or in the form of a separate agreement. On the other hand, 'arbitrator' unless the context otherwise requires, includes an umpire.[24] The umpire could be an individual or a panel of arbitrators.

The formal and functional arrangements of an arbitration agreement in **Brunei Darussalam**[25] have been defined to mean an agreement in writing (including an agreement contained in an exchange of letters, facsimiles or telegrams) to submit to arbitration present or future differences capable of settlement by arbitration whether an arbitrator is named therein or not. In addition, the International Arbitration Order 2009 defines an arbitration agreement as a written agreement referred to in Article 7 of the Model Law and includes an agreement deemed or constituted under subsections (3) or (4). It also defines an award as a decision of the arbitral tribunal on the substance of the dispute and includes any interim, interlocutory or partial award, but excludes any orders or directions made under section 15. Section 2 also refers to an arbitral tribunal as a sole arbitrator, a panel of arbitrators or a permanent arbitral institution. In addition to the above, **Barbados**[26] has defined the following terms: 'arbitral tribunal' or' tribunal' can mean a sole arbitrator or a panel of arbitrators. 'Arbitration' is any arbitration whether or not administered by a permanent arbitral institution.[27] In addition, an 'arbitration·agreement' is an agreement by parties to submit to arbitration all or certain disputes which have arisen or may arise between them in respect of a defined legal relationship, whether contractual or not.

---

[23] Arbitration Act 1976, https://www.regulator.gov.ws/images/2017_CONSOLIDATION_LAWS/A/Arbitration-Act-1976.pdf.

[24] Arbitration Act 2009, https://www.newyorkconvention.org/webcore/search?search=Bahamas section 2.

[25] Arbitration Order 2009 - Chapter 173 Arbitration, https://www.newyorkconvention.org/national+arbitration+law+-+brunei+darussalam.

[26] Arbitration (Foreign Arbitral Awards) - Arbitration 1958-23 http://barbadosparliament-laws.com/en/ShowPdf/110A.pdf and http://barbadosparliament-laws.com/en/ShowPdf/110.pdf 2007, https://www.international-arbitration-attorney.com/wp-content/uploads/2017/02/Barbados-Arbitration-Law.pdf.

[27] Ibid.

In Central Asia, **India** has determined that an 'arbitration agreement' is an agreement referred to in section 7 which constitutes an agreement by the parties to submit to arbitration all or certain disputes which have arisen or which may arise between them in respect of a defined legal relationship, whether contractual or not. An arbitral award includes an interim award. In addition, 'international commercial arbitration' means an arbitration relating to disputes arising out of legal relationships, whether contractual or not, considered as commercial under the law in force in India and where at least one of the parties is (*i*) an individual who is a national of, or habitually resident in, any country other than India; or (*ii*) a body corporate which is incorporated in any country other than India; or (*iii*) an association or a body of individuals whose central management and control is exercised in any country other than India; or (*iv*) the Government of a foreign country.[28]

In the South East Asian nation of **Malaysia** an 'award' means a decision of the arbitral tribunal on the substance of the dispute and includes any final, interim or partial award and any award on costs or interest but does not include interlocutory orders. On the other hand, 'arbitration agreement' is defined in section 9 as an agreement by the parties to submit to arbitration all or certain disputes which have arisen or which may arise between them in respect of a defined legal relationship, whether contractual or not. International arbitration means an arbitration where (a) one of the parties to an arbitration agreement, at the time of the conclusion of that agreement, has its place of business in any State other than Malaysia; (b) one of the following is situated in any State other than Malaysia in which the parties have their places of business: (i) the seat of arbitration if determined in, or pursuant to, the arbitration agreement; (ii) any place where a substantial part of the obligations of any commercial or other relationship is to be performed or the place with which the subject matter of the dispute is most closely connected; or (c) the parties have expressly agreed that the subject matter of the arbitration agreement relates to more than one State.[29]

On the continent of Africa, **Ghana,** arbitration is the voluntary submission of a dispute to one or more impartial persons for a final and binding determination.[30] **Kenya** defines 'arbitration' as any arbitration whether or not administered by a permanent arbitral institution. An arbitration agreement is an agreement by the parties to submit to arbitration all or certain disputes which have arisen or which may arise between them in respect of a defined legal relationship, whether contractual or not. An 'arbitral award' constitutes any award of an arbitral tribunal and includes an interim arbitral award.[31]

---

[28] Arbitration and Conciliation Act 1996, https://www.indiacode.nic.in/bitstream/123456789/1978/1/AAA1996__26.pdf Sections 2 & 7.

[29] Arbitration Act 2005, http://www.arbiter.com.sg/pdf/laws/Malaysia%20Arbitration%20Act%202005%20(Revised%202011).pdf section 2.

[30] Alternative Dispute Resolution Act 2010, https://lawsghana.com/post-1992-legislation/table-of-content/Acts%20of%20Parliament/ALTERNATIVE%20DISPUTE%20RESOLUTION%20ACT,%202010%20(ACT%20798)/28 section 135.

[31] Arbitration Act 2010, https://ncia.or.ke/wp-content/uploads/2021/02/ArbitrationAct4of1995_2.pdf.

India's neighbour, **Pakistan,** in section 2 defines an 'arbitration agreement' as a written agreement to submit present or future differences to arbitration, whether an arbitrator is named therein or not. Additionally, an award is an arbitration award.[32] On the other hand, in **Dominica**[33] according to section 2, only 'an arbitration agreement' has been defined to mean an agreement in writing including an agreement contained in exchange of letters or telegrams, to submit to arbitration present or future differences capable of settlement by arbitration.

In **Singapore**[34] 'arbitral tribunal' means a sole arbitrator or a panel of arbitrators or an arbitral institution, and includes an emergency arbitrator appointed pursuant to the rules of arbitration agreed to or adopted by the parties including the rules of arbitration of an institution or organisation. Arbitration agreement is self-explanatory, and is mentioned in section 4 (an expanded and comprehensive definition). 'Award' is a decision of the arbitral tribunal on the substance of the dispute and includes any interim, interlocutory or partial award but excludes any order or direction made under section 28, which outline the powers of a tribunal. Some states have chosen to provide a more comprehensive meaning of particular terms within the provisions of their legislation. It is argued that Singapore is a country that does this more so than others when defining terms related to arbitration. In **Grenada,**[35] section 2 provides that an award is a written arbitration agreement to submit present or future differences to arbitration whether or not an arbitrator is named therein. This is a much narrower definition.

On the one hand, in **Lesotho**, an 'arbitration agreement' is a written agreement providing for the reference to arbitration of any existing dispute or any future dispute relating to a matter specified in the agreement whether an arbitrator is name or designated therein or not. An 'arbitration tribunal' constitutes arbitrator, arbitrators or umpire acting as such under an arbitration agreement. While 'an award' is an interim award.[36]

On the other hand, in **Sri Lanka**[37] in section 50 defines 'arbitration' as any arbitration whether or not administered by a permanent arbitral institution. An 'arbitration agreement' is an agreement by the parties to submit to arbitration all or certain disputes which have arisen or which may arise between them in respect of a defined legal relationship, whether contractual or not. On the other hand, 'arbitral tribunal' is a panel of one or more arbitrators, while 'an award is a decision of the arbitral tribunal on the substance of the dispute.

---

[32] Arbitration Act 1940, https://www.ma-law.org.pk/pdflaw/Arbitration%20Act,%201940.pdf.

[33] Arbitration Act 1988, https://www.newyorkconvention.org/national+arbitration+law+-+dominica.

[34] Arbitration Act 2001, https://sso.agc.gov.sg/Act/AA2001.

[35] Arbitration Act 1989, https://laws.gov.gd/index.php?option=com_edocman&view=category&id=613&Itemid=181.

[36] Arbitration Act 1980, https://osall.org.za/docs/2011/03/Lesotho-Arbitration-Act-12-of-1980.pdf.

[37] Arbitration Act 1995, https://www.slnarbcentre.com/pdf/ARBITRATION-ACT.pdf or https://webcache.googleusercontent.com/search?q=cache:CBtAZfCjJG0J:https://www.slnarbcentre.com/pdf/ARBITRATION-ACT.pdf&cd=3&hl=en&ct=clnk&gl=sg&client=safari.

Section 2 of the **Malawi** law is limited and only defines 'arbitration agreement' means a written agreement to submit present or future differences to arbitration whether an arbitrator is named therein or not.[38]

Yet, for **Jamaica,** an 'arbitral tribunal' means a sole arbitrator or panel or a panel of arbitrator, arbitration is arbitration whether or not administered by a permanent arbitral institution, and 'arbitration agreement' is a an agreement by the parties to submit to arbitration all or certain disputes which have arisen or which may arise between them in respect of a defined legal relationship whether contractual or not. 'Arbitrator' includes umpire. 'Award' is the decision of the arbitral tribunal on the substance of the disputes and includes any interim interlocutory or partial award.[39]

On the other side, Mauritius[40] has taken a wider view, whereby 'arbitration' means any arbitration, whether or not administered by a permanent arbitral institution. 'Arbitration agreement' means an agreement by the parties to submit to arbitration all or certain disputes which have arisen or may arise between them in respect of a defined legal relationship, whether contractual or not. 'Arbitral tribunal' constitutes a sole arbitrator or a panel of arbitrators. On the other hand, international arbitration is an arbitration where (a) the parties to the arbitration agreement have, at the time of the conclusion of that agreement, their place of business in different States; (b) one of the following places is situated outside the State in which the parties have their place of business (i) the juridical seat of the arbitration, if determined in, or pursuant to, the arbitration agreement; any place where a substantial part of the obligations of the commercial relationship is to be performed or the place with which the subject matter of the dispute is most closely connected; (c) the parties have expressly agreed that the subject matter of the arbitration agreement relates to more than one State or that this Act is to apply to their arbitration; or (d) the arbitration arises under an arbitration clause included in the constitution of a GBL company pursuant to section 3D.

Moreover, Saint Lucia,[41] by taking a narrow approach, only defines an 'arbitration agreement' to mean a written agreement to submit present or future differences to arbitration, whether an arbitrator is named therein or not. In **Kiribati,**[42] section 2 provides that an 'arbitration agreement' constitutes a written agreement to submit present or future differences to arbitration, whether an arbitrator is named therewith or not. Most noteworthy is that **St Kitts and Nevis** have not developed their own laws, but have applied the UK Arbitration Act.[43] There is no better example of full legal harmonisation by adopting another state's national laws in full.

---

[38] Arbitration Act 1967, https://malawilii.org/akn/mw/act/1967/26/eng%402014-12-31.

[39] Arbitration Act 2017, https://japarliament.gov.jm/attachments/article/339/The%20Arbitration%20Act,%202017.pdf.

[40] International Arbitration Act 2008, https://miac.mu/wp-content/uploads/2021/04/mauritian-international-arbitration-legislation-handbook-updated-2016-1.pdf.

[41] Arbitration Act 2001, http://www.oas.org/es/sla/ddi/docs/Santa_Lucia_Arbitration_Act.pdf.

[42] Arbitration Act 1990, http://www.paclii.org/ki/legis/num_act/aa1990137/.

[43] Arbitration Act 2002, www.oas.org › sla › ddi › docs › Saint_Kitt…

In **Namibia,**[44] section 1 provides that an arbitration agreement is similar to most of the other states compared, whereby it means a written agreement providing for the reference to arbitration of any existing dispute or any future dispute relating to a matter specified in the agreement, whether an arbitrator is named or designated therein or not. Further, an arbitration tribunal is the arbitrator, arbitrators or umpire acting as such under an arbitration agreement. Lastly, an award includes an interim award. In the Pacific country of **Nauru**[45] only section 3 defines an 'arbitral award' as the resolution or determination by an arbitrator of a difference or matter referred to arbitration under an arbitration provision, and 'award' is a decision of an Arbitration, Mediation or Tribunal, other than a court.

St Vincent and The Grenadines[46] has adopted a narrow approach, and under section 2 there is only the definition of an 'arbitration agreement', which is a written agreement to submit present and future differences to arbitration, whether an arbitrator is named therein or not.

New Zealand,[47] Australia's neighbour, in section 2 defines an 'a*rbitral tribunal'* as a sole arbitrator, a panel of arbitrators, or an arbitral institution; and includes any emergency arbitrator appointed under the arbitration agreement that the parties have entered into; or the arbitration rules of any institution or organisation that the parties have adopted. '*Arbitration'* means any arbitration whether or not administered by a permanent arbitral institution. '*Arbitration agreement'* means an agreement by the parties to submit to arbitration all or certain disputes which have arisen or which may arise between them in respect of a defined legal relationship, whether contractual or not. While an 'a*ward'* means a decision of the arbitral tribunal on the substance of the dispute and includes any interim, interlocutory or partial award.

Trinidad and Tobago[48] is another state that has taken a minimalist approach and only defines 'arbitration agreement' to mean a written agreement to submit present or future differences to arbitration, whether an arbitrator is named therein or not. A number of other states that have adopted this approach. Similarly, where states have included the definition of an arbitration agreement in their list of definitions, a similar approach has been applied. The question arises, is this an issue for parties? Practically, it would make very little difference, and the definition achieves the same final result that an arbitration agreement is in wirrten form. A further accentuating question is whether the written arbitration agreement is to be signed. This will depend on whether the state has adopted the UNCITRAL Model Law.

[44] Arbitration act 1956, https://www.lac.org.na/laws/annoSTAT/Arbitration%20Act%2042%20of%201965.pdf.

[45] Limitation Act 2017, http://ronlaw.gov.nr/nauru_lpms/files/acts/665725b31f7ba398592d130b557ecb2d.pdf.

[46] Arbitration Act 1971, laws of saint vincent and the grenadines - New York Convention.

[47] Arbitration Act 1996, https://www.legislation.govt.nz/act/public/1996/0099/latest/DLM403277.html.

[48] Arbitration Act 1939, https://rgd.legalaffairs.gov.tt/laws2/alphabetical_list/lawspdfs/5.01.pdf.

In the African nation of **Rwanda**,[49] according to Article 3, 'arbitration' is the procedure applied by parties to the dispute requesting an arbitrator or a jury of arbitrators to settle a legal, contractual dispute or another related issue. Further, an arbitration or a conciliation is international if (a) the parties to an arbitration or a conciliation agreement have, at the time of the conclusion of that agreement, their places of business in different States, of which one shall include the Republic of Rwanda; (b) one of the following places is situated outside the State in which the parties have their places of business the place of arbitration or conciliation if determined in, or pursuant to, the arbitration or conciliation agreement; any place where a substantial part of the obligations of the commercial relationship is to be performed; the place with which the subject-matter of the dispute is most closely connected, the parties have expressly agreed that the subject-matter of the arbitration or conciliation agreement relates to more than one country.

Likewise, **South Africa**[50] in taking a similar approach to its African counterparts, has defined 'arbitration agreement' as a written agreement providing for the reference to arbitration of any existing dispute or any future dispute relating to a matter specified in the agreement, whether an arbitrator is named or designated therein or not. Additionally, 'arbitration tribunal' means the arbitrator, arbitrators or umpire acting as such under an arbitration agreement. While an 'award' includes an interim award.

On the other side, for **Uganda**,[51] and similar to most of the other states compared, in section 2, 'arbitration', 'arbitration agreement', 'arbitral award' and 'arbitral tribunal' have been defined thus:

- arbitration means any arbitration whether or not administered by a domestic or international institution where there is an arbitration agreement;
- arbitration agreement means an agreement by the parties to submit to arbitration all or certain disputes which have arisen or which may arise between them in respect of a defined legal relationship, whether contractual or not;
- arbitral award means any award of an arbitral tribunal and includes an interim arbitral award; and
- arbitral tribunal is a sole arbitrator or a panel of arbitrators, and includes an umpire.[52]

Tanzania,[53] in section 3, goes into some detail more so than the majority of states being examined. First, 'arbitration' is defined as a process by which parties

49 N° 005/2008 of 14/02/2008 Law on arbitration and conciliation in commercial matters, https://www.international-arbitration-attorney.com/wp-content/uploads/2013/07/Rwanda-Arbitration-Law.pdf.

50 Arbitration Act 1965, https://www.gov.za/documents/arbitration-act-14-apr-1965-0000 section 1.

51 *Arbitration and Conciliation Act 2000*, https://arbitrationlaw.com/sites/default/files/free_pdfs/Uganda%20Arbitration%20and%20Conciliation%20Act.pdf.

52 Ibid.

53 *Arbitration Act 2020*, https://www.osg.go.tz/uploads/publications/sw1599657355-Act%20No.%202%20of%202020%20THE%20ARBITRATION%20ACT,%202020%20Final%20chapa.pdf.

submit a dispute to the decision of a neutral person or persons appointed by mutual consent or in accordance with the provisions of this Act. Second, 'arbitrator' means a person who handles arbitration disputes in the manner provided under this Act. Third, 'arbitration agreement' constitutes an agreement by the parties to submit to arbitration all or certain disputes which have arisen or which may arise between them in respect of a defined legal relationship, whether contractual or not. Fourth, 'arbitral award' is a decision of the arbitral tribunal on the substance of a dispute, and includes any interim or interlocutory. Fifth, arbitral tribunal means a sole arbitrator or a panel of arbitrators. Noteworthy too, is the definition of 'international arbitration' which is an arbitration relating to disputes arising out of legal relationships, whether contractual or not, considered as commercial under the law in force in the United Republic and where at least one of the parties is (a) an individual who is a national of, or habitually resident in, any country other than the United Republic; (b) a body corporate which is incorporated in any country other than the United Republic; (c) an association or a body of individuals whose central management and control is exercised in any country other than the United Republic; or (d) the Government of a foreign country.

This and the ensuing chapters do not cover the EU laws applying to arbitration. Instead, the national laws of **Cyprus and Malta** will be examined. Cyprus[54] only defines an 'arbitration agreement' as a written agreement to submit present or future differences to arbitration whether the arbitrator is named therein or not. The International Commercial Arbitration Act 2009, defines arbitral tribunal to be a sole arbitrator or a panel of arbitrators. However, section 2 describes what constitutes international commercial arbitration. On the other hand, in Malta,[55] 'arbitral tribunal' means a sole arbitrator or a number of arbitrators, and an arbitration agreement means an agreement as defined in the Model Law. Finally, the **United Kingdom**[56] under section 82 defines 'arbitrator', unless the context otherwise requires, as an umpire. Section 6 provides that an 'arbitration agreement' is an agreement to submit to arbitration present or future disputes (whether they are contractual or not). This is the same as most other states. The notable difference is the use of brackets to expound on the meaning.

There is a significant divergence in approach to defining the specific terms within nation laws of Arbitration—International Commercial Arbitration; Arbitration Agreement; Foreign arbitral award or Arbitration Award. However, this divergence is probably not crucial to the application of arbitration in resolving disputes within the digital economy. The above is a demonstration of how a much wider and more in depth research is needed to highlight the gaps in the national laws. In making

[54] Arbitration Law 1944, http://www.cylaw.org/nomoi/arith/1944_1_001.pdf and https://thelawreviews.co.uk/title/the-international-arbitration-review/cyprus and Cyprus International Commercial Arbitration Law 101/1987.

https://arbitrationlaw.com/sites/default/files/free_pdfs/Cyprus%20ICAL.pdf

[55] Arbitration Act 1998, https://legislation.mt/eli/cap/387/eng/pdf.

[56] Arbitration Act 1996, https://www.legislation.gov.uk/ukpga/1996/23/contents.

the case for more streamlined harmonised approach to the national laws compared, will make it easier for practitioners and parties to understand the law.

23.2 Conclusion

This chapter has provided a preliminary overview of the differences between the national arbitration laws of Commonwealth states. It has been demonstrated that many countries have not adopted the same definitions for, or defined, international commercial arbitration; arbitration agreement; foreign arbitral award and arbitration award.

Nonetheless, the key themes that have emerged and need to be taken into consideration are evident in the ways that the respective jurisdictions have defined specific terms. While an arbitration agreement is an agreement to submit to arbitration for a present or future dispute, on the other hand, an award is an arbitration award is issued by the tribunal.

Despite the above, conceptually this is not a complicated comparison. The divergence exists in the way the terms have been defined. Some states have taken a narrow approach to defining the terms. Whereas, other states have adopted a much broader approach. Most noteworthy is the approach taken by Tanzania. This country has gone into more detail than other states, particularly in relation to defining arbitration. Firstly they, along with other states have applied a two-stage definition to arbitration. Second, Tanzania in its definitions, distinguishes arbitration from international arbitration. A number of states do not define international arbitration. In another example, Mauritius has taken a four-stage approach to defining international arbitration. This is the most comprehensive definition and addresses: the parties to the arbitration agreement, the place outside of the state, whether there was express agreement between the parties, and the arbitration arises from the national law. This specific definition provides the basis for a transnational arbitration. Given that it is a relatively small state, this is impressive when compared to the definitions provided by India which is much larger in terms of area and population. On the other hand, some states such as the UK do not define arbitration. I do not believe that the different approaches taken by states when defining arbitration and its relevant elements, is critical to arbitration. Where the states have specific laws, it may be beneficial for these definitions to be included if they are absent. In addition, further research is needed to confirm whether the differences and the absence of definitions will, in the long term, inhibit the application of arbitration. Ultimately, it will be the responsibility of the national judiciary to define these terms, if the definitions have been omitted. It is argued that they will likely look to other states' national laws to confirm their position.

A number of states have defined 'arbitration tribunal', while many have not. Again, this is the case for recognition of an arbitral award. That said, the following chapter will reveal that there is a lack of recognition of the long-standing international law on arbitration. This explains why the divergence is so apparent. It will be argued in the next chapter that more Commonwealth members should adopt the UNCITRAL Model on Arbitration.

Chapter 24
UNCITRAL Arbitration Model Law

24.1 Introduction

This history of the United Nations Commission on International Trade Law [UNCITRAL] Model Law on Arbitration (Model Law) has emerged as a significant and successful legal mechanism that has resulted in the harmonisation of international commercial arbitration law.

However, how many of Commonwealth member states have adopted the Model Law within their respective national laws? This chapter addresses this question.

The chapter demonstrates how the respective states have reflected the Model Law in their national law. It further demonstrates that a large number of nation states have not adopted the Model Law in full. Moreover, it shows that there is a lack of formal recognition within the respective national laws. In addition, this chapter will refer to the Model Law.

The United Nations Commission on International Trade Law Model Law on Arbitration[1] has been highly successfully in harmonising commercial arbitration around the world. In 1985, the Model Law was finalised and it was amended in 2006,[2] to take into consideration the rise in technology. The Model Law gives parties the flexibility to decide on the procedural rules. Gary Born reaffirms this point, stating that:

> The Model Law provides, in Article 19(1), that "[s]ubject to the provisions of this Law, the parties are free to agree on the procedure to be followed by the tribunal in conducting the proceedings. More specifically, the parties' freedom to agree upon various matters relating to

[1] United Nations Commission on International Trade Law https://uncitral.un.org and, UNCITRAL Model Law on International Commercial Arbitration 1985 With amendments as adopted in 2006 https://uncitral.un.org/sites/uncitral.un.org/files/media-documents/uncitral/en/19-09955_e_ebook.pdf.

[2] United Nations Commission on International Trade Law, Status: UNCITRAL Model Law on International Commercial Arbitration (1985), with amendments as adopted in 2006, https://uncitral.un.org/en/texts/arbitration/modellaw/commercial_arbitration/status

R. Walters, *Cybersecurity and Data Laws of the Commonwealth*,
https://doi.org/10.1007/978-981-99-3935-0_24

> the presentation of their cases and the taking of evidence is expressly recognised in Articles 18, 19(1) and 24(1) of the Model Law.[3]

This freedom is different from litigation in national courts. The process of litigation restricts parties to abide by what the court has decided. However, there is a degree of flexibility in arbitration. Most noteworthy is the confidentiality and impartiality of arbitration. Simply put, arbitration is a confidential procedure between the parties, unlike litigation that goes through the national courts. This chapter examines the adoption of the Model Law by Commonwealth members. It builds on the work undertaken by the Commonwealth[4] in 2020.

In **Antigua and Barbuda**, there is no reference to the UNCITRAL Model Law in the national laws.[5] The national law is based on the English arbitration laws. At the time of writing, there had been no change in this this state's position, which was the same as that reported by the Commonwealth in 2020. A draft Bill has been developed, which would have brought the national laws in line with the Model Law, but it is still in limbo.

Australia[6] is one of the states that has adopted the UNCITRAL Model Law in full. That is, the reference to Convention is the Convention on the Recognition and Enforcement of Foreign Arbitral Awards adopted in 1958 by the United Nations Conference on International Commercial Arbitration at its twenty-fourth meeting, a copy of the English text of which is set out in Schedule 1. Under the UNCITRAL Model Law[7] the definitions are somewhat limited to Article 2, where 'arbitration' means any arbitration whether or not administered by a permanent arbitral institution, and arbitral tribunal is a sole arbitrator or a panel of arbitrators. Section 15 affirms the adoption and operation of the Model Law in Australia. It states the:

> ***Model Law*** means the UNCITRAL Model Law on International Commercial Arbitration adopted by the United Nations Commission on International Trade Law on 21 June 1985 and amended by the United Nations Commission on International Trade Law on 7 July 2006, the English text of which is set out in Schedule 2.[8]

---

[3] UNCITRAL Model Law on International Commercial Arbitration 1985 With amendments as adopted in 2006 https://uncitral.un.org/sites/uncitral.un.org/files/media-documents/uncitral/en/19-09955_e_ebook.pdf, Article 19. Gary Born, Anniversary Contribution, International Litigation & Arbitration, The Principle of Judicial Non Interference in International Arbitral Proceedings, Ll. P11. j. Int'l L, Vol 30:4, (2009) p. 1007.

[4] The Commonwealth, A Study of International Commercial Arbitration in the Commonwealth, 2020, https://production-new-commonwealth-files.s3.eu-west-2.amazonaws.com/migrated/key_reform_pdfs/A%2BStudy%2Bof%2BInternational%2BCommercial%2BArbitration_PDF_-compressed.pdf.

[5] Arbitration Act 1975, https://www.newyorkconvention.org/webcore/search?search=Antigua+and+Barbuda section 37.

[6] International Arbitration Act 1974, https://www.legislation.gov.au/Details/C2018C00439.

[7] UNCITRAL Model Law on International Commercial Arbitration (As adopted by the United Nations Commission on International Trade Law on 21 June 1985, and as amended by the United Nations Commission on International Trade Law on 7 July 2006).

[8] International Arbitration Act 1974, https://www.legislation.gov.au/Details/C2018C00439, section 15 and schedule 1.

This is the best example of a state adopting the Model Law in full in the national laws. Arguably, Australia is a leader in the adoption of international commercial law. Arbitration is no different. It has served Australian business and the economy of the state very well for more than a decade. Schedule 1 replicates the Model Law. On the other hand, in **Botswana,**[9] there is no reference to the Model Law. This is another state that has had its laws in place for a number of years. The Commonwealth[10] has noted that work was undertaken to prepare a Bill in 2018; however, this has gone nowhere. In **Bangladesh,** while not stated in the same way as Australia, the Commonwealth are of the view that national laws are based on the Model Law.[11] In **Barbados,**[12] section 2 states that UNCITRAL means the United Nations Committee on International Trade Law. Section 2 is more specific and provides Barbados with a comprehensive, modem and internationally recognized framework for international commercial arbitration by adopting the UNCITRAL Model Law.

However, a notable gap across commonwealth member states is the large number that do not adopt the Model Law. For instance, Belize,[13] the **Bahamas,**[14] **Dominica,**[15] **Gambia,**[16] **Grenada,**[17] **Guyana**[18], **Kiribati**[19] **Lesotho**[20] **Malawi,**[21]

[9] Arbitration Law, https://africaarbitration.org/resources/law/Botswana%20Arbitration%20Law.pdf.

[10] The Commonwealth, A Study of International Commercial Arbitration in the Commonwealth, 2020, p. 203.

[11] The Arbitration Act 2001, https://www.newyorkconvention.org/webcore/search?search=Bangladesh. See The Commonwealth, A Study of International Commercial Arbitration in the Commonwealth, 2020, p. 172.

[12] Arbitration (Foreign Arbitral Awards) - Arbitration 1958-23 http://barbadosparliament-laws.com/en/ShowPdf/110A.pdf and http://barbadosparliament-laws.com/en/ShowPdf/110.pdf 2007, https://www.international-arbitration-attorney.com/wp-content/uploads/2017/02/Barbados-Arbitration-Law.pdf.

[13] Arbitration Act 2000, https://www.international-arbitration-attorney.com/wp-content/uploads/2013/07/Belize-Arbitration-Law.pdf.

[14] Arbitration Act 2009, https://www.newyorkconvention.org/webcore/search?search=Bahamas See The Commonwealth, A Study of International Commercial Arbitration in the Commonwealth, 2020, p. 163.

[15] Arbitration Act 1988, https://www.newyorkconvention.org/national+arbitration+law+-+dominica.

[16] Alternative Dispute Resolution Act 2006, https://delosdr.org/wp-content/uploads/2018/06/Gambia-The-Alternative-Dispute-Resolution-2005.pdf

[17] Arbitration Act 1989, https://laws.gov.gd/index.php?option=com_edocman&view=category&id=613&Itemid=181.

[18] Arbitration Act 1916, https://mola.gov.gy/sites/default/files/Cap%20703%20Arbitration%20Act.pdf.

[19] Arbitration Act 1990, http://www.paclii.org/ki/legis/num_act/aa1990137/

[20] Arbitration Act 1980, https://osall.org.za/docs/2011/03/Lesotho-Arbitration-Act-12-of-1980.pdf.

[21] Arbitration Act 1967, https://malawilii.org/akn/mw/act/1967/26/eng%402014-12-31.

Mozambique,[22] **Namibia,**[23] **Pakistan,**[24] **Papua New Guinea**[25] **Seychelles,**[26] **Sierra Leone,**[27] **Saint Lucia,**[28] **Solomon Islands,**[29] **St Vincent and The Grenadines,**[30] **Tonga,**[31] **Trinidad and Tobago,**[32] **Tanzania,**[33] and **Togo**[34] to date, have not adopted the Model Law. It is argued that this is problematic. Professor Kennedy Gastorn makes the point that the arbitral laws are thought to have been heavily influenced by the UN General Assembly's efforts to achieve a recognized standard for arbitral laws and include, amongst others, the UNCITRAL Model Law or the Organisation for the Harmonization of Business Law in Africa's—Uniform Act on Arbitration (UAA).[35] This is an important point because, in my view, the states that have adopted the UAA, have indirectly adopted the Model law, in part. The fact that a large number of Commonwealth states have not adopted the Model Law, is arguably problematic. It is argued that the Commonwealth, while a voluntary organisation, should promote the adoption of the UNCITRAL Model law by these states. It will assist small and medium-sized businesses to resolve disputes.

Nevertheless, there are states such as Brunei Darussalam that have adopted the Model Law[36] and, similar to Australia, have referred to the Model Law within the schedules and defined it under section 2 to be the UNCITRAL Model Law on International Commercial Arbitration adopted by the United Nations Commission on International Trade Law on 21st. June, 1985. The text, in English, is set out in the

---

[22] Law on Arbitration, Conciliation and Mediation Law no. 11/99, https://www.cacm.org.mz/wp-content/uploads/2017/01/Arbitration-Law-11-99.pdf

[23] Arbitration act 1956, https://www.lac.org.na/laws/annoSTAT/Arbitration%20Act%2042%20of%201965.pdf.

[24] Arbitration Act 1940, https://www.ma-law.org.pk/pdflaw/Arbitration%20Act,%201940.pdf.

[25] *Arbitration Act 1951,* http://www.paclii.org/pg/legis/consol_act/aa1951137.pdf *Also see,* https://www.allens.com.au/insights-news/insights/2020/02/png-proposes-a-new-regime-for-arbitration/

[26] Commercial Code Act 1977, https://www.acerislaw.com/wp-content/uploads/2021/03/Seychelles-Arbitration-Law.pdf.

[27] Arbitration Act 2022, https://www.parliament.gov.sl/uploads/acts/THE%20ARBITRATION%20ACT,%202022.pdf.

[28] Arbitration Act 2001, http://www.oas.org/es/sla/ddi/docs/Santa_Lucia_Arbitration_Act.pdf.

[29] Arbitration Act 1996, http://webcache.googleusercontent.com/search?q=cache:rRc_9Ziwe5sJ:www.paclii.org/sb/legis/consol_act/aa137.rtf&cd=1&hl=en&ct=clnk&gl=sg&client=safari.

[30] Arbitration Act 1971, laws of saint vincent and the grenadines - New York Convention.

[31] International Arbitration Act 2020, https://ago.gov.to/cms/images/LEGISLATION/PRINCIPAL/2020/2020-0112/InternationalArbitrationAct2020_1.pdf.

[32] Arbitration Act 1939, https://rgd.legalaffairs.gov.tt/laws2/alphabetical_list/lawspdfs/5.01.pdf.

[33] *Arbitration Act 2020,* https://www.osg.go.tz/uploads/publications/sw1599657355-Act%20No.%202%20of%202020%20THE%20ARBITRATION%20ACT,%202020%20Final%20chapa.pdf.

[34] *Uniform Arbitration Act,* https://www.acerislaw.com/ohada-arbitration-act/

[35] Kennedy Gastorn, Examination of Arbitration Related UNCTIRAL texts and their adoption by African States, (2017) p. 3, https://www.aalco.int/Speech%20by%20SG%20at%20CIRCICA.pdf.

[36] Arbitration Order 2009 - Chapter 173 Arbitration, https://www.newyorkconvention.org/national+arbitration+law+-+brunei+darussalam International Arbitration Order 2009, https://www.agc.gov.bn/AGC%20Images/LAWS/BLUV/INTERNATIONAL%20ARBITRATION%20ORDER,%202009.pdf.

First Schedule. In a further development, in **Cameroon** although the UAA does not specify that the Model Law has been adopted, in part Cameroon's law is based on the UNCITRAL. It has not fully adopted the Model Law.[37] Similarly, **Gabon**[38] has followed the same pathway as that of Cameroon in adopting the UAA. It is not clear whether Gabon has adopted the Model Law, and this requires in country clarification.

Canada[39] has replicated the same by stating that the *Code* means the *Commercial Arbitration Code*, based on the model law adopted by the United Nations Commission on International Trade Law on June 21, 1985, as set out in Schedule 1. The notable absence is a reference to the 2006 version. On the other hand, **Cyprus**[40] has generally adopted the Model Law,[41] even though it does not specify it within the law.

In the Pacific country of **Fiji**[42] section 2 note that Arbitration Model Law" means the Model Law on International Commercial Arbitration adopted by the United Nations Commission on International Trade Law on 21 June 1985 and as amended by the United Nations Commission on International Trade Law on 7 July 2006. The Arbitration Act 1965 is not based on the Model Law, unlike the 2017 legislation. Thus, the following chapter examines only the 2017 International Arbitration Act. **Ghana,** that that does not the Model Law within the laws, Part 1 in particular has been based on the international approach.[43]

The merging economy in Central Asia India has adopted the Model Law, as stated in the Preamble—United Nations Commission on International Trade Law (UNCITRAL) has adopted the UNCITRAL Model Law on International Commercial Arbitration in 1985.[44] This will strengthen India's place in and across the digital

---

[37] Uniform Act on Arbitration 1999, https://www.newyorkconvention.org/national+arbitration+law+-+cameroon see The Commonwealth, A Study of International Commercial Arbitration in the Commonwealth, 2020, p. 220.

[38] Uniform Arbitration Act 1999, https://www.newyorkconvention.org/national+arbitration+law+-+cameroon.

[39] Commercial Arbitration Act 1985, https://laws-lois.justice.gc.ca/eng/acts/c-34.6/fulltext.html.

[40] Arbitration Law 1944, http://www.cylaw.org/nomoi/arith/1944_1_001.pdf and https://thelawreviews.co.uk/title/the-international-arbitration-review/cyprus and, Cyprus International Commercial Arbitration Law 101/1987.

https://arbitrationlaw.com/sites/default/files/free_pdfs/Cyprus%20ICAL.pdf

[41] The Commonwealth, A Study of International Commercial Arbitration in the Commonwealth, 2020, p. 245.

[42] Arbitration Act 1965, https://www.laws.gov.fj/Acts/DisplayAct/2459 and International Arbitration Act 2017 https://www.fiji.gov.fj/getattachment/d9502667-6491-4592-85b2-eff97f245fed/Act-44---International-Arbitration-Act.aspx

[43] Alternative Dispute Resolution Act 2010, https://lawsghana.com/post-1992-legislation/table-of-content/Acts%20of%20Parliament/ALTERNATIVE%20DISPUTE%20RESOLUTION%20ACT,%202010%20(ACT%20798)/28 section 135. See The Commonwealth, A Study of International Commercial Arbitration in the Commonwealth, 2020, p. 295.

[44] Arbitration and Conciliation Act 1996, https://www.indiacode.nic.in/bitstream/123456789/1978/1/AAA1996__26.pdf Sections 2 & 7.

economy as more countries seek to engage in trade and investment with them. India's neighbour **Sri Lanka**[45] has based itsnational laws on the UNCITRAL Model Law.

On the other hand, **Jamaica** has adopted the Model law in full.[46] Section 3 refers to the UNCITRAL Model Law on International Commercial Arbitration adopted by the United Nations Commission on International Trade Law done at Vienna, Austria on the 21st day of June, 1985, and the amendments adopted by the Commission, at New York, United States of America on the 7th day of July, 2006, and any amendments thereto as adopted from time to time by the Government of Jamaica. **Kenya** has generally based its laws on the Model Law, even though there is no reference to UNCITRAL or the Model Law.[47] The **Kingdom of Eswatini**[48] due to the time when the national laws were established in 1904, and having never been revised to include the Model Law, the state has opted not to apply the UNCITRAL arbitration law.

In South East Asia, **Malaysia,**[49] although there is no reference to the Model Law within the national law, the state has adopted the principles of the UNCITRAL Model Arbitration Law.[50] Likewise, **Singapore**[51] has, a format similar to that of Australia and other states, adopted the Model law in full.

The EU member of **Malta**[52] under Part V of the Arbitration Act incorporates the Model Law. Article 55 of the Arbitration Act stipulates that 'the Model Law shall form part of the Laws of Malta and shall be enforceable as such',[53] and provisions of the Model Law are wholly adopted by Malta. However, the amendments made to the Model Law in 2006 have not been reflected in the Arbitration Act. This should be reconciled.

---

[45] Arbitration Act 1995, https://www.slnarbcentre.com/pdf/ARBITRATION-ACT.pdf or https://webcache.googleusercontent.com/search?q=cache:CBtAZfCjJG0J:https://www.slnarbcentre.com/pdf/ARBITRATION-ACT.pdf&cd=3&hl=en&ct=clnk&gl=sg&client=safari

[46] Arbitration Act 2017, https://japarliament.gov.jm/attachments/article/339/The%20Arbitration%20Act,%202017.pdf or https://faolex.fao.org/docs/pdf/jam172060.pdf

[47] Arbitration Act 2010, https://ncia.or.ke/wp-content/uploads/2021/02/ArbitrationAct4of1995_2.pdf See The Commonwealth, A Study of International Commercial Arbitration in the Commonwealth, 2020, p. 343.

[48] Arbitration Act 1904, https://osall.org.za/docs/2011/03/Swaziland-Arbitration-Act-24-of-1904.pdf and https://www.eswatinilii.org/na/judgment/high-court-eswatini/2020/33 Recent high court Case referred to the 1904 Act.

Kingdom of eSwatini, one of the few jurisdictions who still do not apply the New York Convention. See The Commonwealth, A Study of International Commercial Arbitration in the Commonwealth, 2020, p. 351.

[49] Arbitration Act 2005, http://www.arbiter.com.sg/pdf/laws/Malaysia%20Arbitration%20Act%202005%20(Revised%202011).pdf section 2.

[50] The Commonwealth, A Study of International Commercial Arbitration in the Commonwealth, 2020, p. 383.

[51] Arbitration Act 2001, https://sso.agc.gov.sg/Act/AA2001

[52] Arbitration Act 1998, https://legislation.mt/eli/cap/387/eng/pdf

[53] The Commonwealth, A Study of International Commercial Arbitration in the Commonwealth, 2020, p. 393.

Turning to **Mauritius**[54] section 2 states clearly that the law is based on the UNCITRAL Model Law as amended in 2006. **Maldives**[55] has adopted the Model Law. In a similar approach, in **Nauru,**[56] the arbitration legislation applies the English Arbitration Act 1950, which pre-dates (and therefore does not adopt) the United Nations Commission on International Trade Law Model Law of 1985.[57]

In **Nigeria,**[58] section 53 states that notwithstanding the provisions of this Act, the parties to an international commercial agreement may agree in writing that disputes in relation to the agreement shall be referred to arbitration in accordance with the Arbitration Rules set out in the First Schedule to this Act, or the UNCITRAL Arbitration Rules or any other international arbitration rule acceptable to the parties. **New Zealand,**[59] according to section 5, promotes the international consistency of arbitral regimes based on the Model Law on International Commercial Arbitration adopted by the United Nations Commission on International Trade Law on 21 June 1985. Similarly, **Rwandan**[60] national laws are based on the Model Law. **South Africa**[61] has adopted the Model Law. Most noteworthy is that **St Kitts and Nevis** has not developed its own laws, but have applied the UK Arbitration Act.[62] There are a number of other states that have adopted the English law. However, it is out of scope to compare this issue. Finally, **Samoa's**[63] laws are not based on the Model Law. On the other hand, **Uganda**[64] has based its national laws on the Model Law. The **United Kingdom**[65] does not refer to the Model Law within the national laws. However, it is

---

[54] International Arbitration Act 2008, https://miac.mu/wp-content/uploads/2021/04/mauritian-international-arbitration-legislation-handbook-updated-2016-1.pdf

[55] Arbitration Act 2013, https://miac.gov.mv/media/documents/Arbitration%20Act.pdf

[56] Limitation Act 2017, http://ronlaw.gov.nr/nauru_lpms/files/acts/665725b31f7ba398592d130b557ecb2d.pdf

[57] The Commonwealth, A Study of International Commercial Arbitration in the Commonwealth, 2020, p. 427.

[58] Arbitration and Conciliation Act 1990, http://www.commonlii.org/ng/legis/num_act/aac244/ The Act was reformed in 2022.

[59] Arbitration act 1996, https://www.legislation.govt.nz/act/public/1996/0099/latest/DLM403277.html

[60] N° 005/2008 of 14/02/2008 Law on arbitration and conciliation in commercial matters, https://www.international-arbitration-attorney.com/wp-content/uploads/2013/07/Rwanda-Arbitration-Law.pdf See The Commonwealth, A Study of International Commercial Arbitration in the Commonwealth, 2020, p. 482.

[61] Arbitration Act 1965, https://www.gov.za/documents/arbitration-act-14-apr-1965-0000 section 1.

[62] Arbitration Act 2002, www.oas.org › sla › ddi › docs › Saint_Kitt…

[63] Arbitration Act 1976, https://www.regulator.gov.ws/images/2017_CONSOLIDATION_LAWS/A/Arbitration-Act-1976.pdf

[64] *Arbitration and Conciliation Act 2000,* https://arbitrationlaw.com/sites/default/files/free_pdfs/Uganda%20Arbitration%20and%20Conciliation%20Act.pdf

[65] Arbitration Act 1996, https://www.legislation.gov.uk/ukpga/1996/23/contents

noted that it based its arbitration laws[66] on the UNCITRAL Model Law. **Zambia**'s[67] arbitration law is based on the Model Law.

24.2 Conclusion

In transnational commercial disputes, the UNCITRAL Model Law on International Arbitration has emerged as a formidable legal instrument for facilitating a consistent approach across nation states. This chapter has demonstrated that a large number of Commonwealth members have adopted the Model Law. Equally though, there are a number that have not. As the digital economy continues to expand, it is argued that all Commonwealth members should adopt the Model Law in their national legal frameworks. The benefits of doing so will outweigh the negatives. It will provide a level of consistency, reduce costs, and establish efficiencies in resolving commercial disputes related to cybersecurity and data in the digital economy.

Furthermore, the Model Law when coupled with the New York Convention (see Chap. 26), ensures that any Award is binding and enforceable. Importantly, it paves the way for the reconciliation of international commercial disputes, provided that there is a contract or some other agreement to arbitrate.

As the digital economy evolves, areas such as FinTech, primary industries, tourism, health, education, ecommerce amongst others are rapidly changing the way in which commerce is undertaken. The ensuing commercialisation of these activities over the Internet, disputes will arise. Nonetheless, there are a lot of unknowns in and across the digital economy, because it is still developing. As highlighted later in this Part, there are a number of recently-developed areas (such as AI) where arbitration will provide a pathway for resolving commercial disputes that will involve cybersecurity and data either directly or indirectly. Therefore, the earlier work that the Commonwealth has undertaken in relation to arbitration should be extended to encourage members to adopt in full the UNCITRAL Model Law.

---

66 The Commonwealth, A Study of International Commercial Arbitration in the Commonwealth, 2020, p. 264.

67 Arbitration Act, https://www.parliament.gov.zm/sites/default/files/documents/acts/Arbitration%20Act.pdf

Chapter 25
Appointment of Arbitrator, Seat and Arbitration Agreement

25.1 Introduction

This chapter determines whether the relevant laws provide for the appointment of an arbitrator(s). It does not deal with the ability to challenge the appointment of arbitrators under Article 12 of the UNCITRAL Model Law. Furthermore, in some cases, the entire provision has not been dealt with this chapter, due to its size and the number of details. Instead, the key themes thatthat facilitate the appointment of arbitrators have been identified.

The first part of this chapter adopts a descriptive approach. It reconciles the national laws in relation to Article 11 of the Model Law. With the appointment of an arbitrator, other important factors that need to be considered are the place (seat) of arbitration and the arbitration agreement.

The final part of this chapter discusses both the seat of arbitration and the agreement. The establishment of an arbitration agreement is important and will serve those in the digital economy well. It will provide the basis and starting point for establishing the law and procedure of the arbitration.

Without a well- and carefully-constructed arbitration agreement, issues of jurisdiction can arise. This could lead to the final arbitration award being challenged in the domestic courts. As the digital economy continues to develop, the very complexity of governing cybersecurity and data can be problematic when commercial disputes arise, and will be heightened in the SME sector. This sector is the most vulnerable in the digital economy, because it does not have the resources of the larger multinational organisations. Therefore, an arbitration agreement that supports the contractual arrangements through well-constructed dispute resolution clauses, will ensure timely and efficient arbitration. This chapter will identify key difference between the respective national laws.

R. Walters, *Cybersecurity and Data Laws of the Commonwealth*,
https://doi.org/10.1007/978-981-99-3935-0_25

The arbitral tribunal would not exist without the appointment of a single or multiple arbitrators. Simply, an arbitration cannot function without these appointments. Generally, the arbitration agreement provides for the appointment of the arbitrators by the parties. However, a problem arises when an arbitration agreement has not provided for such. The question is whether the national laws can facilitate this process by providing guidelines for the parties involved. Secondly, where the parties have agreed to use the UNCITRAL Model Law, Article 11 provides for the appointment of arbitrators:

(1) No person shall be precluded by reason of his nationality from acting as an arbitrator, unless otherwise agreed by the parties.
(2) The parties are free to agree on a procedure of appointing the arbitrator or arbitrators, subject to the provisions of paragraphs (4) and (5) of this article.
(3) Failing such agreement, *(a)* in an arbitration with three arbitrators, each party shall appoint one arbitrator, and the two arbitrators thus appointed shall appoint the third arbitrator; if a party fails to appoint the arbitrator within thirty days of receipt of a request to do so from the other party, or if the two arbitrators fail to agree on the third arbitrator within thirty days of their appointment, the appointment shall be made, upon request of a party, by the court or other authority specified in article 6; *(b)* in an arbitration with a sole arbitrator, if the parties are unable to agree on the arbitrator, he shall be appointed, upon request of a party, by the court or other authority specified in article 6.
(4) Where, under an appointment procedure agreed upon by the parties, *(a)* a party fails to act as required under such procedure, or *(b)* the parties, or two arbitrators, are unable to reach an agreement expected of them under such procedure, or *(c)* a third party, including an institution, fails to perform any function entrusted to it under such procedure, any party may request the court or other authority specified in article 6 to take the necessary measure, unless the agreement on the appointment procedure provides other means for securing the appointment.
(5) A decision on a matter entrusted by paragraph (3) or (4) of this article to the court or other authority specified in article 6 shall be subject to no appeal. The court or other authority, in appointing an arbitrator, shall have due regard to any qualifications required of the arbitrator by the agreement of the parties and to such considerations as are likely to secure the appointment of an independent and impartial arbitrator and, in the case of a sole or third arbitrator, shall take into account as well the advisability of appointing an arbitrator of a nationality other than those of the parties.[1]

The above facilitates the appointment of an arbitrator who can undertake commercial arbitrations in relation to cybersecurity and data within the digital economy. It sets out the process for the appointment of two arbitrators and the third who will join the panel. It stipulates that the courts have the authority to appoint an arbitrator under certain circumstances. Significantly, the above does not provide for or specify

[1] UNCITRAL model Law on International Commercial Arbitration 1985 (with amendments as adopted in 2006), Article 11.

the timeframes for certain activities to be undertaken, unlike the national laws below. The first part of the chapter provides a detailed description of the national laws of Commonwealth nation states, and how they have addressed the appointment of an arbitrator. However, it deals only with the initial appointment process and does not determine with whether the national laws address a threshold of qualification or otherwise.

In **Antigua** and **Barbuda**, an arbitration agreement provides that the reference shall be to two arbitrators, one to be appointed by each party, then, unless a contrary intention is expressed therein, if either of the appointed arbitrators refuses to act, or is incapable of acting, or dies, the party who appointed him may appoint a new arbitrator in his place. Unless a contrary intention is expressed therein, every arbitration agreement shall, if no other mode of reference is provided, be deemed to include a provision that the reference shall be to a single arbitrator. Where an arbitration agreement provides that the reference shall be to two arbitrators, one to be appointed by each party, then, unless a contrary intention is expressed therein, if either of the appointed arbitrators refuses to act, or is incapable of acting, or dies, the party who appointed him may appoint a new arbitrator in his place. Unless a contrary intention is expressed therein, every arbitration agreement shall, where the reference is to two arbitrators, be deemed to include a provision that the two arbitrators shall appoint an umpire immediately after they are themselves appointed. Where an arbitration agreement provides that the reference shall be to three arbitrators, one to be appointed by each party and the third to be appointed by the two appointed by the parties, the agreement shall have effect as if it provided for the appointment of an umpire, and not for the appointment of a third arbitrator, by the two arbitrators appointed by the parties. The Court appoints an arbitrator or umpire.[2]

In **Australia**,[3] Schedule 1 follows Article 11 of the UNCITRAL Model Law on the appointment of arbitrators. On the surface, it appears that Australia has taken a narrow approach; however, Article 11 of the Model Law is quite comprehensive. In **Botswana**, under section 8, an arbitrator can be appointed by each party, then, unless a contrary intention is expressed if either of the appointed arbitrators refuses to act, or is incapable of acting, or dies, the party who appointed him may appoint a new arbitrator in his place; if, on such reference, one party fails to appoint an arbitrator, either originally, or by way of substitution as aforesaid, for seven clear days after the other party, having appointed his arbitrator, has served the party making default with notice to make the appointment, the party who has appointed an arbitrator may appoint that arbitrator to act as sole arbitrator in the reference and his award shall be binding on both parties as if he had been appointed by consent. Upon two arbitrators being appointed, they can choose the third. Interestingly, an umpire can be used. That is, at any time after the appointment of an umpire, however appointed, the Court may,

[2] Arbitration Act 1975, https://www.newyorkconvention.org/webcore/search?search=Antigua+and+Barbuda section 7, 8, 9, 10, 11.

[3] International Arbitration Act 1974, https://www.legislation.gov.au/Details/C2018C00439.

on the application of any party to the reference and notwithstanding anything to the contrary in the submission, order that the umpire shall enter upon the reference in lieu of the arbitrators and as if he were a sole arbitrator. Finally, the Court has the power to appoint an arbitrator or umpire.[4]

In Central Asia, in **Bangladesh**, according to section 12 deals with the appointment of arbitrators. The parties are free to agree on a procedure for appointing the arbitrator or arbitrators. A person of any nationality may be an arbitrator, unless otherwise agreed to by the parties. If the parties fail to agree on the arbitration within thirty days of the receipt of a request by one party from the other party to so agree, the appointment shall be made upon request of a party by the District Judge in case of arbitration other than international commercial arbitration, and in case of international commercial arbitration with three arbitrators, each party shall appoint one arbitrator, and the two appointed arbitrators shall appoint the third arbitrator who shall be Chairman of the arbitral tribunal. In the case of the appointment of a sole arbitrator or third arbitrator in an international commercial arbitration, the Chief Justice or the Judge of the Supreme Court designated by the Chief Justice, may appoint an arbitrator of a nationality other than the nationalities of the parties.[5]

In the African state of **Cameroon**, Article 5 provides that arbitrators shall be appointed, dismissed or replaced in accordance with the agreement of the parties. Where there is no such arbitration agreement, or where the agreement is not sufficient a) in an arbitration with three arbitrators, each party shall appoint one arbitrator and the two arbitrators thus appointed shah appoint the third arbitrator; if a party fails to appoint the arbitrator within thirty days of receipt of a request to do 50 from the other party, or if the two arbitrators fail to agree on the third arbitrator within thirty days of their appointment, the appointment shall be made upon request of a party, by the competent judge in the Member State in an arbitration with a sole arbitrator. If the parties are unable to agree on the arbitrator, he shall be appointed, upon request of a party. By the competent judge in the Member State. In addition, Article 8 the arbitral Tribunal shall be composed of a sole arbitrator or a panel of three arbitrators. Where the parties designate the arbitrators in even numbers, the arbitral Tribunal shall be completed by one arbitrator, chosen either in accordance with thc agreement of the parties, or, in the absence of such agreement, by the arbitrators appointed or, where they are unable to agree on the arbitrator, by the competent court in the Member State. The same is true in case of challenge, incapacity, death, resignation or revocation

[4] Arbitration Law, https://africaarbitration.org/resources/law/Botswana%20Arbitration%20Law.pdf, sections 8, 9, 10, 11.

[5] The Arbitration Act 2001, https://www.newyorkconvention.org/webcore/search?search=Bangladesh, section 2.

of an arbitrator.[6] In adopting the UAA, **Togo,**[7] **Gabon,**[8] **Tonga**[9] have assumed the same process.

In one of the most comprehensive provisions for the appointment of an arbitrator, **Belize** in section 6 has taken a different approach. It states that when a submission provides that the reference be to a single arbitrator, and all the parties do not after differences have arisen concur in the appointment of an arbitrator; if an appointed arbitrator refuses to act, or is incapable of acting, or dies, and the submission does not show that it was intended that the vacancy should not be supplied, and the parties do not supply the vacancy; where the parties or two arbitrators are at liberty to appoint an umpire or third arbitrator and do not appoint him; where an appointed umpire or third arbitrator refuses to act, or is incapable of acting, or dies, and the submission does not show that it was intended that the vacancy should not be supplied, and the parties or arbitrators do not supply the vacancy, any party may serve the other parties or the arbitrators, as the case may be, with a written notice to appoint an arbitrator, umpire or third arbitrator. If the appointment is not made within seven clear days after the service of the notice, the court or a judge may, on application by the party who gave the notice, appoint an arbitrator, umpire or third arbitrator, who shall have the like powers to act in the reference and make an award as if he had been appointed by consent of all parties. Further, section 7 states that, where there are two arbitrators, one to be appointed by each party, then, unless the submission expresses a contrary intention if either of the appointed arbitrators refuses to act, or is incapable of acting, or dies, the party who appointed him may appoint a new arbitrator in his place, if, on such reference, one party fails to appoint an arbitrator, either originally or by way of substitution as aforesaid, for seven clear days after the other party, having appointed his arbitrator, has served the party making default with notice to make the appointment, the party who has appointed an arbitrator may appoint that arbitrator to act as sole arbitrator in the reference, and his award shall be binding on both parties as if he had been appointed by consent.[10] This departure from the other states and Article 11 is significant. However, it should be noted that Belize has not adopted the Model Law. Hence, the above approach has been adopted.

For **Bahamas** section 26 constitutes the formation of arbitrators to the tribunal, where the parties can agree on the number, and where there is no agreement, there can be a sole arbitrator. In the event that there is a sole arbitrator, the parties are required within 28 days to make that appointment upon being requested. A chairman

---

[6] Uniform Act on Arbitration 1999, https://www.newyorkconvention.org/national+arbitration+law+-+cameroon.

[7] *Uniform Act on Arbitration Act 1999,* https://www.acerislaw.com/ohada-arbitration-act/.

[8] *Uniform Act on Arbitration Act 1999,* https://www.acerislaw.com/ohada-arbitration-act/.

[9] International Arbitration Act 2020, https://ago.gov.to/cms/images/LEGISLATION/PRINCIPAL/2020/2020-0112/InternationalArbitrationAct2020_1.pdf.

[10] Arbitration Act 2000, https://www.international-arbitration-attorney.com/wp-content/uploads/2013/07/Belize-Arbitration-Law.pdf sections 6, 7.

or umpire can be utilized, and the court has the power to remove an arbitrator.[11] It needs to be clarified whether the court has the power to appoint an arbitrator.

In the ASEAN state of **Brunei Darussalam** section 12 provides that the parties are free to determine the number of arbitrators. Failing such determination, there shall be a single arbitrator. Section 13 goes on to say that unless otherwise agreed by the parties, no person shall be precluded by reason of his nationality from acting as an arbitrator. The parties are free to agree on a procedure for appointing the arbitrator or arbitrators. Where the parties fail to agree on a procedure for appointing the arbitrator or arbitrators in an arbitration with 3 arbitrators, each party shall appoint one arbitrator, and the parties shall by agreement appoint the third arbitrator; or in an arbitration with a sole arbitrator, if the parties are unable to agree on the arbitrator, the arbitrator shall be appointed, upon the request of a party, by the appointing authority.[12]

On the other side, in **Barbados,** under section 8, every arbitration agreement shall, where no other mode of reference is provided, be deemed to include a provision that the reference shall be to a single arbitrator. In section 10, the reference is to two arbitrators, be deemed to include a provision that the two arbitrators shall appoint an umpire immediately after they are themselves appointed. Further, section 11 provides that where an arbitration agreement provides that the reference shall be to three arbitrators, one to be appointed by each party and the third to be appointed by the two appointed by the parties, the agreement shall have effect as if it provided for the appointment of an umpire, and not for the appointment of a third arbitrator, by the two arbitrators appointed by the parties. Notably, there is no time limit expressed in the sections for the appointments to be concluded. The court has the power to appoint an arbitrator.[13] Yet, **Dominica** adopts a similar framework for the appointment of an arbitrator.[14]

In **Canada,**[15] under Article 11, no person shall be precluded by reason of his nationality from acting as an arbitrator, unless otherwise agreed by the parties. The parties are free to agree on a procedure of appointing the arbitrator or arbitrators. However, there are considerations according to articles 4 and 5. Failure to obtain agreement, in an arbitration with three arbitrators, each party shall appoint one arbitrator, and the two arbitrators thus appointed shall appoint the third arbitrator; if a party fails to appoint the arbitrator within thirty days of receipt of a request to do so from the other party, or if the two arbitrators fail to agree on the third arbitrator

[11] Arbitration Act 2009, https://www.newyorkconvention.org/webcore/search?search=Bahamas.

[12] Arbitration Order 2009 - Chapter 173 Arbitration, https://www.newyorkconvention.org/national+arbitration+law+-+brunei+darussalam.

[13] Arbitration (Foreign Arbitral Awards) 1980 - Arbitration 1958-23 http://barbadosparliament-laws.com/en/ShowPdf/110A.pdf and http://barbadosparliament-laws.com/en/ShowPdf/110.pdf Section 2. Under the Award Act there is a different version whereby "arbitration agreement" means an agreement in writing to submit to arbitration a present or future difference that is capable of settlement by arbitration. It is argued that they constitute the same.

[14] Arbitration Act 1988, https://www.newyorkconvention.org/national+arbitration+law+-+dominica.

[15] Commercial Arbitration Act 1985, https://laws-lois.justice.gc.ca/eng/acts/c-34.6/fulltext.html.

within thirty days of their appointment, the appointment shall be made, upon request of a party, by the court or other authority. In an arbitration with a sole arbitrator, if the parties are unable to agree on the arbitrator, he shall be appointed, upon request of a party, by the court or other authority. Generally, the same universal approach seems to be taken in regard to number of arbitrators to be appointed. A Tribunal can be a sole arbitrator or three arbitrators.

Ghana is specific and, under section 14, provides a similar process to the other states, although the time period requirement is significantly reduced to only 14 days. This section does not provide for a court to have the power to appoint arbitrators. Section 13 requires that the parties can choose the number of arbitrators but this cannot be an even number, and is three.[16] What has emerged is the time periods related to the appointment of arbitrators upon notice being provided to go to arbitration, vary significantly. Arguably, in practice, this is not a serious issue although a level of consistency across states would simplify the appointment procedure.

In the African state of **Gambia**, specifies the number of arbitrators which is consistent with the above.[17] Section 15, similar to Canada, requires 21 days, and the use of a chairman or umpire is available. Likewise, in **Guyana**, section 6 gives power to the court in certain cases to appoint an arbitrator, umpire, or third arbitrator.[18] Generally, most states provide for an umpire of the court to be engaged when the appointment process has not been finalized within the specified time period.

In the Pacific nation of **Fiji**, section 6 allows the court to appoint an arbitrator, while in section 7, where a submission provides that the reference shall be to 2 arbitrators, one to be appointed by each party, then unless the submission expresses a contrary intention if either of the appointed arbitrators refuses to act, or is incapable of acting, or dies, the party who appointed him or her may appoint a new arbitrator in his or her place; if, on such a reference, one party fails to appoint an arbitrator, either originally or by way of substitution as aforesaid, for seven clear days after the other party, having appointed his or her arbitrator, has served the party making default with notice to make the appointment, the party who has appointed an arbitrator may appoint that arbitrator to act as sole arbitrator in the reference, and his or her award shall be binding on both parties as if he or she had been appointed by consent.[19]

India takes a similar approach to that of the other states compared and, under section 10, the parties are free to determine the number of arbitrators, provided that such number shall not be an even number. Failing the determination of the arbitrators, the arbitral tribunal shall consist of a sole arbitrator. Accordingly, section 11 allows for a person of any nationality may be an arbitrator, unless otherwise agreed by the

---

[16] Alternative Dispute Resolution Act 2010, https://lawsghana.com/post-1992-legislation/table-of-content/Acts%20of%20Parliament/ALTERNATIVE%20DISPUTE%20RESOLUTION%20ACT,%202010%20(ACT%20798)/28 section 135.

[17] Alternative Dispute Resolution Act 2006, https://delosdr.org/wp-content/uploads/2018/06/Gambia-The-Alternative-Dispute-Resolution-2005.pdf

[18] Arbitration Act 1916, https://mola.gov.gy/sites/default/files/Cap%20703%20Arbitration%20Act.pdf.

[19] Arbitration Act 1965, https://www.laws.gov.fj/Acts/DisplayAct/2459.

parties.[20] **Eswatini** adopts a very different approach. It does not specify the number of arbitrators or the period of time for which they are to be appointed.[21] The court can remove an arbitrator or umpire. Although section 8 provides that where there is no agreement on the appointment of an arbitrator within seven days from the service of notice, the court can appoint an arbitrator, third arbitrators or umpire.

India's neighbour, **Pakistan**, according to section 6, allows the court to appoint an arbitrator or umpire, where an arbitration agreement provides that the reference shall be to one or more arbitrators to be appointed by consent of the parties, and all the parties do not, after differences have arisen, concur in the appointment or appointments; or *(b)* if any appointed arbitrator or umpire neglects or refuses to act, or is incapable of acting, or dies, and the arbitration agreement does not show that it was intended that the vacancy should not be supplied, and the parties or the arbitrators, as the case may be, do not supply the vacancy; or *(c)* where the parties or the arbitrators are required to appoint an umpire and do not appoint him; any party may serve the other parties or the arbitrators, as the case may be, with a written notice to concur in the appointment or appointments or in filling the vacancy. The notable difference from other states is that where the appointment is not made within fifteen clear days after the service, the court may, on the application of the party who gave the notice and after giving the other parties an opportunity of being heard, appoint an arbitrator or arbitrators or umpire. Even so, the parties can appoint a new arbitrator under section 7, and generally there are to be three arbitrators. Thus, under section 8, where an arbitration agreement provides that a reference shall be to three arbitrators, one to be appointed by each party and the third by the two appointed arbitrators, the agreement shall have effect as if it provided for the appointment of an umpire, and not for the appointment of a third arbitrator, by the two arbitrators appointed by the parties. While section 9 provides that the court can remove the arbitrator or umpire.[22]

In the ASEAN member country of **Malaysia,** under section 12, and similar to the other states, the parties are free to determine the number of arbitrators. If the parties fail to determine the number of arbitrators, the arbitral tribunal shall in the case of an international arbitration, consist of three arbitrators; and in the case of a domestic arbitration, consist of a single arbitrator. Section 13 stipulates that nationality is not a ground for precluding an arbitrator. Where the parties fail to agree on the procedure referred to in subsection (2), and the arbitration consists of three arbitrators, each party shall appoint one arbitrator, and the two appointed arbitrators shall appoint the third arbitrator as the presiding arbitrator. A party fails to appoint an arbitrator within thirty days of receipt of a request in writing to do so from the other party; or the two arbitrators fail to agree on the third arbitrator within thirty days of their appointment

[20] Arbitration and Conciliation Act 1996, https://www.indiacode.nic.in/bitstream/123456789/1978/1/AAA1996__26.pdf Sections 2 & 7.

[21] Arbitration Act 1904, https://osall.org.za/docs/2011/03/Swaziland-Arbitration-Act-24-of-1904.pdf and https://www.eswatinilii.org/na/judgment/high-court-eswatini/2020/33 Recent high court Case referred to the 1904 Act.

Kingdom of eSwatini, one of the few jurisdictions who still do not apply the New York Convention.

[22] Arbitration Act 1940, https://www.ma-law.org.pk/pdflaw/Arbitration%20Act,%201940.pdf.

or such extended period as the parties may agree, either party may apply to the Director of the Kuala Lumpur Regional Centre for Arbitration for such appointment. However where the Director of the Kuala Lumpur Regional Centre for Arbitration is unable to act or fails to appoint an arbitrator, within thirty days from the request, any party may apply to the High Court for such appointment.[23] On the other hand, in **Kenya**, section 12 provides for three arbitrators and a sole arbitrator, with a 15-day time period. The appointment of a sole arbitrator can be set aside by the court, and the party in default has 14 days to file. Nationality is not a ground for preclusion.[24]

Thus far, several key themes have emerged in relation to the appointment of arbitrators. It is well-settled that there can one arbotrator or three. An even number of arbitrators cannot be appointed. The parties can choose an arbitrator each, and where the third has not been chosen, an umpire or court may step in. A notable difference is the time periods for which appointments are to take place. They diverge significantly from state to state. The remainder of the chapter will not provide a detailed commentary of the provisions of the arbitration laws. Rather, it will highlight where there is a difference or departure amongst the states.

In **Lesotho**, a similar approach has been adopted and there is no change in the number of arbitrators, although the use of an umpire is available. Notably, there is a specified period of time being 7 days under section 11.[25] For **Singapore,** under section 13, there is a similar requirement for the appointment of one or three arbitrators. The notable difference is that there is a 30-day period for failure to appoint. Section 16 allows the court to remove an arbitrator.[26]

Another Central Asian country, **Sri Lanka**, has a similar process, and the number of arbitrators are the same, although there is reference to a third party institution that might be engaged to facilitate the establishment of the arbitration, and where they have not fulfilled their role in appointing arbitrator(s), the High Court can do under take this task. Notably there is a 60-day period available.[27]

On the one hand, **Malawi,** section 8 enables the appointment of both an arbitrator and umpire. They may have distinctly different roles, and this case the court can order an Umpire to take on the role of sole arbitrator. This is not evident in the preceding states compared. Additionally, the number of arbitrators is the same, and the Court can appoint arbitrators, and a 7 day period exists.[28] Likewise in **Jamaica** the same format of the Tribunal exists and the process for the Court to intervene is

---

[23] Arbitration Act 2005, http://www.arbiter.com.sg/pdf/laws/Malaysia%20Arbitration%20Act%202005%20(Revised%202011).pdf section 2.

[24] Arbitration Act 2010, https://ncia.or.ke/wp-content/uploads/2021/02/ArbitrationAct4of1995_2.pdf.

[25] Arbitration Act 1980, https://osall.org.za/docs/2011/03/Lesotho-Arbitration-Act-12-of-1980.pdf.

[26] Arbitration Act 2001, https://sso.agc.gov.sg/Act/AA2001.

[27] Arbitration Act 1995, https://www.slnarbcentre.com/pdf/ARBITRATION-ACT.pdf or https://webcache.googleusercontent.com/search?q=cache:CBtAZfCjJG0J:https://www.slnarbcentre.com/pdf/ARBITRATION-ACT.pdf&cd=3&hl=en&ct=clnk&gl=sg&client=safari

[28] Arbitration Act 1967, https://malawilii.org/akn/mw/act/1967/26/eng%402014-12-31.

also available. The time period for failure of appointment is 30 days.[29] On the other hand, **Mauritius** apply the same process as the UNCITRAL Arbitration Rules.[30] **Saint Lucia has** adopted the same, although there is no time period states and the Court can remove an arbitrator where they have been found not to be impartial or committing fraud.[31]

In a similar development to the other nations, **Kiribati** sections 8–10 provide the same, and the court can intervene, although the time period is tight and there is only 7 days available where a party fails to make an appointment.[32] The same applies in **Namibia,** however there are subtle differences in the requirements between the two states.[33] Most noteworthy, **Nauru** does not provide for the appointment of arbitrators.[34]

In **St Vincent and The Grenadines**, the court can intervene in the appointment of arbitrators, umpire or third arbitrator according to section 8. It also requires only a seven-day period where there has been a failure of the appointment.[35] **New Zealand** has adopted a process similar to that of Australia.[36] **Trinidad and Tobago,** has a seven-day period for non-appointment, and generally has the same procedure as the other states, including the use of an umpire.[37] All states allow the parties to choose the arbitrators; there is no divergence in this regard.

For the African state of **Rwanda,** similarly, the court can intervene, and there are up to three arbitrators or a sole individual, and the time period is limited to 15 days.[38] Notably, there is no umpire, although there is reference to a third party of institution. The term 'third party' would need to be clarified in regard to its application. Likewise, in **South Africa** the same number of arbitrators are allowed, and the court can appoint an umpire of arbitrator. Only seven days are given for an arbitration appointment.[39]

---

[29] Arbitration Act 2017, https://japarliament.gov.jm/attachments/article/339/The%20Arbitration%20Act,%202017.pdf sections 13–14.

[30] International Arbitration Act 2008, https://miac.mu/wp-content/uploads/2021/04/mauritian-international-arbitration-legislation-handbook-updated-2016-1.pdf.

[31] Arbitration Act 2001, http://www.oas.org/cs/sla/ddi/docs/Santa_Lucia_Arbitration_Act.pdf sections 10–14.

[32] Arbitration Act 1990, http://www.paclii.org/ki/legis/num_act/aa1990137/

[33] Arbitration act 1956, https://www.lac.org.na/laws/annoSTAT/Arbitration%20Act%2042%20of%201965.pdf.

[34] Limitation Act 2017, http://ronlaw.gov.nr/nauru_lpms/files/acts/665725b31f7ba398592d130b557ecb2d.pdf.

[35] Arbitration Act 1971, Laws of Saint Vincent and The Grenadines - New York Convention.

[36] Arbitration act 1996, https://www.legislation.govt.nz/act/public/1996/0099/latest/DLM403277.html.

[37] Arbitration Act 1939, https://rgd.legalaffairs.gov.tt/laws2/alphabetical_list/lawspdfs/5.01.pdf.

[38] N° 005/2008 of 14/02/2008 Law on arbitration and conciliation in commercial matters, https://www.international-arbitration-attorney.com/wp-content/uploads/2013/07/Rwanda-Arbitration-Law.pdf

[39] Arbitration Act 1965, https://www.gov.za/documents/arbitration-act-14-apr-1965-0000 section 1.

Most noteworthy is how **St Kitts and Nevis** have not developed their own laws, but have applied the UK Arbitration Act.[40] In **Uganda,** 30 days is provided for the arbitrator appointment, and an umpire can be utilised.[41] The formal arrangements in **Tanzania** are similar, except there is a 28-day timeline for the appointment. Section 18 does differ slightly in that 14 days is the period given for the appointment of two arbitrators, while and the third is to be appointed within 15 days of the service of the written request.[42]

That said, the functional requirements in Cyprus are, by and large, the same as those of other states, although the period is seven days and the court can make an appoint on application by the parties.[43] Malta has assumed the same, albeit with a 30-day period.[44] Because I have not discussed the full provisions in this section of the chapter, further reference and interpretation is required to understand the difference in procedure regarding the court and appointments. Generally, they are very similar. This chapter has not examined the provisions enabling the appointment of arbitrators to be challenged. Most states allow for the appointments to be challenged, which is a procedural step available to the parties.

In the **United Kingdom,** the parties are free to agree on the arbitrators, which must be undertaken within 28 days of service. Section 16 states that if the tribunal is to consist of two arbitrators, each party shall appoint one arbitrator not later than 14 days after service of a request in writing by either party to do so. Section 18 provides that the court can make an appointment.[45]

The most significant departure from the other states is the **Maldives**[46] where, according to Article 16 three arbitrators are appointed if the dispute involves a sum equivalent to or more than MVR 1.5 million (one million, five hundred thousand Maldivian rufiyaa). In addition, where the dispute submitted to arbitration involves a sum less than MVR 1.5 million (one million, five hundred thousand Maldivian rufiyaa), a single arbitrator shall be appointed. Otherwise, the same process of appointment applies. No other state has this unique threshold test. The appointment process requires eight days. Significant too, **Mozambique** has adopted the same provision as the Maldives, except for the monetary threshold test.[47] Notably, in **Nigeria** the composition of the tribunal is the same. However, under sections 6

[40] Arbitration Act 2002, www.oas.org › sla › ddi › docs › Saint_Kitt…

[41] *Arbitration and Conciliation Act 2000,* https://arbitrationlaw.com/sites/default/files/free_pdfs/Uganda%20Arbitration%20and%20Conciliation%20Act.pdf.

[42] *Arbitration Act 2020,* https://www.osg.go.tz/uploads/publications/sw1599657355-Act%20No.%202%20of%202020%20THE%20ARBITRATION%20ACT,%202020%20Final%20chapa.pdf.

[43] Arbitration Law 1944, http://www.cylaw.org/nomoi/arith/1944_1_001.pdf and https://thelawreviews.co.uk/title/the-international-arbitration-review/cyprus.

[44] Arbitration Act 1998, https://legislation.mt/eli/cap/387/eng/pdf.

[45] Arbitration Act 1996, https://www.legislation.gov.uk/ukpga/1996/23/contents.

[46] Arbitration Act 2013, https://miac.gov.mv/media/documents/Arbitration%20Act.pdf.

[47] Law on Arbitration, Conciliation and Mediation Law no. 11/99, https://www.cacm.org.mz/wp-content/uploads/2017/01/Arbitration-Law-11-99.pdf.

and 7, appointments are to be made within 30 days. In the case of failure to do so, the court can undertake to make the necessary appointments.[48]

For the state of **Papua New Guinea**[49] all have a similar appointment process in relation to the number of arbitrators. This commonality does not change. Similarly, the Court can intervene and make the appointment, where the parties have failed to do so. However, in the **Seychelles**[50] the number of appointments is the same, although the time period is one month before the court intervenes if the parties have failed to make an appointment. Thus, this month could be 28, 29, 30 or 31 days, depending on the applicable month. In **Sierra Leone,** the court can intervene if the parties have not appointed an arbitratos within 14 days.[51] In the **Solomon Islands**, the court can intervene if an appointment has not been made within seven days.[52] The same process applies in **Samoa**[53] and in **Zambia.**[54]

Arguably, international arbitration has become attractive to the commercial world because of the parties' ability to have their disputes resolved out of the eye of the public. In other words, where there is a commercial dispute and parties want to proceed to litigation in the courts, the outcome and proceedings are open to the public. Thus, the public can access the disputed information. In addition to this, the concepts of independence and impartiality underpin the application of arbitral proceedings. Importantly, the arbitral tribunal is to be impartial and there must be a high degree of neutrality in the final decision and the award that is issued to resolve the dispute. Simply put, there is a high level of non-bias in arbitration.

Seat [Place of Arbitration]

Commercial arbitration will be undertaken in a designated place, usually agreed between the parties. This section demonstrates that the arbitral seat is an important feature international arbitration. It will compare a selection of eight Commonwealth national laws with the UNCITRAL Model law, and the governance of the seat. This is because a number of national laws are silent on the issue.

---

[48] Arbitration and Conciliation Act 1990, http://www.commonlii.org/ng/legis/num_act/aac244/ The Act was reformed in 2022.

[49] *Arbitration Act 1951,* http://www.paclii.org/pg/legis/consol_act/aa1951137.pdf *Also see,* https:/ /www.allens.com.au/insights-news/insights/2020/02/png-proposes-a-new-regime-for-arbitration/

[50] Commercial Code Act 1977, https://www.acerislaw.com/wp-content/uploads/2021/03/Seychelles-Arbitration-Law.pdf.

[51] Arbitration Act 2022, https://www.parliament.gov.sl/uploads/acts/THE%20ARBITRATION%20ACT,%202022.pdf.

[52] Arbitration Act 1996, http://webcache.googleusercontent.com/search?q=cache:rRc_9Ziwe5sJ:www.paclii.org/sb/legis/consol_act/aa137.rtf&cd=1&hl=en&ct=clnk&gl=sg&client=safari.

[53] Arbitration Act 1976, https://www.regulator.gov.ws/images/2017_CONSOLIDATION_LAWS/A/Arbitration-Act-1976.pdf.

[54] Arbitration Act, https://www.parliament.gov.zm/sites/default/files/documents/acts/Arbitration%20Act.pdf.

The seat of arbitration is the place of arbitration, and is a legal concept referring to location in the legal significance of international commercial arbitration.[55] Generally, the parties involved in an arbitration are free to choose the seat of arbitration. Article 20 of the UNCTIRAL Model Law[56] provides for the place (seat) of arbitration, along with Article 18 of the UNCITRAL Rules.[57] The UNCITRAL Rules[58] provide that a proceeding is not restricted to a particular seat of arbitration or a particular applicable law. Furthermore, the choice-of-law rules, under Article V(1)(a), New York Convention[59] and implied in Article II, give effect to the parties' choice of law governing their agreement to arbitrate, and, in the absence of any express or implied choice by the parties, to apply the law of the arbitral seat, provide essential clarification of the law applicable to the parties' arbitration agreement. The seat of arbitration determines the applicable law when deciding the validity of the arbitration agreement and the arbitration procedure, as well as the nationality of the award. In other words, the difference between the *lex arbitri* and the law governing the substance of the dispute was part of the juridical tradition of continental Europe, but is now firmly established in international arbitration.[60]

Essentially, *lex arbitri* is the law of the arbitration,[61] which consists of the composition and appointment of the tribunal, and the requirements for arbitral procedure and due process, together with the formal requirements for an award.[62] Of importance, Article 19 of the Model Law[63] allows the parties to agree on the procedure to be followed by the arbitral tribunal. *Lex arbitri* includes, but is not limited to, the definition of the agreement to arbitrate, and stipulates whether a dispute is capable

[55] Alan Redfern, Marcus Hunter, *International Arbitration*, Oxford university Press 6th Edt, (2015) p.161.

[56] UNCITRAL Model Law on International Commercial Arbitration 1985 with amendments as adopted in 2006, Article 20.

[57] UNCITRAL Arbitration Rules (2010) (2013), Article 18, Australian Centre for International Commercial Arbitration (ACICA) Arbitration Rules, Article 19.

[58] UNCITRAL Arbitration Rules (2010)-(2013).

[59] New York Convention 1985, Article V, ¶ 1(a); id., art. II. Moreover, the better view is that the Convention also requires application of a validation principle reflecting the parties' implied intentions to give effect to the parties' arbitration agreement. Gary Born, *The New York Convention: A Self-Executing Treaty*, 40 MICH. J. INT'L L. 115 (2018).

[60] Ibid. Where parties to an international arbitration agreement choose a seat of arbitration, they usually choose a place that has no connection with themselves or the commercial relationship. They choose a 'neutral' place and doing so, they do not necessarily intend to choose the law of that place to govern their relationship.

[61] Alistair Henderson, *Lex Arbitri*, Procedural Law and the Seat of Arbitration 26 SAcLJ (2014), pp. 887-895.

[62] Ibid, and regulates such things as, the external relationship between the arbitration and the courts, whose powers may be both supportive and supervisory, such as the grant of interim relief, procuring evidence from third parties and securing the attendance of witnesses, the removal of arbitrators and the setting aside of awards; and the broader external relationship between arbitrations and the public policies of that place, which includes matters such as arbitrability and possibly also—more controversially—the impact on arbitration of social, religious and other fundamental values in each State.

[63] UNCITRAL Model Law, Article 19, *Determination of rules of procedure.*

of being referred to arbitration, and the constitution of the arbitral tribunal. It also includes the entitlement of the arbitral tribunal to rule on its own jurisdiction; the equal treatment of the parties; freedom to agree upon detailed rules of procedure; any interim measures; statements of claim and defence; and hearings as well as the place of arbitration.[64]

In *Sulamrica*, the Court noted the 'proper law of an arbitration agreement in a commercial contract was the governing law of the contract or the law of the seat of the arbitration was a matter of contractual interpretation and terms of the particular contract'.[65] Article V of the New York Convention and Article 36 of the Model Law provide that the recognition and enforcement of the award may be refused, among other grounds, when the award has been set aside or suspended by a competent authority of the country in which, or under the law of which, that award was made. Under the Model Law, the enforcement must be at the seat whereas the enforcement of the award under the New York Convention can be commenced in any court.[66] In regard to the setting aside of an award, in the case of *Nicolay* a 'heavy burden' was imposed on the claimant in seeking to enforce an award that had been set aside at the seat of arbitration.[67] The ensuing process revealed that an award was set aside in Russia. The claimant then sought enforcement in France, the Netherlands and England. France enforced the award, but England did not. Arguably, this highlights the difficulties that a party will face when seeking to enforce an arbitral award in England if it has been set aside at the seat of arbitration.

In the brief comparison of Commonwealth states' administration of the seat, generally, those states that have adopted the Model Law will apply Article 20. **Australia**,[68] by adopting the UNCITRAL Model Law in full, applies Article 20. **Barbados** adopted a similar approach to that of Australia[69]; section 2 states that UNCITRAL means the United Nations Committee on International Trade Law.

---

[64] UNCITRAL Arbitration Rules, Articles 3, 6, 20, 21, 23, 26, 28, and UNCITRAL Model Law, Articles 2, 13, 16, 17, 18, 19, 23, 28.

[65] *Sulamerica CIA Nacional De Seguros SA and others v Enesa Engenharia SA and others [2012] EWHC 42 (Comm); [2012] EWCA Civ 638. 2.* The court noted the law of the arbitration agreement is determined by a three-stage inquiry, (i) express choice, (ii) implied choice' and (iii) closest and most real connection. Three stages to be considered separately and in that order … but it has been said on many occasions that in practice stage (2) often merges into stage (3). See also, *Braes of Doune Wind Farm (Scotland) Ltd v Alfred McAlpine Business Services Ltd [2008] EWHC 426.*

[66] United Nations Conference on International Commercial Arbitration, Convention on the Recognition and Enforcement of Foreign Arbitral Awards 1985. UNCITRAL model Law on International Commercial Arbitration 1985 (with amendments as adopted in 2006), Jurisdiction where assets are located. Both the Model Law and the New York Convention are permissive in nature as both are using the word "may be refused". This indicates that courts still have residual discretion in regard to enforcement of awards.

[67] *Nikolay Viktorovich Maximov v. Open Joint Stock Company "Novolipetsky Metallurgichesky Kombinat* [2017] EWHC 1911 (Comm). See also: Philip Devenish (2018) Enforcement in England and Wales of arbitral awards set aside in their country of origin, Oxford University Commonwealth Law Journal, 18:2, 143-149.

[68] International Arbitration Act 1974, https://www.legislation.gov.au/Details/C2018C00439.

[69] Arbitration (Foreign Arbitral Awards) - Arbitration 1958-23 http://barbadosparliament-laws.com/en/ShowPdf/110A.pdf and http://barbadosparliament-laws.com/en/ShowPdf/110.pdf

Jamaica has adopted the Model law in full[70] under section 3. Similarly, **Canada**[71] **New Zealand**,[72] and **South Africa**[73] have taken the same approach. On the one hand, **St Vincent and The Grenadines**[74] have not adopted the Model Law, and within their national laws there are no specific provisions specifying the seat of arbitration.

On the other hand, **United Kingdom**[75] does not refer to the Model Law in its national laws, however, it is noted that it is based[76] on the UNCITRAL Model Law on Arbitration. However, section 3 of the states being compared has adopted a specific provision, whereby the seat is the juridical seat of the arbitration designated by the parties to the arbitration agreement, or by any arbitral or other institution or person vested by the parties with powers in that regard, or by the arbitral Tribunal if authorised by the parties, or determined, in the absence of any such designation, having regard to the parties' agreement and all the relevant circumstances. However, in relation to Article 20 of the Model Law, in the case of *Dubai*[77] the UK High Court was required to resolve two questions in relation to the seat of arbitration that was based on an appeal arbitration:

- how should the court apply ***section 3*** when determining what is the *"juridical seat of the arbitration"*, if neither the parties to the arbitration agreement nor any arbitral or other institutions have designated the *"seat"* of the arbitration?
- is there a particular point in time during the arbitral process at which the court should consider *"all the relevant circumstances"* in order to determine the *"juridical seat of the arbitration"*?[78]

The Court, in addressing the first question, for the purposes of *sections 2 and 3 of the 1996 Act,* the *"seat of the arbitration"* is in England and Wales?[79] In order to address the above, the Court noted:

> The key circumstance that the Bank relies on is that the actual appeal hearing by the International Board took place at the Board meeting in London on 8 November 1999. The only

2007, https://www.international-arbitration-attorney.com/wp-content/uploads/2017/02/Barbados-Arbitration-Law.pdf.

[70] Arbitration Act 2017, https://japarliament.gov.jm/attachments/article/339/The%20Arbitration%20Act,%202017.pdf or https://faolex.fao.org/docs/pdf/jam172060.pdf.

[71] Commercial Arbitration Act 1985, https://laws-lois.justice.gc.ca/eng/acts/c-34.6/fulltext.html.

[72] Arbitration act 1996, https://www.legislation.govt.nz/act/public/1996/0099/latest/DLM403277.html.

[73] Arbitration Act 1965, https://www.gov.za/documents/arbitration-act-14-apr-1965-0000 section 1.

[74] Arbitration Act 1971, laws of saint vincent and the grenadines - New York Convention.

[75] Arbitration Act 1996, https://www.legislation.gov.uk/ukpga/1996/23/contents.

[76] The Commonwealth, A Study of International Commercial Arbitration in the Commonwealth, 2020, p. 264.

[77] *Dubai Islamic Bank PJSC v. Paymentech*, High Court, England, 24 November 2000, [2001] 1 LLR 65.

[78] Ibid, para 1.

[79] Ibid, para 124.

other "English connections" that the Bank can rely on really have nothing to do with the individual appeal arbitration at all. First, there is the English connection concerning the original agreement between the Bank and VISA. Secondly, there is the fact that the point of contact generally between the Bank and VISA was the VISA centre at Basingstoke. Thirdly, there is the point that, at the start of the payment procedure, the Bank as Issuer would have received a request for authorisation from Basingstoke and (if it had been given) it would have gone to Basingstoke.[80]

Once an arbitration starts and it has a *seat*, then I cannot see how it can be changed, unless it is by one of the mechanisms stipulated in section 3.[81] Therefore, the Court applied the fall-back position of statutory interpretation, in order to better understand section 3, amongst others. The Court made the point that it had:

> to examine the *"agreement of the parties and all the relevant circumstances"* as at May 1999. The reference to the *"parties' agreement"* means, I think, the agreement that contains the original contract to submit disputes to arbitration. That would be consistent with the definition of *"the arbitration agreement"* and *"the agreement"* in *section 5*. The phrase *"the parties' agreement"* cannot mean "what the parties have agreed in relation to the seat of the arbitration" because that is the very point dealt with in *section 3(a)*.[82]

Importantly, the Court drew a connection between the seat and the arbitration agreement itself. An arbitration agreement precedes the arbitration, and is an important means of governing the procedural aspects of the arbitration process. The Court concluded that:

> The *"seat"* of the two appeal arbitrations is not in England and Wales for the purposes of *sections 2 and 3 of the Act*. Accordingly, the Court has no jurisdiction to exercise its powers under *sections 67–69 of Part One of the Act* in relation to those two appeal awards. Therefore, I must set aside the permission of Rix J (made on 31 January 2000) granting the Bank permission to serve the Arbitration Applications on Paymentech. If, contrary to this conclusion, I had found that the *"seat"* of the two appeal arbitrations was in England and Wales, I would have permitted an extension of time to the Bank to allow it to make the Arbitration Applications set out in the Application form dated 24 January 2000.[83]

The point is, that not identifying the place (seat) of arbitration from the outset will pose challenges to the arbitration itself. Where such an arrangement has not be provided for, it is likely that a court may have to make the decision on behalf of the parties. This could be problematic for the technology sector (particularly for newcomers and small-medium sized businesses, which are new to contractual relations and dispute resolution) that has invested significantly in a location through contractual arrangements, and there is an ensuing dispute. Therefore, to reinforce a long-standing practical process, it is important that the contracts or arbitration agreement be clear on where the place of arbitration will be. Additionally, an important issue identified by the Commonwealth in relation to the seat is:

---

[80] Ibid, para 38.

[81] Ibid, para 49(2).

[82] Ibid, para 50.

[83] Ibid, paras 66–67.

> A factor influencing the parties' selection of an arbitral seat is the ease of instructing international counsel. In most international arbitrations, at least one party to the dispute is from somewhere other than the arbitral seat. In many arbitrations, no party is from the arbitral seat. Parties may have established relationships with particular sets of counsel in their local jurisdiction or through previous representations in related or unrelated matters. The ease of being able to instruct international counsel is thus of particular importance to parties foreign to the arbitral seat.[84]

The Commonwealth, in referring to earlier case law from Singapore, noted the shift to open up the restrictions placed on foreign firms bypresenting clients in the states. It noted:

> The liberalisation of the restrictions on instructing international counsel is Singapore. In 1988, the Singapore High Court excluded a well-respected New York law firm from representing a client in an international arbitration seated in Singapore in *Turner (East Asia) Pte Ltd v Builders Federal (HK) Ltd, Josef Gartner & Co, whereby* the decision was extensively criticised internationally. The Singapore Parliament subsequently amended the relevant legislation to permit foreign lawyers to represent parties in international arbitrations seated in Singapore. At first, the amended legislation required the local Singapore counsel to be retained, along with foreign counsel, in matters involving Singaporean law. This requirement of retaining local counsel was subsequently dropped, such that Singapore now respects the parties' full freedom to select their representatives in locally seated international arbitrations.[85]

Noteworthy is that the above case referenced by the Commonwealth was in 1988. More than 30 years on, it is beyond the scope of this book to ascertain whether the national laws of the jurisdictions being compared have implemented the same. Thus, the ensuing question is: where and how can the seat of arbitration be formalised?

Arbitration Agreement

The UNCTIRAL Model Law states that an arbitration agreement according to Article 7, constitutes

(1) *"Arbitration agreement" is an agreement by the parties to submit to arbitration all or certain disputes which have arisen or which may arise between them in respect of a defined legal relationship, whether contractual or not. An arbitration agreement may be in the form of an arbitration clause in a contract or in the form of a separate agreement.*
(2) *The arbitration agreement shall be in writing.*
(3) *An arbitration agreement is in writing if its content is recorded in any form, whether or not the arbitration agreement or contract has been concluded orally, by conduct, or by other means.*
(4) *The requirement that an arbitration agreement be in writing is met by an electronic communication if the information contained therein is accessible so as*

---

[84] The Commonwealth, A Study of International Commercial Arbitration in the Commonwealth, 2020, p. 49 https://production-new-commonwealth-files.s3.eu-west-2.amazonaws.com/migrated/key_reform_pdfs/A%2BStudy%2Bof%2BInternational%2BCommercial%2BArbitration_PDF_-compressed.pdf.

[85] Ibid, p. 49. (1988) 42 BLR 122.

to be useable for subsequent reference; "electronic communication" means any communication that the parties make by means of data messages; "data message" means information generated, sent, received or stored by electronic, magnetic, optical or similar means, including, but not limited to, electronic data interchange (EDI), electronic mail, telegram, telex or telecopy.

(5) *Furthermore, an arbitration agreement is in writing if it is contained in an exchange of statements of claim and defence in which the existence of an agreement is alleged by one party and not denied by the other.*

(6) *The reference in a contract to any document containing an arbitration clause constitutes an arbitration agreement in writing, provided that the reference is such as to make that clause part of the contract.*[86]

An arbitration agreement is an important component, setting the scene for arbitration. Without such an agreement, proceeding to arbitration can be problematic. Put another way, an arbitration agreement provides the basis for the applicable law and appropriate rules for the procedure to apply. In the event that such an agreement is not clear and creates an element of uncertainty, the tribunal itself will need to decide on what law applies, for instance, the arbitration law of the UK. Importantly, the doctrine of separability has been accounted for by Article 16(1) of the Model Law that enshrines this doctrine by providing that:

> The arbitral tribunal may rule on its own jurisdiction, including any objections with respect to the existence or validity of the arbitration agreement. For that purpose, an arbitration clause which forms part of a contract shall be treated as an agreement independent of the other terms of the contract. A decision by the arbitral tribunal that the contract is null and void shall not entail *ipso jure* the invalidity of the arbitration clause.[87]

Arguably, this prevents a party from arguing that the contract has been breached and therefore they want to proceed to court. Redfern and Hunter make the point that an arbitration agreement is essential because it records the consent of the parties to submit to arbitration—a consent that is indispensable to any process of dispute resolution outside national courts. Such processes depend for their very existence upon the agreement of the parties. Redfern and Hunter posit that many attach great importance to the wishes of the parties—to *l'autonomie de la volonté*. Indeed, some go so far as to suggest that this consent, together with an appropriate set of rules, is sufficient to turn international arbitration into an autonomous, delocalised process that takes place independently of national law.[88] The authors also mention that two types of arbitration agreement exist: the 'arbitration clause and the submission agreement. Therefore, an arbitration clause looks to the future, whereas a submission agreement looks to the past. The first, which is most common, is usually contained in the principal agreement between the parties and is an agreement to submit *future* disputes to

[86] UNCITRAL Model Law on https://uncitral.un.org/sites/uncitral.un.org/files/media-documents/uncitral/en/mal-digest-2012-e.pdf.

[87] UNCITRAL Model Law on International Commercial Arbitration 1985 (with amendments as adopted in 2006), Article 16.

[88] Alan Redfern, Marcus Hunter, *International Arbitration*, Oxford university Press 6th Edt, (2015) p. 71.

arbitration. The second is an agreement to submit *existing* disputes to arbitration'.[89] That said, a selection of laws of members of the Commonwealth have been compared below. Noteworthy is that those members who adopted the UNCITRAL Model Law, apply Article 7.

In the development of the above, **Australia,**[90] **Canada,**[91] **India.**[92] **Malaysia,**[93] **Singapore,**[94] **New Zealand,**[95] **South Africa**[96] have by and large all adopted Article 7 of the Model Law. However, Pakistan has not adopted the Model Law and, under section 2, arbitration agreement constitutes a written agreement to submit present or future differences to arbitration, whether or not an arbitrator is named therein. Further, Chapter III provides for an arbitration agreement, in that unless a different intention is expressed therein, it shall be deemed to include the provisions set out in the First Schedule in so far as they are applicable to the reference. Section 4 ensures that an arbitration agreement not to be discharged upon the death of a party.[97]

Most noteworthy is how **St Kitts and Nevis** have not developed their own laws, but have applied the UK Arbitration Act.[98] In the **United Kingdom**[99] section 5 generally follows the Model Law but also has its own characteristics. It states that the expressions "agreement", "agree" and "agreed" shall be construed to actualise an agreement. It further states that, similar to the Model Law, the agreement is to be in writing, and is evidenced in writing if an agreement made otherwise than in writing is recorded by one of the parties, or by a third party, with the authority of the parties to the agreement. However, an exchange of written submissions in arbitral or legal proceedings in which the existence of an agreement otherwise than in writing is alleged by one party against another party and not denied by the other party in his response constitutes as between those parties an agreement in writing to the effect alleged.[100] Section 6 goes further to define such an agreement in anticipation of a future dispute. Further, similar to Article 7, although articulated slightly differently,

---

[89] Ibid, p. 72.

[90] International Arbitration Act 1974, https://www.legislation.gov.au/Details/C2018C00439.

[91] Commercial Arbitration Act 1985, https://laws-lois.justice.gc.ca/eng/acts/c-34.6/fulltext.html.

[92] Arbitration and Conciliation Act 1996, https://www.indiacode.nic.in/bitstream/123456789/1978/1/AAA1996__26.pdf Sections 2 & 7.

[93] Arbitration Act 2005, http://www.arbiter.com.sg/pdf/laws/Malaysia%20Arbitration%20Act%202005%20(Revised%202011).pdf section 2.

[94] Arbitration Act 2001, https://sso.agc.gov.sg/Act/AA2001.

[95] Arbitration act 1996, https://www.legislation.govt.nz/act/public/1996/0099/latest/DLM403277.html.

[96] Arbitration Act 1965, https://www.gov.za/documents/arbitration-act-14-apr-1965-0000 section 1.

[97] Arbitration Act 1940, https://www.ma-law.org.pk/pdflaw/Arbitration%20Act,%201940.pdf.

[98] Arbitration Act 2002, www.oas.org › sla › ddi › docs › Saint_Kitt…

[99] Arbitration Act 1996, https://www.legislation.gov.uk/ukpga/1996/23/contents.

[100] Ibid, section 5.

section 7 ensures that where an arbitration agreement forms part of another agreement, it is to be treated as a distinct agreement. Finally, section 8 provides that unless agreed, the arbitration agreement cannot be discharged on the death of one party. This final point should be addressed in any agreement and, today, it generally should be considered as a standard clause.

Importantly, a party to an arbitration dispute can establish whether it has the capacity to enter into an arbitration agreement.[101] It is generally accepted that parties must have the requisite legal capacity to enter into a contract. The lack of capacity by either person to the agreement makes the arbitration agreement void, inoperative or incapable of being performed.[102]

The UNCITRAL Arbitration Rules[103] provide that the parties to an arbitration agreement fall within the Rules. In *Dallah*,[104] the Court held legal capacity was based on validity of the agreement rather than the parties' domicile or residence. The case is described below:

> claimant commenced an ICC arbitration against the defendant, a ministry of the Government of Pakistan (GoP). The defendant contested jurisdiction, arguing that it was not a party to the arbitration agreement. The arbitrators held that the law applicable to the arbitration clause was "those transnational general principles and usages reflecting the fundamental requirements of justice in international trade and the concept of good faith in business" and found in their first partial award that GoP was a party. In a subsequent final award issued in France the arbitrators ordered GoP to pay the sum of US$20,588,040. GoP did not appeal against the award to the French courts. The claimant sought an order from the English court enforcing the award and the defendant argued that enforcement should be refused on the ground set out in section 103(2)(b) of the Arbitration Act 1996, requiring that it was "not valid under the law to which the parties subjected it, or failing any indication thereon, under the law of the country where the award was made".[105]

However, the case went to appeal in 2010,[106] where the Court noted that:

> The award was made against the Government on the basis that it was "a true party" to an Agreement dated 10 September 1996 expressed to be made between and signed on behalf of Dallah and Awami Hajj Trust ("the Trust"). The Agreement contains an arbitration clause referring disputes or differences between Dallah and the Trust to ICC arbitration. The tribunal in a first partial award dated 26 June 2001 concluded that the Government was a true party to the Agreement and as such bound by the arbitration clause, and so that the tribunal had jurisdiction to determine Dallah's claim against the Government. The central issue before the English courts is whether the Government can establish that, applying French law principles, there was no such "common intention" on the part of the Government and Dallah as would make the Government a party.[107]

---

[101] Edwin Kimani, Peter Mwangi, *A Critique Of The Law Governing Capacity Of Parties To Enter Into An Arbitration Agreement,* Alternative Dispute Resolution Volume 9 Issue 1 (2021), p. 1-2.

[102] UNCITRAL Model Law, Article 8(1), New York Convention, Article II.3.

[103] UNCITRAL Arbitration Rule (revised 2010 and updated 2013), Article 1, 2.

[104] *Dallah Real Estate & Tourism Holding Co v Ministry of Religious Affairs* [2008] EWHC 1901 (Comm).

[105] Ibid.

[106] [2010] UKSC 46.

[107] Ibid, para 2.

In relation to the reliance on the validity of the arbitration agreement the Court argued that:

> The "validity" of the arbitration agreement depends in the present case upon whether there existed between Dallah and the Government any relevant arbitration agreement at all. Dallah's case is that the Government has at all times been an unnamed party to the Agreement containing the arbitration clause. Before the English courts, this case has been founded on a submission that it was the common intention of the parties that the Government should be such a party to the Agreement. Before the arbitral tribunal Dallah put the matter differently. It argued that either the Trust was the alter ego of the Government or the Government was the successor to the Trust or to the rights and obligations which the Trust had under the Agreement prior to its demise. Neither of these ways of putting the case is now pursued. Dallah did not argue before Aikens J that the Trust was the Government's alter ego, and it merely submitted that, if and so far as the Government behaved as if it were a successor to the Trust, this was relevant to the issue of common intention.[108]

Moreover, the Court in referring to the applicable law related to the arbitration agreement, noted that:

> The issue regarding the existence of any relevant arbitration agreement falls to be determined by the Supreme Court as a United Kingdom court under provisions of national law which are contained in the Arbitration Act 1996 and reflect Article V(1)(a) of the New York Convention.[109]

The Court dismissed the appeal ruling that the starting point 'cannot be a review of the decision of the arbitrators that there was an arbitration agreement between the parties. Indeed, no question of a review arose at any stage. The starting point in this case must be an independent investigation by the court of the question whether the person challenging the enforcement of the award can prove that he was not a party to the arbitration agreement under which the award was made. The Court further ruled that the legal position, expressed by the Ministry of Religious Affairs under s103(2)(b) of the 1996 Act/Art V.1(a) NYC, when the issue is initial consent to arbitration, the Court must determine for itself whether or not the objecting party actually consented'.[110] The Court reinforced the original decision that having an arbitration agreement in place is paramount prior to going to an arbitral proceeding. It further confirmed that in this case, no arbitration agreement ever existed, and there were no grounds for the arbitral award to be enforced.

Arbitration agreements are under Chapter II UNCITRAL Model Law along with the Arbitration Rules.[111] In addition, Articles, 1(3), 7, 8, 20, 28 of the Model Law[112] and Article 18 of the Rules provide for performance of the agreement. The Model Law defines: the arbitration agreement; arbitration agreement and substantive claim before

[108] Ibid, para 11.

[109] Ibid, para 12.

[110] Ibid, para 160.

[111] UNCITRAL Arbitration Rules 2010, Article 1, 3, 4, 6, 17, 20, 23.

[112] UNCITRAL Model Law, Article 28, "(1) The arbitral tribunal shall decide the dispute in accordance with such rules of law as are chosen by the parties as applicable to the substance of the dispute.

the court; and arbitration agreement and interim measure by court.[113] Importantly, where the substantive contract contains an express choice of law, but the agreement to arbitrate contains no separate express choice of law, the latter agreement will normally be governed by the body of law expressly chosen to govern the substantive contract.[114] However, arbitration agreements are presumably valid and enforceable, but does not expressly address choice-of-law issues.[115] Articles 34(2)(a)(i) and 36(1)(a)(i) permit non-recognition (or annulment) of an arbitral award if "a party to the arbitration agreement was under some incapacity; or the said agreement is not valid under the law to which the parties have subjected it or, failing any indication thereon, under the law of [the country where the award was relationship between".[116] Importantly, Article 9 expresses the principle that any interim measures of protection that may be obtained from courts under their procedural law are compatible with an arbitration agreement. That provision is ultimately addressed to the courts of any State, and establishes the compatibility between interim measures possibly issued by the court and an arbitration agreement.[117] Moreover, in the case of Jagdish,[118] the Supreme Court of India stated:

> The first respondent filed the application for appointment of an Arbitrator to decide the disputes in regard to dissolution of the said partnership firm and for rendition of accounts. In the said application, the first Respondent arrayed the appellant herein as the first respondent. Respondents 2 to 6 herein were also impleaded as respondents alleging that the two partners entered into an arrangement/agreement with Respondents 2 to 6 in the year 1974 under which Respondents 2 to 6 were to supervise the business of the firm and pay to each of the two partners, a fixed sum, which was increased periodically. According to first Respondent, the arrangement worked satisfactorily for several years, but for some years, the entire amount was being received by the appellant and he was not paying the first Respondent's half share. The appellant resisted the petition, inter alia, on the ground that the partnership had come to an end in the year 1979 and the accounts were all settled. He also contended that the partnership deed did not contain any agreement to refer disputes to arbitration. It was specifically contended that clause 16 of the Deed of Partnership was not an arbitration agreement.[119]

In reconciling the evidence with the statutory requirements under Indian law, the Supreme Court concluded that:

> The existence of an arbitration agreement as defined under section 7 of the Act is a condition precedent for exercise of power to appoint an Arbitrator/Arbitral Tribunal, under section 11 of the Act by the Chief Justice or his Designate. It is not permissible to appoint an Arbitrator to adjudicate the disputes between the parties, in the absence of an arbitration agreement or

---

[113] UNCITRAL Model Law, Articles 7, 8, 9.

[114] *Sonatrach Petroleum Corp (BVI) v Ferrell International Ltd* [2002] 1 All ER (Comm) 627 at [32].

[115] Gary Born, *The Law Governing International Arbitration Agreements: An International Perspective*, 26 SAcLJ, (2014) pp. 827–828.

[116] Ibid.

[117] UNCITRAL Model Law, p. 29.

[118] *Jagdish Chander v. Ramesh Chander & Ors*, Supreme Court, India, on 26 April, 2007, https://indiankanoon.org/doc/1913246/

[119] Ibid, para 3.

mutual consent. The designate of the Chief Justice of Delhi could not have appointed the Arbitrator in the absence of an arbitration agreement.[120]

Arguably, the arbitration agreement is an important step before an arbitration proceeding. It enables the parties to facilitate an arbitration, the appointment of an arbitrator, seat of arbitration and the choice of law, amongst others. In the digital economy, it is paramount that these long-standing principles and concepts of commercial arbitration be developed to ensure that there is a formal and functional dispute resolution process. Failure to make these arrangements right from the outset will only lead to the court possibly having to intervene, which could be costly to the parties.

25.2 Conclusion

This chapter has highlighted a number of variations across the nations compared. It has demonstrated how the law, in responding to and addressing the need for the appointment of arbitrators, has diverged. Notably, the differences in process are not great. Rather, they are related to the time period of appointment. That said, nation states have opted to approach the appointment of an arbitrator on the basis of agreement between the parties, or through and an arbitration agreement. Article 11 of the Model Law does not require an arbitration agreement to be established for an appointment to be made. It only requires agreement between the parties.

In a rare example of full harmonisation, whether or not states have adopted the Model Law, is the number of arbitrators required. All nation states compared have adopted the same number generally expressed as a sole arbitrator or three arbitrators. However, some states have resorted to ensuring there is not an even number of arbitrators appointed. Another common theme that has been all but harmonised is that there be no discrimination on the basis of nationality for the appointment of an arbitrator. That is, a person of any nationality can be appointed. However, and from time to time, it may be subject to specific qualifications. The replacement of arbitrators is usually done by agreement of the parties.

Those states that have not adopted the UNCITRAL Model Law have opted to provide for expanded provision(s) in relation to the appointment of these positions. For instance, in one example, the state requires that if the appointment is not made within seven clear days after the service of the notice, the court or a judge may make the appointment. However, this can be done only if an application has been made by one party. In some cases, the law is silent on most of the requirements.

The court intervention or the appointment of a chairman or umpire varies significantly amongst the states. In addition, a few states make reference to arbitration institutions that may make the appointment of an arbitrator on behalf of the parties. Despite the above, the range from 7 to 30 days for the appointment process, following a notice being provided for arbitration varies. This is an area where the practitioner will need to be aware of those differences.

120 Ibid, para 11.

In a major departure from the other states, one state has attached a monetary threshold for the appointment of arbitrators. Significantly, no other state has adopted for the same provisions as the Maldives, and the Model Law does not promote this threshold test. This approach does not appear to offer any benefit to the parties.

Finally, in relation to the arbitration agreement and the seat of arbitration, the states compared generally take an approach similar to that of the Model Law. While most of the states have adopted the Model Law, it makes sense that those states would follow the same process of harmonisation. However, the remaining states national laws need to be 2 compared as part of future research to confirm whether a similar approach as been adopted. It is argued that a failure to get the arbitration agreement developed to a stage where it addresses the fundamental issues of the arbitration Tribunal procedure itself, places the parties at a disadvantage. While this is well understood amongst arbitrators, it further demonstrates how legal divergence makes the overall process of arbitration more complex. Therefore, adopting the Model Law will elevate the convergence of arbitration law, so as to benefit the digital economy.

Chapter 26
Experts

26.1 Introduction

The technology sector is like no other. It has its own language and consequently there are various experts across the sector. Inevitably, during an arbitration, an individual expert may be required to attend an arbitral proceedings. The list of experts could include, but is not limited to software designers, code developers, infrastructure installers and maintenance personnel, and server specialists, amongst many others in both the government and the private sector, that support ecommerce and transnational trade. Hence, the role of experts in arbitration, in my view, has the potential to be quite topical. This will particularly be the case where experts are drawn from the same entity, which may pose a conflict of interest.

This chapter confirms the importance of dealing with experts in and across the digital economy, under the UNCITRAL Model Law. Article 26 covers experts appointed by an arbitral tribunal, **and** provides that:

Unless otherwise agreed by the parties, the arbitral tribunal.

(a) *may appoint one or more experts to report to it on specific issues to be determined by the arbitral tribunal;*
(b) *may require a party to give the expert any relevant information or to produce, or to provide access to, any relevant documents, goods or other property for his inspection.*

Unless otherwise agreed by the parties, if a party so requests or if the arbitral tribunal considers it necessary, the expert shall, after delivery of his written or oral report, participate in a hearing where the parties have the opportunity to put questions to him and to present expert witnesses in order to testify on the points at issue.[1]

---

[1] UNCITRAL Model Law on International Commercial Arbitration 1985 (with amendments as adopted in 2006).

R. Walters, *Cybersecurity and Data Laws of the Commonwealth*,
https://doi.org/10.1007/978-981-99-3935-0_26

In part, the use of experts by the Tribunal will constitute the use of specialist evidence, which may also fall within the rules of evidence. It is important to note that arbitration institutions may have their own guidelines on the application and use of evidence. This chapter will not compare the way that individual arbitration institutional rules have dealt with this issue, as they form part of another book. It will cite recent court rulings that have been careful to distinguish between the duties of an expert, and whether their role could constitute a conflict of interest.

The new digital economy and the benefits it will bring to the global society has already created in new jobs and experts that were not even considered more than a decade ago. The expertise that will be required in the forthcoming decades may not even be thought of today. The changes in and development of technology are significant. The world is already seeing new business, trade, investment and employment sectors such as Artificial intelligence (AI) cybersecurity and data (privacy, analysists, scientists), perform complex tasks within and across organisations that are multi-national and know no international borders. Put another way, where AI, data and cybersecurity cross over in the technology space, companies are increasingly turning to international arbitration, particularly for disputes involving cryptocurrency, blockchain and artificial intelligence.[2] The acceleration of digital transformation and innovation will continue to affect the disputes landscape, giving rise to new types of commercial conflict. It is argued that this will require technical and legal experts from across the world. On the other hand, legal experts in comparative data and cyber law will be increasingly required in international arbitration.

Importantly, the use and presentation of expert evidence is an important feature of international arbitration. The deployment of experts has raised associated concerns about the best way for parties, and the tribunal, to obtain realistic, objective expert evidence. Although both party-appointed and tribunal appointed experts are used in international arbitration, by far the most expert evidence is provided by party-appointed experts.[3] Doug Jones notes that:

> The legal and factual complexity of disputes requires the involvement of experts who can assist the tribunal by giving specialised evidence in areas with which the tribunal may be unfamiliar. Experts can be broadly divided into three categories, differentiated by the type of expertise and their familiarity with giving expert evidence. The first category are technical experts who are called to assist the tribunal on issues requiring specialist technical knowledge. Their evidence can range from knowledge on specific financial markets to expertise in a range of specialist fields, for example, pharmacology, computer programming and metallurgy. Technical or industry-specific experts often have less experience with giving expert evidence than the other two categories of experts.[4]

[2] International Arbitration 2022 - Exceptional Experts, https://www.financierworldwide.com/power-players-international-arbitration-2022-exceptional-experts#.Y-DG4y9r2CU.

[3] Professor Doug Jones, Redefining the role and Value of Expert Evidence, 2021, pp. 1–4 https://dougjones.info/content/uploads/2021/12/DJ-ICC-Expert-Evidence-Post-Conference-Updated-Chapter.pdf.

[4] Ibid. Also see Jones refers to Brooks W Daly and Fiona Poon, 'Technical and Legal Experts in International Investment Disputes' in Chiara Giorgetti (ed), *Litigating International Investment Disputes* (Brill, 2014) p. 323.

Jones, in describing the second group, states:

> experts can be broadly grouped under the description of 'analysis' experts and comprise delay, disruption and quantum, or damages, experts. These experts collate and express views on masses of material often with the assistance of complex analytical models. Damages experts may specialise in a number of disciplines such as accounting or finance, or possess other technical or scientific skillsets.[5]

Arguably, across the digital economy, these skills are likely to be called upon at some point during an arbitration. Significantly, the two groups above are what Jones is referring to as the technical experts when applied to the technology sector. These groups of experts know the workings and operations of the technology including the capture, use and storage of data. It will also include those specialist experts who secure the systems and infrastructure. That said, Jones goes on to say that a third category pertaining to the law. He takes the position that:

> Lawyers may be called upon to give evidence where the law of a particular legal system is material to the dispute, and neither counsel nor the tribunal are familiar with such laws. However, the actual value of legal experts is problematic when both lawyers and the tribunal are in their own right 'experts' in law; counsel having experience with presenting legal arguments, and arbitrators with assessing them. This is particularly the case in international arbitration where all parties to the arbitration frequently interact with "foreign" law.[6]

In referring to this group of experts, it will be highly relevant to data protection and cybersecurity law (those laws compared in this book). I agree with the position taken by Jones and, as this book has demonstrated, the highly divergent approaches to both data protection and cybersecurity law is significant. It will take a legal specialist in the field to unpack the complex provisions that involve multiple state laws. However, an ensuing problem that can arise is whether an expert may have a conflict of interest. In a recent case involving technology,[7] the UK High Court noted that:

> Disputes arose between the contractor and the claimant concerning delays to the Package A and Package B works. The contractor commenced ICC arbitration proceedings against the claimant, seated in London with an English choice of law clause ("the Works Package Arbitration"). In the Works Package Arbitration, the contractor claims additional costs incurred by reason of delays to its works, including the late release of Issued For Construction ("IFC") drawings.[8]

The application sought to retain the defendants as experts in the proceeding. In relying on a number of email correspondence, case precedents, and examining the role of a fiduciary, and even though the arbitration had not mentioned the UNCITRAL Model Law and was based on institutional rule, the Court ruled that:

---

[5] Ibid.

[6] Ibid, p. 3.

[7] Technology and Construction Court in *A v B* [2020] EWHC 809 (TCC), https://www.zulrafique.com.my/ckfinder/userfiles/files/A%20Company%20v%20X%2C%20Y%20and%20Z%20%5B2020%5D%20EWHC%20809%20(TCC).pdf

[8] Ibid, para 6.

> The defendant group owes a fiduciary duty of loyalty to the claimant arising out of its engagement to provide expert services in connection with the Works Package Arbitration. The defendant group is in breach of that fiduciary duty of loyalty by accepting instructions to provide expert services in connection with the EPCM Arbitration. Pending trial of this matter, the claimant is entitled to a continuation of the interim injunction to restrain the defendants from providing expert services to the third party in connection with the EPCM Arbitration.[9]

Centrally, the Court is saying that experts should avoid a conflict of interest, and will be held to account in the same way as a fiduciary. A year later in 2021, the Court upheld the above position in the case of *Secretariate Consulting*[10] and pointed out that:

> On a proper analysis, the expert's overriding duty to the court could be said to be one of the prime reasons why the expert may indeed owe a duty of loyalty to his client. In many cases, the client instructs an expert to provide extensive pre-trial services and then to give expert evidence at the trial. The client wants a frank and honest appraisal of his case by the expert at the earliest possible opportunity. There is no point in the client spending a good deal of money pursing or defending a claim if his underlying position is hopeless, but none of his other advisors is prepared to tell him so. The client knows that, because an expert has to stand up before the judge or the arbitrators and say that his report is true to the best of his knowledge and belief, and represents his honest opinion, the expert will only be prepared to do that if he or she has first ensured that the pre-trial work has led to the formation of a position which the expert can support. None of that is contrary to any duty of loyalty: on the contrary, complying with the overriding duty to the court is the best possible way in which an expert can satisfy his professional duty to his client.[11]

By and large, on this basis, the appeal was dismissed before the Court provided a comprehensive analysis of the requirements for experts to demonstrate loyalty to their client. In so doing, the Court ruled that 'central plank of the argument advanced was that the existence of a duty of loyalty on the part of the expert to the client would conflict with or negate the expert's (overriding) duty to the court or arbitral tribunal'.[12] Therefore, the point is that the court will examine the level of fiduciary owed by a potential expert as part of their duty to an arbitral tribunal.

---

[9] Ibid, para 66.

[10] *Secretariat Consulting Pte Ltd v A Company* [2021] EWCA Civ 6, https://www.bailii.org/ew/cases/EWCA/Civ/2021/6.html.

[11] Ibid, para 62.

[12] Ibid, para 125.

Given these developments, as highlighted in the previous chapter **Australia,**[13] **Canada,**[14] **India**.[15] **Malaysia,**[16] **Singapore,**[17] **New Zealand,**[18] **South Africa**[19] have by and large adopted the UNCITRAL Model Law. Arguably, Article 26 is applicable.

However, **Pakistan** has not adopted the Model Law, and the national laws do not describe how or when an expert is to be appointed.[20] This, however, does not mean that the Pakistan *Center* for International Investment and Commercial *Arbitration*[21] *does not have its own arbitration rules which facilitate the appointment and management of experts.*

On the other hand, the **United Kingdom**[22] departs from Article 26 of the Model Law. Section 37 provides that unless otherwise agreed by the parties, the tribunal may appoint experts or legal advisers to report to it and the parties, or appoint assessors to assist it on technical matters, and may allow any such expert, legal adviser or assessor to attend the proceedings; and the parties shall be given a reasonable opportunity to comment on any information, opinion or advice offered by any such person. The fees and expenses of an expert, legal adviser or assessor appointed by the tribunal for which the arbitrators are liable are expenses of the arbitrators for the purposes of this Part. The notable difference is that in regard to the fees and expenses of the expert, the arbitrator incurs that cost. In practice, this is a general rule followed by most institutional arbitral rules.

Nonetheless, an Indian court had to grapple with no expert evidence being used because of the expertise of the arbitrators. The Court in National Thermal Power[23] had to reconcile with provisions of the Arbitration and Conciliation Act 1996. The Court noted that:

> disputes between the parties arose from a lump sum contract for 4 Cooling Towers of reinforced cement concrete 120 metres high along with RCC basin for collection of cooled water and arrangement of RCC channels and AC Pipes provided horizontally for sprinkling of hot water through nozzles over layers of PVC serrated sheets, for the purpose of cooling of hot

[13] International Arbitration Act 1974, https://www.legislation.gov.au/Details/C2018C00439.

[14] Commercial Arbitration Act 1985, https://laws-lois.justice.gc.ca/eng/acts/c-34.6/fulltext.html.

[15] Arbitration and Conciliation Act 1996, https://www.indiacode.nic.in/bitstream/123456789/1978/1/AAA1996__26.pdf Sects. 2 & 7.

[16] Arbitration Act 2005, http://www.arbiter.com.sg/pdf/laws/Malaysia%20Arbitration%20Act%202005%20(Revised%202011).pdf Sect. 2.

[17] Arbitration Act 2001, https://sso.agc.gov.sg/Act/AA2001.

[18] Arbitration act 1996, https://www.legislation.govt.nz/act/public/1996/0099/latest/DLM403277.html.

[19] Arbitration Act 1965, https://www.gov.za/documents/arbitration-act-14-apr-1965-0000 Sect. 1.

[20] Arbitration Act 1940, https://www.ma-law.org.pk/pdflaw/Arbitration%20Act,%201940.pdf.

[21] The *Center* for International Investment and Commercial *Arbitration,* https://ciica.org/ciica-council/ *Note, it is out of scope to examine arbitration institutional rules.*

[22] Arbitration Act 1996, https://www.legislation.gov.uk/ukpga/1996/23/contents.

[23] *National Thermal Power Corporation Ltd. v. Wig Brothers Builders and Engineers Ltd.,* High Court of Delhi, India, 17 April 2009 [OMP 16/2003 [2009] INDLHC 1466],

water from 43 to 32°C through natural draft created in the towers. However, the supply of hot water and distribution of cold water from the basin was outside the scope of the contract.[24]

In explaining the contractual dispute between the parties, the Court noted that:

> The contract, inter-alia, provided for foreign collaborators and their design for structural and thermal attributes of the Cooling Towers, for supply of cement and steel free of cost by NTPC, for variation in the quantity of such cement and steel on certain prescribed consideration and for recovery from the contractor for excess consumption of cement and steel, for price adjustment of materials, labour and fuel linked with price indices, for foreign exchange rate protection and other usual conditions found in building and engineering contracts.[25]

Significantly, the Court pointed out that there were allegations of no expert evidence. It noted that:

> Insofar as the issue of PG Tests is concerned, the allegation of the petitioner that no expert evidence was led or no expert evidence was led or no expert opinion was taken is totally misconceived as the arbitrators were themselves experts in the field of construction. Nothing precluded the petitioner from leading expert evidence or citing an expert opinion but it chose not to do so. Therefore, at this stage the petitioner cannot raise an objection on this ground. Further, it is not obligatory for the Arbitral Tribunal to call for expert evidence and particularly in the present case where the Arbitrators were themselves experts in the field. That clause 14, particularly clause 14.3 of the General Terms and Conditions of the contract provided for the conductance of P&G Tests.[26]

Simply put, in determining the level of expertise of the arbitrators, the Court observed:

> Arbitrators were themselves experts in the field or at least had technical knowledge. It was not for the Arbitral Tribunal to call for expert evidence when, in their opinion, they did not require it. However, if the parties wanted to lead expert evidence it was for the parties to lead the evidence and not for the Arbitral Tribunal to secure it for the parties. It is not the case of the petitioner that it applied to the Arbitral Tribunal for being permitted to lead expert evidence but was denied such a request. The claim of the petitioner that no expert evidence was called for by the Arbitral Tribunal and therefore, the Arbitral Award is vitiated, is in my view without any merit particularly where the petitioner itself did not bring any expert's evidence on record.[27]

In weighing up the issues of the level of expertise against the performance guarantee test, the Court made the point that its ensuing obligations had been met. The point is that courts will consider the level of expertise attributed to an arbitrator. It is argued that this is why arbitrators do not necessarily have to come from the legal profession. Arbitration institutions around the world do have non-legal experts appointed to their rosters.

---

[24] Ibid, paras 1, 2, 3.

[25] Ibid.

[26] Ibid, para 56.

[27] Ibid, para 60.

Regarding the above, Article 26 was significantly influenced and inspired by the corresponding article of the 1976 UNCITRAL Arbitration Rules (article 27) and indeed the wording of both articles is very similar.[28] Polkinghorne et al. note that the first drafts of Article 26 adhered even more closely to Article 27 of the UNCITRAL Arbitration Rules, with only minor differences between them. Moreover, the authors state that Article 26 started to develop own form by introducing the principle of the UNCITRAL Arbitration Rules, as Mexico wished to emphasise that the appointment of a tribunal-appointed expert did not preclude parties from producing expert witnesses.[29]

They go on to say that, although also not implemented, India proposed removing the sentence in the final paragraph 'at this hearing either party may present expert party-appointed experts are generally more used. Article 26 was significantly influenced and inspired by the correspond-ability of the tribunal to appoint an expert was subject to the contrary'.[30]

Polkinhorne and others in referring to a 2017 Swiss Court decision noted that the parties have a right to a tribunal-appointed expert subject to certain conditions, namely that:

- timely request for the appointment of a tribunal-appointed expert must be made by either party;
- if required by the tribunal, the requesting party must advance the costs of the appointment of such expert;
- the evidence of the tribunal-appointed expert must relate to facts relevant to the rendering of the award; and
- the evidence of the tribunal-appointed expert must be necessary and proper for proving such relevant facts.[31]

This 2017 decision raised several important points. First, a tribunal-appointed expert must relate to the facts. Therefore, where there is a dispute related to technology, with cybersecurity and data also forming part of the dispute, the appointed expert needs to have the necessary expertise. Second, he or she must be proficient in being able to prove facts related to the technology, cyber or data related matters. Third, the initial steps taken by the Court are procedural and relate only to the appointment of the expert—whereby, it only has to be by one of the parties, not both, along with the costs of that expert, for which the party requesting him/her will bear that cost.

[28] Michael Polkinghorne, Karim Mariey, Tomas Vail, *Expert Appointed by Arbitral Tribunal,* In I Bantekas, P Ortolani, S Ali, M Gomez, M Polkinghorne, UNCITRAL Model Law on International Commercial Arbitration: A Commentary, pp. 697–717.

[29] Ibid.

[30] Ibid.

[31] Ibid.

The facts of this case were that the petitioner and claimant in the arbitration started ICC arbitration proceedings in 2008 based on a contract for four tourism projects concluded in 1977. In a partial award, the tribunal first declared that the respondent had violated the contract by not executing two out of the four tourism projects. In a final award, rendered in 2017, the chairperson of the tribunal in essence rejected all of the parties' claims on quantum, with both co-arbitrators issuing a dissenting opinion.[32] Moreover, it was highlighted that:

> During the arbitration, the petitioner requested the tribunal to appoint an independent expert to evaluate its claim for loss of profit, resulting from the two abandoned tourism projects, which it quantified at more than USD 300 Million. In support of its request, the petitioner submitted four documents: a report by a bank, a feasibility study by a private expert, an update to the aforementioned feasibility study and a further, undated report. The tribunal held that the submitted documents in support of the request for an independent expert were, among other reasons, not to be considered by the tribunal, as they were in its view created after the arbitration had been initiated and with the sole purpose of distracting the tribunal's attention from the real facts of the case. The tribunal further held that the petitioner failed to clearly set out its position with regard to the appointment of the independent expert. The tribunal considered that while on the one hand, the petitioner at times requested the appointment of an expert, on the other hand, it demanded the swift resolution of the case on the merits. Beside this, the tribunal held that it was within its discretionary powers, granted by the applicable arbitration rules, to refrain from appointing an expert if it did not consider it to be necessary.[33]

The Court went further in asking whether there was enough reason for an expert. Voser and Gottlieb note that:

> the tribunal noted the absence of a sufficient factual basis for an expert to render an opinion. The tribunal considered that the negative repercussions for failing to file to the record direct and credible sources of evidence would have to be borne by the petitioner, given that it bore the burden of proving its alleged loss of profit. The petitioner challenged the final award, arguing that its right to be heard was violated in that its right to the appointment of an independent expert to evaluate its claim for loss of profit was denied.[34]

Also, Polkinghorne et al. go further, making the point that the interface between the tribunal-appointed and party-appointed experts should depend on the circumstances of the case, including the technical issues therein.[35] In practice, this issue should be easy to address. However, from time to time there will be a need for the parties to clearly articulate how the expert is to be appointed. This will save a level

---

[32] Professor Dr. Nathalie Voser, Benjamin Gottlieb *Swiss Supreme Court rejects challenge and reiterates principles of right to a tribunal appointed expert*, 2017, https://www.swlegal.com/media/filer_public/b1/3f/b13f1645-9858-464c-a18f-4924a28e5154/2017_nathalie-voser_benjamin-gottlieb_swiss-su-4.pdf.

[33] Ibid.

[34] Ibid.

[35] Michael Polkinghorne, Karim Mariey, Tomas Vail, *Expert Appointed by Arbitral Tribunal,* In I Bantekas, P Ortolani, S Ali, M Gomez, M Polkinghorne, UNCITRAL Model Law on International Commercial Arbitration: A Commentary, p. 717.

of expenditure. The authors present two issues related to costs, from the interface between the tribunal-appointed and party-appointed experts:

(1) during the proceedings (due to duplication of work); and
(2) after the final award (due to any application to set aside the award).[36]

Hence, if technology and legal experts need to be engaged throughout an arbitration, it is important that they be engaged early and through some formal process such as a contract or, as Polkinghorne advises, Terms of Reference. This will ensure that there is a clear line of separation regarding who is responsible for the appointment.

26.2 Conclusion

This short, but important chapter has demonstrated the growing need to include technology experts in international commercial arbitration proceedings. It has also demonstrated how experts can be appointed according to Article 26 of the UNCITRAL Model Law, along with some of the issues that have arisen from the courts. This Article is not often discussed in terms of the wider scope of arbitration, because practicing arbitrators would fully understand the provision. However, it is argued that the sophistication of technology and the law supporting the adoption and use of technology in the digital economy, will require experts to be called upon. Likewise, as I have highlighted in this book, the complexity and divergent responses to data protection and cybersecurity law will require experts from those legal fields to be engaged, rather than a generalist who would find it difficult to deal with these areas.

Notably, this chapter has made only a brief comparison of the national laws of Commonwealth member states, considering only whether these laws provide for the appointment of experts. In limiting the discussion to the appointment of experts, it did not address the issue of how the law responds when an expert's appointment is challenged. This is an area that merits further research.

In a further development, the conflict of interest of an expert has emerged as a source of contention. This is something that individuals will need to consider carefull. As highlighted above, the Courts from time to time will be required to engage an expert to determine the level of conflict or otherwise. Thus, a Tribunal that is made up of experts, needs to consider when using that expertise, whether it constitutes a level of conflict of interest. This could be determined by the Tribunal from the outset. Failure to do so could expose the panel or sole arbitrator and it may border on being a failure to be impartial.

---

[36] Ibid.

Despite this, the recent 2017 decision from Switzerland has provided a pathway forward to ensuring that the appointment of any expert is undertaken to ensure the individuals expertise relates to the facts. This common sense approach is even more justified in the digital economy due to the breadth and depth of technical expertise required to understand servers that store data, to blockchain that captures information, and to software systems. They all are separate pieces of the technology jig-saw puzzle that, will have specific expertise. It is unlikely an expert in blockchain will also be an expert in the operation of a server that stores data.

The life cycle of the data and its ensuing security will need to be understood, along with the law that underpins this economy activity. However, it is acknowledged that data and cybersecurity are by and large only going to be secondary in a dispute that is related to a contract of purchase or technology in regard to data. As highlighted in a previous chapter, data will become a direct issue where it concerns direct access to the system or infrastructure.

Furthermore, the expert must be proficient in being able to prove facts related to the technology, and cyber- or data-related matters. This will also apply to the law. This will reduce the costs to the party requesting the use of the expert. On a final note, it is my view that as technology evolves, so too will the law, which will make the digital economy a distinctive area of expertise that will be needed in arbitration. Carefully considered arbitration clauses will be required, along with memorandums of understanding, or terms of reference for the management of experts and their appointments.

Chapter 27
Enforcement of Arbitration Award

27.1 Introduction

The United Nations Commission for International Trade Law (UNCITRAL) Model Law on Arbitration has served international commercial arbitration well. Once an arbitration award has been handed down by a Tribunal, the decision is final and enforceable on the parties.

That said, *Article 35. Recognition and enforcement provides that:*

(1) *An arbitral award, irrespective of the country in which it was made, shall be recognised as binding and, upon application in writing to the competent court, shall be enforced subject to the provisions of this article and of article 36.*
(2) *The party relying on an award or applying for its enforcement shall supply the original award or a copy thereof. If the award is not made in an official language of this State, the court may request the party to supply a translation thereof into such language.*[1]

Given the above, the question is whether the respective Commonwealth members have adopted the Convention on the Recognition and Enforcement of Foreign Arbitral Awards of 1958 was finalised under the auspices of the United Nations Economic and Social Council at a Conference convened in New York in 1958 (New York Convention-NYC).

This chapter will ascertain whether has been adopted by Commonwealth member countries. It will show the options available to the technology sector engaging in the digital economy, and the provisions in relation to the enforcement of arbitral awards.

The adoption of the UNCITRAL Model Law on Arbitration ensures that an arbitration award handed down by a Tribunal is final and binding. However, under certain circumstances, the award can be challenged. Gary Born, a leading international arbitrator, states that:

---

[1] UNCITRAL Model Law on International Commercial Arbitration 1985 With amendments as adopted in 2006, https://uncitral.un.org/sites/uncitral.un.org/files/media-documents/uncitral/en/19-09955_e_ebook.pdf.

R. Walters, *Cybersecurity and Data Laws of the Commonwealth*,
https://doi.org/10.1007/978-981-99-3935-0_27

> The enforcement of international arbitral awards is subject to a complex legal framework derived from international and national sources. On the national level, national arbitration statutes provide procedural mechanisms and substantive criteria for vacating, confirming, and enforcing international arbitral awards. On the international level, also outlined below, the New York Convention, the Inter-American Convention, and other bilateral and multilateral treaties address.[2]

This chapter examines the Convention on the Recognition and Enforcement of Foreign Arbitral Awards of 1958 was finalised under the auspices of the United Nations Economic and Social Council at a Conference convened in New York in 1958 (New York Convention-NYC).[3] It is considered one of the most widely accepted international legal instruments in relation to international arbitration.[4] Historically, the New York Convention replaced the 1927 Geneva Convention and the 1923 Geneva Protocol.[5] It was prepared by the United Nations in 1958 prior to the establishment of the UNCITRAL in 1969, and seeks to achieve two goals to provide common legislative standards to ensure that:

1. agreements to arbitrate are respected; and
2. foreign and non-domestic arbitral awards will be recognised and enforced.[6]

Put forward as one of the most widely-adopted international legal instruments in transnational commercial law, it has been ratified by 165 states.[7] Arguably, its success has been underpinned by the fact that it has become central to the final process of an arbitration. This chapter will examine a number of Commonwealth member countries to ascertain whether and how they have adopted the New York Convention. Furthermore, Born posits 'equally relevant to the enforcement of international arbitral awards are international arbitration conventions. Particularly significant in this regard is the New York Convention. A principal purpose of the Convention was to make it easier to enforce an arbitral award in one country in other nations'.[8] Also, in referring to the New York Convention, Born states that:

> where the New York Convention is applicable (where its "jurisdictional requirements" are satisfied) , it imposes a general obligation on signatory states to enforce arbitral awards. Article III of the Convention requires signatory states to recognise arbitral awards made in other countries, subject to procedural requirements no more onerous than those for domestic

[2] Gary Born, Intern*ational Commercial Arbitration, Commentary and Materials : Recognition and Enforcement of International Arbitration Awards: Basic Principles,* Brill (2001), p. 706.

[3] The Commonwealth Secretariate, https://uncitral.un.org/sites/uncitral.un.org/files/media-documents/uncitral/en/new-york-convention-commonwealth.pdf.

[4] Ibid.

[5] The Convention on the Recognition and Enforcement of Foreign Arbitral Awards of 1958 was finalised under the auspices of the United Nations Economic and Social Council at a Conference convened in New York in 1958.

[6] N. Blackaby and C. Partasides QC, with Alan Redfern, Michael Hunter, Redfern and Hunter on International Arbitration, Student Edition, 6th ed. Oxford: Oxford University Press, (2015) p. 61.

[7] New York Convention, Contracting States, https://www.newyorkconvention.org/countries.

[8] Gary Born, Intern*ational Commercial Arbitration, Commentary and Materials : Recognition and Enforcement of International Arbitration Awards: Basic Principles,* Brill (2001), p. 706.

> awards. Article III's presumption of enforceability is subject to important jurisdictional limitations, set forth in Article I, and significant exceptions, set forth in Article V. Article V of the Convention sets forth a limited set of grounds for non-recognition of an arbitral award. Importantly, Article V's exceptions are exclusive; outside its country of origin, recognition can be denied a Convention award only on one of the grounds contained in Article V. In light of all these features, national courts have emphasized the "general pro-enforcement bias informing the Convention.[9]

What Born is referring to is that the New York Convention sets out important obligations for those states that have ratified the legal instrument. It has underpinned and supported a high level of legal certainty in commercial disputes. Arguably, without the ability to enforce an arbitration award, then it would make these obligations all but useless and the commercial sector would not take them seriously. The very nature of arbitration being confidential supports the need for a level of enforcement. That said, another important article mentioned by Born is Article V provides:

1. *Recognition and enforcement of the award may be refused, at the request of the party against whom it is invoked, only if that party furnishes to the competent authority where the recognition and enforcement is sought, proof that:*

    (a) *The parties to the agreement referred to in article II were, under the law applicable to them, under some incapacity, or the said agreement is not valid under the law to which the parties have subjected it or, failing any indication thereon, under the law of the country where the award was made; or*
    (b) *The party against whom the award is invoked was not given proper notice of the appointment of the arbitrator or of the arbitration proceedings or was otherwise unable to present his case; or*
    (c) *The award deals with a difference not contemplated by or not falling within the terms of the submission to arbitration, or it contains decisions on matters beyond the scope of the submission to arbitration, provided that, if the decisions on matters submitted to arbitration can be separated from those not so submitted, that part of the award which contains decisions on matters submitted to arbitration may be recognized and enforced; or*
    (d) *The composition of the arbitral authority or the arbitral procedure was not in accordance with the agreement of the parties, or, failing such agreement, was not in accordance with the law of the country where the arbitration took place; or*
    (e) *The award has not yet become binding on the parties, or has been set aside or suspended by a competent authority of the country in which, or under the law of which, that award was made.*

2. *Recognition and enforcement of an arbitral award may also be refused if the competent authority in the country where recognition and enforcement is sought finds that:*

    (a) *The subject matter of the difference is not capable of settlement by arbitration under the law of that country; or*

[9] Ibid, 707.

(b) *The recognition or enforcement of the award would be contrary to the public policy of that country.*[10]

Additionally, as noted by Born, the New York Convention 'applies only to so-called "foreign" and "non-domestic" arbitral awards. Article 1(1) provides that the Convention applies to arbitral awards that either: (l) are "made" outside the country where enforcement is sought (Le., a "foreign" award"), or (2) are "not considered as domestic awards" in the country where enforcement is sought (i.e., a "non-domestic" award)'.[11] Thus, where there is a commercial dispute involving technology, cyber-security and data in the digital economy, parties to the dispute need to be aware of and understand the difference between a domestic and foreign award. For arbitration specialist, this is a basic level of understanding, however, there will be parties in and across the digital economy that have never been exposed to the legal landscape of transnational commercial arbitration. Generally, members of the Commonwealth have embraced in full, or some elements of, the international legal framework for transnational commercial arbitration.

Australia[12] refers to Convention as the Convention on the Recognition and Enforcement of Foreign Arbitral Awards adopted in 1958 by the United Nations Conference on International Commercial Arbitration at its twenty-fourth meeting, a copy of the English text of which is set out in Schedule 1. Under the UNCITRAL Model law[13] the definitions are somewhat limited to Article 2. For instance, 'arbitration' means any arbitration whether or not administered by a permanent arbitral institution, and arbitral tribunal is a sole arbitrator or a panel of arbitrators. In addition to the above, **Canada,**[14] **India,**[15] **Malaysia,**[16] **Kenya,**[17] **Pakistan,**[18] **Singapore,**[19]

[10] The Convention on the Recognition and Enforcement of Foreign Arbitral Awards of 1958 was finalised under the auspices of the United Nations Economic and Social Council at a Conference convened in New York in 1958.

[11] Gary Born, Intern*ational Commercial Arbitration, Commentary and Materials : Recognition and Enforcement of International Arbitration Awards: Basic Principles,* Brill (2001), p. 712.

[12] International Arbitration Act 1974, https://www.legislation.gov.au/Details/C2018C00439.

[13] UNCITRAL Model Law on International Commercial Arbitration (As adopted by the United Nations Commission on International Trade Law on 21 June 1985, and as amended by the United Nations Commission on International Trade Law on 7 July 2006).

[14] Commercial Arbitration Act 1985, https://laws-lois.justice.gc.ca/eng/acts/c-34.6/fulltext.html.

[15] Arbitration and Conciliation Act 1996, https://www.indiacode.nic.in/bitstream/123456789/1978/1/AAA1996__26.pdf Sections 2 & 7.

[16] Arbitration Act 2005, http://www.arbiter.com.sg/pdf/laws/Malaysia%20Arbitration%20Act%202005%20(Revised%202011).pdf section 2.

[17] Arbitration Act 2010, https://ncia.or.ke/wp-content/uploads/2021/02/ArbitrationAct4of1995_2.pdf.

[18] Arbitration Act 1940, https://www.ma-law.org.pk/pdflaw/Arbitration%20Act,%201940.pdf.

[19] Arbitration Act 2001, https://sso.agc.gov.sg/Act/AA2001.

Sri Lanka,[20] **New Zealand**,[21] **South Africa**[22] and the **United Kingdom** are parties to the New York Convention.[23] Generally, most members of the Commonwealth have adopted the New York Convention. It is out of scope to confirm how the respective states have ratified this legal instrument. The importance of the adoption of this legal instrument cannot be underestimated; hence its success. It has a wider reach than merely providing for the enforcement of an award, and on occasion an arbitration agreement can and will determine the outcome of the enforceability of an award, indicating its importance. The next section describes a case from South Africa, in which the court was required to consider the arbitration contract in light of the enforcement of the arbitration award.

South Africa

As highlighted above, an ensuing challenge over the years has been for the courts to reconcile the enforcement of an arbitral award with domestic law. In the case of *Phoenix Shipping*,[24] the Court was required to reconcile the enforcement of a foreign arbitral award with section 2 of the Recognition and Enforcement of Foreign Arbitral Awards Act, 40 of 1977. The Court argued that such an award cannot be enforced if the agreement on the basis of which the award was made is invalid or if the recognition and enforcement of such an award will be contrary to public policy in the Republic. The issue arose from an application for the:

> recognition and enforcement of a foreign arbitral award. The application arises out of an award made on 16 March 2011 when Phoenix Shipping Corporation, a company duly incorporated in accordance with the laws of Delaware, United States of America, obtained a foreign arbitration award pursuant to proceedings conducted in the London Court of International Arbitration, based in London, United Kingdom, under the auspices of the London Maritime Arbitrators Association. The parties to the arbitration proceedings were Phoenix Shipping Corporation, DHL Global Forwarding SA (Pty) Ltd and Bateman Projects Limited, trading as Bateman Engineered Technologies. The latter two companies are South African based companies, having registered places of businesses in the province of Gauteng.[25]

In relation to the domestic arbitration law of South Africa, the Court noted that:

> Bateman resists the relief sought by DHL against it on the basis that it never was a party to any agreement which contained a submission to arbitration; that it is no party to any agreement that seeks to submit the parties to the application of English law; that the arbitrator had no

[20] Arbitration Act 1995, https://www.slnarbcentre.com/pdf/ARBITRATION-ACT.pdf or https://webcache.googleusercontent.com/search?q=cache:CBtAZfCjJG0J:https://www.slnarbcentre.com/pdf/ARBITRATION-ACT.pdf&cd=3&hl=en&ct=clnk&gl=sg&client=safari.

[21] Arbitration act 1996, https://www.legislation.govt.nz/act/public/1996/0099/latest/DLM403277.html.

[22] Arbitration Act 1965, https://www.gov.za/documents/arbitration-act-14-apr-1965-0000 section 1.

[23] Arbitration Act 1996, https://www.legislation.gov.uk/ukpga/1996/23/contents.

[24] *Phoenix Shipping v DHL Global Forwarding SA (Pty) Ltd and Bateman Projects Ltd t/a Bateman Engineered Technologies* (2012) (3) SA 381. https://www.saflii.org/za/cases/ZAWCHC/2012/11.html.

[25] Ibid, para 1.

> jurisdiction to determine the dispute; that the arbitrator had no jurisdiction over Bateman and arising therefrom, Bateman refused to submit to arbitration; and that in view thereof, the enforcement of the arbitral award, as against Bateman, would be contrary to public policy in the Republic as contemplated in section 4(1)(a)(ii) of the Recognition and Enforcement of Foreign Arbitral Awards Act.[26]

From the outset, this case highlights the importance of what was stated in an earlier chapter; that is, that there is a need to look at the arbitration agreement carefully in order to determine the governing agreed rules for arbitration. It also highlights how the enforcement of any arbitration award could become challenging under domestic laws. Thus, the ensuing question is whether the New York Convention was applicable in this matter. The Court noted that on an international level, the enforcement of foreign arbitral awards is governed by the Convention on the Recognition and Enforcement of Foreign Arbitral Awards of 1958, commonly known as the New York Convention.[27] The Court went further and confirmed what this chapter asserts: that South Africa acceded to this convention without reservation in 1976.[28] Another question relates to when South Africa enacted its domestic laws on arbitration. The Court noted that the enactment of the Recognition and the Enforcement of Foreign Arbitral Awards Act in 1977 was to give effect to this ratification.[29] Also, the Court made the following point regarding the international convention:

> The New York Convention recognises the circumstances under which the recognition and enforcement of an award may be refused. It provides as follows in article V(1)(a): (1) Recognition and enforcement of the award may be refused, at the request of the party against whom it is invoked, only if that party furnishes to the competent authority where the recognition and enforcement is sought, proof that: (a) The parties to the agreement referred to in article II were, under the law applicable to them, under some incapacity, or the said agreement is not valid under the law to which the parties have subjected it or, failing any indication thereon, under the law of the country where the award was made; ..." It is worth noting that section 103(2(b) of the English Arbitration Act, 1996 contain words which are identical to the provisions of section 4(1)(b)(i) of the Recognition and Enforcement of Foreign Arbitral Awards Act, as also article V(1)(a) of the New York Convention.[30]

The Court was making a distinction between domestic South African and English law, along with the international legal framework. It highlighted that by adopting the New York Convention, South Africa had all but transposed the wording from Article V into the domestic law. The Court also referred went on to say in referring to the well-known case of *Dallian*[31] where it was contended that:

> In rejecting the contention by Dallah that the Government of Pakistan can only challenge the jurisdictional ruling in France, the Supreme Court held, per Lord Mance, that neither article V(1)(c) of the New York Convention nor section 103(5) of the English Arbitration

---

[26] Ibid, para 5.

[27] Ibid, para 35.

[28] Ibid.

[29] Ibid.

[30] Ibid, paras 35–36.

[31] Ibid, para 55, *Dalian Real Estate & Tourism Holding Company v Government of Pakistan* 2010 4 KSC 46.

> Act, 1996 contain any suggestion that a party resisting recognition or enforcement of an award in any one country has an obligation to seek to set aside the award in the other country where the award was made. Thus, by implication, the English Supreme Court held that the provisions of section 103(f) of the English Arbitration Act, 1996 did not preclude a challenge in England a jurisdictional challenge of a foreign award.[32]

A foreign award can be handed down and challenged, provided there was an agreement in place to arbitrate. In determining how far invalidity extended, the Court made the point that it is not defined in the New York Convention, nor is the term defined in either the English Arbitration Act, 1996 or the Arbitration Act presently applying in South Africa.[33] The framers of the New York Convention thus left it to the signatories to the Convention to determine in their respective countries the meaning to attribute to the term "invalidity". Invalidity, in the circumstances of the matter before this Court, would include a "contract" purportedly concluded between the parties in circumstances where consensus cannot be proved. DHL failed to prove a valid agreement containing a submission to arbitration.[34] In highlighting the importance of an arbitration agreement, in order for it to be binding and enforceable, the Court made the point that:

> An arbitration agreement is based on consensus between the parties. Consensus is a fundamental element of a contract. Consensus is an element of such fundamental importance in the law of contracts which no nation in the civilised world can derogate from. Any contract which does not contain consensus as an element would offend those norms and values which characterise a civilised society. Absent the element of consensus in any alleged or purported contract, the purported agreement or contract is invalid. With these values and norms in mind it was determine that the purported agreement, on the basis of which the tribunal in London found Bateman liable to DHL, is invalid. The recognition and the enforcement of an award derived from such alleged or purported agreement would offend public policy in the Republic.[35]

Thus, a mere booking note does not constitute a contract,[36] and the case further demonstrated and reaffirmed that for an award to be enforced, it must first come with a contract whereby there is agreement between the parties to arbitrate. This element for those operating in the digital economy is significantly important, because of the potential amounts in disputes. Technology, cybersecurity and data combined can generate millions, if not billions, of dollars. Therefore, the contractual terms need to be carefully developed.

Singapore

In addition to the above, the setting aside of an award can often come under Article V (e) of the New York Convention. A recent case from the United States underscored the setting aside of an award. The question that can arise is: what has this got to do

[32] Ibid, para 58.

[33] Ibid, 63, 64, 65.

[34] Ibid.

[35] Ibid.

[36] Ibid, 64.

with technology, data, and cybersecurity within the digital economy? In the case of *Commodities* the[37]:

> Petitioner Commodities and Minerals Enterprise Ltd. sought an order to confirm arbitration award pursuant to Chapter 2 of the Federal Arbitration Act, 9 U.S.C. §§ 201 et seq., and Article III of the United Nations Convention on the Recognition and Enforcement of Foreign Arbitral Awards, June 10, 1958, 330 U.N.T.S. 38 (the "New York Convention"). Specifically, it asks the Court to issue an order to (1) confirm an international arbitration award in favor of Petitioner made by a panel of three arbitrators in an arbitration administered by the Society of Maritime Arbitrators-SMA, sitting in New York, New York, pursuant to the rules of the SMA, (2) direct the Clerk to enter final judgment thereon against Respondent CVG Ferrominera Orinoco, C.A., including interest on $12,655,594.36 at 5.50% per annum from December 20, 2018 until the date of judgment, and at the statutory rate thereafter; and (3) grant Petitioner its costs and expenses, including reasonable attorneys' fees, in this proceeding. For the reasons that follow the Court GRANTS Petitioner's motion.[38]

In relation to Article V, the Court stated that:

> A district court is strictly limited to the seven defenses under the New York Convention when considering whether to confirm a foreign award. *Encyclopaedia Universalis S.A. v. Encyclopaedia Britannica, Inc.*, 403 F.3d 85, 90 (2d Cir. 2005). The party opposing enforcement of an arbitral award has the burden to prove that one of the seven defenses under the New York Convention applies. The burden is a heavy one, as 'the showing required to avoid summary conformance is high'.[39]

The Court went further in relation to a review of 'arbitral awards under the New York Convention is "very limited ... in order to avoid undermining the twin goals of arbitration, namely, settling disputes efficiently and avoiding long and expensive litigation"'.[40] Therefore, those involved in an arbitration cannot simply oppose or seek to have an award set aside. In making limiting how an award can be set aside, it ensures that the arbitration process is as efficient as possible and minimises costs to the organisation. Nonetheless, and while this was a US court decision, courts across the Commonwealth are likely to look to this decision for reference.

Singapore is another Commonwealth member who has adopted the common law, and is considered an arbitration centre.

In the case of CKR[41] in 2021, the Court was required to rule on the setting aside of an arbitration award. It brought together the setting aside of an award and the seat. The Court stated that on '12 July 2016, the Plaintiffs commenced an arbitration against the Defendants, on the basis that the Plaintiffs were entitled to the US$35 million in Earn Out Consideration from the Defendants because their terminations were "Without Cause". The seat of the arbitration was Singapore. A three-member tribunal was

---

[37] United States, U.S. District Court, Southern District of New York/*Commodities & Minerals Enterprise, Ltd v CVG Ferrominera Orrinoco,* C.A./1:19-CV-11654-ALC. https://law.justia.com/cases/federal/district-courts/new-york/nysdce/1:2019cv11654/528772/44/.

[38] Ibid, p. 1–2.

[39] Ibid, p. 6.

[40] Ibid, p. 7.

[41] *CKR and another v CKT and another* [2021] SGHCR 4, https://www.elitigation.sg/gd/s/2021_SGHCR_4.

constituted to hear the arbitration'.[42] In all there were 2 partial awards issues, and a final award, along with an additional final award. The process of application for the setting aside of the award was as follows:

> Shortly after the Tribunal issued the First Partial Award, on 1 June 2018, the Defendants filed Originating Summons No 683 of 2018 in the High Court seeking to challenge the First Partial Award on the following grounds that the Tribunal had jurisdiction to determine whether the respondents were terminated "Without Cause" for the purposes of the SPA pursuant to s 10(3)(b) of the International Arbitration Act (Cap 143A, 2002 Rev Ed); (b) in the alternative pursuant to s 24(b) of the IAA and Art 34(2) of the UNCITRAL Model Law on International Commercial Arbitration.[43]

Importantly, the Court, while not specifying that Singapore had ratified the Model Law, referred to both the domestic and international arrangements allowing for the setting aside of an award. While it is out of scope to confirm whether International Arbitration Act replicates in full the Model Law, the reference "without cause" related to termination letters. Each of the applications was dismissed by the Court, and this indicated the relationship between the domestic and international law. The Court stated that s 101(2) of the 'Arbitration Act 1996, provides that a New York Convention award may, by permission of the court, be enforced in the same manner as a judgment or order of the court to the same effect, and s 101(3) goes on to state that where leave is so given, judgment may be entered in terms of the award'.[44] Moreover, in relation to Article V, the Court in referring to Gary Born[45] noted:

> Other authorities hold that *an award can be "binding" even if it is subject to a pending action to annul in the place where it was made*... This conclusion is decisively supported by Article VI of the Convention, which permits national courts to discretionarily stay recognition proceedings pending the resolution of applications to annul an award in the arbitral seat (i.e., "[i]f an application for the setting aside or suspension of the award" has been made). It is impossible to reconcile Article VI's grant of discretion to suspend recognition proceedings, based on a pending annulment action, with an interpretation of Article V(1)(e) that would treat awards subject to annulment as non-binding; *the premise of Article VI is that an award is subject to recognition, and therefore "binding," even if it is subject to an annulment action, and instead that recognition may be suspended as a consequence of the annulment proceeding.*[46]

In supporting the interpretation of Article V(e), the Court ruled that, pertinent to the above:

> The award made by the tribunal is final and binding on the parties as to the merits of the subject-matter determined under that award. The fact that a party has curial remedies to challenge an award does not affect the final and binding nature of an award. Further, an award is binding on the parties even though there may be pending applications to set aside that award.[47]

---

[42] Ibid, para 8.

[43] Ibid, para 15.

[44] Ibid, para 25.

[45] Ibid, para 34, Gary B. Born in *International Commercial Arbitration* (Kluwer Law International, 3rd Ed, 2020) (at [3613]).

[46] Ibid.

[47] Ibid, para 35.

In conclusion, the Court granted that the Plaintiff was able to enforce all awards. It is a reminder that challenging an award for it to be set aside under national law, will depend on establishing whether the state and the arbitration agreement has accepted the use and application of, for example, the Model Law and the New York Convention. Generally, the courts will view the provisions of the national laws to confirm any divergence from the equivalent international legal instruments. Finally, and while the grounds for 'setting aside as set out in article 34 (2) are almost identical to those for refusing recognition or enforcement as set out in article 36 (1), a practical difference should be noted. An application for setting aside under article 34 (2) may only be made to a court in the State where the award was rendered whereas an application for enforcement might be made in a court in any State. For that reason, the grounds relating to public policy and non-arbitrability may vary in substance with the law applied by the court (in the State of setting aside or in the State of enforcement)'.[48]

United Kingdom

Recently, the UK Court in the 2021 case of *Kabab-Ji SAL*[49] had to decide whether an international arbitration agreement is valid or whether it covers a particular dispute. The first step is to determine which system of law the court must apply to answer this question.[50] In referring to a case a year earlier, the questions of how a court of England and Wales should identify the applicable law was recently considered by this court in *Enka Insaat Ve Sanayi AS v OOO "Insurance Company Chubb"* [2020] USKC 38. In that case:

---

[48] UNCITRAL 2012 Digest of Case Law on the Model Law on International Commercial Arbitration.

https://uncitral.un.org/sites/uncitral.un.org/files/media-documents/uncitral/en/mal-digest-2012-e.pdf Article 34. Application for setting aside as exclusive recourse against arbitral award (1) Recourse to a court against an arbitral award may be made only by an application for setting aside in accordance with paragraphs (2) and (3) of this article. (2) An arbitral award may be set aside by the court specified in article 6 only if: (a) the party making the application furnishes proof that: (i) a party to the arbitration agreement referred to in article 7 was under some incapacity; or the said agreement is not valid under the law to which the parties have subjected it or, failing any indication thereon, under the law of this State; or (ii) the party making the application was not given proper notice of the appointment of an arbitrator or of the arbitral proceedings or was otherwise unable to present his case; or (iii) the award deals with a dispute not contemplated by or not falling within the terms of the submission to arbitration, or contains decisions on matters beyond the scope of the submission to arbitration, provided that, if the decisions on matters submitted to arbitration can be separated from those not so submitted, only that part of the award which contains decisions on matters not submitted to arbitration may be set aside; or (iv) the composition of the arbitral tribunal or the arbitral procedure was not in accordance with the agreement of the parties, unless such agreement was in conflict with a provision of this Law from which the parties cannot derogate, or, failing such agreement, was not in accordance with this Law; or (b) the court finds that: (i) the subject-matter of the dispute is not capable of settlement by arbitration under the law of this State; or (ii) the award is in conflict with the public policy of this State.

[49] *Kabab-Ji SAL (Lebanon) (Appellant) v Kout Food Group (Kuwait) (Respondent)* [2021] UKSC 48.

[50] Ibid, para 1.

> the question of which law governed the validity and scope of an arbitration agreement arose before any arbitration had taken place. In the present case the question of which law governs the validity of an arbitration agreement arises in the different context where an arbitration has already taken place and proceedings have been brought in England to enforce an award made by the arbitral tribunal. The defendant (who took part in the arbitration under protest) maintains that it is not a party to the arbitration agreement and is therefore not bound by the decision of the arbitrators. As in *Enka*, the first question is to identify which system of law the English court must apply to decide whether there is an enforceable arbitration agreement. That is the first issue in this appeal. If the courts below were correct to decide that English law should be applied, two further issues arise. One is whether the Court of Appeal was right to hold that, as a matter of English law, the defendant never became a party to the arbitration agreement. The other is whether, procedurally, the Court of Appeal was right to decide that question and give summary judgment refusing enforcement of the award.[51]

Hence, a 'dispute arose under the Franchise Agreements which the claimant referred to arbitration under the rules of the International Chamber of Commerce in Paris. That arbitration was commenced against KFG alone, and not against Al Homaizi. KFG took part in the arbitration under protest, maintaining that it was not a party to the Franchise Agreements or the arbitration agreements contained in them'.[52] In providing for the operation of an award in the national laws, the Court stated that:

> The operative provisions of the Convention have been transposed into the law of England and Wales by Part III of the Arbitration Act 1996. Section 100(1) of the 1996 Act defines a "New York Convention award" as an award made, in pursuance of an arbitration agreement, in the territory of a state (other than the United Kingdom) which is a party to the New York Convention. Section 101 provides that a New York Convention award may, by leave of the court, be enforced in the same manner as a judgment of the English court and that, where leave is so given, judgment may be entered in the terms of the award. Section 102(1) specifies evidence which a party seeking the recognition enforcement of a New York Convention award must produce. This comprises: the duly authenticated original award or a duly certified copy of it, and the original arbitration agreement or a duly certified copy of it. Section 103 of the 1996 Act replicates article V of the Convention and reads (in relevant part) as follows: Recognition or enforcement of a New York Convention award shall not be refused except in the following cases. Recognition or enforcement of the award may be refused if the person against whom it is invoked proves that a party to the arbitration agreement was (under the law applicable to him) under some incapacity; that the arbitration agreement was not valid under the law to which the parties subjected it or, failing any indication thereon, under the law of the country where the award was made; that the award has not yet become binding on the parties, or has been set aside or suspended by a competent authority of the country in which, or under the law of which, it was made.[53] Nonetheless, Article V comes with inherent challenges, for instance, in regard to the conflict-of-laws rules. The Court noted that:

> article V(1)(a) of the Convention establishes two uniform international conflict of laws rules. The first, and primary, rule is that the validity of the arbitration agreement is governed by "the law to which the parties subjected it"—in other words the law chosen by the parties. The second, default rule, which applies where no choice has been indicated, is that the applicable law is that of "the country where the award was made". Where the parties have chosen the

---

[51] Ibid, para 2.

[52] Ibid, para 5.

[53] Ibid, paras 12, 13, 14.

> seat of arbitration, the place where the award was made will be (or be deemed to be) the place of the seat. In English law this is expressly provided by section 100(2)(b) of the 1996 Act.[54]

Thus, the seat of arbitration becomes crucial to where the award will be made. Similar to many other cases that have been decided based on Article 5, the Court referred to the case of *Dalla*,[55] and all but departed from the position stated in this case. However, in further reconciling the conflict-of-laws issue, the Court stated in relation to Article V that:

> the law applied by the English and French courts to decide that issue is different. For the reasons given earlier, the law which the English court must apply to decide that issue is English law. As described in a joint expert report in these proceedings, however, French law takes a very different approach to the determination of such questions. French case law has abandoned a conflict of laws approach of selecting a national law which governs the existence and validity of the arbitration agreement and has instead created "substantive rules of international arbitration" to govern the issue.[56]

Moreover, and to better understand the difference between the English common law and the French civil law, the Court stated:

> as the substantive rules of international arbitration which the French courts apply are rules of their own creation, the reality is that the French courts determine questions about the existence and validity of an international arbitration agreement by reference to French law (albeit rules of French law which differ from those applicable to domestic agreements). The English court cannot be bound by the decision of the French court because the English court must apply a different system of law to determine the issue.[57]

Essentially, the Court agreed with the Court of Appeal. It confirmed the complex nature of the national laws when they do not converge or harmonise. The case underscores the reach of the New York Convention.

27.2 Conclusion

The Commonwealth should work with bodies such as UNCITRAL to encourage the adoption of the Model Law and the New York Convention. Together, they provide a robust international legal framework for resolving dispute across the digital economy. The enforcement of an award is paramount to ensuring that the arbitration has achieved its desired result. In enforcing an award, the arbitration agreement may be called upon. The concepts and principles of arbitration compared are all elements of the overall binding award.

---

[54] Ibid, para 26.

[55] Ibid, para 77, *Dallah Real Estate and Tourism Holding Co v Ministry of Religious Affairs of the Government of Pakistan* [2008] EWHC 1901, [2009] 1 All ER (Comm) 505.

[56] Ibid, para 88.

[57] Ibid, para 89.

Nevertheless, as stated above, under the New York Convention, an award can be set aside by the courts. However, the process for setting aside an award may vary from state to state in accordance with the national laws. It is well understood that the refusal to enforce an arbitral award under the Model Law is limited, which by and large follows the provisions of Article V of the New York Convention.

This chapter has given only a brief analysis of the New York Convention and there are additional areas of equal importance under Article V that need to be considered such as, incapacity of the party; lack of valid arbitration agreement; procedural unfairness; excess of authority; composition of a tribunal or arbitral procedure not in accordance with the parties' agreement; the award is not yet binding; and annulment of the award at the seat. Moreover, Article V(2) extends the above to include non-arbitrability of the dispute, and a violation of public policy. These areas are all for future research to examine in relation to the formal and functional requirements of an arbitral award.

This chapter has also confirmed the importance of the arbitration agreement since the courts will generally examine the arbitration agreement to determine the reference to the relevant law to be applied in the arbitration. A greater number of countries have adopted the New York Convention rather than the Model Law. This issue needs to be addressed as a matter of urgency. Doing so will enable the small and medium sized business sector in the digital economy to address disputes through well-drafted contracts and arbitration agreements. It will give this sector alone greater access to the benefits of arbitration. Therefore, this book is calling upon the Commonwealth to expand its current work to ensure that this area of arbitration law is addressed by all its members. More importantly, it will ensure that the current rules-based system retains its profile, and it will make it more difficult for others who do not agree with this dispute-resolution framework, to change it.

Finally, the New York Convention has been successful in governing the enforcement of arbitration awards across contracting states. It is widely recognised as one of the most successful conventions in international commercial law.

Chapter 28
International Centre for Settlement of Investment Disputes

28.1 Introduction

The International Centre for Settlement of Investment Disputes (ICSID)[1] and its subsequent Convention have become important tools for resolving investor-state disputes in response to the increase in the amount of global foreign investment. For instance, the energy sector has seen its fair share of foreign investment over the past decade.

This brief chapter is concerned with the recognition of the International Centre for Settlement of Investment Disputes and whether it has been adopted by the respective states. It will not determine whether the respective arbitration laws have incorporated the Convention into their national laws. However, it will draw upon the arbitral decisions to confirm whether cybersecurity and data within the new digital economy form part of investor-state disputes.

Firstly though, Antigua and Barbuda, India, and Kiribati, all of which are Commonwealth members, have not adopted the ICSD. **Belize** signed in 1986 but has not adopted the text. Given that such a small number of states have not signed this important Convention, it is something that the Commonwealth can encourage and play a role in expediting this process as soon as possible. Proportionally, when compared with the take-up of the UNCITRAL Model Law on Arbitration, most states have adopted the Convention. For example, **Australia, Bahamas, Barbados, Botswana, Bangladesh, Brunei Darussalam, Cameroon, Canada, Dominica, Fiji, Gabon, Gambia, Ghana, Guyana, Kenya, Kingdom of Eswatini, Malaysia, Malawi, Pakistan, Togo, Tonga**, have adopted the Convention. In addition, **Singapore, Lesotho, Sri Lanka, Jamaica, South Africa, Maldives, along with the countries of Mauritius, Saint Lucia, Namibia, Nauru, St Vincent and The**

[1] International Centre for Settlement of Investment Disputes https://icsid.worldbank.org/about/member-states/database-of-member-states.

R. Walters, *Cybersecurity and Data Laws of the Commonwealth*,
https://doi.org/10.1007/978-981-99-3935-0_28

Grenadines, New Zealand, Trinidad and Tobago, Rwanda[2] **St Kitts and Nevis, Uganda, Tanzania, Cyprus, Malta, United Kingdom, Mozambique, Nigeria, Papua New Guinea, Seychelles, Sierra Leone, Solomon Islands, Samoa and Zambia**[3] have adopted the Convention. The Convention itself has been in place for more than 4 decades, with Cyprus[4] being one of the earliest adopters back in 1966.

The challenge for nation states is to provide a stable regulatory and policy framework for future investment. With the rapid transition of economic activity to a largely digitally-based economy, disputes involving a state and investor in regard to cybersecurity and data protection are, in my view, inevitable.

The ICSID Convention has become an important feature private sector investment in governments around the world. This brief chapter reveals which of the Commonwealth members have adopted the convention. It presents the history and explains the importance of the Convention on the International Centre for Settlement of Investment Disputes[5] and the evolving practice of investor-state arbitration. It shows the Commonwealth members that have adopted the ICSD, the purpose of which is to 'provide facilities for conciliation and arbitration of investment disputes between Contracting States and nationals of other Contracting States in accordance with the provisions of this Convention'. Further, this chapter discusses how investor state arbitration can be applicable to the digital economy in the areas of cybersecurity and data.

Historically, during the '1950 and 1960s witnessed the emergence of two types of treaties aimed at protecting foreign investment: the substantive and the institutional/procedural'.[6] Christopher Thomas and Harpreet Kaur Dhillon make the point that, in terms of the former, some States had long negotiated treaties, enforceable through state-to-state dispute settlement, which included the affordance of basic protections to aliens and their property. They explain that in 1958, the Federal Republic of Germany and the Islamic Republic of Pakistan concluded the first 'modern era' bilateral investment treaty aimed at ensuring reciprocal protection of investments made by their respective nationals,[7] which was enforceable only at the state-to-state level. From the outset, the objective was to 'confer a right of access to international jurisdiction upon private parties similar to that enjoyed by States when they took their

[2] N° 005/2008 of 14/02/2008 Law on arbitration and conciliation in commercial matters, https://www.international-arbitration-attorney.com/wp-content/uploads/2013/07/Rwanda-Arbitration-Law.pdf.

[3] International Centre for Settlement of Investment Disputes, Member States, https://icsid.worldbank.org/about/member-states/database-of-member-states as at January 2023.

[4] Ibid.

[5] Convention on the International Centre for Settlement of Investment Disputes https://icsid.worldbank.org/sites/default/files/ICSID_Convention_EN.pdf - Convention on the Settlement of Investment Disputes between States and Nationals of Other States (ICSID Convention) 1965, 575 UNTS 159.

[6] J. Christopher Thomas, Harpreet Kaur Dhillon, *The Foundations of Investment Treaty Arbitration: The ICSID Convention, Investment Treaties and the Review of Arbitration Awards, ICSID Review, Foreign Investment Law Journal,* Vol 32, Issue 3, (2017), p. 461.

[7] Ibid.

disputes to international courts and tribunals'.[8] It paved the way for arbitration to be used to settle investment disputes. Essentially, two features emerged that today still remain important to arbitration. First is the voluntary nature of arbitration. Second is the 'once consent to arbitration was given by both parties, a legally enforceable arbitration agreement was formed and neither party could unilaterally prevent the arbitration from proceeding, for example, by declining to appear'.[9] Importantly, the provision of a platform of rules for arbitrating and resolving investment disputes has found its way into investment treaties in the modern era. Simply put, and while not examining every state investment treaty, today, many have specific dispute clauses that, enable or direct the parties to arbitrate. For instance, in the Australian and Singapore Free Trade Agreement of 2003, Chapter 15 on dispute resolution provides that:

> Unless otherwise agreed by the Parties elsewhere in this Agreement, the provisions of this Chapter shall apply with respect to the avoidance or settlement of disputes between the Parties concerning their rights and obligations under this Agreement. The rules and procedures set out in this Chapter may be waived, varied or modified by mutual agreement. Findings and recommendations of an arbitral tribunal cannot add to or diminish the rights and obligations of the Parties under this Agreement. The provisions of this Chapter may be invoked in respect of measures affecting the observance of this Agreement taken by regional or local governments or authorities within the territory of a Party. When an arbitral tribunal has ruled that a provision of this Agreement has not been observed, the responsible Party shall take such reasonable measures as may be available to it to ensure its observance. The provisions of this Chapter relating to compensation and suspension of benefits apply in cases where it has not been possible to secure such observance. 5. Arbitral tribunals shall clarify the provisions of this Agreement in accordance with customary rules of interpretation of public international law.[10]

Thus, the example above demonstrates highlights that the role of arbitration has become a central feature of FTAs. A cause for concern is that, over the past decade, there has been a decrease in direct foreign investment by Commonwealth members,[11] and the resulting effect has seen other nation states who are not members, step in and fill the gap. This, in my view, needs to be addressed. Thus, the ensuing question is: to what extent does data and cybersecurity influence an investment dispute.

Firstly, there is the emerging view that there are 'components of digital operations could qualify as investment and enjoy protection under international investment law'.[12] Secondly in a clear example of what Zhang is referring to can be found in

[8] Ibid, p. 463.

[9] Ibid, p. 464.

[10] Australian-Singapore Free trade Agreement 2003, Chapter 15, Article 1, https://investmentpolicy.unctad.org/international-investment-agreements/treaty-files/2648/download.

[11] Sebastian Shehadi, Ben van der Merwe, Why is investment between Commonwealth countries drying up? Foreign investment inside the Commonwealth has been falling for years, especially from some of its largest economies, which are missing a rich opportunity, 2022, https://www.investmentmonitor.ai/features/investment-commonwealth-countries-members-fdi/.

[12] Sheng Zhang, Protection of Cross-Border Data Flows Under International Investment Law Scope and Boundaries, J. Chaisse et al. (eds.), Handbook of International Investment Law and Policy, Springer Nature Singapore Pte Ltd. 2021 1, https://doi.org/10.1007/978-981-13-5744-2_126-1.

the Australian and Singapore Digital Economic Agreement (DEA). The DEA was established to address the shortcomings of the broader FTAs between the two states, specifically Chapter 14 related to the Digital Economy.[13] Third is defines personal information as any information, including data, about an identified or identifiable natural person. Article 17 deals specifically with personal information, and there is a general recognition that there are significant economic and social benefits to be had by protecting the personal information of persons who conduct or engage in electronic transactions and commerce.[14] Moreover, the DEA requires both parties to take into account the principles and guidelines of relevant international bodies such as the APEC Cross-Border Privacy Rules System[15] and the *OECD Guidelines Governing the Protection of Privacy and Trans-border.* While this is predominantly relevant to cross-border data flows, it is also relevant to disputes of investments. Article 17.3 specifically references the OECD Guidelines requiring each party to take into account, when developing its legal framework, limitation on collection, data quality, purpose specification, use limitation, security safeguards, transparency, individual participation and accountability. Article 17.4 calls for 'non-discriminatory practices to be adopted in order to protect persons who conduct or engage in electronic transactions from personal information protection violations occurring within its jurisdiction'.[16] To provide a greater level of transparency, Article 17.5 requires each 'Party to publish information on the personal information protections along with information on how a data subject can pursue remedies and how businesses can comply with any legal requirements'.[17] To promote transparency and accountability Article 17.6 'encourages enterprises in its territory to publish, including on the Internet, their policies and procedures related to protection of personal information'.[18]

More generally, and not specific to personal information but to wider information that is transferred by electronic means, Article 23 makes it clear that either party has its own regulatory requirements. Every effort should be made to ensure that there is no prohibition or restrictions placed on cross-border transfer of information by electronic means, including personal information, provided the information is in relation to the business.[19] However, Article 23.3 allows a level of restrictions to be established to protect from discrimination but not to disguise any restriction on trade. Further, any restrictions are not to impede transfers of information greater

---

[13] Australian and Singapore Digital Agreement, https://www.dfat.gov.au/sites/default/files/australia-singapore-digital-economy-agreement.pdf This section draws on the work in Robert Walters, *The Digital Economy and International Trade:* Regulation of Transnational Data Flows, Kluwer Law (2022), Chapter 1.

[14] Ibid, Article 17.

[15] Articles, 17.8 and 17.9, The Parties recognise that the CBPR System is a valid mechanism to facilitate cross-border information transfers while protecting personal information. The Parties shall endeavour to jointly promote the CBPR System, with the aim to improving awareness of, and participation in, the CBPR System, including by industry.

[16] Ibid, Article 17.4.

[17] Ibid, Article 17.5.

[18] Ibid, Article 17.6.

[19] Ibid, Article 23.2.

than what is required to achieve the objective. Article 26 promotes the idea of data innovation so as to support the cross-border transfer of information by electronic means and promote data-driven innovation in the digital economy. Additionally, as part of its respective data diplomacy programs, Article 37 encourages cooperation for the purpose of capacity-building throughout the Asia region for: 'digital connectivity; small and medium business sector digital transformation; data protection regimes; and mechanisms to facilitate the cross-border transfer of information'.[20] Arguably, the DEA supports data defined by the respective data laws that have been discussed in Part I of this book. In another development, cybersecurity has also been reflected in the DEA. Importantly, Article 34 directly links cybersecurity, digital trade and the digital economy. It states:

> The Parties have a shared vision to promote secure digital trade to achieve global prosperity and recognise that cybersecurity underpins the digital economy. The Parties recognise the importance of building the capabilities of their government agencies responsible for computer security incident response; using existing collaboration mechanisms to cooperate to identify and mitigate malicious intrusions or dissemination of malicious code that affect the electronic networks of the Parties; and workforce development in the area of cybersecurity, including possible initiatives relating to mutual recognition of qualifications, diversity and equality.[21]

In relation to the above, Chapter 14, Article 1 provides for the definition under Digital Economy. Thus, personal information under Article 1 constitutes any information, including data, about an identified or identifiable natural person. Arguably, this would include the personal information defined by the Australian Privacy Act 1988 and the Personal Data Protection Act 2012 Singapore, which relates to Article 17—as expressed above. Therefore, data and cybersecurity can be part of an investor-state dispute. Under the DEA, this has been reaffirmed in accordance with Article 16 which states that Dispute Settlement shall apply as modified by this Article to the settlement of disputes arising (a) under this Chapter; or (b) in relation to Article 23 (Cross-Border Transfer of Information by Electronic Means) or Article 25 (Location of Computing Facilities for Financial Services) of Chapter 14 (Digital Economy), to the extent that the dispute relates to financial services. Under Chapter 14, arbitration is confined to only financial services. Hence, does data and cyber security apply to Chapter 14? First, Article 16.2 provides for the appointment of an arbitrator by the respective parties. Therefore, it is argued that under the DEA, an arbitration can include issues related to data and cybersecurity within the digital economy. This is just one example, and further examination will need to be undertaken, on a case-by-case basis, of the FTAs current and future laws that have been established by Commonwealth members. Further, because the DEA is a recent agreement, there will be trade agreements in existence that will not provide for the digital economy.

---

[20] Ibid, Article 37.

[21] Ibid, Article 34.

In supporting the above, Article 47 of the ICSID Convention also provides that tribunals may recommend any provisional measures which should be taken to preserve the respective rights of each party.[22] Arguably, in considering Article 47, it can be determined that data law along with cyber security within the digital economy can be used in an arbitration proceeding. To further reaffirm the position taken in this chapter that data and cybersecurity can form part of investor-state disputes that will be resolved through arbitration, the case of *Giovanna*[23] (2010) is cited. This matter, in part concerned the personal data held on a database by one of the parties. In that case, the Tribunal noted that:

> the Tribunal deems that the ICSID Convention and Arbitration Rules do not comprehensively cover the question of the confidentiality/transparency of the proceedings. Thus, in accordance with Article 44 of the ICSID Convention and Rule 19 of the ICSID Arbitration Rules, unless there exist an agreement of the Parties on the issue of confidentiality/transparency, the Tribunal shall decide on the matter on a case by case basis and, instead of tending towards imposing a general rule in favour or against confidentiality, try to achieve a solution that balances the general interest for transparency with specific interests for confidentiality of certain information and/or documents.[24]

The dispute arose between Argentina and Italy following Argentina defaulting on over US$100 billion. The breach was related to the obligations under the *Agreement between the Republic of Argentina and the Republic of Italy on the Promotion and Protection of Investments*, signed in Buenos Aires on 22 May 1990, in two original copies, in the Italian and the Spanish language, both texts being equally authentic in relation to alleged bonds issued by Respondent, allegedly held by Claimants, on which payment Respondent defaulted. Although not directly related to personal data, the procedural history is given below:

> On 14 September 2006, Claimants filed their Request for Arbitration, accompanied by Annexes A through E, which contain information relating to individual Claimants, such as name, address, Database file number, ISIN Code(s) of bondholding, nominal amount, purchase price and purchase date, as well as supporting documentation with respect to such data.[25]

Regarding the above, the reference to names, address, data file number and ISIN Code, could all constitute personal data defined by the respective states data laws. Even though this dispute did not involve members of the Commonwealth, it highlighted the connection between investor-state arbitration and personal data. In a further development, the Tribunal noted that:

[22] Convention on the Settlement of Investment Disputes between States and Nationals of Other States (ICSID Convention) 1965, 575 UNTS 159, Article 47.

[23] *Giovanna A. Beccara and Others v. Argentina*, 27 January 2010, ICSID Case no. ARB/07/5, https://www.italaw.com/sites/default/files/case-documents/ita0002.pdf.

[24] Ibid, para, 73.

[25] Ibid, para 6.

> On 27 March 2008, Claimants responded to Respondent's letter of 19 March 2008 insisting that ICSID Convention and Rules did not sufficiently protect confidentiality of Claimants' personal data under the applicable Italian law and that they already submitted to Respondent all relevant information in a form complying, and even going beyond the requirements of Rules 1 and 2 of ICSID Institution Rules.[26]

During the proceedings there was some conjecture over the need for the Claimant to hand over a database that contained personal information. Moreover, in connecting the personal data with the respective states data-privacy laws, the Tribunal made the point:

> The Database is kept in Italy and is therefore subject to the Italian Legislative Decree of 30 June 2003 n. 196 (hereinafter, the "Italian Privacy Code"), which mandates strict compliance with a set of rules therein established and regulating, under articles 31–36, the electronic management of personal data. The Italian Privacy Code "requires, in particular, that in the case of access to, and use of, private information through electronic means (such as stand-alone personal computers, networked systems, online electronic access systems), the holder of the data adopts specific technological protection measures illustrated under an ad hoc Annex to the Italian Privacy Code, as amended from time to time".

The Tribunal also highlighted that in the case of transmission of private information to third parties or in the case of transfer of the same towards non-EU Countries, the Italian Privacy Code requires that the transmitting entity take steps to ensure that the data are thereafter used only for the purposes for which they were originally intended. More importantly, the Tribunal relied on the ICSID to manage this data. It noted that the:

> ICSID's legal framework (in particular Article 48(5) of the ICISD Convention and Rules 15 and 32(2) of the ICSID Arbitration Rules) would "not provide for the requisite confidentiality for Claimants' data", and it would be "common practice for parties to an ICSID arbitration to conclude a confidentiality agreement to secure protection of private or business confidential information, and for ICSID Tribunals to order the parties to do so (iii) Such protection of Claimants' personal information would not cause any prejudice to Respondent, as "Respondent will be free to use the data as where a party fails to agree to do so.[27]

The Tribunal decided that the personal data could be provided under strict conditions, and noted that elements of the position put forward by the parties relating to the management of personal data, particularly under the ICSID can be problematic, although Article 44 can provide a pathway forward. Moreover, the formal and functional requirements for exhibits were also considered by the Tribunal, and according to Rule 34(1) of the ICSID Arbitration Rules:

> "[t]he Tribunal shall be the judge of the admissibility of any evidence adduced and of its probative value". The Tribunal thus has the power to decide on the admissibility of the Exhibits at stake.[28]

---

[26] Ibid, para 14.

[27] Ibid, para 41(ii).

[28] Ibid, para 138.

This arbitration is an important introduction to potential disputes in the future. It effectively demonstrated the connection between investment and data-related issues, and the reliance upon data laws. While it did not refer specifically to cybersecurity, the Tribunal noted that the data laws required a specific individual to take 'specific security measures preventing certain risks, such as unauthorised access to the data base or processing operations that are either unlawful or inconsistent with the purposes for which the data have been collected'.[29] First this reference has multiple dimensions as it indirectly relates to cybersecurity. Second, it relies on a controller, who is collecting the data, to take responsibility for securing the data. Third, it relates to the purpose for which the data is collected. These elements can be found in the data laws of most states. Most significantly, it drew the connection between the use of data and the unauthorised access to the data base, here by it is argued that there is a direct offence for this type of access, under most Commonwealth member states laws. This sets the scene for data and cybersecurity to become formal aspects of an investor-state dispute. The remaining sections of this chapter will highlight the important principles of regulatory certainty, equal treatment and legitimate expectations, as they relate to investor state arbitrations, and the ensuing ICSID provisions. However, it is noted there are a number of other principles such as proportionality that underpin the above.

Notwithstanding the above, the ICSID Arbitration Rules (the Rules) play an important role in the administration of a hearing. For instance, Rule 32 of the Rules allows the tribunal, unless either party objects, to allow other persons (who are not the parties, their agents, counsels and advocates, witnesses and experts during their testimony or officers of the Tribunal) to attend the hearings.[30] This provision increases the transparency of arbitration.

The ensuing issue is that, the data and cyber laws of Commonwealth countries are significantly different. This means that it will require a panellist and experts within an arbitration to undertake a considerable of work to understand the respective laws of the states. On the one hand, the national data laws are there to provide a level of privacy protection over the Internet, thereby affording individuals an affirmed human right. On the other hand, the data laws themselves are in conflict with each other, particularly in relation to data portability and more so with cross-border data flows. As stated earlier in this book, the data laws alone are in some cases pulling in different directions. When coupled with cybersecurity laws, they are, in some, cases competing with each other. This is challenging enough in the digital economy, without having to deal with laws for investment and international investment disputes The Commonwealth has the role of improving the legal convergence and harmonisation of data, cyber, and investment law.

[29] Ibid, para 127(1).

[30] ICSID Rules of Procedure for Arbitration Proceedings (ICSID Arbitration Rules), April 2006, Rule 32.

Fair and Equitable Treatment [FET]

Government regulation at a national level is relatively benign. Simply put, when assessing the obligations under a single law, in most circumstances, it is straightforward. However, problems may arise when the national laws of more than one state are involved. Arguably, in the digital economy, the data and cybersecurity laws have changed significantly over the past decade as new threats have emerged. Therefore, these changes can pose challenges to investment decisions. Nonetheless, in relation to investment laws, in challenging government regulation, Matthew Porterfield notes that the broad interpretations of the standard for fair and equitable treatment (FET) by investment tribunals have become a source of increasing controversy.[31] Porterfield, in referring to Canada's investment arrangements with the United States, responded by attempting to limit FET to the standard of protection under customary international law (CIL), which is formed through the "general and consistent practice of states" that they follow out of a sense of legal obligation (*opinio juris*).[32] In other jurisdictions such as the EU of which Cyprus and Malta are members, a different approach has been taken to preserving a standard for FET that is not limited to CIL in exercising its new authority over investment under the Lisbon treaty.[33] A decade later, and the FET as a standard has retained its legitimacy. The principle itself can be traced to Article 12 1948 Havana Charter for an International Trade Organisation.[34] For instance, Article 3 of the Australian and Sri Lankan FTA provides for 'investments of investors of either Party shall at all times be accorded fair and equitable treatment and shall, subject to the laws of the other Party'.[35] Similarly in the Australia–India[36] agreement for the Protection of Investments, Article 3 by and large replicates the Australia–Sri Lanka agreement. While it is beyond the scope of this book to examine all Commonwealth members' bilateral investment agreements, it is argued that this principle has become significantly important by providing a level of investment protection. The FET has a wide scope and has been described as assisting arbitrators and the arbitral Tribunal in providing a standard that can be used to invoke additional principles. Robert Ginsburg posits that:

---

[31] Matthew C. Porterfield, *A Distinction Without a Difference? The Interpretation of Fair and Equitable Treatment Under Customary International Law by Investment Tribunals*, Investment Treaty News (2013), https://www.iisd.org/itn/en/2013/03/22/a-distinction-without-a-difference-the-interpretation-of-fair-and-equitable-treatment-under-customary-international-law-by-investment-tribunals/ In Robert Ginsburg, *Investor-State Dispute Settlement in the Digital Economy: The Case for Structured Proportionality*, 39 Northwestern Journal of International Law & Business 171 (2019) p. 187.

[32] Ibid.

[33] Ibid.

[34] Organisation for Economic Co-operation and Development (2004), "Fair and Equitable Treatment Standard in International Investment Law", *OECD Working Papers on International Investment*, 2004/03, OECD Publishing. P. 3, http://dx.doi.org/10.1787/675702255435.

[35] Australia – Sri Lanka Free Trade Agreement, Article 3, http://www.austlii.edu.au/au/other/dfat/treaties/2007/22.html.

[36] Australia – India, Protection of Investments, http://www.austlii.edu.au/au/other/dfat/treaties/2000/14.html.

> The broad scope of the FET enables tribunals to consider a wider range of factors than is possible under the relevant test for direct and indirect expropriations. The analyses of many FET claims focus on investor perspectives of the host governments' actions. Examples of a sub-principles FET analysis include, but are not limited to: good faith; access to justice and due process; regulatory transparency; non-arbitrariness; non-discrimination and reasonableness; and the investor's.[37]

Notwithstanding the above, the FET became central to the negotiations between Australia and Singapore on their trade agreement. That is, in relation to Chapter 8: Investment, Article 4 (Minimum Standard of Treatment), Singapore companies operating in Australia will now have greater certainty that their investments will receive fair and equitable treatment and the full protection and security as required under international law. This includes the right to due process in legal proceedings as well as the provision of police protection required under customary international law.[38] Therefore, the host state has an obligation to treat the investor fairly and equitably. Most noteworthy is the following statement by Julien Chaisse and Cristen Bauer who reinforce the position taken in this chapter and more broadly in the book: that cybersecurity and data will be subject to investor-state claims under the FET. They posit that as states seek to navigate and regulate cybercrime, they face a challenging regulatory dichotomy giving rise to two types of potential FET claims.[39] Thus, stability and transparency of the legal and regulatory framework for conducting business in the host state is a reasonable right expected by investors and key to an investor's ability to function as a business.[40] To put this into context, as governments increasingly require a level of licencing in and across the digital economy, whether for financial services or in other consumer sectors, data and cybersecurity issues can be part of the licensing arrangements, although this will be difficult in the digital economy. In regard to non-Commonwealth members, Chaisse and Bauer make an important point:

> foreign investors operating in another country, could claim that ambiguous and vaguely worded administrative and licensing requirements can drive certain digital service providers, such as cloud computing firms, out of the market. States may change and adapt their policies over time, in order to respond to the changing environment, and cybersecurity and privacy (data) concerns can lead to necessary policy changes [emphasis added].[41]

As observed earlier in this book, the development of data localisation laws is a recent addition to the legal landscape and it is highly divergent across the states compared. In part, most Commonwealth members do not have data localisation

---

[37] Robert Ginsburg, *Investor-State Dispute Settlement in the Digital Economy: The Case for Structured Proportionality*, 39 Northwestern Journal of International Law & Business 171 (2019) p. 188.

[38] Ministry of Trade and Industry Singapore, https://www.nas.gov.sg/archivesonline/data/pdfdoc/20110913003/press_release_2nd_review_for_safta.pdf.

[39] Julien Chaisse, Cristen Bauer, *Cybersecurity and the Protection of Digital Assets: Assessing the Role of International Investment Law and Arbitration,* Vanderbilt Journal of Entertainment and Technology Law (2019), p. 571.

[40] Ibid.

[41] Ibid.

provisions. That said, Chaisse and Bauer posit that data localization can also limit cross-border dataflows and restrict content, which can amount to substantial Internet censorship and fragmentation. The effect of this policy and legal change is an increase in costs and decrease in actual investment in those states.[42] Expanding on Chaisse and Bauer's commentary on the arbitration of *MTD Equity v. Republic of Chile*[43]:

> By letter of June 26, 2001, MTD Equity Sdn, a Malaysian company, and MTD Chile S.A, a Chilean company, (Claimants)filed a request for arbitration with the International Centre for Settlement of Investment Disputes against the Republic of Chile. The request, invoked the ICSID Arbitration provisions of the 1992 Agreement between the Government of Malaysia and the Government of the Republic of Chile for the Promotion and Protection of Investments.[44]

In relation to the FET, the Tribunal noted that Article 2(2) of the BIT requires that Investments of investors of either Contracting Party shall at all times be accorded fair and equitable treatment.[45] In going further, the Tribunal ruled that:

> Chile has not argued that this is how "fair and equitable treatment" should be understood under the BIT. Chile has simply drawn attention to this interpretation and the consequences it had on the application of the standard of fair and equitable treatment by NAFTA arbitral tribunals. The Tribunal further notes that there is no reference to customary international law in the BIT in relation to fair and equitable treatment.[46]

Against the backdrop of the above, in applying a standard to the FET in this arbitration, the Tribunal referred to the threshold test in *Técnicas*[47]*:*

> to provide to international investments treatment that does not affect the basic expectations that were taken into account by the foreign investor to make the investment. The foreign investor expects the host State to act in a consistent manner, free from ambiguity and totally transparently in its relations with the foreign investor, so that it may know beforehand any and all rules and regulations that will govern its investments, as well as the goals of the relevant policies and administrative practices or directives, to be able to plan its investment and comply with such regulations. Any and all State actions conforming to such criteria should relate not only to the guidelines, directives or requirements issued, or the resolutions approved thereunder, but also to the goals underlying such regulations. The foreign investor also expects the host State to act consistently, i.e., without arbitrarily revoking any pre-existing decisions or permits issued by the state that were relied upon by the investor to assume its commitments as well as to plan and launch its commercial and business activities. The investor also expects the state to use the legal instruments that govern the actions of the investor or the investment in conformity with the function usually assigned to such instruments, and not to deprive the investor of its investment without the required compensation.[48]

---

[42] Ibid, p. 573.

[43] MTD Equity Sdn. Bhd. v. Republic of Chile, ICSID Case No. ARB/01/7, Award, 165–66 (May 25, 2004), https://jusmundi.com/en/document/pdf/decision/en-mtd-equity-sdn-bhd-and-mtd-chile-s-a-v-chile-award-tuesday-25th-may-2004.

[44] Ibid, para 1.

[45] Ibid, para 107.

[46] Ibid, para 111.

[47] Ibid, para 114, *Técnicas Medioambientales TECMED S.A. v. The United Mexican States,* ICSID Case No. ARB(AF)00/2, award dated May 29, 2003, para. 154.

[48] Ibid.

This threshold test reaffirms the importance of the FET to cybersecurity and data, whether they apply to a licence or otherwise. The baseline of these developments is that any investor will have great expectation that they will be treated in a consistent manner, and the regulatory framework, along with future policy decisions will provide a level of certainty and dispel any ambiguity. Ambiguity could, in fact, be on the rise as the world experiences a greater level of geopolitical and economic tension. Thus, investor agreements need to be carefully constructed and of the amount of compensation should be included in the relevant clauses, to provide a remedy where states change direction through policy and the law. Moreover, with the relentless evolution of technology, responses from governments are likely to be in the form of policy changes that will lead to regulatory change. It will be important for states that are party to these agreements to develop certainty with respective bilateral agreements.

Legitimate Expectations

The principle of legitimate expectations has been a component of investment law for a number of years. The principle has been described as underpinning the FET principle. Importantly, Article 42 of the ICSID Convention[49] when dealing with the applicable law refers to 'such rules of international law as may be applicable', which is to be read as which is read as including general principles of law.[50] Michele Potestà, is of the view that 'legitimate expectations are also invoked in the context of indirect expropriation, it is under the fair and equitable treatment standard that legitimate expectations have enjoyed more prominence and a greater chance of success'.[51] To reinforce this point, in *Thunderbird v United Mexican States*, the Tribunal noted that there had been:

> ...a significant growth in the role and scope of the legitimate expectation principle, from an earlier function as a subsidiary interpretative principle to reinforce a particular interpretative approach chosen, to its current role as a self-standing subcategory and independent basis for a claim under the 'fair and equitable standard' as under Art. 1105 of the NAFTA. This is possibly related to the fact that it provides a more supple way of providing a remedy appropriate to the particular situation as compared to the more drastic determination and remedy inherent in concept of regulatory expropriation. It is probably partly for these reasons that 'legitimate expectation' has become for tribunals a preferred way of providing protection to claimants in situations where the tests for a 'regulatory taking' appear too difficult, complex and too easily assailable for reliance on a measure of subjective judgment.[52]

---

[49] ICISD Convention, https://icsid.worldbank.org/sites/default/files/ICSID%20Convention%20English.pdf.

[50] Michele Potestà, *Legitimate Expectations in Investment Treaty Law: Understanding the Roots and the Limits of a Controversial Concept, ICSID Review - Foreign Investment Law Journal*, Volume 28, Issue 1, (2013), pp. 96–99.

[51] Ibid, p. 98.

[52] *Thunderbird v United Mexican States (2005), para 37* https://www.italaw.com/sites/default/files/case-documents/ita0432.pdf.

In further considering the above, Michele Potestà argues that:

> the concept of legitimate expectations is particularly useful to describe a situation where the host State has induced an investment by way of certain informal representations or promises, on which the investor has relied at the time of making the investment. If these are both specific and individualized, the doctrine of legitimate expectations will provide a valuable tool to hold the host State liable. This approach is in line with domestic law systems, which typically extend protection to legitimate expectations in these types of situations. It would also be in line with public international law rules on unilateral acts to the extent that those were to be considered applicable by analogy in investor-State relations.[53]

Furthermore, the doctrine itself contains the host state's obligation to:

> act in a consistent manner, free from ambiguity and totally transparently in its relations with the foreign investor, so that it may know beforehand any and all rules and regulations that will govern its investments, as well as the goals of the relevant policies and administrative practices or directives, to be able to plan its investment and comply with such regulations.[54]

Importantly, the doctrine cannot be viewed in isolation. Today it supports the FET principle and regulation. Put another way, the concept of "regulatory fairness" or "regulatory certainty" has been used in this respect. In the light of these criteria, when a State is empowered to fix the tariffs of a public utility, it must do so in such a way that the concessionaire is able to recover its operations costs, amortize its investments, and make a reasonable return over time.[55] Essentially, where the above provides an investor with a high level of certainty, and by doing so constitutes a promise, if the host state changing the regulation without a level of remedy provided to the investor, this could become problematic. Thus, today, legitimate expectation is well-understood to be part of the FET standard. Significantly, if cybersecurity and data-related issues are part of a dispute, they will be subject to these doctrines. There are a number of sub-principles that were not discussed in this chapter that also underscore regulatory certainty and the FET. The brief examination of these principles need further research to expand the knowledge of how important they will become when AI and robotics are mainstream. Combine that with quantum technology and these principles will be very important when governments begin to regulate this technology. This is because this technology will use large amounts of data and require significant levels of cybersecurity.

---

[53] Michele Potestà, *Legitimate Expectations in Investment Treaty Law: Understanding the Roots and the Limits of a Controversial Concept, ICSID Review - Foreign Investment Law Journal*, Volume 28, Issue 1, (2013), p. 122.

[54] Uğur Erman Özgür, *In Search of Consistency and Fairness in Investor-State Arbitration: An "Institutional" Approach to Interpreting the Doctrine of Legitimate Expect*ations, Transnational Dispute Management (2020) p. 10. https://oublegal.com/wp-content/uploads/2020/12/4-In-Search-of-Consistency-and-FairnessEO.pdf

[55] Ibid, p. 21.

28.2 Conclusion

A state's framework for investment in the digital economy is provided by the policy and legal framework of government. It sets a minimum standard to facilitate trade and investment. In nearly every sector of society, there is foreign investment in technology that has the potential to be vulnerable to cybersecurity attacks. Personal data is an integral part of that technology. It is the current, emerging and future that, is collecting, using and storing data. Data is subject to cybersecurity instrusions legal and illegal. This book has made the case that cybersecurity and data are integral components of the digital economy, and thus will be subject to investor-state and commercial disputes. This chapter has departed from the other book chapters by comparing the national laws related to investor state arbitration. This chapter reaffirms the need for greater convergence of data, cyber and arbitration laws across the Commonwealth. This chapter has confirmed that there is a significant connection between investor-state arbitration, data and cybersecurity. The challenge is that nation states have taken very approaches when establishing both their data and cybersecurity laws. This will continue to be problematic. A further challenge is that the data laws are by and large private law. They have been developed to provide a level of privacy protection over the Internet. However, they have evolved to become facilitators of economic activity. This is particularly the case where states have cross-border provisions for data transfer(s), otherwise referred to as data flows.

Data laws are attempting to strike a balance between fostering the expansion of the digital economy while protecting all of us, and our activities, online. On the other hand, cybersecurity law(s) generally fall under the criminal law. They have been developed in isolation from data laws, in order to protect the systems and infrastructure that support the collection and use of data. The primary objective of the criminal law(s) is to protect the economic interests of businesses that have invested in these systems and infrastructure. As demonstrated above, there are a number of consistent provisions that Commonwealth members have included in their national cyber laws. However, this is another area where there is significant divergence.

Arguably, arbitration is emerging as an area that can be used in both commercial and investor state disputes, where data and cybersecurity are involved. On the one hand, the regulatory framework provided by the host state is one of the core elements that can trigger both the FET and legitimate expectations in investment state arbitration. On the other side, this is evaluated at the time of the investment. Hence, the Tribunal will assess the conduct of the state, the objectives of the regulatory framework, and the expectations of the investor based on the information provided by the state.

Notwithstanding the above, Article 14 of the ICISD Convention provides the Tribunal with the flexibility to conduct proceedings in the manner they see fit. It is argued that this enables the Tribunal to consider the important issues related to cybersecurity and data. It must be noted that cybersecurity and data-related issues are likely to emerge in arbitration as a consequence of a wider dispute such as access to a specific data base, or some other technology. Equally, article 32 of the ICSID

Arbitration Rule also becomes important in relation to experts attending a hearing. It provides a level of transparency, which is increasingly important in investor-state arbitrations.

Finally, this is an important area that requires constant vigilance, particularly as the world is moving rapidly towards a fully-integrated digital economy. It is this economy that knows no international border. Nation states will offer and provide incentives through policy and regulation for investors in cyber and data-related technology. They will compete against each other. As this competition intensifies, it is my view that states could find themselves having to defend their earlier policy commitments and regulatory frameworks, which may no longer be relevant because the investment landscape has changed. In part, a way to converge the laws is through the development of ethical concepts and principles for managing the security and use of data by technology. In so doing, Ethics to be considered in the current and future development of these laws, particularly in relation to the use of critical technologies and artificial intelligence that will require high levels of security and use data.

Chapter 29
Ethics, Moving Forward and Conclusion

The digital economy is rapidly changing the way we work and live. It will come with significant policy and legal challenges. At a time when the world is being challenged by competing geopolitical and economic interests, this book has confirmed, that data and cybersecurity will be formidable elements of the new digital economy. The digital economy in and across the Commonwealth will be significant, as its members account for about a third of the world's population. The digital economy is expected to continue to grow, providing the Commonwealth with significant responsibility for conducting research, reaching out to member countries, and engaging with international bodies, particularly other governments.

Most noteworthy are the economic developments in and across the dig ital economy will need to be supported by robust data and cyber laws. However, the highly divergent and fragmented approach currently taken across the Commonwealth is, in my view, an area of concern. These laws will underpin and drive the digital economy. Therefore, the lack of harmonisation, hinders the expansion of this new economic activity. This is further compounded by the need, today, to shift organisations and individuals attitudes, behaviour and thinking to embed *Ethics* into business, legal, codes and standards frameworks. This chapter only briefly discusses the position of Ethics in data and cybersecurity. It calls for further and a more comprehensive research program to be established, to confirm whether ethical principles that should be established in the law. Doing so, will ensure organisations are obliged to adopt them into their everyday activities. Ethics can be considered another form of risk management, or an extension of it.

R. Walters, *Cybersecurity and Data Laws of the Commonwealth*,
https://doi.org/10.1007/978-981-99-3935-0_29

On the one hand, ethics has been included into many governance frameworks, such as, health, food production and the use of agricultural and veterinary chemicals, the legal profession amongst others. On the other hand, it has been discussed in the context of being a moral principle that governs people's behaviour, setting a standard of right and wrong, and used to determine the conduct to be taken when dealing with a moral problem.[1] It has also been described as 'the norms of behavior that promote appropriate judgments and accountability when acquiring, managing, or using data, with the goals of protecting civil liberties, minimizing risks to individuals and society, and maximising the public good'.[2] While this definition comes from the United Sates and applies to federal government departments, it provides another example of the concepts and principles that have been considered to ensure data is managed in an ethical way. The definition is underpinned by what has been described as ethical tenets, which aim to:

1. Uphold Applicable Statutes, Regulations, Professional Practices, and Ethical Standards.
2. Respect the Public, Individuals, and Communities.
3. Respect Privacy and Confidentiality.
4. Act with Honesty, Integrity, and Humility.
5. Hold Oneself and Others Accountable.
6. Promote Transparency.
7. Stay Informed of Developments in the Fields of Data Management and Data Science.[3]

However, the question arises can the above apply to every situation or scenario that data and cybersecurity is going to encounter through technology in the future? In drawing on recent work undertaken by India, they note that with the consent and implementation of artificial intelligence (AI) that, there is both a positive inclusion into the economy there is also a dark side not often discussed. India argues that:

> Everyone should think about the ethics of the work they do, and the work they choose not to do. Artificial Intelligence and robots often seem like fun science fiction, but in fact already affect our daily lives. For example,technology services rekated entities help us find what we want by using AI. They learn both from us and about us when we use them. Many countries and organizations now employ robots in warfare.[4]

[1] Elonnai Hickok, *Ethics and AI in India*, 2018, https://cis-india.org/internet-governance/files/ethics-and-ai.

[2] Federal Data Strategy, Data Ethics Framework, 2019, p. 9, https://resources.data.gov/assets/documents/fds-data-ethics-framework.pdf.

[3] Ibid, p. 10.

[4] Government of India, Ministry of Electronics & Information Technology, pp. 20–22. https://www.meity.gov.in/writereaddata/files/Committes_D-Cyber-n-Legal-and-Ethical.pdf.

The statement above cannot be underestimated and applies to all Commonwealth member countries. Data and cybersecurity are fundamental features or elements of AI and other new and emerging critical technologies.[5] Critical technologies have a sole purpose in supply chains and will be important to the future digital economy in relation to transnational trade and investment. Thus, the challenge will be to develop robust ethical frameworks that support all of these areas, while ensuring that international trade and investment is not restricted by additional regulatory controls. India along with other Commonwealth members have done considerable work in this area. While it is out of scope to fully explore the literature of ethics in data and cyber security, it is argued that ethics will be just as important in the future as data protection and data flows has become to national economies. Similarly, cybersecurity has become just as important if not more important to protect and secure transnational trade and investment. India, further note how:

> Ethics in cyber security must also extend to consumers. Security Intelligence notes that there can't be any delays in letting customers know that a data breach has occurred and their information may have been stolen. While a deeply integrated code of cyber security ethics and conduct is vital, it is also crucial to cultivate ethical teachings among students and young. By promoting awareness of cyber security ethics at the early stages of learning and professional development, we can help ensure that future representatives stay on the right side of the ethical divide.[6]

Thus, this book is calling for the Commonwealth and its members to develop a standard approach towards ethics in data, cyber security, AI and critical technologies. The ensuing challenge is what would constitute core ethic principles and concepts? A further accentuating question is how would, or could the concepts and principles be embedded as standards within the law, and more specifically within organisational business planning frameworks? However, there has been a shift over the past decade from information ethics to data ethics.[7] Floridi and Taddeo make the point that data ethics includes concepts such as trust, transparency, privacy, discrimination (bias). They highlight how:

> data ethics can be defined as the branch of ethics that studies and evaluates moral problems related to data (including generation, recording, curation, processing, dissemination, sharing and use), algorithms (including artificial intelligence, artificial agents, machine learning and robots) and corresponding practices (including responsible innovation, programming,

---

[5] Critical technologies are emerging technologies that, and broadly refers to strategically important technology areas.[1] Australia, for example, defines 'critical technology' as 'technology that can significantly enhance or pose risks to Australia's national interests, including our prosperity, social cohesion and national security'. Australian Strategic Policy Institute, https://www.aspi.org.au/report/benchmarking-critical-technologies See also, https://www.foreignminister.gov.au/minister/marise-payne/speech/launch-international-cyber-and-critical-technology-engagement-strategy Most countries will have a similar definition to that of Australia, however, there may be subtle differences to meet local sovereign needs. United Kingdom, Critical Technologies Strategy, 2021, https://publications.parliament.uk/pa/cm5801/cmselect/cmsctech/450/45006.htm.

[6] Government of India, Ministry of Electronics & Information Technology, pp. 22–24. https://www.meity.gov.in/writereaddata/files/Committes_D-Cyber-n-Legal-and-Ethical.pdf.

[7] Luciano Floridi, Mariarosaria Taddeo, *What is data ethics*? 2016, https://royalsocietypublishing.org/doi/epdf/10.1098/rsta.2016.0360.

hacking and professional codes), in order to formulate and support morally good solutions (e.g. right conducts or right values). Key issues concern possible re-identification of individuals through data-mining, -linking, -merging and re-using of large datasets, as well as risks for so-called 'group privacy', when the identification of types of individuals, independently of the de-identification of each of them, may lead to serious ethical problems, from group discrimination (e.g. ageism, ethnicism, sexism) to group-targeted forms of violence. Trust and transparency are also crucial topics in the ethics of data, in connection with an acknowledged lack of public awareness of the benefits, opportunities, risks and challenges associated with data science.[8]

It is argued that apart from developing a consistent framework of standards for ethics in data and cybersecurity that can also be used for AI and critical technology governance, the data laws could be reviewed to include an Ethics Officer. For example, as this book has demonstrated a number of states require a controller or some other officer to be appointed and responsible for managing data. This role could be expanded upon to also include ethics. In briefly analysing several models, what has emerged is that governments and scholars have developed ethical frameworks on an individual basis. For example, the UK have developed a data ethics framework that focuses on three core principles of transparency, accountability and fairness are considered paramount.[9] While there is no mention of cybersecurity, the framework does make the connection between data and AI. By establishing these three principles, the UK have further developed a series of actions such as, define public benefit and user need, involve diverse expertise, comply with the law, check quality and limitation of the data and model, along with evaluating wider policy implications.[10] However, this framework is predominantly for the public sector. On the other hand the UK Cyber Security Council has taken a different approach to that of data and see that the core principles and concepts of ethics include credibility, integrity, professionalism, responsibility and respect.[11] Notably, this is for the private sector. There is overlap in the principles and concepts that underscore ethics in data

[8] Ibid.

[9] United Kingdom, Data Ethics Framework, 2020, p. 8, https://assets.publishing.service.gov.uk/government/uploads/system/uploads/attachment_data/file/923108/Data_Ethics_Framework_2020.pdf Transparency means that your actions, processes and data are made open to inspection by publishing information about the project in a complete, open, understandable, easily-accessible, and free format. In your work with and on data and AI, use the available guidance. Accountability means that there are effective governance and oversight mechanisms for any project.

Fairness — It is crucial to eliminate your project's potential to have unintended discriminatory effects on individuals and social groups. You should aim to mitigate biases which may infuence your model's outcome and ensure that the project and its outcomes respect the dignity of individuals, are just, non- discriminatory, and consistent with the public interest, including human rights and democratic values.

[10] Ibid, p. 9.

[11] United Kingdom Cyber Security Council, Code of Ethics, 2021, https://www.ukcybersecuritycouncil.org.uk/media/0f1emde3/code-of-ethics-july-2021.pdf Credibility i) maintain the highest standards of objectivity in their service delivery, ii) present the highest standards of advice and conduct, iii) act in ways that are at all times accountable and ethical. Integrity i) be honest and act with integrity in the conduct of their activities and services ii) demonstrate compliance with legislation and regulations. Professionalism i) uphold and improve the professionalism and reputation of the cyber security sector, and be able to evince this by sharing experiences, opportunities, techniques

and cybersecurity. These include but not limited to accountability, transparency and respect. The dilemma that has emerged is the terminology being used to describe the principles and concepts. Problematic in the use of different terminology can result in different meanings, which can translate into different priorities that make up ethics.

In a further development, the ethics in cybersecurity has been described as the harm to privacy, cybersecurity resource allocation and transparency and disclosure.[12] Paul Formosa et al. make the point that it is "apparent that many frameworks succumb to the problem of principle proliferation, whereby new principles are added in an effort to capture the diversity of moral concerns relevant to a particular domain."[13] Formosa and others have developed a model that it includes 5 specific principles of cybersecurity ethics. First, is the principle of beneficence, where cybersecurity technologies should be used to benefit humans, promote human well-being, and make our lives better overall. Second, has been described as non-maleficence, which is the application of cybersecurity technologies that should not be used to intentionally harm humans or to make our lives worse overall. Third, is the principle of autonomy, whereby technologies should be used in ways that respect human autonomy. Humans should be able to make informed decisions for themselves about how that technology is used in their lives. Fourth is the justice principle that involves cybersecurity technologies, which are to be used to promote fairness, equality, and impartiality. It should not be used to unfairly discriminate, undermine solidarity, or prevent equal access. Fifth is the principle of explicability that, involves cybersecurity technologies are to be used in ways that are intelligible, transparent, and comprehensible, and it should also be clear who is accountable and responsible for its use.[14] The authors have taken a security and privacy lead approach. This accords directly with the data laws that have been compared in this book. It is the controls established by the data laws that provide a level of privacy protection over the Internet. Furthermore, the authors focus on the technology that provides a level of cybersecurity.

It is arguable whether cybersecurity technology can and will provide the full foundations of ethical behaviour. It can also be argued that by taking the autonomous approach, and placing the responsibility in each human hands to make the choice

and tools that they consider of merit or which may represent a potential cyber security risk ii) undertake to promote and advance public awareness and understanding of cyber security and its benefits iii) operate from an evidence-based position iv) rebut false or misleading statements concerning the industry or profession and its practices. Responsibility and Respect i) accept appropriate responsibility for what is within their power, control or management ii) apply, at all times, good practice in respect of safeguarding data and information, including but not limited to recognition of potential risks to an ethical principle iii) declare immediately any potential conflict of interest iv) ensure any deliverable is objective, justifiable and defendable v) champion equality of opportunity, diversity and inclusion and support human rights, dignity and respect.

[12] Swiss Cyber Institute; https://swisscyberinstitute.com/blog/a-holistic-approach-to-ethical-issues-in-cyber-security.

[13] *Paul Formosa, Michael Wilson, Deborah Richards,* A principlist framework for cybersecurity ethics, Science Direct, Elsevier, 3.

[14] *Paul Formosa, Michael Wilson, Deborah Richards,* A principlist framework for cybersecurity ethics, Science Direct, Elsevier, 4.

about how the technology is used, in the absence of organisational ethical guidelines– will ensure the technology is not used in a manner that threatens society. Without the ability to undertake an audit of the business community across the Commonwealth members to confirm whether ethics has been embedded into business governance, it could be assumed work is required to establish such a process. This is because currently, the function of cybersecurity ideally should be driven by ethical considerations,[15] that today need to form part of corporate and business operations. There are many ethical challenges which need to be in contemplation in the drafting of a sound incident response plan(s). Arguably the first issue to consider is what are the possible threats or incidents which need to be taken into consideration. On that basis an action plan can be devised importantly reflecting what can be done not what we like to be able to do.[16] What can be done depends on the internal resources of an organisation, and they need to be matched to what must be done. In addition, the question arises have "we adequately considered the risks of 'collateral damage' to innocent parties, or reputational damage to ourselves and our organisation, if our response steps over the ethical line?"[17] It is the understanding of the level of risk that will shape and influence the knowledge and awareness within an organisation. As highlighted earlier in this the Australian Federal Court case of *Australian Securities and Investments Commission v RI Advice Group Pty Ltd*[18] confirmed that not adequately managing the risk of cybersecurity will constitute a breach of a directors fiduciary duty. This important development, in my view, needs to be considered in the context of Directors and Officers having to also consider ethics as part of their obligations to manage risk.

That's said, John Rawls is of the view that ethics comes in two forms. For Rawls, the two main concepts of ethics are those of the right and the good, the concept of a morally worthy person is, I believe, derived from them. The structure of an ethical theory is largely determined by how it is defined and connected to these two basic notions.[19] Therefore, for ethics to be effective in the daily operation and function of an organisation and entity that relies on technology to trade and invest, there needs to be a consistent approach to the development of these concepts and principles.

Ethics "is often formulated in formal codes or standards to which all members of a profession are held, such as those of medical or legal ethics.[20] "Simply put ethics assists everybody to choose the best decision within their work life in any situation including cooperation, productivity, and respect to others. Following along the lines of what is a good life, Hasselbalch referring to Stoddart suggested that one of the

---

[15] Bruno Zeller, Robert Walters, Develop and define an Ethics methodology/framework that is risk-based, forthcoming.

[16] Shannon Vallor, An Introduction to Cybersecurity Ethics, 2. Santa Clara University. https://www.scu.edu/media/ethics-center/technology-ethics/IntroToCybersecurityEthics.pdf, at 15.

[17] Ibid, p. 16.

[18] [2022] FCA 496.

[19] John Rawls. A theory Of Justice, Harvard University:Press, 1999, 21.

[20] Shannon Vallor, An Introduction to Cybersecurity Ethics, 2. Santa Clara University. https://www.scu.edu/media/ethics-center/technology-ethics/IntroToCybersecurityEthics.pdf.

approaches to an ethics process is a "'rights-based' approach, with reference to a body of human rights that demands the accountability of those with the power to watch."[21] Hasselbalch further notes that "the foundation of data ethical governance is an awareness of the very conditions of power between different stakeholders."[22] Yet, this will only partly address the modern day considerations needed to manage the full ethical life cycle between data and cybersecurity, AI, critical and quantum technologies. It is conceivable that a single ethical framework may never be achieved that will address both data (data flows-data protection) and cybersecurity as a collective. Rather, it is more likely than not for separate distinct ethical frameworks to be established, on a sectorial basis. This will be further complicated where states decide to separate any ethical obligations between the public and private sectors. That is, will states develop and oblige different ethic principles and concepts to the public and private sectors? This is up to states to decide, however, in my view they should be identical. Doing so will ensure a higher level of trust and confidence in the management of data and cybersecurity.

Notwithstanding the above, and while there is an overlap between data and cyber security, similarly can also be seen for AI. That said, in India, the concepts and principles for AI that have recently been developed include:

- AI for common and public good;
- Placing humans first and well being;
- Transparency and Explainability;
- Safety and Security;
- Responsibility and Liability;
- Accountability and Oversight;
- Privacy; and
- Fairness, bias, and discrimination.[23]

Again, there is significant overlap between the three areas of law and technology. It is argued that AI technology will drive developments in and support provide another enabler to allow for the illegal access to commercial and personal data. In addition to this dilemma, is the notion of ethical and non-ethical hacking, which has also emerged as a legitimate activity. While it is generally understood that illegal hacking has been connected to cybersecurity law. Ethical hacking is well trained individuals that are employed to undertake this specific activity. As highlighted by David-Olivier Jaquet-Chiffelle and Michele Loi, the activity of ethical hacking involves the conductor to stress and assess the target's IT-security.[24] The authors, rightly make a note that under ethical hacking the conductor operates under a set of rules. The rules have

[21] Gry Hasselbalch, *Data Ethics of Power*, Edward Elgar Publishing (2021), p. 31.

[22] Ibid, p. 36.

[23] Elonnai Hickok, *Ethics and AI in India*, 2018, https://cis-india.org/internet-governance/files/ethics-and-ai.

[24] David-Olivier Jaquet-Chiffelle and Michele Loi, Ethical and unethical Hacking. In Christen, M., Gordijn, B., Loi, M. (eds) The Ethics of Cybersecurity, The International Library if Ethics, Law and Technology, vol 21. Springer (2020), pp. 179–205.

been designed to prevent the ethical hacker from taking any personal advantage of his relationship with his client. Generally, the rules are described by a code, and ensure the ethical hacker will:

- get *written permission* prior to stressing and assessing his or her client's IT-security.
- act *honestly* and stay within the scope of his or her *client's expectations.*
- *respect* his or her client's as well as its employees' *privacy.*
- use *scientific*, state-of-the-art and *documented processes.*
- *transparently communicate* to his or her client all the *findings* as well as a transcript of all his or her *actions.*
- remove his or her traces and will *not introduce* or keep any *backdoor* in the system.
- *inform* software and hardware vendors about *found vulnerabilities* in their products.[25]

In part, these rules can also the principles and concepts of cybersecurity and data protection and data flows alike. The concept of transparency is well understood in data law and practice. It has arguably been the bedrock of ensuring a high level of trust in the modern day data legal framework. Thus, the challenge or yet another dilemma is for regulators and company officers to ensure that the rule applied to ethical hacking activities form part of the broader ethical framework for data and cybersecurity. The question is what will a modern day ethical framework look like? The beginnings can be found in recent research undertaken on behalf of the European Commission. That is, Malta and Cyprus are part of the EU and in a recent White Paper[26] a proposed framework should consider the following principles for cybersecurity outlined in the table below:

Autonomy Beneficence Dignity Equality Fairnes Freedom Justice Privacy Responsibility	Human dignity Freedom Democracy Equality Non-discrimination The rule of law Respect for human rights Pluralism Tolerance Justice Solidarity Protection of EU citizens	Privacy Security Trust Suggested data protection goals: Availability Confidentiality Integrity Intervenability Transparency Unlinkability	Privacy Fairness Autonomy Practical goals of cybersecurity technology: Availability Confidentiality Integrity

The above is looking at the research elements pertaining to cybersecurity only and not data. Column one highlights the ethical values in research. Column two aligns those values in column one with the central values of the EU at the highest level, which can be found in their legal framework. Column three, highlights the ethical values

---

[25] Ibid, p. 193.

[26] Markus Christen, Bert Gordijn, Nadine Kleine, Gwenyth Morgan, Karsten Weber, *Cybersecurity and Ethics,* White Paper 1, 2020, European Commission Erasmus Funding Grant.

in empirical research. While column four are the values in the technical domain. In translating this into business frameworks would be somewhat complex, and would not necessarily be accepted by those states outside of the EU. The above has a heavy emphasis on the values of the supranational polity that the EU has become, outlined in column two. They can be best summarised as the what the EU has built itself on, in creating and establishing a common identity across all member states. They would not be required at the organisational level. Put another way, four major fields of ethics research have been identified. Firstly, meta-ethics, mostly concerning the meaning and reference of normative sentence, and the question how their truth values can be determined. Second, normative ethics, the practical means of determining a moral course of action by examining the standards for right and wrong action and assigning a value to specific actions. Third, descriptive ethics, which aims at an empirical investigation of people's moral behaviour and beliefs. Fourth, applied ethics, concerns what individuals are obligated to do in a specific situation or a particular domain of possibilities for action.[27] Applied ethics deals with real-life situations, where decisions have to be made under time pressure, and often limited rationality.

While not a Commonwealth member, Ishaani Priyadarshini and Chase Cotton from the United States take a higher level approach. They begin by claiming cyberethics as Laws: It refers to the fact that specific laws are derived from ethics. Cyber law and Cyberethics are interconnected and dependent on each other. The need for cyberethics to be strengthened by cyber laws.[28] In agreeing with this position, the principles and concepts, whatever states or the Commonwealth members choose as a collective need to form part of the cyber laws. The authors also believe that cyberethics includes:

- Philosophy;[29]
- Societal Norms;[30]
- Environmental Ethics;[31]

[27] European Commission, Ethics Guidelines for Trustworthy AI, 2019, p. 37 https://www.aepd.es/sites/default/files/2019-12/ai-ethics-guidelines.pdf.

[28] Ibid, pp. 14–15.

[29] Ishaani Priyadarshini, Chase Cotton, *Cybersecurity Ethics, Legal, Risks, and Policies*, CRC Press Taylor Francis (2022), pp. 14–15, It explores the philosophical aspect behind ethics that includes life between birth and death. Gaining unauthorized access to someone's account or compromising the privacy of an account are situations that are unethical and Ethics as Philosophy could avert such situations.

[30] Ibid, It deals with Community Ethics. These underpin questions of bad and good of social media, how it has an impact on the community life and chances of global communication. It also takes into account abuse in terms of cyber bullying, mobbing, etc. It manifests the core values and virtues that usually have their source in the family.

[31] Ibid, It deals with the impact of cyber technology on human-nature relations. It also highlights the environmental negative impact of energy use as well as the positive impact of environmental advantages of weather forecast, scientific research, etc. It deals with questions like whether it is ethical to jeopardize natural resources in order to carry out research.

- Political Ethics;[32]
- Economic Ethics;[33] and
- Religious Ethics.[34]

Against the backdrop of the above, what the authors are putting forward is the need to cascade the ethics approach from society, government to the private sector, and translate these concepts into the law and organisational business process. The above are strategic, and demonstrate the reach that cyberethics has today in the modern world. They confirm the economic (trade and investment) benefits that cybersecurity provides the economy. The authors in proceeding to the next level which could be considered the organisational level described the pillars essential for securing cyberspace include:

- Confidentiality: It refers to protecting the information from disclosure to unauthorised parties. It is associated with the protection of details which should be visible or accessible to people who have appropriate privileges.
- Integrity: It is responsible for ensuring trustworthiness, accuracy, and completeness of the sensitive information. The main objective of integrity is to protect information from being altered by unauthorised or unintended parties and individuals.
- Availability: It is responsible for ensuring that only authorized parties can access the information when at the time of need.
- Authentication: It refers to the process of ensuring and confirming the identity of a user.
- Non-Repudiation: It can be used to ensure that a party involved in a communication cannot deny the authenticity of their signature on a document or the sending of a message that they originated.[35]

The above differ greatly from the approach taken in the EU. It must be noted that the EU approach has to date been focussed on ethical based research. This takes a broader values based approach to that of the EU. In part it captures much of what the EU are considering to adopt. In other words, it provides for a high level of protection of the systems and data, by promoting trust and confidence in the system. What needs to

[32] Ibid, It is concerned with changes in political systems. These may be in the form of elections, security, armies with autonomous weapons, need, and limits of regulation of cyberspace on international and national levels, etc. Elections have been known to get manipulated over cyberspace; Ethics from the political perspective may be one of the ways to avoid it.

[33] Ibid, It explores the positive and negative impacts of cyberspace. The factors taken into account are economic growth, job creation or job losses, financial investments in cybersecurity research, etc. The financial sector is frequently hit by data breaches and monetary losses. Economic Ethics could be followed while dealing with such situations.

[34] Ibid, It looks at the ethical and unethical impact of cyberspace on culture, music, art, dance, language diversity, cultural inclusion or discrimination, religious respect or hate messages through the internet, etc. Social media provides platforms for religious and cultural disputes. Keeping in mind Religious Ethics may be a way of avoiding it.

[35] Ishaani Priyadarshini, Chase Cotton, *Cybersecurity Ethics, Legal, Risks, and Policies*, CRC Press Taylor Francis (2022), p. 5.

be considered is the protection and stability of the systems to ensure property, personal data, privacy, intellectual property, organisations systems and processes are governed by the highest possible level of ethics and risk, while balancing the controls to ensure there is no dilution of trade and investment activity. One model may not address all the related industry sectors. For instance, infrastructure such as telecommunications will have different needs to that of construction, and similar across other professions such as the financial and health sectors. However, the fundamental concepts and principles can be applied across all in that same way as the principles set out in the OECD Privacy Framework (see Chap. 1).[36]

In further drawing upon the work undertaken by Priyadarshini and Cotton who have diligently outlined a number of ethical issues that will need to be considered by regulators, individuals and entities in the future. These include but not limited to privacy, copyright, piracy, intellectual property, computer fraud and misuse, plagiarism, cyberbullying, identify theft and ransomware attacks.[37] The above have a direct connection with the criminal law breaches in relation to cybercrime, such as, identity theft, cyberbullying and ransomware attacks. The authors also identify personal privacy as a key issue in cybersecurity ethics. Thus, indirectly personal data forms part of their ethical considerations. The challenge or decision that will needs to be addressed will be the development of principles for legislation that, can then be translated into operational actions. A further challenge is how, if at all, the principles could be combined for both data and cybersecurity. It will require consultation between legal, business and regulator minds. What the authors have rightly achieved is identifying ethical issues in specific sectors, for instance, health, business, AI, finance amongst others. In confirming the position taken in this book, Priyadarshini and Cotton call for cyber law to be based on cyberethics. They identify ethics as part of a larger risk management framework for preventing and responding to cyber intrusions. The authors do not outline what would constitute an effective ethical framework that, can be adopted by an organisation. On that basis, further research is needed to identify how organisations have developed ethical frameworks.

In making the case for the Commonwealth to take on further work in the data and cyber security area, it also calls for further work to be undertaken in the area of arbitration. The Commonwealth of Nations was established some decades ago, and since then has been involved in some highly important work undertaken to obtain a level of legal convergence and cooperation in terms of data and cyber laws.

However, today there continues to be a significant level of divergence amongst Commonwealth members. This is expected and unavoidable, because of many countries' current state of development, because the Commonwealth itself is a voluntary organisation. That is, there are a large number of member countries that are still developing and do not have the mature legal framework or economy of developed nations.

---

[36] Organisation for Economic Co-operation and Development, Privacy Guidelines, https://www.oecd.org/sti/ieconomy/oecd_privacy_framework.pdf.

[37] Ishaani Priyadarshini, Chase Cotton, *Cybersecurity Ethics, Legal, Risks, and Policies*, CRC Press Taylor Francis (2022), p. 54.

This book is the first of its kind, and has compared the Commonwealth Model Privacy Bill,[38] Model Bill on the Protection of Personal Information[39] along with the Model Bill on Computer Related Crime (Cybersecurity),[40] with the laws established by Commonwealth member countries. It has demonstrated a number of shortcomings and gaps in the laws of the respective jurisdictions. In reconciling the differences between the respective laws, it is argued that data and cyber law are very closely connected, and are important to international trade and the digital economy.

A major theme that has emerged from this comparative research is that the large volume of law examined indicated the extent to which regional and international organisations have influenced the development of national laws. In addition, when comparing multiple provisions, it became clear that terms and terminology have been a major factor contributing to the fragmented approach, particularly in data and cyber law. However, there are states that have yet to develop specific data or cyber laws. This compounds the fragmentation of laws across the Commonwealth. Some states have taken a comprehensive approach and replicated most of the Model Bills, or at least structured their national laws according to these bills.

However, the approach explained above is limited to those states that have adopted their respective laws over the past 15 years. The states who have had their laws in place for more than two decades have structured and applied terms and terminology that, it could be argued, needs to be updated. Nonetheless, these differences are not insurmountable since the national judiciary can address them when handing down a decision. Problematic will be the international flow of commerce over the Internet and the use of data, along with the cybersecurity risks that come from that activity.

On the other hand, there are examples of significantly divergent approaches. The divergences identified should be reconciled with a formal program of law reform across the Commonwealth. Doing so will make it easier to locate and understand the legal provisions. Some states do not have specific cyber laws, in which case these states should reform their respective criminal laws and develop specific legislation for cyber and computer crime, in the same way as the majority of states have done. The economic benefits of doing so will be important for the business community, even though the true financial impact from locating and interpreting and applying the laws is highly complex, and has not been addressed in this book. This is another area requiring further research.

---

[38] The Commonwealth Model Privacy Bill, Office of Civil and Criminal Justice Reform, https://www.asianlaws.org/gcld/cyberlawdb/COM/P15370_9_ROL_Model_Privacy_Bill_0.pdf.

[39] The Commonwealth Model Bill on the Protection of Personal Information, Office of Civil and Criminal Justice Reform, https://www.asianlaws.org/gcld/cyberlawdb/COM/P15370_6_ROL_Model_Bill_Protection_Personal_Information_2.pdf.

[40] Model Law on Computer and Computer Related Crime, Office of Civil and Criminal Justice Reform, 2017, p. 1 https://production-new-commonwealth-files.s3.eu-west-2.amazonaws.com/migrated/key_reform_pdfs/P15370_11_ROL_Model_Law_Computer_Related_Crime.pdf.

Ibid, sections, 5,6,7,8,9.

Most noteworthy is that the Internet, as a highly efficient and critical platform, along with the technology that is supporting the capture and use of data, is changing the way national and international trade and investment is being undertaken. Consumers who have been all but locked out in rural areas, today have access to the Internet via sophisticated, yet easy-to-use, IPhones. Consumers can access knowledge and information across every sector of the economy. The ability to have a laptop and be online anywhere in the world, be it in a restaurant or café or airport is, for the most part, unconstrained. This connectivity has created a new economic activity involving data. However, the data is vulnerable to cyber intrusions and attacks. They can be launched in an instant and, in some cases, without the knowledge of the person or entity who has been intruded upon.

Therefore, and as this book has emphasised, there is a need for urgent reform at a national level and across the Commonwealth. This will ensure that the economic benefits that both cybersecurity and data provide, have the highest level of protection. However, this protection will need to be weighed against the WTO-GAT rules, to ensure they do not impose any unnecessary protectionist laws. Put another way, appropriate laws ensure the growth of the digital economy while simultaneously protecting data. Thus, this book demonstrates the intersection of international trade, investment, criminal and private law. There are a number of areas where it is recommended that the Commonwealth should consider undertaking further research that will enhance and strengthen the respective Model Laws.

The comparison of the data and cyber laws of the Commonwealth, reveals general themes within the laws, particularly in relation to terms and terminology. Even though many of the differences are in some circumstances minor, they become major issues when the laws are being interpreted and applied by the judiciary.

Notwithstanding the above, in drawing the connection between data, cybersecurity, the digital economy and commercial law of arbitration, while not straightforward, the book has successfully navigated the competing outcomes of the respective laws. In so doing, the book has drawn upon a number of judicial examples that have also connected technology and economic benefits this brings, with data and cybersecurity.

A number of examples have shown how the courts have connected commercial data and commercial activity with personal data. Thus, the data laws related to cross-border flows, collection, processing and foremost, the definition of data, that are highly significant.

Arbitration will increasingly be important to the digital economy as it can be applied to data flows, data protection and cybersecurity law. When coupled with the broader digital economy, and the regulatory frameworks of nation states, it has been confirmed that arbitration can play an important role in resolving commercial and investor-state disputes. Additionally, there has been a deliberate focus on the national response to transnational data flows. While there is a long history of regulation that dates back to the 1970s in Europe, with the development of technology, this issue has become more pronounced. Technology has enabled data to be captured and used at an unprecedented rate.

In Chap. 1 discussed the trade and economic agreements that have been established between and amongst countries, and which members of the Commonwealth are party too. These agreements will be highly important in the future, and it is argued that more work in this regard needs to be undertaken at a national level. This is another area where Commonwealth members can become more active. In other words, the Commonwealth could also be involved in developing standards that members could apply when negotiating these agreements. This will help to ensure a better balance between the economic benefits derived from data flows and an adequate level of data protection and security. More importantly, it provides an opportunity for cybersecurity to be aligned with data in trade and investment.

Arguably, in support of international data flows, the OECD Guidelines and Principles have been a valuable reference point for nation states wanting to develop their respective data laws. While these laws have been in circulation since the early 1980s, the Principles have not only stood the test of time, geopolitical and economic competition and shocks; they are still very relevant. Further, in my view, they could be improved and adjusted to take into consideration more ethics related principles that align data with cybersecurity. The purists who understand the Guidelines may well oppose this proposal because security is a core principle. It is argued that the security principle can be strengthened in order to align with cybercrime.

The proposed changes are important as, arguably, they will assist all members of the Commonwealth to further develop and strengthen the delivery of the 4th Industrial Revolution (4IR). On the one hand, the digital economy is a core element of 4IR. On the other hand, it is an emerging area of the economy, where governments and regulators are grappling with how and what regulation should look like. The ensuing question is: do the current data and cyber laws meet the needs of 4IR? In my view, it is too early to determine this. More research is needed. Therefore, the Commonwealth could place itself in a strong position to further identify the regulatory needs of 4IR in relation to data and cybersecurity, and in addition to follow the recommendations proposed in this book.

Apart from the arbitration agreement being critical to the preparation and implementation of an arbitration proceeding, the role of experts will be just as important. That is, it is argued that an expert appointed by a Tribunal must be proficient in being able to provide facts related to the technology, cyber or data, either as single components, or combined. This will apply to both the technology and law.

A significant consideration is that the expert might be knowledgeable only in one area of technology, but not the law. Conversely, an expert might know the law well, but have no idea about the operation of technology. It is the ongoing development and evolution of technology that will challenge experts in arbitration. This can be seen in areas ranging from the storage or data, the development and application of AI, to the collection and use of data, and cybersecurity, each of which requires specific expertise. The Commonwealth has a role here to undertake further work to ensure members adopt the UNCITRAL Model Law, to ensure that the SME sector can benefit from the international commercial legal framework.

Against the back drop of the above, it has been confirmed that data and cybersecurity can be direct or indirectly related to investor-state arbitration. It has been argued that personal data can be a source of direct and indirect arbitration. In my view, in direct arbitration, the data forms part of the arbitration, but, it not the sole reason for the dispute. This issue will only be heightened by the new digital economy which is largely driven by data. Hence, data will drive economic growth. The same can be said for cybersecurity which protects the commercial and economic activity that data facilitates. Thus, the book argues for a greater level of legal convergence. To achieve this, the Commonwealth needs to promote its work through the relevant international institutions and work towards developing international law in the area of data and cybersecurity.

Therefore, the Commonwealth needs to undertake a review of the Model Bill and include data portability in their provisions. In my view, there is a need to improve cross-border data flows with these Bills. In addition, there needs to be agreement on the definition of data and clarification of issues specifically related to data. Further, the right to be forgotten should also be included, and the difference between the Bills should be addressed, particularly in regard to the application of the respective laws to the private and public sectors. It is argued they should apply to both. Another recent addition to the data laws is data retention, and this needs to be included. Also, the various approaches to consent need to be reconciled and made consistent. It is argued that the Model Bill needs to be amended to include the rising areas of data related theft, fraud and ransom-extortion as important provisions.

The reform that has been proposed in this book for the Commonwealth to consider is not easy. However, it is argued that the outcome will encourage and support the growth of the digital economy. All members of the Commonwealth will receive economic and social benefits over the longer term. They will support data in the digital economy as well as provide better security for that data. As data and cyber processes combined become even more embedded in the digital economy, the proposed reforms will bring economic benefits by offering greater transparency, accountability, trust and certainty. These measures will support jobs and ensure that there is a greater balance between facilitating data flows and giving data subjects a high level of control over their own data.

In concluding this book, I come back to the research questions and offer a response based on the comparative study undertaken in this book. Is there an alternative way for the Commonwealth to strengthen relationship between member states through the law and governance of data and cybersecurity? Yes. This book has confirmed that the Commonwealth Model Bills provide the platform for nations to come together and discuss new proposals for law reform. This engagement is already taking place at a national level. It is argued that in order to strengthen and enhance this connectivity, these and other laws underpinning the digital economy should be reviewed and reformed regularly, as this will only benefit members.

Moreover, is a greater level of legal convergence better than the status quo? In my view, this is an area that can and should be improved. It provides an opportunity for the Commonwealth to build on the legal justice program and develop tools to allow members to converge or harmonise these and other commercial laws such as arbitration. In part, the Commonwealth, through its Regulatory Connectivity program discussed in Chap. 1, goes some way to achieving a level of legal convergence. In relation to the comments made by Chief Justice Sundaresh Menon[41] (Singapore, 2016) regarding a greater level of legal convergence of data laws, these should be extended to cybersecurity and arbitration law across the Commonwealth.

On the one hand, this needs to be a measured response so that trade barriers are not erected through and by the law. In part, data laws do create trade barriers, particularly in regard to data localisation. On the other hand, a level of barriers may be introduced through the consideration of Ethics. Stricking a balance will be difficult, but, can be achieved. A significant development that this book has highlighted is that data laws have now found their way into trade and economic agreements. Even though the book did not examine in detail the states' respective agreements, this new development merits further exploration. It is argued that this is an area requiring further research to compare the current provisions of each agreement. This, in my view, is a project that should be given priority by the Commonwealth. It will enable the Commonwealth to be at the forefront of the development of model principles, or law, to ensure that future trade, economic, and investment agreements are appropriately addressing the issue of data localisation. This will ensure that the balance between economic growth in the digital economy is not overly diluted by any actual or perceived controls. The Commonwealth needs to undertake a project focused on data localisation, and ensure that countries fully understand the economic and social benefits, as well as the drawbacks, of enacting data-related restrictions.

While not discussed at length in this book, the EU Data Adequacy program, although limited, has resulted in a greater mutual recognition of data laws. Arguably, this is a level of regulatory connectivity. This program could be explored by the Commonwealth. However, it is far better to achieve legal convergence and harmonisation, because adequacy (even the EU Adequacy framework which Malta and Cyprus are part of) retain[s] gaps in the law. Through legal or regulatory connectivity, which occurs today on various levels such as the judiciary and government, members of the Commonwealth can advance the digital economy significantly.

As stated earlier, the benefits obtained from regulator connectivity can be expanded to include regional and, in particular, international organisations. The Commonwealth is in a unique position where it can establish and develop a regulatory agenda, in the same way as the EU, that can be adopted by its member states. In part, this already occurs. However, the Commonwealth should engage international organisations to develop international data and build on the current international and supranational cyber laws. Notably, the Budapest Convention on Cybercrime and the African Union Convention on CyberSecurity and Personal Data, can both be used as foundations on which to build international laws. The Commonwealth should also engage with these organisations to improve the current commercial laws for data

[41] Asian Business Law Institute, President of SAL sets out his vision for legal convergence and ABLI, 2016, https://abli.asia/NEWS-EVENTS/Whats-New/ID/7.

and cybersecurity to ensure a strong economic outcome that will benefit all states. Nonetheless, it has been put forward that international arbitration will have a role in resolving disputes pertaining to the digital economy. In this regard, more work could be undertaken by states in partnership with the Commonwealth to improve and build on the national laws of arbitration.

Finally, the arguments and proposals put forward throughout this book, if implemented, will bring significant benefits to the Commonwealth: the relationships between member states will be strengthened; trade and investment will be enhanced; economic activity will be generated in new sectors; and areas of the digital economy that could be strengthened in the future can be identified. Failure to do so will continue to add complexity to the already highly-divergent legal landscape in terms of data protection, data flows and cybersecurity, along with arbitration. In order for the digital economy to be fully realised, further work is required to strengthen the law, adopt an international approach and implement new programs of Model Bills, in areas such as arbitration. This will complement data and cybersecurity, and benefit all of the digital economy.

SPRINGER NATURE

GPSR Compliance

The European Union's (EU) General Product Safety Regulation (GPSR) is a set of rules that requires consumer products to be safe and our obligations to ensure this.

If you have any concerns about our products, you can contact us on ProductSafety@springernature.com

In case Publisher is established outside the EU, the EU authorized representative is:

Springer Nature Customer Service Center GmbH
Europaplatz 3
69115 Heidelberg, Germany

The manufacturer's authorised representative in the EU is Springer Nature Customer Service Centre GmbH, Europaplatz 3, 69115 Heidelberg, Germany. If you have any concerns regarding our products, please contact ProductSafety@springernature.com

Printed and bound by CPI Group (UK) Ltd, Croydon, CR0 4YY
05/10/2026
02228122-0016